COST ACCOUNTING
Planning and Control
Eighth Edition

Adolph Matz, PhD
Professor Emeritus of Accounting
The Wharton School
University of Pennsylvania

Milton F. Usry, PhD, CPA
Regents Professor of Accounting
College of Business Administration
Oklahoma State University

Consulting Editor: Lawrence H. Hammer, DBA, CPA
Associate Professor of Accounting
College of Business Administration
Oklahoma State University

Published by

A87 SOUTH-WESTERN PUBLISHING CO.

CINCINNATI   WEST CHICAGO, ILL.   DALLAS   PELHAM MANOR, N.Y.   PALO ALTO, CALIF.

Cover photograph by Thomas Leighton

Material from the Certificate in Management Accounting Examinations, Copyright © 1972 through 1981, by the National Association of Accountants is reprinted (or adapted) with permission.

ISBN: 0-538-01870-4

Library of Congress Catalog Card Number: 83-61249

1 2 3 4 5 6 7 8 D 7 6 5 4 3

Printed in the United States of America

PREFACE

Management's efforts to achieve organizational objectives rest upon the twin functions of planning and control. The *planning function* is essentially a decision-making process dealing with the establishment of desired results, the deployment of resources, and the creation of a communication system that permits the reporting and controlling of actual results and the comparison of these results with plans. The *control function* is the systematic effort by management to organize and marshal natural forces, human behavior, and material objects into a coordinated unit in order to accomplish plans.

The connecting link between the originating planning function and the terminating control function is the cost accounting information system, rightly termed a tool of management. This system permits effective communication, continuous feedback, and managerial flexibility. The processing and reporting of an organization's historical and projected economic data assist management in developing new potentials, improving present opportunities, establishing more aggressive yet flexible control of operations, and enhancing the management process through objective evaluation of the feedback data.

Although the information and underlying data required for the planning and control functions are often quite different, the cost accounting system is expected to provide the answers and respond to the needs of both functions. This dual responsibility of the cost accounting information system strongly influenced the authors in structuring the presentation followed in this textbook.

The textbook has undergone a significant reorganization and rewrite in most chapters to enhance clearness and thoroughness of the coverage. Furthermore, topical flow has been improved by the following:

1. The first five chapters of the previous edition have been completely restructured and rewritten into a modernized three-chapter format.
2. The profit performance measurements, intracompany transfer pricing, and product pricing methods chapter is now located immediately following the marketing cost and profitability analysis chapter.
3. The linear programming chapter is now presented directly after the chapter covering differential cost analysis.

Parts One and Two of this edition fuse planning and control into a harmonious whole by first presenting fundamental cost accounting concepts and objectives, followed by a comprehensive illustration depicting the flow of costs in a manufacturing enterprise, including its interface with the balance sheet and income statement. Cost data accumulation procedures using job order and process costing are then developed as a fundamental means of providing reliable cost data.

Part Three deals with the planning and control of factory overhead and responsibility accounting, while Part Four considers the other two cost elements, materials and labor, from both the planning and control phases.

Part Five elaborates on the heart of the planning function—budgeting—including the flexible budget and cost behavior analysis. This part also treats standard costing, which is basic to effective cost control.

Part Six, the final section, covers the entire spectrum of analysis of costs and profits, including gross profit analysis, direct costing, marketing cost and profitability analysis, profit performance measurements, transfer pricing, product pricing, break-even and cost-volume-profit analysis, differential cost analysis, linear programming, and the planning, evaluating, and controlling of capital expenditures.

Like many other disciplines, cost accounting has been influenced by the development of quantitative techniques and behavioral science concepts. These tools and their applications are presented in a clear and concise manner throughout the textbook as they relate to particular topics. Also, the appropriate consideration of income tax effects is integrated throughout this edition, as is the relevance of inflation's impact on the management process.

The presentation of the fundamental theoretical and practical aspects of cost accounting provides wide flexibility for classroom usage. In addition to its applicability to the traditional two-semester or three-quarter course, the textbook may be used in a one-semester cost course or in a managerial accounting course with emphasis on profit planning and cost analysis. For these alternative courses, a suggested outline, by chapter numbers, follows:

Cost Accounting (one semester)	Profit Planning and Cost Analysis (one semester)
Chapters 1–13	Chapters 1–2
Chapters 16–18	Chapter 11
	Chapters 14–26

Many other chapter combinations can be used effectively, depending on students' needs. The Instructors' Manual includes an outline of possible variations.

Most of the end-of-chapter materials are new or revised and include discussion questions, exercises, problems, and cases. For each topic, these materials afford coverage of relevant concepts and techniques at progressive levels in the learning process, thereby providing a significant student-learning benefit. The end-of-chapter materials include numerous items from the examinations administered by the American Institute of Certified Public

Accountants (designated AICPA adapted), the Institute of Management Accounting of the National Association of Accountants (designated CMA adapted), the Institute of Internal Auditors (designated CIA adapted), the Canadian Institute of Chartered Accountants (designated CICA adapted), and the Certified General Accountants' Association of Canada (designated CGAA adapted). The authors are indebted to these organizations for permission to use their materials.

Three separately printed practice cases are available, coauthored by John H. McMichael of the Wharton School, University of Pennsylvania. Each case — a job order cost case, a process cost case, and a standard cost analysis case — acquaints students with basic procedural characteristics without involving time-consuming details.

A student study guide is also available, prepared by Edward J. VanDerbeck of Xavier University, Cincinnati. This study guide contains a brief summary of each chapter, as well as questions and exercises with answers, thus providing students with immediate feedback on their comprehension of material.

Instructors adopting this edition are supplied with a manual that is devoted to detailed solutions of the end-of-chapter materials. Instructors are also entitled to transparencies of problem solutions (new with this edition), practice case solutions, an examinations booklet (including both multiple-choice questions and problems), and multiple copies of student check sheets for the problems.

The authors wish to express appreciation to the many users of the previous editions who offered helpful suggestions, and to Lane K. Anderson of Texas Tech University, who prepared a detailed critique of the Seventh Edition. Thanks are given to the students and teachers of Oklahoma State University who class-tested new materials and made suggestions for improvements.

Finally, we wish to express special appreciation to Lawrence H. Hammer, of Oklahoma State University, who reviewed and made contributions to the entire textbook in his position as consulting editor.

Adolph Matz
Milton F. Usry

CONTENTS

PART 1

COSTS — CONCEPTS AND OBJECTIVES

PART 2

COST ACCUMULATION PROCEDURES

PART 3

PLANNING AND CONTROL OF FACTORY OVERHEAD

PART 4

PLANNING AND CONTROL OF MATERIALS AND LABOR

PART 5

PLANNING AND CONTROL OF SALES AND COSTS

PART 6

ANALYSIS OF COSTS AND PROFITS

Part One
Costs — Concepts and Objectives

Chapter 1
The Management Concept and the Function of the Controller

The management of a business enterprise is composed of individuals who belong to one of three groups: (1) the operating management group, consisting of foremen and supervisors; (2) the middle management group, represented by department heads, division managers, and branch managers; and (3) the executive management group, consisting of the president, the executive vice-presidents, and the executives in charge of the various functions of marketing, purchasing, engineering, manufacturing, finance, and accounting. Executive management is principally concerned with long-range decisions, middle management with decisions of medium-range impact, and operating managers with short-range decisions.

One of management's chief concerns is the effective use of company capital. This capital is invested in productive facilities, such as factory buildings, tools, and equipment, as well as in circulating capital, or current assets. The use of this capital is determined by management's short- and long-range plans for the future.

The Management Concept

The management concept may be described by such phrases as "making decisions, giving orders, establishing policies, providing work and rewards, and hiring people to carry out policies." Management sets objectives that may be achieved by integrating its knowledge and skills with the ability and experience of the employees. To be successful, management must effectively perform the basic functions of planning, organizing, and controlling. Planning and organizing are basic functions of executive management, while control requires the participation of all levels of the management team.

Planning

Planning refers to the construction of a detailed operating program for all phases of operations. Planning is the process of sensing external opportunities and threats, determining desirable objectives, and employing resources to accomplish these objectives. Planning includes such areas of investigation as the nature of the company's business, its major policies, and the timing of major steps and other factors related to long-range plans. Effective planning is based on analyses of collected facts. Such analyses require reflective thinking, imagination, and foresight.

The establishment of an effective plan also requires the participation of the engineering, manufacturing, marketing, research, finance, and accounting functions. No single group should plan and act independently from other groups. Failure to recognize this fundamental principle may cause unnecessary planning difficulties and may result in financial disaster for the organization.

Closely allied with proper planning is the determination of company objectives. An objective is a target or an end result. In stating the objectives of a business enterprise, many people point to the need for realizing a profit. Although profits are the indispensable element in a successful business, profit is a limited concept in today's economic society. Profits cannot remain the sole objective of a business enterprise. The companies best able to maximize profits are those which produce products or render services in a definite manner, in a volume, at a time, at a cost, and at a price that will, in the long run, assure a profit and also win the cooperation of employees, gain the goodwill of customers, and meet social responsibilities. Business logic and changing public expectations suggest that plans should be formulated within a framework of four major parameters—economic, technological, social, and political.

Organizing

Organizing is essentially the establishment of the framework within which required activities are to be performed. The terms "organize" and "organization" refer to the systematization of various interdependent parts into one unit. Organizing requires (1) bringing the many functional units of an enterprise into a well-conceived structure and (2) assigning authority and responsibility to certain individuals. These organizational efforts include the task of motivating people to work together for the good of the company. Because of the attitudes and ambitions of the many persons involved, the desired organizational structure is developed through instruction and patience.

Creation of an organization involves the establishment of functional divisions, departments, sections, or branches. These units are created for the purpose of dividing tasks, which leads to specialization of labor. A manufacturing enterprise usually consists of at least three large fundamental activities: manufacturing, marketing, and administration. Within these three units, numerous departments are formed according to the nature and the amount of work, the degree of specialization, the number of employees, and the location of the work.

After organizational units have been created, management must assign the work to be done within each unit. The appropriate distribution of work among employees is vital to the attainment of company objectives. Of greater importance to a company's success are the relationships between superiors and subordinates and among managers within the management team.

Controlling

Control is management's systematic effort to achieve objectives by comparing performance to plans. Activities should be continuously supervised if management expects to stay within previously defined boundaries. Actual results of each activity classification are compared with plans, and if significant differences are noted, remedial actions may be taken. The following diagram illustrates the control process:

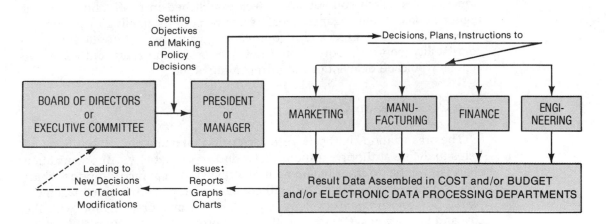

Authority, Responsibility, and Accountability

In a small company, planning and control activities are usually performed by one person, without elaborate analysis. This person will probably be the owner or general manager, who has an intimate knowledge of employees, materials, financing, and customers. In a large company with numerous divisions and a variety of products or services, planning and controlling the activities of individual units is complex. For this reason, large firms assign the planning and control functions to more than one person, so that reports and any corrective actions are closer to the activity.

Authority is the power to command others to perform or not perform activities. Authority is the key to the managerial job and the basis for responsibility. It is the force that binds the organization together.

Authority originates with executive management, which delegates it to the various managerial levels. Such delegation is essential to the existence of an organizational structure. Through delegation, the chief executive's area of operations is extended. However, the chief executive retains overall authority for assigned functions, since delegation does not mean release from responsibility.

Responsibility, or obligation, is closely related to authority. It originates particularly in the superior-subordinate relationship because the superior has the authority to require specific work from other people. As these people accept the obligation to perform the work, they create their own responsibility. The superior, however, is ultimately responsible for the subordinates' performance or nonperformance.

In addition to the aspect of achieving results, another facet of responsibility is *accountability* — reporting results to higher authority. Reporting is important because it makes possible the measurement — in terms of quantity, quality, time, and cost — of the extent to which objectives have been reached.

Accountability is basically an individual rather than a group problem. This principle of single accountability is well established in profit and nonprofit organizations. If the organizational structure permits pooling of judgment, responsibility is diffused and accountability is nullified. Without single accountability, control reports would not only be meaningless, but corrective actions would be delayed or not forthcoming at all.

The Organization Chart

The organization chart sets forth each principal management position and helps to define authority, responsibility, and accountability. An organization chart is essential to the development of a cost system and cost reports which indicate the responsibilities of individuals for implementing management plans. The coordinated development of a company's organization with the cost and budgetary system will lead to an approach to accounting and reporting called *responsibility accounting*.

Generally, an organization chart is based on the line-staff concept, which is especially useful when a company's product lines are simple and not subject to frequent changes. The basic assumption of the line-staff concept is that all positions or functional divisions may be categorized into two groups: the line, which makes decisions and performs the true management functions; the staff, which gives advice or performs any technical functions. A line-staff organization chart is illustrated as follows:

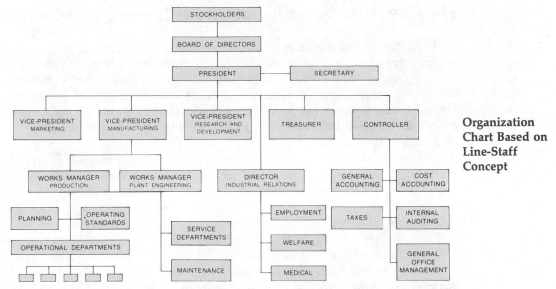

Organization Chart Based on Line-Staff Concept

Another type of organization chart is based on the functional-teamwork concept of management, which is structured to emphasize the most important functions of an enterprise: *resources*, *processes*, and *human interrelations*. The resources function involves the acquisition, disposal, and prudent management of a wide variety of resources — tangible and intangible, human and physical. The processes function deals with activities such as product design, research and development, purchasing, manufacturing, advertising, marketing, and billing. The human interrelations function directs the company's efforts in relation to the behavior of people inside and outside the company. An organization chart based on the functional-teamwork concept is illustrated as follows:

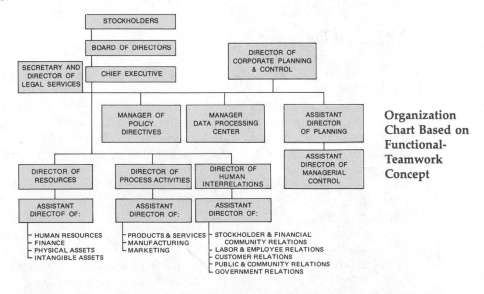

Organization Chart Based on Functional-Teamwork Concept

The Controller's Participation in Planning and Control

The controller is the executive manager responsible for a company's accounting function. The controller coordinates management's participation in the planning and control phases of attaining objectives, in determining the effectiveness of policies, and in creating organizational structures and procedures. The controller is also responsible for observing the methods of planning and control throughout the enterprise and proposing improvements in the planning and control system.

Effective cost control depends upon the proper communication of accounting information to management. Through the issuance of performance reports, the controller advises the various levels of management in regard to activities requiring corrective action. These reports emphasize deviations from a predetermined plan, following the principle of *management by exception.*

Through the conventional accounting system models, the controller provides management with information which it uses in planning a company's future and controlling its daily activities. These models — the balance sheet, the income statement, and the statement of changes in financial position — are based on historical dollars. Management also has access to much information which is outside these models, yet obtainable from the information system.

External users, including stockholders, future investors, and government agencies, must also receive information by which management's effectiveness may be judged. This information is usually communicated to external users via the company's annual report, which includes the basic financial statements of the company. These statements often lack explanatory detail, since it is impossible to include all the data which the large variety of external users would find useful.

The Cost Department

The cost department, under the direction of the controller, is responsible for keeping records of a company's manufacturing and nonmanufacturing activities. This department must also analyze all costs of manufacturing, marketing, and administration. It must issue significant control reports and other decision-making data to those managers who assist in controlling and improving costs and operations. The analysis of costs and the preparation of reports are greatly facilitated through the proper division of functions within the cost department. These functions must be coordinated with other accounting functions, such as general accounting, which are closely tied to cost accounting.

In addition to the cost department, a company may have one or more of the following departments: manufacturing, personnel, treasury, marketing, public relations, and legal. The functions of the cost department are also coordinated with some of the functions of these departments.

The *manufacturing departments,* under the direction of engineers and factory superintendents, design and control production. In research and design, cost estimates for each type of material, labor, and machine process are used in deciding whether to accept or reject a design. Likewise, the scheduling, producing, and inspecting of jobs and products by the manufacturing departments are measured for efficiency in terms of the costs incurred.

The *personnel department* interviews and selects employees for various job classifications. It maintains personnel records, which include the wage rates and the methods of remuneration for each employee. This information forms the basis for the computation of payroll costs.

The *treasury department* is responsible for the financial administration of a company. In scheduling cash requirements and expectations, it relies upon budgets and related reports from the cost department.

The *marketing department* needs a good product at a competitive price in order to attract customers. While prices should not be set merely by adding a predetermined percentage to cost, costs cannot be ignored. Marketing managers use pertinent cost data to determine which products are most profitable and to determine sales policies.

The *public relations department* has the primary function of maintaining good relations between the company and its public, especially its customers and stockholders. Points of friction are most likely to be prices, wages, profits, and dividends. The cost department may be asked to provide basic information for public releases concerning policies in these areas.

The *legal department* uses cost information as an aid in maintaining company affairs according to law. Some of these legal areas include the Equal Pay Act, terms of industry-wide union contracts, the Robinson-Patman Act, social security taxes, unemployment compensation, the Employee Retirement Security Act of 1974, and income tax.

The Role of Cost Accounting

Cost accounting furnishes management with the necessary accounting tools for planning and controlling activities. Specifically, the collection, presentation, and analysis of cost data should help management accomplish the following tasks:

1. Creating and executing plans and budgets for operating under expected competitive and economic conditions.
2. Establishing costing methods and procedures that permit control and, if possible, reductions or improvements of costs.
3. Creating inventory values for costing and pricing purposes and, at times, controlling physical quantities.
4. Determining company costs and profit for an annual accounting period or a shorter period.
5. Choosing from among two or more alternatives which might increase revenues or decrease costs.

Budgeting

The budget is the written expression of management's plan for the future. All levels of management should be involved in creating the budget program and welding it into a homogeneous unit. A workable, realistic budget will not only help promote coordination of people, clarification of policies, and crystallization of plans, but will also create greater internal harmony and unanimity of purpose among managers and workers.

In recent years, considerable attention has been given to the behavioral implications of providing managers with the data required for planning, coordinating, and controlling activities. Cost accounting and budgeting play an important role in influencing individual and group behavior at all stages of the management process, including: (1) setting goals; (2) informing individuals about what they must do to contribute to the accomplishment of these goals; (3) motivating desirable performance; (4) evaluating performance; and (5) suggesting when corrective action should be taken. In short, accountants cannot ignore the behavioral sciences (psychology, social-psychology, and sociology) because the decision-making function of accounting is essentially a behavioral function.

An individual manager's attitude toward the budget will depend greatly upon the existing good relationship within the management group. Guided by the company plan, with an opportunity for increased compensation, greater satisfaction, and eventually promotion, the middle and lower management group might achieve remarkable results. On the other hand, a discordant management group, unwilling to accept the budget's underlying figures, might show such poor performance that the administration would be compelled to defer implementation of the planning and control concept.

The following elements have been suggested as a means for motivating personnel to aim for the goals set forth in the budget:[1]

1. A compensation system that builds and maintains a clearly understood relationship between results and rewards.
2. A system for performance appraisal that employees understand with regard to their individual effectiveness and key results, their tasks and their responsibilities, their degree and span of influence in decision making, as well as the time allowed to judge their results.
3. A system of communication that allows employees to query their superiors with trust and honest communication.
4. A system of promotion that generates and sustains employee faith in its validity and judgment.
5. A system of employee support through coaching, counseling, and career planning.

---

[1]Paul E. Sussman, "Motivating Financial Personnel," *The Journal of Accountancy*, Vol. 141, No. 2, p. 80.

6. A system that not only considers company objectives, but also employees' skills and capacities.
7. A system that will not settle for mediocrity, but which reaches for realistic and attainable standards, stressing improvement and providing an environment in which the concept of excellence can grow.

Controlling Costs

The responsibility for cost control should be assigned to specific individuals, who are also responsible for budgeting the costs under their control. The responsibilities should be limited to controllable costs, and the performance of the individuals should be measured by comparing actual costs with budgeted costs. The responsibility for sales revenues and profits should also be assigned to certain managers.

To aid the process of controlling, the cost accountant may use *standard costs*. These predetermined costs for direct materials, direct labor, and factory overhead are established by using information accumulated from past experience and from scientific research. When standards are used, they form the foundation for the budget and for reports which identify variances between actual and standard costs.

Pricing

Management's pricing policy should assure not only the recovery of all costs but also the securing of a profit, even under adverse conditions. Although supply and demand are usually determining factors in pricing, the establishment of a profitable sales price depends upon consideration of costs.

Determining Profits

One of the primary objectives of cost accounting is the consistent allocation of manufacturing costs to units of products in the ending inventory and to units sold during a period. At the end of a fiscal period, the matching of costs with revenues determines profits for the period. These costs and profits may be reported for segments of the firm or for the entire firm, depending upon management's needs and generally accepted accounting principles.

The matching process requires an identification of short-run and long-run costs and variable and fixed (capacity) costs. Variable manufacturing costs are assigned first to the units manufactured and then matched with the units sold; variable nonmanufacturing costs typically are matched with the units sold. Fixed costs are arbitrarily allocated to units by one of the following alternatives:

1. Matching total fixed costs assigned to a period with revenues of that period (direct costing).

2. Matching manufacturing fixed costs to units of product and matching all other fixed costs with revenues of the period (absorption costing, the generally accepted method).

These alternatives give the same results in the long run, but yield a different profit for individual short periods.

Choosing Among Alternatives

Cost accounting is the source of information concerning the different revenues and different costs which might result from alternative courses of action. Based on this information, management must make long-range decisions that involve such matters as entering new markets, developing new products, discontinuing product lines, and buying or leasing equipment.

The Influence of Private and Governmental Organizations

In the private sector, major research and pronouncements by professional organizations contribute to the development, improvement, and revision of both financial and cost accounting theory and practice. These organizations include the American Institute of Certified Public Accountants (AICPA), the Financial Accounting Standards Board (FASB), the National Association of Accountants (NAA), the American Accounting Association (AAA), and the Financial Executives Institute (FEI). In addition, accounting is influenced by public accounting firms, nonprofit organizations, individuals, and private companies.

The rapid growth of international business activities has led several international organizations to become involved in setting standards of accounting and reporting. These organizations include the International Accounting Standards Committee (IASC) and the Organization for Economic Cooperation and Development (OECD).

In the public sector, federal, state, and local governments prescribe regulations that may often be embodied in the accounting system. At the federal level, the Securities and Exchange Commission (SEC), the Internal Revenue Service (IRS), and the pronouncements of the Cost Accounting Standards Board (CASB) have a significant influence on financial and cost reporting.

Securities and Exchange Commission

The federal government, through the actions of the SEC and other regulatory agencies, is showing an increasing interest in the external reports of private companies. In *Regulation S-X*, requirements are set forth for financial statements filed with the SEC.

Internal Revenue Service

IRS regulations are designed primarily to determine federal income tax liability. However, their influence on financial statements and on cost accounting procedures cannot be ignored. Likewise, any meaningful analysis for planning and decision-making must carefully consider federal as well as state and local tax consequences.

Cost Accounting Standards Board

On August 15, 1970, Congress established the Cost Accounting Standards Board. The purposes of the Board, as outlined in an amendment to Section 719 of the Defense Production Act of 1950, were stated as follows:

> The Board shall from time to time promulgate cost-accounting standards designed to achieve uniformity and consistency in the cost-accounting principles followed by defense contractors and subcontractors under Federal contracts. Such promulgated standards shall be used by all relevant Federal agencies and by defense contractors and subcontractors in estimating, accumulating, and reporting costs in connection with the pricing, administration, and settlement of all negotiated prime contract and subcontract national defense procurements with the United States in excess of $100,000, other than contracts or subcontracts where the price negotiated is based on (1) established catalog or market prices of commercial items sold in substantial quantities to the general public, or (2) prices set by law or regulation. In promulgating such standards... the Board shall take into account the probable costs of implementation... compared to the probable benefits. ... Such regulations shall require defense contractors and subcontractors as a condition of contracting to disclose in writing their cost-accounting principles, including methods of distinguishing direct costs from indirect costs and the basis used for allocating indirect costs, and to agree to a contract price adjustment, with interest, for any increased costs paid to the defense contractor by the United States because of the defense contractor's failure to comply with duly promulgated cost-accounting standards or to follow consistently his disclosed cost-accounting practices in pricing contract proposals and in accumulating and reporting contract performance cost data.

On September 30, 1980, the CASB was dissolved because Congress believed that the Board's purpose of establishing basic cost accounting standards had been accomplished. Legislation assigning the functions of the CASB to the executive branch of the government is being formulated by the Senate Committee on Banking, Housing, and Urban Affairs, but final action has not yet been taken. All of the standards, rules, and regulations promulgated by the Board remain in full force and effect under the oversight of the General Accounting Office.

Significant Standards Issued. During its existence, the CASB issued a series of Cost Accounting Standards (CASs), which govern the determination and allocation of specific costs. These standards were defined as formal statements that (1) enunciate a principle or principles to be followed, (2) establish practices to be applied, or (3) specify criteria to be employed in selecting from alternative principles and practices in estimating, accumulating, and reporting costs of contracts subject to the rules of the Board. To achieve increased uniformity and consistency in accounting for costs of negotiated defense contracts, the standards provide criteria for the allocation of the cost of resources used to cost objectives. *Cost* in this discussion is the monetary value of the resources used. As defined by the Board, a *cost objective* is "a function, organizational subdivision, contract, or other work unit for which cost data are desired and for which provision is made to accumulate and measure the cost of processes, products, jobs, capitalized projects, etc." CASs deal with all aspects of cost allocability, including:

1. The definition and measurement of costs which may be allocated to cost objectives.
2. The determination of the cost accounting period to which such costs are assignable.
3. The determination of the methods by which costs are to be allocated to cost objectives.

The Board's pronouncements adhere to the concept of full costing whenever appropriate. Full allocation of all costs of a period, including general administrative expenses and all other indirect costs, is generally considered to be the basis for determining the cost of negotiated defense contracts.

The CASB's pronouncements are in general harmony with sound accounting concepts and techniques and with generally accepted accounting principles. Yet, the CASB did not hesitate to tackle controversial issues that could be considered in the domain of the Financial Accounting Standards Board. Accordingly, the CASB's influence might be all the more significant and far-reaching.

Although specific CASs are discussed as appropriate in subsequent chapters, it should be noted here that three of the standards—CASs 409, 414, and 417—have the potential for impact far beyond the government contracting area. CAS 409 requires contractors to depreciate their assets for contract costing purposes over lives that are based on documented historical usefulness, irrespective of the lives used for either financial or income tax purposes. CASs 414 and 417 recognize as a contract cost the imputed cost of capital committed to facilities, thereby overturning the government's long-standing practice of disallowing interest and other financing-type costs.

Contractor's Coverage. The CASB standards are to be followed by defense contractors and subcontractors in estimating, accumulating, and reporting costs for negotiated contracts in excess of $100,000. Since all nondefense agencies have also implemented the CASB's standards, rules, and regulations, most negotiated contracts and subcontracts are subject to these standards.

On January 1, 1975, smaller contractors and business units with insignificant amounts of government business were removed from the CASB's coverage. Coverage now extends only to business units (segments or profit centers) of a contractor that has received a covered prime or subcontract in excess of $500,000. Once a business unit receives such a contract, it must comply with applicable standards for all subsequently awarded prime or subcontracts in excess of $100,000 unless otherwise exempt. The coverage ceases only when all covered contracts in excess of $100,000 are completed by a contractor and becomes operative again for contracts in excess of $100,000 upon acceptance of an award exceeding $500,000. A firm qualifying as a small business under the regulations of the Small Business Administration is exempt from the CASB's requirements.

In 1978, the Board issued a rule exempting contracts and subcontracts awarded to foreign concerns and governments from most CASB standards. The exemptions are intended to remove impediments to efficient and successful contracting with foreign groups.

Statement of Disclosure. As a condition of contracting, contractors can be required to disclose in writing their cost accounting practices. For this purpose, the Board provided for a 40-page disclosure statement. The instructions pertaining thereto indicate that a contractor must state the practices of each profit center, division, or similar organizational unit. A *profit center* is defined as "the smallest organizationally independent segment of a company which has been charged by management with profit and loss responsibility."

Although a detailed presentation of the disclosure statement is beyond the scope of this text, it should be noted that the statement requires information regarding the three major elements of direct costs, i.e. direct materials, direct labor, and other direct costs; the methods used to charge out materials (fifo, lifo, standard costs, or others); the accumulation of variances; the method of charging direct labor (individual/actual rates, average rates, standard cost rates, or others) and a description of the types of variances; the method used to cost interorganizational transfers; and the allocation bases used for charging indirect costs to government contracts or similar cost objectives.

DISCUSSION QUESTIONS

1. State the fundamental task in planning and controlling the activities of a company.

2. Enumerate social responsibilities of which management should be aware.

3. What is the meaning of assignment of responsibility?

4. Explain the relationship between assignment of responsibility and control.

5. When an organization or business outgrows direct supervision and management by its owner, authority must be delegated to subordinate managers, and some form of accountability on their part must be provided. Discuss.

6. Is responsibility accounting identical with the concept of accountability? Explain.

7. Why is the budget an essential tool in cost planning?

8. In what manner does the controller exercise control over the activities of other members of management?

9. Discuss the functions of the cost department.

10. Why must the controller be aware of the latest developments in the field of communications?

11. Numerous nonaccounting departments require cost data and must also feed basic data to the cost department. Discuss.

12. How are CASB standards defined and what degree of authority do they have?

Chapter 2
Cost Concepts and the Cost Accounting Information System

Cost accounting is usually considered only as it applies to manufacturing operations. In today's economy, however, every type and size of organization should benefit from the use of cost accounting concepts and techniques. For example, cost accounting principles may be applied by financial institutions, transportation companies (airlines, railroads, bus companies), churches, schools, colleges, universities, and governmental units, as well as the non-manufacturing activities of manufacturing firms. Although these numerous applications of cost accounting are not discussed in depth in this text, they are mentioned in appropriate places.

The Cost Concept

Cost concepts and terms have developed according to the needs of accountants, economists, and engineers. Accountants have defined cost as "an exchange price, a forgoing, a sacrifice made to secure benefit. In financial accounting, the forgoing or sacrifice at date of acquisition is represented by a current or future diminution in cash or other assets."[1]

Frequently the term "cost" is used synonymously with the term "expense." However, an expense may be defined as a measured outflow of goods or services, which is matched with revenue to determine income, or:

> ...the decrease in net assets as a result of the use of economic services in the creation of revenues or of the imposition of taxes by governmental units. Expense is measured by the amount of the decrease in assets or the increase in liabilities related to the production and delivery of goods and the rendering of services... expense in its broadest sense includes all expired costs which are deductible from revenues.[2]

When the term "cost" is used specifically, it should be modified by such descriptions as direct, prime, conversion, indirect, fixed, variable, controllable, product, period, joint, estimated, standard, sunk, or out-of-pocket. Each modification implies a certain attribute which is important in measuring cost, and which may be recorded and accumulated for assigning costs to inventories, preparing financial statements, and planning and controlling costs. The accountant who is involved in planning, analyzing, and decision-making must also work with future, replacement, imputed, differential, or opportunity costs, none of which is recorded.

The Cost Accounting Information System

To manage an enterprise, systematic and comparative cost information as well as analytical cost and profit data are needed. This information helps management set the company's profit goals, establish departmental targets which direct middle and operating management toward the achievement of the final goal, evaluate the effectiveness of plans, pinpoint successes or failures in terms of specific responsibilities, and analyze and decide on adjustments and improvements to keep the entire organization moving forward, in balance, toward established objectives. An integrated and coordinated information system should provide only that information which is needed by each responsible manager. To accomplish these objectives, the system must be designed to provide information promptly. Furthermore, the information must be communicated effectively. Cost control needs and profit opportunities may be delayed or missed because of poor communication.

The accumulation of accounting data requires many forms, methods, and systems due to the varying types and sizes of businesses. A successful information system should be tailored to give the blend of sophistication and simplicity that is most efficient and economical for a specific organization. Designing a cost accounting information system requires a thorough under-

---

[1]Robert T. Sprouse and Maurice Moonitz, *Accounting Research Study No. 3*, "A Tentative Set of Broad Accounting Principles for Business Enterprises," (New York: American Institute of Certified Public Accountants, 1962), p. 25.
[2]*Ibid.*, p. 49.

standing of the organizational structure of the company and the type of cost information required by all levels of management. This interface between the system, management, and employees has significant behavioral implications. The system may enhance or thwart the achievement of desired results, depending on the extent to which sound behavioral judgment is applied in developing, administering, and improving the system and in educating employees to observe cost control procedures.

The cost accounting information system must be closely associated with the division of authority, so that individual managers can be held accountable for the costs incurred in their departments. The system should be designed to promote the concept of management by exception; i.e., it should provide information that enables management to take prompt remedial action. The system should also reflect the manufacturing and administrative procedures of the particular company for which it is designed. The accountant who designs the system must know how employees are paid, how inventories are controlled, how equipment is costed, and other operating information.

Accounting records do not provide all the necessary information for effective management. Other quantifiable and nonquantifiable information, such as machine capacities, may be vital to the decision-making process. Requirements for record keeping and reporting may also be imposed on an organization by external forces, such as the Internal Revenue Code, the Federal Insurance Contributions Act, the Securities and Exchange Commission, Cost Accounting Standards, other governmental regulatory agencies and taxing authorities, as well as creditors and labor unions. These legal and contractual requirements must be met by a system that is designed in a cost-conscious manner. Any sophistication in a system, beyond the basic requirements, must be justified solely on the basis of its value to management.

The Chart of Accounts

Every profit and nonprofit organization, irrespective of its size and complexity, must maintain some type of general ledger accounting system. For such a system to function effectively, data must be collected, identified, and coded for recording in journals and posting to ledger accounts. The prerequisite for efficiently accomplishing these tasks is a well-designed *chart of accounts* for classifying costs and expenses.

In constructing a chart of accounts, the following basic considerations should be observed:

1. Accounts should be arranged and designated to give maximum information with a minimum of supplementary analysis.
2. Account titles should reflect the purpose rather than the nature of expenditures.
3. Manufacturing, marketing, and administrative cost accounts should receive particular attention because these accounts are used to highlight variations in operating efficiency. They should be identifiable with the manager responsible for the costs involved.

A typical chart of accounts is divided into (1) balance sheet accounts for assets, liabilities, and capital, and (2) income statement accounts for sales, cost of goods sold, factory overhead, marketing expenses, administrative expenses, and other expenses and income. The use of numbers to represent these accounts is the simplest form of symbolizing, which is essential to the processing of information, especially when electronic data processing equipment is being used. A condensed chart of accounts is illustrated as follows:

BALANCE SHEET ACCOUNTS (100–299)

Current Assets (100–129)	Current Liabilities (200–219)
Property, Plant, and Equipment (130–159)	Long-Term Liabilities (220–229)
Intangible Assets (170–179)	Capital (250–299)

INCOME STATEMENT ACCOUNTS (300–899)

Sales (300–349)	Administrative Expenses (600–699)
Cost of Goods Sold (350–399)	Other Expenses (700–749)
Factory Overhead (400–499)	Other Income (800–849)
Marketing Expenses (500–599)	Income Taxes (890–899)

Electronic Data Processing

Successful management of a business is essentially a continuous process of decision making. The decision making becomes even more complex when multiple plants are located throughout the nation and in foreign countries; when product lines carry an array of sizes, colors, and options; when various reports are necessary for taxing authorities, regulatory agencies, employees, and stockholders; and when policies and objectives must be communicated from executive management to several operating levels. The information system aids the decision-making process by collecting, classifying, analyzing, and reporting business data. These activities are called *data processing*, and the procedures, forms, and equipment used in the process are called the *data processing system*. Any accounting system, even a cash register in a supermarket, is a data processing system and should be designed to provide pertinent and timely information to management.

The speed and flexibility of computers have led many businesses to convert the processing of data to electronic systems, which replace ledgers with punched cards, reels of magnetic tape, or magnetic disks as media for the recording and storing of account data. These systems can handle routine information easily, verify its accuracy, automatically write checks and remittance statements, classify and post data files, prepare general and subsidiary records and analytical reports, and compute ratios and other statistics for analytical purposes.

An electronic data processing system may be used to recognize and report any circumstances which deviate from a norm or standard. The concept of management by exception is thereby applied efficiently. The system also greatly expands the ability of management to use mathematical models or simulations to plan operations. For example, with a computer, it is possible to simulate a complete operating budget and manipulate product mix, price, cost factors, and the marketing program. By studying alternative combinations of the variables, the uncertainty in making decisions is reduced.

When an electronic data processing system is used, accounting procedures must be carefully programmed for the system. The programming process includes analyzing the procedure, preparing extensive flow charts which reduce the procedure to a logical design for the system, and writing the detailed code of instructions for the system to follow. As a result of the extensive analysis required in programming, an inherent advantage of an electronic data processing system is that possibly vague accounting procedures become more concise and efficient.

In recent years, the use of electronic data processing systems has enabled controllers and their staffs to become the nerve centers of large corporations. With such systems, controllers can assemble data concerning human resources, money, materials, and machines, which may form the basis for proposing alternatives in planning crucial operations. The data are based on (1) the company's historical costs and revenues, (2) management's evaluation of the present and future, and (3) economic forecasts originating outside the company.

Classifications of Costs

Cost classifications are needed for the development of cost data that will aid management in achieving its objectives. These classifications are based on the relationship of costs to:

1. The product
2. Volume of production
3. Manufacturing departments
4. An accounting period

Costs in Relation to a Product

The process of classifying costs and expenses may begin by relating costs to the operations of a business. In a manufacturing concern, total operating cost consists of (1) manufacturing cost and (2) commercial expenses. The chart on the next page illustrates this division of total operating cost and identifies some of the elements included in each division.

Manufacturing Costs. Manufacturing cost, often called production cost or factory cost, is the sum of the three cost elements: direct materials, direct labor, and factory overhead. Direct materials and direct labor may be combined into another classification called *prime cost*. Direct labor and factory overhead may be combined into a classification called *conversion cost*, which represents the cost of converting direct materials into finished products.

| Direct Materials | + | Direct Labor | = | Prime Cost |

+

| Indirect Materials | + | Indirect Labor | + | Other Indirect Costs | = | Factory Overhead |

Includes:
  Factory supplies
  Lubricants

Includes:
  Supervision
  Superintendence
  Inspection
  Salaries of
    factory clerks
  Defective work
  Experimental
    work

Includes:
  Rent
  Insurance — fire
    and liability
  Property tax
  Depreciation
  Maintenance
    and repairs
  Power
  Light
  Heat
  Employer payroll
    taxes
  Miscellaneous
    factory
    overhead
  Small tools

=

| Manufacturing Cost |

+

| Marketing Expenses | + | Administrative Expenses | = | Commercial Expenses |

Includes:
  Sales salaries
  Commissions to sales staff
  Employer payroll taxes
  Advertising
  Samples
  Entertainment
  Travel expenses
  Rent
  Depreciation
  Property tax
  Telephone and telegraph
  Stationery and printing
  Postage
  Freight and cartage out
  Miscellaneous marketing
    expenses

Includes:
  Administrative and office
    salaries
  Employer payroll taxes
  Rent
  Depreciation
  Property tax
  Auditing expenses
  Legal expenses
  Uncollectible accounts
  Telephone and telegraph
  Stationery and printing
  Postage
  Miscellaneous
    administrative expenses

=

| Total Operating Cost |

Direct materials are all materials that form an integral part of the finished product and that can be included directly in calculating the cost of the product. Examples of direct materials are the lumber to make furniture and the crude oil to make gasoline. The ease with which the materials items may be traced to the final product is a major consideration in classifying items as direct materials. For example, tacks to build furniture undoubtedly form part of the finished product, but to cost the furniture expeditiously, such items may be classified as indirect materials.

Direct labor is labor expended to convert direct materials into the finished product. It consists of employees' wages which can feasibly be assigned to a specific product.

Factory overhead — also called manufacturing overhead, manufacturing expenses, or factory burden — may be defined as the cost of indirect materials, indirect labor, and all other manufacturing costs that cannot be charged directly to specific products. Simply stated, factory overhead includes all manufacturing costs except direct materials and direct labor.

Indirect materials are those materials needed for the completion of a product, but the consumption of which is so minimal or so complex that treating them as direct materials is futile. Factory supplies, a form of indirect materials, consist of such items as lubricating oils, grease, cleaning rags, and brushes needed to maintain the working area and machinery in a usable and safe condition.

Indirect labor may be defined as expended labor which does not directly affect the construction or the composition of the finished product. Indirect labor includes the wages of supervisors, shop clerks, general helpers, and employees engaged in maintenance work that is not directly related to production.

Commercial Expenses. Commercial expenses fall into two large classifications: (1) marketing (distribution or selling) expenses and (2) administrative (general and administrative) expenses. *Marketing expenses* begin at the point where the factory costs end, i.e., when manufacturing has been completed and the product is in salable condition. These expenses include the expenses of selling and delivery. *Administrative expenses* include expenses incurred in directing and controlling the organization. Some of these expenses, such as a vice-president's salary, are often allocated to and included in manufacturing costs and marketing expenses.

Costs in Relation to Volume of Production

Some costs vary directly in relation to changes in the volume of production or output, while others remain relatively fixed in amount. The tendency of costs to vary with output must be considered by management if it desires to plan a company's strategy intelligently and control costs successfully.

Variable Costs. In general, *variable costs* have the following characteristics: (1) variability of total amount in direct proportion to volume, (2) relatively constant cost per unit as volume changes within a relevant range, (3) assignable, with reasonable ease and accuracy, to operating departments, and (4) controllable by a specific department head. The costs which have these characteristics generally include direct materials and direct labor. Some factory overhead and nonmanufacturing costs are also variable. The following list identifies overhead costs which are usually classified as variable:

VARIABLE FACTORY OVERHEAD

Supplies	Receiving costs
Fuel	Hauling within plant
Power	Royalties
Small tools	Communication costs
Spoilage, salvage, and	Overtime premium
reclamation expenses	

Fixed Costs. The characteristics of *fixed costs* are: (1) fixed total amount within a relevant output range, (2) decrease in per unit cost as volume increases within a relevant range, (3) assignable to departments on the basis of arbitrary managerial decisions or cost allocation methods, and (4) control responsibility resting with executive management rather than operating supervisors. The following overhead costs are usually classified as fixed:

FIXED FACTORY OVERHEAD

Salaries of production executives	Wages of security guards
Depreciation	and janitors
Property tax	Maintenance and repairs of
Patent amortization	buildings and grounds
Insurance–property and liability	Rent

In some cases, management actions may determine whether a cost is classified as fixed or variable. For example, if a truck is rented at a rate per mile, the cost is variable. If the truck is purchased and subsequently depreciated by the straight-line method, the cost is fixed.

Semivariable Costs. Some costs contain fixed and variable elements. These *semivariable costs* include an amount that is fixed within a relevant range of output and an amount that varies proportionately with output changes. For example, electricity cost may be semivariable. Electricity used for lighting tends to be a fixed cost, since lights will be needed when the plant is operating, regardless of the level of output. Conversely, electricity used as power to operate equipment will vary, depending upon the usage of the equipment. Other examples of semivariable overhead costs are as follows:

SEMIVARIABLE FACTORY OVERHEAD

Supervision	Maintenance and repairs of machinery
Inspection	and plant equipment
Payroll department services	Compensation insurance
Personnel department services	Health and accident insurance
Factory office services	Payroll taxes
Materials and inventory services	Industrial relations expenses
Cost department services	Heat, light, and power

For analytical purposes, all manufacturing and nonmanufacturing costs should be classified as either fixed or variable. Therefore, semivariable costs must be divided into their fixed and variable components. Methods of accomplishing this division are discussed in Chapter 16.

Costs in Relation to Manufacturing Departments

For administrative purposes, a business may be divided into departments, segments, or functions. The division of a factory into departments, cost centers, or cost pools also serves as the basis for classifying and accumulating product costs and assigning responsibility for cost control. As a product passes through a department or cost center, it is charged with direct materials, direct labor, and a share of factory overhead.

To achieve the greatest degree of control, department managers should participate in the development of budgets for their respective departments or cost centers. Such budgets should clearly identify those costs about which the manager can make decisions and for which the manager accepts responsibility. At the end of a reporting period, the efficiency of a department and the manager's success in controlling costs may be measured by comparing actual costs with the budget.

Producing and Service Departments. The departments of a factory generally fall into two categories: (1) producing departments and (2) service departments. In a *producing department,* manual and machine operations, such as forming and assembling, are performed directly upon the product or its parts. The costs incurred by such departments are charged to the product. If two or more different types of machines perform operations on a product within the same department, the accuracy of product costs may be increased by dividing the department into cost centers.

In a *service department,* service is rendered for the benefit of other departments. In some instances, these services benefit other service departments as well as the producing departments. Although a service department does not directly engage in production, its costs are part of the total factory overhead and must be included in the cost of the product. Service departments which are common to many industrial concerns include maintenance, payroll, cost accounting, data processing, and food services.

Direct and Indirect Departmental Charges. In connection with materials and labor, the term "direct" refers to costs which are chargeable directly to the product. Factory overhead is considered "indirect" with regard to the product. The terms "direct" and "indirect" may be used, however, in connection with charging overhead costs to manufacturing departments and in charging expenses to the departments of nonmanufacturing organizations. If an expense is readily identifiable with the department in which it originates, it is referred to as a *direct* departmental expense. The salary of the departmental supervisor is an example of a direct expense. If an expense is shared by several departments that benefit from its incurrence, it is referred to as an *indirect* or *common* cost. Building rent and building depreciation are examples of indirect expenses which are allocated to departments.

Service department expenses are also indirect expenses for other departments. When all service department expenses have been allocated, each producing department's overhead will consist of its own direct and indirect departmental expense and the apportioned charges from service departments.

Common Costs and Joint Costs. *Common costs* are costs of facilities or services employed by two or more operations. Common costs are particularly prevalent in organizations with many departments or segments. The degree of segmentation increases the tendency of costs to be common costs. For example, the salary of the marketing vice-president is not a common cost if the segment is the entire marketing function. If the segment encompasses only the southwestern marketing region, however, the vice-president's salary is a common cost to that region.

Joint costs occur when the production of one product may be possible only if one or more other products are manufactured at the same time. The meatpacking, oil and gas, and liquor industries are excellent examples of production that involves joint costs. In such industries, joint costs can be allocated to joint products only by arbitrary procedures. Therefore, data resulting from joint cost allocation must be analyzed carefully.

Costs in Relation to an Accounting Period

Costs may be classified as capital expenditures or as revenue expenditures. A *capital expenditure* is intended to benefit future periods and is recorded as an asset. A *revenue expenditure* benefits the current period and is recorded as an expense. Ultimately, an asset will flow into the expense stream as it is consumed or when it loses its usefulness.

The distinction between capital and revenue expenditures is essential to the proper matching of costs and revenue and to the accurate measurement of periodic income. However, a precise distinction between the two classifications is not always feasible. In many cases, the initial classification depends upon management's attitude toward such expenditures and the nature of the company's operations. The amount of the expenditure and the number of detailed records required are also factors that influence the distinction between these two classifications.

The Flow of Costs in a Manufacturing Enterprise

Cost accounting neither adds new steps to the familiar accounting cycle nor discards the principles and procedures studied in financial accounting. Cost accounting consists of a system which is concerned with precise recording and measurement of cost elements as they originate and flow through the productive processes. This flow is illustrated in the following diagram:

Flow of
Manufacturing
Costs

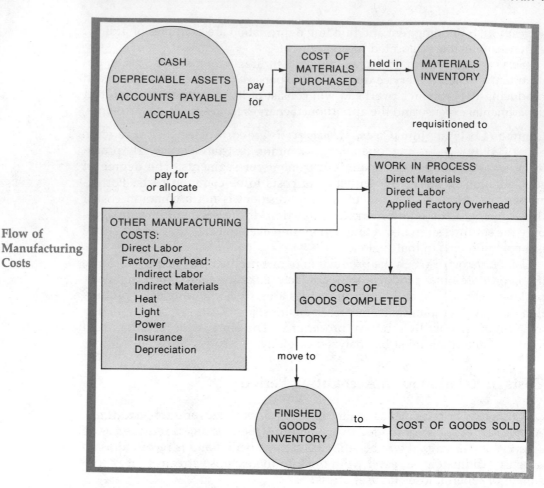

The manufacturing process and the physical arrangement of the factory are the basis for determining cost accumulation procedures. Generally, the accounts which describe manufacturing operations are: Materials, Payroll, Factory Overhead Control, Work in Process, Finished Goods, and Cost of Goods Sold. These accounts are used to recognize and measure the flow of costs in each fiscal period — from the acquisition of materials, through factory operations, to the cost of products sold. Cost accounts are expansions of general accounts and are related to general accounts, as shown in the diagram on the next page. Federal government contractors who are covered by the CASs are required to disclose the extent of this relationship and the type of cost accounting system which is being used.

Cost accounting makes extensive use of a control account-subsidiary record format when detailed information about general ledger accounts is needed. Hundreds of different materials items, for example, may be included in one materials account, and the factory overhead account may include indirect labor, supplies, rent, insurance, taxes, repairs and other factory expenses. The various subsidiary accounts are described and illustrated in later chapters.

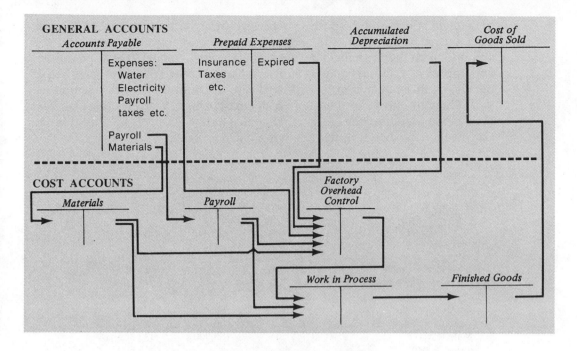

Relationship Between General Accounts and Cost Accounts

The flow of costs to ledger accounts is based on source or transaction documents, which must be checked, verified, and vouchered before they are journalized and posted. These documents are the fundamental evidence of an accounting event. Some of the typical source documents which support transactions involving the elements of manufacturing cost are identified in the following table:

Cost	Source Document
Materials	Purchase invoices, materials requisitions, materials returned slips, etc.
Labor	Time tickets or time sheets, clock cards, job tickets, etc.
Factory overhead	Vouchers prepared to set up depreciation or prepaid expenses, vendors' invoices, utility bills, time sheets, etc.

The flow of accounting information from source document to ledger accounts may be facilitated by using the journal voucher control system.[3] Whether manual, mechanical, or computerized, this system involves the use of journal vouchers on which information from the source documents is summarized and identified according to the chart of accounts. The journal voucher is the basis for the preparation of journal entries which record the transactions

---

[3]The journal voucher control system should not be confused with the voucher register, a basic journal for classifying and summarizing expenditures. The voucher register, also called an accounts payable register, could be part of the system, particularly under a manual system.

for a given period and the posting of these transactions to the ledger accounts. The journal voucher should indicate the voucher number, the date, the accounts with their numbers or codes, the amounts to be debited or credited, and approval. Columns may be added to accommodate the subsidiary ledger details, or these details may be posted directly from the source documents.

To illustrate the flow of costs in a manufacturing enterprise, assume that New Hope Manufacturing Company begins a new fiscal year with the financial position as shown in the following balance sheet:

New Hope Manufacturing Company
Balance Sheet
January 1, 19--

Assets

Current assets:

Cash		$ 183,000	
Marketable securities		76,000	
Accounts receivable (net)		313,100	
Inventories:			
Finished goods	$ 68,700		
Work in process	234,300		
Materials	135,300	438,300	
Prepaid expenses		15,800	
Total current assets			$1,026,200

Property, plant, and equipment:

Land		$ 41,500	
Buildings	$ 580,600		
Machinery and equipment	1,643,000		
	$2,223,600		
Less accumulated depreciation	1,010,700	1,212,900	
Total property, plant, and equipment			1,254,400
Total assets			$2,280,600

Liabilities

Current liabilities:

Accounts payable	$ 553,000	
Estimated income tax payable	35,700	
Due on long-term debt	20,000	
Total current liabilities		$ 608,700
Long-term debt		204,400
Total liabilities		$ 813,100

Stockholders' Equity

Common stock	$ 528,000	
Retained earnings	939,500	
Total stockholders' equity		1,467,500
Total liabilities and stockholders' equity		$2,280,600

During the month of January, New Hope completed the transactions which are summarized, recorded, and posted to the ledger accounts as follows. The revenue and expense accounts are not closed at the end of January, because such formal closing, in practice, is usually done only at year end.

Transactions	Journal Entries

(a) Materials purchased and received on account $100,000

Materials...........................	100,000	
Accounts Payable................		100,000

This is a summary entry. The materials account is an inventory control account; subsidiary records will indicate the details of the materials received.

(b) Materials requisitioned during the month:

For production......................	$ 80,000
For indirect factory use	12,000

Work in Process	80,000	
Factory Overhead Control	12,000	
Materials.......................		92,000

The indirect factory materials are kept in the inventory control account as well as in subsidiary records to control their purchase and usage.

(c) Total gross payroll $160,000
Payroll was paid to employees for the month, after deducting 7% FICA tax and 12% federal income tax withheld* 129,600

*Here and in later chapters, the various tax rates are used for illustration only. Current rates may be found in published government regulations.

Payroll............................	160,000	
Employees' Income Tax Payable ..		19,200
FICA Tax Payable		11,200
Accrued Payroll...................		129,600
Accrued Payroll...................	129,600	
Cash		129,600

The accrued payroll account is used to establish a record until the payroll department has prepared the paychecks to be distributed to the employees.

(d) The distribution of the payroll was:

Direct labor	60%
Indirect factory labor	15
Marketing salaries	18
Administrative salaries...............	7

Work in Process	96,000	
Factory Overhead Control	24,000	
Marketing Expenses Control	28,800	
Administrative Expenses Control.....	11,200	
Payroll..........................		160,000

(e) An additional 10% is recorded for the employer's payroll taxes:

FICA tax	7.0%
Federal unemployment insurance tax ..	.8
State unemployment insurance tax.....	2.2

Payroll taxes are distributed in the same proportion as the distribution of payroll. Payroll taxes related to factory activities (direct and indirect labor) are charged to the factory overhead control account.

Factory Overhead Control	12,000	
Marketing Expenses Control	2,880	
Administrative Expenses Control.....	1,120	
FICA Tax Payable		11,200
Federal Unemployment Tax Payable		1,280
State Unemployment Tax Payable .		3,520

The company is required to pay the same amount of FICA tax as the employees. In addition, the company must pay federal and state unemployment taxes, from which the employee is exempt.

(f) Factory overhead consisting of:

Depreciation	$8,500
Prepaid insurance	1,200

Factory Overhead Control	9,700	
Accumulated Depreciation		8,500
Prepaid Expenses		1,200

(g) General factory overhead costs (not itemized) $26,340
70% of these expenses were paid in cash; the balance was credited to Accounts Payable.

Factory Overhead Control	26,340	
Cash		18,438
Accounts Payable................		7,902

(h) Amount received from customers in payment of their accounts $205,000

Cash	205,000	
Accounts Receivable		205,000

(i) The following liabilities were paid:

Accounts payable	$207,000
Estimated income tax	35,700
Due on long-term debt	20,000

Accounts Payable..................	207,000	
Estimated Income Tax Payable	35,700	
Due on Long-Term Debt	20,000	
Cash		262,700

(j)   Factory overhead accumulated in the factory overhead control account was transferred to the work in process account.

| Work in Process . . . . | 84,040 | |
| Factory Overhead Control . . . . | | 84,040 |

(k)   Work completed and transferred to finished goods $320,000

| Finished Goods . . . . | 320,000 | |
| Work in Process . . . . | | 320,000 |

(l)   Sales $384,000

40% was paid in cash; the balance was charged to Accounts Receivable. The cost of goods sold was 75% of sales.

Cash	153,600	
Accounts Receivable	230,400	
Sales		384,000
Cost of Goods Sold	288,000	
Finished Goods		288,000

(m)   Provision for income tax $26,000

| Provision for Income Tax . . . . | 26,000 | |
| Estimated Income Tax Payable . . . . | | 26,000 |

Cash

1/1	183,000	(c)	129,600
(h)	205,000	(g)	18,438
(l)	153,600	(i)	262,700
	541,600		410,738
	130,862		

Marketable Securities

| 1/1 | 76,000 | | |

Accounts Receivable

1/1	313,100	(h)	205,000
(l)	230,400		
	543,500		
	338,500		

Finished Goods

1/1	68,700	(l)	288,000
(k)	320,000		
	388,700		
	100,700		

Work in Process

1/1	234,300	(k)	320,000
(b)	80,000		
(d)	96,000		
(j)	84,040		
	494,340		
	174,340		

Materials

1/1	135,300	(b)	92,000
(a)	100,000		
	235,300		
	143,300		

Prepaid Expenses

| 1/1 | 15,800 | (f) | 1,200 |
| | *14,600* | | |

Land

| 1/1 | 41,500 | |

Buildings

| 1/1 | 580,600 | |

Machinery and Equipment

| 1/1 | 1,643,000 | |

Accumulated Depreciation

		1/1	1,010,700
		(f)	8,500
			1,019,200

Accounts Payable

(i)	207,000	1/1	553,000
		(a)	100,000
		(g)	7,902
			660,902
			453,902

Accrued Payroll

| (c) | 129,600 | (c) | 129,600 |

Estimated Income Tax Payable

(i)	35,700	1/1	35,700
		(m)	26,000
			61,700
			26,000

Employees Income Tax Payable

| | | (c) | 19,200 |

FICA Tax Payable

		(c)	11,200
		(e)	11,200
			22,400

Federal Unemployment Tax Payable		
	(e)	1,280

State Unemployment Tax Payable		
	(e)	3,520

Due on Long-Term Debt			
(i)	20,000	1/1	20,000

Long-Term Debt		
	1/1	204,400

Common Stock		
	1/1	528,000

Retained Earnings		
	1/1	939,500

Sales		
	(l)	384,000

Cost of Goods Sold		
(l)	288,000	

Factory Overhead Control			
(b)	12,000	(j)	84,040
(d)	24,000		
(e)	12,000		
(f)	9,700		
(g)	26,340		
	84,040		

Payroll			
(c)	160,000	(d)	160,000

Marketing Expenses Control		
(d)	28,800	
(e)	2,880	
	31,680	

Administrative Expenses Control		
(d)	11,200	
(e)	1,120	
	12,320	

Provision for Income Tax		
(m)	26,000	

Reporting the Results of Operations

The results of operations of a manufacturing enterprise are reported in the conventional financial statements. These statements summarize the flow of costs and revenues, and show the financial position at the end of a period of operations.

Income Statement

The following statement shows the revenues and expenses of New Hope Manufacturing Company for the month of January:

New Hope Manufacturing Company Income Statement For January, 19--		
Sales		$384,000
Less cost of goods sold (Schedule 1).		288,000
Gross profit.		$ 96,000
Less commercial expenses:		
Marketing expense	$31,680	
Administrative expense	12,320	44,000
Income from operations		$ 52,000
Less provision for income tax		26,000
Net income		$ 26,000

In the income statement, the cost of goods sold is shown in one figure. Although this procedure is followed in published reports, additional information is necessary for internal uses. Therefore, a supporting schedule of the cost of goods sold is usually produced, illustrated as follows for New Hope:

New Hope Manufacturing Company
Schedule 1
Cost of Goods Sold Statement
For January, 19--

1   Direct materials:

Materials inventory, January 1, 19--.................		$135,300	
Purchases..		100,000	
Materials available for use.........................		$235,300	
Less: Indirect materials used	$ 12,000		
Materials inventory, January 31......	143,300	155,300	
Direct materials consumed			$ 80,000

2   Direct labor...   96,000

3   Factory overhead:

Indirect materials.................................	$ 12,000	
Indirect labor.....................................	24,000	
Payroll taxes.....................................	12,000	
Depreciation......................................	8,500	
Insurance	1,200	
General factory overhead	26,340	84,040

Total manufacturing cost	$260,040
4 Add work in process inventory, January 1	234,300
	$494,340
Less work in process inventory, January 31	174,340
Cost of goods manufactured..........................	$320,000
5 Add finished goods inventory, January 1	68,700
Cost of goods available for sale......................	$388,700
Less finished goods inventory, January 31	100,700
Cost of goods sold	$288,000

1 The direct materials section is comprised of the beginning materials inventory, purchases, and the ending inventory of materials, with an adjustment for the indirect materials that were added to factory overhead. This section identifies the cost of materials that became part of the finished product.

2 The direct labor section indicates the cost of labor which can be identified directly with the products manufactured.

3 Factory overhead includes all costs that are indirectly involved in the manufacturing of the product. (Note: The next chapter and the factory overhead chapters will introduce and demonstrate the use of a predetermined factory overhead rate.)

4 The total manufacturing costs incurred during the period are adjusted for the work in process inventories at the beginning and end of the period.

⑤ The cost of goods manufactured during the period is adjusted for the finished goods inventory at the beginning and end of the period.

Balance Sheet

The balance sheet complements the income statement. Neither statement alone offers a sufficiently clear picture of the status and progress of a company. The following balance sheet shows the financial position of New Hope Manufacturing Company at the end of January:

New Hope Manufacturing Company
Balance Sheet
January 31, 19--

Assets

Current assets:			
Cash		$ 130,862	
Marketable securities		76,000	
Accounts receivable (net)		338,500	
Inventories:			
Finished goods	$ 100,700		
Work in process	174,340		
Materials	143,300	418,340	
Prepaid expenses		14,600	
Total current assets			$ 978,302
Property, plant, and equipment:			
Land		$ 41,500	
Buildings	$ 580,600		
Machinery and equipment	1,643,000		
	$2,223,600		
Less accumulated depreciation	1,019,200	1,204,400	
Total property, plant, and equipment			1,245,900
Total assets			$2,224,202

Liabilities

Current liabilities			
Accounts payable		$453,902	
Estimated income tax payable		26,000	
Other current liabilities		46,400	
Total current liabilities			$ 526,302
Long-term debt			204,400
Total liabilities			$ 730,702

Stockholders' Equity

Common stock		$528,000	
Retained earnings:			
Balance, January 1	$939,500		
January net income	26,000	965,500	
Total stockholders' equity			1,493,500
Total liabilities and stockholders' equity			$2,224,202

DISCUSSION QUESTIONS

1. (a) Explain the meanings of the terms "cost" and "expense" as used for financial reporting in conformity with generally accepted accounting principles. The explanation should indicate distinguishing characteristics of the terms, their similarities and interrelationships.
   (b) Classify each of the following items as a cost, expense, or other category, with an explanation of how the classification of each item may change: (1) cost of goods sold; (2) uncollectible accounts expense; (3) depreciation expense for plant machinery; (4) organization costs; (5) spoiled goods.

2. Define a cost system.

3. Enumerate the requirements of a good information system.

4. What is the purpose of a chart of accounts?

5. What are the advantages of an electronic data processing system?

6. Enumerate the various classifications of costs.

7. (a) What is a service department? Name a few.
   (b) What are some characteristics of a service department in connection with the establishment of a product cost?

8. Expenditures may be divided into two general categories: capital expenditures and revenue expenditures.
   (a) Distinguish between these two categories of expenditures and their treatment in the accounts.
   (b) Discuss the impact on both present and future balance sheets and income statements of improperly distinguishing between capital and revenue expenditures.
   (c) What criteria do firms generally use in establishing a policy for classifying expenditures under these two general categories?

9. Enumerate the five parts of the cost of goods sold section of the income statement.

10. Discuss the complementary relationship between the balance sheet and the income statement.

11. A corporation's annual financial statements and reports were criticized because it was claimed that the income statement does not by any means give a clear picture of annual earning power, and the balance sheet does not disclose the true value of the plant assets. Considering the criticism made, offer an explanation of the nature and purpose of the income statement and of the balance sheet, together with comments on their limitations.

EXERCISES

1. *Journal entries for the cost accounting cycle.* The following transactions pertain to manufacturing operations:
   (a) *Materials were issued as follows: direct, $24,500; indirect, $4,500.*
   (b) *A payroll of $44,000 was recorded. Income tax withheld, $7,000; FICA tax rate, 7%.*
   (c) *The payroll consisted of $30,000 direct labor, $6,000 indirect factory labor, and $8,000 sales salaries. State unemployment insurance is 5.4%, and federal is .8%. The employer's FICA tax rate was 7%.*
   (d) *Miscellaneous factory expenses incurred will require a cash expenditure of $7,500. (Do not journalize the cash payment.)*
   (e) *Factory overhead of $15,000 was charged to production.*
   (f) *Cost of production completed during the period totaled $60,000.*
   (g) *Materials purchased totaled $50,000.*

(h) Goods costing $20,000 were shipped to customers at a sales price of $26,000.

Required: *Prepare journal entries for the above transactions.*

2. *Cost of goods manufactured statement.* Mason Company manufactures special machines made to customer specifications. The following information was available at the beginning of October:

Materials inventory	$16,200
Work in process inventory.	3,600

During October, direct materials costing $20,000 were purchased, direct labor cost totaled $16,500, and factory overhead was $8,580.

October 31 inventories were:

Materials inventory	$17,000
Work in process inventory.	8,120

Required: *Prepare a cost of goods manufactured statement for October, 19A.*

(AICPA adapted)

3. *Manufacturing costs; cost of goods manufactured; cost of goods sold.* The December 31, 19B trial balance of Menges Company showed:

Sales.	$14,000,500	Sales returns and	
Purchases (net)	2,400,000	allowances.	$ 25,200
Transportation in	32,000	Factory overhead.	1,885,600
Direct labor	3,204,000	Advertising expense	155,000
Sales salaries	200,000	Delivery expense	65,000

Inventories:	December 31, 19B	December 31, 19A
Finished goods.	$467,400	$620,000
Work in process	136,800	129,800
Materials	196,000	176,000

Required: *Determine the (1) total manufacturing cost, the (2) cost of goods manufactured, and the (3) cost of goods sold.* *(CGAA adapted)*

4. *Cost of goods sold statement; income statement.* The accounting department of Michaelson Company provided the following data for May: sales, $72,000; marketing expenses, $3,600; administrative expenses, $720; other expenses, $360; purchases, $36,000; factory overhead, $10,000; direct labor, $15,000.

Inventories:	Beginning	Ending
Finished goods.	$7,000	$10,200
Work in process	8,000	15,000
Materials	8,000	8,500

Required: *Prepare the (1) cost of goods sold statement, and the (2) income statement.*

(CGAA adapted)

5. *Cost of goods sold statement.* The following data are provided by the controller of Metaxen Corporation:

Cash.	$240,000
Accounts receivable.	348,000

Inventories:

	January 1	December 31
Finished goods...........................	$44,200	$66,000
Work in process	29,800	38,800
Materials	88,000	64,000

Materials purchased	$	366,000
Sales discount		8,000
Factory overhead (excluding depreciation)		468,400
Marketing and administrative expenses (excluding depreciation).............		344,200
Depreciation (90% manufacturing, 10% marketing and adminis- trative expenses)		116,000
Sales..		1,844,000
Direct labor		523,600
Freight on materials purchased...		6,600
Rental income...		64,000
Interest on bonds payable		16,000

Required: *Prepare a cost of goods sold statement.*   *(CGAA adapted)*

6. **Fixed and variable costs.** *In 19A, the Mercaldo Company had sales of $19,950,000, with $11,571,000 variable and $7,623,000 fixed costs. 19B sales are expected to decrease 15% and the cost relationship is expected to remain constant (the fixed costs will not change).*

Required: *Determine Mercaldo Company's expected operating income or loss for 19B.*

$ Loss 500,850

PROBLEMS

2-1. **Journal entries for the cost accounting cycle.** Selected transactions of the Young Company for February are as follows:
  (a) Materials requisitioned: $18,500 for production and $2,800 for indirect use.
  (b) Work completed and transferred to finished goods amounted to $51,800.
  (c) Materials purchased and received, $32,000.
  (d) The payroll, after deducting 7% FICA tax, 18% federal income tax, and 5% state income tax, was $35,000. The wages due the employees were paid.
  (e) Of the total payroll, 55% was direct labor, 18% indirect factory labor, 17% marketing salaries, and 10% administrative salaries.
  (f) An additional 13.2% is entered for employer's payroll taxes, representing 7% FICA tax, .8% federal unemployment tax, and 5.4% state unemployment tax. Payroll taxes related to factory production are charged to the factory overhead control account.
  (g) Factory overhead of $22,000 was charged to production.
  (h) Other factory overhead consisted of $9,450 depreciation on the factory building and equipment, $600 expired insurance, and $1,250 other unpaid bills.
  (i) Sales on account totaled $92,120, with a markup of 40% on the cost of goods sold.
  (j) Cash collections from accounts receivable totaled $76,000.

Required: Prepare journal entries for these transactions.

2-2. Cost of goods manufactured statement. The following data are from the accounts of Millville Company:

Inventories:	July 1, 19A	June 30, 19B
Finished goods........................	$20,000	$28,000
Work in process......................	60,000	36,000
Materials	40,000	48,000

Sales discounts...	$ 8,000
Purchase discounts.......................................	3,200
Sales..	1,800,000
Purchase returns and allowances	20,000
Depreciation—factory machinery........................	160,000
Factory insurance..	50,000
Freight out	8,000
Other factory expenses	16,000
Bond interest expense	50,000
Sales salaries...	100,000
Freight in...	12,000
Direct factory labor.....................................	800,000
Materials purchases	400,000
Advertising expense.....................................	12,000

Required: Prepare a cost of goods manufactured statement for the year ended June 30, 19B.   (CGAA adapted)

2-3. Cost of goods sold statement. The following information has been taken from the records of Maxwell Company: CGS.- 355,700

Inventories:	January 1	December 31
Finished goods	$ 5,000	$ 7,000
Work in process	15,000	9,000
Materials.................................	10,000	12,000

Materials purchases......................................	$100,000
Direct labor	200,000
Freight in	3,000
Sales salaries and expenses	25,000
Other factory expenses..................................	4,000
Freight out..	2,000
Factory insurance.......................................	12,500
Depreciation–machinery	40,000
Purchase returns and allowances........................	5,000
Sales	350,000
Purchase discounts	800
Sales discounts..	2,000

Required: Prepare a cost of goods sold statement for the year.   (CGAA adapted)

2-4. Manufacturing costs. The payroll records of the Maher Company show payments for labor of $400,000, of which $80,000 is indirect labor. Materials requisitions show $300,000 for materials used, of which $280,000 represents direct materials. Other manufacturing expenses total $124,000. Finished goods on hand at the end of the period are stated at cost, $176,000, of which $40,000 is direct materials cost. Factory overhead is allocated on the basis of direct labor cost.

Required: Determine the amount of direct labor and the amount of factory overhead in Finished Goods.

2-5. Profit planning via income statement. The controller of Moffatt Products, Inc. presented the following income statement for the year ended June 30, 19A, to the board of directors:

Sales...		$12,000,000
Cost of goods sold:		
Direct materials............................	$3,800,000	
Direct labor................................	2,900,000	
Factory overhead...........................	2,450,000	9,150,000
Gross profit....................................		$ 2,850,000
Commercial expenses:		
Marketing expenses	$1,350,000	
Administrative expenses....................	1,000,000	2,350,000
Operating income		$ 500,000

The board discussed the ratio of operating income to sales and decided that for the year ending June 30, 19B, an increase of at least 25% of the present profit is desirable. An expected sales volume increase of 20% will cause all costs except marketing and administrative expenses to increase accordingly. In addition to this increase resulting from the volume change, costs are expected to increase as follows: direct materials, 8%; direct labor, 10%; factory overhead, 3%; marketing expenses, 4%; administrative expenses, 2%. The 3% increase in factory overhead applies to the variable factory overhead only. Fixed factory overhead is considered to remain at the present level of $1,250,000. Ignore income tax.

Required: Prepare a forecast income statement for the year ending June 30, 19B, incorporating all cost increases as well as management's goal for a higher operating income.

2-6. Income statement relationships. The following information is available for three companies at the end of their fiscal years:

Company A:	Finished goods, January 1................................	$ 600,000	
	Cost of goods manufactured.............................	3,800,000	
	Sales	4,000,000	
	Gross profit on sales...................................	20%	
	Finished goods inventory, December 31	?	1,200,00
Company B:	Freight in..	$ 20,000	
	Purchases returns and allowances........................	80,000	
	Marketing expenses.....................................	200,000	
	Finished goods, December 31.............................	90,000	
	Cost of goods sold.....................................	1,400,000	1,490,000
	Cost of goods available for sale	?	
Company C:	Gross profit..	$ 96,000	
	Cost of goods manufactured.............................	340,000	
	Finished goods, January 1..............................	45,000	
	Finished goods, December 31............................	52,000	
	Work in process, January 1	28,000	
	Work in process, December 31...........................	38,000	429,000
	Sales	?	

Required: Determine the amounts indicated by the question marks for each company.

(AICPA adapted)

Part Two
Cost Accumulation
Procedures

Chapter 3
The Factory Ledger;
Job Order Costing

The previous chapter presented an overall view of the flow of costs and expenses, generally known as the manufacturing cost accounting cycle for cost determination. This chapter discusses two refinements in accounting for the flow of costs: (1) the factory ledger, which is used when the general office and the factory are far removed from each other, yet cost accumulation and cost reporting must proceed speedily and promptly; and (2) job order costing, which is used to determine costs and profit for specific jobs or orders.

The Factory Ledger

In the previous chapter, the illustration of the flow of costs through the accounts of New Hope Manufacturing Company was based on the assumption that the factory and general offices were in one location, and that other operating functions were not physically separated. However, a company's administrative offices may be far removed from factory sites, or the company' may operate several factories or offices in different parts of the country. In these situations, some of the accounting functions may be handled at the factory.

The amount of accounting performed at the factory depends upon the organization and operation of the business. If the manufacturing process requires many accounts, the appropriate accounts may be maintained at the factory. If the factory sells products, prepares invoices, and renders statements, the factory may also account for sales and collections. If payrolls are met locally, the factory may record payroll summaries and maintain a bank account for the payroll. The factory may account for income taxes withheld from employees and for payroll taxes. Some factories may account for equipment and accumulated depreciation or for equipment only, while others may not account for any of the plant assets.

Transactions recorded at the factory should be posted to a factory ledger, which is a subsidiary ledger to the general office ledger. The factory ledger includes a control account, General Ledger, which shows the equity of the general office in the factory. A reciprocal control account, Factory Ledger, which shows the investment in the factory, is maintained in the accounting records of the general office. When General Ledger is debited in the factory books, for example, Factory Ledger is credited in the general office books.

To illustrate the use of a factory ledger, selected transactions and entries for Farrington Manufacturing Company are on pages 40-41 and 42-43. These entries are based on assumptions that (1) the materials account is maintained at the factory, while all invoices are vouchered and paid from the general office; (2) the payroll, with deductions, is prepared at the factory, while paychecks and tax liabilities are the treasurer's responsibility at the general office; (3) plant asset accounts are maintained at the general office; and (4) the finished goods account is maintained at the factory, while the general office records the cost of goods sold. Although subsidiary records are shown only for factory overhead, similar records may be maintained for other accounts, as described later in the chapter.

Cost Systems and Cost Accumulation Procedures

Costs which are allocated to units of production may be actual costs or standard costs. In an *actual* or *historical* cost system, costs are collected as they occur, but the presentation of results is delayed until manufacturing operations have been performed or services rendered. In a *standard* cost system, products, operations, and processes are costed using standards for both quantities and dollar amounts. These standards are predetermined in advance of production. Actual costs are also recorded, and variances or differences between actual costs and standard costs are collected in separate accounts.

The actual cost system and the standard cost system may be used with either job order or process cost accumulation procedures. In *job order costing*, costs are accumulated by job or specific order. This method presupposes the possibility of physically identifying the jobs produced and of charging each job with its own cost. Job order costing is applicable to job order work in factories, workshops, and repair shops, as well as to work by builders, construction engineers, and printers.

A variation of the job order cost method is that of costing orders by lots. A lot is the quantity of product which can conveniently and economically be produced and costed. In the shoe manufacturing industry, for example, a contract is typically divided into lots which consist of 100 to 250 pairs of one size and style of shoe. The costs are then accumulated for each lot.

When a job produces a specific quantity for inventory, job order costing permits the computation of a unit cost for inventory costing purposes. When jobs are performed on the basis of customer specifications, job order costing permits the computation of a profit or loss on each order. Since costs are revealed as an order goes through production, these costs may be compared with estimates which were made when an order was taken. Job order costing thereby provides opportunities for controlling costs.

Process costing, which is discussed in Chapters 4, 5, and 6, accumulates costs by production process or by department. This method is used when units are not separately distinguishable from one another during one or more manufacturing processes. Because of the nature of the output, a unit cost must be computed for each process. The following conditions may also exist:

1. The product of one process becomes the material of the next process.
2. Different products, or even by-products, are produced by the same process.

The process cost method is applicable to industries such as flour mills, breweries, chemical plants, and textile factories.

Many companies use both the job order and the process cost methods. For example, a company manufacturing a railway car built according to the customer's specifications uses job order costing to collect the cost per railway car. However, the multiple small metal stampings required are manufactured in a department which uses fast and repetitive stamping machines. The cost of these stampings is accumulated by the process cost method.

Although the textbook discussion of job order and process costing emphasizes manufacturing activity, the job order and process costing methods can also be used by service organizations. For example, an automobile repair shop uses job order costing to accumulate the costs associated with work performed on each automobile. Process costing may be used by an airline to accumulate costs per passenger mile, or by a hospital to accumulate costs per patient day.

When the job order or process cost methods are used, costs must be accumulated for control purposes according to the unit in which the product cost is to be stated. For example, coal is measured by the ton, chemicals by the gallon, and lumber by board feet. Products such as machines, automobiles, and shoes are measured either by the individual unit or by a multiple thereof, such as a dozen or a gross. The unit selected must conform to the type of product and the manufacturing processes, and it should not be too large or too small. If the unit is too large, the averaging of costs may cause significant cost trends to pass unnoticed. If the unit is too small, unnecessarily detailed and expensive clerical work may be required.

Transactions

Materials purchased on account......................... $40,000

Materials requisitioned:
  For production.. $33,000
  For indirect materials................................ 2,000

Payroll prepared at the factory and forwarded to the general office:
  Direct labor $32,000
  Indirect labor 8,000
Deductions:
  12% income tax, 7% FICA tax, and $280 union dues

Factory payroll paid.

Factory payroll allocated to work in process and factory overhead.

Factory payroll tax liability:
  FICA tax.. 7.0%
  Federal unemployment tax............................. .8
  State unemployment tax............................... 2.2

Copies of vouchers showing $18,000 of factory expenses incurred are sent to the factory.

Transfer vouchers sent to the factory show:
  Depreciation of equipment............................ $2,100
  Prepaid factory insurance expired 780
  Accrued plant property taxes......................... 1,250

Factory overhead transferred to work in process account.

General Office			Factory Office			
	Dr.	Cr.		Subsidiary Record	Dr.	Cr.
Factory Ledger	40,000		Materials		40,000	
Accounts Payable		40,000	General Ledger......			40,000
No entry			Work in Process......		33,000	
			Factory Overhead Control		2,000	
			Indirect Materials ..	2,000		
			Materials			35,000
Factory Ledger.............	40,000		Payroll		40,000	
Employees Income Tax Payable		4,800	General Ledger......			40,000
FICA Tax Payable		2,800				
Union Dues Payable		280				
Accrued Payroll		32,120				
Accrued Payroll	32,120		No entry			
Cash....................		32,120				
No entry			Work in Process.......		32,000	
			Factory Overhead Control		8,000	
			Indirect Labor	8,000		
			Payroll			40,000
Factory Ledger.............	4,000		Factory Overhead Control		4,000	
FICA Tax Payable		2,800	Payroll Taxes	4,000		
Federal Unemployment Tax Payable		320	General Ledger......			4,000
State Unemployment Tax Payable		880				
Factory Ledger.............	18,000		Factory Overhead Control		18,000	
Accounts Payable		18,000	Miscellaneous Factory Expenses .	18,000		
			General Ledger......			18,000
Factory Ledger.............	4,130		Factory Overhead Control		4,130	
Accumulated Depreciation .		2,100	Depreciation	2,100		
Prepaid Insurance		780	Insurance Expense	780		
Accrued Property Taxes ...		1,250	Property Tax	1,250		
			General Ledger......			4,130
No entry			Work in Process.......		36,130	
			Factory Overhead Control			36,130

(continued)

Transactions	
Cost of completed production transferred to storage:	
Direct materials......................................	$35,000
Direct labor	30,000
Factory overhead	27,000

Sales of finished goods were $80,000, of which 50% was collected. The cost of goods sold was 75% of the sales price.

Job Order Costing

In job order costing, the cost of each order produced for a given customer or the cost of each lot to be placed in stock is recorded on a *job order cost sheet*, sometimes called simply a *cost sheet*. The cost sheets are subsidiary records which are controlled by the work in process account. Although several jobs or orders may be going through a factory at the same time, each cost sheet is designed to collect the cost of materials, labor, and factory overhead charged to a specific job. Each cost sheet is assigned a job number, which is placed on each materials requisition and labor time ticket used in connection with a job. These forms for materials and labor are totaled daily or weekly by job number, for summary journal entries, and the details are entered on the cost sheets. The factory overhead entered on the cost sheets is computed on the basis of an estimate rather than actual costs incurred. As discussed later in the chapter, the amount computed is referred to as *applied factory overhead*.

Cost sheets differ in form, content, and arrangement in each business. An example is shown on page 44. The upper section of each cost sheet provides space for the job number, the name of the customer, a description of the items to be produced, the quantity, the date started, and the date completed. The lower section summarizes the production costs, the marketing and administrative expenses, and the profit for the job when it is completed on the basis of customer specifications. In the cost sheet for a departmentalized operation, the materials, labor, and factory overhead applied are shown for each department or cost center.

In the remainder of the chapter, job order cost accumulation procedures are described and illustrated for Rayburn Company. The flow of costs for Rayburn Company is summarized in the following diagram:

General Office		Factory Office	
No entry		Finished Goods	92,000
		Work in Process		92,000
Accounts Receivable	80,000	General Ledger	60,000
Sales		80,000	Finished Goods		60,000
Cash	40,000		
Accounts Receivable		40,000		
Cost of Goods Sold	60,000		
Factory Ledger		60,000		

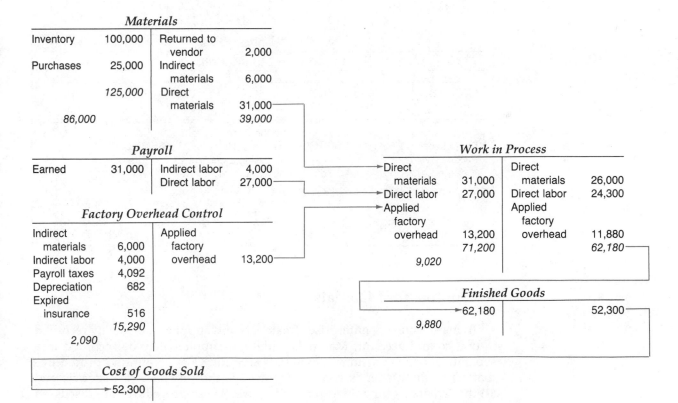

Materials

Inventory	100,000	Returned to vendor	2,000
Purchases	25,000	Indirect materials	6,000
	125,000	Direct materials	31,000
86,000			39,000

Payroll

Earned	31,000	Indirect labor	4,000
		Direct labor	27,000

Factory Overhead Control

Indirect materials	6,000	Applied factory overhead	13,200
Indirect labor	4,000		
Payroll taxes	4,092		
Depreciation	682		
Expired insurance	516		
	15,290		
2,090			

Work in Process

Direct materials	31,000	Direct materials	26,000
Direct labor	27,000	Direct labor	24,300
Applied factory overhead	13,200	Applied factory overhead	11,880
	71,200		62,180
9,020			

Finished Goods

	62,180		52,300
9,880			

Cost of Goods Sold

52,300	

Flow of Costs

Cost Sheet for a Nondepartmentalized Plant

RAYBURN COMPANY	Job Order No.	**5574**

FOR: Lawrenceville Construction Company — DATE ORDERED: 9/10

PRODUCT: #14 Maple Drain Boards — DATE STARTED: 9/14

SPECIFICATION: 12' × 20" × 1" Clear Finishes — DATE WANTED: 9/22

QUANTITY: 100 — DATE COMPLETED: 9/18

DIRECT MATERIALS

DATE	REQ. NO.	AMOUNT	TOTAL
9/14	516	$1,420.00	
9/17	531	780.00	
9/18	544	310.00	
			$2,510.00

DIRECT LABOR

DATE	HOURS	COST	
9/14	40	$ 320.00	
9/15	32	256.00	
9/16	36	288.00	
9/17	40	320.00	
9/18	48	384.00	
	196		$1,568.00

FACTORY OVERHEAD APPLIED

DATE	RATE OF APPLICATION	COST	
9/18	$6 per direct labor hour	$1,176.00	$1,176.00

Direct Materials	$2,510.00	Selling Price	$7,860.00
Direct Labor	1,568.00	Factory Cost $5,254.00	
Factory Overhead		Marketing Expenses ... 776.00	
Applied.............	1,176.00	Admin. Expenses...... 420.00	
Total Factory Cost	$5,254.00	Cost to Make	
		and Sell	6,450.00
		Profit...........................	$1,410.00

Accounting for Materials

In manufacturing enterprises, materials and supplies are usually recorded in one control account, Materials, although supplies may be recorded in a separate supplies or indirect materials account. Cost accounting procedures that affect the materials account involve (1) the purchase of materials and (2) the issuance of materials for factory use. These procedures are discussed in greater detail in Chapters 10 and 11.

Recording the Purchase and Receipt of Materials. Cost accounting techniques for the purchase of materials are similar to those studied in general accounting. As materials are received, the account debited is Materials or Materials Inventory, rather than Purchases, as shown in the following entry:

Materials...	25,000	
Accounts Payable.......................................		25,000

The quantity received, unit cost, and amount of each purchase is also entered on a materials ledger card which is maintained for each materials item. Materials ledger cards function as a subsidiary ledger and provide a perpetual inventory record of each item.

Recording the Issuance of Materials. When a job is started, the necessary materials are issued to the factory on the basis of materials requisitions, which are prepared by production scheduling clerks or other employees. The requisition bears the job order number and specifies the type and quantity of materials required. A copy of the requisition is sent to the storekeeper, who assembles the materials called for on the requisition. The quantity, unit cost, and the total cost of each item is entered on the requisition and posted to the materials ledger cards.

The flow of direct materials from storeroom to factory is recorded as a transfer of materials from the materials account to the work in process account. Materials requisitions are summarized and recorded as follows:

Work in Process	31,000	
Materials...		31,000

A copy of each requisition is also sent to the cost department. In this department, the requisitions are totaled, sorted by job numbers, and entered in the materials section of the cost sheet for the jobs indicated. The quantity and cost of materials used in each job are thereby accumulated.

When materials originally requisitioned for a job are not used, a returned materials report is prepared and the materials are returned to the storeroom. The return requires a journal entry in which Materials is debited and Work in Process is credited. Entries on the materials ledger card and the job order cost sheet are also required.

Materials requisitions are also used to secure indirect materials or supplies from the storeroom. Supplies that will not be used by the factory may be charged to marketing or administrative expense accounts. Supplies to be used by the factory are charged to the factory overhead control account when the supplies are issued, as shown in the following entry:

	Subsidiary Record	Dr.	Cr.
Factory Overhead Control		6,000	
Indirect Materials...........................	6,000		
Materials....................................			6,000

For control purposes, the requisitions for factory supplies must also be recorded in a subsidiary ledger for overhead, which may be a *factory overhead analysis sheet*.

The accounting entries required when materials are purchased and used are illustrated in the following two-stage diagram. In Stage 1, an invoice for

STAGE 1 MATERIALS PURCHASED	STAGE 2 MATERIALS USED

Journal Entry:
  Materials 500
    Accounts Payable 500
	Journal Entries:
	  Work in Process 400
	    Materials......................... 400
	
	  Factory Overhead Control
	  (Indirect Materials) 50
	    Materials 50

Stage 1 — General Ledger:

Materials

500	

Stage 1 — Subsidiary Record:

Materials Ledger Card		
Received	Issued	Balance
500		500

Stage 2 — General Ledger:

Materials

500	400
	50

Work in Process

400	

Factory Overhead Control

50	

Stage 2 — Subsidiary Records:

Materials Ledger Card		
Received	Issued	Balance
500		500
	400	100
	50	50

Job Order Cost Sheet			
Direct Materials Section			
Date	Dept.	Req. No.	Cost
4/25	2	495	400

Factory Overhead Analysis Sheet			
Date			Indirect Materials
4/26			50

Entries Required For Materials Purchased And Used

materials purchased in the amount of $500 is recorded. A materials ledger card is required for each kind of material. In Stage 2, a materials requisition calls for $400 of materials for use on one order. Another requisition for $50 of indirect materials is also recorded.

Accounting for Labor

The accounting procedures for labor may be divided into two distinct phases:

1. Collection of payroll data, computation of earnings, calculation of payroll taxes, and payment of wages.
2. Distribution and allocation of labor costs to jobs, departments, and other cost classifications.

In most factories, time clocks register workers' hours on individual clock cards which the workers punch as they enter and leave the plant. These clock cards are used by the timekeeper for maintaining a record of the days or hours worked by each employee. The clock cards are also the basis for computing the gross earnings of employees who are paid hourly wages.

To compute the direct and indirect labor cost, the time spent on each job during a day must be recorded on labor time tickets for each worker. The time tickets for the various jobs are sorted, priced, and summarized, and the time ticket hours should be reconciled with the clock card hours. These procedures are discussed in more detail in Chapters 12 and 13.

At regular intervals, usually daily or weekly, the labor time and labor cost for each job are entered on the job order cost sheets. For each payroll period — weekly, every two weeks, or monthly — the summary of employees' earnings and the liability for payment is journalized and posted to the general ledger.

To illustrate the recording of labor costs, Rayburn Company incurred $13,800 of labor costs on the 15th of the month and $17,200 of labor costs on the 31st. Of the $31,000 total labor cost incurred during the month, $27,000 was direct labor and $4,000 was indirect labor. Deducted from gross earnings is 15% for employees income tax and 7% for FICA tax. The gross earnings might also be subject to deductions for pension payments, personal insurance policies, savings bonds, union dues, and United Fund contributions. The company incurs additional payroll costs for FICA tax (7%), federal unemployment tax (.8%), and state unemployment tax (5.4%). Entries to record and distribute these payroll costs are shown in the two-stage diagram on the next page.

The payroll account is a clearing account in which labor costs are accumulated, pending their distribution to the proper cost accounts. This distribution is usually recorded on a daily or weekly basis, so that labor costs remain current on the job order cost sheets and are available to operating management. The payroll account and employer payroll taxes account may also include amounts applicable to marketing and administrative personnel. Such costs would be charged to marketing and administrative expense accounts.

STAGE 1	STAGE 2
PAYROLL COMPUTED AND PAID	**PAYROLL COSTS DISTRIBUTED**

STAGE 1 — PAYROLL COMPUTED AND PAID

Journal Entries:

<u>15th</u>

Payroll	13,800	
Employees Income Tax		
Payable		2,070
FICA Tax Payable		966
Accrued Payroll		10,764

Accrued Payroll	10,764	
Cash		10,764

<u>31st</u>

Payroll	17,200	
Employees Income Tax		
Payable		2,580
FICA Tax Payable		1,204
Accrued Payroll		13,416

Accrued Payroll	13,416	
Cash		13,416

Factory Overhead Control		
(Payroll Taxes)	4,092	
FICA Tax Payable		2,170
State Unemployment Tax		
Payable		1,674
Federal Unemployment		
Tax Payable		248

General Ledger:

Factory Overhead Control

4,092	

Subsidiary Records:
  Employees' earnings records
  Employees tax records
  and other deduction records

STAGE 2 — PAYROLL COSTS DISTRIBUTED

Journal Entry:

<u>31st</u>

Work in Process	27,000	
Factory Overhead Control		
(Indirect Labor)	4,000	
Payroll		31,000

General Ledger:

Work In Process

27,000	

Factory Overhead Control

4,092	
4,000	

Subsidiary Records:

Job Order Cost Sheets[1]		
Direct Labor Section		
Date	Hours	Amount
1–31	5,000	$27,000

Factory Overhead Analysis Sheet[2]			
Date	Payroll Taxes	Indirect Labor	Indirect Materials
1/31	4,092	4,000	

[1]There is a separate cost sheet for every job. Entries in the direct labor section of all jobs worked on during the period are made daily and total $27,000, as shown by the work in process account.
[2]There is an analysis sheet for each department or cost center.

Entries Required in Recording Labor Cost

Accounting for Factory Overhead

If a planing mill contracts to make fifty cabinet assemblies for an apartment complex, the materials used and the labor expended can be charged to the cabinets on the basis of requisitions and time tickets. The amount of factory overhead which should be charged to the cabinets is more difficult to determine. Some of the overhead costs, such as rent or depreciation of the factory building, insurance, property taxes, and the plant manager's salary, are fixed regardless of the amount of production. Other expenses, such as power and lubricating oil, vary with the quantity of goods manufactured. To overcome these difficulties, the actual overhead may be charged to jobs by using a rate based on direct labor hours, direct labor cost, machine hours, or some other factor which exhibits a relationship to factory overhead.

Many of the overhead costs may not be known until the end of a fiscal period, long after a job has been completed. Therefore, actual overhead cannot be charged to jobs on a timely basis. To enhance cost control in such cases, it is common to use a *predetermined overhead rate*, which is based on an estimate of factory overhead. For example, assume that an accountant for Rayburn Company determines that a relationship exists between direct labor hours and factory overhead. The accountant estimates that direct labor hours will total 75,000 and factory overhead will total $165,000 for the year. These estimates lead to the assumption that for each hour of direct labor, factory overhead of $2.20 ($165,000 ÷ 75,000 hours) is incurred. The amount of factory overhead for any job, called *applied factory overhead*, is determined by multiplying the direct labor hours during a period by the factory overhead rate.

The applied factory overhead entered on the job order cost sheet for each job is the basis for the following entry:

Work in Process	13,200	
Applied Factory Overhead (6,000 direct labor hours × $2.20) . . .		13,200

At the end of the accounting period, the applied factory overhead account is closed to the factory overhead control account by the following entry:

Applied Factory Overhead	13,200	
Factory Overhead Control		13,200

An applied factory overhead account is used because it keeps applied overhead and actual overhead costs in separate accounts. Some companies do not use the applied factory overhead account, but credit Factory Overhead Control when Work in Process is debited. This procedure eliminates the need to transfer applied overhead to Factory Overhead Control.

Some actual overhead costs, such as indirect materials, indirect labor, and payroll taxes, are charged to Factory Overhead Control as they are incurred. Other overhead costs, such as depreciation and expired insurance, are charged to Factory Overhead Control when adjusting entries are recorded. For example, factory depreciation and expired insurance are recorded at the end of the accounting period by the following entries:

	Subsidiary Record	Dr.	Cr.
Factory Overhead Control		682	
Depreciation	682		
Accumulated Depreciation — Machinery			682

	Subsidiary Record	Dr.	Cr.
Factory Overhead Control		516	
Insurance Expense	516		
Prepaid Insurance			516

These entries are posted to the factory overhead control account shown in the following diagram. This account shows on the debit side the $6,000 of indirect materials, the $4,000 of indirect labor, the $4,092 of payroll taxes on

STAGE 1 ACTUAL FACTORY OVERHEAD INCURRED	STAGE 2 ESTIMATED FACTORY OVERHEAD APPLIED

STAGE 1 — ACTUAL FACTORY OVERHEAD INCURRED

General Ledger:

Factory Overhead Control

6,000	13,200
4,000	
4,092	
682	
516	
2,090 15,290	

Materials

	Indirect materials 6,000

Payroll

	Indirect labor 4,000

Payroll Taxes Payable

	Taxes on factory payroll 4,092

Accumulated Depreciation — Machinery

	682

Prepaid Insurance

	516

Subsidiary Record:

Factory Overhead Analysis Sheet

Date	Depr.	Payroll Taxes	Insurance	Indirect Labor	Indirect Materials
1/31	682	4,092	516	4,000	6,000

STAGE 2 — ESTIMATED FACTORY OVERHEAD APPLIED

General Ledger:

Work in Process

13,200	

Applied Factory Overhead

13,200	13,200

Subsidiary Record:

Job Order Cost Sheets				
Factory Overhead Section				
Job 1	Job 2	Job 3	Job 4	Job 5
$2,420	$2,640	$2,200	$3,300	$2,640

NOTE: The application of overhead to the five jobs is merely for the purpose of illustrating a typical factory overhead section as it appears on job cost sheets.

Flow of Factory Overhead Through Accounting Records

factory labor, the $682 of depreciation, and the $516 of expired insurance. The $13,200 on the credit side is the applied factory overhead.

The $2,090 debit balance in the factory overhead control account indicates that actual expenses exceeded the overhead applied to the job orders. Stated differently, overhead was underapplied by $2,090. The cost control significance and disposition of such a balance, either overapplied or underapplied, are discussed in Chapter 7. Typically, a relatively small balance is charged to the cost of goods sold.

Accounting for Jobs Completed and Products Sold

During a month's operations, the amounts charged to the work in process account represent the total cost of materials placed in process, labor used, and factory overhead applied. As jobs are completed, cost sheets are moved from the in-process category to a finished work file. Completion of a job results in a debit to Finished Goods and a credit to Work in Process, and quantity and cost are recorded on finished goods ledger cards, which are subsidiary records for the finished goods account.

The journal entry to record all the work completed is:

Finished Goods	62,180	
Work in Process		62,180

When finished goods are delivered or shipped to customers, sales invoices are prepared, and the sales and the cost of goods sold are recorded as follows:

Accounts Receivable	70,000	
Sales		70,000
Cost of Goods Sold	52,300	
Finished Goods		52,300

If a job is delivered directly to a customer, the finished goods account may be bypassed. In such a case, Cost of Goods Sold is debited when the work in process account is credited.

DISCUSSION QUESTIONS

1. If a factory is located in one city or state and the general office in another, it is desirable to separate a portion of the records.
   (a) Name four control accounts and the subsidiary ledgers that would likely be kept at the factory.
   (b) How are ledgers kept in balance between the factory and the general office?
   (c) What entry would be made on the factory books when goods are shipped directly to a customer? Assume that inventory records are maintained at the factory.
   (d) What entry would be made on the home office books for transaction (c)?
   (e) A factory sends goods it has produced to another branch factory. What entry would be made on the producing factory's books?

2. (a) When a portion of the accounting is done at the factory and a factory ledger is maintained, what accounts are most likely to be in the factory ledger?

   (b) What is the principal reason for maintaining accounts at the factory?

3. The statement has often been made that an actual product cost does not exist in the sense of absolute authenticity and verifiability. Why?

4. What is the primary objective in job order costing?

5. What is the rationale supporting the use of process costing instead of job order costing for product costing purposes? (AICPA adapted)

6. What is a cost sheet?

7. What is the function of the work in process account in job order costing?

8. How is control over prime costs achieved in job order costing?

9. Distinguish between actual and applied factory overhead.

EXERCISES

1. *Factory ledger entries.* Hewitt Company uses a general ledger and a factory ledger. Inventory accounts, a payroll clearing account for factory employees, and Factory Overhead Control are kept at the factory; plant asset accounts and Accounts Payable are part of the general office books. The following transactions took place:

Mar. 2. Purchased materials for the factory, $20,000. Terms, n/30.
4. Requisitions of $4,000 of direct materials and $2,000 of indirect materials were filled from the stockroom.
8. Factory payroll of $2,000 ($1,880 direct labor; $120 indirect labor) for the week was made up at the home office; $1,680 in cash was sent to the factory. FICA tax was $140 and income tax was $180.
14. Depreciation of $200 for factory equipment was recorded.
14. A job was completed in the factory, with $960 direct labor, $450 of materials, and $640 of factory overhead being previously charged to the job.
15. Miscellaneous factory overhead of $800 was paid by the home office and transferred to the factory.
16. The job completed on the 14th was shipped to Brill Bros. on instructions from the home office. The customer was billed for $2,800.

Required: Prepare journal entries on the factory books and the general office books.

2. *Factory ledger entries.* Electronics Incorporated maintains its factory in Enid, Oklahoma, but its main office is in Stillwater. On September 1, the factory trial balance appeared as follows:

Finished Goods	23,000	
Work in Process.	68,250	
Materials	19,500	
Factory Overhead Control	540,000	
Factory Machinery.	120,000	
Accumulated Depreciation — Factory Machinery		36,000
Applied Factory Overhead		536,400
General Ledger.		198,350
Total	770,750	770,750

The following transactions were completed during September:
(a) *Direct materials of $120,000 were purchased on terms of n/30.*
(b) *The factory payroll for $45,000 direct labor and $9,000 indirect labor was mailed to the home office. The home office payroll was $15,000 for sales salaries and $21,000 for office salaries. Employee payroll deductions were recorded at the home office at these rates: 7% of gross earnings for FICA tax; 18% of gross earnings for income tax.*
(c) *Indirect factory materials and supplies amounting to $26,250 were purchased; terms n/30.*
(d) *Employer payroll tax expense is recorded on the home office books. State unemployment, 3.6%; federal unemployment, .8%; FICA tax, 7%.*
(e) *Analysis of the materials requisitions (all supplies are kept at the factory):*

Production orders..	$60,000
Indirect factory materials and supplies....................	15,000
Shipping supplies.......................................	4,500

(f) *Defective shipping supplies of $900 were returned to the vendor.*
(g) *Accounts payable totaling $142,500, including the accrued payroll, were paid.*
(h) *Depreciation at an annual rate of 10% of the original cost was recorded on the factory machinery.*
(i) *Sundry factory expenses of $6,900 were recorded as liabilities.*
(j) *Factory overhead was applied to production at the rate of $6 per direct labor hour; the factory worked 6,000 hours.*
(k) *Goods completed with a total cost of $126,000 were transferred to finished goods.*
(l) *Sales were $150,000 and cost $96,000 to produce.*

Required:
(1) *Prepare journal entries to record the transactions on the general office books and on the factory office books.*
(2) *Prepare T accounts for the two factory overhead accounts, and prepare journal entries to close the applied factory overhead account and to transfer any over- or underapplied overhead to the cost of goods sold account.*

3. *Factory overhead rate and relationship of cost elements. A schedule of cost of goods manufactured shows:*

Materials used ....,.............	$300,000
Direct labor	800,000
Overhead costs	640,000
Work in process, ending inventory	140,000

Required:
(1) *Calculate the rate of factory overhead to direct labor cost.*
(2) *Determine the cost of direct materials included in the work in process ending inventory, assuming that the direct labor cost included in the inventory of work in process is $50,000.*

4. *Income statement. Hansford, Inc. submits the following data for September:*
Direct labor cost, $30,000.
Cost of goods sold, $111,000, before adjusting for over- or underapplied overhead. Factory overhead is applied at the rate of 150% of direct labor cost. Over- or underapplied factory overhead is closed to the cost of goods sold account.
Inventory accounts showed these beginning and ending balances:

	September 1	September 30
Finished goods.........................	$15,000	$17,500
Work in process......................	9,600	13,000
Materials	7,000	7,400

Other data:

Factory overhead (actual).................................	$ 48,200
Marketing expenses......................................	14,100
General and administrative expenses	22,900
Sales for the month.....................................	182,000

Required: *Prepare an income statement with schedule showing the cost of goods manufactured and sold.*

5. Manufacturing cost computations. *On June 30, 19A, a flash flood damaged the warehouse and factory of Headway Corporation, completely destroying the work in process inventory. There was no damage to either the materials or finished goods inventories. A physical inventory taken after the flood revealed the following valuations:*

Finished goods..	$119,000
Work in process	-0-
Materials	62,000

The inventory on January 1, 19A, consisted of the following:

Finished goods..	$140,000
Work in process	100,000
Materials	30,000

A review of the books and records disclosed that the gross profit margin historically approximates 25% of sales. The sales for the first six months of 19A were $340,000. Materials purchases were $115,000. Direct labor cost for this period was $80,000, and factory overhead has historically been applied at 50% of direct labor.

Required: *Calculate the value of the work in process inventory lost at June 30, 19A.*

(AICPA adapted)

6. Job order cost sheet. *Mullin Machine Works collects its cost data by the job order cost accumulation procedure. For Job 909, the following data are available:*

Direct Materials		Direct Labor	
9/14 Issued................	$600	Week of Sept. 20....	90 hrs. @ $6.20/hr.
9/20 Issued................	331	Week of Sept. 26....	70 hrs. @ $7.30/hr.
9/22 Issued................	200		

Factory overhead is applied at the rate of $5 per direct labor hour.

Required:
(1) Enter the appropriate information on a job order cost sheet.
(2) Determine the sales price of the job, assuming that it was contracted with a markup of 40% of cost.

7. Job order cycle entries. *Brielle Products, Inc. provided the following data for January, 19B:*

Materials and supplies:

Inventory, January 1, 19B	$10,000
Purchases on account	30,000

Labor:

Accrued, January 1, 19B...	$ 3,000
Paid during January (ignore payroll taxes)	25,000

Factory overhead costs:

Supplies (issued from materials)	1,500
Indirect labor	3,500
Depreciation..	1,000
Other factory overhead costs (all from outside suppliers on account).........	14,500

Work in process:

	Job 1	Job 2	Job 3	Total
Work in process, January 1, 19B..............	$1,000	—	—	$ 1,000
Job costs during January, 19B:				
Direct materials...........................	4,000	$6,000	$5,000	15,000
Direct labor..............................	5,000	8,000	7,000	20,000
Applied factory overhead..................	5,000	8,000	7,000	20,000

Job 1 started in December, 19A, finished during January, and sold to a customer for $21,000 cash.

Job 2 started in January, not yet finished.

Job 3 started in January, finished during January, and now in the finished goods warehouse.

Finished goods inventory, January 1, 19B.................................... -0-

Required: *Prepare journal entries, with detail for the respective job orders and factory overhead subsidiary records, to record the following transactions for January:*

(1) Purchases of materials on account.

(2) Labor paid.

(3) Labor cost distribution.

(4) Materials issued.

(5) Depreciation for the month.

(6) Acquisition of other overhead costs on credit.

(7) Overhead applied to production.

(8) Jobs completed and transferred to finished goods.

(9) Sales revenue.

(10) Cost of goods sold.

8. *Calculation of job cost. Hellman Corporation uses job order costing and has two production departments, M and A. Budgeted manufacturing costs for 19-- are as follows:*

	Department M	Department A
Direct materials....................................	$700,000	$100,000
Direct labor.......................................	200,000	800,000
Factory overhead	600,000	400,000

The actual materials and labor costs charged to Job 432 during 19-- were as follows:

Direct materials..		$25,000
Direct labor:		
Department M	$ 8,000	
Department A..	12,000	20,000

Hellman applied factory overhead to production orders on the basis of direct labor cost, using departmental rates predetermined at the beginning of the year on the basis of the annual budget.

Required: *Determine the total manufacturing cost associated with Job 432 for 19--.*

(AICPA adapted)

PROBLEMS

3-1. Factory ledger accounts, journal entries, and trial balances. The Wyoming Company's cost accounting system uses both general and factory ledgers. On December 31, 19A, after closing, the ledgers contained the following account balances:

Dr.		Cr.	
Cash.........................	$20,000	Accounts Payable..............	$15,500
Accounts Receivable...........	25,000	Accrued Payroll...............	2,250
Finished Goods	9,500	Common Stock.................	60,000
Work in Process..............	4,500	Retained Earnings.............	21,250
Materials	10,000	General Ledger	24,000
Machinery....................	30,000		
Factory Ledger	24,000		

Inventory accounts are kept in the factory ledger.

During January, 19B, the following transactions were completed:
- (a) Materials purchased, $92,000.
- (b) Miscellaneous factory overhead incurred, $18,500.
- (c) Labor was consumed as follows: for direct production, $60,500; indirect labor, $12,500; sales salaries, $8,000; administrative salaries, $5,000. 10% of the wages is withheld for income tax. The state and federal unemployment tax rates are 3.2% and .8%, respectively; the employer FICA tax rate is 7%. The total accrued payroll was paid. A payroll account is maintained at the factory for factory employees only.
- (d) Materials were consumed as follows: direct materials, $82,500; indirect materials, $8,300.
- (e) Factory overhead charged to production was $47,330.
- (f) Work finished and placed in stock cost $188,000.
- (g) All but $12,000 of the finished goods were sold, terms 2/10, n/60. The markup was 30% above production cost.
- (h) Of the accounts receivable, 80% was collected, less 2% discount.
- (i) A liability was recorded for various marketing and administrative expenses amounting to $30,000. Of this amount, 60% was marketing and 40% was administrative.
- (j) The check register showed payments of $104,000 for liabilities other than payrolls.

Required:
- (1) Prepare trial balances of the general ledger and the factory ledger as of January 1, 19B.
- (2) Prepare general ledger and factory ledger T accounts, with balances from the January 1 trial balances.
- (3) Post January transactions directly into the ledger accounts, without journal entries and with new accounts opened whenever necessary.
- (4) Prepare trial balances of the general ledger and the factory ledger as of January 31, 19B.

3-2. Factory ledger entries. The following transactions were completed by Hyden Corporation, which maintains both a factory ledger and a general ledger:
  (a) Materials purchased and received at the factory..................... $13,500
  (b) Requisitions received and filled in the storeroom:
       For direct materials... $12,300
       For manufacturing supplies.....................................   4,000
  (c) Factory payroll paid for the week, as follows:
       Direct labor... $10,000
       Indirect labor...   3,200
       Superintendence..   1,000
       (A factory payroll book is maintained at the factory. At the end of each week, the factory payroll is reported to and paid by the general office. Provision for employee FICA tax in the amount of $994 and 10% income tax is made on the general office books. The only payroll entry on the factory books is one distributing the payroll to the appropriate accounts and crediting General Ledger. The employer factory payroll taxes are treated as factory overhead. The state unemployment insurance rate is 3.6%, the federal unemployment insurance rate is .8%, and the employer FICA tax is $994.)
  (d) Direct materials returned to the storeroom, $800.
  (e) A transfer voucher from the general office showed the following expenses to be recorded:
       Insurance on factory building and equipment
       (prepaid account on general books)............................. $ 250
       Heat, light, and power...   325
       Property tax on factory building...............................   75
       Depreciation of machinery......................................   240
       Depreciation of factory building..............................   100
                                                                        $ 990

  (f) Factory overhead charged to production, $10,468.
  (g) Work completed during the week, $28,000.
  (h) Goods costing $32,500 to produce were sold for $42,000.

Required: Prepare journal entries to record the above transactions on the general office books and on the factory books, using only one work in process account and assuming that all inventory accounts and Factory Overhead are a part of the factory ledger, while liability accounts, Sales, and Cost of Goods Sold are a part of the general ledger.

3-3. Bid calculations. The Davies Equipment Company manufactures machines to customers' specifications. Two requests for bids have been received, each calling for the delivery of one machine with the following shop and cost specifications:

	Bid No. 1	Bid No. 2
Parts to be purchased.........................	$550	$900
Materials: bar, strip, and sheet metal.........	130	190
Pig metal for castings.........................	56	80

	Direct Labor Hours	
	Bid No. 1	Bid No. 2
Foundry	6 hrs.	8 hrs.
Machining	8	20
Electroplating and painting	6	12
Assembly	40	70
Installing....................................	0	16

Labor and overhead hourly rates:

	Foundry	Machining	E & P	Assembly	Installing
Direct labor rate per hour	$8.25	$7.50	$8.40	$8.00	$7.00
Factory overhead rate per direct labor hour...........	3.25	3.00	2.50	2.60	1.80

Allowance for estimating error, 5% of direct labor and materials cost (including parts purchased).

Allowance for marketing and administrative expenses and profit, 35% of sales.

Required: Determine the bids for the two possible orders.

3-4. Income statement; cost of goods sold statement; factory overhead analysis. On October 1, the accountant of the Tempe Company prepared a trial balance from which these accounts were extracted:

Finished Goods (2,800 units)	9,800	
Work in Process (1,200 units).....................................	4,070	
Materials and Supplies	40,700	
Buildings	48,000	
Accumulated Depreciation—Buildings		6,000
Machinery and Equipment	96,000	
Accumulated Depreciation—Machinery and Equipment		37,500
Office Equipment	3,200	
Accumulated Depreciation—Office Equipment		1,000
Accrued Payroll..		650

The following transactions and other data have been made available for October:

Purchased materials and supplies..................................	$ 24,800
Paid factory overhead	20,100
Paid marketing expenses	25,050
Paid administrative expenses......................................	19,700
Requisitions for:	
Direct materials	29,800
Indirect materials	3,950
Depreciation:	
Building, 5% (75% to manufacturing, 15% to marketing, and 10% to administrative expenses)	
Machinery and equipment, 10%	
Office equipment, 15% (40% to marketing and 60% to administrative expenses)	
Sales (20,700 units)	144,900
Sales returns and allowances	1,300
Cash payments for:	
Accounts payable	75,000
Payroll	21,800
Distribution of payroll earned:	
Direct labor...	18,600
Indirect labor	4,400
Cash collected from customers	116,900
Applied factory overhead	27,450

Units transferred to finished goods, 20,400.

Cost of goods sold is calculated on the fifo basis.

Work in process inventory on October 31, $4,440.

Required:

(1) Prepare the cost of goods sold section of the income statement for October in detail, assuming that over- or underapplied factory overhead is deferred until the end of the calendar year.   *CGS $76,030*   *mat. consumed 29,800*

(2) Prepare the income statement for October.   *NI $22,730*

(3) Calculate the amount of over- or underapplied factory overhead for October.   *$1,950*

3-5. Balance sheet; income statement. On December 31, 19A, Morrisville Canning Company, with outstanding common stock of $30,000, had the following assets and liabilities:

Cash	$ 5,000
Accounts receivable	10,000
Finished goods	6,000
Work in process	2,000
Materials	4,000
Prepaid expenses	500
Property, plant, and equipment (net)	30,000
Current liabilities	17,500

During 19B, the retained earnings account increased 50% as a result of the year's business. No dividends were paid during the year. Balances of accounts receivable, prepaid expenses, current liabilities, and common stock were the same on December 31, 19B, as they had been on December 31, 19A. Inventories were reduced by exactly 50%, except for the finished goods inventory, which was reduced by 33⅓%. Plant assets (net) were reduced by depreciation of $4,000, charged ¾ to factory overhead and ¼ to administrative expenses. Sales of $60,000 were made on account, costing $38,000. Direct labor cost was $9,000. Factory overhead was applied at a rate of 100% of direct labor cost, leaving $2,000 underapplied that was closed into the cost of goods sold account. Total marketing and administrative expenses amounted to 10% and 15%, respectively, of the gross sales.

Required:

(1) Prepare a balance sheet as of December 31, 19B.

(2) Prepare an income statement for the year 19B, with details of the cost of goods manufactured and sold.   (AICPA adapted)

3-6. Journal entries for a job order cost cycle. During the month, the following transactions took place in the factory of the Wissahickon Valley Manufacturing Company:

(a) Materials purchased on account, $53,400.

(b) Materials issued during the month as follows: to fill requisitions on job orders, $31,750; supplies issued to the factory, $1,700.

(c) Materials issued to complete defective units, $150. (Charge to Factory Overhead Control.)

(d) Freight paid for materials received, $900. (Freight is not added to unit costs on materials inventory cards.)

(e) Materials not yet paid for were returned to the vendor during the month, $185.

(f) Materials were returned to the storeroom during the month as follows: from job orders, $990; from supplies issued to the factory, $200.

(g) Total payroll for the month was as follows:

Recorded as liability, then paid by check to workers, $44,500.

Withheld for income tax, $8,120.

Withheld for hospitalization plan, $1,005.

Withheld for FICA tax, $4,036.   *accrued pay (d.) 44,500*   *payroll*   *57,661(cr)*

(h) Taxes were recorded for the employer's FICA tax. State unemployment insurance for the company is 2.6% of total payroll, and the federal rate is .8%. These taxes were charged to Factory Overhead Control.

(i) The payroll was distributed as follows: direct labor, $41,250; indirect labor, balance of payroll.

(j) Depreciation for the month: buildings, $3,500; machinery, $4,500.

(k) Property taxes accrued during the month, $800; insurance expired with a credit to the prepaid account, $750.

(l) Factory overhead is charged to production at a rate of $1.50 per direct labor hour. Records show 20,000 direct labor hours used during the month. (Credit Applied Factory Overhead.)

(m) Close out the over- or underapplied factory overhead to Cost of Goods Sold.

(n) Cost of job orders completed during the month, $82,750.

(o) Goods costing $75,000 were sold on account during the month at a sales price of $95,000.

Required:

(1) Prepare journal entries to record the transactions. Subsidiary ledger accounts need not be included.

(2) Why does over- or underapplied factory overhead occur, and what is the effect of closing it to Cost of Goods Sold?

3-7. Job order costing. Topper, Inc. had the following inventories on March 1:

Finished goods	$15,000
Work in process	19,070
Materials	14,000

The work in process account controls three jobs:

	Job 621	Job 622	Job 623
Materials	$2,800	$3,400	$1,800
Labor	2,100	2,700	1,350
Applied factory overhead	1,680	2,160	1,080
Total	$6,580	$8,260	$4,230

The following information pertains to March operations:

(a) Materials purchased and received, $22,000; terms, n/30.

(b) Materials requisitioned for production, $21,000. Of this amount, $2,400 was for indirect materials; the difference was distributed: $5,300 to Job 621; $7,400 to Job 622; and $5,900 to Job 623.

(c) Materials returned to the storeroom from the factory, $600, of which $200 was for indirect materials, the balance from Job 622.

(d) Materials returned to vendors, $800.

(e) Payroll, after deducting 7% for FICA tax and 12% for employees' income tax, was $30,780. The payroll amount due the employees was paid during March.

(f) Of the payroll, direct labor represented 55%; indirect labor, 20%; sales salaries, 15%; and administrative salaries, 10%. The direct labor cost was distributed: $6,420 to Job 621; $8,160 to Job 622; and $6,320 to Job 623.

(g) An additional 13.2% was entered for employer payroll taxes, representing the employer's 7% FICA tax, 5.4% state unemployment insurance tax, and .8% federal unemployment insurance tax. Employer payroll taxes related to direct labor are charged to the factory overhead control account.

(h) Factory overhead, other than any previously mentioned, amounted to $5,500. Included in this figure were $2,000 for depreciation of factory building and equipment and $250 for expired insurance on the factory. The remaining overhead, $3,250, was unpaid at the end of March.

(i) Factory overhead applied to production: 80% of the direct labor cost to be charged to the three jobs based on the labor cost for March.

(j) Jobs 621 and 622 were completed and transferred to the finished goods warehouse.

(k) Both Jobs 621 and 622 were shipped and billed at a gross profit of 40% of the cost of goods sold.

(l) Cash collections from accounts receivable during March were $69,450.

Required:

(1) Prepare job order cost sheets to post beginning inventory data.

(2) Journalize the March transactions with current postings to general ledger inventory accounts and to job order cost sheets.

(3) Prepare a schedule of inventories on March 31.

M - 14,800   WIP - 21,506
FG - 15,000

3-8. Job orders; factory overhead subsidiary ledger; cost of goods manufactured statement. At the beginning of September, certain ledger accounts in the books and records of the Detroit Products Company had these balances:

Work in Process...	$2,020 (debit)
Materials	7,380 (debit)
Accrued Payroll...	1,436 (credit)

The balance in the work in process account is supported by these details appearing in the job order cost sheets:

Direct materials	$ 640
Direct labor (150 hours)..	900
Applied factory overhead	480
Total...	$2,020

Certain columnar totals in the accounts payable register at the end of September show:

Accounts Payable	$13,820 (credit)
Discounts Lost...	108 (debit)
Materials	10,600 (debit)
Accrued Payroll...	8,704 (debit)
Employees Income Tax Payable.............................	956 (credit)

Materials requisitions indicate:

For production...	$ 8,540
For repairs and maintenance	500
For factory supplies	1,200

The labor distribution sheet shows:

Direct labor (for job orders), 2,000 hours....................		$12,000
Factory overhead:		
Supervisor's salary	$ 1,600	
Repairs and maintenance	360	
Indirect labor	1,200	3,160
Total...		$15,160

The finished orders for the month consist of:

Direct materials	$ 8,060
Direct labor (1,910 hours)	11,460
Applied factory overhead	6,112
Total	$25,632

The following subsidiary accounts and their balances controlled by the factory overhead control account appear in the ledger as of September 30:

Supervisor's Salary	$1,600	Factory Insurance	$ 300
Repairs and Maintenance	860	Light and Power	320
Indirect Labor	1,200	Water and Heat	300
Factory Supplies	1,200	Payroll Taxes	1,500
Depreciation—Factory Equipment	240	Rent—Factory	400

At the end of the month, the three incomplete production (job) orders can be summarized as follows:

Materials	$1,120
Direct labor (240 hours)	1,440
Applied factory overhead	768
Total	$3,328

Required:

(1) Prepare a statement of the cost of goods manufactured for September.
(2) Determine the over- or underapplied factory overhead for September.

[handwritten: dm used 8540 / cogm 25,632 / 9#6400]

3-9. Job order costing; general and factory ledger. On December 31, 19A, after closing, the ledgers of Tri-State Machine Company contained these accounts and balances:

Cash	$47,000	Accounts Payable	$ 59,375
Accounts Receivable	50,000	Common Stock	100,000
Finished Goods*	32,500	Retained Earnings	34,925
Work in Process*	7,500	Factory Ledger	62,000
Materials*	22,000	General Ledger*	62,000
Machinery	35,300		

*Maintained in the factory ledger.

Details of the three inventories are:

Finished goods inventory:	Item X—1,000 units @ $12.50	$12,500
	Item Y—2,000 units @ 10.00	20,000
	Total	$32,500

	Job 101	Job 102
Work in process inventory:		
Direct materials:		
500 units of A @ $5.00	$2,500	
200 units of B @ 3.00		$ 600
Direct labor:		
500 hours @ $4.00	2,000	
200 hours @ 5.00		1,000
Factory overhead applied at the rate of $2.00 per hour	1,000	400
Total	$5,500	$2,000

Materials inventory: Material A—2,000 units @ $5.00	$10,000
Material B—4,000 units @ 3.00	12,000
Total	$22,000

During January, 19B, these transactions were completed:

(a) Purchases on account: Material A, 10,000 units @ $5.20; Material B, 12,000 units @ $3.75; indirect materials, $17,520.

(b) Payroll totaling $110,000 was paid. Of the total payroll, $20,000 was for marketing and administrative salaries. Payroll deductions consisted of $15,500 for employees' income tax and 7% for FICA tax.

(c) Payroll is to be distributed as follows: Job 101, 5,000 direct labor hours @ $4; Job 102, 8,000 direct labor hours @ $5; Job 103, 6,000 direct labor hours @ $3; indirect labor, $12,000; marketing and administrative salaries, $20,000. Employer's payroll taxes are: FICA, 7%; state unemployment, 5.4%; federal unemployment, .8%.

(d) Materials were issued on a fifo basis as follows: Material A, 10,000 units (charged to Job 101); Material B, 12,000 units (charged to Job 102); Material A, 1,000 units, and Material B, 2,500 units (charged to Job 103). (*Note:* Transactions are to be taken in consecutive order.) Indirect materials amounting to $7,520 were issued.

(e) Factory overhead was applied to Jobs 101, 102, and 103 based on a rate of $2.25 per direct labor hour.

(f) Jobs 101 and 102 were completed and sold on account for $120,000 and $135,000, respectively.

(g) After allowing a 5% cash discount, a net amount of $247,000 was collected on accounts receivable.

(h) Marketing and administrative expenses (other than salaries) paid during the month amounted to $15,000. Miscellaneous factory overhead of $10,800 was paid and transferred to the factory. Depreciation on machinery was $2,000.

(i) Payments on account, other than payrolls paid, amounted to $85,000.

(j) The over- or underapplied factory overhead is to be closed to the cost of goods sold account.

Required:

(1) Prepare trial balances of the general ledger and of the factory ledger as of January 1, 19B.

(2) Open general ledger and factory ledger accounts and record balances from the January 1 trial balances.

(3) Journalize the January transactions.

(4) Post January transactions to the general ledger, factory ledger, and subsidiary ledgers for materials, work in process, finished goods, and factory overhead incurred.

(5) Prepare trial balances of the general ledger and the factory ledger as of January 31, 19B, reconciling control accounts with subsidiary ledgers.

(6) Prepare a statement of cost of goods sold for January, 19B.

Chapter 4
Process Costing: Cost of Production Report; Lost Unit Calculations

Cost accumulation procedures used by manufacturing concerns are classified as either (1) job order costing or (2) process costing. In this chapter, the basic aspects of process costing are discussed. These aspects include the cost of production reports for producing departments, the calculation of departmental unit costs, the computation of cost transferred to other departments or to the finished goods storeroom, the costing of work in process, and the effect of lost units on unit costs. Chapter 5 discusses the effect of adding materials in departments other than the first and beginning work in process inventories. Chapter 6 discusses the problem of assigning costs to by-products and joint products.

Process Cost Accumulation Procedures

The objective of either job order or process costing is to match costs of a period with units produced in the same period. The type of manufacturing operations performed determines the cost procedures that must be used. For example, a company manufacturing custom machinery will use job order cost procedures, whereas a chemical company will use process cost procedures. In the case of the machinery manufacturer, a job order cost sheet accumulates materials, labor, and factory overhead costs for each order. In contrast, the chemical company cannot identify materials, labor, and factory overhead with each order, which is part of a batch or a continuous process. The individual order identity is lost, and the cost of a completed unit must be computed by dividing the total cost incurred during a period by total units completed.

Process costing is used when products are manufactured under conditions of continuous processing or under mass production methods. These conditions exist in industries that produce such commodities as plastics, petroleum, textiles, steel, flour, and sugar. Process costing is used by firms that manufacture bolts and small electrical parts, and by assembly-type industries (automobiles, airplanes, and household appliances). Some utilities (gas, water, and heat) cost their products by using process costing methods.

The characteristics of process costing are:

1. Costs are charged to departmental work in process accounts.
2. A cost of production report is used to collect, summarize, and compute total and unit costs. Unit costs are determined by dividing the total cost charged to a department by the total production of the department for a specific period.
3. Production in process at the end of a period is restated in terms of equivalent units.
4. Costs of completed units of a department are transferred to the next processing department in order to arrive eventually at the total cost of the finished products during a period, and costs are assigned to units still in process.

Costing by Departments

In manufacturing firms, production may take place in several departments. Each department performs a specific operation or process leading to the completion of the product. In a process costing situation, for example, the first department performs the starting phase of work on the product and transfers the units to a second department. The second department completes its work and transfers the units to a third department which completes them and sends them to the finished goods storeroom. When the units are transferred from one producing department to another, the accumulated costs are transferred to the subsequent department. The costs of materials, labor, and factory overhead are charged to work in process accounts which are maintained for each department.

In process costing, departmental total and unit costs are summarized in a cost of production report, which is described and illustrated in this chapter. The cost of a completed unit is used in determining the cost of units still in process. This breakdown of costs for units transferred and departmental work in process inventories is useful for cost control purposes.

Product Flow

A product can move through a factory in a variety of ways. Three product flow formats associated with process costing—sequential, parallel, and selective—are illustrated here to indicate that the same basic costing procedures can be applied to all types of product flow situations.

Sequential Product Flow. In a sequential flow, each product is processed in the same series of steps. In a company with three departments, such a flow may be illustrated as follows:

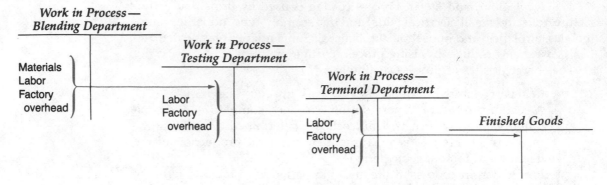

The processing of materials begins in the Blending Department, and labor and factory overhead costs are added. When the work is finished in this department, it moves to the Testing Department. Any succeeding processes may add more materials or simply work on the partially completed input from the preceding process, adding only labor and factory overhead, as in this example. After the product has been processed by the Terminal Department, it is complete and becomes a part of Finished Goods.

Parallel Product Flow. In a parallel product flow, certain portions of the work are done simultaneously and then brought together in a final process or processes for completion and transfer to Finished Goods. The following accounts illustrate a parallel flow for a production process in which materials are added in subsequent departments:

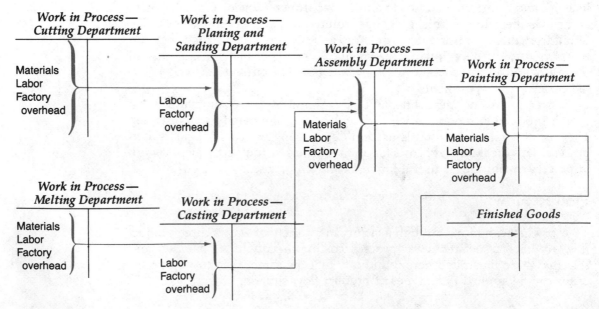

Selective Product Flow. In a selective flow, the product moves to different departments within the plant, depending upon the desired final product. The accounts below illustrate a selective flow in a meat processing plant. After the initial butchering process is completed, some of the product goes directly to the Packaging Department and then to Finished Goods; some goes to the Smoking Department and then to the Packaging Department and Finished Goods; some to the Grinding Department, then to the Packaging Department and finally to Finished Goods.

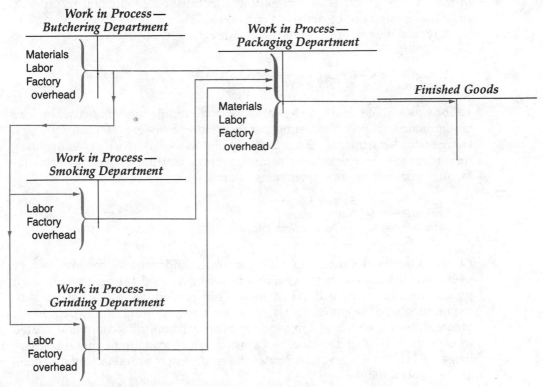

Procedures for Materials, Labor, and Factory Overhead Costs

The details involved in process cost procedures are usually fewer than those in job order costing, where accumulation of costs for many orders may become unwieldy. The job order procedures for accumulating materials, labor, and factory overhead costs generally apply, however, to process costing. Costs are charged to departments or processes by appropriate journal entries.

Materials Costs. In job order costing, materials requisitions are the basis for charging direct materials to specific jobs. If requisitions are used in process costing, the details are considerably reduced because materials are charged to departments rather than to jobs and the number of departments using materials is usually less than the number of jobs which a firm handles at a given time. Frequently materials are issued only to the process-originating department; subsequent departments add labor and factory overhead.

Materials requisition forms may be useful for materials control purposes. If the requisitions are not priced individually, the cost of materials used may be determined at the end of the production period through inventory difference procedures; i.e., adding purchases to beginning inventory and deducting ending inventory. Consumption reports which state the cost or quantity of materials put into process by various departments may also be used. The costs or quantities charged to departments may be based on formulas or prorations. These formulas specify the type and quantity of materials required in the various products and are applied to finished production in order to calculate the amount of materials consumed.

A typical journal entry to record the direct materials used during a period is as follows:

issuance of raw mat. into Blending

Work in Process—Blending Department......................	24,500	
Materials..		24,500

Labor Costs. The detailed clerical work of accumulating labor costs by jobs is eliminated in process costing because labor costs are identified by and charged to departments. Daily time tickets or weekly clock cards are used instead of job time tickets. A summary entry distributes the direct manufacturing payroll to departments, as follows:

Work in Process—Blending Department......................	29,140	
Work in Process—Testing Department	37,310	
Work in Process—Terminal Department......................	32,400	
Payroll..		98,850

Factory Overhead Costs. In both job order and process costing, factory overhead should be accumulated in a factory overhead subsidiary ledger for producing and service departments. This procedure is consistent with requirements for responsibility accounting and reporting. As expenses are incurred, they are recorded in a factory overhead control account and posted to departmental expense analysis sheets, which constitute the subsidiary ledger. The following entry illustrates the recording of actual factory overhead in the general ledger:

Factory Overhead Control.....................................	81,500	
Accounts Payable..		24,500
Accumulated Depreciation—Machinery......................		42,500
Prepaid Insurance...		8,000
Indirect Materials and Supplies		4,500
Indirect Labor..		2,000

At the end of each period, either actual overhead or applied overhead is charged to the producing departments. When overhead is applied in process costing, the rates are multiplied by the respective actual activity base (e.g., direct labor hours) for each producing department. The following entry illustrates this procedure for Clonex Corporation:

Work in Process—Blending Department......................	28,200	
Work in Process—Testing Department	32,800	
Work in Process—Terminal Department......................	19,800	
Applied Factory Overhead		80,800

The Cost of Production Report

In process costing, all costs chargeable to a department are summarized in a departmental cost of production report. This report is a device for presenting the amount of costs accumulated and disposed of during a month. It is also the source of information for preparing summary journal entries which record activity in the cost accounts.

A cost of production report for a department shows (1) total and unit costs transferred from a preceding department; (2) materials, labor, and factory overhead added by the department; (3) unit costs added by the department; (4) total and unit costs accumulated at the end of operations in the department; (5) the cost of the beginning and ending work in process inventories, which are in various stages of completion; and (6) cost transferred to a succeeding department or to the finished goods storeroom. The cost section of the report is usually divided into two parts: one showing total costs for which the department is accountable, the other showing the disposition of these costs. The cost of production report or a supporting schedule should indicate the cost elements for each department because these detailed data are needed for cost control and for determining the cost of the ending work in process inventories.

The cost of production report also includes a quantity schedule which shows the total number of units for which a department is accountable and the disposition of these units. Information in this schedule, adjusted for equivalent production, is used to determine the unit costs added by a department, the costing of the ending work in process inventory, and the cost to be transferred out of the department.

To illustrate the details involved in the preparation of cost of production reports, the cost procedures of Clonex Corporation are discussed on the following pages. This company manufactures one product in three producing departments: Blending, Testing, and Terminal. The Clonex reports are condensed to show the total materials, labor, and factory overhead charged to departments. Unit costs are computed for each cost element rather than for each item.

Blending Department

The cost of production report of the Blending Department, the originating department of Clonex Corporation, is on page 70. The quantity schedule of this report shows that the Blending Department put 50,000 units in process. Of these 50,000 units for which the department was responsible, 45,000 units were transferred to the next department (Testing), 4,000 units are still in process, and 1,000 units were lost in processing.

The units reported by the Blending Department are assumed to be measured in gallons. Generally, each department should report units in terms of the finished product. If materials issued to a department are stated in pounds, for example, and the finished product is reported in gallons, units in

Clonex Corporation
Blending Department
Cost of Production Report
For January, 19--

Quantity Schedule

Units started in process...		50,000
Units transferred to next department...........................	45,000	
Units still in process (all materials— ½ labor and factory overhead)	4,000	
Units lost in process..	1,000	50,000

Cost Charged to the Department	Total Cost	Unit Cost
Cost added by department:		
Materials..	$24,500	$ .50
Labor..	29,140	.62
Factory overhead	28,200	.60
Total cost to be accounted for............................	$81,840	$1.72

Cost Accounted for as Follows		
Transferred to next department (45,000 × $1.72)................		$77,400
Work in process—ending inventory:		
Materials (4,000 × $.50).....................................	$ 2,000	
Labor (4,000 × ½ × $.62)	1,240	
Factory overhead (4,000 × ½ × $.60).........................	1,200	4,440
Total cost accounted for		$81,840

Additional computations:

Equivalent production: Materials = 45,000 + 4,000 = 49,000 units

$$\text{Labor and factory overhead} = 45,000 + \frac{4,000}{2} = 47,000 \text{ units}$$

Unit costs: $\text{Materials} = \dfrac{\$24,500}{49,000} = \$.50 \text{ per unit}$

$\text{Labor} = \dfrac{\$29,140}{47,000} = \$.62 \text{ per unit}$

$\text{Factory overhead} = \dfrac{\$28,200}{47,000} = \$.60 \text{ per unit}$

the quantity schedule should be stated in gallons by using a product conversion table.

Equivalent Production. To assign costs equitably to the ending work in process inventory and to transferred units, the stage of completion of the in-process inventory must be analyzed by a supervisor or by the use of formulas. Units still in process must be restated in terms of completed units and added to units actually completed in order to arrive at the equivalent production figure for the period. Units in process at the beginning of the period must also be restated and included in equivalent production. The discussion of this procedure is deferred to Chapter 5.

The equivalent production figure represents the number of units for which materials, labor, and overhead issued or used during a period were sufficient to complete those units. To compute unit costs by elements, the equivalent production figure is divided into the materials, labor, and overhead costs.

If the cost elements are at different stages of completion with respect to units in process, then separate equivalent production figures must be computed for each element. In many manufacturing processes, all materials are issued at the start of production. Unless stated otherwise, the illustrations in this discussion assume such a procedure. The 4,000 units still in process in the Clonex factory have all the materials needed for their completion, but only 50 percent of the labor and factory overhead needed to complete the units has been used. In terms of equivalent production, labor and factory overhead in process are sufficient to complete 2,000 units.

Unit Costs. Department cost of production reports indicate the cost of units as they leave each department. These individual departmental unit costs are accumulated into a completed unit cost for the period. The report for the Blending Department shows a materials cost of $24,500, labor cost of $29,140, and factory overhead of $28,200. The materials cost of $24,500 is sufficient to complete 49,000 units (the 45,000 units transferred out of the department as well as the work in process for which enough materials are in process to complete 4,000 units). The unit materials cost is $.50 ($24,500 ÷ 49,000). To determine the number of units actually and potentially completed with the labor and overhead costs, the 2,000 equivalent units in process are added to the 45,000 units completed and transferred. When this production figure of 47,000 units is divided into the labor cost of $29,140 for the month, a unit cost of $.62 ($29,140 ÷ 47,000) for labor is computed. The unit cost for factory overhead is $.60 ($28,200 ÷ 47,000).

The departmental unit cost, or the cost added by the department, is $1.72, which is the sum of the materials, labor, and overhead unit costs. This departmental unit cost figure cannot be determined by dividing total departmental costs of $81,840 by a single equivalent production figure. No such figure exists, since units in process are at different stages of completion as to materials, labor, and factory overhead.

Disposition of Departmental Costs. In the departmental cost report, the section titled "Cost Charged to the Department" shows a total departmental cost of $81,840. The section titled "Cost Accounted for as Follows" shows the disposition of this cost. The 45,000 units transferred to the next department have a cost of $77,400 (45,000 units multiplied by the departmental completed unit cost of $1.72). The balance of the cost to be accounted for, $4,440 ($81,840 − $77,400), is the cost of the work in process.

The work in process inventory must be broken down into its component parts. The $2,000 cost of materials in process is obtained by multiplying 4,000 total units in process by the materials unit cost of $.50. The costs of labor and factory overhead in process are similarly calculated by multiplying equivalent units by unit cost. Since the amount of labor and overhead in process is sufficient to complete only 50 percent of the units in process, the cost of labor in process is $1,240 (2,000 × $.62) and the cost of factory overhead in process is $1,200 (2,000 × $.60).

Lost Units. Continuous operating and processing lead to the possibility of waste, seepage, shrinkage, and other factors which cause loss or spoilage of production units. Lost units, units reported as complete, and units still in process must be reconciled with the quantities put in process. One method of making such reconciliations is to establish the expected process yield; i.e., the finished production that should have resulted from processing the various materials. This yield is computed as follows:

$$\text{Percent Yield} = \frac{\text{Weight of finished product}}{\text{Weight of materials charged in}} \times 100$$

Various yields are established as normal. Yields below normal are measures of inefficiencies and are sometimes used to compute lost units. The yield figure is useful in controlling materials consumption and ties in closely with a firm's quality control procedures.

When units are lost during processing in the first department, the total cost must be spread over a reduced number of units. Therefore, the effect of losing units is an increase in the unit cost of the remaining good units. If 1,000 units had not been lost in the Blending Department, the equivalent production figure would have been 50,000 units for materials and 48,000 units for labor and factory overhead. The unit cost for materials would have been $.49 instead of $.50; labor, $.607 instead of $.62; and factory overhead, $.588 instead of $.60.

Testing Department

The Blending Department transferred 45,000 units to the Testing Department, where labor and factory overhead were added before the units were transferred to the Terminal Department. Costs incurred by the Testing Department resulted in additional departmental as well as cumulative unit costs.

The cost of production report of the Testing Department, shown on page 73, differs from that of the Blending Department in several respects. Several additional calculations are made, for which space has been provided on the report. The additional information includes (1) costs received from the preceding department, (2) an adjustment of the preceding department's unit cost because of lost units, and (3) costs received from the preceding department to be included in the cost of the ending work in process inventory.

The quantity schedule for the Testing Department shows that the 45,000 units received from the Blending Department were accounted for as follows: 40,000 units were sent to the Terminal Department, 3,000 units are still in process, and 2,000 units were lost. An analysis of the work in process indicates

The Clonex Corporation
Testing Department
Cost of Production Report
For January, 19--

Quantity Schedule

Units received from preceding department		45,000
Units transferred to next department	40,000	
Units still in process (⅓ labor and factory overhead)	3,000	
Units lost in process	2,000	45,000

Cost Charged to the Department	Total Cost	Unit Cost
Cost from preceding department:		
Transferred in during the month (45,000 units)	$ 77,400	$1.72
Cost added by department:		
Labor..	$ 37,310	$ .91
Factory overhead	32,800	.80
Total cost added	$ 70,110	$1.71
Adjustment for lost units		$ .08
Total cost to be accounted for	**$147,510**	**$3.51**

Cost Accounted for as Follows

Transferred to next department (40,000 × $3.51)		$140,400
Work in process—ending inventory:		
Adjusted cost from preceding department [3,000 × ($1.72 + $.08)]	$ 5,400	
Labor (3,000 × ⅓ × $.91)	910	
Factory overhead (3,000 × ⅓ × $.80)	$ 800	7,110
Total cost accounted for		**$147,510**

Additional computations:

Equivalent production: Labor and factory overhead $= 40,000 + \dfrac{3,000}{3} = 41,000$ units

Unit costs: Labor $= \dfrac{\$37,310}{41,000} = \$.91$ per unit

Factory overhead $= \dfrac{\$32,800}{41,000} = \$.80$ per unit

Adjustment for lost units:

Method No. 1 — $\dfrac{\$77,400}{43,000} = \$1.80; \$1.80 - \$1.72 = \$.08$ per unit

Method No. 2 — 2,000 units × $1.72 = $3,440; $\dfrac{\$ 3,440}{43,000} = \$.08$ per unit

that units in process are only one-third complete as to labor and factory overhead. Therefore, equivalent production of the Testing Department is 41,000 units [40,000 + (⅓ × 3,000)], the labor unit cost is $.91 ($37,310 ÷ 41,000), and the factory overhead unit cost is $.80 ($32,800 ÷ 41,000). No materials were added by the department, so the departmental unit cost is the sum of the labor unit cost of $.91 and the factory overhead unit cost of $.80, or $1.71.

The cost of production report for the Testing Department indicates that this department is also responsible for the cost of units received from the Blending Department. This cost is included in the section titled "Cost Charged to the Department." The cost transferred in was $77,400, which was previously shown in the cost report of the Blending Department as cost transferred out of that department. This cost was charged to the Testing Department by the following entry:

Work in Process—Testing Department......................	77,400	
Work in Process—Blending Department....................		77,400

Since the work in process account of the Testing Department is also charged with $70,110 of departmental labor and factory overhead, a total cost of $147,510 must be accounted for by the department.

Units Lost in Departments Subsequent to the First. The Blending Department's unit cost was $1.72 when 45,000 units were transferred to the Testing Department. However, because 2,000 of these 45,000 units were lost during processing in the Testing Department, the $1.72 unit cost figure must be adjusted. The total cost of the units transferred remains at $77,400, but 43,000 units must now absorb this total cost, causing an increase of $.08 in the cost per unit.

The lost unit cost may be computed by either of two methods. Method No. 1 determines a new unit cost for work done in the preceding department and subtracts the preceding department's old unit cost figure from the adjusted unit cost figure. The difference between the two figures is the additional preceding department unit cost due to the lost units. In the Testing Department, the new adjusted unit cost for work done in the preceding department is $1.80. This figure is obtained by dividing the remaining good units, 43,000 (45,000 − 2,000), into the cost transferred in, $77,400. The old unit cost figure of $1.72 is subtracted from the revised unit cost of $1.80 to arrive at the adjustment of $.08.

Method No. 2 determines the lost units' share of total cost and allocates this cost to the remaining good units. The total cost previously absorbed by the units lost is $3,440, which is the result of multiplying the 2,000 lost units by their unit cost of $1.72. The $3,440 cost must now be absorbed by the remaining units. Therefore, the additional cost to be picked up by each remaining unit is $.08 ($3,440 ÷ 43,000).

The lost unit cost adjustment is entered on the "Adjustment for lost units" line in the cost report. The $1.72 unadjusted unit cost for work done in the preceding department, the $1.71 departmental unit cost, and the $.08 adjustment for lost units are totaled to obtain the $3.51 cumulative unit cost for work done up to the end of operations in the Testing Department. The departmental unit cost of $1.71 does not have to be adjusted for units lost, since the cost of any Testing work on lost units has automatically been absorbed in the departmental unit costs by using the equivalent production figure of 41,000 instead of 43,000 units.

Disposition of Testing Department Costs. The cost of production report on page 73 shows a total cost of $147,510 to be accounted for by the Testing Department. The department completed and transferred 40,000 units to the Terminal Department at a cost of $140,400 (40,000 × $3.51). The remaining cost is assigned to the work in process inventory and is broken down by the various costs in process. When the cost of the ending work in process inventory of any department subsequent to the first is computed, costs received from preceding departments must be included.

The 3,000 units still in process but completed by the Blending Department at a unit cost of $1.72 were later adjusted by $.08 (to $1.80) because of the loss of some of the units transferred. Therefore, the Blending Department's cost of the 3,000 units still in process is $5,400 (3,000 × $1.80). The separate cost elements in this $5,400 figure are not identified, since such information is not pertinent to the Testing Department's operations. However, the amount is listed separately in the cost of production report because it is part of the Testing Department's ending work in process inventory.

Materials (if any), labor, and factory overhead added by a department are costed separately to arrive at the total work in process. Since the Testing Department added no materials to the units received, the ending inventory shows no materials in process. However, labor and factory overhead costs were incurred. The work in process analysis indicates that labor and factory overhead used on the units in process were sufficient to complete 1,000 units. The cost of labor in process is $910 (1,000 × $.91) and factory overhead in process is $800 (1,000 × $.80). The total cost of the 3,000 units in process is $7,110 ($5,400 + $910 + $800). This cost and the $140,400 transferred to the Terminal Department accounts for the $147,510 total cost charged to the Testing Department.

Terminal Department

The cost of production report of the Terminal Department of Clonex Corporation is illustrated on page 76. Total and unit cost figures were derived by using procedures discussed for the cost of production report of the Testing Department (page 73). Costs charged to the Terminal Department come from the payroll distribution and the department's expense analysis sheet. These costs include costs transferred from the Testing Department when the following journal entry was recorded:

Work in Process—Terminal Department	140,400	
Work in Process—Testing Department		140,400

Since the Terminal Department is the final processing department, the work completed is transferred to the finished goods storeroom. This transfer is recorded as follows:

Finished Goods	176,750	
Work in Process—Terminal Department		176,750

Clonex Corporation
Terminal Department
Cost of Production Report
For January, 19--

Quantity Schedule

Units received from preceding department		40,000
Units transferred to finished goods storeroom	35,000	
Units still in process (¼ labor and factory overhead)	4,000	
Units lost in process	1,000	40,000

Cost Charged to the Department	Total Cost	Unit Cost
Cost from preceding department:		
Transferred in during the month (40,000 units)	$140,400	$3.51
Cost added by department:		
Labor..	$ 32,400	$ .90
Factory overhead	19,800	.55
Total cost added	$ 52,200	$1.45
Adjustment for lost units		$ .09
Total cost to be accounted for	**$192,600**	**$5.05**

Cost Accounted for as Follows

Transferred to finished goods storeroom (35,000 × $5.05)		$176,750
Work in process—ending inventory:		
Adjusted cost from preceding department [4,000 × ($3.51 + $.09)]	$ 14,400	
Labor (4,000 × ¼ × $.90)	900	
Factory overhead (4,000 × ¼ × $.55)	550	15,850
Total cost accounted for................................		**$192,600**

Additional computations:

Equivalent production: Labor and factory overhead $= 35,000 + \dfrac{4,000}{4} = 36,000$ units

Unit costs: Labor $= \dfrac{\$32,400}{36,000} = \$.90$ per unit

Factory overhead $= \dfrac{\$19,800}{36,000} = \$.55$ per unit

Adjustment for lost units:

Method No. 1 — $\dfrac{\$140,400}{39,000} = \$3.60;\ \$3.60 - \$3.51 = \$.09$ per unit

Method No. 2 — 1,000 units × $3.51 = $3,510; $\dfrac{\$ 3,510}{39,000} = \$.09$ per unit

Combined Cost of Production Report

The three cost of production reports for Clonex Corporation have been discussed and computed separately. These reports would most likely be consolidated in a single report summarizing manufacturing operations of the firm for a specified period. Such a report, as illustrated below, emphasizes the interrelationship of the various departmental reports.

	Blending		Testing		Terminal	
Clonex Corporation Cost of Production Report All Producing Departments For January, 19--						
Quantity Schedule						
Units started in process	50,000					
Units received from preceding department			45,000		40,000	
Units transferred to next department	45,000		40,000			
Units transferred to finished goods storeroom					35,000	
Units still in process	4,000		3,000		4,000	
Units lost in process	1,000	50,000	2,000	45,000	1,000	40,000
	Total Cost	Unit Cost	Total Cost	Unit Cost	Total Cost	Unit Cost
Cost Charged to the Department						
Cost from preceding department:						
Transferred in during the month			$ 77,400	$1.72	$140,400	$3.51
Cost added by department:						
Materials	$24,500	$ .50				
Labor	29,140	.62	$ 37,310	$ .91	$ 32,400	$ .90
Factory overhead	28,200	.60	32,800	.80	19,800	.55
Total cost added	$81,840	$1.72	$ 70,110	$1.71	$ 52,200	$1.45
Adjustment for lost units				$ .08		$ .09
Total cost to be accounted for . .	$81,840	$1.72	$147,510	$3.51	$192,600	$5.05
Cost Accounted for as Follows						
Transferred to next department		$77,400		$140,400		
Transferred to finished goods storeroom						$176,750
Work in process—ending inventory:						
Adjusted cost from preceding department			$ 5,400		$ 14,400	
Materials	$ 2,000					
Labor	1,240		910		900	
Factory overhead	1,200	4,440	800	7,110	550	15,850
Total cost accounted for		$81,840		$147,510		$192,600

Other Factors in Accounting for Lost Units

In the Testing Department as well as in the Blending and Terminal Departments of Clonex Corporation, it was assumed that the loss of units applied to all good units and was within normal tolerance limits. Thus, the loss of units resulted in an increase in the unit cost of the remaining good units, i.e., the units completed and the units still in process. Other lost unit situations require the application of the procedures that are discussed in the following paragraphs.

Timing of Lost Units

Situations may arise in which the cost of lost units does not pertain to the ending work in process inventory, because the identification of lost units occurs at a point beyond the stage of completion of the units still in process. Thus, any measured loss pertains only to units completed. No part of the loss is charged to units still in process.

To illustrate, assume that the 2,000 units lost by the Testing Department of Clonex Corporation were the result of spoilage which was discovered by the Quality Control Department at its final inspection. The cost of these units would be charged only to the 40,000 finished units, as illustrated in the cost of production report for the Testing Department, on page 79.

Since the lost units were discovered after completion in the Testing Department, unit costs are based on equivalent production for good units plus lost units. Therefore, no adjustment of the preceding department unit cost is required, and none of the cost of the spoiled units is included in the cost assigned to the ending work in process inventory. Only the cost transferred to the next department includes the full cost of the spoiled units.

The differences between the two cost of production reports for the Testing Department (pages 73 and 79) as to amounts for costs of units transferred and work in process inventory are shown below. A comparison of the differences indicates that the increases and decreases are offsetting.

Cost of units transferred:		Work in process inventory:	
On page 73	$140,400	On page 73	$7,110
On page 79	140,720	On page 79	6,790
Increase	$ 320	Decrease	$ 320

In this illustration, the 2,000 lost units identified at the end of the process were assumed to be complete as to all costs. However, lost units may not be entirely complete when the loss actually occurs, even though the loss is not identified until the end of the process. In other instances, the loss may be discovered when production checks are made prior to the end of the process, but the loss cannot be associated with units still in process. In both of these cases, the lost units should be adjusted for their equivalent stage of completion. For instance, 2,000 units lost at the 90 percent stage of conversion in the Testing Department would appear as 1,800 equivalent units with regard to labor and factory overhead costs.

The Clonex Corporation
Testing Department
Cost of Production Report
For January, 19--

Quantity Schedule

Units received from preceding department		45,000
Units transferred to next department	40,000	
Units still in process (⅓ labor and factory overhead)	3,000	
Units lost in process (at end of process)	2,000	45,000

Cost Charged to the Department	Total Cost	Unit Cost
Cost from preceding department:		
Transferred in during the month (45,000 units)	$ 77,400	$1.72
Cost added by department:		
Labor	$ 37,310	$ .87
Factory overhead	32,800	.76
Total cost added	$ 70,110	$1.63
Total cost to be accounted for	$147,510	$3.35

Cost Accounted for as Follows

Transferred to next department [40,000 units × ($3.35 + $.1675)]*		$140,720
Work in process—ending inventory:		
From preceding department (3,000 × $1.72)	$ 5,160	
Labor (3,000 × ⅓ × $.87)	870	
Factory overhead (3,000 × ⅓ × $.76)	760	6,790
Total cost accounted for		$147,510

Additional computations:

Equivalent production: Labor and factory overhead $= 40,000 + \dfrac{3,000}{3} + 2,000$ lost units

$$= 43,000 \text{ units}$$

Unit costs: Labor $= \dfrac{\$37,310}{43,000} = \$.87$ per unit

Factory overhead $= \dfrac{\$32,800}{43,000} = \$.76$ per unit

Lost unit cost $= \$3.35 \times 2,000$ units $= \$6,700$; $\$6,700 \div 40,000$ units $= \$.1675$ per unit to be added to $3.35 to make the transfer cost $3.5175.

*40,000 units × $3.5175 = $140,700. To avoid a decimal discrepancy, the cost transferred is computed: $147,510 − $6,790 = $140,720.

Normal vs. Abnormal Loss of Units

Units are lost through evaporation, shrinkage, substandard yields, spoiled work, poor workmanship, or inefficient equipment. In many instances, the nature of operations makes certain losses normal or unavoidable. When such losses are determined to be within normal tolerance limits for human and machine errors, the cost of the lost units does not appear as a separate item of cost but is spread over the remaining good units.

A different situation is created by abnormal or avoidable losses that are not expected to arise under normal, efficient operating conditions. Again, the procedure involves computing unit costs based on equivalent production for good units plus lost units. The lost units are multiplied by the resulting unit costs to determine the cost applicable to the abnormal loss. This cost is charged to Factory Overhead or to a current-period expense account which is reported as a separate item in the cost of goods sold statement. Such a procedure assumes that a predetermined overhead rate is used. Charging abnormal spoilage cost to a current-period expense account would be mandatory if a predetermined factory overhead rate is not used. Otherwise, the actual factory overhead rate would include this cost, thereby assigning it to the cost of units produced.

If the cost of the abnormal loss is charged to Factory Overhead, as shown in the following entry, it will be reported as an additional unfavorable factory overhead variance, since abnormal spoilage is not included in the overhead rate.

	Subsidiary Record	Dr.	Cr.
Factory Overhead Control		6,700	
Abnormal Lost Units	6,700		
Work in Process—Testing Department			6,700

The cost of production report would show the abnormal spoilage or loss as follows:

Transferred to next department (40,000 units × $3.35) $134,020*
Transferred to factory overhead—cost of abnormal loss
  (2,000 lost units × $3.35)   6,700

*40,000 units × $3.35 = $134,000. To avoid decimal discrepancy, the cost transferred is computed: $147,510 − $6,790 ending inventory − $6,700 = $134,020.

When the lost units are only partially complete, their stage of completion should be considered, and the costing of the abnormal loss should be weighted accordingly.

If one part of a loss is normal and another part abnormal, each portion should be treated in accordance with the above illustrations and discussion. The critical factor in distinguishing between the normal and abnormal portions of a loss is the degree of controllability. Normal or unavoidable loss is produced under efficient operating conditions and is uncontrollable. Abnormal or avoidable loss is considered unnecessary, because the conditions resulting in the loss are controllable. For this reason, within the limits set by the refinement of the production process, the difference is a short-run condition. In the long run, management would attempt to adjust and control all factors of production and eliminate all abnormal conditions.

DISCUSSION QUESTIONS

1. What is the primary objective in process costing?

2. Job order and process costing procedures are used by different types of industries. Discuss the procedure appropriate for each type.

3. For the following products, indicate whether job order or process cost procedures would be required:

   (a) Gasoline   (e) Dacron yarn
   (b) Sewing machines   (f) Cigarettes
   (c) Chocolate syrup   (g) Space capsules
   (d) Textbooks   (h) Men's and women's
                                   suits

4. What are the distinguishing characteristics of process cost procedures?

5. Discuss three product flow formats.

6. Compare the cost accumulation and summarizing procedures of job order costing and process costing.

7. Can predetermined overhead rates be used in process costing?

8. Would one expect to find service departments in a firm using process costing? If so, how would they be handled? Would cost of production reports be used for service departments?

9. What is the purpose of a cost of production report?

10. What are the various sections of a cost of production report?

11. Separate cost of production reports are prepared for each producing department. Why is this method used in preference to one report for the entire firm?

12. Are month-to-month fluctuations in average unit costs computed in a cost of production report meaningful data in attempting to control costs?

13. What is equivalent production? Explain in terms of its effect on computed unit costs.

14. Describe the difference between units started in process for a period and equivalent units for a period when there is no beginning work in process inventory and the ending work in process inventory is 50% complete.
    (AICPA adapted)

15. Describe the difference between units completed for a period and equivalent units for a period when there is no beginning work in process inventory and the ending work in process inventory is 50% complete.   (AICPA adapted)

16. In process costing, physical inventories of work in process must be taken at the end of each accounting period. Ordinarily, all department heads are responsible for their own inventories, and the methods they use to determine such data are crude by comparison with procedures used for determining year-end physical inventory. It is not unusual for a department head to estimate rather than count inventory in process. Consequently, figures are bound to have errors. Is this good practice or should more accurate methods be used, such as having inventory teams determine inventories?

17. What is the justification for spreading the cost of lost units over the remaining good units? Should the cost of these units ever be charged to overhead? Will the answer be different if units are lost (a) in the originating department, (b) at the beginning of a department's operations, (c) during operations, or (d) at the end of operations?

18. (a) Distinguish between normal (unavoidable) spoilage and abnormal (avoidable) spoilage. (b) Explain how both should be reported for management purposes.   (AICPA adapted)

EXERCISES

1. *Equivalent production.* During April, 20,000 units were transferred in from Department A at a cost of $39,000. Materials cost of $6,500 and conversion cost of $9,000 were

added in Department B. On April 30, Department B had 5,000 units of work in process 60% complete as to conversion cost. Materials are added in the beginning of the process in Department B.

Required:

(1) Compute equivalent production for materials and conversion cost.

(2) Calculate the cost per equivalent unit for conversion cost.   (AICPA adapted)

2. Costing of units transferred; lost units. Rude, Inc. instituted a new process in October, during which it started 10,000 units in Department A. Of the units started, 1,000 units, a normal number, were lost during the process; 7,000 were transferred to Department B; and 2,000 remained in work in process inventory at the end of the month, 100% complete as to materials and 50% complete as to conversion cost. Materials and conversion cost of $27,000 and $40,000, respectively, were charged to the department in October.

Required: Compute the total cost transferred to Department B.   (AICPA adapted)

3. Equivalent production. The Felix Manufacturing Company uses a process cost system to account for the cost of its only product, known as Nino. Production begins in the Fabrication Department, where units of raw material are molded into various connecting parts. After fabrication is complete, the units are transferred to the Assembly Department. There is no material added in the Assembly Department. After assembly is complete, the units are transferred to the Packaging Department, where the units are packaged for shipment. At the completion of this process, the units are complete and are transferred to the Shipping Department.

At year end, December 31, the following inventory of Nino is on hand:

(a) No unused raw material or packaging material.

(b) Fabrication Department: 6,000 units, 25% complete as to raw material and 40% complete as to direct labor.

(c) Assembly Department: 10,000 units, 75% complete as to direct labor.

(d) Packaging Department: 3,000 units, 60% complete as to packaging material and 75% complete as to direct labor.

(e) Shipping Department: 8,000 units.

Required: As of December 31, compute:

(1) The number of equivalent units of raw material in all inventories.

(2) The number of equivalent units of Fabrication Department direct labor in all inventories.

(3) The number of equivalent units of Packaging Department material and direct labor in the Packaging Department inventory.   (AICPA adapted)

4. Cost of production report. A company's Department 2 costs for June were:

Cost from Department 1	$16,320
Cost added in Department 2:	
Materials	43,415
Labor	56,100
Factory overhead	58,575

The quantity schedule shows 12,000 units were received during the month from Department 1; 7,000 units were transferred to finished goods; and 5,000 units in process at the end of June were 50% complete as to materials cost and 25% complete as to conversion cost.

Required: Prepare a cost of production report.

5. Cost of production report; normal loss. *For December, the Production Control Department of Loren Chemical, Inc. reported the following production data for Department 2:*

Transferred in from Department 1..................................	55 000 liters
Transferred out to Department 3....................................	39 500 liters
In process at end of December (with ⅓ labor and factory overhead) ...	10 500 liters

All materials were put into process in Department 1. The Cost Department collected these figures for Department 2:

Unit cost for units transferred in from Department 1	$1.80
Labor cost in Department 2	$27,520
Applied factory overhead	15,480

Required: *Prepare a cost of production report for Department 2 for December.*

6. Cost of production report; abnormal loss. *During February, the Assembly Department received 60,000 units from the Cutting Department at a unit cost of $3.54. Costs added in the Assembly Department were: materials, $41,650; labor, $101,700; and factory overhead, $56,500. There was no beginning inventory. Of the 60,000 units received, 50,000 were transferred out; 9,000 units were in process at the end of the month (all materials, ⅔ converted); 1,000 lost units were ½ complete as to materials and conversion costs. The entire loss is considered abnormal and is to be charged to factory overhead.*

Required: *Prepare a cost of production report.*

7. Cost of production report; normal and abnormal spoilage. *Farniente Company uses process costing. In Department B, conversion costs are incurred uniformly throughout the process. Materials are added following inspection, which occurs at the 90% stage of completion. Normal spoilage is discovered during the inspection and is expected to be 5% of good output.*

The following information related to Department B for January:

	Units	Dollars
Received from Department A	12,000	$84,000
Transferred to finished goods	9,000	
Ending inventory (70% complete).................	2,000	
Cost incurred:		
Materials......................................		18,000
Labor and factory overhead.....................		45,200

Required: *Prepare a cost of production report for Department B.*

8. Cost of production report; normal and abnormal spoiled units. *Kraker Company uses process costing in accounting for its production department, which uses two materials. Material A is added at the beginning of the process. Inspection is at the 90% stage. Material B is then added to the good units. Normal spoilage units amount to 5% of good output. Company records contain the following information for January:*

Started during the period..	10,000 units
Material A..	$13,370
Material B..	$ 4,500
Direct labor cost	$37,580
Factory overhead	$46,975
Transferred to finished goods....................................	7,000 units
Ending inventory (95% complete, and includes all Material B)	2,000 units

Required: *Prepare a cost of production report.*

PROBLEMS

4-1. Cost of production report; normal spoilage. Moffo Company uses process costing. All materials are added at the beginning of the process. The product is inspected when it is 80% converted, and spoilage is identified only at that point. Normal spoilage is expected to be 5% of good output.

During March, 10,500 units were put into process. Current costs were $52,500 for materials; $39,770 for labor; and $31,525 for factory overhead. The 3,000 units still in process at the end of March were estimated to be 90% complete. A total of 7,000 units were transferred to finished goods.

Required: Prepare a cost of production report for March.

4-2. Cost of production report; normal spoilage. Navarro Milling Company produces one product, processed in three departments. During May, 110,000 units were completed in Department One at a total cost of $176,000 and were transferred to the next department. From this quantity, Department Two completed and transferred out 85,000 units. The May 31 work in process inventory of Department Two is 22,000 units, ¼ completed as to labor and factory overhead. Department Two's labor and factory overhead costs for May were $26,245 and $12,670, respectively, and the department's spoilage was normal and occurred during processing.

Required: Prepare a cost of production report for Department Two. Compute the adjustment for lost units to five decimal places.

4-3. Quantity and equivalent production schedules; adjustment for lost units. Fleming Laboratories, Inc. produces an antibiotic product in its three producing departments. The following quantitative and cost data have been made available:

	Department		
	Blending	Testing	Terminal
Production data:			
Started into production................	8 000 kg	5 400 kg	3 200 kg
Transferred to next department........	5 400	3 200	
Transferred to finished goods storeroom.			2 100
In process (100% materials, ⅓ labor and			
overhead)	2 400	1 800	
In process (100% materials, ⅔ labor and			
overhead)			900
Cost charged to departments:			
Materials	$20,670	$ 7,980	$14,400
Labor	11,160	5,016	11,520
Factory overhead	5,580	2,280	5,040
Total................................	$37,410	$15,276	$30,960

Lost units are normal and apply to all production.

Required:
(1) Prepare a quantity schedule for each of the three departments.
(2) Prepare an equivalent production schedule for each of the three departments.
(3) Compute the unit cost of factory overhead in the Blending Department.
(4) Compute the lost unit cost adjustment in the Testing Department if the unit cost transferred in from the Blending Department is $5.35.

4-4. Cost of production report; normal spoilage. Popovich, Inc. uses process costing in its two producing departments. Materials are added after quality control inspection, which occurs at the 90% stage of completion. No abnormal spoilage occurred during the month.

During October, 2,500 units were received from Department 1 at a cost of $50,000. Costs incurred by Department 2 during October were:

Materials	$ 8,000
Conversion costs	35,700

A total of 2,000 units were transferred to finished goods inventory.

The 300 units still in process at the end of October were ⅔ complete as to conversion costs.

Required: Prepare a cost of production report for Department 2.

4-5. Cost of production report; units lost at end, all normal. Campbell Milling Company manufactures a product requiring processing in three departments, with all materials put into process in the first department. During May, 110,000 units were completed in Department One at a total cost of $176,000 and were transferred to the next department. From this lot, Department Two completed and transferred out 85,000 units, incurring labor cost of $26,180 and factory overhead cost of $13,090. The May 31 work in process inventory of Department Two is 22,000 units, ¼ completed as to labor and factory overhead. Department Two spoilage occurs at the end of processing and is normal.

Required: Prepare a cost of production report for Department Two, rounding unit costs to the nearest cent.

4-6. Cost of production report; spoiled units — normal and abnormal. Menninger, Inc. uses process costing in its two producing departments. In Department 2, inspection takes place at the 96% stage of completion, after which materials are added to good units. A spoilage rate of 3% of good output is considered normal.

Department 2 records for April show:

Received from Department 1..................................	30,000 units
Cost	$135,000
Materials ....:	$ 12,500
Conversion cost	$139,340
Transferred to finished goods	25,000 units
Ending work in process inventory (50% complete)................	4,200 units

Required: Prepare a cost of production report for Department 2.

4-7. Cost of production report; normal and abnormal spoilage. Gross Company uses process costing in its two producing departments. The following information pertains to Department 2 for November.

Normal spoilage is 5% of good output; inspection and identification of spoilage take place at the 90% stage of completion; materials are added after inspection.

Department 2 received 14,000 units from Department 1 at a cost of $140,000. Department 2 costs were $12,000 for materials and $89,250 for conversion costs.

A total of 8,000 units were completed and transferred to finished goods. At the end of the month, 5,000 units were still in process, estimated to be 60% complete as to conversion costs.

Required: Prepare a cost of production report for Department 2.

Chapter 5
Process Costing: Addition of Materials; Average and Fifo Costing

The previous process costing chapter discussed the fundamentals of the cost of production report and lost unit calculations. The discussion of process costing is now continued to include the effect of adding materials in departments other than the first, and the effect of beginning work in process inventories.

Addition of Materials

The addition of materials in departments subsequent to the first has two possible effects on units and costs in process:

1. The additional materials increase the unit cost, since these materials become a part of the product manufactured, but do not increase the number of final units. For example, in a finishing plant of a textile company, the material added is often a bleach; in a wire company, a plating mixture; in an automobile assembly plant, additional parts. These materials are needed to give the product certain specified qualities, characteristics, or completeness; or

2. The added materials increase the number of units and also cause a change in unit cost. For example, in processing a chemical, water is often added to a mixture. As a result, the number of units increases and costs are spread over a greater number of units.

Increase in Unit Cost

In the simplest case, added materials, such as parts of an automobile, do not increase the number of units but increase the total cost and unit costs. A materials unit cost must be computed for the department, and a materials cost must be included in the work in process inventory.

The cost of production report of the Terminal Department of Clonex Corporation (page 76) is used to illustrate the different effects of the addition of materials on total and unit costs of a department. Assume that additional materials costing $17,020 are placed in process and charged to the Terminal Department. Assume further that these materials are sufficient to complete 2,000 of the 4,000 units; that is, units are 50 percent complete as to materials cost. The effect of the additional materials cost is shown in the following cost report:

Clonex Corporation
Terminal Department
Cost of Production Report
For January, 19--

Quantity Schedule

Units received from preceding department		40,000
Units transferred to finished goods storeroom	35,000	
Units still in process (½ materials — ¼ labor and factory overhead)	4,000	
Units lost in process.....................................	1,000	40,000

Cost Charged to the Department	Total Cost	Unit Cost
Cost from preceding department:		
Transferred in during the month (40,000 units).............	$140,400	$3.51
Cost added by department:		
Materials..	$ 17,020	$ .46
Labor..	32,400	.90
Factory overhead	19,800	.55
Total cost added	$ 69,220	$1.91
Adjustment for lost units		$ .09
Total cost to be accounted for	**$209,620**	**$5.51**

Cost Accounted for as Follows

Transferred to finished goods storeroom (35,000 × $5.51)		$192,850
Work in process — ending inventory:		
Adjusted cost from preceding department (4,000 × $3.60) ...	$ 14,400	
Materials (4,000 × ½ × $.46)	920	
Labor (4,000 × ¼ × $.90)	900	
Factory overhead (4,000 × ¼ × $.55)....................	550	16,770
Total cost accounted for..............................		**$209,620**

Additional computations:

Equivalent production: Materials $= 35,000 + \dfrac{4,000}{2} = 37,000$ units

Labor and factory overhead $= 35,000 + \dfrac{4,000}{4} = 36,000$ units

Unit costs: Materials $= \dfrac{\$17,020}{37,000} = \$.46$ per unit

Labor $= \dfrac{\$32,400}{36,000} = \$.90$ per unit

Factory overhead $= \dfrac{\$19,800}{36,000} = \$.55$ per unit

Adjustment for lost units:

Method No. 1 — $\dfrac{\$140,400}{39,000} = \$3.60$; $\$3.60 - \$3.51 = \$.09$ per unit

Method No. 2 — 1,000 units $\times \$3.51 = \$3,510$; $\dfrac{\$\,3,510}{39,000} = \$.09$ per unit

The only differences in the two cost reports (pages 76 and 87) are the $17,020 materials cost charged to the department and the $.46 materials unit cost ($17,020 ÷ 37,000). The additional materials cost is also reflected in the total cost to be accounted for, in the cost of units transferred to finished goods, and in the ending work in process inventory.

Increase in Units and Change in Unit Cost

When additional materials result in additional units, different computations are necessary. The greater number of units causes a decrease in unit cost, which necessitates an adjustment of the preceding department's unit cost, since the increased number of units will absorb the same total cost transferred from the preceding department.

To illustrate this situation, assume Terminal Department costs for labor and factory overhead of $32,400 and $19,800, respectively, an additional materials cost of $17,020, and an increase of 8,000 units as the result of added materials. The effect of these assumptions on the Terminal Department's cost of production report is shown on page 89.

The additional 8,000 units are entered in the department's quantity schedule as "Additional units put into process." The quantity schedule reports that 44,000 units were completed and transferred to the finished goods storeroom and that 4,000 units are still in process, 50 percent complete as to materials and 25 percent complete as to labor and factory overhead. Therefore, equivalent production is 46,000 units for materials and 45,000 units for labor and factory overhead. Dividing departmental materials, labor, and factory overhead costs for the period by these production figures results in a unit cost of $.37 ($17,020 ÷ 46,000) for materials, $.72 ($32,400 ÷ 45,000) for labor, and $.44 ($19,800 ÷ 45,000) for factory overhead.

Clonex Corporation
Terminal Department
Cost of Production Report
For January, 19--

Quantity Schedule

Units received from preceding department	40,000	
Additional units put into process	8,000	48,000
Units transferred to finished goods storeroom	44,000	
Units still in process (½ materials — ¼ labor and factory overhead)	4,000	48,000

Cost Charged to the Department	Total Cost	Unit Cost
Cost from preceding department:		
Transferred in during the month (40,000 units).	$140,400	$3.510
Cost added by department:		
Materials	$ 17,020	$ .370
Labor	32,400	.720
Factory overhead	19,800	.440
Total cost added	$ 69,220	$1.530
Adjusted unit cost of units transferred in during the month		2.925
Total cost to be accounted for	$209,620	$4.455

Cost Accounted for as Follows

Transferred to finished goods storeroom (44,000 × $4.455). . . .		$196,020
Work in process — ending inventory:		
Adjusted cost from preceding department (4,000 × $2.925). .	$ 11,700	
Materials (4,000 × ½ × $.370)	740	
Labor (4,000 × ¼ × $.720)	720	
Factory overhead (4,000 × ¼ × $.440).	440	13,600
Total cost accounted for.		$209,620

Additional computations:

$$\text{Equivalent production: Materials} = 44,000 + \frac{4,000}{2} = 46,000 \text{ units}$$

$$\text{Labor and factory overhead} = 44,000 + \frac{4,000}{4} = 45,000 \text{ units}$$

$$\text{Unit costs: Materials} = \frac{\$17,020}{46,000} = \$.370 \text{ per unit}$$

$$\text{Labor} = \frac{\$32,400}{45,000} = \$.720 \text{ per unit}$$

$$\text{Factory overhead} = \frac{\$19,800}{45,000} = \$.440 \text{ per unit}$$

$$\text{Adjustment for additional units: } \frac{\$140,400}{48,000} = \$2.925 \text{ per unit}$$

These computations do not differ from those already discussed. Peculiar to this situation of additional materials is the adjustment of the preceding department's unit cost. Total cost charged to the Terminal Department as cost transferred in from the preceding department must now be allocated over a greater number of units, thereby reducing the unit cost of work done in the preceding department.

In the illustration on page 87, the $140,400 cost transferred to the Terminal Department was absorbed by 40,000 units, resulting in a unit cost of $3.51. Because of the increase in units, the $140,400 cost must now be spread over 48,000 units, resulting in a unit cost of $2.925 for the preceding department. This adjusted cost is inserted in the production report on page 89 as "Adjusted unit cost of units transferred in during the month" and is added to departmental unit costs to arrive at the unit cost accumulated to the end of operations in the Terminal Department.

When additional materials increase the number of units being processed, it is still possible to have lost units. However, if both an increase and a loss occur, no separate calculation is required for the lost units; only net units added are used. In the illustration above, 8,000 additional units resulted from added materials. It is quite possible, though, that the materials added should have yielded 10,000 additional units. If 2,000 units were lost in processing, the effect is similar to that of units lost in the first department; that is, the cost is absorbed within the department as an increase in unit costs. However, if desired, it is also possible to report separately the effect of the loss, which can be determined as follows: (1) compute the unit cost of work done in preceding departments and in the Terminal Department as if no loss had occurred; (2) compute the loss by multiplying the unit cost obtained in the preceding computation by the 2,000 lost units.

Beginning Work in Process Inventories

The cost of production reports illustrated in Chapter 4 list ending work in process inventories. These inventories become beginning inventories of the next period. Two of the possible methods of accounting for these beginning inventory costs are:

1. *Average costing.* Beginning inventory costs are added to the costs of the new period.
2. *First-in, first-out (fifo) costing.* Beginning inventory costs are kept separate from the new costs necessary to complete the work in process inventory.

Average Costing

The average costing method of accounting for beginning work in process inventory costs involves merging these costs with the costs of the new period.

To accomplish this relatively simple task, representative average unit costs must be determined.

The February cost reports of the three departments reviewed in Chapter 4 are used to illustrate the treatment of beginning work in process inventory and to show the relationship of costs from one period to the next. Ending inventories in January departmental cost reports become beginning work in process inventories for February and are summarized as follows:

	Blending	Testing	Terminal
Units...	4,000	3,000	4,000
Cost from preceding department....................	—	$5,400	$14,400
Materials in process..............................	$2,000	—	—
Labor in process..................................	1,240	910	900
Factory overhead in process	1,200	800	550

Blending Department. The February 1 work in process inventory of the Blending Department shows a $2,000 materials cost, a $1,240 labor cost, a $1,200 factory overhead cost, and 4,000 units in process. During February, additional charges to the department are: materials, $19,840; labor, $24,180; and factory overhead, $22,580. The additional materials put into process are for the production of 40,000 units. Therefore, units to be accounted for total 44,000 (4,000 + 40,000). Of the total units put into process, 39,000 are completed, with 38,000 units transferred to the Testing Department and 1,000 units awaiting transfer. At month end, 3,000 units are in process, 100 percent complete as to materials but only 66⅔ percent complete as to labor and overhead. During the month, 2,000 units were lost. In the Blending Department as well as in the subsequent departments in this illustration, it is assumed that the loss applies to all good units and that the loss is within normal tolerance limits. The above facts are illustrated in the cost of production report on page 92.

The unit cost of work done in the Blending Department is $1.72, consisting of $.52 for materials, $.62 for labor, and $.58 for factory overhead. The $.52 unit cost for materials is computed by adding the materials cost in the beginning work in process inventory to the materials cost for the month ($2,000 + $19,840) and dividing the $21,840 total by the equivalent production figure of 42,000 units. These units include the 38,000 units completed and transferred, the 1,000 units completed but still on hand, and the 3,000 units in process, which are complete as to materials. The cost of materials already in process is added to the materials cost for the month before dividing by the equivalent production figure. This method results in an average unit cost for work done in the current and preceding periods.

The same procedure is followed in computing unit costs for labor and factory overhead. The $.62 unit cost for labor is the result of dividing equivalent production of 41,000 units [39,000 + (2/3 × 3,000)] into the sum of the beginning inventory labor cost of $1,240 and the departmental labor cost of $24,180 for the month. The factory overhead unit cost is $.58 [($1,200 + $22,580) ÷ 41,000].

Clonex Corporation
Blending Department
Cost of Production Report—Average Costing
For February, 19--

Quantity Schedule

Units in process at beginning (all materials—½ labor and factory overhead)..	4,000	
Units started in process.....................................	40,000	44,000
Units transferred to next department........................	38,000	
Units completed and on hand..............................	1,000	
Units still in process (all materials—⅔ labor and factory overhead)..	3,000	
Units lost in process.......................................	2,000	44,000

Cost Charged to the Department	Total Cost	Unit Cost
Cost added by department:		
Work in process—beginning inventory:		
Materials...	$ 2,000	
Labor..	1,240	
Factory overhead	1,200	
Cost added during period:		
Materials...	19,840	$ .52
Labor..	24,180	.62
Factory overhead	22,580	.58
Total cost to be accounted for	**$71,040**	**$1.72**

Cost Accounted for as Follows

Transferred to next department (38,000 × $1.72)		$65,360
Work in process—ending inventory:		
Completed and on hand (1,000 × $1.72)	$ 1,720	
Materials (3,000 × $.52)	1,560	
Labor (3,000 × ⅔ × $.62)	1,240	
Factory overhead (3,000 × ⅔ × $.58).....................	1,160	5,680
Total cost accounted for.............................		**$71,040**

Additional computations:

Equivalent production: Materials = 38,000 + 1,000 + 3,000 = 42,000 units

Labor and factory overhead = 38,000 + 1,000 + (⅔ × 3,000)
= 41,000 units

Unit costs: Materials = $2,000 + $19,840 = $21,840; $\dfrac{\$21,840}{42,000}$ = $.52 per unit

Labor = $1,240 + $24,180 = $25,420; $\dfrac{\$25,420}{41,000}$ = $.62 per unit

Factory overhead = $1,200 + $22,580 = $23,780; $\dfrac{\$23,780}{41,000}$ = $.58 per unit

Of the total cost charged to the department, $65,360 is transferred to the Testing Department when the following entry is recorded:

Work in Process—Testing Department......................   65,360
    Work in Process—Blending Department   65,360

The cost remaining in the Testing Department, $5,680, is assigned to the ending work in process inventory. The work in process inventory consists of $1,720 (1,000 units × $1.72) for units completed and on hand and of the following costs assigned to units still in process: $1,560 (3,000 units × $.52) for materials; $1,240 (2,000 units × $.62) for labor; and $1,160 (2,000 units × $.58) for factory overhead. The 1,000 units completed but on hand are listed as work in process in the Blending Department because this department is still responsible for these units.

Testing Department. Accounting for the beginning work in process inventory cost in a department other than the first requires additional analysis. When the prior period's ending work in process inventory was computed, part of the cost of this inventory came from costs added by the preceding department. Because costs assigned to the beginning work in process inventory are added to costs incurred during the period and the total is divided by equivalent production, the beginning work in process inventory of departments other than the first must be split into the following two parts:

1. Cost transferred from preceding departments.
2. Cost added by the department itself.

The portion of the beginning work in process inventory cost from preceding departments is entered in the section of the cost report entitled "Cost from preceding department." It is added to the cost of transfers received from the preceding department during the current period. An average unit cost for work done in preceding departments is then computed. The other portion of the beginning inventory cost, which was added by the Testing Department, is entered as a departmental cost to be added to other departmental costs incurred during the current period. Average unit costs are then computed.

The cost of production report of the Testing Department presented on page 94 illustrates these procedures. The analysis of the beginning work in process inventory of this department (page 91) lists 3,000 units in process with a cost of $5,400 from the preceding department, a labor cost of $910, and $800 for factory overhead. The following costs pertain to February: cost from the preceding department, $65,360; labor, $34,050; factory overhead, $30,018. Units completed and transferred to the Terminal Department totaled 36,000; 4,000 units are in process, 50 percent complete as to labor and factory overhead; 1,000 units were lost in process.

The $5,400 portion of the beginning work in process inventory, which is cost from the preceding department, is entered in the current month's cost report as work in process—beginning inventory. It is added to the $65,360 of cost transferred from the Blending Department to the Testing Department

Clonex Corporation
Testing Department
Cost of Production Report—Average Costing
For February, 19--

Quantity Schedule

Units in process at beginning (⅓ labor and factory overhead) . .	3,000	
Units received from preceding department	38,000	41,000
Units transferred to next department.	36,000	
Units still in process (½ labor and factory overhead).	4,000	
Units lost in process	1,000	41,000

Cost Charged to the Department		Total Cost	Unit Cost
Cost from preceding department:			
Work in process—beginning inventory (3,000 units)		$ 5,400	$1.800
Transferred in during this period	(38,000 units)	65,360	1.720
Total	(41,000 units)	$ 70,760	$1.726
Cost added by department:			
Work in process—beginning inventory:			
Labor		$ 910	
Factory overhead		800	
Cost added during period:			
Labor		34,050	$ .920
Factory overhead		30,018	.811
Total cost added		$ 65,778	$ 1.731
Adjustment for lost units			$ .043
Total cost to be accounted for		**$136,538**	**$ 3.500**

Cost Accounted for as Follows:

Transferred to next department (36,000 × $3.500)		$126,000
Work in process—ending inventory:		
Adjusted cost from preceding department [4,000 × ($1.726 + $.043)]	$ 7,076	
Labor (4,000 × ½ × $.920)	1,840	
Factory overhead (4,000 × ½ × $.811)	1,622	10,538
Total cost accounted for		**$136,538**

Additional computations:

Unit cost from preceding department $= \dfrac{\$70,760}{41,000} = \$1.726$ per unit

Equivalent production: Labor and factory overhead $= 36,000 + \dfrac{4,000}{2} = 38,000$ units

Unit costs: Labor $= \$910 + \$34,050 = \$34,960; \dfrac{\$34,960}{38,000} = \$.920$ per unit

Factory overhead $= \$800 + \$30,018 = \$30,818; \dfrac{\$30,818}{38,000} = \$.811$ per unit

Adjustment for lost units:

Method No. 1 $— \dfrac{\$70,760}{40,000} = \$1.769; \$1.769 - \$1.726 = \$.043$ per unit

Method No. 2 $—1,000$ units $\times \$1.726 = \$1,726; \dfrac{\$ 1,726}{40,000} = \$.043$ per unit during the month. The average unit cost for work done in the preceding department is $1.726, computed by dividing total cost received from the Blending Department, $70,760 ($5,400 + $65,360), by 41,000 units. These units consist of 3,000 units in the beginning work in process inventory and 38,000 units received during the month. The unit cost is a weighted average, since it considers all units and costs received from the preceding department. It is not the average of the two unit costs, $1.80 and $1.72. A simple average would not be accurate, since there are more units with a unit cost of $1.72 (38,000 units) than with a unit cost of $1.80 (3,000 units).

Departmental unit costs for labor and factory overhead are computed as explained in discussing the cost report of the Blending Department. The $910 of labor in process at the beginning is added to labor put in process during the month, $34,050. The total of these two labor costs, $34,960, is divided by an equivalent production figure of 38,000 units [36,000 + (4,000 × 1/2)] to arrive at a unit cost of $.920. The factory overhead unit cost of $.811 is the result of dividing total factory overhead, $30,818 ($800 + $30,018), by equivalent production of 38,000 units. The departmental unit cost is the sum of these two unit costs, $.920 + $.811, or $1.731.

The lost unit cost is computed on the assumption that units lost cannot be identified as coming from either units in process at the beginning or from units received during the period, but proportionately from both sources. The lost unit cost adjustment of $.043 is computed by dividing total preceding department cost, $70,760, by remaining good units, 40,000, and subtracting from this adjusted unit cost of $1.769 the previous average unit cost of $1.726. The lost unit adjustment can also be determined by multiplying the 1,000 lost units by the preceding department's average unit cost of $1.726, and dividing the $1,726 result by the 40,000 remaining good units. The lost unit cost adjustment is added to the $1.731 departmental unit cost and the unadjusted average preceding department unit cost of $1.726 to give a cumulative unit cost figure of $3.50.

The total cost to be accounted for is $136,538. Of this total, $126,000 is the cost of the 36,000 units completed and transferred. The balance is cost assigned to the ending work in process inventory. The following entry transfers the cost of the 36,000 units to the next department:

Work in Process — Terminal Department	126,000	
Work in Process — Testing Department		126,000

Terminal Department. To complete this discussion of operations for February, the cost of production report of the Terminal Department is shown on page 96. The following entry transfers the cost of the 36,000 finished units to finished goods:

Finished Goods	182,160	
Work in Process — Terminal Department		182,160

Combined Cost of Production Report — Average Costing. Although the cost reports of each department are presented separately, operations for the month would also be combined in a single cost report as illustrated on page 97.

Clonex Corporation
Terminal Department
Cost of Production Report—Average Costing
For February, 19--

Quantity Schedule

Units in process at beginning (¼ labor and factory overhead) . .	4,000	
Units received from preceding department	36,000	40,000
Units transferred to finished goods storeroom	36,000	
Units still in process (⅓ labor and factory overhead).	3,000	
Units lost in process.	1,000	40,000

Cost Charged to the Department	Total Cost	Unit Cost
Cost from preceding department:		
Work in process—beginning inventory (4,000 units)	$ 14,400	$ 3.60
Transferred in during this period (36,000 units)	126,000	3.50
Total (40,000 units)	$140,400	$ 3.51
Cost added by department:		
Work in process—beginning inventory:		
Labor.	$ 900	
Factory overhead	550	
Costs added during period:		
Labor.	33,140	$ .92
Factory overhead	19,430	.54
Total cost added	$ 54,020	$ 1.46
Adjustment for lost units		$ .09
Total cost to be accounted for.	194,420	$ 5.06

Cost Accounted for as Follows

Transferred to finished goods storeroom (36,000 × $5.06)		$182,160
Work in process—ending inventory:		
Adjusted cost from preceding department [3,000 × ($3.51 +		
$.09)]	$ 10,800	
Labor (3,000 × ⅓ × $.92)	920	
Factory overhead (3,000 × ⅓ × $.54).	540	12,260
Total cost accounted for.		$194,420

Additional computations:

$$\text{Unit cost from preceding department} = \frac{\$140,400}{40,000} = \$3.51 \text{ per unit}$$

$$\text{Equivalent production: Labor and factory overhead} = 36,000 + \frac{3,000}{3} = 37,000 \text{ units}$$

$$\text{Unit costs: Labor} = \$900 + \$33,140 = \$34,040; \frac{\$34,040}{37,000} = \$.92 \text{ per unit}$$

$$\text{Factory overhead} = \$550 + \$19,430 = \$19,980; \frac{\$19,980}{37,000} = \$.54 \text{ per unit}$$

Adjustment for lost units:

$$\text{Method No. 1} - \frac{\$140,400}{39,000} = \$3.60; \$3.60 - \$3.51 = \$.09 \text{ per unit}$$

$$\text{Method No. 2} - 1,000 \times \$3.51 = \$3.510; \frac{\$3,510}{39,000} = \$.09 \text{ per unit}$$

Clonex Corporation
All Producing Departments
Cost of Production Report — Average Costing
For February, 19--

	Blending		Testing		Terminal	
Quantity Schedule						
Units in process at beginning.........	4,000		3,000		4,000	
Units started in process..............	40,000	44,000				
Units received from preceding department			38,000	41,000	36,000	40,000
Units transferred to next department...	38,000		36,000			
Units transferred to finished goods storeroom					36,000	
Units completed and on hand.........	1,000					
Units still in process	3,000		4,000		3,000	
Units lost in process.................	2,000	44,000	1,000	41,000	1,000	40,000

	Blending Total Cost	Blending Unit Cost	Testing Total Cost	Testing Unit Cost	Terminal Total Cost	Terminal Unit Cost
Cost Charged to the Department						
Cost from preceding department:						
Work in process — beginning inventory......................			$ 5,400	$ 1.800	$ 14,400	$3.60
Transferred in during this period			65,360	1.720	126,000	3.50
Total.............................			$ 70,760	$ 1.726	$140,400	$3.51
Cost added by department:						
Work in process — beginning inventory:						
Materials......................	$ 2,000					
Labor..........................	1,240		$ 910		$ 900	
Factory overhead	1,200		800		550	
Cost added during period:						
Materials......................	19,840	$ .52				
Labor..........................	24,180	.62	34,050	$ .920	33,140	$ .92
Factory overhead	22,580	.58	30,018	.811	19,430	.54
Total cost added	$71,040	$ 1.72	$ 65,778	$ 1.731	$ 54,020	$1.46
Adjustment for lost units				$ .043		$ .09
Total cost to be accounted for ..	$71,040	$ 1.72	$136,538	$ 3.500	$194,420	$5.06
Cost Accounted for as Follows						
Transferred to next department		$65,360		$126,000		
Transferred to finished goods storeroom						$182,160
Work in process — ending inventory:						
Completed and on hand		$ 1,720				
Adjusted cost from preceding department.....................				$ 7,076		$ 10,800
Materials........................		1,560				
Labor...........................		1,240		1,840		920
Factory overhead		1,160		1,622		540
Total cost accounted for		5,680 $71,040		10,538 $136,538		12,260 $194,420

First-In, First-Out (Fifo) Costing

The first-in, first-out method may be used to account for beginning work in process inventory costs in process costing. Under this method, the beginning work in process inventory costs are separated from costs incurred in the current period and are not averaged with the additional new costs. This procedure gives one unit cost for units completed from the beginning work in process inventory and another for units started and finished in the same period. The cost of completing units in process at the beginning of the period is computed first, followed by the computation of the cost of units started and finished within the period.

To illustrate the fifo method, the February cost of production reports for Clonex Corporation are presented on the following pages. A comparison of these reports with those illustrated for the average costing method indicates that the two methods do not result in significantly different unit costs, since in general, manufacturing operations in process cost type industries are more or less uniform from period to period.

Blending Department. The February cost of production report of the Blending Department, using the fifo method, is shown on pages 99 and 100. When the report is compared to the average costing report on page 92, the following differences are apparent:

1. Under fifo costing, the beginning work in process inventory cost of $4,440 is kept separate and is not broken down into its component parts.
2. Under fifo costing, the degree of completion of the beginning work in process inventory must be stated in order to compute completed unit costs.

Under fifo costing, the cost of completing the 4,000 units in process at the beginning of February must be computed first. No additional materials were needed; but since these units were only 50 percent complete as to labor and factory overhead, more labor and overhead cost must be added.

To determine costs expended in completing the units in the beginning inventory and to arrive at the cost of units started and finished within the current period, unit costs are computed for materials, labor, and factory overhead added during the period. Materials added during February, costing $19,840, were sufficient to complete an equivalent production of 38,000 units. Of these 38,000 units, 34,000 were started and completed during the period, 3,000 units are in process at month end, with all the necessary materials, and 1,000 units were complete but still on hand. Therefore, the unit cost for materials is $.522 ($19,840 ÷ 38,000).

The labor cost for February is $24,180, and the overhead cost is $22,580. The labor and overhead unit costs are computed after determining the number of units that could have been completed from these total costs. The labor cost and the overhead cost were sufficient to complete (1) 50 percent or 2,000 of the 4,000 units in the beginning inventory; (2) 34,000 units started and completed

Clonex Corporation
Blending Department
Cost of Production Report—Fifo Costing
For February, 19--

Quantity Schedule

Units in process at beginning (all materials—½ labor and factory overhead)	4,000	
Units started in process	40,000	44,000
Units transferred to next department	38,000	
Units completed and on hand	1,000	
Units still in process (all materials—⅔ labor and factory overhead)	3,000	
Units lost in process	2,000	44,000

Cost Charged to the Department	Total Cost	Unit Cost
Work in process—beginning inventory	$ 4,440	
Cost added by department:		
Materials	$19,840	$ .522
Labor	24,180	.620
Factory overhead	22,580	.579
Total cost added	$66,600	1.721
Total cost to be accounted for	$71,040	

Cost Accounted for as Follows

Transferred to next department—		
From beginning inventory:		
Inventory cost	$4,440	
Labor added (4,000 × ½ × $.620)	1,240	
Factory overhead added (4,000 × ½ × $.579)	1,158	$ 6,838
From current production:		
Units started and finished (34,000 × $1.721)	58,517*	$65,355
Work in process—ending inventory:		
Completed and on hand (1,000 × $1.721)	$ 1,721	
Materials (3,000 × $.522)	1,566	
Labor (3,000 × ⅔ × $.620)	1,240	
Factory overhead (3,000 × ⅔ × $.579)	1,158	5,685
Total cost accounted for		$71,040

Additional computations:

Equivalent production:	Materials	Labor and Factory Overhead
Transferred out	38,000	38,000
Less beginning inventory (all units)	4,000	4,000
Started and finished this period	34,000	34,000
Add beginning inventory (work this period)	-0-	2,000
Add ending inventory:		
Completed and on hand	1,000	1,000
Still in process (work this period)	3,000	2,000
	38,000 units	39,000 units

*34,000 units × $1.721 per unit = $58,514. To avoid a decimal discrepancy, the cost transferred from current production is computed as follows: $71,040—($6,838 + $5,685) = $58,517.

$$\text{Unit costs: Materials} = \frac{\$19,840}{38,000} = \$.522 \text{ per unit}$$

$$\text{Labor} = \frac{\$24,180}{39,000} = \$.620 \text{ per unit}$$

$$\text{Factory overhead} = \frac{\$22,580}{39,000} = \$.579 \text{ per unit}$$

this period; (3) 1,000 units still on hand; and (4) 2/3 or 2,000 of the 3,000 units still in process. Therefore, the equivalent production for labor and overhead is 39,000 units. The unit cost for labor is $.620 ($24,180 ÷ 39,000), and the unit cost for factory overhead is $.579 ($22,580 ÷ 39,000).

In average costing, the cost of the units transferred to the next department was computed by multiplying the number of units transferred by the final unit cost. Under fifo costing, units in process at the beginning must be completed first and will usually have a completed unit cost that is different from the unit cost for work started and finished during the period. Two separate computations determine the total cost transferred to the next department.

No additional materials were needed to complete the beginning work in process inventory. The cost of labor and factory overhead used during the period in completing the beginning inventory units is added to the $4,440 already included as a cost of these units. Labor and overhead were added at unit costs of $.620 for labor and $.579 for factory overhead to complete the equivalent of 2,000 of the 4,000 units in process. The labor cost added was $1,240 (2,000 × $.620), and factory overhead was $1,158 (2,000 × $.579). The total cost of the 4,000 units completed and transferred was $6,838 ($4,440 + $1,240 + $1,158). The other 34,000 units were transferred at a unit cost of $1.721, or at a total of $58,517. The remaining $5,685 cost to be accounted for is in work in process at the end of the period and is computed as shown on the cost of production report on page 99.

The following entry transfers the total cost of the 38,000 units sent to the next department:

Work in Process—Testing Department 65,355
Work in Process—Blending Department.....................   65,355

Testing Department. The cost report of the Testing Department is illustrated on pages 101 and 102. Although the cost transferred out of the Blending Department was the result of two separate computations, the total cost transferred into the Testing Department is shown as only one amount in its cost report. The unit cost of $1.72 is obtained by dividing the 38,000 total units received into the total cost received of $65,355 ($6,838 + $58,517). This procedure seems to cancel out the apparent advantages of the fifo method and has been criticized by some writers.

The balance of the Testing Department report is consistent with the fifo method of costing. The beginning work in process inventory, valued at $7,110, is shown in total and is not broken down into its component parts. Labor and factory overhead costs needed to complete the units in the beginning inven-

Clonex Corporation
Testing Department
Cost of Production Report—Fifo Costing
For February, 19--

Quantity Schedule

Units in process at beginning (⅓ labor and factory overhead) . . .	3,000	
Units received from preceding department	38,000	41,000
Units transferred to next department	36,000	
Units still in process (½ labor and factory overhead)	4,000	
Units lost in process	1,000	41,000

Cost Charged to the Department	Total Cost	Unit Cost
Work in process—beginning inventory	$ 7,110	
Cost from preceding department:		
Transferred in during the month (38,000 units)	$ 65,355	$ 1.720
Cost added by department:		
Labor	$ 34,050	$ .920
Factory overhead	30,018	.811
Total cost added	$ 64,068	$ 1.731
Adjustment for lost units		$ .046
Total cost to be accounted for	$136,533	$ 3.497

Cost Accounted for as Follows

Transferred to next department—			
From beginning inventory:			
Inventory cost	$7,110		
Labor added (3,000 × ⅔ × $.920)	1,840		
Factory overhead added (3,000 × ⅔ × $.811)	1,622	$ 10,572	
From current production:			
Units started and finished (33,000 × $3.497)		115,435*	$126,007
Work in process—ending inventory:			
Adjusted cost from preceding department [4,000 × ($1.72			
+ $.046)]		$ 7,064	
Labor (4,000 × ½ × $.920)		1,840	
Factory overhead (4,000 × ½ × $.811)		1,622	10,526
Total cost accounted for			$136,533

Additional computations:

Equivalent production:	Labor and Factory Overhead
Transferred out	36,000
Less beginning inventory (all units)	3,000
Started and finished this period	33,000
Add beginning inventory (work this period)	2,000
Add ending inventory (work this period)	2,000
	37,000 units

*33,000 units × $3.497 per unit = $115,401. To avoid a decimal discrepancy, the cost transferred from current production is computed as follows: $136,533 − ($10,572 + $10,526) = $115,435.

$$\text{Unit costs: Labor} = \frac{\$34,050}{37,000} = .920 \text{ per unit}$$

$$\text{Factory overhead} = \frac{\$30,018}{37,000} = \$.811 \text{ per unit}$$

Adjustment for lost units:

$$\text{Method No. 1} - \frac{\$65,355}{38,000 - 1,000} = \$1.766; \$1.766 - \$1.720 = \$.046 \text{ per unit}$$

$$\text{Method No. 2} - 1,000 \text{ units} \times \$1.720 = \$1,720; \frac{\$1,720}{37,000} = \$.046 \text{ per unit}$$

tory are added to this figure to determine the completed cost of these units which are transferred to the next department. The $.920 unit cost for labor and the $.811 unit cost for factory overhead are computed by dividing the equivalent production figure of 37,000 units for labor and factory overhead into the labor cost of $34,050 and factory overhead of $30,018, respectively. The equivalent production figure of 37,000 units consists of (1) 2,000 units of beginning inventory completed; (2) 33,000 units started and finished this period; and (3) 2,000 of the 4,000 units in the ending work in process inventory. The labor cost added to the beginning work in process inventory was $1,840 (2,000 × $.920), and factory overhead added was $1,622 (2,000 × $.811). These two amounts are added to the beginning inventory cost of $7,110 to give a total cost of $10,572. This is the completed cost of the 3,000 units in the beginning inventory transferred to the Terminal Department.

The department unit cost is $1.731. Because 1,000 units were lost during February, computation of the cost accumulated to the end of operations in the Testing Department requires an adjustment of $.046 for lost units. This adjustment is determined by dividing the previous department's total cost of $65,355 by the good units (37,000) of the period, and subtracting the old unit cost of $1.720 from the new unit cost of $1.766. In fifo costing, the lost units must be identified as all units from the beginning inventory, all new units started during the period, or a portion in each of these two categories. The identification is needed to determine which unit cost(s) should be adjusted. In any case, as a result of lost units, total costs incurred must be spread over a smaller number of units. In both the Testing and Terminal Departments, it is assumed that units lost came entirely from those started in process during the period.

The Testing Department completed and transferred 36,000 units, of which 3,000 units came from those in process at the beginning of the period. The cost of the 3,000 units is $10,572. The remaining 33,000 units came from units started and finished during the month. These units are transferred at a cumulative unit cost of $3.497 and a total cost of $115,435. The following entry transfers the cost of the 36,000 units to the next department:

Work in Process — Terminal Department	126,007	
Work in Process — Testing Department		126,007

The remaining $10,526 cost to be accounted for is the ending work in process inventory, which is computed in the conventional manner.

Terminal Department.   To complete the illustration of fifo costing, the cost of production report of the Terminal Department is presented below.

Clonex Corporation
Terminal Department
Cost of Production Report — Fifo Costing
For February, 19--

Quantity Schedule

Units in process at beginning (¼ labor and factory overhead) . . .	4,000	
Units received from preceding department	36,000	40,000
Units transferred to finished goods storeroom	36,000	
Units still in process (⅓ labor and factory overhead)	3,000	
Units lost in process	1,000	40,000

Cost Charged to the Department	Total Cost	Unit Cost
Work in process — beginning inventory	$ 15,850	
Cost from preceding department:		
Transferred in during the month (36,000 units)	$126,007	$ 3.500
Cost added by department:		
Labor	$ 33,140	$ .921
Factory overhead	19,430	.540
Total cost added	$ 52,570	$ 1.461
Adjustment for lost units		$ .100
Total cost to be accounted for	**$194,427**	$ 5.061

Cost Accounted for as Follows

Transferred to finished goods storeroom —			
From beginning inventory:			
Inventory cost	$15,850		
Labor added (4,000 × ¾ × $.921)	2,763		
Factory overhead added (4,000 × ¾ × $.540)	1,620	$ 20,233	
From current production:			
Units started and finished (32,000 × $5.061)		161,933*	$182,166
Work in process — ending inventory:			
Adjusted cost from preceding department [3,000 × ($3.50			
+ $.10)]		$ 10,800	
Labor (3,000 × ⅓ × $.921)		921	
Factory overhead (3,000 × ⅓ × $.540)		540	12,261
Total cost accounted for			**$194,427**

Additional computations:	Labor and Factory Overhead
Equivalent production:	
Transferred out	36,000
Less beginning inventory (all units)	4,000
Started and finished this period	32,000
Add beginning inventory (work this period)	3,000
Add ending inventory (work this period)	1,000
	36,000 units

*32,000 × $5.061 per unit = $161,952. To avoid a decimal discrepancy, the cost transferred from current production is computed as follows: $194,427 − ($20,233 + $12,261) = $161,933.

Unit costs: Labor $= \dfrac{\$33,140}{36,000} = \$.921$ per unit

Factory overhead $= \dfrac{\$19,430}{36,000} = \$.540$ per unit

Adjustment for lost units:

Method No. 1 — $\dfrac{\$126,007}{36,000 - 1,000} = \$3.60; \$3.60 - \$3.50 = \$.100$ per unit

Method No. 2 — $1,000 \times \$3.50 = \$3,500; \dfrac{\$3,500}{35,000} = \$.100$ per unit

Based on this report, the entry to transfer the cost of the 36,000 finished units is:

Finished Goods...	182,166	
Work in Process—Terminal Department...................		182,166

Combined Cost of Production Report—Fifo Costing. The illustration on page 105 is a combined cost of production report for February, using fifo costing. This report should be compared with the report (page 97) in which average costing is used.

Average Costing vs. Fifo Costing

Both average costing and fifo costing have certain advantages. It would be arbitrary to state that one method is either simpler or more accurate than the other. The selection of either method depends entirely upon management's opinion regarding the most appropriate and practical cost determination procedures. Each firm should select the method which offers reliable figures for managerial guidance.

The basic difference between the two methods concerns the treatment of beginning work in process inventory. The averaging method adds beginning work in process inventory cost to the cost from the preceding department and to materials, labor, and factory overhead costs incurred during the period. Unit costs are determined by dividing these costs by equivalent production figures. Units and costs are transferred to the next department as one cumulative figure.

The fifo method retains the beginning work in process inventory cost as a separate figure. Costs necessary to complete the beginning inventory units are added to this total cost. The sum of these two cost totals is transferred to the next department. Units started and finished during the period have their own unit cost, which is usually different from the completed unit cost of units in process at the beginning of the period. The fifo method thus separately identifies for management the current period unit cost originating in a department. Unfortunately, these costs are averaged out in the next department, resulting in a loss of much of the value associated with the use of the fifo method.

Clonex Corporation
All Producing Departments
Cost of Production Report — Fifo Costing
For February, 19--

	Blending		Testing		Terminal	
Quantity Schedule						
Units in process at beginning	4,000		3,000		4,000	
Units started in process	40,000	44,000				
Units received from preceding department			38,000	41,000	36,000	40,000
Units transferred to next department	38,000		36,000			
Units transferred to finished goods storeroom					36,000	
Units completed and on hand	1,000					
Units still in process	3,000		4,000		3,000	
Units lost in process	2,000	44,000	1,000	41,000	1,000	40,000
	Total Cost	Unit Cost	Total Cost	Unit Cost	Total Cost	Unit Cost
Cost Charged to the Department						
Work in process — beginning inventory	$ 4,440		$ 7,110		$ 15,850	
Cost from preceding department:						
Transferred in during the month			$ 65,355	$ 1.720	$126,007	$ 3.500
Cost added by department:						
Materials	$19,840	$ .522				
Labor	24,180	.620	$ 34,050	$ .920	$ 33,140	$ .921
Factory overhead....................	22,580	.579	30,018	.811	19,430	.540
Total cost added	$66,600	$ 1.721	$ 64,068	$ 1.731	$ 52,570	$ 1.461
Adjustment for lost units................				$ .046		$ .100
Total cost to be accounted for	$71,040	$ 1.721	$136,533	$ 3.497	$194,427	$ 5.061
Cost Accounted for as Follows						
Transferred to next department —						
From beginning inventory:						
Inventory cost......................	$ 4,440		$ 7,110		$ 15,850	
Labor added	$ 1,240		1,840		2,763	
Factory overhead added	1,158	$ 6,838	1,622	$ 10,572	1,620	$ 20,233
From current production:						
Units started and finished		58,517		115,435		161,933
		$65,355		$126,007		$182,166
Work in process — ending inventory:						
Completed and on hand.............	$ 1,721					
Adjusted cost from preceding department			$ 7,064		$ 10,800	
Materials	1,566					
Labor	1,240		1,840		921	
Factory overhead....................	1,158	5,685	1,622	10,526	540	12,261
Total cost accounted for		$71,040		$136,533		$194,427

If the fifo method is used, units lost during a period must be identified as to whether they came from units in process at the beginning or from units started or received during the period. Also, in computing equivalent production figures in fifo costing, the degree of completion of both the beginning and ending work in process inventories must be considered.

The principal disadvantage of fifo costing is that if several unit cost figures are used at the same time, extensive detail is required within the cost of production report, which can lead to complex procedures and even inaccuracy. Whether the extra detail yields more representative unit costs than the average costing method is debatable, especially in a firm where production is continuous and more or less uniform, and appreciable fluctuations in unit costs are not expected to develop. Under such conditions, the average costing method leads to more satisfactory cost computations.

Difficulties Encountered in Process Cost Accounting Procedures

The following difficulties in using process costing may be encountered in actual practice:

1. The determination of production quantities and their stages of completion presents problems. Every computation is influenced by these figures. Since the data generally come to the cost department from operating personnel often working under circumstances that make a precise count difficult, a certain amount of doubtful counts and unreliable estimates are bound to exist. Yet, the data submitted form the basis for the determination of inventory costs.
2. Materials cost computations frequently require careful analysis. In the illustrations, materials cost is generally part of the first department's cost. In certain industries, materials costs are not even entered on production reports. When materials prices are influenced by fluctuating market quotations, the materials cost may be recorded in a separate report designed to facilitate management decisions in relation to the materials market.
3. When units are lost by shrinkage, spoilage, or evaporation, the time when the loss occurs influences the final cost calculation. Different assumptions concerning the units to which the loss pertains would result in different departmental unit costs which, in turn, affect inventory costs, the cost of units transferred, and the completed unit cost. Another consideration involves the treatment of cost attributable to avoidable loss as an expense of the current period.
4. Industries using process cost procedures are generally of the multiple product type. Joint processing cost must be allocated to the products resulting from the processes. Weighted unit averages or other bases are used to prorate the joint cost to the several products. If units manufactured are used as a basis for cost allocation, considerable difficulties arise in determining unit costs.

Management must decide whether economy and low operational cost are compatible with increased information, based on additional cost computations and procedures. Some companies use both job order and process costing procedures for various purposes in different departments. The basis for using either method should be reliable production and performance data which, when combined with output, budget, or standard cost data, will provide the foundation for effective cost control and analysis.

DISCUSSION QUESTIONS

1. What are the possible effects on units and costs in process when materials are added in subsequent departments?

2. Distinguish between the fifo and average methods of process costing.

3. Why are units completed and on hand in a processing department included in the department's work in process?

4. How are equivalent production figures computed when fifo costing is used?

5. The Wiring Department is the second stage of Flem Company's production cycle. On May 1, the beginning work in process contained 25,000 units which were 60% complete as to conversion costs. During May, 100,000 units were transferred in from the first stage of Flem's production cycle. On May 31, the ending work in process contained 20,000 units which were 80% complete as to conversion costs. Material costs are added at the end of the process. Using the average method, compute the equivalent units of production.   (AICPA adapted)

6. Ace Company computed the flow of physical units for Department A for April, as follows:

Units completed:
  From work in process on
    April 1 10,000
    From April production................... 30,000
                                            40,000

Materials are added at the beginning of the process. Units of work in process at April 30 were 8,000. The work in process at April 1 was 80% complete as to conversion costs and the work in process at April 30 was 60% complete as to conversion costs. What are the equivalent units of production for April, using the fifo method?   (AICPA adapted)

7. What are some of the disadvantages of the fifo costing method?

8. Enumerate several of the basic difficulties frequently encountered in process costing.

9. Express an opinion as to the usefulness of data, derived from process costing, for the control of costs.

EXERCISES

1. **Cost of production report; materials added.** *Oloroso, Inc. produces a cologne, Mi Sudor, which requires processing in three departments. In the third department, materials are added, doubling the number of units. The following data pertain to the operations of Department 3 for March:*

Units received from Department 2	20,000
Units transferred to finished goods storeroom	32,000

The balance of the units are still in process—100% complete as to materials, 50% complete as to labor and overhead.

Cost transferred from Department 2		$30,000
Cost added by the department:		
Materials	$8,800	
Labor	9,000	
Factory overhead	7,200	$25,000

There was no beginning work in process inventory.

Required: *Prepare a cost of production report for Department 3 for March.*

2. *Computation of equivalent production—fifo method; materials added.* *Poore, Inc. produces a chemical compound in two departments, A and B, using the following procedure: The chemical compound requires one pound of Chemical X and one pound of Chemical Y. One pound of Chemical X is processed in Department A and transferred to Department B, where one pound of Chemical Y is added when the process is 50% complete. When the processing is complete in Department B, the finished chemical compound is transferred to finished goods. The process is a continuous 24-hour-a-day operation. Normal spoilage occurs in Department A, where 5% of Chemical X is lost in the first few minutes of processing. Department A's conversion cost is incurred uniformly throughout the process and is allocated to good pounds produced, since spoilage is normal. Department B's conversion cost is allocated equally to each equivalent pound of output. No spoilage occurs in Department B.*

Data available for October are:

	Department A	Department B
Work in process, October 1	8,000 pounds	10,000 pounds
Stage of completion of beginning inventory (one batch per department)	¾	³⁄₁₀
Started or transferred in	50,000 pounds	?
Transferred out	46,500 good pounds	?
Work in process, October 31	?	12,000 pounds
Stage of completion of ending inventory (one batch per department)	⅓	⅕
Total equivalent pounds of material added in Department B		44,500 pounds

Required:

(1) Prepare a quantity schedule for each department.

(2) Prepare an equivalent production schedule for each department, using the fifo method.   (AICPA adapted)

3. *Computation of equivalent production.* *The following data originate from three different situations:*

(a) Beginning inventory, 6,600 units, ⅓ complete as to materials, labor, and factory overhead; started in process, 10,200 units; in process at end of period, 4,800 units, ½ complete as to materials and ¼ complete as to labor and factory overhead; transferred 12,000 units to next department.

(b) Started in process, 9,200 units; completed and on hand, 700 units; in process at end of period, 1,000 units, complete as to materials and ⁴⁄₁₀ complete as to labor and factory overhead; transferred 7,500 units to next department.

Avge   *FIFO*

M.-22500   *Units 21500*

cc. 21250   *20850*

(c) *Beginning inventory, 2,000 units, ½ complete as to materials, ⅕ complete as to labor and factory overhead; transferred out, 20,000 units; units lost at beginning of production, 500, a normal quantity; in process at end of period, 2,500 units, complete as to materials, ½ complete as to labor and factory overhead.*

Required: *Compute the equivalent production figures in each situation, using (1) average costing and (2) fifo costing.*

4. Computation of equivalent production. *The following data originate from three different situations:*

(a) *Started in process, 18,000 units; in process at end of period, 6,000 units, complete as to materials, ½ complete as to conversion cost; transferred 12,000 units to finished goods.*

(b) *Beginning inventory, 11,000 units, ¼ complete as to materials, ⅛ complete as to conversion cost; transferred out, 12,000 units; units lost at end of production, 1,500; in process at end of period, 6,200 units, ⅛ complete as to materials, ¼ complete as to conversion cost.*

(c) *Beginning inventory, 4,500 units, complete as to materials, ¼ complete as to conversion cost; started in process, 12,500 units; in process at end of period, 2,100 units, complete as to materials, ⅓ complete as to conversion cost, and 1,700 units, ½ complete as to materials, ¼ complete as to conversion cost; units lost when units ¼ converted, 1,100, a normal amount.*

Required: *Compute the equivalent production figures in each situation, using (1) average costing and (2) fifo costing.*

5. Computation of equivalent production. *T & A Company operates two producing departments, whose quantity reports appear as follows:*

	Department 1	Department 2
Beginning inventory..........................	200	80
Department 1—all materials, 25%		
conversion cost		
Department 2—60% conversion cost		
Started in process	2,260	2,160
	2,460	2,240
Transferred out...............................	2,160	2,000
Ending inventory	300	240
Department 1—all materials, 60%		
conversion cost		
Department 2—80% conversion cost		
	2,460	2,240

Required: *Compute equivalent production figures for each department, using (1) average costing and (2) fifo costing.*

6. Average costing. *Information concerning Department B of Toby Company is as follows:*

Units in beginning inventory	5,000
Units transferred in	35,000
	40,000
Units completed	37,000
Units in ending inventory	3,000

| | Costs | | | |
	Trans-ferred In	Materials	Conversion	Total Cost
Beginning inventory..............	$ 2,900	—	$ 3,400	$ 6,300
Units transferred in	17,500	$25,500	15,000	58,000
	$20,400	$25,500	$18,400	$64,300

Conversion costs were 20% complete as to the beginning inventory and 40% complete as to the ending inventory. All materials are added at the end of the process. Toby uses average costing.

Required:
(1) Compute the cost per equivalent unit for conversion costs, rounded to the nearest penny.
(2) Determine the portion of the total cost of ending inventory attributable to transferred-in cost.   *(AICPA adapted)*

7. *Cost of production report–average costing.* A product called Aggregate is manufactured in one department of West Corporation. Materials are added at the beginning of the process. Shrinkage of 10% to 14%, all occurring at the beginning of the process, is considered normal. Labor and factory overhead are added continuously throughout the process.

The following information relates to November production:

Work in process, November 1 (4,000 pounds, 75% complete):
Materials	$ 22,800
Labor	24,650
Factory overhead.......................................	21,860

November costs:
Materials (fifo costing):
Inventory, November 1, 2,000 pounds......................	10,000
Purchase, November 3, 10,000 pounds	51,000
Purchase, November 18, 10,000 pounds	51,500
Released to production during November, 16,000 pounds	
Labor	103,350
Factory overhead.......................................	93,340

Transferred out, 15,000 pounds
Work in process, November 30, 3,000 pounds, 33⅓% complete (average costing)

Required: *Prepare a cost of production report for November.*   *(CMA adapted)*

8. *Cost of production report — average costing.* Culpepper Corporation is a manufacturer that uses average costing to account for costs of production. Culpepper manufactures a product that is produced in three separate departments: Molding, Assembling, and Finishing. The following information was obtained for the Assembling Department for June:
Work in process, June 1 — 2,000 units, composed of:

	Amount	Degree of Completion
Transferred in from the Molding Department	$32,000	100%
Cost added by the Assembling Department:		
Direct materials	20,000	100
Direct labor	7,200	60
Factory overhead...................................	5,500	50

The following activity occurred during June:
(a) 10,000 units were transferred in from the Molding Department at a cost of $160,000.
(b) $150,000 of costs were added by the Assembling Department: direct materials, $96,000; direct labor, $36,000; and factory overhead, $18,000.
(c) 8,000 units were completed and transferred to the Finishing Department.

At June 30, 4,000 units were still in work in process, with the following degrees of completion: direct materials, 90%; direct labor, 70%; and factory overhead, 35%.

Required: Prepare the June cost of production report for the Assembling Department.
(AICPA adapted)

9. Process Costing—fifo method. Ohm Motors is engaged in the production of a standard type of electric motor. Manufacturing costs for April totaled $66,000. At the beginning of April, inventories appeared as follows:

Motors in production, estimated 80% complete (2,500 units) $32,000
Motors on hand and in finished goods (1,200 units)   19,200

During the month, 5,500 completed units were placed in finished stock. At the end of April, inventories were:

Motors in production, estimated 50% complete . . . . 1,000 units
Motors on hand, completed and in finished goods   1,400

The company uses fifo costing for production and goods sold. In costing finished goods, the unit cost for units completed from beginning work in process inventory is kept separate from the unit cost of motors started and completed during the month.

Required:
(1) Compute the cost assigned to the ending work in process inventory.
(2) Compute the cost assigned to the ending finished goods inventory.
(3) Compute the cost of goods sold.   (CGAA adapted)

10. Cost of production report—fifo costing. Dentex Plastics Corporation produces non-breakable containers for cosmetics, using three departments: Mixing, Molding, and Finishing. On July 1, the work in process inventory in the Molding Department was 1,000 units, 50% complete as to materials and conversion costs, while the July 31 work in process inventory consisted of 2,800 units, 75% complete as to materials and conversion costs. During July, the Finishing Department received 20,000 units from the Molding Department. In the Molding Department, 800 units, a normal quantity, were lost during processing. Fifo costing is used.

Relevant cost data are as follows:

Work in process, July 1	$ 3,000
July costs:	
Cost from Mixing Department	97,632
Materials	16,200
Labor	26,568
Factory overhead	19,872

Required: Using the fifo costing method, prepare the cost of production report for the Molding Department for July. Round unit costs to the nearest cent.

PROBLEMS

5-1. Cost of production report; materials added. Ferry, Inc. manufactures a product in two departments. Materials are added in each department, increasing the number of units manufactured. A summary of the cost information for the company's first month of operations (January) is as follows:

	Dept. 1	Dept. 2
Materials	$ 90,000	$ 67,500
Labor	39,000	41,400
Factory overhead	7,800	20,700
Total	$136,800	$129,600

The production supervisor reports that 300,000 units were put into production in Department 1. Of this quantity, 75,000, a normal number, were lost in production, and 180,000 were completed and transferred to Department 2. The units in process at the end of the month were complete as to materials, but only one-third complete as to labor and factory overhead.

In Department 2, 45,000 units of materials were purchased outside and added to the units received from Department 1; 195,000 units were completed and transferred to finished goods inventory. The units in process at the end of the month were complete as to materials, but only 40% complete as to labor and factory overhead.

Required: Prepare a cost of production report for January for both departments. (Carry unit cost computations to three decimal places.)

5-2. Cost of production report–fifo costing; materials added. Adept Company manufactures a product known as Prep. The manufacturing process covers two departments, Grading and Saturating, in which fifo costing is used.

The manufacturing process begins in the Grading Department, where raw materials are started in process. The output is transferred to the Saturating Department for the final phase of production, where water is added at the beginning of the production process, resulting in a 50% gain in weight of the materials in production.

The following information is available for November:

	November 1		November 30
	Quantity (pounds)	Amount	Quantity (pounds)
Work in process inventories:			
Grading Department	—	—	—
Saturating Department	1,600	$17,600	2,000

	Materials	Labor and Factory Overhead
November costs of production:		
Grading Department	$259,200	$86,400
Saturating Department	—	86,000

The work in process inventory in the Saturating Department is estimated to be 50% complete as to conversion costs at both the beginning and end of November. The material used in the Grading Department during November weighed 28,800 pounds.

Required: Prepare a cost of production report for each department for November.

(AICPA adapted)

5-3. Cost of production report—average costing. Edmonton Company uses average costing in accounting for its three manufacturing departments. Department 2 receives units from Department 1 and applies conversion costs to these units at a uniform rate. When the units are 80% complete, they are inspected and material is then added to the good units. A Department 2 spoilage rate of 5% is considered normal.

For December, the following information is available:
- (a) 3,000 units were in process on December 1, estimated to be 30% complete, with cost from Department 1 of $16,000 and Department 2 costs of $2,600.
- (b) 32,000 units were received from Department 1 at a cost of $180,000.
- (c) Department 2 costs were: materials, $12,000; conversion, $96,700.
- (d) 30,000 units were completed and transferred to Department 3.
- (e) 4,500 units were in process December 31, estimated to be 60% complete.

Required:
- (1) Prepare the Department 2 cost of production report for December.
- (2) Prepare the journal entry to record the transfer of cost from Department 2 to Department 3.   (CGAA adapted)

5-4. Cost of production report—average costing. Sporific Company produces sleeping pills in two departments: Mixing, and Compounding and Packaging. The company uses average costing. For February, in the Mixing Department, the ending inventory is complete as to materials and ½ complete as to labor and factory overhead, and lost units occur at the end of the department's processing. In the Compounding and Packaging Department, the ending inventory is ⅔ complete as to labor and factory overhead.

	Mixing Department	Compounding and Packaging Department
Production data:		
Beginning inventory	1,000 units	500 units
Started in process	15,000	
Received from prior department		12,500
Transferred out	12,500	11,500
Ending inventory	3,000	1,500
Lost units (all normal)	500	
Cost summary:		
Beginning inventory:		
Cost from prior department		$ 650
Materials	$ 980	
Labor	230	175
Factory overhead	400	100
Cost for February:		
Materials	15,020	
Labor	5,570	6,700
Factory overhead	8,300	4,275

Required: Prepare a cost of production report for both departments for February.

5-5. Process costing—average method. Chatam Paper Company manufactures a high-quality paper box. The Box Department applies two separate operations—cutting and folding. The paper is first cut and trimmed to the dimensions of a box form by one machine group. One square foot of paper is equivalent to four box forms. The trimmings from this process have no scrap value. Box forms are then creased and folded (i.e., completed) by a second machine group. Any partially processed boxes in the Box Department are cut box forms that are ready for creasing and folding. These partly processed boxes are considered 50% complete as to labor and factory overhead. The Materials Department maintains an inventory of paper in sufficient quantities to permit continuous processing, and transfers to the Box Department are made as needed. Immediately after folding, all satisfactory boxes are transferred to the Finished Goods Department.

During June, the Materials Department purchased 1,210,000 square feet of unprocessed paper for $244,000. Conversion cost for June was $226,000. A quantity equal to 30,000 boxes was spoiled during paper cutting, and 70,000 boxes were spoiled during folding. All spoilage has a zero salvage value, is considered normal, and cannot be reprocessed. All spoilage loss is allocated between the completed units and partially processed boxes. The company applies the weighted average costing method to all inventories. Inventory data for June are:

| | | June 1 | | |
Inventory	Physical Unit	Units on Hand	Cost	June 30 Units on Hand
Materials Department:				
Paper	square feet	390,000	$76,000	200,000
Box Department:				
Boxes cut (not folded)	number	800,000	55,000*	300,000
Finished Goods Department:				
Completed boxes on hand	number	250,000	18,000	50,000
*Materials	$35,000			
Conversion cost	20,000			
	$55,000			

Required: Prepare the following:
(1) A report of cost of paper used in June by the Materials Department.
(2) A schedule showing the physical flow of units (including beginning and ending inventories) in the Materials Department, in the Box Department, and in the Finished Goods Department.
(3) A schedule showing the computation of equivalent units produced in June for materials and conversion cost in the Box Department.
(4) A schedule of the computation of unit costs for the Box Department.
(5) A report of inventory cost and cost of completed units for the Box Department.
(6) A schedule showing the computation of unit costs for the Finished Goods Department. (Carry computation to five decimal places.)
(7) A report of inventory cost and cost of units sold for the Finished Goods Department.   (AICPA adapted)

5-6. Inventory costing; average method. In attempting to verify the costing of the December 31, 19A inventory of work in process and finished goods recorded on Spirit Corporation's books, the auditor finds:

Finished goods, 200,000 units	$1,009,800
Work in process, 300,000 units, 50% complete as to labor and	
factory overhead	660,960

The company uses average costing. Materials are added to production at the beginning of the manufacturing process and factory overhead is applied at the rate of 60% of direct labor cost. Spirit's inventory cost records disclosed zero finished goods on January 1, 19A, and the following additional information for 19A:

	Units	Costs Materials	Labor
Work in process, January 1 (80% complete as to labor and factory overhead)	200,000	$ 200,000	$ 315,000
Units started in production......................	1,000,000		
Materials cost.....................................		$1,300,000	
Labor cost			$1,995,000
Units completed...............................	900,000		

Required:

(1) Compute the equivalent units of production.

(2) Compute the unit production costs of materials, labor, and factory overhead.

(3) Cost the ending finished goods and work in process inventories and compare to book balances.

(4) Prepare the necessary journal entry to correctly state the finished goods and work in process ending inventories.   (AICPA adapted)

5-7. Cost of production report—fifo vs average costing. Deterra, Inc. uses three departments to produce a detergent. The Finishing Department is the third and last step before the product is transferred to storage.

All materials needed to give the detergent its final composition are added at the beginning of the process in the Finishing Department. Any lost units occur only at this point and are considered to be normal.

The company uses fifo costing. The following data for the Finishing Department for October have been made available:

Production data:

In process, October 1 (labor and factory overhead, ¾ complete)	10,000 gals.
Transferred in from preceding department.........................	40,000 gals.
Finished and transferred to storage	35,000 gals.
In process, October 31 (labor and factory overhead, ½ complete)	10,000 gals.

Additional data:

Work in process inventory, October 1:	
Cost from preceding department....................................	$ 38,000
Cost from this department:	
Materials	21,500
Labor	39,000
Factory overhead..	42,000
Total work in process inventory, October 1	$140,500
Transferred in during October......................................	$140,000
Cost added in this department:	
Materials	$ 70,000
Labor	162,500
Factory overhead..	130,000
Total cost added...	$362,500
Total cost to be accounted for.....................................	$643,000

Required:

(1) Prepare a cost of production report for the Finishing Department for October, using fifo costing.

(2) Prepare a cost of production report for the Finishing Department for October, using average costing. (Carry unit cost computations to three decimal places, and round up the digit "5" in the fourth decimal place.)   (AICPA adapted)

5-8. Cost of production report—fifo vs average costing. Zaranka Corporation has two producing departments, Fabricating and Finishing. In the Fabricating Department, Polyplast is prepared from Miracle Mix and Bypro. In the Finishing Department, each unit of Polyplast is converted into six Tetraplexes and three Uniplexes. Service departments provide services to both producing departments.

The Fabricating and Finishing Departments use process cost procedures. Actual production costs, including factory overhead, are allocated monthly.

Service department expenses are allocated to producing departments as follows:

Expenses	Fabricating	Finishing
Building maintenance................	$30,000	$15,000
Timekeeping and personnel..........	16,500	11,000
Others	19,500	19,500

Materials inventory and work in process are costed on a fifo basis.
The Fabricating Department's records for December show:

Quantities (units of Polyplast):

In process, December 1	3,000
Started in process	25,000
Total units to be accounted for...............................	28,000
Transferred to Finishing Department..........................	19,000
In process, December 31	6,000
Normal losses throughout the process.........................	3,000
Total units accounted for.....................................	28,000

Cost of work in process, December 1:

Materials	$ 13,000
Labor	17,500
Factory overhead..	21,500
	$ 52,000
Direct labor cost...	$154,000
Departmental factory overhead (excluding service department allocation)	$132,000

Polyplast work in process at the beginning and end of the month was partially completed as follows:

	Materials	Labor and Factory Overhead
December 1.......................	66⅔%	50%
December 31.....................	100%	75%

Materials inventory records for December indicate:

	Miracle Mix		Bypro	
	Quantity	Amount	Quantity	Amount
Balance, December 1...........	62,000	$62,000	265,000	$18,550
Purchases:				
December 12................	39,500	49,375		
December 20................	28,500	34,200		
Fabricating Department usage ..	83,200		50,000	

Required:

(1) Compute the equivalent number of units of Polyplast for materials and conversion costs.

(2) (a) Determine the total Fabricating Department cost to be accounted for.
(b) Compute the unit costs for materials, labor, and factory overhead for the Fabricating Department.
(c) Compute the cost of units transferred to the Finishing Department, and the cost of the ending work in process inventory in the Fabricating Department.
(3) Complete requirements (1) and (2) above, assuming that work in process inventory is costed using the average method. (Round unit costs to the nearest cent.)

(AICPA adapted)

5-9. Cost of production report—average and fifo methods. Relaxo Company manufactures tranquilizers. Production is divided into three processes: Mixing, Compounding, and Packaging. Average costing is used in the first two departments, and fifo costing is used in the Packaging Department.

The following data are available for September:

Quantity schedule:

	Mixing	Compounding	Packaging
Units in process at beginning	4,000	2,000	2,000
Units started in process	60,000	—	—
Units received from preceding department	—	50,000	46,000
	64,000	52,000	48,000
Units transferred to next department	50,000	46,000	
Units transferred to finished goods			41,600
Units lost during process*	2,000		4,000**
Units still in process	12,000	6,000	2,400
	64,000	52,000	48,000

*Losses are within normal tolerance limits.
**Loss is assumed to be entirely from units transferred in this period.

	Mixing	Compounding	Packaging
Stage of completion of units in process at beginning of period:			
Materials	1/1	—	1/2
Labor and factory overhead	5/6	2/3	1/2
Stage of completion of units in process at end of period:			
Materials	1/1	—	1/6
Labor and factory overhead	1/2	2/3	1/6
Cost data:			
Work in process—beginning inventory:			
Cost from preceding department	—	$ 2,260	$3,000
Materials	$ 1,960	—	60
Labor	770	350	130
Factory overhead	1,060	200	100
Cost added during period:			
Materials	29,040	—	1,230
Labor	10,430	13,400	2,870
Factory overhead	15,740	8,550	2,460

Required:
(1) Compute the equivalent units of production for each department.
(2) Prepare a combined cost of production report for September. (Carry unit cost computations to five decimal places.)

Chapter 6
Costing By-Products and Joint Products

Many industrial concerns are confronted with the difficult and often rather complicated problem of assigning costs to their by-products and/or joint products. Chemical companies, petroleum refineries, flour mills, coal mines, lumber mills, dairies, canners, meat packers, and many others produce in their manufacturing or conversion processes a multitude of products to which some costs must be assigned. Assignment of costs to these various products is required for inventory costing for income determination and financial statement purposes. An even more important aspect of by-product and joint product costing is that it furnishes management with data for use in planning maximum profit potentials and evaluating actual profit performance.

By-Products and Joint Products Defined

The term *by-product* is generally used to denote one or more products of relatively small total value that are produced simultaneously with a product of greater total value. The product with the greater value, commonly called the "main product," is usually produced in greater quantities than the by-products. Ordinarily, the manufacturer has only limited control over the quantity of the by-product that comes into existence. However, the introduction of more advanced engineering methods, such as in the petroleum industry, has permitted greater control over the quantity of residual products. For example, one company, which formerly paid a trucker to haul away and dump certain waste materials, discovered that the waste was valuable as fertilizer, and this by-product is now an additional source of income for the entire industry.

Joint products are produced simultaneously by a common process or series of processes, with each product possessing a more than nominal value in the form in which it is produced. The definition emphasizes the point that the manufacturing process creates products in a definite quantitative relationship. An increase in one product's output will bring about an increase in the quantity of the other products, or vice versa, but not necessarily in the same proportion. To the point of split-off or to the point where these several products emerge as individual units, the cost of the products forms a homogeneous whole.

Nature of By-Products and Joint Products

The accounting treatment of by-products necessitates a reasonably complete knowledge of the technological factors underlying their manufacture, since the origins of by-products may vary. By-products arising from the cleansing of the main product, such as gas and tar from coke manufacture, generally have a residual value. In some cases, the by-product is leftover scrap or waste, such as sawdust in lumber mills. In other cases, the by-product may not be the result of any manufacturing process but may arise from preparing raw materials before they are used in the manufacture of the main product. The separation of cotton seed from cotton, cores and seeds from apples, and shells from cocoa beans are examples of this type of by-product.

By-products can be classified into two groups according to their marketable condition at the split-off point: (1) those sold in their original form without need of further processing and (2) those which require further processing in order to be salable.

The classic example of joint products is found in the meat-packing industry, where various cuts of meat and numerous by-products are processed from one original carcass with one lump-sum cost. Another example of joint product manufacturing is the production of gasoline, where the derivation of gasoline inevitably results in the production of such items as naphtha, kerosene, and distillate fuel oils. Other examples of joint product manufacturing are the simultaneous production of various grades of glue and the processing of soybeans into oil and meal. Joint product costing is also found in industries that must grade raw material before it is processed. Tobacco manufacturers (except in cases where graded tobacco is purchased) and virtually all fruit and vegetable canners face the problem of grading. In fact, such manufacturers have a dual problem of joint cost allocation: (1) materials cost is applicable to all grades; (2) subsequent manufacturing costs are incurred simultaneously for all the different grades.

Joint Costs

A *joint cost* may be defined as that cost which arises from the common processing or manufacturing of products produced from the same process. Whenever two or more different joint or by-products are created from a single cost factor, a joint cost results. A joint cost is incurred prior to the point at which separately identifiable products emerge from the same process.

The chief characteristic of a joint cost is the fact that the cost of several different products is incurred in an indivisible sum for all products, rather than in individual amounts for each product. The total production cost of multiple products involves both joint cost and separate, individual product costs. These separable product costs are identifiable with the individual product and, generally, need no allocation. However, a joint production cost requires allocation or assignment to the individual products.

Difficulties in Costing By-Products and Joint Products

By-products and joint products are difficult to cost because a true joint cost is indivisible. For example, an ore might contain both lead and zinc. In the raw state, these minerals are joint products, and until they are separated by reduction of the ore, the cost of finding, mining, and processing is a joint cost; neither lead nor zinc can be produced without the other prior to the split-off stage. The cost accumulated to the split-off stage must be borne by the difference between the sales price and the cost to complete and sell each mineral after the split-off point.

Joint costs are frequently confused with common costs. However, there is a significant difference between the two: a joint cost is indivisible and common costs are divisible. *Common costs* are allocable among products or services because each of the products or services could have been obtained separately. Therefore, any shared costs of obtaining them can be allocated on the basis of relative usage of common facilities. For example, the cost of fuel or power may be allocated to products on the basis of production volumes or metered usage. The indivisibility characteristic of a joint cost is not always easy to comprehend, since in some cases a joint cost can be divided among joint products in accordance with a common cost-causing characteristic. However, the result of such a division is of limited use to management for decision making.

Because of the indivisibility of a joint cost, cost allocation and apportionment procedures used for establishing the unit cost of a product are far from perfect and are, indeed, quite arbitrary. The costing of joint products and by-products highlights the problem of assigning costs to products whose origin, use of equipment, share of raw materials, share of labor costs, and share of other facilities cannot truly be determined. Whatever methods of allocation are employed, the total profit or loss figure is not affected — provided there are no beginning or ending inventories — by allocating costs to the joint products or by-products, since these costs are recombined in the final income statement. However, a joint cost is ordinarily allocated to the products on some acceptable basis to determine product costs needed for inventory carrying costs. For this reason, there is an effect on periodic income, because different amounts may be allocated to inventories of the numerous joint products or by-products under various allocation methods. In addition, product costs may be required for such special purposes as justifying sales prices before governmental regulatory bodies. However, the validity of splitting a joint cost to determine fair, regulated prices for products has been questioned by both accountants and economists.

Methods of Costing By-Products

The accepted methods for costing by-products fall into two categories:

1. A joint production cost is not allocated to the by-product. Any revenue resulting from sales of the by-product is credited either to income or to cost of the main product. In some cases, costs subsequent to split-off may be offset against the by-product revenue. For inventory costing, an independent value may be assigned to the by-product. The methods most commonly used in industry are:

   Method 1. Revenue from sales of the by-product is listed on the income statement as:
   a. Other income.
   b. Additional sales revenue.
   c. A deduction from the cost of goods sold of the main product.
   d. A deduction from the total manufacturing cost of the main product.

   Method 2. Revenue from sales of the by-product less the costs of placing the by-product on the market (marketing and administrative expenses) and less any additional processing cost of the by-product is shown on the income statement in a manner similar to that indicated in Method 1.

   Method 3. The replacement cost method.

2. Some portion of the joint production cost is allocated to the by-product. Inventory costs are based on this allocated cost plus any subsequent processing cost. In this category, the following method is used:

   Method 4. The market value (reversal cost) method.

Method 1: Recognition of Gross Revenue

Method 1 is a typical noncost procedure in which the final inventory cost of the main product is overstated to the extent that some of the cost belongs to the by-product. However, this shortcoming is somewhat removed in Method 1 (d), although a sales value rather than a cost is deducted from the production cost of the main product.

By-Product Revenue as Other Income. To illustrate this procedure, the following income statement is presented:

Sales (main product, 10,000 units @ $2)		$20,000
Cost of goods sold:		
Beginning inventory (1,000 units @ $1.50)............	$ 1,500	
Total production cost (11,000 units @ $1.50).........	16,500	
Cost of goods available for sale	$18,000	
Ending inventory (2,000 units @ $1.50)	3,000	15,000
Gross profit		$ 5,000
Marketing and administrative expenses.................		2,000
Operating income.....................................		$ 3,000
Other income: Revenue from sales of by-product........		1,500
Income before income tax		$ 4,500

By-Product Revenue as Additional Sales Revenue. In this case, the income statement above would show the $1,500 revenue from sales of the by-product as an addition to sales of the main product. As a result, total sales revenue would be $21,500, and gross profit and operating income would increase accordingly. All other figures would remain the same.

By-Product Revenue as a Deduction from the Cost of Goods Sold. In this case, the $1,500 revenue from the by-product would be deducted from the $15,000 cost of goods sold figure, thereby reducing the cost and increasing the gross profit and operating income. The income before income tax remains at $4,500.

By-Product Revenue Deducted from Production Cost. In this case, the $1,500 revenue from by-product sales is deducted from the $16,500 total production cost, giving a net production cost of $15,000. This revised cost results in a new average unit cost of $1.3625 for the main product. The final inventory will consequently be $2,725 instead of $3,000. The income statement would appear as follows:

Sales (main product, 10,000 units @ $2)................			$20,000
Cost of goods sold:			
Beginning inventory (1,000 units @ $1.35)		$ 1,350	
Total production cost (11,000 units @ $1.50) ...	$16,500		
Revenue from sales of by-product............	1,500		
Net production cost................................		15,000	
Cost of goods available for sale (12,000 units			
@ $1.3625 average cost)		$16,350	
Ending inventory (2,000 units @ $1.3625)..............		2,725	13,625
Gross profit...			$ 6,375
Marketing and administrative expenses			2,000
Operating income			$ 4,375

The preceding methods require no complicated journal entries. The revenue received from by-product sales is debited to Cash (or Accounts Receivable). In the first three cases, Income from Sales of By-Product is credited; in the fourth case, the production cost of the main product is credited.

Method 2: Recognition of Net Revenue

Method 2 recognizes the need for assigning some cost to the by-product. It does not attempt, however, to allocate any main product cost to the by-product. Any expenses involved in further processing or marketing the by-product are recorded in separate accounts. All figures are shown on the income statement, following one of the procedures described in Method 1.

Journal entries in Method 2 would involve charges to by-product revenue for the additional work required and perhaps for factory overhead. The marketing and administrative expenses might also be allocated to the by-product on some predetermined basis. Some firms carry an account called By-Product, to which all additional expenses are debited and all income is credited. The balance of this account would be presented in the income statement, following one of the procedures outlined in Method 1. However, accumulated manufacturing costs applicable to by-product inventory should be reported on the balance sheet.

Method 3: Replacement Cost Method

The replacement cost method ordinarily is applied by firms whose by-products are used within the plant, thereby avoiding the necessity of purchasing certain materials and supplies from outside suppliers. The production cost of the main product is credited for such materials, and the offsetting debit is to the department that uses the by-product. The cost assigned to the by-product is the purchase or replacement cost existing in the market. In the steel industry, for example, many by-products are sold in the open market. Other products, such as blast furnace gas and coke oven gas, are mixed and used for heating in open-hearth furnaces. The waste heat from open hearths is used again in the generation of steam needed by the various producing departments. The resourceful use of these by-products and their accounting treatment are indicated by the following procedure used by a steel company:

1. Coke oven by-products are credited to the cost of coke at the average sales price per unit for the month.
2. Coke oven and blast furnace gas are credited respectively to the cost of coke and the cost of pig iron at a computed value based on the cost of fuel oil yielding equivalent heat units.
3. Tar and pitch used as fuel are credited respectively to the cost of coke at a computed value based on the cost of fuel oil yielding equivalent heat units.
4. Scrap steel remelted is credited to the cost of finished steel at market cost of equivalent grades purchased.
5. Waste heat from furnaces used to generate steam is credited to the steel ingot cost at a computed value based on the cost of coal yielding equivalent heat units.[1]

---

[1]Howard C. Greer, "Accounting for By-Products and Joint Products," *NA(C)A Bulletin*, Vol. XVII, No. 24, Section 1, p. 1413.

Method 4: Market Value Method

The market value (reversal cost) method is basically similar to the last technique illustrated in Method 1. However, it reduces the manufacturing cost of the main product, not by the actual revenue received, but by an estimate of the by-product's value at the time of recovery. This estimate must be made prior to split-off from the main product. Dollar recognition depends on the stability of the market as to price and salability of the by-product; however, control over quantities is important as well. The by-product account is charged with this estimated amount and the production (manufacturing) cost of the main product is credited. Any additional costs of materials, labor, or factory overhead incurred after the by-product is separated from the main product are charged to the by-product. Marketing and administrative expenses might also be allocated to the by-product on some equitable basis. The proceeds from sales of the by-product are credited to the by-product account. The balance in this account can be presented on the income statement in one of the ways outlined for Method 1, except that the manufacturing cost applicable to by-product inventory should be reported in the balance sheet.

The market value (reversal cost) method of ascertaining main product and by-product costs may be illustrated as follows:

Item	Main Product	By- Product	
Materials................................	$ 50,000		
Labor.....................................	70,000		
Factory overhead	40,000		
Total production cost (40,000 units)	$160,000		
Market value (5,000 units @ $1.80)			$9,000
Estimated gross profit consisting of:			
Assumed operating profit			
(20% of sales price).................		$1,800	
Marketing and administrative expenses			
(5% of sales price)..................		450	2,250
			$6,750
Estimated production costs after split-off:			
Materials.............................		$1,000	
Labor.................................		1,200	
Factory overhead		300	2,500
Estimated value of by-product at split-off			
to be credited to main product...........	4,250		$4,250
Net cost of main product..................	$155,750		
Add back *actual* production cost after			
split-off			2,300
Total			$6,550
Total number of units	40,000		5,000
Unit cost	$ 3.894		$ 1.31

This illustration indicates that an estimated value of the by-product at the split-off point results when estimated gross profit and production cost after split-off are subtracted from the by-product's ultimate market value. Alternatively, if the by-product has a market value at the split-off point, the by-product account is charged with this market value, less its estimated gross profit, and the main product's production cost would be credited. It is also possible to use the total market values of the main product and the by-product at the split-off point as a basis for assigning a share of the prior-to-split-off cost to the by-product, applying the offsetting credit to the production cost of the main product. In any event, subsequent-to-split-off cost related to the by-product would be charged to the by-product.

Method 4 is based on the theory that the cost of a by-product is related to its sales value. It is a step toward the recognition of a by-product cost prior to its split-off from the main product. It is also the nearest approach to methods employed in joint product costing.

Methods of Allocating Joint Production Cost to Joint Products

Joint production cost, incurred up to the split-off point, can be allocated to joint products by using one of the following methods:

1. The market or sales value method, based on the relative market values of the individual products.
2. The quantitative or physical unit method, based on some physical measurement unit such as weight, linear measure, or volume.
3. The average unit cost method.
4. The weighted average method, based on a predetermined standard or index of production.

Market or Sales Value Method

This method enjoys great popularity because of the argument that the market value of any product is a manifestation of the cost incurred in its production. The contention is that if one product sells for more than another, it is because more cost was expended to produce it. Therefore, the way to prorate the joint cost is on the basis of the respective market values of the items produced. The method is really a weighted market value basis using the total market or sales value of each unit (quantity produced times the unit sales price).

To illustrate, assume that joint products A, B, C, and D are produced at a total joint production cost of $120,000. Quantities produced are: A, 20,000 units; B, 15,000 units; C, 10,000 units; and D, 15,000 units. Product A sells for $.25; B, for $3; C, for $3.50; and D, for $5. These prices are market or sales values for the products at the split-off point; i.e., it is assumed that they can be sold at that point. Management may have decided, however, that it is more profitable to process certain products further before they are sold. Nevertheless, this condition does not destroy the usefulness of the sales value at the split-off point for the allocation of the joint production cost. The proration of this joint cost is made in the following manner:

Product	Units Produced	Market Value per Unit	Total Market Value	Ratio of Product Value to Total Market Value	Apportionment of Joint Production Cost
A	20,000	$ .25	$ 5,000	3.125%	$ 3,750
B	15,000	3.00	45,000	28.125	33,750
C	10,000	3.50	35,000	21.875	26,250
D	15,000	5.00	75,000	46.875	56,250
Total			$160,000	100.000%	$120,000

The same results can be obtained if the total joint production cost ($120,000) is divided by the total market value of the four products ($160,000). The resulting 75 percent is the percentage of joint cost in each individual market value. By multiplying each market value by this percentage, the joint cost will be apportioned as shown in the preceding table.

Proponents of the market or sales value method state that the joint cost should be assigned to products in accordance with their sales value because, were it not for such a cost, a sales value would not exist. Under this method, each joint product yields the same unit gross profit percentage, assuming that the units are sold without further processing. This can be illustrated as follows, assuming no beginning inventories:

	Total	A	B	C	D
Sales — units	52,000	18,000	12,000	8,000	14,000
Ending inventories	8,000	2,000	3,000	2,000	1,000
Sales — dollars	$138,500	$ 4,500	$36,000	$28,000	$70,000
Production cost	$120,000	$ 3,750	$33,750	$26,250	$56,250
Less ending inventory	16,125	375*	6,750	5,250	3,750
Cost of goods sold	$103,875	$ 3,375	$27,000	$21,000	$52,500
Gross profit	$ 34,625	$ 1,125	$ 9,000	$ 7,000	$17,500
Gross profit percentage	25%	25%	25%	25%	25%

*$3,750 production cost ÷ 20,000 units produced = $.1875; $.1875 × 2,000 units in ending inventory = $375.

Consideration of Cost After Split-Off. Products not salable in their stage of completion at the split-off point and therefore without any market value require additional processing to place them in marketable condition. In such cases, the basis for allocation of the joint production cost is a hypothetical market value at the split-off point. To illustrate the procedure, the assumptions listed below are added to the preceding example:

Product	Ultimate Market Value per Unit	Processing Cost After Split-off
A	$ .50	$ 2,000
B	5.00	10,000
C	4.50	10,000
D	8.00	28,000

To arrive at the basis for the apportionment, it is necessary to use a working-back procedure, whereby the after-split-off processing cost is subtracted from the ultimate sales value to find a hypothetical market value. After-split-off marketing and administrative expenses traceable to specific products and an allowance for profit should also be considered if their amounts are proportionately different among the joint products, because the joint cost apportionment would be affected. The following table indicates the steps to be taken:

Product	Ulti-mate Market Value per Unit	Units Pro-duced	Ultimate Market Value	Processing Cost After Split-Off	Hypo-thetical Market Value*	Apportion-ment of Joint Production Cost**	Total Production Cost	Total Production Cost Percent-age***
A	$ .50	20,000	$ 10,000	$ 2,000	$ 8,000	$ 4,800	$ 6,800	68.0
B	5.00	15,000	75,000	10,000	65,000	39,000	49,000	65.3
C	4.50	10,000	45,000	10,000	35,000	21,000	31,000	68.8
D	8.00	15,000	120,000	28,000	92,000	55,200	83,200	69.3
Total			$250,000	$50,000	$200,000	$120,000	$170,000	68.0

*At the split-off point
**Percentage to allocate joint production cost (using the joint cost total determined on page 126):

$$\frac{\text{Total joint production cost}}{\text{Total hypothetical market value}} = \frac{\$120,000}{\$200,000} = .60 = 60\%;$$

60% × hypothetical market value = apportionment of joint production cost
***The production cost percentage is calculated by dividing total production cost by the ultimate market value; e.g.,

$\frac{\$49,000}{\$75,000} = .653 = 65.3\%$ for Product B, and $\frac{\$170,000}{\$250,000} = .68 = 68\%$ for all products combined.

If in a given situation, certain of the joint products are salable at the split-off point while others are not, the market values at the split-off point would be used for the former group; for the latter group, hypothetical market values would be required.

The following gross profit statement uses the same number of units sold as was used in the preceding illustration, but the sales prices have been increased as a result of additional processing.

	Total	A	B	C	D
Sales—units	52,000	18,000	12,000	8,000	14,000
Ending inventories	8,000	2,000	3,000	2,000	1,000
Sales—dollars	$217,000	$ 9,000	$60,000	$36,000	$112,000
Cost of goods sold:					
Joint production cost	$120,000	$ 4,800	$39,000	$21,000	$ 55,200
Further processing cost	50,000	2,000	10,000	10,000	28,000
Total	$170,000	$ 6,800	$49,000	$31,000	$ 83,200
Less ending inventory	22,227	680*	9,800	6,200	5,547
Cost of goods sold	$147,773	$ 6,120	$39,200	$24,800	$ 77,653
Gross profit	$ 69,227	$ 2,880	$20,800	$11,200	$ 34,347
Gross profit percentage	32%	32%	35%	31%	31%

*$6,800 production cost ÷ 20,000 units produced = $.34; $.34 × 2,000 units in ending inventory = $680.

Since the statement has often been made that every joint product should be equally profitable, the sales value technique may be modified by using the overall gross profit percentage to determine the gross profit for each product.

In the following table, the gross profit (32 percent) is deducted from the sales value to find the total cost, which is reduced by each product's further processing cost to find the joint cost allocation for each product.

	Total	A	B	C	D
Ultimate sales value	$250,000	$10,000	$75,000	$45,000	$120,000
Less 32% gross profit	80,000	3,200	24,000	14,400	38,400
Total cost	$170,000	$ 6,800	$51,000	$30,600	$ 81,600
Further processing cost	50,000	2,000	10,000	10,000	28,000
Joint cost	$120,000	$ 4,800	$41,000	$20,600	$ 53,600

If sales value, gross profit percentage, or further processing costs are estimated, the balance labeled "Joint cost" would serve as the basis for allocating the actual joint cost to the four products.

Quantitative Unit Method

This method attempts to distribute the total joint cost on the basis of some unit of measurement, such as pounds, gallons, tons, or board feet. However, if the joint products are not measurable by the basic measurement unit, the joint units must be converted to a denominator common to all units produced. For instance, in the manufacture of coke, products such as coke, coal tar, benzol, sulfate of ammonia, and gas are measured in different units. The yield of these recovered units is measured on the basis of the quantity of product extracted per ton of coal.

The following table illustrates the use of weight as a quantitative unit method of joint cost allocation:

Product	Yield in Pounds of Recovered Product per Ton of Coal	Distribution of Waste to Recovered Products	Revised Weight of Recovered Products	Materials Cost of Each Product per Ton of Coal
Coke..........	1,320.0 lbs.	69.474 lbs.*	1,389.474 lbs.	$27.790**
Coal tar	120.0	6.316	126.316	2.526
Benzol	21.9	1.153	23.053	.461
Sulfate of ammonia	26.0	1.368	27.368	.547
Gas...........	412.1	21.689	433.789	8.676
Waste (water) ..	100.0			
Total	2,000.0 lbs.	100.000 lbs.	2,000.000 lbs.	$40.000

*[1,320 ÷ (2,000 − 100)] = 69.474
**(1,389.474 ÷ 2,000) × $40 = $27.790

Average Unit Cost Method

This method attempts to apportion the total joint production cost to the various products on the basis of an average unit cost obtained by dividing the total number of units produced into the total joint production cost. As long as all units produced are measured in terms of the same unit and do not differ greatly, the method can be used without too much misgiving. When the units produced are not measured in like terms or differ markedly, the method should not be applied. Using figures in the market value example, the procedure can be illustrated as follows:

$$\frac{\text{Total joint production cost}}{\text{Total number of units produced}} = \frac{\$120,000}{60,000} = \$2 \text{ per unit}$$

Product	Units Produced	Apportionment of Joint Production Cost
A	20,000	$ 40,000
B	15,000	30,000
C	10,000	20,000
D	15,000	30,000
	60,000	$120,000

Companies using this method argue that all products turned out by the same process should receive a proportionate share of the total joint production cost based on the number of units produced.

Weighted Average Method

In many industries, the previously described methods do not give a satisfactory answer to the joint cost apportionment problem. For this reason, weight factors are often assigned to each unit, based upon size of the unit, difficulty of manufacture, time consumed in making the unit, difference in type of labor employed, amount of materials used, etc. Finished production of every kind is multiplied by weight factors to apportion the total joint cost to individual units.

Using figures from the previous example, weight factors assigned to the four products might be as follows:

Product A— 3   points
Product B— 12   points
Product C— 13.5 points
Product D— 15   points

The joint production cost allocation would result in the following values:

Product	Units Produced	× Points	=	Weighted Units	×	Cost Per Unit*	=	Apportionment of Joint Production Cost
A	20,000	3		60,000		$.20		$ 12,000
B	15,000	12		180,000		.20		36,000
C	10,000	13.5		135,000		.20		27,000
D	15,000	15		225,000		.20		45,000
				600,000				$120,000

$$* \frac{\text{Total joint production cost}}{\text{Total number of weighted units}} = \frac{\$120,000}{600,000} = \$.20 \text{ per unit}$$

Federal Income Tax Laws and the Costing of Joint Products and By-Products

Federal income tax laws concerning the costing of joint products and by-products are not numerous. Legislators recognize the impossibility of establishing a specific code of law for every conceivable situation involving this type of cost problem. Consequently, the written pronouncement of the law does not precisely establish the boundaries of acceptable procedures. A digest of legal viewpoint is given in the Federal Income Tax Regulations, which state the following:

> *Inventories of miners and manufacturers.* *A taxpayer engaged in mining or manufacturing who by a single process or uniform series of processes derives a product of two or more kinds, sizes, or grades, the unit cost of which is substantially alike, and who in conformity to a recognized trade practice allocates an amount of cost to each kind, size, or grade of product, which in the aggregate will absorb the total cost of production, may, with the consent of the Commissioner, use such allocated cost as a basis for pricing inventories, provided such allocation bears a reasonable relation to the respective selling values of the different kinds, sizes, or grades of product.*[2]

The above quotation does not fully and unequivocally authorize the utilization of the market value theory of costing joint products and by-products. The words "in conformity to a recognized trade practice" and "with the consent of the Commissioner" clearly imply that the multiplicity of conceivable situations is far too great to be covered by definite rules that allow or prohibit a particular costing procedure. Thus, when the size of the business warrants the trouble and expense and before any joint product and by-product inventories are assigned costs for income tax purposes, the commissioner must study the proposed costing program and inform the producer whether it will be allowed. It is a genuine problem for the commissioner to decide whether a cost policy conforms closely enough to the accepted standards of the industry, or whether the alleged cost of a joint product or a by-product is reasonably related to the market values. So much depends upon the judgment of the commissioner that a person might justifiably claim that in joint product and by-product costing disputes, the commissioner is virtually the enactor of the law. Of course, decisions may be appealed, but the higher tribunals find themselves beset by the same vague, general statute. Thus, they too must rely almost entirely upon their own independent discretion and practically make the law.

Clearly, tax laws have not solved the problem of costing joint products and by-products for the accountant and the manufacturer. Tax officials find themselves in exactly the same predicament as any coke producer, petroleum refiner, or chemical manufacturer, even though their immediate objective may be limited to collecting a proper tax. The necessity of defining and interpreting accepted practices in a given industry proves, at least partially, that if the present income tax law on joint product and by-product costing — with its implication that the market value method is desirable — is unfair or manifestly

---

[2]*Regulations,* Section 1.471-7.

inaccurate and illogical, it can and will be changed if industry and the accounting profession can offer better reasons for the use of other procedures.

Joint Cost Analysis for Managerial Decisions and Profitability Analysis

The Securities and Exchange Commission requires that annual reports to stockholders include data by lines of business. The Financial Accounting Standards Board requires business enterprises, excluding nonpublic enterprises, to report in their annual external financial statements the revenue, operating profit or loss (revenue less operating expense), as well as identifiable assets of each significant industry segment of their operations. "Significant" generally means 10 percent or more of the total of the respective amounts. Aggregate depreciation, depletion, amortization expenses, and the amount of capital expenditures must also be reported for each segment. Furthermore, the FASB requires information about foreign operations, export sales, and major customers, who need not be identified. Also, methods used for cost allocations to segments must be disclosed. Interim financial statements are exempt from these requirements.[3] The SEC's disclosure requirements are consistent with the provisions contained in FASB statements, yet they call for more information than the FASB.

Companies generally resist such requirements. One of their main arguments is that cost allocation today is fraught with great danger of improper interpretation caused by an arbitrarily allocated joint cost. Of course, as this chapter indicates, there are acceptable ways of allocating joint product cost. Yet, the choice of method makes a difference. The decision determines the degree of profitability of the various individual products.

Joint cost allocation methods indicate only too forcefully that the amount of the cost to be apportioned to the numerous products emerging at the point of split-off is difficult to establish for any purpose. Furthermore, the acceptance of an allocation method for the assignment of the joint production cost does not solve the problem. The thought has been advanced that no attempt should be made to determine the cost of individual products up to the split-off point; rather, it seems important to calculate the profit margin in terms of total combined units. Of course, costs incurred after the split-off point will provide management with information needed for decisions relating to the desirability of further processing to maximize profits.

[3]*Statement of Financial Accounting Standards, No. 14*, "Financial Reporting for Segments of a Business Enterprise" (Stamford: Financial Accounting Standards Board, 1976); *Statement of Financial Accounting Standards, No. 18*, "Financial Reporting for Segments of a Business Enterprise—Interim Financial Statements" (Stamford: Financial Accounting Standards Board, 1977); and *Statement of Financial Accounting Standards, No. 21*, "Suspension of the Reporting of Earnings per Share and Segment Information by Nonpublic Enterprises" (Stamford: Financial Accounting Standards Board, 1978).

Production of joint products is greatly influenced by both the technological characteristics of the processes and by the markets available for the products. This establishment of a product mix which is in harmony with customer demands appears profitable but is often physically impossible. It is interesting to note that cost accounting in the meat-packing industry serves primarily as a guide to buying, for aggregate sales realization values of the various products that will be obtained from cutting operations are considered in determining the price that a packer is willing to pay for livestock. Sales realization values are also considered when deciding to sell hams or other cuts in a particular stage or to process them further.

A joint cost is often incurred for products that are either interchangeable or not associated with each other at all. Increasing the output of one will in most joint cost situations unavoidably increase to some extent the output of the other. These situations fall into the category of the cost-volume-profit relationship and differential cost analysis (Chapters 23 and 24). Evaluation of many alternative combinations of output can lead to time-consuming computations. Often such evaluations are carried out on a computer using sophisticated simulation techniques. Developments in operations research procedures have provided techniques helpful in solving such problems (Chapter 25 on linear programming).

For profit planning, and perhaps as the only reliable measure of profitability, management should consider a product's contribution margin after separable or individual costs are deducted from sales. This contribution margin allows management to predict the amount that a segment or product line will add to or subtract from company profits. This margin is not the product's net profit figure. It only indicates relative profitability in comparison with other products. "Net profit determined by allocating to segments an 'equitable' share of all costs, both separable and joint, associated with the group of segments is not a reliable guide to profit planning decisions because these data cannot be used for predicting the outcome of decisions in terms of the change in aggregate net profit."[4] For these reasons, attempts to allocate joint marketing cost to products and customers by time studies of salespersons' activities, as well as attempts to allocate the joint production cost, often yield results which are unreliable for appraising segment profitability.

---

[4]Walter B. McFarland, *Concepts for Management Accounting* (New York: National Association of Accountants, 1966), p. 49.

DISCUSSION QUESTIONS

1. Distinguish between joint products and by-products.

2. How may the revenue from the sale of by-products be shown on the income statement?

3. Does the showing of revenue from by-products on the income statement influence the unit cost of the main product?

4. By what method can production cost be relieved of the value of a by-product that can be further utilized in production processes? Explain.

5. By-products which require no additional processing after the point of separation are often accounted for by assigning to them a cost of zero at the point of separation and crediting the cost of production of the main product as sales are made.
   (a) Justify the above method of treating by-products.
   (b) Discuss the possible shortcomings of the treatment.   (AICPA adapted)

6. Are by-products ever charged with any cost? Explain.

7. Describe methods for allocating the total joint production cost to joint products.

8. Discuss the advantages and disadvantages of the market value and average unit cost methods of joint cost allocation.

9. When is it necessary to allocate joint costs to joint products?

10. Does the Internal Revenue Service prescribe any definite joint product or by-product cost allocation methods for tax purposes? Explain.

11. Oregon Logging Company obtains its cost information by dividing total cost by the number of board feet of lumber produced. The president states that money is lost on every foot of low grade lumber sold but is made up on the high grades. Appraise the statement.

12. In making a decision about the further processing of joint products, what costs are relevant?

EXERCISES

1. **By-product costing and entries.** Okalala Soap Company produces a product known as Okay. In the manufacturing of Okay, a by-product results which can be sold as is for $.36 per pound or processed further and sold for $1.30 per pound. The additional processing for each pound of by-product requires $.125 for materials, $.075 for labor, and $.05 for factory overhead.

For May, production costs of the main product and by-product up to the point of separation were: materials, $250,000; labor, $200,000; and factory overhead, $170,000. These costs were charged to the main product. During the month, 315,000 pounds of Okay and 80,000 pounds of by-product were produced.

Required: *Prepare journal entries for the by-product when it is:*

(1) Stored without assigning it any cost and later sold on account at $.36 per pound, with no additional costs incurred.

(2) Stored and costed at $.36 per pound, reducing the main product cost by the amount allocated to the by-product.

(3) Further processed and stored, with no cost prior to separation allocated to it.

(4) Further processed and stored, with the market value method being used to allocate the cost prior to separation, the cost of the main product being reduced by the cost allocated to the by-product, and the main product selling at $2 per pound.

2. By-product costing — market value (reversal cost) method. Fisher Company manufactures one main product and two by-products, A and B. For April, the following data are available:

	Main Product	By-Product A	By-Product B	Total
Sales.....................	$75,000	$6,000	$3,500	$84,500
Manufacturing cost after separation	$11,500	$1,100	$ 900	$13,500
Marketing and administrative expenses	6,000	750	~~500~~ 550	7,300
Manufacturing cost before separation				37,500

Profit allowed for A and B is 15% and 12%, respectively.

Required:

(1) Calculate manufacturing cost before separation for by-products A and B, using the market value (reversal cost) method.

(2) Prepare an income statement, detailing sales and costs for each product.

3. Joint cost allocation — market value method; by-product allocation — market value (reversal cost) method. Whatley Company manufactures joint products X and Y as well as by-product Z. Cumulative joint cost data for the period show $204,000, representing 20,000 completed units processed through the Refining Department at an average cost of $10.20. Costs are assigned to X and Y by the market value method, which considers further processing costs in subsequent operations. To determine the cost allocation to Z, the market value (reversal cost) method is used. Additional data:

	Z	X	Y
Quantity processed	2,000 units	8,000 units	10,000 units
Sales price per unit	$6	$20	$25
Further processing cost per unit	2	5	7
Marketing and administrative expenses per unit...............	1	—	—
Operating profit per unit	1	—	—

Required: *Compute the joint cost allocated to Z, then the amount to X and Y.*

4. Joint cost allocation — market value method. Helen Corporation manufactures products W, X, Y, and Z from a joint process. Additional information follows:

Product	Units Produced	Market Value at Split-Off	If Processed Further Additional Cost	If Processed Further Market Value
W..........	6,000	$ 80,000	$ 7,500	$ 90,000
X..........	5,000	60,000	6,000	70,000
Y..........	4,000	40,000	4,000	50,000
Z..........	3,000	20,000	2,500	30,000
Total	18,000	$200,000	$20,000	$240,000

Required: *Assuming that total joint cost of $160,000 is allocated using the market value method, allocate the joint cost to each product.* (AICPA adapted)

5. Market values at the split-off point for joint cost allocation. *As the result of a joint process, JKL Company manufactures three products, J, K, and L. Every 100 kilograms of raw material input results in output of six units of J, three units of K, and two units of L. In the past month, 100 000 kilograms of raw material costing $80,000 were put into production, and joint processing costs were $88,000. Unit sales prices are: J, $50; K, $40; and L, $20. However, before the products could be sold at these prices, further processing was done: cost for J, $30,000; for K, $6,000; and for L, $4,000.*

Required: *Allocate the joint cost to each product, using the market value method.*

6. Joint cost allocation — market value method. *Faran Company manufactures three different products from a single raw material. A summary of production costs shows:*

	Product S	Product K	Product Y	Total
Output in kilograms	80 000	200 000	160 000	440 000
Sales price per kilogram...........	$.75	$1.00	$1.50	—

	Separable Costs S	Separable Costs K	Separable Costs Y	Total Cost
Production costs:				
Materials	—	—	—	$ 90,000
Direct labor	$ 3,000	$20,000	$30,000	80,000
Variable factory overhead........	2,000	10,000	16,000	45,000
Fixed factory overhead..........	15,000	34,000	30,000	115,000

All separable costs have been assigned to products but the joint cost has not been allocated. All of the year's output was sold.

Required: *Compute the gross profit for each product, allocating the joint cost by the market value method.* (CGAA adapted)

7. Joint cost allocation — market value method. *Bryant Company spent $158,400 on raw materials, then processed this material at a cost of $171,600, resulting in three products: 6,000 units of B, 4,000 units of R, and 3,000 units of Y.*

To make these products salable, an additional $50,000 is spent on B, $30,000 on R, and $40,000 on Y. Unit sales prices are: B, $40; R, $50; and Y, $60.

Required:
   (1) *Compute a unit cost for each product for inventory costing, using the market value method for joint cost allocation.*

(2) The company has an opportunity to sell all of its B output at the split-off point for $34 per unit. Advise management as to whether B output should be sold at the split-off point or after further processing.   (CGAA adapted)

8. *Joint cost allocation — market value method.* CBA Company produces three joint products, C, B, and A. During February, the following information was recorded:

	C	B	A	Total
Joint materials..............	—	—	—	$ 5,000
Joint processing	—	—	—	$23,000
Separable processing	$8,000	$5,000	$2,000	$15,000
Output in kilograms	2 000	5 000	3 000	10 000
Sales in kilograms	1 500	4 200	2 400	8 100
Sales price per kilogram........	$10	$6	$7	—

Required:

(1) Compute the total cost for each product, using the market value method.
(2) What is the justification for treating a joint product as a by-product?

9. *Market value at the split-off point for joint cost allocation.* Miller Company buys Zeon for $.80 a gallon. At the end of processing in Department 1, Zeon splits off into Products A, B, and C. A is sold at the split-off point with no further processing; B and C require further processing before they can be sold; B is processed in Department 2; and C is processed in Department 3. The following is a summary of costs and other related data for the year ended June 30, 19B:

	Department		
	1	2	3
Cost of Zeon.............................	$96,000	—	—
Direct labor	14,000	$45,000	$65,000
Factory overhead.........................	10,000	21,000	49,000

	Product		
	A	B	C
Gallons sold	20,000	30,000	45,000
Gallons on hand at June 30, 19B............	10,000	—	15,000
Sales....................................	$30,000	$96,000	$141,750

There were no inventories on hand at July 1, 19A, and there was no Zeon on hand at June 30, 19B. All gallons on hand at June 30, 19B, were complete as to processing. There were no factory overhead variances. Miller uses the market value at split-off point to allocate joint cost.

Required:

(1) Compute the market value at the split-off point for Product A total units produced for the year.
(2) Compute the total joint cost for the year ended June 30, 19B, to be allocated.
(3) Compute the cost of Product B sold for the year ended June 30, 19B.
(4) Compute the cost assigned to the Product A ending inventory. (AICPA adapted)

10. *Joint cost allocation — market value and weighted average methods.* Buildon Company produces three joint products: Buildon, Buildeze, and Buildrite. Total joint production cost for November was $21,600.

The units produced and unit sales prices at the split-off point were:

Product	Units	Unit Sales Price
Buildon..........................	6,000	$2.20
Buildeze.........................	8,000	1.25
Buildrite	10,000	1.28

In determining costs by the weighted average method, each unit is weighted as follows:

Product	Per-Unit Weighting
Buildon......................................	3
Buildeze.....................................	2
Buildrite	2

Required: Allocate the production cost, using (1) the market value method, and (2) the weighted average method.

11. **Joint cost allocation — weighted average method.** A department's production schedule shows 10,000 units of Article X and 8,000 units of Article Y. Both articles are made from the same raw materials, but units of Article X and Article Y require estimated quantities of materials in the ratio of 3 : 2, respectively. Both articles pass through the same conversion process, but Article X and Article Y require estimated production times per unit in the ratio of 5:4, respectively.

Required: Compute the unit materials and conversion costs for each product if the total costs are: materials, $92,000; conversion cost, $123,000.

PROBLEMS

6-1. Joint cost allocation. Mowen Company produces four joint products, which have a manufacturing cost of $112,000 at the split-off point. Data pertaining to these products are as follows:

Product	Per Unit Market Value at Split-Off	Units Produced	Weight Factors
Kim	$6.00	10,000	3.0
Lim	1.75	16,000	5.5
Mim	3.00	18,000	5.0
Nim	2.75	12,000	6.0

Required: Allocate the joint cost under each of the following methods:
(1) Market or sales value method.
(2) Average unit cost method.
(3) Weighted average method.

6-2. Joint cost allocation — market value method. Charlottetown Company produces three products jointly. During May, joint cost totaled $200,000, and the following individual product information was available:

	C	L	T
Production.	15,000	10,000	20,000
Sales units.	13,000	9,000	16,000
Sales price.	$ 20.00	$ 15.00	$ 9.50
Separable processing cost	$75,000	$25,000	$40,000

Required:
(1) Compute the May gross profit for each product and in total, using the market value allocation method.
(2) A customer has offered to buy all of Product T output at the split-off point for $7 per unit. Advise the Charlottetown management.

6-3. Cost allocation—joint products and by-product. Jefferson Corporation produces three products, Alpha, Beta, and Gamma. Alpha and Gamma are joint products, while Beta is a by-product of Alpha. No joint cost is to be allocated to the by-product. The production processes for a given year are as follows:
(a) In Department 1, 110,000 pounds of material, Rho, are processed at a total cost of $120,000. After processing, 60% of the units are transferred to Department 2 and 40% of the units (now Gamma) are transferred to Department 3.
(b) In Department 2, the material is further processed at a total additional cost of $38,000. Seventy percent of the units (now Alpha) are transferred to Department 4 and 30% emerge as Beta, the by-product, to be sold at $1.20 per pound. The marketing expense related to Beta is $8,100.
(c) In Department 4, Alpha is processed at a total additional cost of $23,660. After processing, Alpha is ready for sale at $5 per pound.
(d) In Department 3, Gamma is processed at a total additional cost of $165,000. In this department, a normal loss of units of Gamma occurs, which equals 10% of the good output of Gamma. The remaining good output is sold for $12 per pound.

Required:
(1) Prepare a schedule showing the allocation of the $120,000 joint cost between Alpha and Gamma, using the market value at split-off point and treating the net realizable value of Beta as an addition to the sales value of Alpha.
(2) Prepare a statement of gross profit for Alpha, independent of the answer to requirement (1), assuming that:
   (a) $102,000 of total joint cost was appropriately allocated to Alpha.
   (b) 48,000 pounds of Alpha and 20,000 pounds of Beta were available for sale.
   (c) During the year, sales of Alpha were 80% of the pounds available for sale. There was no beginning inventory.
   (d) The net realizable value of Beta available for sale is to be deducted from the cost of producing Alpha. The ending inventory of Alpha is to be based on the net cost of production.
   (e) All other costs, sales prices, and marketing expenses are those presented in the facts of the original problem.   (AICPA adapted)

6-4. Cost allocation—joint products and by-product. Madison Chemical Company manufactures several products in its three departments:
(a) In Department 1, the raw materials amanic acid and bonyl hydroxide are used to produce Amanyl, Bonanyl, and Am-Salt. Amanyl is sold to others, who use it as a raw material in the manufacture of stimulants. Bonanyl is not salable without further processing. Although Am-Salt is a commercial product for which there is

a ready market, the company does not sell this product, preferring to submit it to further processing.

(b) In Department 2, Bonanyl is processed into the marketable product, Bonanyl-X. The relationship between Bonanyl used and Bonanyl-X produced has remained constant for several months.

(c) In Department 3, Am-Salt and the raw material colb are used to produce Colbanyl, a liquid propellant. As an inevitable part of this process, Demanyl is also produced. Demanyl was discarded as scrap until discovery of its usefulness as a catalyst in the manufacture of glue. For two years, Madison has been able to sell all of its Demanyl production.

In its financial statements, the company states inventory at the lower of cost (on the first-in, first-out basis) or market. Unit costs of the items most recently produced must therefore be computed. The cost allocated to Demanyl is computed so that after allowing $.04 per pound for packaging and selling costs, no profit or loss will be recognized on sales of this product.

Raw materials	Pounds Used	Total Cost
Amanic acid	6,300	$5,670
Bonyl hydroxide	9,100	6,370
Colb	5,600	2,240

Conversion costs (labor and factory overhead)	Total Cost
Department 1................................	$33,600
Department 2................................	3,306
Department 3................................	22,400

		Inventories in Pounds		
	Pounds Produced	September 30	October 31	Sales Price per Pound
Amanyl	3,600	—	—	$ 6.65
Bonanyl	2,800	210	110	—
Am-Salt	7,600	400	600	6.30
Bonanyl-X	2,755	—	—	4.20
Colbanyl	1,400	—	—	43.00
Demanyl	9,800	—	—	.54

Required: Prepare schedules for the following items for October, with supporting computations prepared in good form and answers rounded to the nearest cent:

(1) Cost per pound of Amanyl, Bonanyl, and Am-Salt produced, using the market or sales value method.

(2) Cost per pound of Amanyl, Bonanyl, and Am-Salt produced, using the average unit cost method.

(3) Cost per pound of Colbanyl produced, assuming that the cost per pound of Am-Salt produced was $3.45 in September and $3.55 in October.

(AICPA adapted)

6-5. Cost of production report—fifo process costing method; joint products and by-product. The following data were gathered from the records of Rodomontade Company for February:

	Process		
	1	2	3
Unit data:			
Beginning work in process inventory			
(⅓ completed in Processes 2 and 3)	—	3,000	3,000
Started or received	32,000	10,000	20,000
	32,000	13,000	23,000
Transferred to Process 2.........................	10,000	—	—
Transferred to Process 3.........................	20,000	—	—
Transferred to finished goods storeroom...........	—	9,000	20,000
Transferred out as by-product	2,000	—	—
Normal loss.....................................	—	—	1,000
Ending work in process inventory (¼ completed in			
Process 2 and ½ completed in Process 3)	—	4,000	2,000
	32,000	13,000	23,000
Partial summary of costs:			
Beginning work in process inventory............	—	$ 8,000	$14,500
Cost added by department:			
Materials	$58,000	—	—
Labor and factory overhead	30,000	18,000	60,000
	$88,000		
Less market value of by-product..............	4,000		
	$84,000		

Materials are issued in Process 1. At the end of processing in Process 1, the by-product appears and the balance of production is transferred to Process 2 for additional processing of one main product and to Process 3 for additional processing of the other main product.

The joint cost of Process 1, less the market value of the by-product, is apportioned to the main products using the market value method at the split-off point. Sales prices for the finished products of Processes 2 and 3 are $10 and $15, respectively. The by-product sells for $2. The company uses the fifo costing method.

Required: Prepare a departmental cost of production report for February. (Carry unit cost computations to four decimal places and round off the unit cost adjustment for lost units to the nearest cent.)

6-6. Cost of production report—fifo process costing method; joint products and by-product. Colloid Chemical Company produces two principal products known as XO and MO. Incidental to the production of these products, it produces a by-product known as Bypo. The company has three producing departments, which it identifies as Departments 101, 201, and 301. Raw materials A and B are started in process in Department 101. Upon completion of processing in that department, one fifth of the material is by-product and is transferred directly to stock. One third of the remaining output of Department 101 goes to Department 201, where it is made into XO, and the other two thirds goes to Department 301, where it becomes MO. The processing of XO in Department 201 results in a 50% gain in weight of materials transferred into the department due to the addition of water at the start of the processing. There is no gain or loss of weight in the other processes.

The company considers the income from Bypo, after allowing $.05 per pound for estimated selling and delivery costs, to be a reduction of the costs of the two principal products. The company assigns Department 101 costs to the two principal products in proportion to their net sales value at the point of separation, computed by deducting costs to be incurred in subsequent processes from the sales value of the products.

The following information concerns operations during April:

Inventories	March 31		April 30
	Quantity (Pounds)	Cost	Quantity (Pounds)
Department 101	—	—	—
Department 201	800	$17,160	1,000
Department 301	200	2,340	360
Finished stock — XO.....................	300	7,260	80
Finished stock — MO	1,200	18,550	700
Finished stock — Bypo	—	—	—

Inventories in process are estimated to be one-half complete in Departments 201 and 301, both at the beginning and at the end of the month. The company uses the fifo method for inventory costing.

Costs	Materials Used	Labor and Factory Overhead
Department 101	$134,090	$87,418
Department 201	—	31,950
Department 301	—	61,880

The materials used in Department 101 weighed 18,000 pounds.

Sales Prices
    XO — $29.50 per pound
    MO — 17.50 per pound
    Bypo—   .50 per pound

Prices as of April 30 are unchanged from those in effect during the month.

Required: Prepare a departmental cost of production report for April. (Carry unit cost computations to three decimal places and round off total amounts to the nearest dollar.)

(AICPA adapted)

Part Three
Planning and Control of Factory Overhead

Chapter 7
Factory Overhead: Planned, Actual, and Applied; Variance Analysis

The use of a predetermined factory overhead rate for the purpose of charging a fair share of factory overhead to products was introduced briefly in earlier chapters. This chapter (1) discusses the methods, procedures, and bases available for applying factory overhead; (2) describes methods and procedures for classifying and accumulating actual factory overhead; (3) shows computations for over- or underapplied factory overhead; and (4) analyzes the total net variance, showing the spending and idle capacity variances. Chapter 8 discusses (1) the departmentalization of factory overhead, (2) the creation and use of separate departmental overhead rates, and (3) departmentalization in nonmanufacturing businesses and nonprofit organizations. Chapter 9 discusses (1) the relationship of product costing to responsibility accounting, (2) monthly overhead variance analysis for use in responsibility accounting and reporting for producing and service departments, and (3) responsibility reporting fundamentals and systems.

The Nature of Factory Overhead

Factory overhead is generally defined as indirect materials, indirect labor, and all other factory expenses that cannot conveniently be identified with nor charged directly to specific jobs or products or final cost objectives, such as government contracts. Other terms used for factory overhead are *factory burden, manufacturing expense, manufacturing overhead, factory expense,* and *indirect manufacturing cost.*

Factory overhead possesses two characteristics that require consideration if products are to be charged with a fair share of this expense. These characteristics deal with the particular relationship of factory overhead to (1) the product itself and (2) the volume of production. Unlike direct materials and direct labor, factory overhead is an invisible part of the finished product. There is no materials requisition or labor time ticket to indicate the amount of overhead, such as factory supplies or indirect labor, that enters into a job or product. Yet factory overhead is as much a part of a product's manufacturing cost as direct materials and direct labor.

The second characteristic deals with the change in cost that many items of overhead undergo with a change in production volume; i. e., overhead may be fixed, variable, or semivariable. Fixed overhead remains relatively constant regardless of changes in production volume, while the fixed overhead per unit of output varies inversely with production volume. Variable overhead varies proportionately with production output. Semivariable overhead varies but not in proportion to units produced. As production volume changes, the combined effect of these different overhead patterns can cause unit manufacturing cost to fluctuate considerably, unless some method is provided to stabilize overhead charged to the units produced. The following chart illustrates the relationship of overhead and volume:

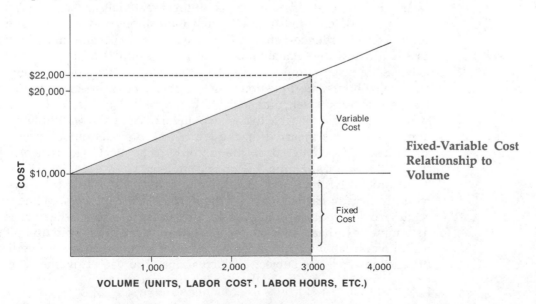

Fixed-Variable Cost Relationship to Volume

The Use of a Predetermined Factory Overhead Rate

The various overhead expenses must be charged to all work done during any period. The problem is how to make such a charge. It is possible to allocate actual overhead to all work completed during the month, using a base such as actual direct labor dollars, direct labor hours, or machine hours. As long as the volume of work completed each month is the same, and costs are within control limits, this method would result in a consistent charge to production each period. As variations occur, work completed during different months would receive a greater or smaller charge—an inequitable situation. For example, costing problems would result if actual costs incurred for repairs and maintenance are charged directly to a job or product when repairs are made. Ordinarily, repairs are necessary because of wear and tear over a much longer period than one month and are made to permit continuous operations in any month. Moreover, since overhead cost needs to be assigned promptly to production and inefficiencies need to be identified, it is argued that factory overhead should be charged to work done on an estimated basis. However, the use of estimates can cause certain difficulties because underlying data are the result of opinions and judgments. Consequently, estimates must be the outcome of careful studies.

Because of the impossibility of tracing all items of factory overhead to specific jobs or specific products, an arbitrary overhead allocation must be made. A predetermined factory overhead rate permits an equitable and logical allocation. For both job order and process cost accumulation procedures, it provides the only feasible method of computing product overhead costs promptly enough to serve management needs, identify inefficiencies, and smooth out uncontrollable and somewhat illogical month-to-month fluctuations in unit costs.

In job order costing, actual costs of direct materials and direct labor used on a job are determined from materials requisitions and time cards and are entered on job order cost sheets. Overhead costs are predetermined from cost data to arrive at the total amount of overhead estimated for the activity level to be used in computing the rate. This total cost is then related to estimated direct labor hours, machine hours, direct labor dollars, or some other base for the same activity level, ultimately to be expressed in a rate. For example, factory overhead applicable to a job would be calculated by multiplying actual direct labor hours incurred on the job by the predetermined rate, and the amount would be entered on the job order cost sheet. The cost of a job is thereby known at the time the job is completed.

In process costing, unit costs are computed by dividing total weekly or monthly costs of each process by the output of that process. While process costing could produce product costs without the use of overhead rates, predetermined overhead rates are recommended, since they speed up unit product cost calculations and offer other distinct advantages when overhead or production levels are subject to fluctuations. The use of overhead rates for process costing is similar to that for job order costing.

Factors To Be Considered in the Selection of Overhead Rates

The types of overhead rates used differ not only from company to company but also from one department, cost center, or cost pool to another within the same company. The type, significance, and use of factory overhead items must be considered when deciding upon applicable rates. At least five main factors influence the selection of overhead rates. The first three of these factors, which are identified as follows, are discussed in this chapter. The last two factors are discussed in Chapters 8 and 9.

I. Base To Be Used

    a. Physical output
    b. Direct materials cost
    c. Direct labor cost
    d. Direct labor hours
    e. Machine hours

II. Activity Level Selection

    a. Normal capacity
    b. Expected actual capacity

III. Including or Excluding of Fixed Overhead

    a. Absorption costing
    b. Direct costing

IV. Use of a Single Rate or Several Rates

    a. Plant-wide or blanket rate
    b. Departmental rates
    c. Cost center or cost pool rates

V. Use of Separate Rates for Service Activities

Base To Be Used

Selection of the most appropriate base for applying overhead is of utmost importance if a cost system is to provide reasonably proper costs and if management is to receive meaningful and valuable data. Therefore, the primary objective in selecting a base is to ensure the application of factory overhead in a reasonable proportion to the beneficial or causal relationship to jobs, products, or work performed. Since factory overhead rates are also used for estimating purposes, the overhead distribution base quantity needed can be translated easily and efficiently into a factory overhead cost to arrive at total estimated production cost.

Ordinarily, the base selected should be closely related to functions represented by the overhead cost being applied. If, for example, factory overhead is predominantly labor-oriented, such as supervision and indirect labor, the proper base is probably direct labor cost or direct labor hours. If overhead items are predominantly investment-oriented, related to the ownership and operation of machinery, then a machine-hour base is probably most appropriate. If overhead is mainly materials-oriented, such as costs associated with the purchasing and handling of materials, then the materials cost might be considered as the base.

A secondary objective in selecting a base is to minimize clerical cost and effort. When two or more bases provide approximately the same applied overhead cost to specific units of production, the simplest base should be used. Although the cost of administering the various methods differs from one company to another, the direct labor cost base and the direct materials cost base seem to cause the least clerical effort and cost. The labor and machine-hour bases generally require additional clerical work and expense.

CAS 418, "Allocation of Direct and Indirect Costs," specifies allocation bases to be used in a variety of circumstances. These instructions are in harmony with the criteria set forth for the various bases discussed in the following paragraphs.

Physical Output. The *physical output* or *units of production* base, the simplest and most direct method of applying factory overhead, is computed as follows:

$$\frac{\text{Estimated factory overhead}}{\text{Estimated units of production}} = \text{Factory overhead per unit}$$

If the estimated expense is $300,000 and the company intends to produce 250,000 units during the next period, each completed unit would be charged with $1.20 ($300,000 ÷ 250,000 units) as its share of factory overhead. An order with 1,000 completed units would be charged with $1,200 (1,000 units × $1.20) of factory overhead.

The physical output base is satisfactory when a company manufactures only one product; otherwise, the method is either unsatisfactory or subject to arbitrary allocation procedures. However, if the several products manufactured are alike or closely related, their difference being merely one of weight or volume, application of factory overhead can be made on a weight, volume, or point base. The weight base applies overhead according to the weight of each unit of product as follows:

	Product		
	A	B	C
Estimated number of units manufactured	20,000	15,000	20,000
Unit weight of product.	5 lbs.	2 lbs.	1 lb.
Estimated total weight produced.	100,000 lbs.	30,000 lbs.	20,000 lbs.
Estimated factory overhead per pound ($300,000 ÷ 150,000).	$2	$2	$2
Estimated factory overhead for each product.	$200,000	$60,000	$40,000
Estimated factory overhead per unit.	$10	$4	$2

If the weight or volume base does not seem to yield a just apportionment of overhead, the method can be improved by assigning a certain number of points to each unit to compensate for differences. For example, a company manufacturing Products L, S, M, and F computes an overhead rate per product as follows:

Product	Estimated Quantity	Points Assigned	Estimated Total Points	Estimated Factory Overhead per Point	Estimated Factory Overhead for Each Product	Estimated Factory Overhead Cost per Unit
L	2,000	5	10,000	$3	$ 30,000	$15
S	5,000	10	50,000	3	150,000	30
M	3,000	8	24,000	3	72,000	24
F	4,000	4	16,000	3	48,000	12
			100,000		$300,000	

If products are different in any respect, such as time to produce or method of production not considered in the allocation base, a uniform charge based on physical output may result in incorrect costing. Other methods must be adopted in such instances.

Direct Materials Cost Base. In some companies, a study of past costs will reveal a correlation between direct materials cost and factory overhead. The study might show that factory overhead has remained approximately the same percentage of direct materials cost. Therefore, a rate based on materials cost might be applicable. In such instances, the charge is computed by dividing total estimated factory overhead by total direct materials cost expected to be used in the manufacturing processes:

$$\frac{\text{Estimated factory overhead}}{\text{Estimated materials cost}} \times 100 = \frac{\text{Percentage of overhead}}{\text{per direct materials cost}}$$

If the estimated overhead is $300,000 and the estimated materials cost is $250,000, each job or product completed would be charged with an additional 120 percent [($300,000 ÷ $250,000) × 100] of its materials cost as its share of factory overhead. For example, if the materials cost of an order is $5,000, the order would receive an additional charge of $6,000 ($5,000 × 120%) for factory overhead.

The materials-related cost base has only limited use, because in most cases no logical relationship exists between the direct materials cost of a product and factory overhead used in its production. One product might be made from high-priced materials, another from less expensive materials; yet, both products might require the same manufacturing process and thus use approximately the same amount of factory overhead. If the materials cost base is used to charge overhead, the product using expensive materials will, in this case, be charged with more than its share. To overcome this unfairness, two overhead rates might be calculated: one for items that are materials-oriented, such as purchasing, receiving, inspecting, handling, and storage costs; the other for the remaining overhead costs.

Direct Labor Cost Base. The direct labor cost base seems to be the most widely used method of applying overhead to jobs or products. Estimated factory overhead is divided by estimated direct labor cost to compute a percentage:

$$\frac{\text{Estimated factory overhead}}{\text{Estimated direct labor cost}} \times 100 = \text{Percentage of direct labor cost}$$

If estimated factory overhead is $300,000 and total direct labor cost for the next period is estimated at $1,200,000, the overhead rate would be 25 percent [($300,000 ÷ $1,200,000) × 100]. A job or product with a direct labor cost of $12,000 would be charged with $3,000 ($12,000 × 25%) for factory overhead.

Analysis of this method of applying factory overhead indicates a step in the direction of charging overhead equitably to products manufactured. Factory overhead items that are used over a period of time must be taken into consideration. The direct labor cost base does so, since the labor cost is computed by multiplying the number of work-hours by an hourly wage rate. The more hours worked, the higher the labor cost, the greater the use of time-related items, and the greater the charge for factory overhead.

The direct labor cost base is relatively easy to use, since information needed to apply overhead is readily available. Its use is particularly favored when (1) a direct relationship between direct labor cost and factory overhead exists and (2) the rates of pay per hour for similar work are comparable. The weekly payroll provides the direct labor cost without any additional record keeping. As long as economy in securing underlying information remains a main prerequisite, the direct labor cost base can be accepted as the best and quickest of the available methods of applying factory overhead.

On the other hand, this method can be objected to for two reasons:

1. Factory overhead must be looked upon as adding to the value of a job or product. The added value often comes about through depreciation charges of high-cost machinery, which might not bear any relationship to direct labor payroll.
2. Total direct labor cost represents the sum of wages paid to high- and low-wage production workers. By applying overhead on the basis of direct labor cost, a job or product is charged with more overhead when a high-wage operator performs work. Such a method can lead to incorrect distribution of factory overhead, particularly when numerous operators, with different hourly rates in the same department, perform similar operations on different jobs or products.

Direct Labor Hour Base. The direct labor hour base is designed to overcome the second disadvantage of using the direct labor cost base. The overhead rate based on direct labor hours is computed as follows:

$$\frac{\text{Estimated factory overhead}}{\text{Estimated direct labor hours}} = \text{Rate per direct labor hour}$$

If estimated factory overhead is $300,000 and total direct labor hours are estimated to be 200,000, an overhead rate based on direct labor hours would be $1.50 per hour of direct labor ($300,000 ÷ 200,000 hours). A job or product that required 400 direct labor hours would be charged with $600 (400 hours × $1.50) for factory overhead.

The use of this method requires accumulation of direct labor hours by job or product. Timekeeping forms and records must be organized to provide the additional data. The use of the direct labor hour base requires, first, a direct relationship between direct labor hours and factory overhead and, second, different rates of pay per hour for similar work, caused by seniority rather than increased output. As long as labor operations are the chief factor in production processes, the direct labor hour method is acceptable as the most equitable base for applying overhead. However, if shop or factory departments use machines extensively, the direct labor hour method might lead to an inaccurate costing.

Machine Hour Base. When machines are used extensively, the machine hour method may be appropriate. This method is based on time required to perform identical operations by a machine or group of machines. Machine hours expected to be used are estimated, and a machine hour rate is determined as follows:

$$\frac{\text{Estimated factory overhead}}{\text{Estimated machine hours}} = \text{Rate per machine hour}$$

If factory overhead is estimated to be $300,000 and 50,000 machine hours are estimated, the rate is $6 per machine hour ($300,000 ÷ 50,000 machine hours). Work that required 120 machine hours would be charged with $720 (120 hours × $6) for factory overhead.

This method requires additional clerical work. A reporting system must be designed to assure correct accumulation of all required data for proper overhead accounting. Generally, shop personnel, supervisors, or timekeepers collect machine hour data needed to charge overhead to jobs, products, or work performed. The machine hour method is considered the most accurate method of applying overhead if the overhead cost is comprised predominantly of facility-related costs, such as depreciation, maintenance, and utilities.

Activity Level Selection

In calculating an overhead rate, a great deal depends on the activity level selected. The greater the assumed activity, the lower the fixed portion of the overhead rate, because fixed overhead will be spread over a greater number of direct labor dollars, hours, etc. The variable portion of the rate will tend to remain constant at various activity levels. Determination of estimates used in deriving a factory overhead rate depends on whether a long- or a short-range viewpoint is adopted, i.e., whether the activity level used is normal capacity, expected actual capacity, or some other capacity level (Chapter 16).

Normal Capacity. The long-range or long-term planning and control approach, the *normal capacity concept*, advocates an overhead rate in which expenses and production are based on average utilization of the physical plant over a time period long enough to level out the highs and lows that occur in every business venture. The normal capacity rate is based on the concept that the overhead rate should not be changed because existing plant facilities are used to a greater or lesser degree in different periods; therefore, a more useful unit cost results. A job or product should not cost more to produce in any one accounting period just because production was lower and fixed charges were spread over a fewer number of units. The rate will be changed, however, when prices of certain expense items change or when fixed costs increase or decrease.

As a result of the use of normal production figures for estimating factory overhead and the selected bases, applied overhead will usually differ from actual overhead incurred. The possibility of such a difference or variance must be recognized, but should not serve to discourage the use of an overhead rate nor encourage the change of this rate. In fact, when this variance, generally called over- or underapplied factory overhead, is further analyzed, it reveals useful management information (pages 154–160).

Expected Actual Capacity. The short-range or short-term planning and control approach, the *expected actual capacity* concept, advocates a rate in which overhead and production are based on the expected actual output for the next production period. This method usually results in the use of a different predetermined rate for each period, depending on increases or decreases in estimated factory overhead and production figures. The use of a predetermined rate based on expected actual production is often due to the difficulty of judging current performance on a long-range or normal capacity level.

The fact that at times the factory overhead charged to production approaches the overhead expense actually incurred often makes the use of the expected actual factory overhead rate seem logical and acceptable, even though the overhead expense is not representative of normal operations. To illustrate, assume that the normal capacity for a company is 150,000 direct labor hours. For the past year, the actual capacity attained was 116,000 hours. The management believes that 120,000 hours will be worked during the coming year. The fixed overhead for either capacity level is $120,000, and the variable overhead is $.50 per direct labor hour. The predetermined factory overhead rate based on normal capacity is $1.30 per direct labor hour, and the overhead rate based on expected actual capacity is $1.50 per direct labor hour. These rates are calculated as follows:

	Normal Capacity	Expected Actual Capacity
Fixed overhead	$120,000	$120,000
Variable overhead:		
150,000 hours × $.50	75,000	
120,000 hours × .50		60,000
Total estimated overhead	$195,000	$180,000
Estimated direct labor hours	150,000	120,000
Factory overhead rate per hour	$1.30	$1.50
Fixed overhead rate per hour	$ .80	$1.00

The difference in the two rates lies in the fixed overhead rate. The expected actual capacity method increases the rate by $.20 per hour, resulting in a greater product cost than with the normal capacity rate. Since fixed expenses are the same for both levels, it must be assumed that management anticipated a volume of business requiring such an amount of fixed cost.

Including or Excluding of Fixed Overhead Items

Ordinarily, cost accounting procedures apply all factory costs to the output of a period. Under these procedures, called *absorption costing, conventional* costing, or *full costing*, both fixed and variable expenses are included in overhead rates. Another method of costing, termed *direct costing*, is sometimes used, chiefly for internal management purposes. Under this method of costing, only variable overhead is included in overhead rates. The fixed expense does not become a product cost but is treated as a period cost, meaning that it is charged off in total each period as are marketing and administrative expenses. It is not included in either work in process or finished goods inventories. Direct costing is discussed in detail in Chapter 20.

Absorption costing and direct costing are the results of two entirely different cost concepts with respect to product cost, period cost, gross profit, and operating income. Although the two methods result in different inventory costs and different period profits, each of the various bases discussed for applying overhead may be used with absorption costing or direct costing.

The Calculation of a Factory Overhead Rate

The first step in calculating the overhead rate is to determine the activity level to be used for the base selected and then estimate or budget each individual expense at the estimated activity level in order to arrive at the total estimated factory overhead. To illustrate, assume that DeWitt Products estimates a normal capacity level of 200,000 direct labor hours. The total factory overhead is estimated to be $300,000. This overhead is classified into fixed or variable categories, as follows:

DeWitt Products Estimated Factory Overhead for 19--			
Expense	Fixed	Variable	Total
Supervisors	$ 70,000		$ 70,000
Indirect labor	9,000	$ 66,000	75,000
Overtime premium		9,000	9,000
Factory supplies	4,000	19,000	23,000
Repairs and maintenance	3,000	9,000	12,000
Electric power	2,000	18,000	20,000
Fuel	1,000	5,000	6,000
Water	500	500	1,000
FICA tax	3,000	15,000	18,000
Unemployment taxes	1,500	3,500	5,000
Workmen's compensation	500	2,500	3,000
Hospitalization insurance	500	1,500	2,000
Pensions	2,000	13,000	15,000
Vacations and holidays	2,000	10,000	12,000
Group insurance	1,000	3,000	4,000
Depreciation — building	5,000		5,000
Depreciation — equipment	13,000		13,000
Property tax	4,000		4,000
Insurance (fire)	3,000		3,000
Total estimated factory overhead	$125,000	$175,000	$300,000

The classification of expenses according to changes in volume attempts to establish a variability pattern for each expense item. This classification must, in turn, consider certain specific assumptions regarding plant facilities, prices (including inflation estimates), managerial policy, and the state of technology. Once the classification has been decided upon, the expense may remain in this category for a limited period of time. Should underlying conditions change, the original classification must be reviewed and expenses reclassified as necessary.

Variable expenses change with production volume and are considered a function of volume; that is, the amount of variable expense per unit is constant. Fixed expenses, on the other hand, are just the opposite. The total amount is fixed, but the expense per unit is different for each production level. Increased production causes a decrease in fixed expense per unit. Knowledge of the effect of fixed and variable expenses on the product unit cost is highly important in any study of factory overhead. A knowledge of the behavior of all costs is fundamental to the planning and analytical processes for decision-making purposes as well as for cost control.

An examination of fixed and variable expenses indicates the difficulty of segregating all expenses as either fixed or variable. Some expenses are partly fixed and partly variable; some are fixed to a certain production level and then increase as production increases. Also, costs may change in step-like fashion at various production levels. Such expenses are classified as semivariable.

Because expenses are to be classified as either fixed or variable, the fixed portion of any semivariable expense and the degree of change in the variable part must be determined. Several methods are available to aid in finding the constant portion and the degree of variability in the variable portion. These procedures determine the relationship between increases in production and increases in total and individual expenses. For example, when production is expected to increase 10 percent, it is possible to determine the corresponding increase in total expense as well as the increase in individual expenses such as supplies, power, or indirect labor. A detailed illustration and discussion of such procedures are presented in Chapter 16.

After the activity level for the selected base and the factory overhead have been estimated, the overhead rates can be computed. Assuming that the direct labor hour base is used and direct labor hours for the coming year are estimated to be 200,000 (normal capacity level) for DeWitt Products, the factory overhead rate at this selected activity level would be:

$$\text{Factory overhead rate} = \frac{\text{Estimated factory overhead}}{\text{Estimated direct labor hours}} = \frac{\$300,000}{200,000} = \frac{\$1.50 \text{ per}}{\text{direct labor}}$$

This rate should be used to charge overhead to jobs, products, or work performed. Amounts applied are first entered in subsidiary ledgers such as job order cost sheets and cost of production reports. Direct labor hours, direct labor cost, or other similar data already recorded determine the amount of overhead chargeable to each job or product.

The factory overhead rate can be further broken down into its fixed and variable components as follows:

$$\frac{\$125,000 \text{ Estimated fixed factory overhead}}{200,000 \text{ Estimated direct labor hours}} = \$ \text{ .625 fixed portion of the factory overhead rate}$$

$$\frac{\$175,000 \text{ Estimated variable factory overhead}}{200,000 \text{ Estimated direct labor hours}} = \$ \text{ .875 variable portion of the factory overhead rate}$$

Total factory overhead rate = $\underline{\$1.500}$ per direct labor hour

Actual Factory Overhead

Deciding upon the base and activity level to be utilized, estimating the factory overhead, and calculating the overhead rate take place prior to the incurrence or recording of the actual expenses. Factory overhead is applied as soon as the necessary data, such as direct labor hours, have been made available. Each day, however, actual overhead transactions are journalized and posted to general and subsidiary ledgers, independent of the application of factory overhead based on the predetermined overhead rate.

A basic objective for accumulating factory overhead is the gathering of information for purposes of control. Control, in turn, requires (1) reporting costs to the individual department heads responsible for them and (2) making comparisons with amounts budgeted for the level of operations achieved. The mechanics for collecting overhead items are based on the chart of accounts, which indicates the accounts to which various factory overhead items are to be charged.

The principal source documents used for recording overhead in the journals are (1) purchase vouchers, (2) materials requisitions, (3) labor time tickets, and (4) general journal vouchers. These documents provide a record of the overhead information which must be analyzed and accumulated in proper accounts. To obtain accurate and useful information, each transaction must be properly classified at its inception. Those responsible for this identification must be thoroughly familiar with names and code numbers of cost accounts as well as with the purpose and function of each account.

Factory overhead includes numerous items which can be classified in many different ways. Every firm, because of its own manufacturing peculiarities, will devise its own particular accounts and methods of classifying them. However, regardless of these possible variations, expenses are summarized in a factory overhead control account kept in the general ledger. Details of this general ledger account are kept in a subsidiary overhead ledger. This subsidiary ledger also can take many forms, and it may be difficult to recognize it as such, particularly when electronic data processing equipment is used. A subsidiary ledger will group various expense items together under significant selective titles as to kinds of expenses and may also detail the expenses chargeable to individual producing and service departments (discussed in Chapter 8), thereby permitting stricter control over factory overhead.

The accumulation of factory overhead in accounting records presents several distinct problems. Due to the many varied potential requests and uses of factory overhead data for managerial decision-making purposes, it is almost impossible to set up an all-purpose system for accumulating factory overhead.

Applied Factory Overhead — Over- or Underapplied and Variance Analysis

At the end of the month or year, applied factory overhead and actual factory overhead are analyzed. The comparison between actual and applied figures leads to computation of the spending variance and the idle capacity variance. The following paragraphs present the mechanics of applying factory overhead, determining the over- or underapplied overhead, and analyzing the overhead variances.

The Mechanics of Applying Factory Overhead

The job order cost sheets or the departmental cost of production reports receive postings as soon as direct materials or direct labor data become available. Factory overhead is applied to the work done after the direct materials and the direct labor costs have been recorded. If direct labor hours or machine hours are the basis for overhead charges, these data must also be available to the cost department.

To continue the illustration for DeWitt Products, assume that actual direct labor hours worked totaled 190,000, and actual factory overhead totaled $292,000. The overhead applied during the period is $285,000 (190,000 hours × $1.50 per hour). The journal entry for summarizing factory overhead applied is:

```
Work in Process .........................................  285,000
    Applied Factory Overhead ..................................        285,000
```

Charges made to subsidiary records (the job order cost sheets or departmental cost of production reports) list in detail applied factory overhead charged to jobs or process costing departments. The debit to the work in process control account brings total applied overhead into the general ledger or into the factory ledger, if factory cost accounts are kept there.

The applied factory overhead account would subsequently be closed to the factory overhead control account by the following entry:

```
Applied Factory Overhead ..................................  285,000
    Factory Overhead Control ..................................        285,000
```

It is common practice to use an applied factory overhead account because it keeps applied costs and actual costs in separate accounts. However, some companies post the credit directly to Factory Overhead Control.

After the actual and applied overhead have been recorded, the factory overhead control account for DeWitt Products appears as follows:

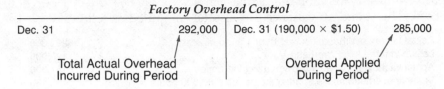

Factory Overhead Control

Dec. 31	292,000	Dec. 31 (190,000 × $1.50)	285,000

Total Actual Overhead   Overhead Applied
Incurred During Period   During Period

Over- or Underapplied Factory Overhead

Debits to the factory overhead control account are for actual expenses incurred during the period, while credits are for applied expenses. There may also be credit adjustments (e.g., the return of supplies to the storeroom) which reduce the total actual factory overhead. Since the debits and credits are seldom equal, there is usually a debit or credit balance in the account. A debit balance indicates that overhead has been underapplied; a credit balance means that overhead has been overapplied. These over- or underapplied balances must be analyzed carefully, because they are the source of much information needed by management for controlling and judging the efficiency of operations and the use of available capacity during a particular period.

For DeWitt Products, applied factory overhead for the period is $7,000 less than the actual factory overhead incurred. Therefore, factory overhead for the period was $7,000 underapplied. This difference must be analyzed to determine the reason or reasons for the underapplied overhead.

Variance Analysis

Two separate variances are computed in analyzing over- or underapplied overhead:

1. Spending variance—a variance due to budget or expense factors.
2. Idle capacity variance—a variance due to volume or activity factors.

The analysis can be made in the following manner, using the factory overhead data given on pages 151–153:

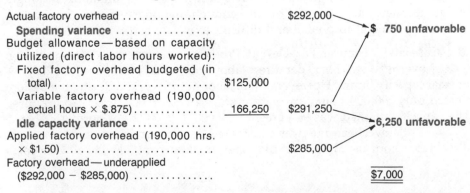

Actual factory overhead $292,000
   Spending variance ....   **$ 750 unfavorable**
Budget allowance—based on capacity
   utilized (direct labor hours worked):
   Fixed factory overhead budgeted (in
     total) $125,000
   Variable factory overhead (190,000
     actual hours × $.875) 166,250 $291,250
   Idle capacity variance ....   **6,250 unfavorable**
Applied factory overhead (190,000 hrs.
   × $1.50) $285,000
Factory overhead—underapplied
   ($292,000 − $285,000) $7,000

Spending Variance. The $750 spending variance is the difference between the actual factory overhead incurred and the budget allowance estimated for the capacity utilized, i.e., for the actual activity of 190,000 direct labor hours worked. The spending variance can also be computed as follows:

Actual factory overhead incurred during the period....................	$292,000
Less budgeted fixed overhead.......................................	125,000
Actual variable expense incurred during the period	$167,000
Variable overhead applied during the period (190,000 hours × $.875)...	166,250
Spending variance—unfavorable	$ 750

If actual overhead had been less than budgeted, the spending variance would have been favorable. Any difference between actual and budgeted fixed overhead would be included as part of the spending variance or separately identified as an additional variance.

A breakdown of the $750 spending variance, as well as a comparison of each actual expense with its budgeted figure, is useful. Details of the actual expenses are recorded in the factory overhead subsidiary ledger. The comparison of actual with budgeted overhead for capacity worked (190,000 direct labor hours) is illustrated for DeWitt Products on page 157.

The budgeted figures utilize the concept of the flexible budget discussed in Chapter 16. Basically, the budget figures represent the budget for the level of activity attained. For example, from the estimates for indirect labor on page 151, fixed overhead is $9,000; the variable part of the overhead cost is $.33 per hour ($66,000 estimated variable indirect labor ÷ 200,000 estimated direct labor hours). The budgeted indirect labor for the activity level attained is $9,000 fixed overhead plus $62,700 ($190,000 direct labor hours × $.33) variable overhead.

Some of the actual expenses exceed while others are less than the budgeted figures. Each difference must be analyzed, the reason for the difference must be determined, and discussion must be initiated with the individual responsible for its incurrence. Corrective action should be taken where called for; likewise, effective and efficient performance should be recognized and rewarded. Observe that even underexpenditures may be undesirable. For example, the $1,350 underspent repairs and maintenance amount may suggest insufficient attention to preventive maintenance.

Some of the spending variance may be attributable to inflation. Although budget estimates are intended to incorporate inflationary effects, the level of inflation is difficult to predict and difficult to isolate as part of a variance.

Idle Capacity Variance. For DeWitt Products, the rate used for applying factory overhead was $1.50 per direct labor hour, which was based on 200,000 normal capacity hours. However, direct labor hours worked during the period totaled only 190,000 hours; capacity not used was 10,000 direct labor hours. The capacity attained was 95 percent (190,000 ÷ 200,000) of normal.

The $1.50 overhead rate was considered the proper costing price for each direct labor hour used. The fact that operations were at a level below normal

DeWitt Products
Comparison of Actual and Budgeted Factory Overhead for 19--
(Capacity Utilized: 190,000 Direct Labor Hours = 95% of Normal)

	Budgeted	Actual	Over	Under
Variable overhead:				
Indirect labor......................	$ 62,700	$ 63,550	$ 850	—
Overtime premium.................	8,550	8,700	150	—
Factory supplies...................	18,050	18,720	670	—
Repairs and maintenance	8,550	7,200	—	$1,350
Electric power....................	17,100	17,650	550	—
Fuel	4,750	4,300	—	450
Water	475	500	25	—
FICA tax	14,250	14,450	200	—
Unemployment taxes	3,325	3,425	100	—
Workmen's compensation	2,375	2,400	25	—
Hospitalization insurance	1,425	1,435	10	—
Pensions	12,350	12,550	200	—
Vacations and holidays.............	9,500	9,300	—	200
Group insurance	2,850	2,820	—	30
Total	$166,250	$167,000	$2,780	$2,030
Fixed overhead:				
Supervisors.......................	$ 70,000	$ 70,000	—	—
Indirect labor.....................	9,000	9,000	—	—
Factory supplies...................	4,000	4,000	—	—
Repairs and maintenance	3,000	3,000	—	—
Electric power....................	2,000	2,000	—	—
Fuel	1,000	1,000	—	—
Water	500	500	—	—
FICA tax	3,000	3,000	—	—
Unemployment taxes	1,500	1,500	—	—
Workmen's compensation	500	500	—	—
Hospitalization insurance	500	500	—	—
Pensions	2,000	2,000	—	—
Vacations and holidays.............	2,000	2,000	—	—
Group insurance	1,000	1,000	—	—
Depreciation—building	5,000	5,000	—	—
Depreciation—equipment	13.000	13,000	—	—
Property tax	4,000	4,000	—	—
Insurance (fire)	3,000	3,000	—	—
Total	$125,000	$125,000	—	—
Total overhead	$291,250	$292,000	$2,780	$2,030
Spending variance—unfavorable			$ 750	

should not increase the factory overhead cost of each unit. The cost of idle capacity should be recorded separately and considered a part of total manufacturing cost. The $6,250 idle capacity variance arises because 10,000 available hours were not used. It is computed as follows:

Budget allowance (based on capacity utilized)................... $291,250
Applied factory overhead 285,000
　　Idle capacity variance—unfavorable .... $ 6,250

The idle capacity variance can also be computed by multiplying the 10,000 idle hours by the $.625 fixed expense rate or by multiplying the total budgeted fixed expense of $125,000 by 5 percent (100% − 95%).

Responsibility for the idle capacity variance rests with executive management, since this variance indicates the under- or overutilization of plant and equipment. The cause of a capacity variance, whether favorable or unfavorable, should always be determined and possible reasons for the variance discovered. One cause may be a lack of proper balance between production facilities and sales. On the other hand, it might be due to a favorable sales price that recovers fixed overhead at an unusually low volume level.

Disposition of Over- or Underapplied Factory Overhead. Because of its importance, the analysis of the over- or underapplied factory overhead is presented in detail. Disposition of this figure is generally quite simple. Although total over- or underapplied overhead is analyzed, showing spending and idle capacity variances, it need not be journalized and posted in two parts. At the end of the fiscal period, overhead variances may be (1) treated as a period cost or (2) allocated between inventories and the cost of goods sold.

For financial reporting purposes, the procedure often used for disposing of over- or underapplied overhead is to close it directly to Income Summary or to Cost of Goods Sold, thereby treating the over- or underapplied overhead as a period cost. The entries are:

Income Summary	7,000	
Factory Overhead Control		7,000

or

Cost of Goods Sold	7,000	
Factory Overhead Control		7,000

In the second case, the $7,000 is subsequently closed to the income summary account as a part of the total cost of goods sold account balance.

The over- or underapplied figure is closed to the cost of goods sold account if the variances are considered a manufacturing function responsibility; if not, the balance is closed to Income Summary. If it is closed to the income summary account, it will appear in the income statement as follows:

DeWitt Products
Income Statement
For Year Ended December 31, 19--

Sales		$1,600,000
Less: Cost of goods sold at normal	$1,195,000	
Underapplied factory overhead	7,000	1,202,000
Gross profit		$ 398,000
Less: Marketing expense	$ 150,000	
Administrative expense	100,000	250,000
Operating income		$ 148,000

If the over- or underapplied overhead is closed to the cost of goods sold account, it will appear in the cost of goods sold statement. This statement and the income statement would appear as follows:

DeWitt Products
Cost of Goods Sold Statement
For Year Ended December 31, 19--

Direct materials used	$ 400,000
Direct labor used	500,000
Applied factory overhead	285,000
Total manufacturing cost	$1,185,000
Less work in process inventory change	20,000
Cost of goods manufactured at normal	$1,165,000
Plus finished goods inventory change	30,000
Cost of goods sold at normal	$1,195,000
Plus underapplied factory overhead	7,000
Cost of goods sold at actual	$1,202,000

DeWitt Products
Income Statement
For Year Ended December 31, 19--

Sales		$1,600,000
Less cost of goods sold at actual		1,202,000
Gross profit		$ 398,000
Less: Marketing expense	$150,000	
Administrative expense	100,000	250,000
Operating income		$ 148,000

Over- or underapplied overhead may be allocated between inventories and the cost of goods sold. This procedure has the effect of restating applied overhead at amounts approximating actual overhead.

Internal Revenue Service regulations require that inventories include an allocated portion of significant annual overhead variances. When the amount involved is not significant in relation to total actual factory overhead, an allocation is not required, unless such allocation is made for financial reporting purposes. Also, the taxpayer must treat both over- and underapplied overhead consistently. The regulations, however, do permit expensing of the idle capacity variance.[1]

Regardless of the disposition made of the over- or underapplied figure, the computation, analysis, and reporting of both the spending and idle capacity variances are significant and important. In the disposition of over- or underapplied factory overhead for financial reporting purposes, companies should generally follow the same procedures at interim dates as are followed at year end. Variances that occur at an interim date and that are expected to be absorbed prior to year end should be deferred rather than disposed of immediately. Further discussion of the disposition of variances is reserved for the standard cost chapters (17 and 18).

---

[1]*Regulations*, Section 1.471-11 (d) (3).

Changing Overhead Rates

Overhead rates are usually reviewed annually. This procedure helps level out costing through the year and ties overhead control in with budget control. If rates are changed during a fiscal or budget period, meaningful comparisons will be difficult. Changes in production methods, prices (because of inflation or for other reasons), efficiencies, and sales expectancy make review and, possibly, revision of overhead rates necessary at least annually. Revisions should be based on a complete review of all factors involved. The extent to which a company revises its overhead rates depends on the frequency of changes, on factors which affect overhead rates, and on management's need and desire for current costs and realistic overhead variance information.

An overhead rate may be incorrect because of misjudgments regarding estimated overhead or anticipated activity. A large over- or underapplied overhead figure does not necessarily mean that the overhead rate was wrong. As mentioned, use of a normal overhead rate is purposely designed to show spending variances as well as the extent to which normal capacity is or is not used. Likewise, when an overhead rate based on expected actual conditions is used, seasonal variations may result in a large amount of over- or under-absorbed overhead, which will tend to even itself out during a full year. The best way to detect an incorrect overhead rate is to analyze the factors used in its predetermination. Since a rate is an estimate, small errors should be expected, and the rate need not be changed for such errors.

Summary of Factory Overhead

This chapter's discussion of estimating, accounting for, and analyzing factory overhead is summarized diagrammatically on page 161.

DISCUSSION QUESTIONS

1. List some of the main expenses that are considered to be factory overhead.

2. Why will factory overhead vary from month to month?

3. When and why must predetermined factory overhead rates be used? Indicate the impracticalities and inaccuracies of charging actual overhead to jobs and products.

4. Name five bases used for applying overhead. What factors must be considered in selecting a particular base?

5. Why is the selection of a proper predetermined rate so essential to accurate costing? Explain.

6. How does the selection of normal or maximum capacity affect operating profit in setting the factory overhead rate?

7. What are the steps involved in accounting for actual factory overhead?

8. The factory overhead control account has a credit balance at the end of the period. Was overhead over- or underapplied?

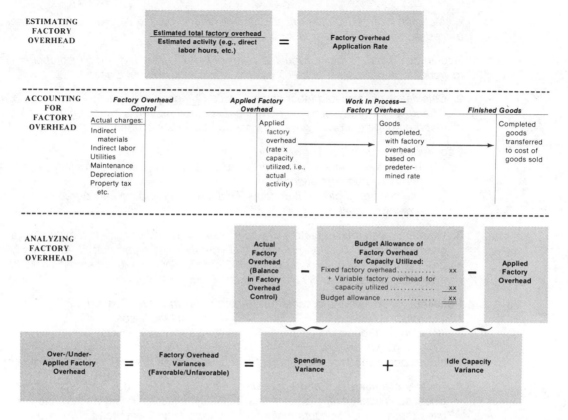

9. Over- or underapplied overhead can be analyzed into two parts called variances. Name these variances, state the reason(s) for their titles, and show their computations.

10. A company applies factory overhead to production on the basis of direct labor dollars. At the end of the year, factory overhead has been overapplied to the extent of $60,000. What factors could cause this situation?

11. Describe two methods for disposing of over- or underapplied factory overhead and explain how the decision to use one of these methods rather than the other would affect net income.

12. If large underabsorbed (underapplied) factory overhead variances occur month after month, the factory overhead rate should be revised to make unit costs more accurate. Comment.

EXERCISES

1. *Factory overhead application.* On November 30, the work in process account of Watkins Company showed:

	Work In Process		
Materials	23,800	Finished	
Direct		goods	48,600
labor	20,160		
Factory			
overhead	15,840		
	59,800		

Materials charged to the work still in process amounted to $4,560. Factory overhead is a fixed percentage of direct labor cost.

Required: Compute the individual amounts of factory overhead and direct labor charged to work still in process. (Round off all amounts to four decimal places.)

2. **Calculation of estimated labor hours.** Venice Company employs 150 people, who work 8 hours a day, 5 days a week. Normal capacity for the firm is based on the assumption that the equivalent of 47 weeks of work can be expected from an employee.

Required: Calculate the following:
  (1) The number of direct labor hours to be used in setting up the firm's factory overhead rate based on normal capacity.
  (2) The number of direct labor hours if management and workers agree on a 10-hour, 4-day workweek.

3. **Various predetermined factory overhead rates.** Colossal Corporation estimates factory overhead of $207,000 for the next fiscal year. It is estimated that 52,100 units will be produced at a materials cost of $500,000. Conversion will require an estimated 85,000 labor hours at a cost of $9 per hour, with 69,000 machine hours.

Required: Calculate the predetermined factory overhead rate based on:
  (1) Materials cost. *41 %*   (4) Direct labor cost. *27 %*
  (2) Units of production. *3.97*   (5) Direct labor hours. *2.44*
  (3) Machine hours. *3.00*
Compute percentages to the nearest percent and dollar amounts to the nearest cent.

4. **Factory overhead rate and application.** Faye Company produces electric hairdryers. Because variable overhead expense is closely related to hours worked, the company uses the direct labor hours method of applying factory overhead. The following data pertain to a recent accounting period:

	Estimated	Actual
Per hour labor cost	$10.00	$9.75
Factory overhead....................	$67,500	$69,000
Labor hours........................	15,000	16,000

Required: Determine the following:
  (1) The predetermined factory overhead rate. *4.50*
  (2) The applied factory overhead. *72000*
  (3) The over- or underapplied factory overhead. *3000*

5. **Entries for factory overhead.** Garfield Co. assembles and sells electric mixers. All parts are purchased and labor is paid on the basis of $32 per mixer assembled. The cost of the parts per mixer totals $40. Since the company handles only this one product, the unit cost basis for applying factory overhead is used. Estimated factory overhead for the coming period, based on a production of 30,000 mixers, is as follows:

Indirect materials	$220,000
Indirect labor.....................................	240,000
Light and power	30,000
Depreciation	25,000
Miscellaneous....................................	55,000

During the period, 29,000 mixers were assembled and actual factory overhead was $559,600. These units were completed but not yet transferred to the finished goods storeroom.

Required:
  (1) Prepare the journal entries to record the above information.
  (2) Determine the amount of over- or underapplied factory overhead.

6. Applied factory overhead and variance analysis. Normal annual capacity for Maddax Company is 36,000 units, with fixed factory overhead budgeted as $16,920 and an estimated variable factory overhead rate of $2.10 per unit. During October, actual production was 2,700 units, with a total overhead of $7,959.

Required: Compute (1) the applied factory overhead and (2) the spending and idle capacity variances.

7. Variance analysis. Starflite Company's normal operating capacity is rated at 47,500 machine hours per month. At this operating level, fixed factory overhead is estimated to be $17,100 and variable factory overhead is estimated to be $20,900. During November, the company operated 50,000 machine hours. Actual factory overhead for the month totaled $39,300.

Required: Compute (1) the over- or underapplied factory overhead and (2) the spending and idle capacity variances.

8. Variance analysis. The Heinrich Company made the following data available from its accounting records and reports:

  (a) $\dfrac{\$600,000 \text{ estimated factory overhead}}{200,000 \text{ estimated direct labor hours}} = \$3$ predetermined factory overhead rate
  (b) Further analysis indicates that one third of the rate is variable-cost oriented.
  (c) During the year, the company worked 210,000 direct labor hours, and actual factory overhead expenditures were $631,000.

Required: Compute the spending and idle capacity variances.

9. Variance analysis procedure. The Kornbrant Company was totally destroyed by fire during June. However, certain fragments of its cost records with the following data were recovered: idle capacity variance, $1,266 favorable; spending variance, $879 unfavorable; and applied factory overhead, $16,234.

Required: Determine (1) the budget allowance, based on capacity utilized, and (2) the actual factory overhead.

PROBLEMS

7-1. Factory overhead accumulation and application. Bullock Company uses job order cost accumulation procedures. Manufacturing-related costs for November were:

Work in process, November 1 (Job 50).............	$54,000
Materials and supplies requisitioned for:	
Job 50......................................	$45,000
Job 51......................................	37,500
Job 52......................................	25,500
Supplies....................................	2,000
Factory direct labor hours:	
Job 50......................................	3,500
Job 51......................................	3,000
Job 52......................................	2,000
Labor costs:	
Direct labor wages...........................	$102,000
Indirect labor wages.........................	15,000
Supervisory salaries	6,000
Building occupancy costs.........................	3,500
Factory equipment costs	6,000
Other factory costs	5,000

Jobs 50 and 51 were completed during November. The predetermined factory overhead rate is $4.50 per direct labor hour.

Required:
    (1) Compute the total cost of Job 50.
    (2) Determine the factory overhead costs applied to Job 52 during November.
    (3) Compute the total factory overhead costs applied during November.
    (4) Determine the actual November factory overhead incurred.
    (5) How should Bullock dispose of any over- or underapplied factory overhead, assuming that the amount is not significant in relation to total factory overhead?
                                               (CMA adapted)

7-2. Journal entries for monthly transactions. Shapiro, Inc. uses job order costing and applies factory overhead on the basis of direct labor hours. Transactions for September were:

    (a) Materials purchased on account, $20,000.
    (b) Shop supplies purchased on account, $5,000.
    (c) Materials requisitioned, $10,000, of which $7,000 was direct materials.
    (d) Recorded liability, paid, and distributed payroll: direct labor, $15,000; indirect labor, $5,000; employee income tax withheld, $2,000; FICA tax, $1,200.
    (e) Employer factory payroll taxes for the month, $1,800.
    (f) Factory overhead paid: repairs, $175; rent, $300; power and light, $400.
    (g) Depreciation of machinery and equipment, $625.
    (h) Expired insurance on machinery, $50.
    (i) Paid marketing and administrative expense, $1,100.
    (j) Factory overhead applied to production at the rate of 80% of direct labor cost.
    (k) Inventories at the end of the month: work in process, $9,000; finished goods, $6,000.
    (l) Sales on account, $50,000.

The trial balance as of September 1 is shown at the top of page 165.

Required: Prepare the journal entries to record the transactions (a) through (l), using a factory overhead control account (not closed until the end of the year) to record both actual and applied overhead.

Cash	20,000	
Notes Receivable	10,000	
Accounts Receivable	28,000	
Allowance for Doubtful Accounts		1,900
Finished Goods	5,000	
Work in Process	10,000	
Materials	15,000	
Prepaid Insurance on Machinery	500	
Factory Overhead Control	8,500	
Machinery and Equipment	75,000	
Accumulated Depreciation — Machinery and Equipment		25,000
Accounts Payable		10,000
Employees Income Tax Payable		2,000
Accrued Payroll Taxes		900
Common Stock		100,000
Retained Earnings		32,200
Total	172,000	172,000

7-3. Factory overhead costing; job order cost accumulation. The following manufacturing cost data are available for Department 203:

Work in process — beginning of period:

Job No.	Materials	Labor	Factory Overhead	Total
1376	$17,500	$22,000	$33,000	$72,500

Costs for 19--:

Incurred by Jobs	Materials	Labor	Other	Total
1376	$ 1,000	$ 7,000	—	$ 8,000
1377	26,000	53,000	—	79,000
1378	12,000	9,000	—	21,000
1379	4,000	1,000	—	5,000

Not Incurred by Jobs	Materials	Labor	Other	Total	
Indirect materials and supplies	15,000	—	—	15,000	
Indirect labor	—	53,000	—	53,000	
Employee benefits	—	—	23,000	23,000	*123000*
Depreciation	—	—	12,000	12,000	
Supervision	—	20,000	—	20,000	
Total	$58,000	$143,000	$35,000	$236,000	

Factory overhead rate for 19--:

Budgeted overhead:

Variable — Indirect materials and supplies	$ 16,000	
Indirect labor	56,000	*96/80 = 100%*
Employee benefits	24,000	
Fixed — Depreciation	12,000	
Supervision	20,000	
Total	$128,000	
Budgeted direct labor cost	$ 80,000	
Overhead rate per direct labor dollar ($128,000 ÷ $80,000)	160%	

Required:

(1) Compute the actual factory overhead.

(2) Determine the over- or underapplied factory overhead.

(3) Calculate the spending variance.

(4) Calculate the amount included in cost of goods sold for Job 1376, which was the only job completed and sold in 19—.

(5) Determine the cost assigned to the work in process account at the end of 19—, unadjusted for any over- or underapplied factory overhead.

(6) Assume that factory overhead was $14,000 underapplied. Compute the underapplied factory overhead charged to the ending work in process inventory if it was distributed between this account and cost of goods sold.   (CMA adapted)

7-4. Variance analysis. Following are eight sets of partial factory overhead data, with favorable variances shown in parentheses:

	Actual Factory Overhead	Applied Factory Overhead	Budget Allowance (Based on Capacity Utilized)	Spending Variance	Idle Capacity Variance
(a)	$30,000	$29,000	$32,000	$? (3000)F	$? 3000 u
(b)	? 23000	15,000	? 22000	1,000	7,000
(c)	24,000	24,000	32000	(6,000)	? 6000
(d)	? 19000	? 16000	18,000	1,000	2,000
(e)	18,000	20,000	? 15000	3,000	? (5000)
(f)	27,000	? 35000	? 33000	(6,000)	(2,000)
(g)	16,000	16,000	? 16000	–0–	? 0

Required: Compute the missing figures.

7-5. Variance analysis. Allied Goods Company set normal capacity at 60,000 direct labor hours. The expected operating level for the period just ended was 45,000 hours. At this expected actual capacity, variable expenses were estimated to be $29,250 and fixed expenses, $18,000. Actual results show that 47,000 hours were worked and that actual factory overhead totaled $49,400 during the period.

Required:

(1) Compute the predetermined factory overhead rate based on normal capacity.

(2) Compute the predetermined factory overhead rate based on expected actual capacity.

(3) Compute the amount of factory overhead charged to production if the company used the normal capacity rate.

(4) Compute the amount of factory overhead charged to production if the company used the expected actual capacity rate.

(5) Would there be a favorable idle capacity variance if the normal capacity rate were used? Illustrate by variance computation.

(6) Would there be a favorable idle capacity variance if the expected actual capacity rate were used? Illustrate by variance computation.

(7) Determine the difference in the amount of the spending variance, depending on whether normal or expected actual capacity was used. Illustrate by variance computation.

7-6. Variance analysis. In June, the factory overhead idle capacity variance for Silvoso Company was $800 favorable and the spending variance was zero. In July, the factory overhead idle capacity variance was zero, but the spending variance was $500 unfavorable. June actual factory overhead was $9,000 for an output of 700 tons, while July factory overhead was $7,500 for a 500-ton output. In August, output was 400 tons, actual factory overhead was $5,900, and the budget allowance was $6,000.

Required: Complete the variance analysis for each of the three months.

7-7. Variance Analysis. The June idle capacity variance was zero, and the spending variance was $600, unfavorable. The July idle capacity variance was $800, unfavorable, and the spending variance was zero. June overhead was $7,000 for an output of 800 tons, while July overhead was $5,600, and output was 600 tons. In August, output was 900 tons and actual factory overhead was $7,100.

Required: Prepare a columnar analysis, indicating actual, budget allowance, applied, total variance, spending variance, and idle capacity variance for each month.

7-8. Inventory costing; overhead analysis; statement of cost of goods sold. The Cost Department of Ingot Company received the following monthly data, pertaining solely to manufacturing activities, from the general ledger clerk:

Work in process inventory, January 1	$ 32,500
Materials inventory, January 1	21,000
Direct labor	256,000
Materials purchased	108,000
Materials returned to suppliers	5,050
Supervision	18,500
Indirect labor	29,050
Heat, light, and power	22,800
Depreciation — factory buildings	7,500
Property tax	4,000
Insurance on factory buildings	3,000
Transportation in (factory overhead)	6,500
Repairs and maintenance — factory equipment	8,250
Depreciation — factory equipment	7,500
Miscellaneous factory overhead	9,900
Finished goods inventory, January 1	18,000
Applied factory overhead	115,200

Additional data:
  (a) Physical inventory taken January 31 shows $9,000 of materials on hand.
  (b) The January 31 work in process and finished goods inventories show the following direct materials and direct labor contents:

	Direct Materials	Direct Labor
Work in process	$ 9,000	$16,000 (2,000 hrs.)
Finished goods	10,000	40,000 (5,000 hrs.)

  (c) Factory overhead is applied to these two ending inventories on the basis of a factory overhead rate of $3.60 per direct labor hour.

Required:
  (1) Determine the cost assigned to the ending work in process and finished goods inventories, including factory overhead.
  (2) Prepare a schedule of the total actual factory overhead for the month.
  (3) Prepare an analysis of the over- or underapplied factory overhead, assuming that the predetermined factory overhead rate was based on the following data:

Variable factory overhead	$70,875
Fixed factory overhead............................	$42,525
Direct labor hours	31,500

(4) Prepare a detailed cost of goods sold statement, assuming that over- or under-applied overhead is closed to the cost of goods sold account.

CASE

A. Factory overhead rate bases. Herbert Manufacturing Company, a manufacturer of custom designed restaurant and kitchen furniture, uses job order costing. Actual factory overhead costs incurred during the month are applied to the products on the basis of actual direct labor hours required to produce the products and consist primarily of supervision, employee benefits, maintenance costs, property tax, and depreciation.

Herbert recently won a contract to manufacture the furniture for a new fast food chain which is expanding rapidly in the area. In general, this furniture is durable but of a lower quality than the company normally manufactures. To produce this new line, Herbert must produce more molded plastic parts for the furniture than for its current line. Through innovative industrial engineering, an efficient manufacturing process for this new furniture has been developed, requiring only a minimum capital investment. Management is optimistic about the profit improvement the new product line will bring.

At the end of October, the start-up month for the new line, and again in November, the controller prepared a separate income statement for the new product line. On a consolidated basis, the gross profit percentage was normal; however, the profitability for the new line was less than expected. Management is concerned that knowledgeable stockholders will criticize the decision to add this lower-quality product line at a time when profitability appeared to be increasing with their standard product line. Gross profit results for the first nine months, for October, and for November are as follows:

Herbert Manufacturing Company
Statement of Gross Profit
(000s omitted)

	First Nine Months			October			November		
	Fast Food Furniture	Custom Furniture	Consolidated	Fast Food Furniture	Custom Furniture	Consolidated	Fast Food Furniture	Custom Furniture	Consolidated
Sales...................	—	$8,100	$8,100	$400	$900	$1,300	$800	$800	$1,600
Direct materials	—	$2,025	$2,025	$200	$225	$ 425	$400	$200	$ 600
Direct labor:									
Forming	—	758	758	17	82	99	31	72	103
Finishing..............	—	1,314	1,314	40	142	182	70	125	195
Assembly.............	—	558	558	33	60	93	58	53	111
Factory overhead........	—	1,779	1,779	60	180	240	98	147	245
Cost of goods sold.......	—	$6,434	$6,434	$350	$689	$1,039	$657	$597	$1,254
Gross profit	—	$1,666	$1,666	$ 50	$211	$ 261	$143	$203	$ 346
Gross profit percentage...........	—	20.6%	20.6%	12.5%	23.4%	20.1%	17.9%	25.4%	21.6%

The controller contends that the factory overhead allocation based solely on direct labor hours is inappropriate and that only supervision and employee benefits should use this base, with the balance of factory overhead allocated based on machine hours. In the controller's judgment, the increase in custom design furniture profitability is partially a result of overhead misallocation.

The actual direct labor hours and machine hours for the past two months are as follows:

	Fast Food Furniture	Custom Furniture		Fast Food Furniture	Custom Furniture
Machine hours:			Machine hours:		
October:			November:		
Forming	660	10,700	Forming	1,280	9,640
Finishing	660	7,780	Finishing	1,280	7,400
Assembly	—	—	Assembly	—	—
	1,320	18,480		2,560	17,040
Direct labor hours:			Direct labor hours:		
October:			November:		
Forming	1,900	9,300	Forming	3,400	8,250
Finishing	3,350	12,000	Finishing	5,800	10,400
Assembly	4,750	8,700	Assembly	8,300	7,600
	10,000	30,000		17,500	26,250

The actual factory overhead costs for the past two months were:

	October	November
Supervision	$ 13,000	$ 13,000
Employee benefits	95,000	109,500
Maintenance	50,000	48,000
Depreciation	42,000	42,000
Property tax	8,000	8,000
All other	32,000	24,500
Total	$240,000	$245,000

Required:
(1) Reallocate actual factory overhead for October and November, following the controller's preference. (Round allocated costs to the nearest $100)
(2) Present support or criticism of the controller's contention, based on requirement (1) results, and including revised statements of gross profit for October and for November.
(3) The controller has also recommended that consideration be given to using predetermined factory overhead rates calculated on an annual basis rather than allocating actual cost over actual volume each month. The controller stated that this is particularly applicable now that the company has two distinct product lines. Discuss the advantages of predetermined factory overhead rates.

(CMA adapted)

Chapter 8
Factory Overhead: Departmentalization

The preceding chapter discussed the establishment and use of one factory-wide predetermined overhead rate, the accumulation of actual factory overhead, and the analysis of over- or underapplied factory overhead. These phases are now expanded through the use of predetermined departmental factory overhead rates, which improves the charging of overhead to jobs and products, leads to cost control via responsibility accounting, and provides useful data for planning and analytical decision-making processes.

The computation of predetermined overhead rates requires a series of departmental allocation processes with respect to estimated expenses. These allocations are limited to those necessary for computing overhead rates prior to the beginning of the fiscal period. Actual overhead accumulated during the month or year should remain with the individual department until the end of the accounting period.

Computing complete product costs involves recognizing all manufacturing costs, regardless of their direct or indirect relationship to a given department or product. In addition to its direct costs, each product must bear an equitable share of indirect costs such as utilities, materials handling, inspection, storage, and general factory expenses. The selection of the best overhead allocation methods is important in determining product costs.

The Concept of Departmentalization

Methods for the control of materials and labor costs are discussed in other chapters. However, because each product manufactured requires a certain minimum amount of materials and labor, there is a limit to the amount of cost reduction for materials and labor which can be realized through the use of such methods. The control potential and control methods are different for factory overhead.

Departmentalization of factory overhead means dividing the plant into segments, called departments, cost centers, or cost pools, to which expenses are charged. For accounting purposes, dividing a plant into separate departments provides more accurate costing of jobs and products and responsible control of overhead costs, which is necessary if unit and total costs are to stay within predetermined or budgeted ranges.

More accurate costing of jobs and products is possible because departmentalization uses different departmental overhead rates for applying factory overhead. A job or product going through a department is charged with factory overhead for work done in that department, using the department's predetermined overhead rate. Depending on the type and number of departments through which they pass, jobs or products are charged with varying amounts of factory overhead, rather than with a single plant-wide overhead rate.

Responsible control of overhead costs is possible because departmentalization makes the incurrence of expenses the responsibility of a supervisor or manager. Expenses which originate directly and completely in a department are identified with the individual responsible for the supervision of the department.

The entire process of departmentalizing factory overhead is an extension of methods previously discussed. Estimating or budgeting expenses and selecting a proper basis for applying them is still necessary; but, in addition, departmentalizing overhead requires separate estimates or budgets for each department. Actual expenses of a period must still be recorded in a factory overhead control account and a factory overhead subsidiary ledger for each department, according to the nature of the expense. This procedure permits comparison of actual departmental expenses with departmentally applied factory overhead. Over- or underapplied factory overhead is computed departmentally and analyzed separately to determine departmental spending and idle capacity variances.

Producing and Service Departments

Departments are classified as either producing or service departments. A *producing department* engages in the actual manufacture of the product by changing the shape, form, or nature of the material worked upon, or by assembling the parts into a finished article. A *service department* renders a service that contributes in an indirect manner to the manufacture of the product but which does not itself change the shape, form, or nature of the material that is converted into the finished product. The following table lists examples of producing and service departments:

PRODUCING		SERVICE	
Cutting	Mill Room	Utilities	Shipping
Planing	Plating	Materials Handling	Medical
Assembly	Knitting	Inspection	Production Control
Upholstery	Mixing	Storage	Personnel
Finishing	Refining	Plant Security	Maintenance
Machining		Purchasing	Cafeteria
		Receiving	General Factory Cost Pool

Selection of Producing Departments

A manufacturing company is usually organized along departmental lines for production purposes. Manufacturing processes dictate the type of organization needed to handle the different operations efficiently, to obtain the best production flow, and to establish responsibility for physical control of production.

The cost information system is designed to fit the departmentalization required for production purposes. The system accumulates manufacturing costs according to such departmentalization, whether operations are of the job type or the continuous process type. Factors to be considered in deciding the kinds of departments required for establishing accurate departmental overhead rates with which to control costs are:

1. Similarity of operations, processes, and machinery in each department.
2. Location of operations, processes, and machinery.
3. Responsibilities for production and costs.
4. Relationship of operations to flow of product.
5. Number of departments or cost centers.

The establishment of producing departments for the purpose of costing and controlling expenses is a problem for the management of every company. Although no hard and fast rules can be given, the most common approach divides the factory along lines of functional activities, with each activity or group of activities constituting a department. Division of the factory into separate, interrelated, and independently governed units is important for the proper control of factory overhead and the accurate costing of jobs and products.

The number of producing departments used depends on the emphasis the cost system puts on cost control and the development of overhead rates. If the emphasis is on cost control, separate departments might be established for the plant manager and for each superintendent or supervisor. When the development of departmental overhead rates emphasizes accurate costing, fewer departments might be used. Sometimes the number of departments needed for cost control is larger than that needed for overhead rates. In such cases, the cost control system can be adapted to proper overhead rates by combining departments, thus reducing the number of rates used without sacrificing control of costs.

In certain instances, particularly when different types of machines are used, departments are further subdivided for cost control and overhead rate purposes. This results in a refinement in applying and controlling overhead with respect to the jobs or products passing through a department.

Selection of Service Departments

The selection and designation of service departments has considerable bearing on effective costing and control. Services available for the benefit of producing departments and other service departments can be organized in several ways by (1) establishing a separate service department for each function, (2) combining several functions into one department, or (3) placing service costs in a department called "general factory cost pool." The specific service is not identified if service costs applicable to producing and service functions are accumulated in a general factory cost pool.

Determination of the kinds and number of service departments should consider the number of employees needed for each service function, the cost of providing the service, the importance of the service, and the assignment of supervisory responsibility. Establishing a separate department for every service function is rarely done, even in large companies. When relatively few employees are involved and activities are closely related, service functions are generally combined for the sake of economy and expediency. Decisions with respect to combining service functions are governed by the individual circumstances existing in each company. Since factory overhead rates for job and product costing are generally calculated for producing departments only, service department expenses are transferred ultimately to producing departments for rate setting and variance analysis.

CAS 418, "Allocation of Direct and Indirect Costs," states that a department should be homogeneous and specifies that this criterion is met ". . . if each significant activity whose costs are included therein has the same or a similar beneficial or causal relationship . . . as the other activities whose costs are included in the [department]."

Direct Departmental Expenses in Producing and Service Departments

The majority of direct departmental overhead costs can be categorized as follows:

1. Supervision, indirect labor, and overtime.
2. Labor fringe benefits.
3. Indirect materials and factory supplies.
4. Repairs and maintenance.
5. Equipment depreciation.

These expense categories are generally readily identified with the originating department, whether producing or service. In the discussion that follows, detailed attention is given to each of the categories.

Supervision, Indirect Labor, and Overtime

These factory labor categories, in contrast to direct labor, do not alter the shape or content of a product; they are auxiliary to its manufacture. It is important to realize that any factory labor not classified as direct labor is automatically classified as factory overhead.

Since overhead is allocated to all products, a lax or incorrect classification would cause direct labor that applies to only one product to be allocated as indirect labor in the form of overhead to other products, thereby understating the one product cost and overstating the others. Thus, decisions on whether or not to classify costs as direct labor can have an important effect on overhead rates, since direct labor cost is often used as the base for determining the rates. In such a case, a decision to classify certain labor as indirect reduces the denominator and increases the numerator of the ratio (factory overhead ÷ direct labor cost) used to compute overhead rates. The following illustration points out the possible effect of incorrect identification of $1,000 of direct labor as indirect labor:

	Correctly Identified as Direct Labor	Incorrectly Identified as Indirect Labor
Direct labor	$6,000	$5,000
Factory overhead:		
Indirect labor	$5,000	$6,000
Other overhead	1,000	1,000
Total factory overhead	$6,000	$7,000

$$\text{Factory overhead rates} = \frac{\text{Factory overhead}}{\text{Direct labor cost}} \qquad \frac{\$6,000}{\$6,000} = 100\% \qquad \frac{\$7,000}{\$5,000} = 140\%$$

The premium portion of overtime paid should generally be charged as overhead to the departments in which the overtime occurred. This method should be followed for all labor except for special cases, which are discussed in the labor chapters. However, the straight-time portion of overtime paid to direct labor employees should be charged to direct labor.

Labor Fringe Benefits

Labor fringe benefits include such costs as vacation and holiday pay, FICA tax, state and federal unemployment taxes, workmen's compensation insurance, pension costs, hospitalization benefits, and group insurance. In theory, these labor fringe benefits are additional labor costs and should—when they pertain to direct labor employees—be added to the direct labor cost. In practice, such a procedure is usually impractical; therefore, these costs that pertain to direct as well as to other factory workers are generally included in factory overhead and become part of the factory overhead rate.

Indirect Materials and Factory Supplies

Incorrectly distinguishing between direct and indirect materials (the latter being part of overhead) has the same adverse effects on product costing as failure to make proper distinction between direct and indirect labor. However, distinguishing between direct and indirect materials is usually not as difficult. In a manufacturing operation, direct materials are those which are changed in form through processing and become an integral part of the end product. Indirect materials, often referred to as factory supplies, are auxiliary to the processing operations and do not become an essential part of the end product. Although insignificant amounts of direct materials may be distinguishable, they may be charged to overhead as an expediency.

There are two basic methods of accounting for the cost of supplies: (1) as a direct departmental charge or (2) as a charge to inventory.

Direct Departmental Charge. An easy, though not the most effective, way to account for factory supplies is to charge the expense to the department that originated the purchase request. This procedure assumes that the department supervisor has the authority to purchase and that the cost of the purchase stays within departmental budget limits. At the end of the accounting period, an adjusting entry should be made, so that the cost of any unused supplies is deferred as inventory on the balance sheet. This adjusting entry would be reversed at the beginning of the next accounting period.

Charge to Inventory. When closer control of supplies is required or when more than one department uses certain supplies, it is not practical or correct to charge only one department at the time of purchase. In such cases, supplies purchased are charged to an inventory account at the time of purchase, and departments using the supplies are charged when supplies are issued.

When an inventory account is used, consumption may be determined by one of two methods. First, if the supply is used only in one department, it is possible to determine the amount to be charged to that department by (1) taking a physical inventory at the end of each month, (2) adding purchases for the month to the cost of the beginning inventory, and (3) from this total, subtracting the final cost assigned to physical inventory at month end to determine the usage for the month.

A second method of accounting for the cost of supplies through an inventory account involves the use of materials requisitions. Requisitions approved by authorized employees permit charging a department with the proper cost and thereby provide better control over the use of materials than the physical inventory method. However, additional clerical work is required, since requisitions must be prepared, priced, and summarized.

Repairs and Maintenance

With respect to repairs and maintenance costs, it is essential to establish control over the total cost incurred by the repairs and maintenance department and to devise effective means for charging maintenance costs to departments receiving the service.

As a rule, the work of repair and maintenance crews is supervised by a maintenance superintendent. If possible and practical, all actual maintenance costs should be charged to a maintenance department, so that the total cost is controlled by the maintenance superintendent and kept within a maintenance budget. However, since maintenance is a service function, its costs must be distributed to departments that receive the service.

Most maintenance work performed for departments is generally of a recurring nature, and charges are incurred evenly throughout the year. However, certain types of maintenance work, such as breakdowns and overhauls, occur at irregular intervals and often involve large expenditures. In such cases, companies using departmental budgets may spread major repair costs over the year by making monthly charges to operations, based on a predetermined rate. These rates are commonly derived from previous years' experience. Monthly provisions are charged to Maintenance Expense and credited to an allowance account. Actual repair costs are charged to the allowance account. In this manner, large maintenance costs are charged to operations in direct proportion to the operating rate and presumably approximate the actual deterioration of the equipment.

Equipment Depreciation

Depreciation is usually a cost not controllable by departmental supervisors. However, their use of equipment influences maintenance and depreciation costs. This is true with respect to all types of depreciable assets — machinery and equipment, buildings, vehicles, and furniture and fixtures. For effective costing and controlling, depreciation is usually identified with the departments using the assets, and the cost is charged directly to departments. The recommended method is to compute depreciation by departments, based on the cost of equipment as recorded on detailed plant asset records. When no records are available or equipment is used by more than one department, depreciation is frequently accumulated in the general factory cost pool.

For assets acquired in earlier years, depreciation of historical costs results in failure to consider both price-level changes and/or current values, especially as they relate to inflationary trends. The result is a mingling of these older costs with other costs acquired with more current dollars. Inflation accounting, while not incorporated in the historical-cost accounting records, should be considered by management in using accounting data for planning and decision making. Discussion of the related adjustment procedures is left to financial accounting textbooks.

Indirect Departmental Expenses in Producing and Service Departments

Expenses such as power, light, rent, and depreciation of factory buildings, when shared by all departments, are not charged directly to a department. These expenses do not originate with any specific department. They are incurred for all to use and must, therefore, be prorated to any or all departments using them.

Selecting appropriate bases for the distribution of indirect departmental expenses is difficult and, in some instances, rests on an arbitrary decision. To charge every department with its fair share of an expense, a base using some factor common to all departments must be found. For example, square footage may be used for prorating such expenses as rent. In plants with departments occupying parts of the factory with ceilings of unequal height, cubic measurement rather than square footage might be used. Areas occupied by stairways, elevators, escalators, corridors, and aisles must also be considered. Some of the indirect departmental expenses that require prorating, together with the bases most commonly used, are:

Indirect Departmental Expenses	Distribution Bases
Factory rent	Square footage
Property tax	Square footage
Depreciation — buildings	Square footage
Insurance (fire)	Square footage
Building repairs	Square footage
Heat	Square footage
Superintendence	Number of employees
Telephone and telegraph	Number of employees or number of telephones
Workmen's compensation insurance	Department payroll
Light	Kilowatt-hours
Freight in	Materials used
Power	Horsepower-hours

At times a service that could be obtained separately by each of several departments can be obtained centrally at a lower aggregate cost. In such cases, the cost if each department obtained the service separately, i.e., the "stand-alone" cost, may be the most equitable base for allocation of the centralized cost.[1] For example, assume that individual departments can obtain necessary rental space separately as follows:

---

[1]Richard B. Troxel, "Corporate Cost Allocation Can be Peaceful...Is Sharing the Key?" *Management Focus*, Vol. 28, No. 1, pp. 3-5.

Department	Cost of Rental Space Obtained Separately
A	$ 500,000
B	500,000
C	250,000
D	50,000
	$1,300,000

Assume further that the rental space can be provided under a consolidated rental agreement for a total cost of $1,030,000. Proration of the aggregate cost on a "stand-alone" base would yield the following result:

Department	Aggregate Cost		Allocation Base		Allocated Aggregate Cost
A.......	$1,030,000	×	$500,000/$1,300,000	=	$ 396,154
B.......	1,030,000	×	500,000/1,300,000	=	396,154
C.......	1,030,000	×	250,000/1,300,000	=	198,077
D.......	1,030,000	×	50,000/1,300,000	=	39,615
					$1,030,000

The Cost Accounting Standards Board Disclosure Statement requires that covered federal government contractors identify and describe allocation bases for all factory overhead, service center, and general and administrative cost pools used by the contractor. CAS 418 sets forth guidance for accumulating as well as for allocating indirect costs.

Establishing Departmental Overhead Rates

Factory overhead is usually applied on the basis of direct labor cost or hours when one factory overhead rate is used for the entire plant, since this procedure is considered most convenient and acceptable. The use of departmental rates requires a distinct consideration of each producing department's overhead, which often results in the use of different bases for applying overhead for different departments. For example, it is possible to use a direct labor hour rate for one department and a machine hour rate for another. A further refinement might possibly lead to different bases and rates for cost centers within the same producing department.

Since all factory overhead, whether from producing departments or from service departments, is included in producing departments, the establishment of departmental factory overhead rates proceeds in the following manner:

1. Estimate or budget total direct factory overhead of producing departments and total direct expenses of service departments at the selected activity levels; determine, if possible, the fixed and variable nature of each expense category.
2. Prepare a factory survey for the purpose of distributing indirect factory overhead and service department costs.
3. Estimate or budget total indirect factory overhead, such as electric

power, fuel, water, building depreciation, property tax, and fire insurance at the selected activity levels; allocate these costs, based on selected methods.
4. Distribute service department costs.
5. Calculate departmental factory overhead rates.

These procedures are illustrated with the total estimated factory overhead for DeWitt Products (page 151), which has now been departmentalized. The figures have been modified for ease in calculating departmental rates, but the fixed-variable cost classification has been retained. The illustration uses four producing departments: Cutting, Planing, Assembly, and Upholstery; and four service departments: Materials Handling, Inspection, Utilities, and General Factory.

Materials handling involves the operation of equipment such as cranes, trucks, forklifts, and loaders. Since many departments are served by this function, a preferred method of organization establishes a separate service department for materials handling activities. All handling costs are charged to this department, with a supervisor responsible for their control. Costs charged to such a service department are the same as those charged to any department and include wages and labor fringe costs of the department's employees; supplies, such as batteries and gasoline; and repairs and maintenance of the equipment. In addition to centralizing responsibility for materials handling operations, departmentalization has the advantage of collecting all materials handling costs in one place.

For cost control, inspection costs are treated in the same manner as other service department costs. However, in certain instances, a special work order may require additional inspection or testing. This type of inspection cost is chargeable to the order and must be so identified. To accumulate these specific charges, separate cost centers may be established for the purpose of charging time and materials for special inspections.

Power and fuel are consumed for two major purposes: for operating manufacturing facilities such as machines, electric welders, and cranes, and for what might be termed "working condition" purposes, such as lighting, cooling, and heating. Although a single billing is common for electric power or natural gas, a direct departmental allocation is often possible. To make such an allocation possible, separate meters to measure power or fuel consumed by specific types of equipment may be installed. In other instances, separate power sources (fuel, natural gas, coal, or electricity) may be used for different facilities or equipment in order to determine an individual utility cost by department.

For purposes of departmental and product costing, two methods of accounting for costs of utilities are recommended:

1. Charge all power and fuel costs to a separate utilities department; then allocate to the benefiting departments.
2. Charge specific departments with power or fuel cost if separate meters are provided, and charge the remaining power and fuel costs to

a separate utilities department or to a general factory account; this remainder is then allocated to the benefiting departments.

Allocation of utilities costs to specific departments is based on special studies that determine such information as each department's horsepower of machines and the number of machines.

Certain expenses other than those discussed above come under the category "general factory," because they represent a variety of miscellaneous factory services. Therefore, a separate general factory cost pool is established to accumulate and control such expenses. Such an organizational unit is usually the direct responsibility of the plant superintendent. Salaries of management personnel directly concerned with production are charged to this cost pool if they cannot be charged to specific departments except by arbitrary allocations. Janitor labor and supplies may be charged to general factory unless charged to maintenance or to a department called "building occupancy." Unless separate service departments for plant security and yard operation are established, these costs are also examples of charges to general factory services.

Estimating Direct Departmental Expenses

Estimating or budgeting the direct expenses of producing and service departments (Exhibit 1, page 181) is a joint undertaking of department heads, supervisors, and members of the budget or cost department of the company. Labor fringe costs are calculated by the office personnel, since the individual supervisor has little influence or knowledge with respect to the underlying rates and figures. Costs of indirect labor and indirect materials are of greater interest to the supervisor. Repairs and maintenance costs are often disputed items unless a definite maintenance program has been established. Departmental depreciation charges are based on management's decision regarding depreciation methods and rates. In the illustration, depreciation of equipment is charged directly to the departments on the basis of asset values and rates set by the controller. The plant manager, working with budget personnel, estimates and supervises the general factory costs.

Factory Survey

Before indirect departmental and service department expenses can be prorated to benefiting and ultimately to producing departments, certain underlying data must be obtained. A survey of factory facilities and records usually produces the information needed, such as rated horsepower of equipment in each department, estimated kilowatt-hour consumption, number of employees in each department, estimated payroll costs, square footage, estimated materials consumption, and asset values. Functions performed by each service department must be studied carefully to determine the most

DeWitt Products
Estimated Departmental Factory Overhead
For the Year 19—

Cost Accounts	F or V	Total	Producing Departments				Service Departments			
			Cutting	Planing	Assembly	Upholstery	Materials Handling	Inspection	Utilities	General Factory
Direct departmental exp.:										
Supervisors	F	$ 70,000	$ 9,000	$ 8,000	$ 8,000	$ 8,000	$10,000	$ 6,000	$ 9,000	$12,000
Indirect labor	F	9,000	1,000	2,000	1,000	1,500	1,000	500	1,000	1,000
Labor fringe costs	V	66,000	9,000	3,000	5,000	5,500	11,000	8,500	10,000	14,000
	F	10,000	1,500	1,000	1,000	1,000	2,000	1,000	1,500	1,000
	V	47,000	10,500	11,800	9,400	8,200	1,800	1,400	1,900	2,000
Indirect materials	F	4,000	500	500	800	1,200	300	200	200	300
	V	19,000	2,500	2,500	3,200	4,800	1,700	800	1,800	1,700
Repairs and maintenance	F	3,000	600	500	700	600			300	300
	V	9,000	1,400	1,500	1,300	1,800	500	200	1,700	600
Depreciation — equipment	F	13,000	1,500	3,500	1,000	3,000				4,000
Total direct departmental expenses		$250,000	$37,500	$34,300	$31,400	$35,600	$28,300	$18,600	$27,400	$36,900
Indirect departmental exp.:										
Electric power	F	$ 2,000							$ 2,000	
	V	20,000							20,000	
Fuel	F	1,000							1,000	
	V	10,000							10,000	
Water	F	1,000							1,000	
	V	4,000							4,000	
Depreciation — buildings	F	5,000	1,250	1,000	1,500	1,250				
Property tax	F	4,000	1,000	800	1,200	1,000				
Insurance (fire)	F	3,000	750	600	900	750				
Total indirect departmental expenses		$ 50,000	$ 3,000	$ 2,400	$ 3,600	$ 3,000			$38,000	
Total departmental factory overhead		$300,000	$40,500	$36,700	$35,000	$38,600	$28,300	$18,600	$65,400	$36,900
Total fixed factory overhead		$125,000	$17,100	$17,900	$16,100	$18,300	$13,300	$ 7,700	$16,000	$18,600
Total variable factory overhead		$175,000	$23,400	$18,800	$18,900	$20,300	$15,000	$10,900	$49,400	$18,300

Exhibit 1

equitable basis for distributing their expenses. The factory survey for DeWitt Products appears as follows:

DEWITT PRODUCTS
SCHEDULE A—FACTORY SURVEY PREPARED AT THE BEGINNING OF THE YEAR

Producing Departments	Number of Employees	%	Kilo-watt-Hours	%	Horse-power-Hours	%	Floor Area (Sq. Ft.)	%	Cost of Materials Requisitioned	%
Cutting	30	20	12 800	20	200,000	40	5,250	25	$180,000	45
Planing	25	17	6 400	10	120,000	24	4,200	20	40,000	10
Assembly	45	30	19 200	30	80,000	16	6,300	30	40,000	10
Upholstery	50	33	25 600	40	100,000	20	5,250	25	140,000	35
Total	150	100	64 000	100	500,000	100	21,000	100	$400,000	100

Estimating and Allocating Indirect Expenses

Indirect departmental expenses, such as heat, electric power, fuel, water, and building depreciation, must be estimated and then allocated to either producing and service departments or perhaps only to producing departments. The method depends upon management's decision. In Exhibit 1, indirect departmental expenses are prorated in two ways: (1) electric power, fuel, and water are charged to Utilities, from which a distribution is made to producing departments only; (2) depreciation of building, property tax, and fire insurance are prorated only to producing departments on the basis of floor area as shown in the Factory Survey (Schedule A); e.g., 25 percent of $5,000, or $1,250, is charged to the Cutting Department for building depreciation. However, as an alternative, these costs could be allocated to service departments as well as to producing departments. This procedure would more completely measure the total cost for individual service departments and thus provide information needed for cost planning and control.

Distributing Service Department Costs

The number and types of service departments in a company depend on its operations and the degree of expense control desired. As shown in Exhibit 1, each service department of DeWitt Products is charged with its direct expenses. These costs and any indirect departmental expenses charged to the service departments should be distributed equitably to either producing departments and service departments or just to producing departments, again depending on management's decision. The distribution might be based on number of employees, kilowatt-hour consumption, horsepower-hour consumption, floor space, asset value, or cost of materials to be requisitioned. The expenses of service departments are ultimately transferred to producing departments to establish predetermined factory overhead rates and to analyze variances.

General Procedures for Distributing Service Department Overhead. Various procedures are followed for the transfer of service department overhead to benefiting departments. In some companies (as illustrated in Exhibit 2, page 184), service department expenses are transferred only to producing departments. This direct procedure avoids much clerical work. It can be justified for product costing if there is no material difference in the final costs of a producing department when the expenses of a service department are not prorated to other service departments. However, again this procedure fails to measure the total cost for individual service departments when such information is needed for cost planning and control.

An alternative procedure is to transfer, by steps, the expenses of service departments on the basis of producing and other service departments' use of the respective services. To use this procedure, a decision must be made with respect to the service department which should be closed first, because no further distributions are made to a service department, once its costs have been distributed. Usually, expenses are transferred in the order of the amount of service rendered, with the expenses of the department rendering the greatest amount of service transferred first. When service rendered by a department cannot be determined accurately, however, the expenses of the service department which has the largest total expense may be distributed first. With this procedure, it is assumed that the department with the largest amount of expense rendered the greatest amount of service.

The distribution of estimated service department costs for DeWitt Products is shown in Exhibit 2, page 184. Since the illustration shows no transfer of service department costs to other service departments, the order of distribution does not matter. The distribution is made by starting with Materials Handling. The overhead of this department is distributed on the basis of the estimated cost of materials requisitioned per Schedule A; e.g., 45 percent of $28,300, or $12,735, is transferred to the Cutting Department. The Inspection cost is transferred to the producing departments Assembly and Upholstery on a 50-50 basis, because these two departments are the only ones receiving this type of service and they receive it in equal amounts.

The Utilities cost is transferred in a threefold manner: 20 percent of the cost based on kilowatt-hours; 50 percent, on horsepower-hours; and 30 percent, on floor area. The amount of $13,080 represents 20 percent of $65,400, the total cost of the department. According to Schedule A, 20 percent of $13,080, or $2,616, is distributed to the Cutting Department. The same method is followed for the other costs and departments. General Factory is distributed on the basis of number of employees, e.g., 20 percent of $36,900, or $7,380, is distributed to the Cutting Department.

The distribution of these service department costs is based on percentages in the Factory Survey, page 182. Some accountants proceed in a different manner by calculating a rate per square foot, per kilowatt-hour, or per employee. For example, the amount of General Factory cost transferred to the Cutting Department may be determined as shown at the top of page 185.

DeWitt Products
Distribution of Estimated Service Department Costs
and
Calculation of Departmental Factory Overhead Rates
For the Year 19--

Cost Accounts	Total	Producing Departments				Service Departments			
		Cutting	Planing	Assembly	Upholstery	Materials Handling	Inspection	Utilities	General Factory
Total departmental factory overhead before distribution of service depts.	$300,000	$40,500	$36,700	$ 35,000	$38,600	$28,300	$18,600	$65,400	$36,900
Distribution of service department costs:									
Materials handling (Base: estimated cost of materials requisitioned)		$12,735	$ 2,830	$ 2,830	$ 9,905	(28,300)			
Inspection (Base: equally to assembly and upholstery departments)				9,300	9,300		(18,600)		
Utilities: (Bases: 20% on kwh .... 50% on hph .... 30% on floor area ....)		2,616 13,080 4,905	1,308 7,848 3,924	3,924 5,232 5,886	5,232 6,540 4,905			(13,080) (32,700) (19,620)	
General factory (Base: no. of employees)		7,380	6,273	11,070	12,177				(36,900)
Total service dept. costs distributed		$40,716	$22,183	$ 38,242	$48,059				
Total departmental factory overhead after distribution of service depts.	$300,000	$81,216	$58,883	$ 73,242	$86,659				
Bases: Direct labor hours ... Machine hours ... Direct labor cost ...		40,608	18,400	$122,000	48,140				
Rates		$2.00 per direct labor hour	$3.20 per machine hour	60% of direct labor cost	$1.80 per direct labor hour				

Exhibit 2

$$\frac{\$36,900 \text{ General Factory cost}}{150 \text{ employees}} = \$246 \text{ per employee}$$

$$\$246 \times 30 \text{ employees in the Cutting Department} = \underline{\$7,380}$$

Algebraic Method for Overhead Distribution. The proration of service department expenses to other service departments may be incomplete if a department provides service to a department from which it receives service. The incompleteness in proration arises because, using the procedures discussed earlier, one department would be closed out before the other and therefore before receiving any expense proration from the other. To illustrate, consider the following situation in which Service Department Y provides service to Service Department Z and, in turn, Z renders service to Y:

Department	Factory Overhead Before Distribution of Service Departments	Services Provided Dept. Y	Services Provided Dept. Z
Producing—A	$ 6,000	40%	20%
Producing—B	8,000	40	50
Service—Y	3,630	—	30
Service—Z	2,000	20	—
Total factory overhead...	$19,630	100%	100%

If greater reciprocal exactness is desired, the expenses of Y and Z should be allocated simultaneously. The following algebraic technique can be followed:[2]

Let: $Y = \$3,630 + .30Z$

            $Z = \$2,000 + .20Y$

Substituting: $Y = \$3,630 + .30(\$2,000 + .20Y)$

Solving: $Y = \$3,630 + \$600 + .06Y$

        $.94Y = \$4,230$

           $Y = \$4,500$

Substituting: $Z = \$2,000 + .20(\$4,500) = \$2,000 + \$900 = \$2,900$

Distribution of Service Department Expenses

	Producing Departments A	Producing Departments B	Service Departments Y	Service Departments Z	Total
Factory overhead before distribution of service departments	$6,000	$ 8,000	$3,630	$2,000	$19,630
Distribution of:					
Department Y	1,800	1,800	(4,500)	900	
Department Z	580	1,450	870	(2,900)	
Total factory overhead.......	$8,380	$11,250			$19,630

---

[2]Matrix algebra can also be used, and it is especially efficient when there is a large number of service departments and the allocation is done by computer. See Thomas H. Williams and Charles H. Griffin, "Matrix Theory and Cost Allocation," *The Accounting Review*, Vol. XXXIX, No. 3, pp. 671–678 and John L. Livingstone, "Matrix Algebra and Cost Allocation," *The Accounting Review*, Vol. XLIII, No. 3, pp. 503–508.

Calculating Departmental Overhead Rates

After service department expenses have been distributed, producing department overhead rates can be calculated in terms of direct labor hours, direct labor cost, machine hours, or some other appropriate base. In Exhibit 2, three different bases are used: direct labor hours, machine hours, and direct labor cost.

This discussion has described procedures by which all factory overhead costs, for both producing and service departments, are assigned to work in process by ultimate accumulation of factory overhead in producing departments and then by use of overhead rates for producing departments only. However, it is possible to assign certain service department costs directly from the service department to work in process. For example, materials handling costs might be accumulated in a materials handling department and a materials-cost-oriented rate used for assigning these costs directly to work in process, with any difference between actual and applied costs analyzed into spending and idle capacity variances.

Use of Departmental Factory Overhead Rates

During the fiscal year, as information becomes available at the end of each week or month, factory overhead is applied to a job or product by inserting the applied overhead figure in the overhead section of a job sheet or production report. Amounts applied must be summarized periodically for entry in the general journal. The summary entry applicable to DeWitt Products is illustrated as follows:

Work in Process	285,000	
Applied Factory Overhead—Cutting Department (42,010 actual direct labor hours × $2)		84,020
Applied Factory Overhead—Planing Department (17,000 actual machine hours × $3.20)		54,400
Applied Factory Overhead—Assembly Department ($111,700 actual direct labor cost × 60%)		67,020
Applied Factory Overhead—Upholstery Department (44,200 actual direct labor hours × $1.80)		79,560

Actual Factory Overhead — Departmentalized

Actual factory overhead is summarized in the factory overhead control account in the general ledger. Details are entered in the factory overhead subsidiary ledger. Departmentalization of actual factory overhead also involves the detailed adaptation of previously outlined procedures for handling actual factory overhead. The extra detail can become quite extensive and unduly burdensome unless care is taken to organize the flow of work efficiently.

Departmental Expense Analysis Sheets

Departmentalization of factory overhead requires that each expense be charged to a department as well as to a specific expense account. Such charges are collected on departmental expense analysis sheets. A portion of the form used for both producing and service departments is reproduced below:

DEPARTMENTAL EXPENSE ANALYSIS SHEET									
Department No. 1 — Cutting					For		March, 19--		
Explanation	Date	411	412	413	421	433	451	453	Summary

In this form, each column represents a certain class of factory overhead that will be charged to the department. For example, the column coded 411 represents supervisors, and 412 represents indirect labor. Entries to departmental expense analysis sheets are facilitated by combining department numbers and expense codes. A code such as 1412 indicates that Department No. 1 (Cutting) is charged with indirect labor (Code 412). Similar combinations are used for other departments. The chart of accounts establishes the codes.

The subsidiary ledger must also include a sheet for each indirect factory expense not originally charged to a department, so that the total of the subsidiary overhead ledger will equal the total in the factory overhead control account.

Steps and Procedures at End of Fiscal Period

At the end of the fiscal period, actual costs of producing and service departments, as well as those of a general indirect nature, are again assembled in the same manner as for estimated factory overhead at the beginning of the year. When all overhead has been assembled in the producing departments, it is then possible to compare actual with applied overhead and to determine the over- or underapplied factory overhead. The procedures are summarized as follows:

1. Prepare a summary of the actual direct departmental factory overhead of producing departments and the actual direct expenses of service departments. (See Exhibit 3 on page 188.)
2. Prepare a second factory survey based on the actual data experienced during the year. (See Schedule B on page 189.)
3. Allocate actual indirect factory overhead based on the results of the factory survey at the end of the year. (See Exhibit 3 and Schedule B.)

DeWitt Products
Actual Departmental Factory Overhead
For the Year 19--

Cost Accounts	F or V	Total	Producing Departments				Service Departments			
			Cutting	Planing	Assembly	Upholstery	Materials Handling	Inspection	Utilities	General Factory
Direct departmental expenses:										
Supervisors	F	$ 70,000	$ 9,000	$ 8,000	$ 8,000	$ 8,000	$10,000	$ 6,000	$ 9,000	$12,000
Indirect labor	F	9,000	1,000	2,000	1,000	1,500	1,000	500	1,000	1,000
Labor fringe costs	V	63,000	9,800	2,800	4,200	6,000	10,000	7,300	9,000	13,900
	F	10,000	1,500	1,000	1,000	1,000	2,000	1,000	1,500	1,000
Indirect materials	V	45,000	10,000	11,400	9,700	8,000	1,700	1,300	1,600	1,300
	F	4,000	500	500	800	1,200	300	200	200	300
Repairs and maintenance	V	23,000	4,300	3,600	2,900	5,400	1,800	1,200	2,100	1,700
	F	3,000	600	500	700	600			300	300
Depreciation — equipment	V	12,000	1,700	1,800	2,000	2,100	600	300	2,500	1,000
	F	13,000	1,500	3,500	1,000	3,000				4,000
Total direct departmental expenses		$252,000	$39,900	$35,100	$31,300	$36,800	$27,400	$17,800	$27,200	$36,500
Indirect departmental expenses:										
Electric power	F	$ 2,000							$ 2,000	
	V	14,000							14,000	
Fuel	F	1,000							1,000	
	V	7,000							7,000	
Water	F	1,000							1,000	
	V	3,000							3,000	
Depreciation — buildings	F	5,000	$ 1,250	$ 1,000	$ 1,500	$ 1,250				
Property tax	F	4,000	1,000	800	1,200	1,000				
Insurance (fire)	F	3,000	750	600	900	750				
Total indirect departmental expenses		$ 40,000	$ 3,000	$ 2,400	$ 3,600	$ 3,000			$28,000	
Total actual departmental factory overhead before distribution of service departments		$292,000	$42,900	$37,500	$34,900	$39,800	$27,400	$17,800	$55,200	$36,500

Exhibit 3

DEWITT PRODUCTS
SCHEDULE B—FACTORY SURVEY—DECEMBER 31, 19--

Producing Departments	Number of Employees	%	Kilo-watt-Hours	%	Horse-power-Hours	%	Floor Area (Sq. Ft.)	%	Cost of Materials Requisi-tioned	%
Cutting	35	24	16 978	26	210,000	42	5,250	25	$193,500	45
Planing	25	17	5 224	8	110,000	22	4,200	20	43,000	10
Assembly	40	28	16 325	25	90,000	18	6,300	30	47,300	11
Upholstery	45	31	26 773	41	90,000	18	5,250	25	146,200	34
Total	145	100	65 300	100	500,000	100	21,000	100	$430,000	100

4. Distribute actual service department costs on the basis of the end-of-the-year factory survey. (See Exhibit 4 on page 190 and Schedule B.)
5. Compare actual total and departmental factory overhead with the total and departmental factory overhead applied to jobs and products during the year, and determine the total and departmental over- or underapplied factory overhead. (See Exhibit 4.)

Over- or Underapplied Factory Overhead

With the year-end overhead distribution sheet completed, total actual departmental factory overhead can now be transferred to the individual departmental factory overhead control accounts. Using the figures provided by the overhead distribution sheet (Exhibit 4), the following entry can be made:

Factory Overhead—Cutting Department	82,592	
Factory Overhead—Planing Department	56,712	
Factory Overhead—Assembly Department	69,730	
Factory Overhead—Upholstery Department	82,966	
Factory Overhead Control		292,000

A comparison of actual and applied overhead of each producing department as well as of the total overhead of the company results in the following (over-) underapplied factory overhead:

Total	Cutting	Planing	Assembly	Upholstery
$7,000	$(1,428)	$2,312	$2,710	$3,406

Spending and Idle Capacity Variance Analysis

In the previous chapter, page 155, the $7,000 underapplied factory overhead was analyzed and a $750 unfavorable spending variance and a $6,250 unfavorable idle capacity variance were determined. The $1.50 overhead rate used there and based on 200,000 direct labor hours is not applicable for the departmentalized illustration. New rates with different bases have been created. However, it is possible to analyze each departmental over- or underapplied figure and determine a departmental spending and idle capacity variance. What is particularly needed is the amount of overhead budgeted for

DeWitt Products
Distribution of Actual Service Department Costs
and
Computation of Departmental Over- or Underapplied Factory Overhead
For the Year 19—

Cost Accounts	Total	Producing Departments				Service Departments			
		Cutting	Planing	Assembly	Upholstery	Materials Handling	Inspection	Utilities	General Factory
Total actual departmental factory overhead before distribution of service departments	$292,000	$42,900	$37,500	$34,900	$39,800	$27,400	$17,800	$55,200	$36,500
Distribution of service department costs:									
Materials handling (Base: actual cost of materials requisitioned)		$12,330	$ 2,740	$ 3,014	$ 9,316	(27,400)			
Inspection (Base: equally to assembly and upholstery departments)				8,900	8,900		(17,800)		
Utilities: (Bases: 20% on kwh / 50% on hph / 30% on floor area)		2,870 / 11,592 / 4,140	883 / 6,072 / 3,312	2,760 / 4,968 / 4,968	4,527 / 4,968 / 4,140			(11,040) / (27,600) / (16,560)	
General factory (Base: number of employees)		8,760	6,205	10,220	11,315				(36,500)
Total service department costs distributed		$39,692	$19,212	$34,830	$43,166				
Total actual departmental factory overhead after distribution of service departments		$82,592	$56,712	$69,730	$82,966				
Total applied factory overhead	285,000	84,020	54,400	67,020	79,560				
(Over-) or underapplied factory overhead	$ 7,000	$(1,428)	$ 2,312	$ 2,710	$ 3,406				

Exhibit 4

the level of operation attained (capacity utilized), which, in turn, requires a knowledge of the fixed and variable overhead in each producing department. To develop the budget allowance, the estimates shown in the summaries of the departmental factory overhead (Exhibit 1) and the distribution of service department costs (Exhibit 2) are examined. Exhibit 1 indicates the fixed and variable departmental costs at the bottom line of the estimates. The service department costs distributed to the producing departments, as shown in Exhibit 2, are considered variable costs for the producing departments. The fixed-variable classification does not apply after the distribution.

The following spending and idle capacity variance analysis is prepared for executive management on the basis of the actual annual data after the books have been closed. However, the middle- and operating-management levels require current cost control information at least once a month. With ever greater emphasis placed upon the control of costs by responsible supervisory personnel, control information must be communicated to all levels of management in a manner that permits the charging and discharging of responsibility of cost incurrence. This is discussed in Chapter 9.

CALCULATION OF ESTIMATED FIXED AND VARIABLE OVERHEAD RATES

	Producing Departments			
	Cutting	Planing	Assembly	Upholstery
Fixed departmental overhead.........	$17,100	$17,900	$ 16,100	$18,300
Variable departmental overhead	$23,400	$18,800	$ 18,900	$20,300
Variable service department costs.....	40,716	22,183	38,242	48,059
Total variable overhead	$64,116	$40,983	$ 57,142	$68,359
Bases:				
Direct labor hours	40,608			48,140
Machine hours....................		18,400		
Direct labor cost			$122,000	
Fixed overhead rate	$ .42	$ .97	13%	$ .38
Variable overhead rate..............	1.58	2.23	47	1.42
Total overhead rate:				
Per direct labor hour...............	$2.00			
Per machine hour		$3.20		
Of direct labor cost...............			60%	
Per direct labor hour..............				$1.80

CALCULATION OF BUDGET ALLOWANCES*

	Producing Departments			
	Cutting	Planing	Assembly	Upholstery
Fixed overhead	$17,100	$17,900	$ 16,100	$18,300
Variable overhead:				
42,010 direct labor hours × $1.58...	66,376			
17,000 machine hours × $2.23		37,910		
$111,700 direct labor cost × 47%...			52,499	
44,200 direct labor hours × $1.42...				62,764
Total budget allowance	$83,476	$55,810	$ 68,599	$81,064

*Based on capacity utilized, i.e., actual activity.

SPENDING AND IDLE CAPACITY VARIANCE ANALYSIS						
Producing Departments	(1) Actual Overhead	(2) Budget Allowance	(3) Applied Overhead	Total Variance (1)–(3)	Spending Variance (1)–(2)	Idle Capacity Variance (2)–(3)
Cutting	$ 82,592	$ 83,476	$ 84,020	$(1,428)	$ (884)	$ (544)
Planing	56,712	55,810	54,400	2,312	902	1,410
Assembly	69,730	68,599	67,020	2,710	1,131	1,579
Upholstery	82,966	81,064	79,560	3,406	1,902	1,504
Total	$292,000	$288,949	$285,000	$7,000	$3,051	$3,949

Overhead Departmentalization in Nonmanufacturing Businesses and Nonprofit Organizations

The responsible control of departmental expenses is equally essential in nonmanufacturing activities. The following large complex entities should be divided into administrative and supervisory departments, sections, or service units for cost planning and control:

Nonmanufacturing segments of manufacturing concerns (e. g., marketing departments — see Chapter 21)
Retail or department stores
Financial institutions (banks, savings and loan associations, and brokerage houses)
Insurance companies
Educational institutions (school systems, colleges, and universities)
Service organizations (hotels, motels, hospitals, and nursing homes)
Federal, state, and local governments (and their agencies)

Retail or department stores have practiced departmentalization for many years by grouping their organizations under the following typical headings: administration, occupancy, sales promotion and advertising, purchasing, selling, and delivery. These groups incur costs similar to those in manufacturing businesses. The group "Occupancy" is almost identical with General Factory, and includes such expenses as building repairs, rent and property taxes, insurance on buildings and fixtures, light, heat, power, and depreciation on buildings and fixtures. Again, similar to factory procedures, group costs are prorated to revenue-producing sales departments via a charging or billing rate.

Financial institutions (banks, savings and loan associations, and brokerage houses) should departmentalize their organizations in order to control expenses and establish a profitability rating of individual activities. The size of the institution and the types of services offered determine the number of departments. The accumulation of departmental costs again follows factory procedure: (1) direct expenses, such as salaries, supplies, and depreciation of equipment, are charged directly; (2) general expenses, such as light, heat, and air conditioning, are prorated to the departments on appropriate bases. As income and expenses are ascertained, it is possible to create a work cost unit that permits the charging of accounts for services rendered and the analysis of an account's profitability.

The work of insurance companies is facilitated by dividing the office into departments. Some departments have several hundred clerks, and the work is highly organized. Insurance companies were one of the first businesses to install computers to reduce the clerical costs connected with the insurance business and to calculate new insurance rates and coverage on a more expanded basis for greater profitability. This quite detailed departmentalization might include actuarial, premium collection, group insurance, policyholders' service, registrar, medical, and legal information. While some costs are unique to the individual group, most are identical with expenses experienced in any office.

Educational institutions (such as public and private school systems, colleges, and universities) and service organizations (such as hotels, motels, hospitals, and nursing homes) find it increasingly necessary to budget their expenses on a departmental basis in order to control expenses and be able to charge an adequate cost recovering fee for their services. The services of social security via Medicare make a knowledge of costs mandatory in hospitals and nursing homes. Departmentalization will assist management in creating a costing or charging rate for short- or long-term care, for special services, for nurses' instruction, and for professional services (surgical, medical, X-rays, laboratory examinations, and filling of prescriptions).

The federal government employs a great number of people in a vast number of departments and agencies. A similar situation exists in state and local governments. This discussion uses the municipality as an example, since its varied services are better known to the public. Some common services or departments are street cleaning, street repairing and paving, public works projects, police and fire departments, city hospitals, sewage disposal plants, and trash and garbage collection. These services should be budgeted and their costs controlled on a responsibility accounting basis. Since the costs incurred are generally not revenue- but service-benefit-oriented, an attempt should be made to measure the operating efficiency of an activity based on some unit of measurement such as per capita (police), per mile (street paving and cleaning), and per ton (trash and garbage collection). Increasing costs require additional revenue, which means additional taxes. Taxpayers, however, expect efficient service in return for their tax money.

The state and federal governments must be made equally aware of the need for responsible cost control methods, so that services may be rendered at the lowest cost with greatest efficiency. With their many departments and agencies and huge sums budgeted for all of these units, governments must ensure that these activities are being administered by cost-conscious and service-minded people. The departmentalization process helps to assure the achievement of such a goal in any governmental unit.

DISCUSSION QUESTIONS

1. State reasons for the preference of departmental overhead rates over a single plant-wide rate.

2. The statement has been made that the entire process of departmentalizing factory overhead is an extension of methods used when a single overhead rate is used. Explain.

3. A company uses departmental factory overhead rates based on direct labor hours. Would the sum of departmental over- or underapplied overhead be any different if a plant-wide or blanket rate were used? Would the costs of goods sold and inventory be different?

4. What is a producing department? A service department? Give illustrations of each.

5. What are some of the factors that must be considered in deciding the kinds and number of departments required to control costs and to establish accurate departmental overhead rates?

6. For effective control of overhead, a supervisor, superintendent, manager, or department head can be held accountable for more than one cost center; but responsibility for a single cost center should not be divided between two or more individuals. Discuss.

7. State reasons for using a general factory cost pool for certain types of overhead instead of allocating it directly to producing and service departments.

8. Justify classifying overtime premiums as factory overhead. List some of the difficulties in estimating this item in the creation of predetermined overhead rates.

9. Most companies keep plant asset records to identify equipment and its original cost by location or department. However, charges for depreciation, property tax, and fire insurance are often accumulated in general factory accounts and charged to departments on the basis of equipment values. Is this the best method for controlling such costs? If not, suggest possible improvements.

10. What are the important factors involved in selecting the rate to be used for applying the factory overhead of a producing department?

11. What are the several steps followed in establishing departmental factory overhead rates?

12. What questions must be resolved in allocating service department costs to benefiting departments, and how can cost information aid in service department cost control?

13. What methods can be used for allocating service department costs to producing departments? Which is recommended?

14. Procedures followed in computing departmental factory overhead rates determine the accounting for actual factory overhead. Explain.

15. Describe how departmental over- or underapplied overhead is determined, and explain the computations of departmental spending and idle capacity variances.

16. Overhead control in a nonmanufacturing business can be achieved through departmentalization. Explain.

17. Federal, state, and local governments should practice cost control via responsibility accounting. Discuss.

EXERCISES

1. *Entries with overhead subsidiary ledger.* The general ledger of Skotts Company contains a factory overhead control account supported by a subsidiary ledger showing details by departments. The plant has one service department and three producing departments. The following table shows details with respect to these departments:

	Machining Dept.	Painting Dept.	Assembly Dept.	General Factory Cost Pool
Building space (sq. ft.)......................	10,000	4,000	4,000	2,000
Cost of machinery..........................	$300,000	$100,000	$60,000	$20,000
Horsepower rating..........................	1,000	–0–	100	150
Workmens' compensation insurance rate (per $100)...............................	$1.50	$1.50	$1.00	$1.00

During January, certain assets expired and some liabilities accrued as follows:

(a) Depreciation on buildings, $1,500.
(b) Depreciation on machinery, $9,600.
(c) Property tax for the year ending December 31 is estimated to be $12,000 (60% on buildings and 40% on machinery).
(d) Workmen's compensation insurance for January is based on the following earnings of factory employees: Machining Department, $30,000; Painting Department, $12,000; Assembly Department, $16,000; and General Factory Cost Pool, $6,000.
(e) The power meter reading at January 31 shows 12 500 kilowatt-hours consumed. The rate is $.06 per kilowatt-hour.
(f) The heat and light bill for January is $900.
(g) Supplies requisitions show $1,800 used in the Machining Department, $2,300 in the Assembly Department, and $410 in the General Factory Cost Pool.

Required: Prepare journal entries, with details entered in the departmental factory overhead subsidiary ledger columns.

2. Overhead distribution sheet and rate calculation. Epsilon Company's factory is divided into four departments—two producing departments, Cutting and Finishing, serviced by the Buildings and Grounds and the Factory Administration departments. Service department costs are allocated to producing departments only—Buildings and Grounds based on square feet, and Factory Administration based on direct labor hours. In calculating predetermined overhead rates, machine hours are used as the base in Cutting, and direct labor hours as the base in Finishing.

	Cutting	Finishing	Buildings and Grounds	Factory Administration
Budgeted factory overhead	$200,000	$300,000	$40,000	$60,000
Direct labor hours..............	100,000	50,000		
Machine hours	212,000			
Square feet..................	50,000	30,000	1,000	2,000

The following data pertain to Job 2375:

Cutting: Direct materials $35
Direct labor, 3 hrs. @ $6......................... 18
Machine hours, 7
Finishing: Direct materials $10
Direct labor, 5 hrs. @ $8........................ 40

Required:
(1) Calculate predetermined factory overhead rates for the producing departments.
(2) Determine the total cost of Job 2375.   (CGAA adapted)

3. Hospital cost allocation. Beaumont Municipal Hospital uses the step method for allocating nonrevenue-generating departments to revenue departments. This method is approved for Medicare reimbursement computation purposes, and requires that the nonrevenue department serving the greatest number of other revenue and nonrevenue departments and receiving services from the smallest number be allocated first. Once the cost of a nonrevenue department has been allocated, no costs from any other department may be allocated to it, even though services may have been provided.

Beaumont Municipal Hospital has received approval to use the following order of allocation: Depreciation, Maintenance and Utilities, Laundry. June's costs are:

Total
_122,016_

Department	Original Departmental Cost
Operating Room	$100,000
Radiology	65,000
Laboratory	45,000
Patient Rooms	250,000
Depreciation	100,000
Maintenance and Utilities	50,000
Laundry	20,000
	$630,000

Cost allocation data (expressed as percentages) have been determined as follows:

Department	Depreciation*	Maintenance and Utilities**	Laundry***
Operating Room	7%	10.7%	21.2%
Radiology	5	9.3	3.0
Laboratory	10	6.7	—
Patient Rooms	50	60.0	75.8
Depreciation	—	—	—
Maintenance and Utilities	25	—	—
Laundry	3	13.3	—
	100%	100.0%	100.0%

*Buildings on the basis of square footage; equipment on the basis of dollar value.
**On the basis of square footage.
***On the basis of pounds used in each department.

Required: Allocate the June costs to final revenue departments.

(Based on an article in **Management Accounting**)

4. Distribution of service department expenses. Inhofe Company has two producing departments, A and B, and four service departments, C, D, E, and F. Expenses are distributed from Department F first, D second, C third, and E fourth. The company assigns some service department expenses to other service departments; however, after a department's expenses have been allocated, no expenses are assigned back to it.

Department F distributes one half of its expenses to A and the remainder, on the basis of the number of employees, to Departments D and E. Department D distributes its expenses on the basis of the investment in equipment. C's expenses are assigned to B, and E's expenses are distributed on the basis of floor space.

The following information for March is available:

Department	Actual Expenses	Square Feet	Employees	Investment in Equipment (000s omitted)
A	$100,000	1,500	20	$12,500
B	80,000	2,500	10	6,000
C	120,000	3,000	10	10,000
D	56,000	1,500	15	5,000
E	15,000	1,000	10	4,000
F	30,000	1,200	5	2,000
Total	$401,000	10,700	70	$39,500

Required: Distribute service department expenses, based on the data given.

5. Algebraic distribution of factory overhead. Sherlock Company has decided to distribute the costs of service departments by the algebraic method. The producing departments are P1 and P2, the service departments are S1 and S2, and the monthly data are:

	Actual Factory Overhead Costs Before Distribution	Services Provided By	
		S1	S2
P1	$94,000	40%	50%
P2	85,000	50	30
S1	20,000	—	20
S2	17,600	10	—

Required: Compute the total factory overhead of producing department P1 after distribution of service department costs.

6. Algebraic distribution of factory overhead. The estimated departmental factory overhead for Producing Departments S and T and the estimated expenses of Service Departments E, F, and G (before any service department allocations) are:

Producing Departments		Service Departments	
S	$60,000	E	$20,000
T	90,000	F	20,000
		G	10,000

The interdependence of the departments is as follows:

Department	Services Provided		
	E	F	G
Producing — S....................	—	30%	40%
Producing — T....................	50%	40	30
Service — E......................	—	20	—
Service — F......................	20	—	—
Service — G......................	30	10	—
Marketing........................	—	—	20
General Office....................	—	—	10
	100%	100%	100%

Required:
(1) Compute the final amount of estimated overhead of each service department after reciprocal transfer costs have been calculated algebraically.
(2) Compute the total factory overhead of each producing department and the amount of Department G cost assigned to the Marketing Department and to General Office.

7. Transfer entries and variance analysis. The distribution of a company's actual factory overhead for the past year is given as follows. Budgeted factory overhead for the four producing departments (including apportioned service department expenses) is also given for two levels of activity.

Actual Factory Overhead

	A	B	C	D	X	Y	Z	Total
Actual expenses.............	$11,000	$16,000	$4,000	$8,000	$3,000	$5,000	$6,000	$53,000
Z's expenses...............	1,500	750	1,250	500	1,000	1,000	(6,000)	
Y's expenses..............	1,800	1,200	1,800	600	600	(6,000)		
X's expenses..............	2,000	1,000	1,200	400	(4,600)			
Total	$16,300	$18,950	$8,250	$9,500				$53,000

Budgeted Factory Overhead

	20,000 hours (Normal)	16,000 Hours
Department A	$17,800	$15,000
Department B	20,200	17,800
Department C	10,600	9,400
Department D	10,600	9,400
Total	$59,200	$51,600

The company uses a predetermined rate for each producing department, based on labor hours at the normal capacity level. Actual hours worked last year were 17,000 for Department A and 18,000 for B.

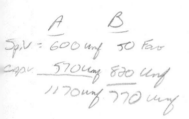

Required:
(1) Prepare entries to record:
  (a) The transfer of the actual factory overhead to producing departments, assuming that the actual factory overhead was accumulated in a single factory overhead control account.
  (b) The applied factory overhead for Department A and for B.
(2) Compute the spending and idle capacity variances for Department A and for B.

8. Overhead analysis and causes for variances. Beachmont Company uses predetermined departmental overhead rates. The rate for the Fabricating Department is $4 per direct labor hour. Direct labor employees are paid $10.50 per hour. A total of 15,000 direct labor hours were worked in the department during the year. Total overhead charged to the department for supervisors' salaries, indirect labor, labor fringe benefit costs, indirect materials, and service department costs was $65,000.

Required:
(1) Determine the over- or underapplied factory overhead.
(2) Determine the effect on the amount of over- or underapplied factory overhead in each of the following situations. Discuss each item separately as though the other factors had not occurred.
  (a) Direct laborers worked one hundred overtime hours for which time-and-a-half was paid. Overtime premium, the amount in excess of the regular rate, is charged as overhead to the department in which the overtime is worked.
  (b) A $.35 per hour wage increase was granted November 1. Direct labor hours worked in November and December totaled 2,500.

(c) *The company cafeteria incurred a $1,500 loss, which was distributed to produc-*
ing departments on the basis of number of employees. Nine of the 120 employ-
ees work in the Fabricating Department. No loss was anticipated when prede-
termined overhead rates were computed.

PROBLEMS

8-1. Journal entries; revision of overhead rates. De Jongheer Furniture Company manufactures laboratory benches in three producing departments: Cutting, Assembling, and
Finishing. All overhead costs are charged directly to producing departments without the
use of auxiliary or service departments.

For the first six months of the calendar year, management had approved the following
predetermined factory overhead rates:

> Cutting............................$1.50 per machine hour
> Assembling........................ 1.90 per direct labor hour
> Finishing .... 100% of direct labor cost

Factory overhead costs for the first six months were:

> Cutting... $16,950
> Assembling.. 12,143
> Finishing 8,405

For the same period, the following data were also accumulated:

> Cutting........................... 12,900 machine hours
> Assembling....................... 8,100 direct labor hours
> Finishing .... $9,100 direct labor

As of June 30, the company revised its annual budget in the light of experience to that
date and projections for the remainder of the year. Data on factory overhead from the new
budget follow:

	Cutting	Assembling	Finishing
Total budgeted factory overhead.......	$26,975	$20,160	$14,805
Application basis (estimated)	20,750 machine hours	12,600 direct labor hours	$16,450 direct labor

Required: Prepare journal entries to record:
 (1) Incurred and applied overhead for the first six months.
 (2) Adjustment of the applied overhead based on the new rates, retroactive to January 1.
 Analysis of the job cost sheets shows the total overhead adjustment should be
 distributed 10% to work in process, 30% to finished goods, and 60% to cost of
 goods sold.

8-2. Overhead distribution. Bash, Inc. has two producing departments and three service
departments. A summary of costs and other data for each department prior to allocation
of service department costs for the year ended June 30, 19--, shows:

	Producing Departments		Service Departments		
	Fabrication	Assembly	General Factory Cost Pool	Mainte- nance	Cafeteria
Direct labor cost.....................	$2,100,000	$4,100,000	$180,000	$164,200	$174,000
Direct materials cost	3,130,000	950,000	—	67,700	91,000
Factory overhead cost...............	1,650,000	1,850,000	70,000	56,100	62,000
Direct labor hours...................	562,500	437,500	31,000	27,000	42,000
Number of employees	280	200	12	8	20
Square footage occupied	88,000	72,000	1,750	2,000	4,800

The costs of General Factory Cost Pool, Maintenance, and Cafeteria are allocated on the basis of direct labor hours, square footage occupied, and number of employees, respectively. There are no factory overhead variances.

Required:
(1) Compute the amount of Maintenance cost allocated to Fabrication, assuming that the company elects to distribute service department costs directly to the producing departments without inter-service-department cost allocation.
(2) Compute the amount of General Factory Cost Pool cost allocated to Assembly, assuming the same policy of allocating service departments to producing departments only.
(3) Assuming that the company elects to distribute service department costs to other service departments (starting with the service department with the greatest total cost) as well as to the producing departments and that once a service department's cost has been allocated, no subsequent service department cost is recirculated back to it, compute (a) the amount of Cafeteria cost allocated to Maintenance and (b) the amount of Maintenance cost allocated to Cafeteria.   (AICPA adapted)

8-3. Overhead distribution sheet and rate calculation. The president of Mellow Products Company has been critical of the product costing methods whereby factory overhead is charged to products by a factory-wide overhead rate. The chief accountant suggested a departmentalization of the factory for the purpose of calculating departmental factory overhead rates. The following estimated direct departmental overhead data on an annual basis were accumulated:

Overhead Items	Producing Departments			Service Departments		
	Dept. 10	Dept. 12	Dept. 14	Store- room	Repairs and Maintenance	General Factory Cost Pool
Supervision......................	$20,500	$16,000	$14,000	$ 7,200	$ 8,000	$24,000
Indirect labor	5,400	6,000	8,000	6,133	7,200	18,000
Indirect supplies	4,850	5,600	5,430	1,400	3,651	1,070
Labor fringe benefits.............	6,872	9,349	10,145	640	760	2,100
Equipment depreciation...........	6,000	8,000	10,000	560	1,740	1,100
Property tax, depreciation of buildings, etc.						20,000
Total..........................	$43,622	$44,949	$47,575	$15,933	$21,351	$66,270

The annual light and power bill is estimated at $9,300 and is allocated on the basis of electricity usage.

The order and bases of distribution of service department expenses are as follows:

(a) General Factory Cost Pool—area occupied
(b) Storeroom—estimated requisitions
(c) Repairs and Maintenance—estimated repairs and maintenance hours

The following departmental information is provided:

	Dept. 10	Dept. 12	Dept. 14	Store-room	Repairs and Maintenance	General Factory Cost Pool
Percentage of usage of electricity ..	20%	25%	30%	3%	12%	10%
Area occupied (sq. ft.)	21,000	25,200	29,400	3,360	5,040	—
Estimated number of requisitions ..	124,200	81,000	40,500	—	24,300	—
Estimated number of repairs and maintenance hours	4,800	4,200	6,000	—	—	—
Estimated direct labor hours	80,000	90,000	80,000	—	—	—

Required: Prepare a factory overhead distribution sheet, with calculation of overhead rates for the producing departments based on direct labor hours.

8-4. Allocation of Personnel Department costs. Bracken, Inc. has 1,000 employees—600 factory workers, 300 clerks, and 100 managers. Of that number, Department A, a producing department, has 60 factory, 30 clerical, and 10 managerial employees.

During the past year, Bracken's Personnel Department incurred the following expenses, charged to six functional categories:

			Expenses			
Functional Category	Salaries	Advertising and Recruiting	Rent	Depreciation	Supplies and Miscellaneous	Total
Placement and separation	$ 30,000	$12,800	$ 2,400	$ 168.00	$ 600	$ 45,968.00
Labor relations	17,625	200	1,530	153.25	275	19,783.25
Benefits	22,875	1,000	1,890	142.00	745	26,652.00
Management development	30,000	500	2,640	182.25	185	33,507.25
Safety	13,375	500	1,110	94.25	70	15,149.25
Wage and salary administration	26,125	-0-	2,430	260.25	125	28,940.25
Total	$140,000	$15,000	$12,000	$1,000.00	$2,000	$170,000.00

The following criteria are used for allocating the functionally categorized costs to benefiting departments:

(a) Placement and separation—90% placement related, 10% separation related. Cost of placing and separating a manager is five times that for other employees.
(b) Labor relations—the average number of factory workers.
(c) Benefits—the average number of employees.
(d) Management development—the average number of managers.
(e) Safety—90% factory worker related; 10% clerical and managerial related.
(f) Wage and salary administration—the average number of employees.

The past year was stable in terms of the total work force, with the same number of employees at the end of the year as at the beginning. During the year, Bracken placed and separated 60 factory, 30 clerical, and 10 management employees. Of this number, 20% of the factory workers, 20% of the clerical employees, and one manager were from Department A.

Required: Allocate Personnel Department costs to Department A. (Round off all amounts to the nearest cent.)

8-5. Cost accounting records; overhead distribution; ledger accounts. Lankford, Inc. uses job order costing that has been kept rather inadequately by the former accountant, who left in the middle of September. The company's president asks for assistance in getting the books and records in an acceptable order. The company's cost system includes a general ledger and a factory ledger with reciprocal control accounts. A trial balance of the factory ledger at September 1 is as follows:

Materials	30,000	
Store Supplies	10,000	
Work in Process	20,000	
General Ledger Control		60,000
	60,000	60,000

After reviewing the work done up to September 1, information is gathered for September from the following sources:

				Work in Process				
					Service Depts.		Producing Depts.	
Sources of Information	General Ledger Control	Materials	Store Supplies	Total	Power Plant	General Plant	Pattern Foundry	Machine Shop
From cash payments journal:								
Purchases	$(27,150)*	$20,000	$ 7,150					
Direct labor	(6,150)			$ 6,150	$300	$ 350	$ 2,200	$ 3,300
Direct factory overhead	(2,300)			2,300	50	175	730	1,345
Assets acquired	(9,400)							
Prepaid insurance	(3,000)							
From general ledger entries:								
Depreciation	(1,100)			1,100	140	80	**	**
Property tax	(250)			250	40	20	**	**
Expired insurance	(500)			500	100	25	**	**
Repairs to power plant	(320)			320	320			
From requisitions:								
Materials		(27,000)		27,000	500	1,000	15,500	10,000
Store supplies	150		(15,150)	15,000	150	1,350	9,000	4,500
From cost of finished jobs report:								
Shipped to customers	45,000			(45,000)				
For company's own use	2,460			(2,460)				

Bases for distribution of costs:

Power plant							50%	50%

General plant on the basis of store supplies issued to producing departments.
Indirect costs of producing departments on the basis of each department's direct labor cost.

*( ) denotes credit balance
**Balance on the basis of direct labor cost.

Required: On a work sheet, using the same headings as those appearing in this information, determine:
  (1) The direct, indirect, and total costs that should be debited to the work in process account for September.
  (2) Distribution of service department costs to the producing departments as per instructions.

(3) The September 30 balances of the following factory ledger accounts: General Ledger Control; Materials; Store Supplies; Work in Process.   (AICPA adapted)

8-6. Algebraic distribution of actual factory overhead. The controller of Margan Corporation instructs the cost supervisor to use an algebraic procedure for allocating service department costs to producing departments. The corporation's three producing departments are served by three service departments, each of which consumes part of the services of the other two. After primary but before reciprocal distribution, the account balances of the service departments and the interdependence of the departments were tabulated as follows:

Department	Departmental Overhead Before Distribution of Service Departments	Services Provided		
		Powerhouse	Personnel	General Factory
Mixing	$200,000	25%	35%	25%
Refining..............	90,000	25	30	20
Finishing	105,000	20	20	20
Powerhouse	16,000	—	10	20
Personnel	29,500	10	—	15
General Factory	42,000	20	5	—
	$482,500	100%	100%	100%

Required:
1. (1) Compute the final amount of overhead of each service department after reciprocal transfer costs have been calculated algebraically.
2. (2) Compute the total factory overhead of each producing department.

8-7. Algebraic distribution; make-or-buy decision for a service department. Capuccini Company has three service departments (Water, Steam, and Electric Power) and one producing department. The technical relationships between the service departments are that it requires .8 kilowatt-hours of electricity to pump one gallon of water, .5 gallons of water to generate one cubic foot of steam, and .15 cubic feet of steam to generate one kilowatt-hour of electricity. Each unit of producing department output requires .6 gallons of water, .9 cubic feet of steam, and 4.8 kilowatt-hours of electricity. The output of the producing department is 100,000 units.

Cost data before service department cost allocations are:

Department	Variable Cost per Unit of Service Department Output	Fixed Costs at Various Service Department Output Levels			
		0–50,000	50,001–100,000	100,001–300,000	300,001–800,000
Water	$.0266	$4,000	$ 6,000	$ 8,000	Not Applicable
Steam	.2000	5,000	10,000	12,000	Not Applicable
Electric Power	.0200	6,000	8,000	8,500	$9,000

The company can purchase electric power externally for $.06 per kilowatt-hour.

Required: Develop calculations (with the aid of the algebraic method for allocating service department costs) to support a recommendation as to whether the company should continue generating electric service internally or acquire it externally.

8-8. Cost center rates and variance analysis. The Cost Department of Wilton Co. applies factory overhead to jobs and products on the basis of predetermined cost center overhead rates. In each of the two producing departments, two cost centers have been set up. For the coming year, the following estimates and other data have been made available:

Department 10	Estimated Annual Factory Overhead			Estimated Annual Hours
	Fixed	Variable	Total	
Cost Center 10-1	$14,040	$23,400	$37,440	15,600
Cost Center 10-2	26,910	43,290	70,200	23,400
Department 20				
Cost Center 20-1	$ 8,320	$21,580	$29,900	26,000
Cost Center 20-2	6,240	19,760	26,000	20,800

Required:

(1) Compute the annual normal cost center overhead rates, based on the estimated machine hours in Department 10 and the estimated direct labor hours in Department 20.

(2) Apply factory overhead to the four cost centers on the basis of these actual machine or labor hours used or worked during February:

Cost Centers	10-1	10-2	20-1	20-2
Machine hours..........	1,220	2,000		
Labor hours			2,250	1,650

(3) Compute the spending and the idle capacity variances for the two producing departments. Actual factory overhead in Department 10 amounted to $9,430 and in Department 20 to $4,005.

(4) Analyze the total idle capacity variance of Department 10, determining the idle capacity variances of the two cost centers. Use $\frac{1}{12}$ of the total annual estimated hours as normal monthly hours.

CASES

A. Types of factory overhead rates. Vukovich, Inc. engages the services of a CPA firm for the installation of a job order cost system. Preliminary investigation of manufacturing operations discloses these facts:

(a) The company makes a line of light fixtures and lamps. The materials cost of any particular item ranges from 15% to 60% of total factory cost, depending on the kind of metal and fabric used.

(b) The business is subject to wide cyclical fluctuations, since the sales volume follows new housing construction.

(c) About 60% of the manufacturing is normally finished during the first quarter of the year.

(d) For the whole plant, the direct labor wage rates range from $6.50 to $12 an hour. However, within each of the eight individual departments, the spread between the high and low wage rate is less than 5%.

(e) Each product requires the use of all eight of the manufacturing departments, but not proportionately.

(f) Within the individual manufacturing departments, factory overhead ranges from 30% to 80% of conversion cost.

Required: Prepare a letter to the president of Vukovich, Inc., explaining whether its cost system should use the following procedures, and including the reasons supporting each of these recommendations:

(1) A predetermined overhead rate or an actual overhead rate—departmental or plant-wide.

(2) A method of factory overhead distribution based on direct labor hours, direct labor cost, or prime cost.   (AICPA adapted)

B. Assigning costs to activity centers in a data processing department. Fitzgerald Associates recently reorganized its computer and data processing activities. In the past, small computer units were located in accounting departments at the firm's plants and subsidiaries. These units have been replaced with a single Electronic Data Processing Department at corporate headquarters. The new department has been in operation for two years, regularly producing reliable and timely data for the past twelve months.

Because the department has focused its activities on converting applications to the new system and producing reports for the plant and subsidiary managements, little attention has been devoted to data processing costs. Now that the department's activities are operating relatively smoothly, company management has requested that the departmental manager recommend a cost accumulation system to facilitate cost control and the development of suitable service charging rates.

For the past two years, the data processing costs have been recorded in one account. The costs have then been allocated to user departments on the basis of computer time used. Following are the costs and charging rate for the current year:

(a) Salaries and benefits	$ 622,600
(b) Supplies	40,000
(c) Equipment maintenance contract	15,000
(d) Insurance	25,000
(e) Heat and air conditioning	36,000
(f) Electricity	50,000
(g) Equipment and furniture depreciation	285,400
(h) Building improvement depreciation	10,000
(i) Building occupancy and security	39,300
(j) Corporate administrative charge	52,700
Total cost	$1,176,000
Computer hours for user processing*	2,750
Hourly rate ($1,176,000 ÷ 2,750)	$428

*Use of available computer hours:	
Testing and debugging programs	250
Setup of jobs	500
Processing jobs	2,750
Downtime for maintenance	750
Idle time	742
Total	4,992

The department manager recommends that the data processing costs be accumulated by five activity centers within the department: Systems Analysis, Programming, Data Preparation, Computer Operations (processing), and Administration. The Administration activity cost should be allocated to the other four activity centers before a separate rate for charging users is developed for each of the first four activities.

The manager noted that the subsidiary accounts within the department contained the following charges:

- (a) Salaries and benefits — the salary and benefit costs of all employees in the department.
- (b) Supplies — punch card cost, paper cost for printers, and a small amount for miscellaneous other costs.
- (c) Equipment maintenance contracts — charges for maintenance contracts covering all equipment.
- (d) Insurance — cost of insurance covering the equipment and the furniture.
- (e) Heat and air conditioning — a charge from the corporate Heating and Air Conditioning Department estimated to be the differential costs which meet the special needs of the Electronic Data Processing Department.
- (f) Electricity — the charge for electricity, based upon a separate meter within the department.
- (g) Equipment and furniture depreciation — the depreciation charges for all owned equipment and furniture within the department.
- (h) Building improvement depreciation — the depreciation charges for the building changes which were required to provide proper environmental control and electrical service for the computer equipment.
- (i) Building occupancy and security — the department's share of the depreciation, maintenance, heat, and security costs of the building; these costs are allocated to the department on the basis of square feet occupied.
- (j) Corporate administrative charge — the department's share of the corporate administrative cost which is allocated to the department on the basis of number of employees in the department.

Required:
- (1) State whether each of the ten cost items (lettered a through j) should be allocated to the five activity centers. For each cost item which should be distributed, specify the basis upon which the distribution should be made. Justify your answer in each case, including an indication as to whether the cost would be included in a rate designed to include only variable costs as opposed to a full cost rate.
- (2) Calculate the total number of hours that should be employed to determine the charging rate for Computer Operations, using the analysis of computer utilization shown as a footnote to the department cost schedule, and assuming that the Computer Operations activity cost will be charged to the user departments on the basis of computer hours. Explain.   (CMA adapted)

Chapter 9
Factory Overhead: Responsibility Accounting and Reporting

Factory overhead creates two distinct problems:

1. Allocation to products for the purpose of inventory costing and profit determination, and
2. Control of factory overhead with the aid of responsibility accounting.

The well-designed information system should yield product costs for inventory costing and profit determination. It should also provide a control mechanism encompassing *responsibility accounting* and make meaningful cost data available for setting policies and making decisions. The predetermined or budgeted revenue and expense items form the foundation for comparison with actual results, leading to variance analysis or the management by exception principle.

The establishment of such a system allows and maintains the most efficient and profitable balance between manufacturing and marketing. On the one hand, management needs to decide the kinds and costs of its products; on the other hand, it must decide the prices of its products. The greatest profit results from the proper balance of these considerations. For these reasons, product costs must be fairly accurate, include all relevant costs, and recognize cost differentials between products.

Responsibility Accounting and Control of Factory Overhead

Webster's dictionary defines being *responsible* as "liable to be called upon to answer." Kohler's *A Dictionary for Accountants* defines *responsibility* as "the obligation prudently to exercise assigned or imputed authority attaching to the assigned or imputed role of an individual or group participating in organizational activities or decisions." The N. A.(C.)A. Research Series, No.22, says: "A responsibility may be defined as an organizational unit having a single head accountable for activities of the unit."

Responsibility Accounting — Basic Concepts

The following concepts are prerequisites to the initiation and maintenance of a responsibility accounting system:

1. Responsibility accounting is based on a classification of managerial responsibilities (departments) at every level in the organization for the purpose of establishing a budget for each. The individual in charge of each responsibility classification should be responsible and accountable for the expenses of his or her activity. This concept introduces the need for the classification of costs into controllable and not controllable by a department head. Generally, costs charged directly to a department, with the exception of fixed costs, are controllable by the department's manager.
2. The starting point for a responsibility accounting information system rests with the organization chart in which the spheres of jurisdiction have been determined. Authority leads to the responsibility for certain costs and expenses which, with the knowledge and cooperation of the supervisor, department head, or manager, are presented in the budget.
3. Each individual's budget should clearly identify the costs controllable by that person. The chart of accounts should be adapted to permit recording of controllable or accountable expenses within the jurisdictional framework.

Factors Influencing Responsible Cost Control

The fundamental tenet of responsibility accounting limits the individual's control effort to controllable costs. Yet, studies have shown that in departmental situations, several factors may influence the extent of controllability and the effectiveness of the departmental control efforts. These factors are summarized in the following performance model:[1]

---

[1]David C. Hayes, "The Contingency Theory of Managerial Accounting," *The Accounting Review*, Vol. LII, No. 1, pp. 22-39.

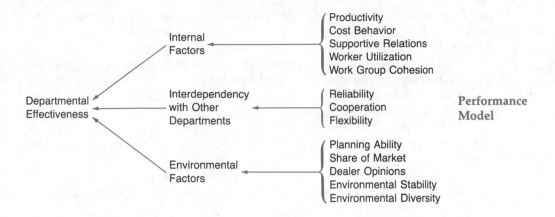

Human Behavior in Responsibility Accounting

A program to develop management accounting controls must be considered a prime responsibility of executive management, with the accounting department providing technical assistance. To assure the follow-through of the program and its ultimate success, management must provide a complete clarification of the objectives and responsibilities of all levels of the organization. This prerequisite requires an understanding by middle and operating management of executive management's goals. The acceptance of responsibility for certain costs and expenses does not always follow the issuance of directives and orders. Supervisory personnel, particularly at the foreman level, need guidance and training to achieve the control and/or profit results expected from them. Control responsibility does not happen naturally, but requires a certain fundamental attitude or frame of mind for the task.

One of the most beneficial influences is executive management's own exemplary adherence to the cost-and-profit responsibility it created. Of equal importance is the motivation for corrective action by the responsible individual. The issuance of reports based on the organization's responsibility concept is not sufficient. The successful achievement of effective management control depends upon the lines of communication between the accounting department, the responsible supervisors, and their superiors. Responsibility accounting requires teamwork in the truest sense of the word.

Responsibility for Overhead Costs

As the preceding factory overhead chapters indicate, many overhead items are directly chargeable to a given department and become the direct responsibility of the departmental supervisor. Other overhead items must be allocated or distributed in order to calculate a departmental factory overhead rate that will charge all costs to a job, a product, or the work performed. This allocation procedure, however, is not necessary or useful for cost control, i.e., for responsibility accounting. For responsibility accounting purposes, any allocated charges should be limited to those expenses for which control and responsibility have been assumed by the originating department. However, the assignment of responsibility depends a great deal upon the methods of cost accumulation and allocation used by a firm.

In some firms, the cost system provides for a normal volume distribution of service hours, use hours, and/or maintenance hours to producing or other service departments. The distribution can be looked upon as a purchase by the recipient department and a sale by the providing service department. The distribution to the recipient department is based on what is termed a *billing rate*, a *sold-hour rate*, a *charging rate*, or a *transfer rate*. The method is based on the idea that these departments purchase the services in the same manner as direct materials and direct labor.

The determination of the billing rate follows the procedures discussed in the previous factory overhead chapters:

1. Estimate or budget the costs of any service department according to their nature (supervision, supplies, electricity, etc.).
2. Classify costs as fixed or variable. This classification often leads to the realization that many costs of service departments are fixed over fairly wide ranges of service volume.
3. Determine a rate by dividing total estimated departmental cost by the number of hours the service is expected to be needed.
4. Compare actual service department costs with estimated or budgeted costs.

The establishment of the use hours is as important for billing rates as it is for factory overhead rates. The hours can be based either on past experience in a representative period or on future activity or volume as expressed in the budget. A refinement of the rate is the apportionment of fixed costs to cost centers on the basis of service capacity, i.e., readiness or ability to provide services, as defined for each benefiting department. The variable cost is then assigned on the basis of actual usage.[2]

The comparison of actual and budgeted costs is made (1) in the service department to which the expenses are originally charged, by comparing actual costs with charged-out or sold-out amounts; and (2) in the benefiting (recipient) departments in which the charges for service departments' services are linked with the budget allowances. This step is the control phase of the service department's charging-out procedure. The supervisor of the service department is responsible for the actual cost versus the cost for services charged out to benefiting departments. The benefiting department supervisor is responsible for the number of service department hours purchased, and the resulting cost charged to his or her department. Variances for service and producing departments are calculable.

---

[2]An example of more sophisticated allocation procedures is found in Daniel L. Jensen's "A Class of Mutually Satisfactory Allocations," *The Accounting Review,* Vol. LII, No. 4, pp. 842-856.

Billing Rates for Electronic Data Processing Services. Electronic data processing (EDP) services offer an excellent illustration of the need for careful attention to the use of appropriate billing rates. EDP services usually start as a support group, with costs classified as general overhead. These costs may be allocated to broad functional classifications, such as manufacturing (factory overhead), marketing, and administrative expenses. As data processing matures and becomes an integral part of the organization's operations, more precise cost accounting mechanisms are considered. The EDP center might apportion costs to users on the basis of a percentage of general utilization; e.g., assigning ten percent of the costs to one department, fifteen percent to another, and so forth. This approach has limitations, because it fails to contribute to efficient use of the EDP facility and does not aid the recipient in making selective judgments about the application requested. Users need to understand the cost and value of the services which they require.

The electronic data processing department should develop a price (charge) for the services which users can include in their departmental budgets. The price of a given system is usually a fixed amount plus a variable amount per transaction, the volume of which would affect the total processing time. The difference between actual price and actual cost provides one measure of the data processing department's efficiency.[3]

The general, one-rate allocation to functional classifications may be superseded by the partitioning of the computer into cost centers, with major expenses classified as direct expenses to a cost center. To illustrate, a budget for a data processing department which has been partitioned into eight cost centers is shown on page 212.[4]

The "percent utilization expected" is important to a data processing department. Experience indicates that available hours are often utilized at only a 70 to 80 percent rate. The difference between utilized and available hours represents nonproductive activity which, for a systems analyst or a programmer, consists of vacation, holiday, illness, training, staff meetings, administrative tasks, professional societies, initial examination of requests, and other miscellaneous tasks. Time recording procedures established in all cost centers would allow the data processing administration to:

1. Keep a close watch over the productive utilization percentage and take action if and when it gets out of line.
2. Calculate the cost of each project or system, based on actual time incurred multiplied by the budgeted hourly rates.
3. Compare the actual productive hours to budgeted productive hours, and be aware of variances on a weekly or monthly basis.
4. Note the variance between total actual monthly data processing cost and the summation of project and system costs.
5. For subsequent years, estimate more accurately the expected productive hours by cost centers.

---

[3]Adapted from "The Fair Measure," *Data Processor*, Vol. 18, No. 2, pp. 10-13.
[4]Adapted from "Costing in the Data Processing Department" by John E. Finney, *Management Accounting*, Vol. LVI, No. 4, pp. 29-35.

DATA PROCESSING BUDGET BY COST CENTER

Item	Annual Budget	Systems	Programming	Computer Background	Computer Foreground 1	Computer Foreground 2	Off-Line Devices	Data Entry	Data Control
Data processing administration...	$ 48,000	$ 7,400	$ 5,200	$ 4,700	$ 8,900	$ 5,600	$ 500	$ 13,000	$ 2,700
Group managers and secretaries.	82,000	20,000	15,000	5,000	10,000	10,000	2,000	10,000	10,000
Other salaries and fringe benefits.	528,300	114,000	84,000	10,000	23,000	15,000	4,000	230,000	48,300
Training costs	11,000	3,500	3,500	300	900	500	200	1,600	500
Supplies	34,600	2,300	1,700	1,000	8,000	12,600	2,000	6,000	1,000
Travel expenses	7,700	4,000	2,000	500	700	500			
Consulting fees	9,000	6,000	3,000						
Rent, insurance, and utilities	78,000	13,500	13,500	8,000	11,000	9,000	2,000	17,000	4,000
Equipment rental and depreciation	356,000			80,000	150,000	77,000	1,000	47,000	1,000
Equipment maintenance	30,700			8,000	12,000	10,000	500		200
Depreciation on furniture and fixtures	6,100	1,700	1,700	200	400	400	300	400	1,000
Employment agency fees	7,000	4,000	3,000						
Dues and subscriptions	1,600	1,000	600						
Total budgeted cost	$1,200,000	$177,400	$133,200	$117,700	$224,900	$140,600	$ 12,500	$325,000	$ 68,700
Available or purchased hours	14,560	14,560	14,560	7,488	7,488	7,488	1,040	60,320	12,480
Percent utilization expected	70	70	80	35	60	20	85	86	80
Expected productive hours	10,192	10,192	11,648	2,621	4,493	1,498	884	51,875	9,984
Budgeted hourly rate	$ 17.41	$ 17.41	$ 11.44	$ 44.91	$ 50.06	$ 93.86	$ 14.14	$ 6.27	$ 6.88

The use of a "budgeted hourly rate" provides the following benefits:

1. Aids in controlling or reducing data processing costs.
2. Permits accurate and realistic costing of all work performed by project, system, user department, and/or line of business served.
3. Provides realistic rates to be used in estimating the cost of requested or proposed projects.
4. Permits a comparison of actual costs of processing a system to those costs which were estimated prior to implementation.
5. Aids in the evaluation of operating efficiency of a data processing installation.
6. Provides one measure of profitability for each data processing cost center and for the entire department in those cases where services are charged to a user or customer.

Maintenance Costs. Maintenance expense, like any other indirect factory cost, must be charged to producing departments in order to be included in the calculation of overhead rates. The basic problem is assigning cost responsibility for this expense. Maintenance supervisors often believe that their department really incurs no cost at all, since any cost incurrence is for the benefit and at the request of other departments. Factory supervisors, on the other hand, may argue that they have no influence on either personnel or machinery costs of the maintenance department. The control is in reality twofold: the factory supervisors control the amount of maintenance work, while maintenance engineers or supervisors control the quantity of people and materials required to serve the various departments. Since maintenance work is done at the request of production supervisors, the problem arises as to whether control should be exercised at the source level or the recipient level.

At the source level, maintenance labor is organized and supervised. Control at this point requires predetermination of labor-hour requirements in each of the producing and service departments for each maintenance function. At the recipient level, the cost system establishes budget allowances for this indirect cost. Budget allowances based on planned levels of production permit the determination of the labor-hour budgets and advance scheduling of the work force of each shop service or maintenance unit. Preplanning is the heart of the control, providing an opportunity for corrective action before the hours are worked. Maintenance department supervisors are apprised of the maintenance allowance or budgeted service for individual recipient cost centers, but the distribution or scheduling of the work is left largely to their discretion.[5]

---

[5]For additional discussion and illustration of responsibility accounting for maintenance, see James H. Bullock, *Maintenance Planning and Control* (New York: National Association of Accountants, 1979), pp. 29-33.

One major problem, however, is how much maintenance or repair work is needed in a department. Up to a point, the costs of preventive maintenance services generally will be more than offset by reductions in cost due to fewer equipment failures. Beyond this point, costs of providing additional preventive maintenance services will outweigh the benefits gained and total cost will increase. A basic problem of maintenance, therefore, is the determination of the balance — in terms of both effectiveness and cost — between prevention of equipment failure and correction of equipment failure.[6]

The solution may be determined by the executive management group. When a factory is laid out and the machinery installed, a maintenance program should be planned. The size of the maintenance department, the type or class of workers (carpenters, plumbers, electricians, pipefitters, masons, millwrights, machinists, etc.), and the kind of equipment and tools are greatly influenced by early decisions. On the other hand, experience indicates that such maintenance objectives are lacking in many companies due to management's own lack of interest as well as alleged difficulties in planning, measuring, and controlling the maintenance function. Although many organizations engage the services of outside firms for part or all of their maintenance, the need for careful planning and control of maintenance cost is not negated.

When management and the supervisors of the producing, service, and maintenance engineering departments agree on a preventive maintenance program, their objective is to keep equipment in such condition that breakdowns and the need for emergency repairs are within control. Preventive maintenance facilitates the scheduling of maintenance work and helps to obtain better utilization of the maintenance work force and the productive equipment.

A preventive maintenance program can work automatically so that inspection, minor repairs, adjustments, and lubrication are completed as a matter of course. The method further provides for a check on the effectiveness of the maintenance work by the supervisor of the serviced or buying unit. The maintenance supervisor, in turn, is responsible for the inspection and the upkeep of the facilities.

Responsibility for Other Factors

The discussion has intentionally focused on factory overhead items, since their assignment and control occupies the attention of many executives, department heads, and supervisors. However, other cost elements as well as functions in administration and marketing also require supervision and control by responsible managers.

Basically, the best approach to assigning responsibility for any cost element is to identify those individuals who are in the most favored position to keep the costs under control. The assignment of responsibility for overhead ex-

---

[6]*Ibid*., p.14.

penses to supervisors and department heads provides a certain degree of control. Admittedly, however, certain expenses (e.g., maintenance expenses) are often troublesome. In the direct materials and direct labor areas, many individuals may be assigned the responsibility for costs incurred, and this responsibility often becomes very obscure and nearly impossible to identify. Of course, it seems advisable to insist upon the assignment on the basis of relative control rather than absolute control.

In the direct materials area, the variances or deviations from a predetermined norm or standard will result in (1) materials price variances, (2) materials quantity, or mix and yield variances, and/or (3) excessive defective work, rejects, or scrap costs. In the direct labor area, the variances or deviations from a predetermined norm or standard will result in (1) pay rate variations, (2) efficiency variations, (3) and/or overtime costs.

Other factors also may be subject to change for which a manager may be held responsible. In later chapters, the deviations from budgeted gross or net profit figures require explanation. The changes in sales prices, sales volume, and sales mix are the responsibility of the marketing department. Yet the gross profit and net profit figures contain elements of cost as well, so that a further investigation is warranted.

Cost Control Characteristics

An effective cost control system has two major characteristics:

1. A sound technical design with goals set at a challenging but attainable performance level and with a reporting system that distinguishes controllable costs within each managerial responsibility from costs controllable elsewhere in the organization.
2. A managerial style sensitive to the behavior of people in a particular organizational setting. This requires a proper blend of:
   (a) Involvement by managers in setting goals for their own activities.
   (b) Leadership provided by executive management.
   (c) Open communication channels through which individual managers feel their views receive serious consideration.
   (d) Review procedures which disclose and discourage suboptimization and individual gains at the expense of the whole organization.

Cost control techniques are effective only with sufficient managerial appreciation of the behavioral aspects of control systems.[7]

Variance Analysis for Responsibility Accounting

Today with the emphasis on responsible control of financial results via the return-on-capital-employed concept, assets, liabilities, net worth, revenue, and

---

[7]Walter B. McFarland, *Manpower Cost and Performance Measurement* (New York: National Association of Accountants, 1977), p. 101.

costs form a vast area in which the entire management spectrum, from the top executive to the supervisor, holds some share of responsibility. Like blocks within a pyramid (page 223), the responsibility travels from the lowest to the highest level of supervision. All supervisors are responsible for costs incurred by their subordinates.

To exercise this control, the cost and/or budget department should issue monthly reports that compare actual results with predetermined amounts or budget allowances. An analysis prepared at the end of the annual fiscal period, as shown in Chapter 8, is not very helpful for immediate control actions. Reports on a monthly or more frequent basis are advisable to allow short-range comparisons of those costs for which operating management is responsible.

In general, variable expenses are controllable at the departmental level, while fixed expenses are not. In some circumstances, however, certain variable expenses may be controlled at a higher level in the organization; e.g., employee fringe benefits may be determined by negotiations between executive management and the labor union or by government regulations. Such costs should be analyzed and separately identified to relieve a department manager of this responsibility. Conversely, a department manager may have some control over certain fixed costs—those that involve a long-term commitment (sometimes called *committed fixed expenses*), such as equipment depreciation or lease expense, and those that can be readily changed in the short run (sometimes called *programmed fixed expenses*), such as the number of supervisors in the department. These costs should be individually identified as controllable by the manager of the department. Whether fixed or variable, some costs may be joint with respect to two or more departments and thus may require arbitrary allocation. Accordingly, their controllability by a single department manager is restricted.

Attention must be called to the fact that in the long run, all costs are controllable. Variable costs are generally controllable over short time periods. Some fixed costs, such as supervisory labor or equipment rental, can also be altered on short notice. Other fixed costs, such as depreciation of plant assets or a long-term lease agreement, involve a fixed commitment over a long period of time. Finally, some costs possess a dual short- and long-run controllability characteristic. For example, a five-year contract as to the price of a raw material, representing a long-term commitment, is not immediately controllable and the contract may be negotiable only at a higher management level. However, waste and spoilage of the same material is immediately controllable by the department. Generally, department managers should be well enough informed to explain cost variances, even though the control or certain aspects of the control do not fall within their scope of authority and responsibility.

To illustrate monthly variance analysis on a departmental basis, the DeWitt Products data used in Chapter 8 are modified to accommodate a monthly comparison, and only one service department, Utilities, is used. The four departmental factory overhead rates computed in Chapter 8 are maintained as follows:

Cutting Department. . . . . $2.00 per direct labor hour
Planing Department . . . . $3.20 per machine hour
Assembly Department . . . . 60% of direct labor cost
Upholstery Department . . . . $1.80 per direct labor hour

At the end of January, the following actual data for DeWitt Products are assembled:

Department	Actual Hours (Labor or Machine) or Labor Cost	Actual Consumption for the Month — kwh	Actual Consumption for the Month — hph	Actual Departmental Overhead Before Billing Out Utilities
Cutting	3,046 direct labor hours	1 180	19,000	$3,575
Planing.	1,620 machine hours	700	10,800	3,125
Assembly.	$11,400 direct labor cost	1 700	7,000	2,900
Upholstery	4,100 direct labor hours	1 980	8,000	3,570
Utilities				5,860
		5 560	44,800	

Based on the actual production and cost data, the cost department would apply the following amounts of factory overhead to products passing through the four departments:

Cutting Department, 3,046 direct labor hours × $2.00 . . . . $6,092
Planing Department, 1,620 machine hours × $3.20   5,184
Assembly Department, $11,400 direct labor cost × 60%   6,840
Upholstery Department, 4,100 direct labor hours × $1.80   7,380

To determine and analyze the amount of over- or underapplied factory overhead, service department costs must be added to the actual direct and indirect departmental overhead to put actual and applied figures on a comparable basis. These procedures were presented in Chapter 8.

Spending Variance. In responsibility accounting, the emphasis rests upon the comparison of actual departmental expenses with budgeted or estimated costs before service department costs are allocated, because it is at these departmental points of origin that costs are best controlled. Furthermore, many accountants believe that only the variable portion of these point-of-origin costs should be compared and not the total overhead, since these variable costs tend to be the most readily controllable at the department level. Naturally, the procedures for different organizations vary.

In this example, both procedures are illustrated for the four producing departments and one service department. The first computation shows total actual departmental overhead, both fixed and variable, compared with budgeted or predetermined departmental overhead. The second computation shows only variable actual departmental overhead compared with its budgeted or predetermined amount. In both situations, the analysis is made for producing and service departments prior to any service department cost allocation.

PROCEDURE 1

	Departments				
	Cutting	Planing	Assembly	Upholstery	Utilities
Actual departmental overhead....	$3,575	$3,125	$2,900	$3,570	$5,860
Budget allowances:					
Fixed expenses (¹⁄₁₂ annual fixed costs; e.g., $17,100* ÷ 12 = $1,425)....	$1,425	$1,492	$1,342	$1,525	$1,333
Variable expenses:					
3,046 hours × $.5762**	1,755				
1,620 hours × $1.0217**		1,655			
$11,400 × 15.5%**			1,767		
4,100 hours × $.4217**				1,729	
5 560 kwh × $.1544**					858
44,800 hph × $.0494**					2,213
1,750 sq. ft.*** × $.7057**					1,235
Budget allowances........	$3,180	$3,147	$3,109	$3,254	$5,639
Spending variances.......	$ 395	$ (22)	$ (209)	316	$ 221
	unfav.	fav.	fav.	unfav.	unfav.

*Estimated fixed cost for the Cutting Department, page 181.
**Variable cost rate, as calculated on page 191.
***1,750 sq. ft. is ¹⁄₁₂ of 21,000 sq. ft. (to convert to a one-month period), as shown on page 182.

PROCEDURE 2

	Departments				
	Cutting	Planing	Assembly	Upholstery	Utilities
Actual variable departmental overhead (e.g., $3,575 − $1,425 fixed costs)............	$2,150	$1,633	$1,558	$2,045	$4,527
Budgeted variable expenses	1,755	1,655	1,767	1,729	4,306
Spending variances.............	$ 395	$ (22)	$ (209)	$ 316	$ 221
	unfav.	fav.	fav.	unfav.	unfav.

The variable cost rates for the producing departments are calculated by dividing the variable departmental overhead, before service department distribution, by the predetermined or estimated direct labor hours, direct labor cost, or machine hours, using data from pages 181 and 184:

	Estimated Variable Departmental Overhead	÷	Estimated			=	Variable Departmental Cost Rates
			Direct Labor Hours	Direct Labor Cost	Machine Hours		
Cutting	$23,400		40,608				$ .5762
Planing..............	$18,800				18,400		$1.0217
Assembly............	$18,900			$122,000			15.5%
Upholstery	$20,300		48,140				$ .4217

In the producing departments, actual hours or actual costs for the month are multiplied by the variable cost rate to arrive at the budgeted or estimated variable cost.

The variable rates for Utilities (using data from pages 181 and 184) are calculated as follows:

Total departmental expense $65,400
Less fixed expense..................... 16,000
Total variable expense $49,400

$49,400 × 20% = $9,880 ÷ 64 000 kwh = $.1544 variable rate per kwh
$49,400 × 50% = $24,700 ÷ 500,000 hph = $.0494 variable rate per hph
$49,400 × 30% = $14,820 ÷ 21,000 sq. ft. = $.7057 variable rate per sq. ft.

The estimated allowance for Utilities is based on the actual monthly consumption figures multiplied by the corresponding variable rates.

Idle Capacity Variance. Responsibility accounting stresses the control of variable expenses and the calculation of the departmental spending variance. It is possible, however, to continue the analysis and calculate an idle capacity variance based entirely on departmental costs without any allocation of service department costs or charges. To illustrate, the data from page 181 are used in determining the idle capacity variance for the Cutting Department, as shown in the following table.

(1) Actual Overhead	(2) Budget Allowance	(3) Applied Overhead	(4) Total Variance (1)–(3)	(5) Spending Variance (1)–(2)	(6) Idle Capacity Variance (2)–(3)
$3,575	$3,180	$3,038*	$537 unfav.	$395 unfav.	$142** unfav,

*3,046 actual hours × $.9973 = $3,038
**3,384 (40,608 hours ÷ 12 months) predetermined hours − 3,046 actual hours = 338 idle hours × $.4211

The Cutting Department's total estimated overhead cost is $40,500, with $17,100 fixed and $23,400 variable. The variable overhead rate is $.5762 and the fixed rate is $.4211 ($17,100 ÷ 40,608 estimated hours), providing a total of $.9973. In the Cutting Department, a factory overhead rate of $2 per direct labor hour is used for product costing purposes. The difference of $1.0027 ($2.00 − $.9973) is accounted for by service department costs assigned to this department.

A similar analysis can be made as follows for the service department, Utilities:

(1) Actual Cost	(2) Budget Allowance	(3) Utilities Cost Charged Out	(4) Total Variance (1)–(3)	(5) Spending Variance (1)–(2)	(6) Idle Capacity Variance (2)–(3)
$5,860	$5,639	$5,701*	$159 unfav.	$221 unfav.	$(62) fav.

*The amount of cost charged out is based on the total predetermined cost of $65,400, which was to be distributed 20% or $13,080 based on kwh, 50% or $32,700 on hph, and 30% or $19,620 on floor area, resulting in these charging rates: $.2044 ($13,080 ÷ 64 000 kwh); $.0654 ($32,700 ÷ 500,000 hph); and $.9343 ($19,620 ÷ 21,000 sq. ft.). The $5,701 is the result of:

5 560 actual kwh × $.2044 = $1,136
44,800 actual hph × $.0654 = 2,930
1,750 sq. ft. converted to a one-month period (1/12 of 21,000 sq. ft.) × $.9343 = 1,635
$5,701

Responsibility for Service Department Variances. While the responsibility for the cost incurred is, generally speaking, easily identifiable in the producing departments, a service department's cost variances need a great deal of additional investigation. With a service department such as Utilities, the analysis is not so easy because:

1. Utilities can be charged accurately to consuming departments only when departmental or cost center meters are used.
2. Even with meters, the quantity used might differ from the quantity produced, due to line losses. The pinpointing of the responsibility for these losses is often impossible.
3. Since any utility can often be either purchased from outside or manufactured inside, it could be possible that the interchangeable use of one source with another will give rise to variances for which the cause is also difficult to detect.

Similar difficulties regarding the pinpointing of responsibility for the cost incurrence and the resulting variance are experienced with any service department. The maintenance department has already been cited as an example. In many instances, service department costs are largely fixed, at least over a relevant range of activity or volume. For this reason, responsibility is difficult to establish. The idle capacity variance is particularly troublesome when calculated on a monthly basis. The spending variance is somewhat more meaningful, since actual and budgeted costs can be compared with their increases and decreases.

As a rule, the manager of the service department is responsible for the variance between the actual cost and the cost based on the number of hours or service units charged out or sold. The manager of the producing or services received department, together with the service department supervisor, is responsible for the number of hours or service units consumed in the department. This statement indicates that a kind of dual responsibility exists between the charges to the services received departments and the credits to the services rendered departments. The consuming department's cost must be compared with the allowed or budgeted service cost to determine the cost increase or decrease in that department, while the service department must examine its cost on the basis of the quantity consumed or sold.

Responsibility Reporting

Responsibility accounting is a program encompassing all operating management for which the accounting, cost, or budget divisions provide technical assistance in the form of daily, weekly, or monthly control reports. Responsibility reporting includes the reporting phase of responsibility accounting. In fact, the terms, "responsibility accounting" and "responsibility reporting" are generally considered synonymous.

Reporting to the various levels of management can be divided into responsibility-performance reporting and information reporting. A clear distinction between the two is important; each serves different goals or objectives. *Responsibility-performance reports* are accountability reports with two purposes:

1. To inform managers and superiors of their performance in responsible areas.
2. To motivate managers and superiors to generate the direct action necessary to improve performance.

Information reports are issued for the purpose of providing managers with information relevant to their areas of interest, although not necessarily associated directly with their specific responsibility for performance. Information reports serve a broader and different set of goals than performance reports. In the short view, responsibility-performance reports are more important than information reports because of the immediate and pressing needs to keep the business on course. However, from the long view, information reports bearing on the progress and growth of the business are also important.

Fundamentals of Reports

Reports should be based on the following fundamental qualities and characteristics:

1. Reports should fit the organization chart; that is, they should be addressed primarily to the individuals responsible for controlling the items covered by the reports. Managers must be educated to use the results of the reporting system.
2. Reports should be consistent in form and content each time they are issued. Changes should be made only for good reasons and with clear explanations to users.
3. Reports should be prompt and timely. Prompt issuance of a report requires that cost records be organized so that information is available when it is needed.
4. Reports should be issued with regularity. Promptness and regularity are closely tied in with the mechanical aids used to assemble and issue reports.
5. Reports should be easy to understand. Often they contain accounting terminology that managers with little or no accounting training find difficult to understand, and vital information may be incorrectly communicated. Therefore, accounting terms should be explained or modified to fit the user. Management should have some knowledge of the kind of items chargeable to an account as well as

the methods used to compute overhead rates, allocate costs, and analyze variances.

6. Reports should convey sufficient but not excessive detail. The amount and nature of the detail depend largely on the management level receiving the report. Reports to management should neither be flooded with immaterial facts nor so condensed that management lacks vital information essential to carrying out its responsibilities.

7. Reports should give comparative figures (a comparison of actual with budgeted figures, or of predetermined standards with actual results) and should isolate variances.

8. Reports should be analytical. Analysis of underlying papers, such as time tickets, scrap tickets, work orders, and materials requisitions, provides reasons for poor performance which might have been due to power failure, machine breakdown, an inefficient operator, poor quality of materials, or other similar factors.

9. Reports for operating management should be stated in physical units as well as in dollars, since dollar information may be irrelevant to a supervisor not trained in the language of the accountant. Also, dollars may be more difficult to compare over time because of the impact of inflation.

10. Reports may tend to highlight supposed departmental efficiencies and inefficiencies. Care should be exercised to see that such reports do not encourage departmental activities aimed at "making a good showing" regardless of the effect on the entire organization.

To be of value, information must be used; to be used, it must be understood by both accounting and nonaccounting personnel. Effective information usage depends on the form and method of the reporting techniques, whether written, oral, or visual.

The two principal written reporting techniques are charts or graphs and tabular presentation. Narrative reports are useful for conveying qualitative information that is difficult to quantify. Supplementary oral and visual presentations have been used effectively to enhance opportunities for individuals and groups to receive information, raise questions, and voice opinions.

Responsibility-Reporting Systems Illustrated

The first step in a responsibility-reporting system is the establishment of lines of responsibility and responsibility areas. Each block in a company's organization chart represents a segment (cost center, division, department, etc.) that is reported upon and that receives reports on the functions responsible to it. Any report prepared according to this concept easily fits into one of the blocks illustrated in the following organization chart for a manufacturing concern:

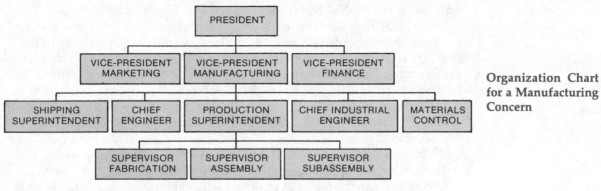

Organization Chart for a Manufacturing Concern

The following reports illustrate the factory overhead reporting structure for each level of responsibility and the relationship of each report to the next higher echelon of responsibility.[8] Starting with Report D (bottom of the pyra-

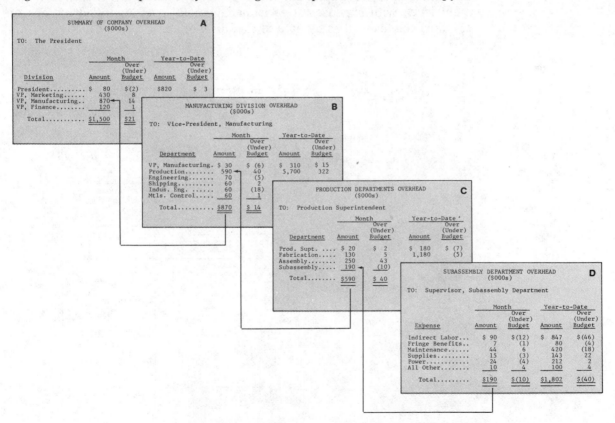

Flow of Responsibility Reporting in a Manufacturing Concern

[8]James D. Wilson, "Human Relations and More Effective Reporting," *NAA Bulletin*, Vol. XLII, No. 9, pp. 13-24.

mid), the Subassembly Department supervisor is provided with the factory overhead expenses for this area. The supervisors for the Fabrication and Assembly Departments also receive similar reports. The supervisors of these three departments are responsible to the production superintendent. Report C summarizes the overhead expenses for the production superintendent and the three departments for which the production superintendent is accountable. Report B provides the vice-president of manufacturing with performance figures for this office and for the five responsibility areas within this division. Finally, the president receives a summary, Report A, indicating overhead expenses not only for the president's own area but also for the three divisions (Marketing, Manufacturing, Finance) reporting to that office.

The following illustration depicts responsibility reporting in a bank, utilizing a reporting system that accurately identifies and reports expenses along the bank's organizational lines.[9] This permits effective expense control through the proper assignment of responsibility and control at each management level, with expenses at each management level identified by area of responsibility as well as by natural classification.

Flow of Responsibility Reporting in a Bank

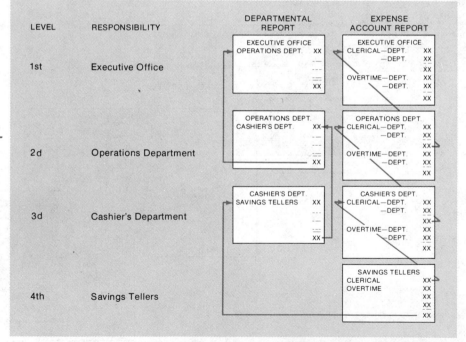

Reviewing the Reporting Structure

To provide all levels of management with all the facts when needed, the reporting system should be geared to the requirements of all managerial personnel. Each report should be so arranged that exceptions are highlighted and brought to the attention of the responsible manager without too much searching and extensive reading. The number of reports issued and sent to a manager also needs constant examination. Too many times a reporting system is cluttered with old, detailed, and voluminous reports, without consideration of the cost of their preparation or their justification. No reporting system is ever perfect. It requires continuous checking and examination in the light of changing times and the vicissitudes of business itself.

DISCUSSION QUESTIONS

1. Explain responsibility accounting and the classification of revenues and expenses under this concept.

2. Responsibility accounting does not involve a drastic change in accounting theory or principles. Discuss.

3. What is the significance of controllable as compared to uncontrollable costs?

4. Enumerate general requirements that are absolutely necessary for a successful responsibility accounting system.

5. Enumerate the benefits that should result from responsibility accounting.

6. Why is some knowledge of human behavior important to responsibility accounting?

7. The departmentalization of factory overhead is essential for maximum control of overhead. Explain in terms of responsibility reporting.

8. Overhead control reports received by department heads should include only those items over which they have control. Explain.

9. Why are service department costs included in the overhead rates? Why should actual service department costs be accumulated in service department accounts instead of being charged directly to production department accounts?

10. Although service department costs are included in departmental overhead rates, actual costs of these departments need not be distributed to departments serviced each period. Explain.

11. The following charges are found on the monthly report of a division which manufactures and sells products primarily to outside companies. State which, if any, of these charges are consistent with the responsibility accounting concept. Support each answer with a brief explanation.
    (a) A charge for general corporation administration at 10% of division sales.
    (b) A charge for the use of the corporate computer facility. The charge is determined by taking the actual annual Computer Department cost and allocating an amount to each user on the ratio of its use to total corporation use.
    (c) A charge for goods purchased from another division. (The charge is based upon the competitive market price for the goods.)   (CMA adapted)

12. The electric bill of the Emmons Company increased from $5,000 to $7,500 between January

and February. As a bill is received, its cost is allocated to various departments on the basis of actual usage.
(a) What factors may have caused the increase?
(b) Is this an effective way of handling this cost? If not, suggest a better procedure.

13. A charging rate is frequently used to charge Maintenance Department cost to departments using its services. The charge is determined by multiplying the number of labor hours of service by a charging rate which is computed by the following formula:

$$\frac{\text{Total actual Maintenance Department cost}}{\text{Total labor hours worked}}$$

The superintendent of the Stamping Department was upset by a $15,000 maintenance charge for work that involved approximately the same number of labor hours as work done in a previous month when the charge was $12,000.

(a) What factors may have caused the increased charge?
(b) What improvements can be made in the distribution of this company's Maintenance Department cost?

14. Discuss the information which a well-designed cost report should give to the management from the point of view of production and of control. Is there any other information with which the cost figures should be amplified? In what terms should such information be given?

15. On what fundamentals should the method of presenting cost data to management be based?

16. Why is usefulness of the figures so important in accounting?

17. A frequent complaint made by management is that cost reports arrive too late to be of any value to the executives. What are the main contributing causes of this condition, and how can it be remedied?

EXERCISES

1. *Billing rates; variance analysis.* Applegate Company uses predetermined departmental overhead rates to apply factory overhead. In computing these rates, every attempt is made to transfer service department costs to producing departments on the most equitable bases. Budgeted cost and other data for Applegate's two service departments, Maintenance and General Factory, are as follows:

	Maintenance	General Factory
Monthly fixed cost	$7,500	$30,000
Variable cost	$8.50 per maintenance labor hour	$20 per employee (producing departments only)
Normal level of activity	15,000 maintenance hours per month	1,000 producing department employees
Actual November results:		
Total cost.............................	$132,000	$48,000
Actual level of activity	14,000 maintenance hours	980 producing department employees

Required:

(1) Compute the charging or billing rates to be used to transfer estimated maintenance and general factory costs to other departments, together with a description of the method used.

(2) Compute the spending and idle capacity variances for the service departments.

2. Sold-hour rates; variance analysis. *A company's two service departments provide the following data:*

Service Center	Monthly Budget	Service-Hours Available	Actual Monthly Expense
Carpenter Shop	$20,000	2,000	$19,300
Electricians	30,000	2,500	28,400

The two service departments serve three producing departments that show the following budgeted and actual cost and service-hours data:

Department No.	Estimated Services Required		Actual Services Used	
	Carpenter Shop	Electricians	Carpenter Shop	Electricians
1	600 hrs.	900 hrs.	400 hrs.	1,000 hrs.
2	750 hrs.	1,000 hrs.	800 hrs.	850 hrs.
3	650 hrs.	600 hrs.	450 hrs.	550 hrs.

Required:

(1) Compute the sold-hour rates for the two service departments.

(2) Compute the amounts charged to the producing departments for services rendered.

(3) Compute the spending variances for the two service departments, assuming that 70% of the budgeted expense is fixed in Carpenter Shop and 80% in Electricians.

3. Billing rates; variance analysis. *The management of Bale Company wishes to secure greater control over service departments and decides to create a billing rate for the Maintenance and Payroll Departments. For September, the following predetermined and actual operating and cost data have been made available:*

Maintenance Department

Predetermined data (beginning of the month):

Normal level of maintenance hours per month 3,200

Average hourly rate for maintenance worker $8.70

Other maintenance costs:

	Fixed Cost per Month	Variable Cost per Maintenance Labor Hour
Supervision	$9,800	$.50
Tools and supplies...........	2,300	.75
Other miscellaneous items	700	.05

Actual data (end of the month):

Maintenance hours worked 3,355

Maintenance workers' earnings $29,610

Other costs (supervision, etc.) $17,390

Payroll Department

Predetermined data (beginning of the month):

Average number of employees in factory and office 1,200

Budgeted cost for department..................... $12,000 *plus* $2 for each employee in factory and office

Actual data (end of the month):

Number of employees in factory and office   1,165

Total cost in the Payroll Department $14,875

Required:

(1) Compute the billing rate for the two departments.

(2) Compute the variances for the two departments for September.

4. Readiness-to-serve and billing rates. During November, the actual expense of operating a power plant was $11,800, of which $5,000 was considered a fixed cost. The schedule of horsepower-hours for the producing and service departments is as follows:

	Producing Departments		Service Departments	
	A	B	X	Y
Needed at capacity production ..	10,000	20,000	12,000	8,000
Used during November	8,000	13,000	7,000	6,000

Required:

(1) Compute the dollar amounts of the power plant expense to be allocated to each producing and service department. The fixed cost is assigned on the basis of the power plant's readiness to serve.

(2) State reasons for allocating one service department's cost to other service departments as well as to producing departments.

5. Readiness-to-serve and billing rates; variance analysis. Bulloch Company operates its own power plant. Cost of energy is distributed to the producing departments by charging the fixed cost based on the readiness-to-serve capacity provided, and the variable cost on the basis of a predetermined rate multiplied by actual consumption. The rated readiness-to-serve capacity of the three departments, Cutting, Grinding, and Polishing, is 70 000, 52 500, and 17 500 kwh per month.

The following information relative to the producing departments and the power plant for April, May, and June is available:

	Consumption in Kilowatt-Hours			Actual Power Plant Costs	
	Cutting	Grinding	Polishing	Fixed	Variable
April	45 000	40 000	12 000	$28,000	$21,800
May	55 000	35 000	10 000	28,000	21,400
June	47 500	42 000	11 000	28,000	23,000

The predetermined variable power cost rate is $.22 per kwh.

Required:

(1) Separately identify the fixed and variable power cost charged to each department for each of the three months.

(2) Compute the over- or underdistributed variable cost of the power plant for each of the three months.

6. Overhead analysis; report to supervisor. The cost and operating data on April factory overhead for Department 10 are shown at the top of page 229.

Required:

(1) Prepare a variance analysis of the factory overhead for Department 10.

(2) Prepare a departmental report for the supervisor of Department 10, with explanations regarding the format used.

	Budgeted Factory Overhead	Actual Factory Overhead
Variable departmental overhead:		
Supplies..............................	$ 2,000	$ 1,700
Repairs and maintenance	800	600
Indirect labor..........................	4,000	3,600
Power and light	1,200	1,150
Heat	400	350
Subtotal	$ 8,400	$ 7,400
Fixed departmental overhead:		
Building expense	$ 800	$ 840
Depreciation—machinery	2,400	2,400
Property tax and insurance	400	420
Subtotal	$ 3,600	$ 3,660
Total	$12,000	$11,060
Operating data:		
Normal capacity hours	8,000	
Factory overhead rate per hour	$1.50	
Actual hours		6,400

PROBLEMS

9-1. Variance analysis of producing and service departments overhead. Brock Products, Inc. decided to push for a greater amount of cost consciousness and cost responsibility among its departmental supervisors. The allocation of service department costs to the producing departments, using predetermined rates, has been in use for some time. Now the management asks the Cost Department, with the cooperation of the departmental supervisors, not only to prepare departmental budgets but also to give the supervisors monthly reports for cost control information.

The company operates with three producing departments, A, B, and C, and two service departments, Repairs and Maintenance, and Utilities. For the year 19--, the Cost Department prepared the following departmental factory overhead budgets and determined the factory overhead rates based on direct labor hours:

	Producing Departments			Service Departments	
	A	B	C	Repairs and Maintenance	Utilities
Total budgeted expense......................	$52,000	$52,450	$41,900	$56,000	$49,000
Allocation of service depts.:					
Utilities (based on kilowatt-hours)	14,000	15,750	12,250	7,000	(49,000)
Repairs and maintenance (based on direct labor hours)	18,000	27,900	17,100	(63,000)	
Total	$84,000	$96,100	$71,250		
Bases:					
Kilowatt-hours...........................	40 000	45 000	35 000	20 000	
Direct labor hours.........................	20,000	31,000	19,000		
Service department allocation rates				$.90 per direct labor hour	$.35 per kilowatt-hour
Departmental overhead rates..................	$4.20 per direct labor hour	$3.10 per direct labor hour	$3.75 per direct labor hour		

Actual cost and operating data before allocation of service department costs at the end of the budget period are:

	Producing Departments			Service Departments	
	A	B	C	Repairs and Maintenance	Utilities
Total actual expense	$56,220	$52,850	$42,580	$56,320	$50,240
Operating data:					
Direct labor hours	20,480	29,850	20,100		
Kilowatt-hours	39 300	46 200	35 800	18 950	

Required:

(1) Compute the amount of factory overhead applied for each of the three producing departments.

(2) Compute the amount of over- or underapplied factory overhead for each of the three producing departments, charging them with service department costs on the basis of actual kilowatt-hours or labor hours multiplied by the billing rate.

(3) Compute the total variance for each of the two service departments.

9-2. Billing rates; estimated factory overhead and variance analysis. Toledo Tool Co. has two producing departments, Planers and Radial Drills, and two service departments, Maintenance and Utilities. The Cost Department collected the following data:

	Producing Departments		Service Departments	
	Planers	Radial Drills	Maintenance	Utilities
Estimated data for 19--:				
Fixed overhead	$18,000	$15,000	$ 6,000	$ 4,800
Variable overhead	15,000	9,000	4,500	3,600
Total	$33,000	$24,000	$10,500	$ 8,400
Direct labor hours	12,000	7,500		
Maintenance hours	2,500	1,000	3,500	
Kilowatt-hours	45 000	25 000		70 000
Actual data for January 19--:				
Fixed overhead	$ 1,500	$ 1,250	$ 500	$ 400
Variable overhead	1,620	1,050	670	310
Total	$ 3,120	$ 2,300	$ 1,170	$ 710
Direct labor hours	1,020	680		
Maintenance hours	320	80	400	
Kilowatt-hours	4 000	2 000		6 000

Required:

(1) Compute the billing (or charging) rate for each of the two service departments.

(2) Calculate the total predetermined factory overhead for each of the two producing departments and their departmental factory overhead rates based on direct labor hours. Service department expenses are to be distributed on the basis of the billing rates calculated in (1). (Carry all computations to three decimal places.)

(3) Prepare an analysis of the over- or underapplied factory overhead of each of the two producing departments for January, including the spending and idle capacity variances. Service department expenses are to be charged on the basis of actual hours (maintenance or kilowatt) multiplied by the billing rate. This method treats these expenses as being wholly variable.

(4) Prepare a calculation and analysis of the over- or underdistributed factory overhead in each of the two service departments, including the spending and idle capacity variances. (Round off all amounts to four decimal places.)

(5) Prepare a reconciliation of the total variances.

9-3. Budget allowance; variance analysis based on responsibility reporting. The controller of Ushco Corporation prepared the following forecast income statement for the year:

	Amount	Unit
Sales (60,000 units)	$600,000	$10.00
Cost of goods sold (Schedule I)	384,000	6.40
Gross profit	$216,000	$ 3.60
Operating expenses:		
Marketing expense	$80,000	
Administrative expense	70,000	
	150,000	2.50
Income before income tax	$ 66,000	$ 1.10
Schedule I—Estimated cost of goods sold:		
Direct materials	$102,000	$ 1.70
Direct labor	162,000	2.70
Factory overhead	120,000	2.00
Total	$384,000	$ 6.40

The product's manufacturing processes require two producing departments that make use of the services of Department 76, Maintenance, and Department 95, Janitorial. To charge the products moving through the two departments, the cost accountant has prepared an overhead distribution sheet and calculated predetermined factory overhead rates for product costing, as follows:

	Producing Departments		Service Departments	
	Dept. 10	Dept. 12	Dept. 76 Maintenance	Dept. 95 Janitorial
Production units	60,000	60,000		
Direct labor hours	15,000	12,000		
Direct labor cost	$90,000	$72,000		
Factory overhead:				
Variable overhead	$27,000	$22,800	$ 5,100	$2,700
Fixed overhead	17,520	34,230	8,400	7,200
			$13,500	$9,900
Share of Department 76	7,500	6,000	(13,500)	
Share of Department 95	1,980	2,970		(4,950)
Total factory overhead	$54,000	$66,000		
To marketing and administrative expenses				(4,950)
Factory overhead rate (based on direct labor hours)	$3.60	$5.50		

Actual hours and costs at the end of the month:

	Dept. 10	Dept. 12	Dept. 76	Dept. 95
Hours worked	1,340	1,030		
Actual factory overhead:				
Variable overhead	$2,700	$2,240	$595	$440
Fixed overhead	1,500	3,000	700	600

The Department 76 cost was allocated to the two producing departments on the basis of the direct labor hours. The Department 95 cost was prorated 50% to the factory and 50% to the general offices. The two producing departments shared the 50% factory allocation on a 40:60 basis, respectively.

For January, the Planning Department scheduled 5,000 units. At the end of the month, sales and production showed the following results:

Sales..	4,900 units
Production—completed in both departments......................	5,200 units

Required:
     (1) Compute the budget allowance for each of the two producing departments for January, based on (a) scheduled production hours and (b) actual production hours.
     (2) Compute the spending and idle capacity variances for each of the two producing departments, based on actual production hours.
     (3) Compute the spending variance for each of the two service departments. (Round off all amounts to three decimal places.)

9-4. Overhead rates; variance analysis in producing and service departments. Dentan Products Co. prepared the following budgeted and actual data:

	Budgeted Data, 19--			Actual Data March, 19--	
	Direct Labor Hours	Factory Overhead		Direct Labor Hours	Factory Overhead Cost
Departments		Fixed	Variable		
Machining....................	22,000	$12,840	$14,400	2,130	$3,586*
Assembly	28,000	14,100	18,300	2,310	3,341*
Tools and Supplies	-0-	3,600	5,600	-0-	919
Materials Handling	-0-	5,700	6,000	-0-	1,080

*Includes service departments

The fixed cost of the service departments is apportioned to the producing departments on a 60:40 basis and the variable cost at a predetermined rate on the basis of direct labor hours. Budgeted direct labor hours are based on normal capacity utilization. Factory overhead is applied on the basis of direct labor hours.

Required:
     (1) Compute the departmental factory overhead rates for the producing departments. (Round off all amounts to three decimal places.)
     (2) Compute the spending and idle capacity variances of producing and service departments for March. (Round off calculations to three decimal places.)

9-5. Setting sewage treatment usage charge rates. The city of Commerce, Texas, estimates its sewage treatment costs for next year as follows:

Fixed

Debt service cost associated with excess capacity....................	$350,000
Costs attributable to infiltration and inflow (basically rain water and sub-surface ground water):	
Debt service	150,000
Operating and maintenance......................................	140,000
Administration and office overhead................................	250,000
Remaining debt service	110,000

Variable

Sewage volume and strength processing costs	$1,000,000

Its user census profile is estimated to be:

User Class	Number of Users	Volume/Strength Units
Wet industry	3	80,000
Commercial and dry industry	150	50,000
Residential	8,675	120,000
Total	8,828	250,000

Required:
(1) Compute the user charging rate, based on volume/strength units.
(2) Compute the fixed and variable user charging rates, assuming that:
   (a) Excess capacity cost and infiltration and inflow debt service cost are excluded from rates and recovered through property tax, and
   (b) All other fixed costs are charged to industry/commercial users and residential users at a per user ratio of 25:1, based on the user's relative size of lateral pipe.
(3) Calculate allocations to user classes, based on (1) and (2), and identify the more equitable method, giving reasons.

CASES

A. Cost responsibility and the attitude of managers. Declining profits compelled the management of the Olinvelte Corporation to approach employees to work for production economy and increased productivity. Production managers were promised a monetary incentive based on cost reductions.

The production managers responded with (1) an increased rate of production; (2) a higher rejection rate for quantities of raw materials and parts received from the storeroom; (3) a postponement of repairs and maintenance work; and (4) a reliance on quick emergency repairs to avoid breakdowns.

The repair and maintenance policy is causing serious conflicts. The maintenance supervisor argues that the postponement of certain repairs in the short run and the use of emergency repair techniques could result in increased costs later and, in some instances, could reduce the life of machines as well as machine safety.

Even more serious is the growing bitterness caused by pressures placed on the maintenance managers by individual production managers to obtain service. Also, in several instances, some production departments whose production has been halted due to machine breakdown have had to wait while another production department, with an aggressive manager, has received repair service on machines not needed in the current production run. Furthermore, the demand for immediate service sometimes results in substandard repair work.

The production departments are charged with the actual cost of the repairs. A record of the repair work conducted in individual production departments is prepared by the maintenance managers. This record, when completed in the Accounting Department, shows the repair hours, the hourly rate of the maintenance worker, the maintenance overhead charge, and the cost of any parts. The record serves as the basis for the charges to production departments. Production managers have complained about the charging system, claiming that charges depend upon which maintenance worker does the work (hourly rate and efficiency), when the work is done (the production department is charged for the overtime premium), and how careful the worker is in recording the time on the job.

Required:
  (1) Identify and briefly explain the motivational factors which may cause friction between the production and maintenance managers.
  (2) Develop a plan which revises the system employed to charge production departments for repair costs, so that the production departments' complaints are eliminated or reduced.   (CMA adapted)

B. Maintenance cost control. Stevenson Company is a medium-sized manufacturer in a capital-intensive industry. The corporation's profitability is low at the moment and, as a result, investment funds are limited and hiring is restricted. These consequences of the corporation's problems have placed a strain on the plant's repair and maintenance program. The result has been a reduction in work efficiency and cost control effectiveness in the repair and maintenance area.

The controller proposes the installation of a maintenance work order system to overcome these problems. This system would require a work order to be prepared for each repair request and for each regular maintenance activity. The maintenance superintendent would record the estimated time to complete a job and would send one copy of the work order to the department in which the work was to be done. The work order would also serve as a job cost sheet. The actual cost of the parts and supplies used on the job as well as the actual labor costs incurred in completing the job would be recorded directly on the work order. A copy of the completed work order with the actual costs would be the basis of the charge to the department in which the repair or maintenance activity occurred.

The maintenance superintendent opposes the program on the grounds that the added paperwork will be costly and nonproductive. He states that the departmental clerk who now schedules repair and maintenance activities is doing a good job without all the extra forms the new system would require. The real problem, in the superintendent's opinion, is that the Maintenance Department is understaffed.

Required:
  (1) Discuss how the maintenance work order system would aid cost control.
  (2) Explain how the maintenance work order system might aid the maintenance superintendent in obtaining authorization to employ more mechanics.   (CMA adapted)

C. Reviewing the reporting structure. Wright Company employs a computer-based data processing system for maintaining all company records. The present system was developed in stages over the past five years and has been fully operational for the last 24 months.

When the system was being designed, all department heads were asked to specify the types of information and reports they would need for planning and controlling operations. The Systems Department attempted to meet the specifications of each department head. Company management specified that certain other reports be prepared for department heads. During the five years of systems development and operations, there have been changes in the department head positions due to attrition and promotions. New department heads have often requested additional reports according to their specifications; the Systems Department has complied with all of these requests. Consequently, the data processing system has generated a large quantity of reports each reporting period. Occasionally, a report has been discontinued upon request by a department head, but only if it was not a standard report required by executive management.

Company management became concerned about the quality of information being produced by the system, and the Internal Audit Department was asked to evaluate the effectiveness of these reports. The audit staff noted the following reactions to this information overload:

   (a) Many department heads would not act on certain reports during periods of peak activity. The department head would let these reports accumulate with the hope of catching up during a subsequent lull.

   (b) Some department heads had so many reports that they did not act at all upon the information or made incorrect decisions because of misuse of the information.

   (c) Frequently, action required by the nature of the report data was not taken until the department head was reminded by someone who needed the decision. These department heads did not appear to have developed a priority system for acting on the information produced by the data processing system.

   (d) Department heads often would develop the information they needed from alternative, independent sources, rather than utilize the reports generated by the data processing system. This was often easier than trying to search among the reports for the needed data.

Required:

   (1) Explain whether each of the observed reactions is a functional or dysfunctional behavioral response.

   (2) Recommend procedures that the company could employ to eliminate any dysfunctional behavior and to prevent its recurrence.   (CMA adapted)

Part Four
Planning and Control of Materials and Labor

Chapter 10
Materials: Controlling and Costing

Effective materials management is essential in order to (1) provide the best service to customers, (2) produce at maximum efficiency, and (3) manage inventories at predetermined levels to stabilize investments in inventories. Successful materials management requires the development of a highly integrated and coordinated system involving sales forecasting, purchasing, receiving, storage, production, shipping, and actual sales. Both the theory of costing materials and other inventories and the practical mechanics of cost calculations and record keeping must be considered.

Costing materials presents some important, often complex, and sometimes highly controversial questions concerning the costing of materials used in production and the cost of inventory remaining to be consumed in a future period. In financial accounting, the subject is usually presented as a problem of inventory valuation; in cost accounting, the primary problem is the determination of the cost of various materials consumed in production and a proper charge to cost of goods sold. The discussion of materials management in this chapter deals with:

1. Procedures for materials procurement and use.
2. Materials costing methods.
3. Inventory valuation at cost or market, whichever is lower.
4. Inventory pricing and interim financial reporting.
5. Costing procedures for scrap, spoiled goods, and defective work.

Procedures for Materials Procurement and Use

Although production processes and materials requirements vary according to the size and type of industry, the cycle of procurement and use of materials usually involves the following steps:

1. *Engineering, planning,* and *routing* determine the design of the product, the materials specifications, and the requirements at each stage of operations. Engineering and planning not only determine the maximum and minimum quantities to run and the bill of materials for given products and quantities, but also cooperate in developing standards where applicable.
2. The *production budget* provides the master plan from which details concerning materials requirements are eventually developed.
3. The *purchase requisition* informs the purchasing agent concerning the quantity and type of materials needed.
4. The *purchase order* contracts for appropriate quantities to be delivered at specified dates to assure uninterrupted operations.
5. The *receiving report* certifies quantities received and may report results of inspection and testing for quality.
6. The *materials requisition* notifies the storeroom or warehouse to deliver specified types and quantities of materials to a given department at a specified time or is the authorization for the storeroom to issue materials to departments.
7. The *materials ledger cards* record the receipt and the issuance of each class of materials and provide a perpetual inventory record.

Procedures for materials procurement and use involve forms and records necessary for general ledger financial accounting as well as those necessary for costing a job, process, or department, and for maintaining perpetual inventories and other statistical summaries. Some of these forms and records are identified in the flowchart on page 238, which shows procedures for purchasing, receiving, recording, and paying for materials, i.e., the procurement phase.

Purchases of Productive Materials

The actual purchase of all materials is usually made by the purchasing department headed by a general purchasing agent. In some small and

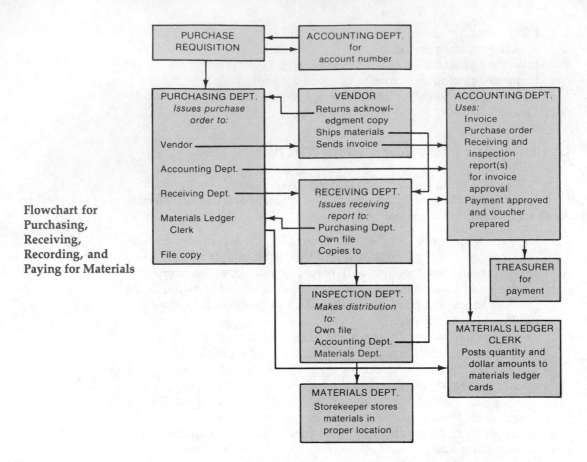

Flowchart for Purchasing, Receiving, Recording, and Paying for Materials

medium-size companies, however, department heads or supervisors have authority to purchase materials as the need arises. In any case, systematic procedures should be in writing in order to fix responsibility and to provide full information regarding the ultimate use of materials ordered and received.

The purchasing department should (1) receive purchase requisitions for materials, supplies, and equipment; (2) keep informed concerning sources of supply, prices, and shipping and delivery schedules; (3) prepare and place purchase orders; and (4) arrange for adequate and systematic reports between the purchasing, the receiving, and the accounting departments. An additional function of the purchasing department in some enterprises is to verify and approve for payment all invoices received in response to purchase orders placed by the department. This procedure has the advantage of centralizing the verification and approval of invoices in the department that originates the purchases and that has complete information concerning items and quantities ordered, prices, terms, shipping instructions, and other conditions and details of the purchases. However, invoice verification and approval by the purchasing department may violate sound procedures and principles of internal control, particularly if the same individual prepares an order and later approves the invoice. Consequently, invoice audit and approval in many instances have been made a function of the accounting department, which receives a copy of the purchase order. The purchase order carries all necessary information regarding price, discount agreement, and delivery stipulations, as well as the number of the account to which the order is to be charged. Furthermore, the centralization of invoice approval in the accounting department helps avoid delaying payments beyond the discount period.

Purchases of Supplies, Services, and Repairs

The procedure followed in purchasing productive materials should apply to all departments and divisions of a business. Purchase requisitions, purchase orders, and receiving reports are appropriate for accounting department supplies and equipment, the company cafeteria, the first aid unit, and the treasurer's office, as well as all other departments. If, for example, the accounting department needs new forms printed, a requisition should be sent to the purchasing department in the usual manner, and a purchase order should be prepared and sent to the printer.

In the case of magazine subscriptions, trade and professional association memberships for company officials, and similar services, the official or department head may send in a requisition in the usual manner. A requisition, an order, and an invoice for all goods and services purchased are a necessity in properly controlling purchases.

Repair contracts on an annual basis for typewriters, calculators, electronic data processing equipment, and some types of factory equipment may be requisitioned and ordered in the usual manner. In other cases, a department head or other employee may telephone for service and shortly thereafter may have a machine repaired and back in operation. In such cases, the purchasing agent issues a so-called blanket purchase order that amounts to approval of all repair and service costs of a specific type without knowing the actual amount charged. When the repair bill is received, the invoice clerk checks the amount of the bill with the head of the department where the repairs took place and then approves the invoice for payment.

Purchasing Forms

The principal forms required in purchasing are the purchase requisition and the purchase order.

Purchase Requisition. The *purchase requisition* originates with (1) a stores or warehouse clerk, who observes that the quantity on hand is at a set ordering minimum, (2) a materials ledger clerk, who may be responsible for notifying the purchasing agent when to buy, (3) a works manager, who foresees the need for special materials or unusual quantities, (4) a research, engineering, or other department employee or supervisor, who needs materials or supplies of a special nature, or (5) a computer that has been programmed to produce replenishment advice for the purchasing department. One copy remains with the originator, and the original is sent to the purchasing department for execution of the request. For standard materials, the requisition may indicate only the stock number of an item, and the purchasing agent uses judgment and established policy concerning where to buy and the quantity to order. For other purchase requests, it may be necessary to give meticulous descriptions, blueprints, catalog numbers, weights, standards, brand names, exact quantities to order, and suggested prices.

Purchase Order. The *purchase order,* signed by the purchasing agent or other official, is a written authorization to a vendor to supply specified quantities of described goods at agreed terms and at a designated time and place. As a convenience, the vendor's order forms may be used. In typical practice, however, the order forms are prepared by the purchasing company, and the form is adapted to the particular needs of the purchaser. As a matter of record and for accounting control, a purchase order should be issued for every purchase of materials, supplies, or equipment. When a purchase commitment is made by mail, telephone, or a sales representative, the purchase order serves as confirmation to the vendor and places the required documents in the hands of those concerned in the purchasing company.

The purchase order gives the vendor a complete description of the goods and services desired, the terms, the prices, and the shipping instructions. When necessary, the description may refer to attached blueprints and specification pages. The original and an acknowledgment copy are sent to the vendor. Other copies are distributed as shown in the flowchart on page 238. The vendor is asked to sign and return the acknowledgment copy to the purchaser, indicating that the order was received and will be delivered according to the specifications enumerated in the purchase order.

Receiving

The function of the receiving department is to: unload and unpack incoming materials; check quantities received against the shipper's packing list; identify goods received with descriptions on the purchase order; prepare a receiving report; notify the purchasing department of discrepancies discovered; arrange for inspection when necessary; notify the traffic department and the purchasing department of any damage in transit; and route accepted materials to the appropriate factory location.

The *receiving report* shows the purchase order number, the account number to be charged, the name of the vendor, details relating to transportation, and the quantity and type of goods received. The form also provides a space for the inspection department to note either the complete approval of the shipment or the quantity rejected and the reason for the rejection. If inspection does not take place immediately after receipt of the materials, the receiving report is distributed as follows: (1) the receiving department keeps one copy and sends another copy to the purchasing department as notice of the arrival of the materials; (2) all other copies go to the inspection department, and are distributed when inspection is completed. After inspection, one copy of the receiving report, with the inspection result noted thereon, is sent to the accounting department, where it is matched with the purchase order and the vendor's invoice and then paid. Other copies go to various departments such as materials and production planning. One copy accompanies the materials, so that the storekeeper knows the quantity and the kind of materials received.

Invoice Approval and Data Processing

By the time materials reach the receiving department, the company usually will have received the invoice from the vendor. This invoice and a copy of the purchase order are filed in the accounting department. When the receiving report with its inspection report arrives, the receiving report and the invoice are compared to see that materials received meet purchase order specifications as to items, quantities, prices, price extensions, discount and credit terms, shipping instructions, and other possible conditions. If the invoice is found to be correct or has been adjusted because of rejects as noted by the inspection department, the invoice clerk approves it, attaches it to the purchase order and the receiving report, and sends these papers to another clerk for the preparation of the voucher.

Invoice approval is an important step in materials control procedure, since it verifies that the goods have been received as ordered and that payment can be made. The verification procedure is handled by responsible invoice clerks, thus assuring systematic examination and handling of the paper work necessary for adequate control of materials purchases.

The preparation of a voucher is based on an approved invoice. The voucher data are entered first in the purchases journal and are posted to the subsidiary records. They are then entered in the cash payments journal according to the due date for payment. The original voucher and two copies are sent to the treasurer for issuance of the check. The treasurer mails the check with the original voucher to the vendor, files one copy of the voucher, and returns another copy to the accounting department for the vendor's file. Purchase transactions entered in the purchases journal affect the control accounts and the subsidiary records as shown in the chart on page 242.

Correcting Invoices

When the purchase order, receiving report, and invoice are compared, various adjustments may be needed as a result of the following circumstances:

1. Some of the materials ordered are not received and are not entered on the invoice. In this case no adjustment is necessary, and the invoice may be approved for immediate payment. On the purchase order the invoice clerk will make a notation of the quantity received in place of

TRANSACTION	GENERAL LEDGER CONTROL		SUBSIDIARY RECORDS
	Debit	Credit	
Materials purchased for stock	Materials	Accounts Payable	Entry in the Received section of the materials ledger card
Materials purchased for a particular job or department	Work in Process	Accounts Payable	Entry in the Direct Materials section of the production report or job order cost sheet
Materials and supplies purchased for factory overhead purposes	Materials	Accounts Payable	Entry in the Received section of the materials ledger card
Supplies purchased for marketing and administrative offices	Materials Marketing Expenses Control Administrative Expenses Control	Accounts Payable	Entry in the Received section of the materials ledger card or in the proper columns of the marketing or administrative expense analysis sheets
Purchases of services or repairs	Factory Overhead Marketing Expenses Control Administrative Expenses Control	Accounts Payable	Entry in the proper account columns of the expense analysis sheets
Purchases of equipment	Equipment	Accounts Payable	Entry on the equipment ledger card

the quantity ordered. If the vendor is out of stock or otherwise unable to deliver specified merchandise, an immediate ordering from other sources may be necessary.

2. Items ordered are not received but are entered on the invoice. In this situation the shortage is noted on the invoice and is deducted from the total before payment is approved. A letter to the vendor explaining the shortage is usually in order.

3. The seller ships a quantity larger than called for on the purchase order. The purchaser may keep the entire shipment and add the excess to the invoice, if not already invoiced; or the excess may be returned or held, pending instructions from the seller. Some companies issue a supplementary purchase order that authorizes the invoice clerk to pay the overshipment.

4. Materials of a wrong size or quality, defective parts, and damaged items are received. If the items are returned, a correction on the invoice should be made before payment is approved. It may be advantageous to keep damaged or defective shipments if the seller makes adequate price concessions, or the items may be held subject to the seller's instructions.

5. It may be expedient for a purchaser to pay transportation charges, even though delivered prices are quoted and purchases are not made on this basis. The amount paid by the purchaser is deducted on the invoice, and the paid freight bill is attached to the invoice as evidence of payment.

Electronic Data Processing for Materials Purchases

The preceding description of invoice approval and payment was for a manual operation performed by an accounts payable clerk or an invoice clerk. In an electronic data processing (EDP) system, the computer—to a great extent—replaces the clerk. Upon receipt of the invoice (the source document), the accounts payable clerk enters the account distribution on the invoice. The data are then directly inputted from the invoice to the computer data bank via a terminal device. The data are edited, audited, and merged with the purchase order and the receiving order data, both of which have been stored in the computer data bank. The common matching criterion on all documents is the purchase order number. Quantities, dollar values, due dates, terms, and unit prices are matched. When in agreement, the cost data are entered in the accounts payable computer file with a date for later payment, or a printout of a check is transmitted for payment.

The above procedure deals with the accounts payable phase of a purchase transaction. Of equal importance is the need for posting the data in quantities and dollar values to the materials inventory file in the EDP system. The information enters the EDP system from either the invoice or the invoice approval form, which would have to include all computer-necessary data. The internal computer program updates the materials inventory file. The withdrawal of materials could also be programmed, so that manual postings to the materials inventory file would be eliminated.

Cost of Acquiring Materials

A guiding principle in accounting for the cost of materials is that all costs incurred in entering a unit of materials into factory production should be included. Acquisition costs, such as the vendor's invoice price and transportation charges, are visible costs of the purchased goods. Less obvious costs of materials entering factory operations are costs of purchasing, receiving, unpacking, inspecting, insuring, storing, and general and cost accounting.

Controversial concepts and certain practical limitations result in variations in implementing the principles of costing materials, even with respect to easily identified acquisition costs. Calculating a number of cost additions and adjustments to each invoice involves clerical expenses which may be greater than benefits derived from the increased accuracy. Therefore, materials are commonly carried at the invoice price paid the vendor, although all acquisition costs and price adjustments affect the materials cost. As a result, acquisition costs are generally charged to factory overhead when it is not practical to follow a more accurate costing procedure.

Purchases Discount. The handling of discounts on purchases is a problem in accounting for materials costs. Trade discounts and quantity discounts normally are not on the accounting records but are treated as price reductions. Cash discounts should be handled as price adjustments but at times are accounted for as other income, although income is not produced by buying. A lower purchase cost may well widen the margin between sales price and cost, but it takes the sale to produce income. When the vendor quotes terms such as 2/10, n/30 on a $100 invoice, is the sales price $100 or $98? The purchaser has two dates to make payment: on the tenth day, which allows time to receive, unpack, inspect, verify, voucher, and pay for the goods; or twenty days later. For the additional twenty days, an additional charge or penalty of 2 percent is assessed. If regarded as interest, the extra charge is 36 percent per year [(360 days ÷ 20 days) × 2%]. On these terms the seller is pricing on essentially a cash basis, and the purchaser has no reasonable choice except to buy on the cash basis.

Although the nature of a purchases discount is readily understood, for practical reasons the gross materials unit cost of the invoice may be recorded in the materials account and the cash discount recorded as a credit account item. Otherwise it would be necessary to compute the discount on each item, with unit costs having four or more decimal places.

Freight In. Freight or other transportation charges on incoming shipments are obviously costs of materials, but differences occur in the allocation of these charges. A vendor's invoice for $600 may show 25 items, weighing 1,700 pounds, shipped in five crates, with the attached freight bill showing a payment of $48. The delivered cost is $648. But how much of the freight belongs to each of the invoice items, and what unit price should go on the materials ledger card? When the purchased units are not numerous and are large in size and unit cost, computation of actual amounts of freight may be feasible; otherwise, some logical, systematic, and expedient procedure is necessary.

If freight charges are debited to Materials, the total amount should be added proportionately to each materials card affected. This might be done by assuming that each dollar of materials cost carries an equal portion of the freight. For example, freight of $48 on materials costing $600 would add $.08 ($48 ÷ $600) to each dollar on the invoice. The relative weight of each item on the invoice might be determined and used as a basis for calculating the applicable freight. If an invoice item is estimated to weigh 300 pounds, then $8.47 [(300 ÷ 1,700) × $48] would be added for freight. This procedure is also likely to result in unit costs having four or more decimal places on the materials ledger cards.

To simplify procedures, all freight costs on incoming materials and supplies may be charged to Freight In. As materials are issued for production, an applied rate for freight in might be added to the unit price on the ledger cards. The same amount is included in the debit to Work in Process or Factory Overhead (Indirect Materials), and Freight In is credited. Any balance in Freight In at the end of a period is closed to Cost of Goods Sold or prorated to Cost of Goods Sold and inventories.

Another method of accounting for incoming freight costs on materials is to estimate the total for an accounting period and include this amount in computing the factory overhead rate. Freight In would then become one of the accounts controlled by Factory Overhead. For materials or supplies used in marketing and administrative departments, freight, transportation, or delivery costs should be charged to the appropriate nonmanufacturing account.

Applied Acquisition Costs. If it is decided that the materials cost should include other acquisition costs as well, an applied rate might be added to each invoice and to each item, instead of charging these costs directly to factory overhead. A single rate for these costs could be used, but a more accurate method would be to use separate rates for each class of costs, as follows:

$$\frac{\text{Estimated purchasing department cost for budget period}}{\text{Estimated number of purchases or estimated amount of purchases}} = \text{Rate per purchase or rate per dollar purchased}$$

$$\frac{\text{Estimated receiving department cost for budget period}}{\text{Estimated number of items to be received during period}} = \text{Rate per item}$$

$$\frac{\text{Estimated materials department cost for budget period}}{\text{Estimated number of items, feet of space, dollar value, etc.}} = \text{Rate per item, cubic foot, dollar value, etc.}$$

$$\frac{\text{Estimated applicable accounting department cost for budget period}}{\text{Estimated number of transactions}} = \text{Rate per transaction}$$

This procedure results in the following accounting treatment:

Materials...	xxx	
Applied Purchasing Department Expenses...................		xxx
Applied Receiving Department Expenses....................		xxx
Applied Materials Department Expenses.....................		xxx
Applied Accounting Department Expenses..................		xxx

Actual expenses incurred by each of the departments for which applied rates are used will be debited to the applied accounts. Differences between the expenses incurred by the departments during the period and the expenses applied to the materials cost would represent over- or underapplied expenses and would be closed to Cost of Goods Sold or prorated to Cost of Goods Sold and inventories.

Storage and Use of Materials

Materials, together with a copy of the receiving report, are forwarded to the storeroom from the receiving or inspection department. The storekeeper and assistants are responsible for safeguarding the materials, which means that materials and supplies are placed in proper bins or other storage spaces, that they are kept safely until required in production, and that all materials taken from the storeroom are properly requisitioned. It is good policy to restrict admittance to the storeroom to employees of that department only and to have these employees work behind locked doors, issuing materials through cage windows.

Since the cost of storing and handling materials may be a substantial amount, careful design and arrangement of storerooms can result in significant cost savings. Materials can be stored according to (1) the materials account number; (2) the frequency of use of the item; (3) the factory area where the item is used; or (4) the nature, size, and shape of the item. In practice, no single base is likely to be suitable, but the size and shape of materials usually dictate the basic storeroom arrangement. Variations can then be introduced, such as placing the most frequently used items nearest the point of issue and locating materials used primarily in one factory area nearest that area.

Bin cards or *stock cards* are effective ready references that may be attached to storage bins, shelves, racks, or other containers. Bin cards usually show quantities of each type of material received, issued, and on hand. They are not a part of the accounting records as such, but they show the quantities on hand in the storeroom at all times and should agree with the quantities on the materials ledger cards in the accounting department.

Issuing and Costing Materials

To control the quantity and cost of materials, supplies, and services requires a systematic and efficient system of purchasing, recording, and storing. Equally necessary is a systematic and efficient procedure for issuing materials and supplies.

Materials Requisition. The *materials requisition* is a written order to the storekeeper to deliver materials or supplies to the place designated or to give the materials to the person presenting a properly executed requisition. It is drawn by someone who has the authority to requisition materials for use in the department. The authorized employee may be a production control clerk, a department head, a supervisor, a group leader, an expediter, or a materials release analyst.

The materials requisition is the basic form used to withdraw materials from the storeroom. Its preparation results in entries in the Issued section of the materials ledger cards and in postings to the job order cost sheets, production reports, or the various expense analysis sheets for individual departments. All withdrawals result in debits to Work in Process or to control accounts for factory overhead, marketing expenses, or administrative expenses, and in credits to Materials. A materials requisition is illustrated as follows:

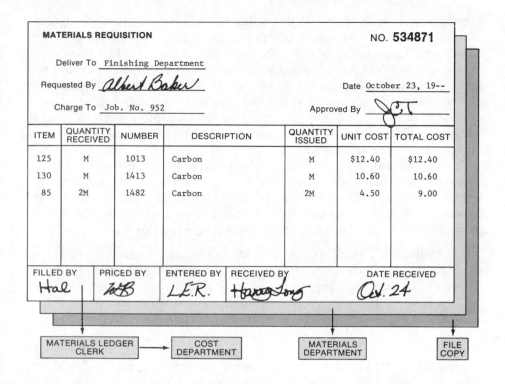

Materials Requisitioned Journal. With the posting to the materials ledger cards, the job order cost sheets, the production reports, and the expense analysis sheets completed, it is still necessary to post the materials withdrawals to the proper ledger control accounts. This task is greatly facilitated by the use of a *materials requisitioned journal*. This journal, illustrated as follows, is a form of materials summary. At the end of the month, the totals of the various columns are posted directly to the ledger accounts, except for the Sundries column, from which items are posted individually.

MATERIALS REQUISITIONED JOURNAL

Date		Credit Materials	Description	Req. No.	Job or Acct. No.	Work in Process	Factory Overhead Control	Marketing Expenses Control	Administrative Expenses Control	Sundries Acct. No.	Sundries Post. Ref.	Sundries Amount
19-- Oct.	1	600 00	Direct materials......	4101	5317	600 00						
	1	225 00	Indirect materials	4102	411		225 00					
	3	1,800 75	Direct materials......	4103	5318	1,800 75						
	3	195 50	For installation.......	4104						135	√	195 50
	4	75 00	Supplies.............	4105	630				75 00			
	4	112 80	Supplies.............	4106	530			112 80				
		41,160 90				36,400 00	2,280 00	1,525 40	760 00			195 50

Tabulating Cards as Materials Requisitions. In a computerized system, the computer program will often prepare the requisition in the form of a tabulating card. To produce the card, the computer is instructed by the console operator to perform certain materials issuance transactions for jobs or products. The card serves as authority for the storekeeper to issue the materials. Internal computer operations will update the materials data bank and job or product cost detail, and will eventually produce output reports. The totals included in these reports will be entered in the general ledger accounts, unless those accounts are also part of the EDP system.

Indirect materials or supplies for factory use will also be stored in the inventory data bank of the computer. When such materials are needed, a request will inform the computer as to type, quantity, and requesting department. Supplies requisitioned for marketing and administrative departments would be charged to their respective departments.

Bill of Materials. The *bill of materials,* a kind of master requisition, is a printed or duplicated form that lists all materials and parts necessary for a typical job or production run. Time is saved and efficiency is promoted through the use of a bill of materials. When a job or production run is started, all the materials listed on the bill of materials are sent to the factory or are issued on a prearranged time schedule. Since the bill of materials is a rather cumbersome medium for posting purposes, however, data processing improves the procedure by simultaneously preparing tabulating cards for materials requisitions. While the storekeeper issues the materials as stated on the bill of materials, the tabulating cards can be processed in the materials ledger section and in the cost department at almost the same time as the materials are used in the factory. A computer program will provide the printouts of the bill of materials and process the information internally to update the accounting records.

Materials Ledger Card — Perpetual Inventory

As purchased materials go through the systematic verification of quantities, prices, physical condition, and other checks, the crux of the accounting procedure is to establish a perpetual inventory — maintaining for each type of materials a record showing quantities and prices of materials received, issued, and on hand. In a perpetual inventory system, an entry is made each time the inventory is increased or reduced.

Materials ledger cards or stock ledger sheets constitute a subsidiary materials ledger controlled by the materials or inventory accounts in the general ledger or in the factory ledger. Materials ledger cards commonly show the account number, description or type of material, location, unit measurement, and maximum and minimum quantities to carry. These cards are the *materials ledger,* with new cards prepared and old ones discarded as changes occur in the types of materials carried in stock. The ledger card arrangement is basically the familiar debit, credit, and balance columns under the description of Received, Issued, and Balance, and is illustrated as follows:

MATERIALS LEDGER CARD

Piece or Part No. _____   Reorder Point _____

Description _____   Reorder Quantity _____

Maximum Quantity _____

Received				Issued				Balance		
Date	Rec. No.	Qty.	Amount	Date	Req. No.	Qty.	Amount	Quantity	Unit Cost	Amount

The approved invoice with supporting documents, such as the purchase order and receiving report, goes to the materials ledger clerk. These documents enable the clerk to make the necessary entries in the Received section of the materials ledger card. Each receipt increases the balance on hand, and the new balance is extended upon entry of the receipt.

Unsatisfactory goods or defective units should be detected by the inspection department before being stored or even paid for. The receiving report should show materials actually accepted, and the ledger entries are made after all adjustments. However, goods accepted in the storeroom may be found unsatisfactory after part of a shipment has been used in the factory, and the balance may then be returned to the vendor. Since these units were entered in the Received and Balance sections of the materials ledger card when they were placed in the storeroom, an adjustment must be made. The recommended procedure is to enter the quantity and the cost of the returned shipment in red in the Received section and to reduce the balance accordingly.

When the storekeeper issues materials, a copy of the requisition is sent to the materials ledger clerk, who then makes an entry in the Issued section of the materials ledger card, showing the date, requisition number, job, lot, or department number, quantity, and cost of the issued materials. The new balance is computed and entered in the Balance column. As already explained, these manual operations can be performed in an EDP system based on the computer program designed for materials transactions.

Physical Inventory. The alternative to a perpetual inventory system is the periodic inventory system, whereby purchases are added to the beginning inventory, the ending (remaining) inventory is counted and costed, and the difference is considered the cost of materials issued. Regardless of whether a periodic or a perpetual inventory system is used, periodic physical counts are necessary to discover and eliminate discrepancies between the actual count and the balances on materials ledger cards. These discrepancies may be due to: errors in transferring invoice data to the cards; mistakes in costing requisitions; unrecorded invoices or requisitions; or spoilage, breakage, and theft. In some enterprises, plant operations are suspended periodically during a seasonal low period or near the end of the fiscal year while a physical inventory is taken. In others, an inventory crew or members of the internal audit department make a count of one or more stock classes every day throughout the year, presumably on a well-planned schedule, so that every materials item will be inventoried at least once during the year.

Adjusting Materials Ledger Cards and Accounts to Conform to Inventory Count. When the inventory count differs from the balance on the materials ledger card, the ledger card is adjusted to conform to the actual count. If the ledger card balance shows more materials units than the inventory card, an entry is made in the Issued section, and the Balance section is reduced to equal the verified count. In case the materials ledger card balance is less than the physical count, the quantity difference may be entered in the Received section or may be entered in red in the Issued section, with the Balance section being increased to agree with the actual count.

In addition to the corrections on the materials ledger cards, the materials account must be adjusted for the increase or decrease. For example, if the inventory count is less than that shown on the materials ledger card, the following entry should be recorded:

	Subsidiary Record	Dr.	Cr.
Factory Overhead Control		xxxx	
Inventory Adjustment to Physical			
Count	xxxx		
Materials			xxxx

Materials Costing Methods

The ultimate objective in cost accounting is to produce accurate and meaningful figures for the cost of goods sold. These figures can be used for purposes of control and analysis and are eventually matched against revenue produced in order to determine operating income.

After the unit cost and total cost of incoming materials are entered in the Received section of a materials ledger card, the next step is to cost these materials as they move either from storeroom to factory as direct or indirect materials or from storeroom to marketing and administrative expense accounts as supplies. The more common methods of costing materials issued and inventories are:

1. First-in, first-out (fifo).
2. Average cost.
3. Last-in, first-out (lifo).
4. Other methods — such as market price at date of issue or last purchase price, and standard cost.

These methods relate to assumptions as to the flow of costs. The physical flow of units may coincide with the method of cost flow, though such a condition is not a necessary requirement. Although this discussion deals with materials inventory, the same costing methods are also applicable to work in process and finished goods inventories.

Previous discussion as well as the following illustrations assume a perpetual inventory system. Such a procedure is especially useful in enhancing materials control and is needed to accurately identify the various general and subsidiary ledger accounts to which materials issued should be charged. Cost flow assumptions other than fifo, however, may result in unit costs that differ, depending on whether the perpetual or periodic inventory system is used.

First-In, First-Out (Fifo) Method of Costing

The first-in, first-out (fifo) method of costing is used to introduce the subject of materials costing. This illustration is based on the following transactions:

Feb. 1. Beginning balance: 800 units @ $6 per unit.
    4. Received 200 units @ $7 per unit.
  10. Received 200 units @ $8 per unit.
  11. Issued 800 units.
  12. Received 400 units @ $8 per unit.
  20. Issued 500 units.
  25. Returned 100 excess units from the factory to the storeroom — to be recorded at the latest issued price (or at the actual issued price if physically identifiable).
  28. Received 600 units @ $9 per unit.

Calculations for these transactions would be as follows:

FIFO COSTING METHOD ILLUSTRATED

Feb.	1. Beginning balance	800 units @ $6 =	$4,800	
	4. Received	200 @ $7 =	1,400	
	10. Received	200 @ $8 =	1,600	$7,800
	11. Issued..............................	800 @ $6 =		4,800
	Balance........................	{200 @ $7 =	1,400	
		{200 @ $8 =	1,600	3,000
	12. Received	400 @ $8 =	3,200	6,200
	20. Issued..............................	{200 @ $7 =	1,400	
		{300 @ $8 =	2,400	3,800
	Balance........................	300 @ $8 =	2,400	
	25. Returned to storeroom...............	100 @ $8 =	800	
	28. Received	600 @ $9 =	5,400	8,600
	Balance........................	{400 @ $8 =	3,200	
		{600 @ $9 =	5,400	$8,600

The fifo method of costing issued materials follows the principle that materials used should carry the actual experienced cost of the specific units used. The method assumes that materials are issued from the oldest supply in stock and that the cost of those units when placed in stock is the cost of those same units when issued. However, fifo costing may be used even though physical withdrawal is in a different order. Advantages claimed for the fifo costing method are:

1. Materials used are drawn from the cost records in a logical and systematic manner.
2. Movement of materials in a continuous, orderly, single-file manner represents a condition necessary to and consistent with efficient materials control, particularly for materials subject to deterioration, decay, and quality or style changes.

The fifo method is recommended whenever (1) the size and cost of materials units are large, (2) materials are easily identified as belonging to a particular purchased lot, and (3) not more than two or three different receipts of the materials are on a materials card at one time. Fifo costing is definitely awkward if frequent purchases are made at different prices and if units from several purchases are on hand at the same time. Added costing difficulties arise when returns to vendors or to the storeroom occur.

Average Costing Method

Issuing materials at an average cost assumes that each batch taken from the storeroom is composed of uniform quantities from each shipment in stock at the date of issue. Often it is not feasible to mark or label each materials item with an invoice price in order to identify the used unit with its acquisition cost. It may be reasoned that units are issued more or less at random as far as the specific units and the specific costs are concerned and that an average cost of all units in stock at the time of issue is a satisfactory measure of materials cost. However, average costing may be used even though the physical withdrawal is in an identifiable order. If materials tend to be made up of numerous small items low in unit cost and especially if prices are subject to frequent change, average costing is advantageous because:

1. It is a realistic costing method useful to management in analyzing operating results and appraising future production.
2. It minimizes the effect of unusually high or low materials prices, thereby making possible more stable cost estimates for future work.
3. It is a practical and less expensive perpetual inventory system.

The average costing method divides the total cost of all materials of a particular class by the number of units on hand to find the average price. The cost of new invoices is added to the total in the Balance column; the units are added to the existing quantity; and the new total cost is divided by the new quantity to arrive at the new average cost. Materials are issued at the established average cost until a new purchase is recorded. Although a new average cost may be computed when materials are returned to vendors and when excess issues are returned to the storeroom, for practical purposes it seems sufficient to reduce or increase the total quantity and cost, allowing the unit price to remain unchanged. When a new purchase is made and a new average is computed, the discrepancy created by the returns will be absorbed.

Using the data of the fifo illustration (page 251), the transactions can be summarized as follows:

AVERAGE COSTING METHOD ILLUSTRATED

					Average Cost
Feb.	1. Beginning balance	800 units @ $6	= $4,800		
	4. Received	200 @ $7	= 1,400		
	Balance.	1,000		6,200	$6.20
	10. Received	200 @ $8	= 1,600		
	Balance.	1,200		7,800	6.50
	11. Issued	800 @ $6.50	= 5,200		
	Balance.	400		2,600	6.50
	12. Received	400 @ $8	= 3,200		
	Balance.	800		5,800	7.25
	20. Issued	500 @ $7.25	= 3,625		
	Balance.	300		2,175	7.25
	25. Returned to storeroom.	100		725	
	Balance.	400		2,900	7.25
	28. Received	600 @ $9	= 5,400		
	Balance.	1,000		$8,300	8.30

To insure quick costing and early reporting of completed jobs or products, some companies at the close of each month establish an average cost for each kind of material on hand and use this cost for all issues during the following month. When perpetual inventory costing procedures are not used, a variation of this method is to wait until the end of a costing period to compute the cost of materials consumed. The cost used is obtained by adding both quantities and dollars of purchases to beginning inventory figures, thus deriving an average cost.

Last-In, First-Out (Lifo) Method of Costing

The last-in, first-out (lifo) method of costing materials issued is based on the premise that materials units issued should carry the cost of the most recent purchase, although the physical flow may actually be different. The method assumes that the most recent cost (the approximate cost to replace the consumed units) is most significant in matching cost with revenue in the income determination procedure.

Under lifo procedures, the objective is to charge the cost of current purchases to work in process or other operating expenses and to leave the oldest costs in the inventory. Several alternatives can be used to apply the lifo method. Each procedure results in different costs for materials issued and the ending inventory, and consequently in a different profit. It is mandatory, therefore, to follow the chosen procedure consistently.

The fifo data on page 251 are used to illustrate lifo costing, as follows:

LIFO COSTING METHOD ILLUSTRATED

Feb.	1. Beginning balance	800 units	@ $6 =	$4,800	
	4. Received	200	@ $7 =	1,400	
	10. Received	200	@ $8 =	1,600	$7,800
	11. Issued........................... {	200	@ $8 =	1,600	
		200	@ $7 =	1,400	
		400	@ $6 =	2,400	5,400
	Balance	400	@ $6 =	2,400	
	12. Received	400	@ $8 =	3,200	5,600
	20. Issued........................... {	400	@ $8 =	3,200	
		100	@ $6 =	600	3,800
	Balance........................	300	@ $6 =	1,800	
	25. Returned to storeroom..............	100	@ $6 =	600	
	28. Received	600	@ $9 =	5,400	7,800
	Balance........................ {	400	@ $6 =	2,400	
		600	@ $9 =	5,400	$7,800

In this illustration, a new inventory balance is computed after each issue of materials, with the ending inventory consisting of 1,000 units valued at $7,800. If, however, a periodic rather than a perpetual inventory procedure is used, whereby the issues are determined at the end of the period by ignoring day-to-day issues and subtracting total ending inventory from the total of the beginning balance plus the receipts, the ending inventory would consist of:

800 units @ $6, on hand in the beginning inventory......................	$4,800
200 units @ $7, from the oldest purchase, Feb. 4........................	1,400
1,000 units, lifo inventory at the end of February	$6,200

Both procedures are often referred to as the *item-layer identification method* of applying lifo and are acceptable variations of the lifo method, even though the cost of materials used and the ending inventory figures differ.

Regardless of the cost flow assumption, the latter procedure is particularly appropriate in process costing where individual materials requisitions are seldom used and the materials move into process in bulk lots, as in flour mills, spinning mills, oil refineries, and sugar refineries. The procedure also functions smoothly for a company that charges materials to work in process from month-end consumption sheets which provide the cost department with quantities used.

Lifo Advantages and Disadvantages. The advantages of the lifo costing method are:

1. Materials consumed are priced in a systematic and realistic manner. It is argued that current acquisition costs are incurred for the purpose of meeting current production and sales requirements; therefore, the most recent costs should be charged against current production and sales.
2. Unrealized inventory gains and losses are minimized, and reported operating profits are stabilized in industries subject to sharp materials price fluctuations.

3. Inflationary prices of recent purchases are charged to operations in periods of rising prices, thus reducing profits, resulting in a tax saving, and therewith providing a cash advantage through deferral of income tax payments. The tax deferral creates additional working capital as long as the economy continues to experience an annual inflation rate increase.

The disadvantages of the lifo costing method are:

1. The election of lifo for income tax purposes is binding for all subsequent years unless a change is authorized or required by the Internal Revenue Service (IRS).[1]

2. Lifo is a "cost only" method, with no write-down to the lower of cost or market allowed for income tax purposes. Furthermore, the IRS requires that when lifo is adopted, an adjustment must be made to restore any previous write-downs from actual cost. Should the market decline below lifo cost in subsequent years, the business would be at a tax disadvantage. When prices drop, the only option may be to charge off the older (higher) costs by liquidating the inventory. However, liquidation for income tax purposes must take place at year end. According to IRS regulations, liquidation during the fiscal year is not acceptable if the inventory returns to its original level at the end of the year.[2]

3. Lifo must be used in financial statements if it is elected for income tax purposes. However, for financial reporting purposes, the lower of lifo cost or market can be used without violating IRS lifo conformity rules.[3]

4. Record keeping requirements under lifo, as well as fifo, are substantially greater than those under alternative costing and pricing methods.

5. Under lifo, the balance sheet reflects the earliest inventory costs incurred. Consequently, in periods of rising prices, the company's inventory, current and total assets, and stockholders' equity are understated.

Since the use of lifo reduces profits during periods of rising prices, managers whose rewards are based on immediate profits may not be inclined to use lifo. Therefore, if lifo is in the best interests of the firm, it may be necessary to modify the management reward system.

Dollar-Value Lifo. The item-layer identification method and the previous illustrations of the characteristics of lifo costing are generally not practicable for a company that has a wide variety of inventory items. The item-layer identification method is also particularly unsuitable for a company whose range or mix of inventory frequently changes. Use of this method under such

---

[1]*Internal Revenue Code,* Section 472 (e).
[2]*Regulations,* Section 1.472-2(b), (c), and (d).
[3]*Regulations,* Section 1.472-2(e) (1) and (7).

conditions virtually ensures frequent liquidation of lifo layers and a corresponding loss of the benefits from using lifo. As a result, companies in using lifo usually employ some version of the *dollar-value lifo method* for financial reporting and for income tax purposes.[4] This method reduces the cost of administering lifo and reduces the likelihood of liquidating lifo layers. Also, the income tax savings during periods of rising prices is greater if dollar-value lifo is used, rather than the item-layer identification method. Thus, units issued to jobs or products are costed according to the company's established cost flow assumptions, whatever they may be, and inventories are adjusted to dollar-value lifo figures.

The distinguishing feature of the dollar-value method is that similar inventory items are grouped into a pool and layers are determined, based upon the pool's total dollar changes. Under this method, the unit of measurement is the dollar rather than the quantity of goods.[5]

Other Materials Costing Methods

Although fifo, average cost, and lifo are commonly used methods of costing materials units into work in process, various other methods exist.

Market Price at Date of Issue or Last Purchase Price. Materials precisely standardized and traded on commodity exchanges, such as cotton, wheat, copper, or crude oil, are sometimes costed into production at the quoted price at date of issue. In effect, this procedure substitutes replacement cost for experienced or consumed cost and has the virtue of charging materials into production at a current and significant cost. This method of materials costing and that of using the last purchase price are often used for small, low-priced items.

Standard Cost. This method charges issued materials at a predetermined or estimated cost reflecting a normal or an expected future cost. Receipts and issues of materials are recorded in quantities only on the materials ledger cards or in the computer data bank, thereby simplifying the record keeping and reducing clerical or data processing costs.

For materials purchases, the difference between actual and standard cost is recorded in a purchase price variance account. The variance account enables management to observe the extent to which actual materials costs differ from planned objectives or predetermined estimates. Materials are charged into production at the standard price, thereby eliminating the erratic costing inherent in the actual cost methods. Standard quantities for normal production runs at standard prices enable management to detect trouble areas and take corrective action immediately. Materials pricing under standard costs is discussed in Chapters 17 and 18.

---

[4]*Regulations*, Section 1.472-8.

[5]For a detailed discussion of dollar-value lifo, retail-dollar-value lifo, and other simplifying procedures, see Jay M. Smith, Jr. and K. Fred Skousen, *Intermediate Accounting*, 8th ed. (Cincinnati: South-Western Publishing Co., 1984), Chapter 9.

Analysis and Comparison of Costing Methods

The several methods of costing materials represent industry's intense effort to measure costs. Undoubtedly, there is no one best method applicable to all situations. Methods may vary even within the same company, since the same method need not be used for the entire inventory of a business. Whatever method of costing is chosen, it should be followed consistently from period to period.

The various costing methods represent different views of the cost concept. The best method to use is the one that most clearly reflects periodic income when consumed cost is subtracted from current revenue. Perhaps no costing method will reflect consumed materials cost with complete accuracy at all times in all situations. The most appropriate method will, as nearly as possible, (1) relate current cost to current sales; (2) reflect the procurement, manufacturing, and sales policies of a particular company; and (3) carry forward to the new fiscal period a previously incurred residual cost which will be consumed in subsequent periods.

Adequate comparison of the various methods of costing is difficult and involved. However, certain generalizations can be made relative to the use of fifo, average cost, and lifo. In periods of rising prices, fifo costing will result in materials being charged out at lowest costs; lifo will result in materials being charged out at highest costs; and average costing will result in a figure between the two. In a period of falling prices, the reverse situation will develop, with fifo showing the highest cost of materials consumed, lifo showing the lowest cost of materials used, and average cost showing a result between the other two methods.

CASB Costing of Materials

In accounting for government contracts to which CASB regulations apply, materials may be charged directly to a contract if the contract is specifically identified at the time of purchase or manufacture. Materials drawn from company-owned inventory can be priced using fifo, lifo, average, or the standard costing method. However, the method(s) selected must be used consistently for similar categories of materials. Furthermore, the contractor must prepare in writing the procedure for accumulating and allocating the cost of materials.[6]

Transfer of Materials Cost to Finished Production

The ultimate, intended destination of direct materials is finished products delivered to customers. The cost of materials used on each job or in each department is transferred from the materials requisition to the job order cost

---

[6]*Standards, Rules and Regulations, Part 411*, "Accounting for Acquisition Costs of Materials" (Washington, D. C.: Cost Accounting Standards Board, 1975), p. 226.

sheet or to the cost of production report. When the job or process is completed, the effect of materials used, as well as labor distributed and factory overhead applied, is expressed in the following entry:

```
Finished Goods . . . . . . . . . . . . . . . . . . . . . . . . . . . . . . . . . . . . . . . . . . . . . . . . . . . .   xxxx
    Work in Process . . . . . . . . . . . . . . . . . . . . . . . . . . . . . . . . . . . . . . . . . . . . . . .         xxxx
```

In production devoted to filling specific orders, cost sheets should provide sufficient information relative to the cost of goods sold. If a considerable portion of production is to be used for stock, a finished goods ledger is advantageous in maintaining adequate and proper control over the inventory. The finished goods ledger, controlled by the finished goods account in the general ledger, is similar in form and use to materials ledger cards.

Some production may consist of components manufactured for use in subsequent manufacturing operations. If the units move directly into these operations, the transfer is simply from one departmental work in process account to the next. However, if the components must be held in inventory, their cost should be debited to Materials and credited to Work in Process.

Inventory Valuation at Cost or Market, Whichever Is Lower

American accounting tradition follows the practice of pricing year-end inventories (materials as well as work in process and finished goods) at *cost or market, whichever is lower.* This departure from any experienced cost basis is generally defended on the grounds of conservatism. A more logical justification for cost or market inventory valuation is that a full stock is necessary to expedite production and sales. If physical deterioration, obsolescence, and price declines occur, or if stock when finally utilized cannot be expected to realize its stated cost plus a normal profit margin, the reduction in inventory value is an additional cost of the goods produced and sold during the period when the decline in value occurred.

AICPA Cost or Market Rules

The American Institute of Certified Public Accountants (AICPA) takes the position that cost may properly be determined by any of the common methods already discussed in this chapter. The AICPA then says that cost must be abandoned in valuing inventory when the usefulness of goods is no longer as great as cost. This principle of *cost or residual useful cost, whichever is lower,* is described as follows:

> *Where there is evidence that the utility of goods, in their disposal in the ordinary course of business, will be less than cost, whether due to physical deterioration, obsolescence, changes in price levels, or other causes, the difference should be recognized as a loss of the current period. This is generally accomplished by stating such goods at a lower level commonly designated as* <u>market</u>.

As used in the phrase <u>lower of cost or market</u>, the term "market" means current replacement cost (by purchase or by reproduction, as the case may be) except that:
1. *Market should not exceed the net realizable value (i.e., estimated selling price in the ordinary course of business less reasonably predictable costs of completion and disposal); and*
2. *Market should not be less than net realizable value reduced by an allowance for an approximately normal profit margin.[7]*

In the AICPA's cost or market approach to inventory valuation, it is clear that the Institute does not hold that a replacement cost should be used for inventory value merely because it is lower than the acquisition cost figure. The real test is the usefulness of the inventory (whether it will sell at its cost). The position of the AICPA in regard to inventory valuation may be interpreted as follows:

1. In principle, inventories are to be priced at cost.
2. Where cost cannot be recovered upon sale in the ordinary course of business, a lower figure is to be used.
3. This lower figure is normally market replacement cost, except that the amount should not exceed the expected sales price less a deduction for costs yet to be incurred in making the sale. On the other hand, this lower market figure should not be less than the expected amount to be realized in the sale of the goods, reduced by a normal profit margin.

To illustrate, assume that a certain commodity sells for $1; the marketing expense is 20 cents; the normal profit is 25 cents. The lower of cost or market as limited by the foregoing concepts is developed in each case as follows:[8]

| | | | Market | | | |
Case	Cost	Replacement Cost	Floor (Estimated Sales Price Less Costs of Completion and Disposal and Normal Profit)	Ceiling (Estimated Sales Price Less Costs of Completion and Disposal)	Market (Limited by Floor and Ceiling Values)	Lower of Cost or Market
A	$.65	$ .70	$.55	$.80	$.70	$.65
B	.65	.60	.55	.80	.60	.60
C	.65	.50	.55	.80	.55	.55
D	.50	.45	.55	.80	.55	.50
E	.75	.85	.55	.80	.80	.75
F	.90	1.00	.55	.80	.80	.80

A: Market is not limited by floor or ceiling; cost is less than market.
B: Market is not limited by floor or ceiling; market is less than cost.
C: Market is limited to floor; market is less than cost.
D: Market is limited to floor; cost is less than market.
E: Market is limited to ceiling; cost is less than market.
F: Market is limited to ceiling; market is less than cost.

[7]*Accounting Research and Terminology Bulletins—Final Edition* (New York: American Institute of Certified Public Accountants, 1961), pp. 30–31.
[8]Adapted from Jay M. Smith, Jr. and K. Fred Skousen, *Intermediate Accounting,* 8th ed. (Cincinnati: South-Western Publishing Co., 1984), Chapter 9.

The lower of cost or market procedure may be applied to each inventory item, to major inventory groupings, or to the inventory as a whole. Application of this procedure to the individual inventory items will result in the lowest inventory value. However, application to inventory groups or to the inventory as a whole may provide a sufficiently conservative valuation with less effort. The application method selected by a company must be followed consistently from period to period. The mix within a group or within the total inventory should not change erratically from period to period, so that inventory value is not distorted by the mix changes.

Adjustments for Cost or Market, Whichever Is Lower

The problem of year-end inventory valuation is primarily a question of the materials cost consumed in products manufactured and sold to customers and the cost assignable to goods in inventory ready to move into production and available for sales the next fiscal period. This question is important, because the materials ledger cards would have to be adjusted for any change in unit prices if there is a departure from cost. However, the detailed task of changing hundreds and even thousands of cards may not be possible or at least may be cumbersome and time-consuming, since the lower of cost or market procedure may be applied to inventory groups or to the inventory as a whole, and since the new unit price generally is not available to the materials ledger clerk until some time after the year-end inventory is priced. Instead of adjusting the ledger cards, companies may create an inventory valuation account, as illustrated by the following journal entry:

	Subsidiary Record	Dr.	Cr.
Cost of Goods Sold (or Factory Overhead Control)...............................		5,000	
Inventory Adjustment—Lower of Cost or Market...................	5,000		
Materials—Allowance for Inventory Decline to Market			5,000

If the debit is to Factory Overhead Control, the effect is to increase the amount of the unfavorable factory overhead variance.

Use of the valuation account retains the cost of the inventory and at the same time reduces the materials inventory for statement purposes to the desired cost or market, whichever is lower valuation, without disturbing the materials ledger cards. The preceding entry should result in the following balance sheet presentation:

Materials, at cost...	$100,000	
Less allowance for inventory decline to market	5,000	
Materials, at cost or market, whichever is lower...............		$95,000

The net charge to Cost of Goods Sold may be shown in the cost of goods sold statement or deducted from the ending inventory at cost, thus increasing the cost of materials used. In the subsequent fiscal period, Materials—Allowance for Inventory Decline to Market is closed out to Cost of Goods Sold to the extent necessary to bring the materials consumed that are still carried at a higher cost to the desirable lower cost level.

Whenever the lower of cost or market procedure is applied to each inventory item and the adjustment of materials ledger cards to a lower market figure is not burdensome and the data are available early in the next year, the adjustment should be accomplished by dating the entry with the last day of the fiscal period just ended and entering in the Balance section the units on hand at the unit price determined for inventory purposes. In such a case, the credit portion of the adjusting entry would be to the materials account.

Inventory Pricing and Interim Financial Reporting

Companies should generally use the same inventory pricing methods and make provisions for write-downs to market at interim dates on the same basis as used at annual dates when preparing published financial statements. However, the following exceptions are appropriate at interim reporting dates:

1. Some companies use estimated gross profit rates to determine the cost of goods sold during interim periods or use other methods different from those used at annual inventory dates. These companies should disclose the method used at the interim date and any significant adjustments that result from reconciliations with the annual physical inventory.
2. Companies that use the lifo method may encounter a liquidation of base period inventories at an interim date that is expected to be replaced by the end of the annual period. In such cases the inventory at the interim reporting date should not give effect to the lifo liquidation, and cost of sales for the interim reporting period should include the expected cost of replacement of the liquidated lifo base.
3. Inventory losses from market declines should not be deferred beyond the interim period in which the decline occurs. Recoveries of such losses on the same inventory in later interim periods of the same fiscal year through market price recoveries should be recognized as gains in the later interim period. Such gains should not exceed previously recognized losses. Some market declines at interim dates, however, can reasonably be expected to be restored in the fiscal year. Such *temporary* market declines need not be recognized at the interim date since no loss is expected to be incurred in the fiscal year.[9]

The second exception indicates that if the liquidation of base period inventories is considered temporary and is expected to be replaced prior to year

---

[9]*Opinions of the Accounting Principles Board, No. 28,* "Interim Financial Reporting" (New York: American Institute of Certified Public Accountants, 1973), par. 14.

end, the company should charge Cost of Goods Sold at current prices. The difference between the carrying value of the inventory and its current replacement cost is a current liability for replacement of temporarily depleted lifo base inventory. When the liquidated inventory is replaced, inventory is debited for the original lifo value, and the liability is removed from the books.

Costing Procedures for Scrap, Spoiled Goods, and Defective Work

Generally, manufacturing operations cannot escape the occurrence of certain losses or output reduction due to scrap, spoilage, or defective work. Management and the entire personnel of an organization should cooperate to reduce such losses to a minimum. As long as they occur, however, they must be reported and controlled.

Scrap and Waste

In many manufacturing processes, waste and scrap result from (1) the processing of materials, (2) defective and broken parts, (3) obsolete stock, (4) revisions or abandonment of experimental projects, and (5) worn out or obsolete machinery. This scrap should be collected and placed in storage for sale to scrap dealers. At the time of sale, the following entry may be made:

Cash (or Accounts Receivable)	xxxx	
Scrap Sales (or Factory Overhead Control)		xxxx

The amount realized from the sale of scrap and waste can be treated in two ways with respect to the income statement:

1. The amount accumulated in Scrap Sales may be closed directly to Income Summary and shown on the income statement under Other Income.
2. The amount may be credited to Factory Overhead Control, thus reducing the total factory overhead expense and thereby the cost of goods manufactured.

When scrap is collected from a job or department, the amount realized from the sale of scrap is often treated as a reduction in the materials cost charged to the individual job or product. In this case, the entry to record the sale would be:

Cash (or Accounts Receivable)	xxxx	
Work in Process		xxxx

When the quantity and value of scrap material is relatively high, it should be stored in a designated place under the supervision of a storekeeper. One of the following procedures may then be used:

1. The materials ledger clerk may open a materials ledger card, filling in the quantity only. The dollar value would not be needed. When the scrap is sold, the entries and treatment of the income item might be handled as discussed previously.

2. The quantity as well as the dollar value of the scrap delivered to the storekeeper may be recorded. The value would be based on scrap prices quoted on the market at the time of entry. The entry would be:

Scrap Materials	xxxx	
Scrap Sales (or Work in Process or Factory Overhead		
Control)		xxxx

When the scrap is sold, the entry would be:

Cash (or Accounts Receivable)	xxxx	
Scrap Materials		xxxx

[handwritten margin note: Scrap in inventoried value @ LCM]

Any difference between the price at the time the inventory is recorded and the price realized at the time of sale would be a plus or minus adjustment in the scrap sales account, the work in process account, or the factory overhead control account, consistent with the account credited in the first entry.

To reduce accounting for scrap to a minimum, often no entry is made until the scrap is actually sold. At that time, Cash or Accounts Receivable is debited while Scrap Sales is credited. This method is expedient and is justified when a more accurate accounting becomes expensive and burdensome, the scrap value is relatively small, or the price is uncertain.

Proceeds from the sale of scrap are in reality a reduction in production cost. As long as the amounts are relatively small, the accounting treatment is not a major consideration. What is important is an effective scrap control system based on periodic reporting to responsible supervisory personnel. Timely scrap reports for each producing department call attention to unexpected items and unusual amounts and should induce prompt corrective action.

Spoiled Goods

Cost accounting should provide product costs and cost control information. In the case of spoilage, the first requirement is to know the nature and cause of the spoiled units. The second requirement, the accounting problem, is to record the cost of spoiled units and to accumulate spoilage costs and report them to responsible personnel for corrective action.

Attaining the degree of materials and machine precision and the perfection of labor performance necessary to eliminate spoiled units entirely would involve costs far in excess of a normal or tolerable level of spoilage. In job order costing, if spoilage is normal and happens at any time and at any stage of the productive process, its cost should be treated as factory overhead, included in the predetermined factory overhead rate, and prorated over all production of a period. If, on the other hand, normal spoilage is caused by exacting specifications, difficult processing, or other unusual and unexpected factors, the spoilage cost should be charged to that order. In either case, the cost of abnormal spoilage should be charged to factory overhead and, since abnormal spoilage is not included in the overhead rate, an unfavorable factory overhead variance is created.

The following discussion of accounting for spoiled goods pertains to job order costing. The appropriate procedures for process costing were covered in Chapter 4.

Spoiled Materials Charged to Total Production. Nevada Products Company has a monthly capacity to manufacture 125,000 three-inch coil springs for use in mechanical brakes. Production is scheduled in response to orders received. Spoilage is caused by a variety of unpredictable factors and averages $.05 per spring. During November, 100,000 springs were produced, with a materials cost of $.40 per unit, a labor cost of $.50 per unit, and factory overhead charged to production at a rate of 150% of the direct labor cost. This rate is based on an estimate that includes $.05 per spring for spoilage. The entry to record work put into production during the month is:

Work in Process	165,000	
Materials		40,000
Payroll		50,000
Applied Factory Overhead		75,000

On the last working day of the month, the entire day's production of 4,000 units is spoiled due to improper heat treatment; however, these units can be sold for $.50 each in the secondhand market. To record this normal loss on spoiled goods and the possible resale value, the entry that charges all production during the period with a proportionate share of the spoilage is:

	Subsidiary Record	Dr.	Cr.
Spoiled Goods		2,000	
Factory Overhead Control		4,600	
Loss on Spoiled Goods	4,600		
Work in Process			6,600

The materials, labor, and factory overhead in the spoiled units, reduced by the recovery or sales value of these units ($1,600 materials + $2,000 labor + $3,000 factory overhead − $2,000 cost recovery = $4,600 spoilage loss) is transferred from Work in Process to Factory Overhead Control. Each of the 96,000 good units produced during the month has a charged-in cost of $.05 for spoilage (96,000 × $.05 = $4,800); the actual spoilage during the period is $4,600).

The good units produced during the week or on the order where spoilage did occur carry a cost of $.40 for materials, $.50 for labor, and $.75 for overhead because spoilage is charged to all production — not to the lot or order which happens to be in process at the time of spoilage. In other words, the $165,000 monthly production cost less the $6,600 credit resulting from spoiled units leaves $158,400 to be divided by the 96,000 good units manufactured during the month at a cost of $1.65 per good unit. The entry transferring the good units to Finished Goods is:

Finished Goods	158,400	
Work in Process		158,400

During the month, the amounts charged to Factory Overhead Control represent the depreciation, insurance, taxes, indirect materials, and indirect labor actually experienced, along with the $4,600 spoilage cost. All production during the month is charged with overhead of $.75 per unit. Overhead analysis reveals a $200 favorable variance ($4,600 actual minus $4,800 applied) attributable to the spoilage units. Any difference between the price when the inventory was recorded and the price realized at the time of sale would be a plus or minus adjustment to Factory Overhead Control (Loss on Spoiled Goods).

Spoiled Materials Charged to a Particular Job. Nevada Products Company has a contract to manufacture 10,000 heavy-duty coil springs for the Tri-State Supply Company. This order requires a steel wire that is harder and slightly heavier than stock normally used, but the production process, as well as labor time and overhead factors, is identical with the standard product. Materials cost for each of these springs is $.60. This special order requires exacting specifications, and normal spoilage is to be charged to the order. The $.05 per unit spoilage factor is now eliminated from the overhead rate, and 140% of direct labor cost, or $.70 per unit, is the rate used on this job. The order is put into production the first day of December, and sampling during the first hour of production indicates that eleven units of production are required to secure ten good springs. The entry to record costs placed into production for 11,000 units is:

Work in Process	19,800		
Materials		6,600	11,000 × .60
Payroll		5,500	11,000 × .50
Applied Factory Overhead		7,700	140% × 5500

One thousand units, a normal number, did not meet specifications and are spoiled but can be sold as seconds for $.45 per unit. The entry to record the spoilage is:

Spoiled Goods	450	
Work in Process		450

The entry transferring the completed order to Finished Goods would be:

Finished Goods	19,350	
Work in Process		19,350

The net result of this treatment is to charge the spoilage loss of $1,350 ($1,800 − $450 cost recovery) to the 10,000 good units that are delivered at the original contract price. The unit cost of completed springs is $1.935 ($19,350 ÷ 10,000 units).

Any difference between the price when the inventory was recorded and the price realized at the time of sale should be an adjustment to Work in Process, Finished Goods, or Cost of Goods Sold, depending on the completion status of the particular job order. As an expedient, the difference might be closed to Factory Overhead Control.

Defective Work

In the manufacturing process, imperfections may arise because of faults in materials, labor, or machines. If the unit can be reprocessed in one or more stages and made into a standard salable product, it is often profitable to rework the defective unit. Although spoiled work cannot usually be made into a first-class finished unit without uneconomical expenditures, defective work can be corrected to meet specified standards by adding materials, labor, and factory overhead.

Two methods of accounting for the added cost to upgrade defective work are appropriate, depending upon the circumstances:

1. If defective work is experienced in regular manufacturing, the additional cost to correct defective units (based on previous experience) is included in the predetermined factory overhead and in the resulting factory overhead rate, actual rework cost is charged to Factory Overhead Control, and any difference appears as a factory overhead variance.

   To illustrate, assume that a company has an order for 500 units of a product that has direct production costs of $5 for materials and $3 for labor, with factory overhead charged to production at 200% of labor cost, including a 5% allowance for reworking defective units. Fifty units are found to be defective and are to be reworked at a total cost of $30 for materials, $60 for labor, and overhead at 200% of direct labor cost. The entries are:

	Subsidiary Record	Dr.	Cr.
Work in Process		7,000	
Materials			2,500
Payroll			1,500
Applied Factory Overhead			3,000
Factory Overhead Control		210	
Defective Work	210		
Materials			30
Payroll			60
Applied Factory Overhead			120
Finished Goods		7,000	
Work in Process			7,000

The unit cost of the completed units is $14 ($7,000 ÷ 500 units).

2. Suppose, however, that the same company received a special order for 500 units, with the agreement stating that any defective work is chargeable to the contract. During production, 50 units are improperly assembled. The total cost to correct these defective units is $30 for materials, $60 for labor, and 195% of the direct labor cost for factory overhead. Observe that the factory overhead rate has been reduced by the 5% allowance for reworking defective units, because the rework cost is to be charged directly to the job instead of to factory overhead. The entries in this case are:

Work in Process	6,925	
Materials..		2,500
Payroll..		1,500
Applied Factory Overhead...............................		2,925
Work in Process	207	
Materials..		30
Payroll..		60
Applied Factory Overhead...............................		117
Finished Goods...	7,132	
Work in Process		7,132

rework is charged to the job.

The unit cost is $14.264 ($7,132 ÷ 500 units) instead of $14.

Summary of Materials Management

Materials managers are constantly confronted with these problems and requirements:

1. Inventories account for a large portion of the working capital requirements of most businesses. This fact makes materials and/or inventory management a major problem requiring constant attention by all three management levels.
2. At present, the problem of materials management has become even more acute due to market conditions and inflation.
3. Effective materials management and materials control is found in an organization in which individuals have been vested with responsibility for, and authority over, the various details of procuring, maintaining, and disposing of inventory. Such a person or persons must have the ability to obtain, coordinate, and evaluate the necessary facts and to take action when and where needed.

DISCUSSION QUESTIONS

1. List the forms most frequently used in the procurement and use of materials.

2. Should formal purchase requisitions and purchase orders be prepared for the purchase of incidental supplies, services, and repairs? Explain.

3. How is an invoice approved for payment?

4. If a firm purchases raw materials from its supplier on a 2/10, n/60 cash discount basis, what is the equivalent annual interest rate (using a 360-day year) of forgoing the cash discount?

5. A client who wishes to include as a part of the cost of materials all of the cost of acquiring and handling incoming materials wants to know:
   (a) The principal items that may enter into the cost of materials acquisition and handling.
   (b) The arguments favoring the inclusion of these items as a part of materials in storage.
   (c) The arguments against inclusion of these items as a part of the cost of materials in storage.   (AICPA adapted)

6. A company's own power plant uses coal as the principal fuel. Coal is delivered by rail and stored in an open field close to the powerhouse, from which it is fed into furnaces by conveyor belts. What method should be used to determine coal consumption during a time period and the coal on hand at the end of the period?

7. A company using a periodic inventory system neglected to record a purchase of materials on account at year end. These materials were omitted from the year-end physical count. How will these errors affect assets, liabilities, and stockholders' equity at year end, and operating income for the year?

8. Describe the fundamental cost flow assumptions of the average cost, fifo, and lifo inventory costing methods.

9. Discuss the reasons for using lifo in an inflationary economy.

10. Proponents of lifo and fifo procedures ascribe certain merits to each. Identify the inventory procedure, lifo or fifo, to which the following features are attributed:
    (a) Matches actual physical flow of goods.
    (b) Matches old costs with new prices.
    (c) Costs inventory at approximate replacement cost.
    (d) Matches new costs with new prices.
    (e) Emphasizes the balance sheet.
    (f) Emphasizes the income statement.
    (g) Opens door for profit manipulation.
    (h) Understates the current ratio in a period of inflation.
    (i) Overstates inventory turnover in a period of inflation.
    (j) Gives higher profits in a period of inflation.
    (k) Matches current cost with current revenue.
    (l) Reflects more accurately the profit available to owners.
    (m) Gives lower profits in a period of deflation.
    (n) Results in a procession of costs in the same order as incurred.   (CGAA adapted)

11. Does the method of inventory costing have its principal effect on the balance sheet or on the income statement?

12. When there is evidence that the utility of goods, in their disposal in the ordinary course of business, will be less than cost, what is the proper accounting treatment and under what concept is that treatment justified?
       (AICPA adapted)

13. Several methods of accounting for scrap materials are discussed in this chapter. Which method could be regarded as most accurate?

14. In the control of materials cost, why is the knowledge that there is excessive waste likely to be of greater value than the income derived from the sale of scrap?

15. In some situations, labor and materials costs incurred on defective work are treated as factory overhead. In other cases the cost of perfecting defective work is charged directly to the job. Explain the appropriate use of each accounting treatment.

EXERCISES

1. *Freight-in allocation.* An invoice for Pepto, Lenco, and Bilco is received from Wellright Company. Invoice totals are: Pepto, $1,125; Lenco, $1,350; Bilco, $1,575. The freight charges on this shipment of 1,800 pounds total $162. Weights for the respective materials are 450, 600, and 750 pounds.

Required:
   (1) Allocate freight to materials, based on cost.
   (2) Allocate freight to materials, based on shipping weight.

2. *Materials costing methods.* Seltzer Company made the following materials purchases and issues during January:

Inventory: January 1.—500 units @ $1.20	Issues: January 15.—560
Receipts: January 6.—200 @ 1.25	27.—400
10.—400 @ 1.30	
25.—500 @ 1.40	

Required: Compute the cost of materials consumed and the cost assigned to the inventory at the end of the month, using a perpetual inventory system and:
   (1) Average costing, rounding unit costs to the nearest cent.
   (2) Fifo costing.
   (3) Lifo costing.

3. *Materials costing methods.* The following information is to be used in costing inventory on October 31:

   October 1. Beginning balance: 800 units @ $6
            5. Purchased 200 units @ $7
            9. Purchased 200 units @ $8
           16. Issued 400 units
           24. Purchased 300 units @ $9
           27. Issued 500 units

Required: Compute the cost of materials used and the cost assigned to the October 31 inventory by each of these perpetual inventory costing methods:
   (1) First-in, first-out.
   (2) Last-in, first-out.
   (3) Average, using a materials ledger card and rounding unit costs to the nearest cent.
   (4) Market price at date of issue.

4. *Average costing method—perpetual and periodic inventory costing.* The following information was available from Alexander Company's January inventory records:

	Units	Unit Cost	Total Cost
Balance at January 1	2,000	$ 9.775	$19,550
Received			
January 6	1,500	10.300	15,450
January 26	3,400	10.750	36,550
Issued			
January 7	1,800		
January 31	3,200		
Balance at January 31	1,900		

Required: *Compute the cost of materials used and the cost assigned to the January 31 inventory, using (a) perpetual inventory records and the average costing method, and (b) the periodic inventory costing system at average cost. For (b), round the unit cost to the nearest cent and add the rounding difference to the cost of materials used.*

(AICPA adapted)

5. Materials costing methods. *Lee Company, a wholesaler, made the following purchases of Material X during 19A:*

January 7.................	8,000 units	@	$12.00	$ 96,000
March 30	8,800	@	12.40	109,120
May 10....................	12,000	@	12.00	144,000
July 5	16,000	@	12.60	201,600
September 2...............	6,400	@	12.80	81,920
December 14	7,200	@	12.68	91,296
	58,400			$723,936

The December 31, 19A inventory was 15,200 units, and on January 1, 19A, 4,000 units at $11.92 each were on hand. The sales price during the year was stable at $16.

Required:
(1) Prepare a schedule of December 31, 19A inventory, assuming a periodic inventory system and lifo as the costing method.
(2) Prepare a statement showing Material X's sales, cost of goods sold, and gross profit for 19A, assuming the fifo costing method.   *(CGAA adapted)*

6. Inventory costing method related to income computation. *Ajax Company uses lifo in costing inventory. During its first three years of operations, the year-end inventory, computed by different methods for comparative purposes, was as follows:*

	Ending Inventory		
	19A	19B	19C
Lifo	$360,000	$400,000	$320,000
Fifo	300,000	320,000	280,000
Average cost	340,000	420,000	300,000

Operating income computed using the lifo method was: 19A, $80,000; 19B, $140,000; 19C, $60,000.

Required: *Determine operating income, using the (a) fifo method and (b) average cost method.*   *(CGAA adapted)*

7. Fifo, lifo, and cash flow. *Due to rising prices for materials, the problem of using the most appropriate inventory costing method has become acute. With the wide variety of methods available to account for inventories, it is important to select one that will be the most beneficial for a company. To illustrate, assume that two companies are almost identical, except that one uses fifo and the other lifo costing. Both companies have a beginning inventory of 200 units @ $2 per unit. The ending inventory is 240 units. The price paid for all purchases during the fiscal period was $2.40, and sales totaled 180 items at a sales price of $3.60. The income tax rate is 50% for both companies.*

Required:
(1) Compute the amount of total materials available for sale.
(2) Prepare income statements showing aftertax earnings for both companies.
(3) Compute the cost assigned to the ending inventory, based on the fifo and lifo

costing methods.

(4) *Determine the cash position at the end of the fiscal year, assuming that all trans-actions, materials purchases, sales, and income tax were paid in cash.*

(5) *Write a brief evaluation of the results.*

8. *Inventory valuation at cost or market, whichever is lower.* The following pertinent factors and simplified figures are available for five situations:

	Situation				
	1	2	3	4	5
Cost..	$100	$100	$100	$40	$100
Net realizable value	80	80	80	80	80
Net realizable value less normal profit	50	50	50	50	50
Market (replacement cost)	60	90	40	30	110

Required: *Determine the inventory value for each situation, based on the AICPA rule.*

9. *Inventory valuation at cost or market, whichever is lower.* The following information has been gathered for four inventory items:

Item	Original Cost	Replacement Cost	Sales Price	Estimated Cost to Complete and Sell	Normal Profit Margin
Delta	$ .67	$ .62	$ .72	$ .04	$ .08
Sigma	2.20	2.12	2.22	.12	.08
Beta	.19	.20	.24	.03	.01
Nu	.93	.87	.97	.05	.04

Required: *Determine the unit value that would be assigned to each item for inventory valuation purposes, using the lower of cost or market as defined by the AICPA.*

10. *Journal entries to correct materials accounts.* The following transactions were completed by the Patterson Company:

(a) *The inventory of materials on the average costing basis was $4,200 and repre-sented a book quantity of 8,000 units. An actual count showed 7,780 units.*

(b) *Materials of $150 issued to Job 182 should have been charged to the Repair Department.*

(c) *Excess materials returned from the factory amounted to $382 for Job 257.*

(d) *Materials returned to vendor amounted to $165. Freight out on this shipment, to be borne by the Patterson Company, was $14, paid in cash.*

(e) *Finished goods returned by customers: cost, $1,500; sales price, $2,100.*

(f) *Materials requisitions totaled $4,814.50, of which $214.50 represented supplies used.*

(g) *Materials purchased and placed in stockroom, $6,150, of which $500 represented supplies. Freight in paid, applicable to direct materials, was $70.*

(h) *Supplies returned to the storeroom, $150.*

(i) *Scrap materials sent to the storeroom, valued at sales price (debit Scrap Materials):*

> From direct materials $190
> From supplies 10

(j) *Spoiled work received in storeroom: original cost, $60; sales value, $20. Loss is charged to total production.*

(k) *Scrap was sold for $250 cash; the book value of the scrap was $200 [see (i)].*

Required: Prepare the general ledger entries or adjustments, if any, for each of the above transactions. Carry all computations to three decimal places. Indicate the appropriate subsidiary ledger account for debits or credits to Factory Overhead Control.

11. Accounting for spoiled work. Quitman Company had a production run of 4,000 pairs of jeans during the last week of June, with these unit costs:

Direct materials	$ 5.00
Direct labor	4.00
Factory overhead (includes a $.50 allowance for spoiled work)	3.50
	$12.50

Final inspection revealed that 300 pairs, a normal number, did not meet quality standards, but can be sold as seconds at a price of $6 a pair.

Required: Prepare journal entries for all of the described transactions if:
(1) The loss is charged to all production.
(2) The loss is due to exacting specifications and charged to the production run.

12. Journal entries to correct defective work. Columbus Fabricators manufacture golf carts and other recreational equipment. One order from Wisconsin Wholesale Company for 1,000 carts showed the following costs per unit: direct materials, $40; direct labor, $20; and factory overhead applied at 140% of direct labor cost if defective work is charged to a specific job and 150% if it is not.

Final inspection revealed that wheels were assembled with improper bearings. The wheels were disassembled and the proper bearings inserted. The cost of correcting each defective cart consists of $2 added cost for bearings, $4 for labor, and factory overhead at the predetermined rate.

Required: Prepare journal entries to record correction of the defective units and transfer of the work in process to finished goods if:
(1) The Wisconsin Wholesale Company order is to be charged with the cost of defective units.
(2) The cost of correcting the defective work is not charged to Wisconsin Wholesale Company order.

PROBLEMS

10-1. Applied acquisition costs. Zang Industries, Inc. records incoming materials at invoice price less cash discounts plus applied receiving and handling cost. For product Zingo, the following data are available:

	Budgeted for the Month	Actual Cost for the Month
Freight in and cartage in	$ 1,500	$ 1,580
Purchasing Department cost	4,800	4,500
Receiving Department cost	3,900	4,200
Storage and handling	4,200	3,800
Testing, spoilage, and rejects	2,600	3,120
Total	$17,000	$17,200

The purchasing budget shows estimated net purchases of $136,000 for the month; actual invoices net of discounts total $141,500 for the month.

Required:

(1) Determine the applied acquisition costing rate for the month.

(2) Determine the amount of applied cost added to materials purchased during the month.

(3) Indicate the possible disposition to be made of the variance.

10-2. Materials costing methods. A corporation that uses a perpetual inventory system had the following transactions during June:

> June 1. Beginning balance: 200 units @ $3.00 per unit.
> 2. Purchased 500 units @ $3.20 per unit.
> 7. Issued 400 units.
> 11. Purchased 300 units @ $3.30 per unit.
> 14. Issued 400 units.
> 17. Purchased 400 units @ $3.20 per unit.
> 21. Issued 200 units.
> 24. Purchased 300 units @ $3.40 per unit.
> 26. Purchased 400 units @ $3.50 per unit.
> 29. Issued 600 units.

Sales were 1,600 units @ $7 per unit; marketing and administrative expenses totaled $2,100.

Required:

(1) Prepare comparative income statements based on the transactions for June, using the lifo and fifo methods and a 40% income tax rate.

(2) For each costing method, determine the cash position at the end of June, assuming that all transactions, purchases, sales, and nonmanufacturing expenses were paid in cash.

10-3. Materials costing methods. During 19A, the records of Redgrave Trading Company show the following information about Item A:

Balance on January 1, 200 units @ $10 per unit.

	Purchased Units	Purchase Price per Unit	Sales Units
January 12......................	100	$11	
February 1			200
April 16......................	200	12	
May 1........................			100
July 15	100	14	
November 10			100
December 5	200	17	
	600		400

The Item A selling price throughout 19A was $20.

Required:

(1) Determine the cost of the ending inventory under the fifo method when a periodic inventory system is followed.

(2) Determine the cost of the ending inventory under the lifo method when perpetual inventory records are maintained.

(3) Prepare the required journal entry or entries to record the sale on account and the cost of the goods sold on February 1, assuming that perpetual inventory records are maintained and the lifo method is used.   (CGAA adapted)

10-4. Inventory costing and valuation. Alberta, Ltd. uses perpetual inventory costing for inventory Item 407, which it purchases for resale. The company began its operations on January 1 and is in the process of preparing its first financial statements.

Upon examining the inventory ledger and other accounting records, the following information was gathered pertaining to the first four months of operations:

Purchases			Sales	
	Units	Cost per Unit		Units
January 2..........	2,000	$5	January 15...............	500
February 2	1,200	6	January 31...............	700
March 2...........	1,500	8	February 15	600
April 2	1,900	7	February 28	900
			March 15	600
			March 31	800
			April 15	700
			April 30	700

On April 30, the following additional information was obtained:

(a) Current replacement cost, $6.50 per unit.
(b) Net realizable value, $8 per unit.
(c) Net realizable value reduced by a normal profit margin, $5 per unit.

Management has not decided which of the following three inventory costing methods should be selected to evaluate the cost of goods sold:

(a) Average method.
(b) First-in, first-out method.
(c) Last-in, first-out method.

Required:
(1) Prepare the perpetual inventory ledger for Item 407, using each of the above methods. (Carry all computations to three decimal places.)
(2) Prepare a comparative statement showing the effect of each method on gross profit. The sales price is $10 per unit.
(3) Prepare the necessary adjusting journal entry under each of the three inventory costing methods, assuming that the company decides to show its April 30 inventory at the lower of cost or market. (CGAA adapted)

10-5. Inventory valuation at cost or market, whichever is lower. The following information is available for five cases:

	Case				
	1	2	3	4	5
Cost.................................	$2.00	$2.00	$2.00	$2.00	$2.00
Net realizable value....................	1.30	2.05	1.80	2.40	1.90
Net realizable value less normal profit ...	1.10	1.85	1.60	2.20	1.70
Market (replacement cost)	1.20	2.10	1.85	2.15	1.60

Required:
(1) Determine the proper inventory price per unit for each case, using the AICPA lower of cost or market rules.
(2) Determine the proper inventory price per unit in Case 5, assuming that the item is also in stock at the end of the next fiscal period and that the four values are $2.00, $1.90, $1.70, and $2.05, respectively.

(3) Indicate the circumstances under which freight in might be excluded from the determination of inventory cost, with comments on the propriety of the exclusions.

(4) List other materials-related costs that might similarly be excluded from inventory cost.

10-6. Fifo and cost or market, whichever is lower. Kenny Company, a food wholesaler, supplies independent grocery stores in the immediate region. The company has a fifo inventory system for all of its food products. Kenny records all purchases net of purchase discounts and takes all purchase discounts. The following transactions and other related information regarding two items (instant coffee and sugar) are given for October, the last month of Kenny's fiscal year:

	Instant Coffee	Sugar
Standard unit of packaging:	Case containing 24 one-pound jars	Baler containing 12 five-pound bags
Inventory, October 1:	1,200 cases @ $53.22 per case	600 balers @ $6.50 per baler
Purchases (before purchase discount):	October 10–1,600 cases @ $56.40 per case plus freight of $480.	October 5–640 balers @ $5.76 per baler, plus freight of $320.
	October 20–1,600 cases @ $57 per case plus freight of $480.	October 16–640 balers @ $5.40 per baler, plus freight of $320.
		October 24–640 balers @ $5.04 per baler, plus freight of $320.
Purchase terms:	2/10, net/30, FOB shipping point	Net 30 days, FOB shipping point
October sales:	3,400 cases @ $76 per case	2,200 balers @ $7.80 per baler
Sales terms:	1/10, net/30, FOB shipping point	1/10, net/30, FOB shipping point
Returns and allowances:	A customer returned 50 cases which had been shipped by error. The customer's account was credited for $3,800.	As the October 16 purchase was unloaded, 20 balers were discovered to be damaged. A representative of the trucking firm confirmed the damage and the balers were discarded. Credit of $108 for the merchandise and $10 for the freight was received by Kenny.
October 31:		
Most recent quoted price (before deducting purchase discount; excluding freight)	$56.65 per case	$5.30 per baler
Net realizable value	$60.80 per case	$5.20 per baler
Net realizable value less a normal markup	$53.20 per case	$4.55 per baler

Required:
(1) Compute the number of units in inventory and the related unit cost for instant coffee and sugar as of October 31.
(2) Compute the total dollar amount of the October 31 instant coffee and sugar inventory, applying the AICPA lower of cost or market rule on an individual product basis.
(3) State whether or not the company could apply the lower of cost or market rule to groups of products or to the inventory as a whole, rather than on an individual product basis.   (CMA adapted)

10-7. Journal entries for spoiled work. Fashioncraft Company had a production run of 8,000 pairs of slacks during the last week of June, at the following costs:

	Per Pair
Materials	$5
Labor	4
Factory overhead (includes $.70 allowance for spoiled work)	3

Final inspection revealed 600 pairs as not meeting quality standards, salable as seconds at $4 a pair.

Required: Prepare the journal entries to record all related costs if:
(1) The loss is to be charged to the production run.
(2) The loss is to be charged to all production of the fiscal period.

10-8. Journal entries to correct defective work. Los Angeles Fabricators manufactures jacks and other lifting equipment. One order from Seattle Supply House for 1,000 jacks showed the following costs per unit: materials, $5; labor, $1.75; factory overhead applied at 160% of direct labor cost (150% in cases in which any defective unit costs are to be charged to a specific order).

Final inspection revealed that 75 of the units were improperly riveted. To correct each defective unit requires $.20 for materials, $.30 for labor, and factory overhead at the appropriate rate.

Required: Prepare entries to record all costs related to the order when the:
(1) Order is charged with the cost of defective work.
(2) Cost of correcting defective work is not charged to a specific order.

CASES

A. Purchasing procedures. Long, CPA, has been engaged to examine and report on the financial statements of Maylou Corporation. During the review phase of the study of Maylou's system of internal accounting control over purchases, Long was given the following document flowchart for purchases:

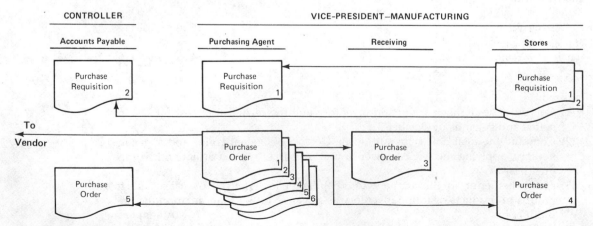

Required: Specify the procedures, relating to purchase requisitions and purchase orders, that Long would expect to find if Maylou's system of internal accounting control over purchases were effective. For example, purchase orders should be prepared only after giving proper consideration to the time to order and quantity to order. Do not comment on the effectiveness of the flow of documents as presented in the flowchart or on separation of duties.   (AICPA adapted)

B. Procedures for materials procurement and use. Jameson Co. produces a variety of chemical products for use by plastics manufacturers. The plant operates on two shifts, five days per week, with maintenance work performed on the third shift and on Saturdays as required.

An audit conducted by the staff of the new corporate Internal Audit Department has recently been completed, and the comments on inventory control were not favorable. Audit comments were particularly directed to the control of raw materials and maintenance materials and supplies.

Raw Materials. Raw materials are received at the back of the plant, signed for by one of the employees of the Batching Department and stored near the location of the initial batching process. During the day, receiving tallies are given to the supervisor, who forwards the tallies to the Inventory Control Department at the end of the day. The Inventory Control Department calculates raw materials usage, using weekly reports of actual production and standard formulas. Physical inventories are taken quarterly. Purchase requisitions are prepared by the Inventory Control Department and rush orders are frequent. In spite of the need for rush orders, the production superintendent regularly gets memos from the controller, stating that there must be excess inventory because the raw materials inventory dollar value is too high.

Maintenance Materials and Supplies. Maintenance materials and supplies are received and stored in a storeroom to which a clerk is assigned for each operating shift. A requisition is to be filled out for items taken from the storeroom, but this practice is not always followed. Because of the need to obtain parts quickly, the storeroom is not locked when the clerk is out. The storeroom is also open during the third shift and on Saturdays, so that maintenance crews can get needed materials and supplies. Purchase requisitions are prepared by the storeroom clerk and rush orders are frequent. A physical inventory is taken on a cycle-count basis.

Required: Identify weaknesses and recommended improvements in the procedures used for (1) the raw materials and (2) the maintenance materials and supplies inventories.

(CMA adapted)

Chapter 11
Materials:
Quantitative Models
for Planning and Control

The planning and control of inventory from product design to final delivery are of considerable strategic significance to management. Inventories serve as a cushion between the production and consumption of goods and exist in various forms: materials awaiting processing; partially completed products or components; and finished goods at the factory, in transit, at warehouse distribution points, and in retail outlets. At each of these stages, a sound economic justification for the inventory should exist, since each additional unit carried in inventory generates some additional costs.

Inventory investment varies with the type of industry and the characteristics of a company. On the average, inventory accounts for about one third of total assets, and for many manufacturers the cost of materials represents about one half of total product cost. Any inventory planning and control method should have but one goal that might be expressed in two ways: (1) to minimize total cost or (2) to maximize profit within specified time and resource allocations. For example, the size of inventory at production sites should reflect the profitability inherent in large production runs, in the economic ordering, handling, and shipping of lots, and in the need for flexibility to meet uncertain future demand.

Planning Materials Requirements

Materials planning begins with the design of a product. Whether it is a regular product or a special contract, a series of planning stages is necessary to get materials into production. In the preliminary stages, the engineering department studies the proposal, design, blueprints, and other available specifications and prepares a product requirement statement. The tooling department studies the work details necessary to manufacture the product in a particular plant. The manufacturing control department examines production in terms of existing and contemplated production schedules. The materials planning and cost estimating departments study the cumulative information and submit a cost estimate for the production proposal. The long-range or economic planning section suggests a product price based on considerations of present product lines, economic conditions and expectations, company policies, and expansion plans. Executive management must finally decide whether to proceed with, reject, or modify the proposal.

To plan manufacturing requirements, every stock item or class of items must be analyzed periodically to:

1. Forecast demand for the next month, quarter, or year.
2. Determine acquisition lead time.
3. Plan usage during the lead time.
4. Establish quantity on hand.
5. Place units on order.
6. Determine reserve or safety stock requirements.

These six steps are illustrated below in determining the quantity to order in September for a November delivery. In this illustration, the *lead time*, the time between the order and delivery, is two months. The desired inventory cushion, or *safety stock*, is approximately a two weeks' supply.

Planned or forecast usage from review date:		Units
September production		2,500
October production		2,000
November production		2,500
Desired inventory, November 30		1,000
Total to be provided		8,000
Quantity on hand, September 1	1,600	
On order for September delivery	2,000	
On order for October delivery	2,000	5,600
Quantity to order for November delivery		2,400

Future requirements for each purchased or produced item play a central role in materials control. If usage requirements are not accurately planned, even the most elaborate control system will result in the wrong level of inventory during and at the end of a future period.

Materials planning deals with two fundamental factors—the quantity and the time to purchase. Determination of how much and when to buy involves two conflicting kinds of cost—the cost of carrying inventory and the cost of inadequate carrying. The nature of these conflicting costs is indicated in the following comparison:

Cost of Carrying Inventory	Esti-mate	Cost of Inadequate Carrying
Interest on investment in working capital	10.00%	Extra purchasing, handling, and transportation costs
Property tax and insurance	1.25	Higher prices due to small order quantities
Warehousing or storage	1.80	Frequent stockouts resulting in disruptions of production
Handling	4.25	schedules, overtime, and extra setup time
Deterioration and shrinkage of stocks.	2.60	Additional clerical costs due to keeping customer back-order
Obsolescence of stocks	5.20	records
Total.	25.10%	Inflation-oriented increases in prices when inventory purchases are deferred
		Lost sales and loss of customer goodwill

Inventory Carrying and Ordering Costs for Economic Order Quantity Calculations

The *economic order quantity (EOQ)* is the amount of inventory to be ordered at one time for purposes of minimizing annual inventory cost. If a company buys in large quantities, the cost of carrying the inventory is high because of the sizable investment. If purchases are made in small quantities, frequent orders with correspondingly high ordering costs will result. Therefore, the quantity to order at a given time must be determined by balancing two factors: (1) the cost of possessing (carrying) materials and (2) the cost of acquiring (ordering) materials.

The cost factors of carrying an inventory, listed at the top of this page, are expressed as percentages of the average inventory investment and can be estimated and measured. These cost factors should include only those costs that vary with the level of inventory. For example, in the case of warehousing or storage, only those costs that will vary with changes in the number of units ordered should be included. The cost of labor and equipment used in the storeroom is normally a fixed cost and should not be considered a part of the carrying charge. Similarly, the insurance cost is included only when the company has a monthly reporting type of policy with premiums charged on the fluctuating inventory value. A standard insurance policy for one year or more should be considered a fixed cost that is irrelevant to the decision.

It is difficult to determine the costs of not carrying enough inventory; yet they must be considered in deciding upon order quantities and order points. Such costs include ordering costs, although the fixed cost of placing an order is not relevant. Only the variable or out-of-pocket cost of procuring an order should be included. Ordering costs include preparing the requisition and the purchase order, handling the incoming shipment and preparing a receiving report, communicating in case of quantity/quality errors or delays in receipts of materials, and accounting for the shipment and the payment. Other costs of not carrying enough inventory relate to such questions as savings in freight and quantity discounts as well as to the question of when to order, including an appropriate allowance for safety stock.

Depending upon many factors, it may cost from $2 to $20 or more to process an order and from 10 to 35 percent of the average inventory investment to hold materials. Techniques for analyzing cost behavior, described and illustrated in Chapter 16, should facilitate the determination of realistic carrying and ordering cost estimates, provided due consideration is given to current costs, including the impact of inflation. Mathematical and statistical techniques permit improved planning and control in an endeavor to maximize profits and minimize costs.

Tabular Determination of the Economic Order Quantity

A tabular arrangement of data relative to a materials item allows the determination of an approximate economic order quantity, and thereby the number of orders that need to be placed annually. To illustrate, assume the following data:

Estimated requirements for next year	2,400 units
Cost of the item per unit	$ 1.50
Ordering cost (per order)	$20.00
Inventory carrying cost (% of average inventory investment)	10%

Based on these data, various possible order sizes can be evaluated:

QUANTITATIVE DATA

Order size in units	300	400	800	1,200	2,400
Number of orders	8	6	3	2	1
Average inventory (order size ÷ 2) . . .	150	200	400	600	1,200

COST DATA

Average inventory investment	$225.00	$300	$600	$900	$1,800
Total carrying cost (10% of average inventory)	$ 22.50	$ 30	$ 60	$ 90	$ 180
Total ordering cost	160.00	120	60	40	20
Cost to order and carry	$182.50	$150	$120	$130	$ 200

Of the order sizes calculated, 800 is the most economical; thus, an order should be placed every four months. However, the most economical order size may not have been calculated; there may be some unit quantity between 400 and 800 or between 800 and 1,200 with a cost to order and carry that is lower than $120.

Graphic Determination of the Economic Order Quantity

The following graph shows the lowest point of the total-cost-to-order-and-carry curve, about $120, and the most economic order quantity of about 800 units. The ideal order size is the point where the sum of the ordering and carrying costs is at a minimum, i.e., where the total cost curve is at its lowest. This point generally occurs where the annual carrying charges equal the ordering charges, i.e., where these two cost lines intersect.

Graphic Determination of the Economic Order Quantity

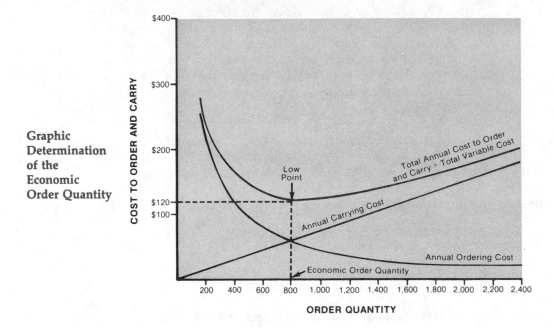

The Economic Order Quantity Formula

To determine the economic order quantity by a tabular or graphic method is lengthy and may not provide the most accurate answer. Companies using order-point calculations based upon economic order quantities usually prefer to use a formula. With information such as quantity required, unit price, inventory carrying cost percentage, and cost per order, differential calculus makes it possible to compute economic order quantity by formula. One formula variation follows:

$$\text{Economic order quantity} = \sqrt{\frac{2 \times \text{Annual required units} \times \text{Cost per order}}{\text{Cost per unit of material} \times \text{Carrying cost percentage}}}$$

$$OR \quad EOQ = \sqrt{\frac{2 \times RU \times CO}{CU \times CC}}$$

Given the terms EOQ, RU, CO, CU, and CC as specified, the formula is based on the following relationships:

$$\frac{RU}{EOQ} = \text{Number of orders placed annually}$$

$$\frac{RU \times CO}{EOQ} = \text{Annual ordering cost}$$

$$\frac{EOQ}{2} = \text{Average number of units in inventory at any point in time}$$

$$\frac{CU \times CC \times EOQ}{2} = \text{Annual carrying cost}$$

$$\frac{RU \times CO}{EOQ} + \frac{CU \times CC \times EOQ}{2} = \begin{array}{l}\text{Total annual cost of ordering and} \\ \text{carrying inventory, designated as AC}\end{array}$$

This latter equation is then solved, utilizing differential calculus to determine the minimum total annual cost of inventory:

$$AC = \frac{RU \times CO}{EOQ} + \frac{CU \times CC \times EOQ}{2}$$

$$AC = RU \times CO \times EOQ^{-1} + \frac{CU \times CC \times EOQ}{2}$$

$$\frac{dAC}{dEOQ} = -RU \times CO \times EOQ^{-2} + \frac{CU \times CC}{2}$$

$$\frac{dAC}{dEOQ} = \frac{-RU \times CO}{EOQ^2} + \frac{CU \times CC}{2}$$

$$\text{Let } \frac{dAC}{dEOQ} = 0 ; \quad \frac{-RU \times CO}{EOQ^2} + \frac{CU \times CC}{2} = 0$$

$$\frac{CU \times CC}{2} = \frac{RU \times CO}{EOQ^2}$$

$$EOQ^2 \times CU \times CC = 2 \times RU \times CO$$

$$EOQ^2 = \frac{2 \times RU \times CO}{CU \times CC}$$

$$EOQ = \sqrt{\frac{2 \times RU \times CO}{CU \times CC}}$$

The formula for the economic order quantity, or least-cost order quantity in units, is the square root of a fraction whose numerator is twice the product of the annual unit demand and the cost per order and whose denominator is the product of the unit price and the annual carrying rate. The formula assumes a constant rate of materials usage. Using the formula, the EOQ for the data on page 281 is:

$$EOQ = \sqrt{\frac{2 \times 2,400 \times \$20}{\$1.50 \times 10\%}} = \sqrt{\frac{96,000}{.15}} = \sqrt{640,000} = 800 \text{ units}$$

It is also possible to express EOQ in dollars rather than in units. The following formula is employed:

$$EOQ = \sqrt{\frac{2 \times RU \times CU \times CO}{CC}}$$

Using the data from the previous illustration, the EOQ in dollars is computed as follows:

$$EOQ = \sqrt{\frac{2 \times 2,400 \times \$1.50 \times \$20}{10\%}} = \sqrt{\frac{\$144,000}{.10}} = \sqrt{\$1,440,000} = \$1,200 \text{ total cost}$$

The EOQ can be converted to units by dividing the EOQ total cost by the cost per unit ($1,200 ÷ $1.50 = 800 units).

The following example is given to indicate the results when new cost data enter the formula, since any shift in cost data will affect the answer. Again, only those cost components that vary directly with order or production quantities should be used, i.e., the variable costs.

RU = 2,400 units of materials used per year (200 units per month)
CO = $10 ordering cost per order
CU = $1.50 cost per unit of materials
CC = 20% carrying cost as a percent of average inventory investment

$$EOQ = \sqrt{\frac{2 \times 2,400 \times \$10}{\$1.50 \times 20\%}} = \sqrt{\frac{48,000}{.30}} = \sqrt{160,000} = 400 \text{ units}$$

The economic order quantity for the stock item is 400 units, or six orders per year. Other order quantities resulting in more or less than six orders per year are not so economical, as proven by the following table, which is based on $3,600 (2,400 units × $1.50 cost per unit) annual usage of materials:

Orders per Year	Units per Order	Value per Order	Ordering Cost	Carrying Cost	Total Cost
1	2,400	$3,600	$10	$360	$370
2	1,200	1,800	20	180	200
3	800	1,200	30	120	150
4	600	900	40	90	130
5	480	720	50	72	122
6	400	600	**60**	**60**	120
7	343	515	70	52	122
8	300	450	80	45	125

Quantity Price Discounts. By purchasing in quantities larger than the minimum, quantity price discounts and/or freight savings may be realized, resulting in a lower cost per unit and altering the economic order quantity. Buying in larger quantities also alters the frequency of orders, and thus changes the total ordering cost. At the same time, it involves a larger investment in inventories.

To illustrate, assume that annual usage of an inventory item is 3,600 units, costing $1 each, with no quantity discount available. The carrying cost is 20 percent of the average inventory investment, and the cost to place an order is $10. The EOQ is:

$$\sqrt{\frac{2 \times 3,600 \times \$10}{\$1 \times 20\%}} = \sqrt{\frac{72,000}{.20}} = \sqrt{360,000} = 600 \text{ units}$$

Now assume the availability of the following quantity discounts:

Order Size	Quantity Discount
3,600 units	8%
1,800	6
1,200	5
900	5
720	4½
600	4
450	4

The following table considers the effect of quantity price discounts, using a cost-comparison approach. Observe that the order quantity that minimizes total cost (900 units per order) differs from the EOQ computed when no quantity discount is available (600 units per order).

	Number of orders per year						
	1	2	3	4	5	6	8
List price per unit..........	$1	$1	$1	$1	$1	$1	$1
Quantity discount...........	8%	6%	5%	5%	4½%	4%	4%
Discount price per unit	$.92	$.94	$.95	$.95	$.955	$.96	$.96
Size of order in units........	3,600	1,800	1,200	900	720	600	450
Average inventory in units ...	1,800	900	600	450	360	300	225
Cost of average inventory ...	$1,656.00	$ 846.00	$ 570.00	$ 427.50	$ 343.80	$ 288.00	$ 216.00
Cost of materials.........(a)	$3,312.00	$3,384.00	$3,420.00	$3,420.00	$3,438.00	$3,456.00	$3,456.00
Carrying cost							
(20% of average).......(b)	$ 331.20	$ 169.20	$ 114.00	$ 85.50	$ 68.76	$ 57.60	$ 43.20
Cost to order.............(c)	$ 10.00	$ 20.00	$ 30.00	$ 40.00	$ 50.00	$ 60.00	$ 80.00
Total cost per year							
(a) + (b) + (c)	$3,653.20	$3,573.20	$3,564.00	$3,545.50	$3,556.76	$3,573.60	$3,579.20

With quantity discounts, the cost of materials is not constant but is affected by the quantity discount. Therefore, the objective becomes the identification of an order quantity that minimizes not only the sum of the ordering and carrying costs [(b) + (c) in the table], but the sum of these costs *plus* the cost of the materials, i.e., (a) + (b) + (c). Since variable carrying cost is assumed to fluctuate directly with and is expressed as a percentage of the average inventory investment, carrying cost is also affected by the quantity discount, because the cost per unit contained in the average inventory investment is reduced.

The EOQ Formula and Production Runs. The EOQ formula is equally appropriate in computing the optimum size of a production run, in which case CO represents an estimate of the setup cost and CU is the variable manufacturing cost per unit. To illustrate, assume that stock item A87 is manufactured rather than purchased; the setup cost (CO), such as the cost of labor to rearrange and adjust machines, is $62; variable manufacturing cost (CU) is $2 per unit; annual required units total 6,000; and the carrying cost is 20 percent. The optimum size of a production run is computed as follows:

$$\sqrt{\frac{2 \times 6,000 \text{ units} \times \$62 \text{ setup cost}}{\$2 \text{ variable manufacturing cost} \times 20\%}} = \sqrt{\frac{744,000}{.4}} = \sqrt{1,860,000} = 1,364 \text{ units}$$

Determining the Time to Order

The EOQ formula answers the quantity problem of inventory control. However, the question of when to order is equally important. This question is controlled by three factors: (1) time needed for delivery, (2) rate of inventory usage, and (3) safety stock. Unlike the economic order quantity, the order point has no generally applicable and acceptable formula. Determining the order point would be relatively simple if *lead time* — the interval between placing an order and having materials on the factory floor ready for production — and the usage pattern for a given item were definitely predictable. For most stock items, there is a variation in either or both of these factors, which almost always causes one of three results: (1) if lead time or usage is below expectation during an order period, the new materials will arrive before the existing stock is consumed, thereby adding to the cost of carrying inventory; (2) if lead time or usage is greater than expected, a *stockout* will occur, with the resultant incurrence of costs associated with not carrying enough inventory; (3) if average lead time is used to determine an order point, a stockout could be expected on every other order.

Forecasting materials usage requires the expenditure of time and money. In materials management, forecasts are an expense as well as an aid to balancing the cost to acquire and the cost to carry inventory. Since perfect forecasts are rarely possible, an inventory cushion or safety stock is often the least costly device for protecting against a stockout. The basic problem is to determine the safety stock quantity. If the safety stock is greater than needed, the carrying cost will be too high; if too small, frequent stockouts will occur and inconveniences, disruptions, and additional costs will result. The optimum safety stock is that quantity which results in minimal total annual cost of stockouts and safety stock carrying cost. This carrying cost is determined in the same manner as in calculating the economic order quantity. The annual cost of stockouts depends upon their probability and the actual cost of each stockout.

To illustrate, assume that a company uses an item for which it places 10 orders per year, the cost of a stockout is $30, and the carrying cost is $.50 per unit. The following probabilities of a stockout have been estimated for various levels of safety stock:

Probability	Safety Stock Level
40%	0 units
20	50
10	100
5	200

The total carrying cost and stockout cost at each level of safety stock is determined as follows:

Expected Annual Stockouts (Probability × Number of Orders)	Total Stockout Cost	Total Carrying Cost	Total Stockout and Carrying Cost
4.0	$120	-0-	$120
2.0	60	$ 25	85
1.0	. 30	50	80
.5	15	100	115

In this illustration, the optimum level of safety stock is 100 units, since the total stockout and safety stock carrying cost is minimized at this level. Such an analysis of important stock items leads to smooth operations and effective materials management.

Order Point Formula

Order points are based on usage during the time necessary to requisition, order, and receive materials, plus an allowance for protection against stockout. The *order point* is reached when inventory on hand and quantities due in are equal to the lead time usage quantity plus the safety stock quantity. In equation form, the order point may be expressed as:

$$I + QD = LTQ + SSQ, \text{ when:}$$

I = Inventory balance on hand

QD = Quantities due in from orders previously placed, materials transfers, and returns to stock

LTQ = Lead time quantity equals average lead time in months, weeks, or days multiplied by average month's, week's, or day's use

SSQ = Safety stock quantity

The following situations are illustrated, both of which are solved mathematically and graphically:

1. Usage and lead time are known with certainty; therefore, no safety stock is provided.
2. A safety stock is injected into the calculation.

Order Point Illustrated—No Safety Stock. Assume the weekly use of 175 units of a stock item (35 units each, Monday through Friday, or 25 units, seven days a week) and that a lead time of four weeks establishes an order point at 700 units (175 units × 4 weeks). Assuming that the unit cost is $.50, the carrying cost is 20%, the order cost is $24, and annual usage is 9,100 units (175 units × 52 weeks), then the EOQ is computed as follows:

$$EOQ = \sqrt{\frac{2 \times 9,100 \times \$24}{\$.50 \times 20\%}} = \sqrt{\frac{436,800}{.10}} = \sqrt{4,368,000} = 2,090 \text{ units}$$

Each order provides a 12 weeks' supply (2,090 ÷ 175). Figure 1 shows the control pattern of this item if usage and lead time are definitely known. It is apparent that (1) if lead time is more than four weeks, a stockout will result;

and (2) if usage exceeds 700 units in any four-week period following an order point, a stockout is inevitable. Since perfect prediction of usage and lead time is usually unrealistic, a safety stock allowance is needed.

Figure 1—Rate of Usage and Lead Time Known with Certainty

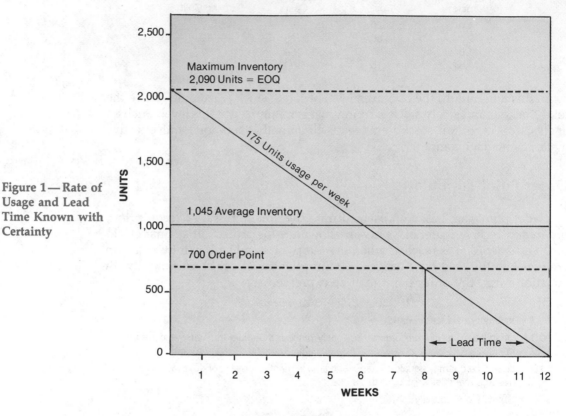

Order Point Illustrated — Safety Stock. Assuming the same usage of 175 units per week, shown in Figure 1, with a lead time of normally four weeks but possibly as long as nine weeks, the order point would be 1,575 units: 700 units usage during normal lead time (175 units × 4 weeks) plus 875 units of safety stock (175 units × 5 weeks). Assuming a beginning inventory of 2,800 units and no orders outstanding, the usage, order schedule, and inventory levels would be:

2,800	units in beginning inventory
<u>1,225</u>	usage to order point (1,225 ÷ 175 weekly usage = 7 weeks)
1,575	order point
<u>700</u>	usage during normal lead time (700 ÷ 175 weekly usage = 4 weeks)
875	maximum inventory or safety stock at date of delivery, assuming normal lead time and usage
<u>2,090</u>	EOQ units received
<u>2,965</u>	maximum inventory, assuming normal lead time and usage

The average inventory, assuming normal lead time and usage, is 1,920 units [(2,090 EOQ ÷ 2) + 875 units of safety stock]. Figure 2 depicts materials planning under the above assumptions and shows that a stockout would not occur unless lead time exceeds nine weeks, assuming normal usage.

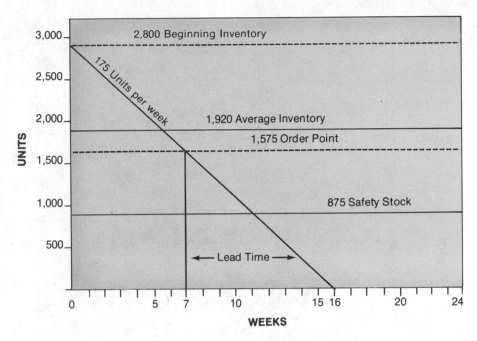

Figure 2—Rate of Usage Known with Certainty and Lead Time Known but Variable

In most businesses, a constant normal usage is not likely to occur because usage depends upon production schedules, and production depends upon sales. For instance, if the usage rate is as high as 210 units per week, with lead time normally four weeks or possibly as long as nine weeks, the safety stock would be 1,190 units and the order point 1,890 units, calculated as follows:

Normal usage for normal lead time of four weeks
   (175 units × 4 weeks) . . . .   700 units
Safety stock:
   Normal usage for five weeks' delay (175 units × 5 weeks)   875
   Usage variation [(210 − 175) × 9 weeks]   315   <u>1,190</u>
   Order point . . . .   <u>1,890</u> units

Assuming a beginning inventory of 2,800 units, with no orders outstanding, the usage, order schedule, and inventory levels would be:

2,800 units in beginning inventory
  <u>910</u> usage to order point (910 ÷ 210 maximum weekly usage = 4.3 weeks)
1,890 order point
  <u>700</u> normal usage for normal lead time (700 ÷ 175 normal weekly usage = 4 weeks)
1,190 maximum inventory or safety stock at date of delivery, assuming normal lead time
     and usage
<u>2,090</u> EOQ units received
<u>3,280</u> maximum inventory, assuming normal lead time and usage

The average inventory, assuming normal lead time and usage, is 2,235 units [(2,090 EOQ ÷ 2) + 1,190 units of safety stock]. Figure 3 shows materials planning under the assumptions that the rate of usage and lead time are known but variable.

Figure 3—
Rate of Usage
and Lead Time
Known but
Variable

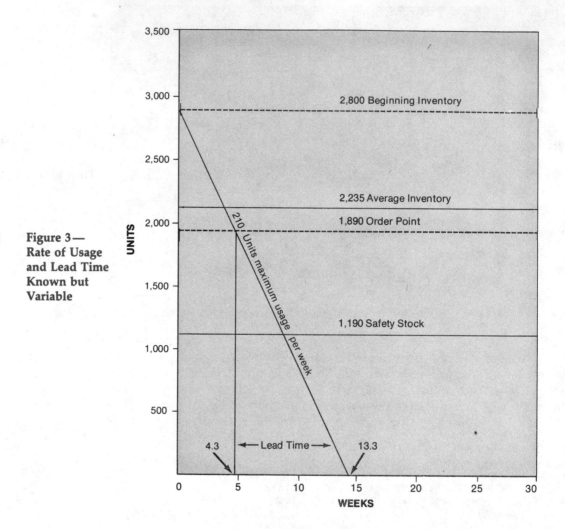

Safety Stock Calculations by Statistical Methods

The preceding situations tend to provide a safety stock for the extreme boundaries of usage and lead time variability. In other situations, the amount of safety stock is often calculated by traditional rules of thumb, such as a two weeks' supply. These approaches have given way to statistical techniques which minimize the combined costs of stockouts and carrying additional safety stock inventory. With any increasing complexity of calculations, computer application is inevitable.

The tabulation of an eight months' actual consumption of Material J-2, together with the forecast monthly usage, forms the basis for one possible statistical approach. This technique assumes that variations between future forecast and actual lead time demands are represented by the variations experienced during the sample period. The technique is illustrated as follows:

	(1) Forecast	(2) Units Consumed	(3) Forecast Minus Units Consumed	(4) Column 3 Squared
January............	260	250	10	100
February...........	218	225	− 7	49
March	260	275	−15	225
April...............	230	240	−10	100
May	275	280	− 5	25
June	270	260	10	100
July	245	240	5	25
August	270	280	−10	100
			−22	724

In Column 3, the differences between forecast requirements and actual usage are derived and totaled. In Column 4, these differences are squared and totaled. The Column 3 total is squared and divided by the number of time periods (8 months) and the quotient is subtracted from the Column 4 total:

$$724 - \frac{(-22)^2}{8} = 724 - \frac{484}{8} = 724 - 60.5 = 663.5$$

The result is divided by the number of time periods minus one, and the square root is computed, giving the standard deviation:

$$\sqrt{\frac{663.5}{8-1}} = \sqrt{94.786} = 9.74$$

The average difference between forecast requirements and actual usage is computed next by dividing the Column 3 total by the number of time periods (months):

$$\frac{-22}{8} = -2.75$$

Based on a normal probability distribution, two times the standard deviation minus the average difference, 22.23 units [2(9.74) − (−2.75)], or 22 when rounded to the nearest unit, would protect against a stockout about 97.5 percent of the time (a safety stock of 22 units).[1] This percentage is referred to as the *confidence level*.

Here the average difference of −2.75 increases the safety stock because the actual usage is, on the average, greater than the forecast usage. A positive

---

[1]The 97.5 percent figure includes all of the area under the normal curve, except for the 2.5 percent right tail of the curve, which represents the probability of a stockout.

average difference would indicate that, on the average, the actual usage is less than the forecast, thus reducing the safety stock figure.

In January, with a forecast usage of 260 units, a lead time of one month, and a safety stock of 22 units, the order point is 282 units for Material J-2. Of course, an additional safety stock allowance may be needed if lead time varies, again giving consideration to the degree of protection desired by management. When the stock reaches the order point level, it should trigger an order for the most economical order quantity.

Lead time units must be the same time period units of measure as those used in computing the standard deviation, e.g., days, weeks, or months. This illustration uses months as time period units and assumes a lead time of one month. When the lead time is not one time period, proper computation of the safety stock requires the multiplication of the desired number of standard deviations, the standard deviation, and the square root of the number of time period units. From this product, the average difference multiplied by the number of time period units is subtracted. Assuming the same standard deviation and average difference as computed on page 291, two standard deviations and a lead time of four months, the safety stock would be computed as follows:

$$
\begin{aligned}
\text{Safety stock} &= (2 \times 9.74 \times \sqrt{4}) - (-2.75 \times 4) \\
&= (19.48 \times 2) + 11 \\
&= 38.96 + 11 \\
&= 49.96 = \text{approximately 50 units for safety stock}
\end{aligned}
$$

The normal probability distribution assumed in the previous illustration is appropriate for samples of approximately 30 or more, which would often be available in an actual application. For small samples, however, the Student's t distribution is a more appropriate assumption than is the standard normal distribution. Thus, the safety stock would be computed for a sample of size n by multiplying the standard deviation by the t value for n − 1 degrees of freedom at the desired confidence level. The table of selected t values on page 293 is based on the assumption that only one tail of the distribution is of concern, i.e., the possibility of a stockout.

Given a sample size of 8, as used in the previous illustration, the 8 − 1 = 7 line in the table indicates that for a 97.5 percent confidence level, 2.365 rather than 2 should be multiplied by the standard deviation. Assuming a lead time of one month, the safety stock should be 26 units [2.365 (9.74) − (−2.75)]. As shown in the table, the Student's t distribution approaches the normal distribution as the sample size increases; i.e., a 97.5 percent confidence level is about 2 (precisely 1.960) standard deviations for somewhat larger sample sizes.

Forecasting Usage

The number of units needed during the lead time and the lead time itself are the two variables which influence the when-to-order decision. It is usually

Degrees of Freedom	Desired Confidence Level			
	95%	97.5%	99%	99.5%
1	6.314	12.706	31.821	63.657
2	2.920	4.303	6.965	9.925
3	2.353	3.182	4.541	5.841
4	2.132	2.776	3.747	4.604
5	2.015	2.571	3.365	4.032
6	1.943	2.447	3.143	3.707
7	1.895	2.365	2.998	3.499
8	1.860	2.306	2.896	3.355
9	1.833	2.262	2.821	3.250
10	1.812	2.228	2.764	3.169
11	1.796	2.201	2.718	3.106
12	1.782	2.179	2.681	3.055
13	1.771	2.160	2.650	3.012
14	1.761	2.145	2.624	2.977
15	1.753	2.131	2.602	2.947
20	1.725	2.086	2.528	2.845
25	1.708	2.060	2.485	2.787
30	1.697	2.042	2.457	2.750
40	1.684	2.021	2.423	2.704
60	1.671	2.000	2.390	2.660
120	1.658	1.980	2.358	2.617
∞	1.645	1.960	2.326	2.576

possible to estimate fairly accurately the time required to receive materials. It is seldom possible to forecast exactly the materials needed even for a short future period; and when thousands of items are involved, the task becomes prodigious even with the aid of a computer. Some forecasting techniques are briefly mentioned in order to indicate the scope and complexity of the task:

1. Factor listing or barometric methods.
2. Statistical methods.
3. Forecasting surveys.

Factor listing involves enumerating the favorable and unfavorable conditions likely to influence sales of the various divisions or products of a company and relies upon the forecaster's judgment to evaluate the degree of the influence factor. *Barometric methods* result in systematized factor listing.

Statistical methods describe historical patterns in time series. The methods may be simple or complex, but the purpose is to reveal patterns that have occurred in the past and project them into the future. The usual procedure results in plotting time series data (such as total sales, sales of specific lines or products, inventory units or dollars, labor hours, or machine hours) on a graph, thus revealing a trend or a seasonal or cyclical pattern. A moving average may be used to smooth a series and remove irregular fluctuations, but the intent is to describe mathematically the growth or decline over a period of time. Regression analysis usually employs the least-squares method (see Chapter 16) to determine economic relationships between a dependent variable and one or more independent variables, such as sales territory, family incomes, advertising expenditures, and price of the product.

Forecasting surveys are used to avoid complete dependence on historical data. They are commonly made in order to determine consumer buying intentions, opinions, or feelings about the business outlook, and capital investment plans.

General Observations

The primary key to good inventory planning is sufficient knowledge of the fundamental techniques to develop enough self-confidence to permit their practical adaptation to the specific needs of the company. Basically, economic order quantity and computed order points assume:

1. Relatively uniform average demand.
2. Uniform rate of inventory usage.
3. Normal distribution of demand forecast errors.
4. Constant purchase price per unit, regardless of order size.
5. Available funds when the order point is reached.
6. Statistical independence of demand for all inventory items.

Aside from the technical and mathematical steps, it is important to remember that the following fundamentals largely determine the success of inventory planning procedures:

1. The order point is a significant factor affecting inventory planning, since it establishes the inventory level. It determines the investment in inventories and the ability to provide satisfactory customer service. The order point depends primarily on the accuracy of the sales or usage forecast.
2. Of equal importance is the establishment of unit costs, carrying and ordering costs, and the investment factor. They are involved in determining the economic order quantity.
3. The inventory model should be sensitive and adaptive to seasonal usage variations and other nonstatic data influencing order point quantity computations.

Materials Control

Materials control is accomplished through functional organization, assignment of responsibility, and documentary evidence obtained at various stages of operations. These stages begin with the approval of sales and production budgets and with the completion of products which are ready for sale and shipment to warehouse stocks or to customers.

Two levels of inventory control exist: unit control and dollar control. Purchasing and production managers are primarily interested in unit control; they think, order, and requisition in terms of units instead of dollars. Executive management is primarily interested in the financial control of inventories.

These executives think in terms of an adequate return on capital employed; i.e., dollars invested in inventory must be utilized efficiently and effectively. Inventory control is operating successfully when inventory increases or decreases follow a predetermined and predictable pattern, related in amount and time to sales requirements and production schedules.

The control of materials must meet two opposing needs: (1) maintenance of an inventory of sufficient size and diversity for efficient operations and (2) maintenance of a financially favorable inventory. A basic objective of materials control is the ability to place an order at the appropriate time with the best source to acquire the proper quantity at the right price and quality. Effective inventory control should:

1. Provide a supply of required materials and parts for efficient and uninterrupted operations.
2. Provide ample stocks in periods of short supply (seasonal, cyclical, or strike), and anticipate price changes.
3. Store materials with a minimum of handling time and cost and protect them from loss by fire, theft, elements, and damage through handling.
4. Keep inactive, surplus, and obsolete items to a minimum by systematic reporting of product changes which affect materials and parts.
5. Assure adequate inventory for prompt delivery to customers.
6. Maintain the amount of capital invested in inventories at a level consistent with operating requirements and management's plans.

Control Principles

Inventory control systems and techniques should be based on the following principles:

1. Inventory is created by purchasing (a) materials and parts and (b) additional labor and overhead to process the materials into finished goods.
2. Inventory is reduced through sales and spoilage.
3. Accurate sales and production schedule forecasts are essential for efficient purchasing, handling, and materials investment.
4. Management policies, which attempt to balance size and diversity of inventory for efficient operations and cost of maintaining that inventory, are the greatest factor in determining inventory investment.
5. Ordering materials is a response to forecasts; scheduling production controls inventory.
6. Inventory records alone do not achieve inventory control.
7. Control is comparative and relative, not absolute. It is exercised by people with varying experiences and judgment. Rules and procedures guide these individuals in making evaluations and decisions. For example, by establishing closer controls, experts in the field of

materials control commonly expect to reduce inventory by 15 percent or more without significantly affecting customer service or production scheduling.

Organizing for Materials Control

Materials control is commonly centralized in one department called the materials management or materials control department. Size of the company, number of purchased items in a finished product, time required to manufacture a product, and physical size, weight, and unit value of items are factors that influence the organization and personnel required for effective materials control. A materials management organization may include some or all of the following sections:

Planning and Scheduling	Finished Goods
Purchasing	Warehousing
Receiving	Packing
Inspection	Traffic
Stores	Shipping
Materials Handling	Statistical Analysis

Materials Control Methods

Materials control methods differ primarily in the care and cost expended. Critical items and high-value items require greater attention than do low-value items. For example, for low-cost items, large safety stocks and large orders of three to six months' supply are appropriate, since carrying costs are usually low and the risk of obsolescence is often negligible. Control methods include order cycling and the min-max method.

The *order cycling* or *cycle review method* examines periodically (e.g., each 30, 60, or 90 days) the status of quantities on hand of each item or class. Different companies use different time periods between reviews and may use different cycles for different types of materials. High-value items and items that would tie up normal operations if out of stock usually require a short review cycle. On low-cost and noncritical items, a longer review cycle is common, since these materials would be ordered in large quantities and a stockout would not be as costly. At each review period in the order cycling system, orders are placed to bring quantities up to some determined and desired level. This quantity is often expressed as a number of days' or weeks' supply and can be adjusted to projected sales for seasonal items.

The *min-max method* is based on the premise that the quantities of most stock items are subject to definable limits. A maximum quantity for each item is established. A minimum level provides the margin of safety necessary to prevent stockouts during a reorder cycle. The minimum level sets the order point, and the quantity to order will usually bring inventory to the maximum level.

Min-max procedures may be based on physical observation or they may be keyed to the accounting system. Physical observation that a reorder point has been reached is illustrated by the two-bin procedure, which separates each stock item into two bins, piles, or bundles. The first bin contains enough stock to satisfy usage that occurs between receipt of an order and the placing of the next order; the second bin contains the normal amount used from order date to delivery date plus the safety stock. When the first bin is empty and the second bin is tapped, a requisition for a new supply is prepared. The second bin or reserve quantity is determined originally by estimating usage requirements and adding a safety stock adequate to cover the time required for replenishing the materials. For example, if monthly usage of an item is ten dozen, a one-month safety stock is desired; and if 30 days are required to place an order and receive delivery, the second bin should contain 20 dozen units. A purchase order must be written when the reserve stock is tapped; otherwise, a stockout is likely to occur. The two-bin or "last bag" system requires little paper work, since reordering takes place when the "last bag" is opened.

The min-max method may be implemented through the accounting system by triggering an order when a materials ledger card shows that the balance on hand has dropped to the order point. The system is especially advantageous in companies using electronic data processing equipment. The materials control department reviews materials items, forecasts usage and lead time, establishes safety stock requirements, and determines economic order quantities. Thereafter, subject to quarterly or semiannual review, receipts and issues are machine-recorded on the materials cards. When the quantity on hand drops to the established order point, the materials cards are automatically machine-sorted and are routed to order clerks who activate orders for the quantity specified. Companies with computers may go even further in their use of the automatic order system. The computer reviews and updates order points, recalculates economic order quantities, and even writes purchase orders.

Selective Control — The ABC Plan

Segregation of materials for *selective control*, called the *ABC plan*, is an analytical approach based upon statistical averages. The ABC plan measures the cost significance of each materials item. "A," or high-value, items would be under the tightest control and the responsibility of the most experienced personnel. "C" items would be under simple physical controls, such as the two-bin system with safety stocks. The plan provides an impressive saving in materials cost.

The ABC plan concentrates on important items and is also known as *control by importance and exception (CIE)*. Because it is impractical to give equal attention to all items in inventory, stock items are classified and ranked in descending order on the basis of the annual dollar value of each item, thus providing a proportional value analysis. In most situations, an arbitrary number of items can be selected on a percentage basis to approximate:

10% of the items to equal 70% of the dollar cost of materials used
30% of the items to equal 25% of the dollar cost of materials used
60% of the items to equal 5% of the dollar cost of materials used

The following table suggests the handling of high-, middle-, and low-value items to achieve effective control:

	High-Value Items (A)	Middle-Value Items (B)	Low-Value Items (C)
Quality of personnel	Best available	Average	Low
Records needed	Complete	Simple	Not essential
Order point and quantity used ..	As guides, frequent review	Infrequent review	Strictly used
Number of orders per year	Generally high	Two to six	One or two
Replacement time	As short as possible	Normal	Can be long
Amount of safety stock	Low	Moderate	High
Inventory turnover	High	Moderate	Low

The procedure for segregating materials for selective control consists of six steps:

1. Determining future use in units over the review forecast period— month, quarter, or year.
2. Determining the price per unit for each item.
3. Multiplying the projected price per unit by the projected unit requirement to determine the total cost of that item during the period.
4. Arranging the items in terms of total cost, listing first the item with the highest total cost.
5. Computing for each item its percentage of the total for (a) units— number of units of each item divided by total units of all items, and (b) total cost—total cost of each item divided by total cost of all materials.
6. Plotting the percentages on a graph.

The following table and graph demonstrate ABC inventory classification:

Item	Units	% of Total		Unit Cost	Total Cost	% of Total	
1	800	8 } 12%		$20.00	$16,000	32.0 } 56%—A	
2	400	4		30.00	12,000	24.0	
3	1,600	16 } 42%		4.50	7,200	14.4 } 38%—B	
4	1,400	14		5.00	7,000	14.0	
5	1,200	12		4.00	4,800	9.6	
6	2,000	20 } 46%		1.00	2,000	4.0 } 6%—C	
7	1,600	16		.50	800	1.6	
8	1,000	10		.20	200	.4	
Total	10,000	100			$50,000	100.0	100%

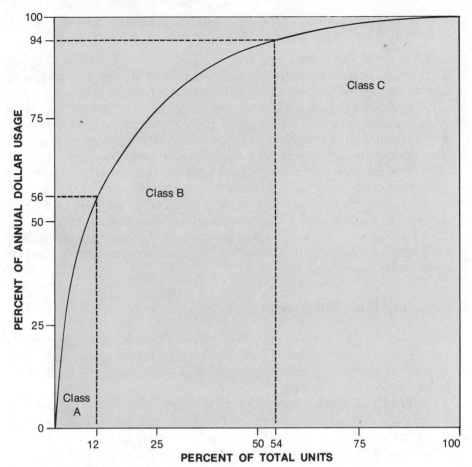

Distribution of Inventory Usage Values (Cumulative Percentages)

Controlling Materials in Process

The materials cost control responsibility is not ended when materials are requisitioned for production. Until goods are finished, packed, sold, and shipped, inventory control problems and cost savings potentials exist. This is particularly true of in-process inventories, which are intimately related to production processes and schedules but often are not controlled. Generally, the objective is to maintain inventory levels based either on maximum production or the lowest unit cost.

Work in process inventory investment is largely determined by the time necessary for goods to pass through the production process. The time involved includes:

1. Setup time—preparing to run a job on a machine.
2. Running time—actually performing the work.
3. Queue time—the amount of time that the job spends waiting to be worked on.

4. Move time — transporting the goods to the next processing location.
5. Wait time — time spent waiting to be moved.

In most job shops, queue time accounts for 70 to 90 percent of the total time. Therefore, a large portion of the dollars invested in in-process inventory is tied up in nonproductive, idle goods. Although cutting queue time can result in significant reductions in inventory investment, some minimum level of queues is required in order to keep operations from running out of work.[2]

The computation of turnover rates aids in identifying inventory problems and measuring the effectiveness of control procedures. A computation is usually made for each manufacturing department, cost center, or process by dividing the cost of units transferred to the next department by the average inventory cost of the transferring department. Turnover rates vary from one department to another; hence the focus is on turnover rate changes. Scheduling or production problems are often indicated by a declining turnover rate. For cost control purposes, the downtrend in turnover rates should suggest analysis and induce corrective action.

Controlling Finished Goods

An accurate sales forecast is the key to effectively managing finished goods inventories and meeting delivery dates. This forecast must be communicated to production control departments in order to develop production schedules for meeting sales commitments.

To meet customer preferences and competition, many product lines feature a growing array of colors, sizes, and optional equipment. This results in added inventory items, more work in process inventory and finished subassemblies, and the need for tighter control.

Control of Obsolete and Surplus Inventory

Almost every organization is faced with the problem of surplus and obsolete inventory at one time or other. Whatever the many possible reasons for such conditions, some action is required in order to reduce or eliminate these items from inventory and free the related capital. To accomplish a reduction, management should first make certain that the buildup will not continue due to present ordering policies, and should then take steps to dispose of stock. Accurate perpetual inventory records showing acquisition and issue quantities and dates, as well as periodic review of the records, are necessary to identify obsolete and surplus items. Obsolete inventory usually results from changing a design or dropping a product. Prompt sale of the inventory for the first reasonable offer is usually the best policy.

---

[2]Jay Severance and Ronald R. Bottin, "Work-in-Process Inventory Control Through Data Base Concepts," *Management Accounting*, Vol. LX, No. 7, pp. 37–38.

DISCUSSION QUESTIONS

1. How can a firm benefit from economic order quantity and order point techniques?

2. Explain each of the following terms: (a) economic order quantity, (b) order point, (c) lead time, and (d) safety stock.

3. What are the costs of carrying inventories? Explain. How does overstocking add to the cost of carrying inventories?

4. What are the consequences of maintaining inadequate inventory levels? What are the difficulties of measuring precisely the costs associated with understocking?

5. An inventory planning and control system is designed to minimize the total cost of ordering and carrying inventory. Therefore, inventory control is good as long as the investment in inventory is declining. Discuss.

6. Is general management concerned primarily with unit control or financial control of inventory?

7. The control of materials must meet two opposing needs. What are they?

8. In what situation are selective control and automatic control of materials effective?

9. What is the key to controlling finished goods inventory in a manufacturing company?

EXERCISES

1. *Quantity to order.* Franklin Company's production schedule calls for 5,200 units of Material B for January operations, 4,950 for February, and 5,550 for March. On January 1, the Material B inventory is 5,600 units, with 4,100 on order for January delivery and 5,100 for February delivery. The desired inventory level to begin second-quarter production is 75% of the January 1 inventory.

Required: Compute the number of Material B units to order for March delivery.

2. *Usage forecast and inventory balances.* On January 1, a materials analyst is asked to determine the number of units of Material Z to order for March delivery. The production schedule calls for 4,800 units of this material for January operations, 5,000 units for February, and 5,600 units for March. On January 1, the Material Z inventory is 5,500 units, 3,800 units are on order for January delivery, and 4,600 units are on order for February delivery. The desired inventory level to begin second-quarter production is 80% of the January 1 inventory.

Required:
   (1) Compute the quantity to order for March delivery.
   (2) If the planned usage occurs and outstanding orders are received on expected delivery dates, compute the number of units on hand (a) March 1 and (b) March 31.

3. *Computations and applications of the EOQ formula.* (Round off all answers to the nearest whole number.)
   (a) Shilders, Inc. has an annual usage of 100 units of Item M, with a purchase price of $55 per unit. The following data are applicable to Item M:

Ordering cost . . . . $5 per order
Carrying cost percentage . . .   15%

Required: *Compute the economic order quantity.*

(b) *Henry Company has developed the following information for one of its inventory items: units required per year, 30,000; cost of placing an order, $100; unit carrying cost per year, $600.*

Required: *Compute the economic order quantity.*

(c) *Modern Equipment Company estimates a need for 2,250 Ajets next year at a cost of $3 per unit. The estimated carrying cost is 20%, and the cost to place an order is $12.*

Required: *Compute the economic order quantity.*

(d) *Trefoil, Inc. requires 6,750 containers next year at a list price of $12 per container. The estimated carrying cost is 25% of average inventory, and the cost to place an order is $20.*

Required: *Compute the economic order quantity.*

(e) *Shubert Company estimates that it will need 12,500 cartons next year at a cost of $8 per carton. The estimated carrying cost is 25% of average inventory investment, and the cost to place an order is $20.*

Required: *Compute (1) the economic order quantity and (2) the frequency in days that orders should be placed, based on a 365-day year.*

(f) *Brown Sporting Goods, Inc. buys baseballs at $20 per dozen from its wholesaler. Brown will sell 48,000 dozen balls evenly throughout the year. The firm incurs interest expense of 10% on its average inventory investment. In addition, rent, insurance, and property tax for each dozen baseballs in the average inventory is $.40. The cost involved in handling each purchase order is $10.*

Required: *Compute (1) the economic order quantity and (2) the total annual inventory expense to sell 48,000 dozen baseballs, if orders of 800 dozen each are placed evenly thoughout the year.*

(g) *Stocks Company manufactures 10,000 blades annually for its electric lawn mower division. Blades are used evenly throughout the year. The setup cost each time a production run is made is $80, and the cost to carry a blade in inventory is $.40. Management's objective is to produce the blades at the lowest possible cost.*

Required: *Compute the most economical number of annual production runs, if each run is scheduled for the same number of blades.*

(h) *A customer has been ordering 5,000 specially designed metal columns at the rate of 1,000 per order during the past year. The variable production cost is $8 per unit: $6 for materials and labor, and $2 for factory overhead. It costs $1,000 to set up for one run of 1,000 columns, and the inventory carrying cost is 20%. Since this customer may buy at least 5,000 columns per year, the company would like to avoid making five different production runs.*

Required: *Compute the most economical production run.*

(i) Collins, Inc. manufactures a line of walnut office products. Management estimates the annual demand for the double walnut letter tray at 6,000 units. The tray sells for $80. The costs relating to the letter tray are: manufacturing cost per tray, $50; cost to initiate a production run, $300; annual cost of carrying the tray in inventory, 20%. In prior years, the production of the tray has been scheduled in two equal production runs.

Required: Find the expected annual cost savings the company could experience if it employed the economic order quantity model to determine the number of production runs which should be initiated during the year.

4. Ordering and carrying costs, economic order quantity, and quantity discount. Patterson Company buys 500 boxes of Item X-100 every 2 months. Order costs are $380 per order; carrying costs are $1 per unit, and vary directly with inventory investment. Currently the company purchases the item for $5 each.

Required:
(1) Determine ordering and carrying costs under current policy.
(2) Determine the economic order quantity and the related ordering and carrying costs.
(3) What is the order-size decision Patterson should make, if the supplier offers a 5% discount for order sizes of 3,000 units?   (CGAA adapted)

5. Economic order quantity, order point, safety stock. LeMaster Company has obtained the following costs and other data pertaining to one of its materials:

Working days per year	250
Normal use per day	500 units
Maximum use per day	600 units
Minimum use per day	100 units
Lead time	5 days
Variable cost of placing one order	$36
Variable carrying cost per unit per year	$4

Required: Compute the following:
(1) Economic order quantity.
(2) Safety stock (maximum).
(3) Order point.
(4) Normal maximum inventory.
(5) Absolute maximum inventory.
(6) Average inventory, assuming normal lead time and usage.   (CGAA adapted)

6. Safety stock. Herringbone & Sons, Inc. would like to determine the safety stock to maintain for a product, so that the lowest combination of stockout cost and carrying cost would result. Each stockout will cost $75; the carrying cost for each safety stock unit will be $1; the product will be ordered five times a year. The following probabilities of running out of stock during an order period are associated with various safety stock levels:

Safety Stock Level	Probability of Stockout
10 units	40%
20	20
40	10
80	5

Required: Determine the combined stockout and safety stock carrying cost associated with each level and the recommended level of safety stock.   (AICPA adapted)

7. Safety stock calculation by statistical method. Fargo Company has been experiencing stockouts in one of its important materials, even though deliveries which arrive one month from the date of an order are dependable. Records provide the forecast usage and the actual consumption on this item for the previous nine months. The sum of the deviations is zero, while the sum of the deviations squared is 2,048. A 97.5% protection against stockout is deemed adequate.

Required:
- (1) Compute the safety stock. Use the Student's t table on page 293.
- (2) Compute the order point if average usage is 250 units per month.
- (3) Compute the safety stock for 97.5% safety if 120 days are required from order to delivery.

8. ABC plan of control. Dumas Industries, Inc. is considering a system of selective control of materials, using the following data:

Materials Stock No.	Quarterly Usage in Units	Unit Cost	Total Cost
24	2,000	$20.00	$ 40,000
25	20,400	.25	5,100
26	5,600	10.50	58,800
27	1,000	30.00	30,000
28	18,600	1.00	18,600
29	7,560	2.50	18,900
30	8,880	3.25	28,860
31	4,920	2.00	9,840
32	6,840	2.00	13,680
33	30,000	.50	15,000
34	9,980	1.50	14,970
35	8,220	2.50	20,550
Total	124,000		$274,300

Required:
- (1) Prepare an arrangement of the data for presentation to management, assuming that the ABC plan of selective control is indicated. (Round off all percentages to two decimal places.)
- (2) Construct a graph to depict the situation.

PROBLEMS

11-1. Economic order quantity and quantity discount. McCormick Company, a regional supermarket chain, orders 480,000 cans of frozen orange juice per year from a California distributor. A 24-can case of frozen juice delivered to McCormick's central warehouse costs $4.80, including freight charges. The company borrows funds at a 10% interest rate to finance its inventories.

McCormick Company's purchasing agent has calculated that it costs $15 to place an order for frozen juice and that the annual variable storage expense (electricity, insurance, handling) is $.08 for each can of juice.

Required:
(1) Compute the number of cases of frozen juice that McCormick Company should request in each order.
(2) Determine the order-size decision that McCormick should make, if the California distributor offers a 10% discount off the delivery price for minimum orders of 72,000 cans.   (CGAA adapted)

11-2. EOQ; order point; graphic illustration of materials management. The new financial vice-president of Coolidge Products Corporation is directing an intensive analysis of working capital management. The objective is to attain more efficient resource allocation and higher earnings from each dollar of assets.

Materials cost of one important manufactured product is $12 per unit; sales average 100 units per month; and the lead time is one month. Calculations show that the variable cost of placing an order and handling the incoming shipment is $50, and the cost of holding units in stock is 25% of the average inventory.

Required:
(1) Compute the economic order quantity.
(2) Determine the order point.
(3) Construct a graphic presentation of materials management.

11-3. Optimum production run size. A manufacturer expects to produce 100,000 Widgets during the year ending June 30, to supply a demand which is uniform throughout the year. The setup cost for each production run of Widgets is $144 and the variable cost of producing each Widget is $5. The cost of carrying one Widget in inventory is $.20 per year. After a batch of Widgets is produced and placed in inventory, it is sold at a uniform rate, and inventory is exhausted when the next batch of Widgets is completed.

Management would like to have an equation to describe the above situation and determine the optimal quantity of Widgets in each production run in order to minimize total production and inventory carrying costs.

Let: AC = Total annual cost of producing and carrying Widgets in inventory.
     X = Number of Widgets to be produced in each production run.

Required: Using the above notation, show (1) the derivation, dAC/dX, of the equation which determines the optimal quantity of Widgets produced during each production run in the fiscal year, and (2) the quantity of Widgets (to the nearest whole number) that should be produced in each production run in the fiscal year in order to minimize total cost.   (AICPA adapted)

11-4. EOQ formula and safety stock. Strickland Company sells a number of products to many restaurants in the area. One product is a special meat cutter with a disposable blade. Blades are sold in a package of 12 at $20 per package. It has been determined that the demand for the replacement blades is at a constant rate of 2,000 packages per month. The packages cost the company $10 each from the manufacturer and require a three-day lead time from date of order to date of delivery. The ordering cost is $1.20 per order, and the carrying cost is 10% per annum. The company uses the economic order quantity formula.

Required:
(1) Compute the economic order quantity.

    (2) Compute the number of orders needed per year.

    (3) Compute the cost of ordering and of carrying blades for the year.

    (4) Determine the date on which the next order should be placed, assuming that there is no reserve (safety stock) and that the present inventory level is 200 packages. (360 days = 1 year.)

    (5) Discuss the difficulties that most firms would have in attempting to apply the EOQ formula to their inventory problems.   (CMA adapted)

11-5. Determining the EOQ and time to order. Montreal Company has developed the following costs and other data pertaining to one of its raw materials:

Normal use per day	400 units
Maximum use per day	600 units
Minimum use per day	100 units
Working days per year	250
Lead time	8 days
Cost of placing one order	$20.00
Cost per unit of material	$ 2.50
Carrying cost percentage	10%

Required: Compute the following:

    (1) Economic order quantity.

    (2) Safety stock.

    (3) Reorder point.

    (4) Normal maximum inventory.

    (5) Absolute maximum inventory.

    (6) Average normal inventory.   (CGAA adapted)

11-6. Safety stock. For Product D, ordered 5 times per year, stockout cost per occurrence is $80 and safety stock carrying cost is $2 per unit. Available options are:

Units of Safety Stock	Probability of Running Out of Safety Stock
10	50%
20	40
30	30
40	20
50	10
55	5

Required: Compute the safety stock resulting in the lowest cost.   (AICPA adapted)

11-7. Establishing safety stock. Ledbetter Products Company has been experiencing stockouts on one of its important materials, even though deliveries are dependable within one month from the date of an order. Management asks that a safety stock for this item be established and provides the following record of actual and forecast usage during the past nine months.

Month	Usage	Forecast	Month	Usage	Forecast
January	475	490	June	520	510
February	480	490	July	500	510
March	490	475	August	490	510
April	500	485	September	485	500
May	510	500			

It is believed that a 97.5% protection against a stockout is adequate.

Required:

(1) Prepare a schedule showing the safety stock required, using the statistical method and the Student's t table on page 293. (Round off all amounts to two decimal places.)

(2) Compute the safety stock required if the normal lead time is three months.

CASES

A. Estimating ordering and carrying costs. Evans Inc., a large wholesale distributor, deals exclusively in baby shoes. Due to substantial ordering and storing costs, management decided to use the EOQ model to help determine the optimum quantities to order from the different manufacturers.

As a starting point, management has decided to develop values for the ordering cost and carrying cost by using data from the most recent fiscal year. The company had placed 4,000 purchase orders during the year, the largest of which was 400 orders in June and the smallest, 250 in December. Selected cost data for these two months and for the year were:

	Cost for High Activity Month (June — 400 Orders)	Cost for Low Activity Month (December — 250 Orders)	Annual Cost
Purchasing Department:			
Purchasing manager	$ 1,750	$ 1,750	$ 21,000
Buyers	2,500	1,900	28,500
Clerks	2,000	1,100	20,600
Supplies	275	150	2,500
Accounts Payable Department:			
Clerks	2,000	1,500	21,500
Supplies	125	75	1,100
Data processing	2,600	2,300	30,000
Warehouse:			
Supervisor	1,250	1,250	15,000
Receiving clerks	2,300	1,800	23,300
Receiving supplies	50	25	500
Shipping clerks	3,800	3,500	44,000
Shipping supplies	1,350	1,200	15,200
Freight out	1,600	1,300	16,800
Total	$21,600	$17,850	$240,000

The Purchasing Department is responsible for placing all orders. The costs listed for the Accounts Payable Department relate only to the processing of purchase orders for payment. The Warehouse costs reflect two operations, receiving and shipping. The receiving clerks inspect all incoming shipments and place the orders in storage. The shipping clerks are responsible for processing all sales orders to retailers.

The company leases space in a public warehouse where the rental fee is priced according to the square feet occupied during a month. The annual charges during the year totaled $34,500. Annual insurance and property tax on the shoes stored in the warehouse were $5,700 and $7,300, respectively. The company pays 8% a year for a small amount of short-term, seasonal bank debt. Long-term capital investments are expected to produce a rate of return of 12% after income tax; the effective income tax rate is 40%.

The inventory balances tend to fluctuate during the year, depending upon the demand for baby shoes. Selected data on inventory balances for the year are:

Inventory, January 1	$160,000
Inventory, December 31	120,000
Highest inventory balance (June)	220,000
Lowest inventory balance (December)	120,000
Average monthly inventory	190,000

The boxes in which the baby shoes are stored are all approximately the same size and occupy about the same amount of storage space in the warehouse.

Required:
  (1) Estimate values appropriate for (a) the cost of placing an order (CO), and (b) the annual carrying cost per dollar of average investment in inventory (CC).
  (2) Explain whether the costs should be developed solely from the historical data used in the EOQ model.   (CMA adapted)

B. Setup cost. Pointer Furniture Company manufactures and sells office desks. For efficiency and quality control reasons, the desks are manufactured in batches. For example, 10 high-quality desks might be manufactured during the first two weeks in October and 50 units of a lower-quality desk during the last two weeks. Because each model has its own unique manufacturing requirement, the change from one model to another requires the factory's equipment to be adjusted. Pointer management wishes to determine the most economical production run for each of the items in its product lines by adapting the economic order quantity inventory model.

One of the cost parameters that must be determined before the model can be employed is the setup cost incurred when there is a change to a different furniture model. As an example, the Accounting Department has been asked to determine the setup cost for Model JE 40 in its junior executive line.

The Equipment Maintenance Department is responsible for all of the changeover adjustments on production lines, in addition to the preventive and regular maintenance of all the production equipment. The equipment maintenance employees are paid $9 per hour and employee benefits average 20% of wage costs. The other departmental costs, which include such items as supervision, depreciation, and insurance, total $50,000 per year. Two people from the Equipment Maintenance Department are required to make the production change for Model JE 40. Each person spends an estimated 5 hours in setting up the equipment, as follows:

Machinery changes	3 hours
Testing	1 hour
Machinery readjustments	1 hour
Total	5 hours

The production line on which Model JE 40 is manufactured is operated by five workers. During the changeover, these workers assist the maintenance workers when needed and operate the line during the test run. However, they are idle for approximately 40% of the time required for the changeover, and cannot be assigned to other jobs. The production workers are paid a basic wage of $7.50 per hour. Two factory overhead bases are used to apply the indirect costs because some of the costs vary in proportion to direct labor hours, while others vary with machine hours. The factory overhead rates applicable for the current year are as follows:

	Based on Direct Labor Hours	Based on Machine Hours
Variable	$2.75	$ 5.00
Fixed.	2.25	15.00
	$5.00	$20.00

These department overhead rates are based on an expected activity of 10,000 direct labor hours and 1,500 machine hours for the current year. This department is not scheduled to operate at full capacity because production capability currently exceeds sales potential.

The estimated cost of the direct materials used in the test run totals $200. Salvage materials from the test run should total $50.

Required:
    (1) Estimate Pointer's setup cost for desk Model JE 40, for use in the economic production run model.
    (2) Identify cost items to include in estimating Pointer's inventory carrying cost.
(CMA adapted)

Chapter 12
Labor: Controlling and Accounting for Costs

Labor cost represents the human contribution to production and is an important cost factor requiring constant measurement, control, and analysis. Labor cost consists of basic pay and fringe benefits. The basic pay for work performed is called the *base rate* or *job rate*. A base rate should be established for each operation in a plant or office and grouped by class of operation. An equitable wage rate or salary structure requires an analysis, description, and evaluation of each job within the plant or office. The value of all jobs must relate to wages and salaries paid for similar work in the community and in the industry or business as a whole. Maintaining competitive wage rates and salaries facilitates the acquisition and retention of quality personnel.

Fringe benefits also form a substantial element of labor cost. Fringe costs, such as the employer's share of FICA tax, unemployment taxes, holiday pay, vacation pay, overtime premium pay, pension costs, and cost of living adjustments, must be added to the base rate in order to arrive at the full labor cost. While these fringe costs are generally included in overhead, they should not be overlooked in management's planning and control responsibilities, in decision-making analyses, or in labor-management wage negotiations. Workers' demands for a 50¢ per hour increase in pay may result in far greater expenditures by the company when related fringe costs are considered.

Productivity and Labor Costs

All wage payments are directly or indirectly based on and limited by the productivity and skill of the worker. Therefore, proper motivation, control, and accounting for this human cost factor is one of the most important problems in the management of an enterprise. A cooperative and enthusiastic labor force, loyal to the company and its policies, can contribute greatly toward efficient, low-cost operations. Wages are only one element in employer-employee relations, however. Adequate records, easily understood and readily available, are an equally important factor in harmonious relations between management, employees, labor unions, government agencies, and the general public.

Productivity may be defined as the measurement of production performance using the expenditure of human effort as a yardstick. It is the amount of goods and services a worker produces. Perhaps productivity could also be described as the efficiency with which resources are converted into commodities and/or services. Greater productivity can be achieved by better processes, improved or modern equipment, or any other factor that improves the utilization of the work force. Changes in the utilization of a labor force often require changes in methods of compensating labor, followed by changes in accounting for labor costs.

The objective of productivity measurement is to provide management with a concise and accurate index for the comparison of actual results with a standard of performance. Productivity measurement should recognize the individual contribution of factors such as employees (including management), plant and equipment used in production, products and services utilized in production, capital invested, and government services utilized (as indicated by taxes). However, the most generally utilized measurement has been physical output per labor hour, which takes into account only one element of input — labor. Thus, productivity measurement ratios are, at their best, crude statistical devices that ignore such essential factors as capital and land.

Setting a standard of labor performance is not easy, since it is often accompanied by serious disputes between management and unions. The pace at which the observed person is working is noted and referred to as a *rating* or *performance rating*. The rating factor is applied to the selected task to obtain a *normal time*, i.e., the time it should take a person working at a normal pace to do the job. Allowances are added for personal time, rest periods, and possible delays. The final result is the *standard time* for the job, expressed in minutes per piece or in units to be produced per hour.

The *productivity-efficiency ratio* measures the output of an individual, relative to the performance standard. This ratio can also be used to measure the relative operating achievement of a machine, an operation, a department, or an entire organization. To illustrate, if 4,000 hours is standard for a department and if 4,400 hours are used, then there is an unfavorable ratio of 90.9 percent (4,000 ÷ 4,400).

When productivity increases, business profits and the real earnings of workers should also increase. In recent years, productivity has generally been increasing, resulting in more available goods and services. However, the normal productivity gain has fallen below the average gain of earlier years. This slowdown has given rise to increased costs. Whenever output does not keep pace with costs, unit costs—and, therefore, prices—go up. Wage increases, often excessive, have been a significant factor in this wage-price spiral because labor cost forms such a large part of total cost. If prices are to be kept from rising, then wage increases should not exceed an amount that reflects the unit cost reduction resulting from increased productivity. In recent years, employment costs—wages, salaries, and fringe benefits—have risen more than output or production per labor hour, leading to higher prices to meet higher unit labor costs.

In 1980, the Congressional Joint Economic Committee issued a report, *Productivity and Inflation*, in which the role of productivity in reducing the nation's rate of inflation was assessed. The report states that each increase of 1 percent in productivity growth would reduce inflation by at least 2.1 percent two years after the change and 2.8 percent four years later. The report further states that productivity growth should be considered in designing any wage and price standards, and that wage settlements which would otherwise be inflationary might not be, if accompanied by large productivity gains.

Incentive Wage Plans

In the modern industrial enterprise with mass production and many employees, a worker's wage is based on negotiated labor contracts, productivity studies, job evaluations, profit sharing, incentive wage plans, and guaranteed annual wages. Because all wages are paid for work performed, an element of incentive is present in all wage plans. In contrast with pay by the hour, week, or month, an incentive wage plan should reward workers in direct proportion to their increased output. A fair day's work standard should be established so that the worker can meet and even exceed it with a reasonable effort, thereby receiving full benefit from the incentive wage plan.

The installation and operation of incentive wage plans require not only the combined efforts of the personnel department, labor unions, factory engineers, and accountants, but also the cooperation and willingness of each worker. To be successful, an incentive wage plan must: (1) be applicable to situations in which a worker can increase output, (2) provide for proportionately more pay for output above standard, (3) set fair standards so that extra effort will result in bonus pay, and (4) result in immediate reward every payday. Along with these essentials, the plan needs to be reasonably simple and understandable to workers as well as to managers.

Purpose of an Incentive Wage Plan

The primary purpose of an incentive wage plan is to induce a worker to produce more, to earn a higher wage, and at the same time to reduce unit costs. The plan seeks to insure greater output, to increase control over labor cost by insuring more uniform unit costs, and to change the basis for reward from hours served to work accomplished. Naturally, producing more in the same period of time should result in higher pay for the worker. Because of the greater number of units produced, it should also result in a lower cost per unit for factory overhead and labor cost combined.

To illustrate, assume that a factory operation takes place in a building that is rented for $2,400 per month ($80 per day or $10 per hour) and that depreciation, insurance, and property tax amount to $64 per day or $8 per hour. Assume further that 10 workers on an 8-hour day are paid $6 per hour and that each worker produces 40 units of product per day (an individual production rate of 5 units per hour). The workers and the management agree that a rate of $6.60 per hour will be paid if a worker produces 48 units per day, thereby increasing the hourly output from 5 to 6 units.

The following table shows the cost per hour and cost per unit for the two systems, and indicates how a wage incentive can reduce unit costs and at the same time provide the worker with a higher income.

Cost Factor	Original System, $6 Per Hour (10 workers)			New System, $6.60 Per Hour (10 workers)		
	Amount Per Hour	Units Per Hour	Unit Cost	Amount Per Hour	Units Per Hour	Unit Cost
Labor	$60	50	$1.20	$66	60	$1.1000
Rent	10	50	.20	10	60	.1667
Depreciation, insurance, and property tax....	8	50	.16	8	60	.1333
Total	$78	50	$1.56	$84	60	$1.4000

Effect of an Incentive Wage Plan on Unit Costs

Although the hourly labor cost of the work crew increases from $60 to $66, the cost of a complete unit of product is reduced from $1.56 to $1.40. The unit cost decrease is caused by two factors: (1) unit output per worker is increased 20 percent, with a 10 percent increase in wages, and (2) the same amount of factory overhead is spread over 60 instead of 50 units of product an hour. For greater precision, such an analysis should also include labor-related costs, such as employer's payroll taxes, as well as any other relevant factory overhead that would influence the unit cost.

The lowering of conversion or manufacturing cost resulting from an incentive wage plan, illustrated here on a cost per unit basis, should also be analyzed in terms of differential (marginal or incremental) cost (Chapter 24). The marginal revenue associated with the additional output and the marginal cost of administering an incentive wage plan are two factors that may influence management's decision to install a plan.

Types of Incentive Wage Plans

In actual practice, time wages and output wages are not clear-cut and distinct. Incentive plans typically involve wage rates based upon various combinations of output and time. Many wage incentive systems retain the names of the industrial engineers and efficiency experts who originated the plans—the Taylor differential piece-rate plan, the Halsey premium plan, the Bedaux point system, the Gantt task and bonus plan, and the Emerson efficiency bonus plan. Most of these plans are no longer used, but many adaptations are still in use. To demonstrate the operation of incentive wage plans, the straight piecework plan, the 100 percent bonus plan, and the group bonus plan are discussed as representative examples.

Straight Piecework Plan. The *straight piecework plan,* one of the simplest incentive wage plans, pays wages above the base rate for production above the standard. The production standard is computed in minutes per piece and is then translated into money per piece. If time studies determine that 2.5 minutes is to be the standard time required for producing one unit, the standard rate is 24 pieces per hour. If a worker's base pay rate is $7.44 per hour, the piece rate is $.31. Workers are generally guaranteed a base pay rate, even if they fail to earn that amount in terms of output. If a worker's production exceeds 24 pieces per hour, the $.31 per unit still applies. In the following table, the labor cost per unit of output declines until the standard is reached and then remains constant at any level of output above standard.

	Units per Hour	Guaranteed Hourly Rate	Piece Rate	Earned per Hour	Labor Cost per Unit	Over-head per Hour	Over-head per Unit	Conversion Cost per Unit
Straight Piecework Plan	20	$7.44	$ 0	$7.44	$.372	$4.80	$.240	$.612
	22	7.44	0	7.44	.338	4.80	.218	.556
	24	7.44	.31	7.44	.310	4.80	.200	.510
	26	7.44	.31	8.06	.310	4.80	.185	.495
	28	7.44	.31	8.68	.310	4.80	.171	.481
	30	7.44	.31	9.30	.310	4.80	.160	.470
	32	7.44	.31	9.92	.310	4.80	.150	.460

While piece rates reflect an obvious cause-effect relationship between output and pay, the incentive is effective only when workers can control their rates of output. Piece rates would not be effective when output is machine-paced. Also, modification of production standards and labor rates becomes necessary when increases in output are the result of the installation of new and better machines.

100 Percent Bonus Plan. The *100 percent bonus plan* is a variation of the straight piecework plan. It differs in that standards are stated not in terms of money, but in time per unit of output. Instead of a price per piece, a standard time is allowed to complete a job or unit, and the worker is paid for the standard time at the hourly rate if the job or unit is completed in standard time or less. Thus, if a worker produces 100 units in an 8-hour shift and the standard time is 80 units per shift (or 10 units per hour), the worker would be paid the hourly rate for 10 hours. In other variations of the 100 percent bonus plan, savings are shared with the supervisor and/or the company.

Each payroll period, an efficiency ratio must be figured for every worker before earnings can be computed. Production standards in units of output per hour are set by industrial engineers. Hours of work and units produced are reported to the payroll department, where the reported hours worked are multiplied by the hourly production standard to determine the standard units. The worker's production is then divided by the standard quantity, resulting in the efficiency ratio. The efficiency ratio multiplied by the worker's base rate results in the hourly earnings for the period. The following table illustrates how earnings are computed, assuming that standard production is 15 units per hour.

Worker	Hours Worked	Output Units	Standard Units	Efficiency Ratio	Base Rate	Base × Efficiency Ratio	Total Earned	Labor Cost per Unit	Overhead per Hour	Overhead per Unit	Conversion Cost per Unit
Abrams	40	540	600	.90	$7.50	—*	$300.00	$.5556	$5.40	$.4000	$.9556
Gordon	40	660	600	1.10	7.50	$ 8.250	330.00	.5000	5.40	.3273	.8273
Hanson	40	800	600	1.33	7.50	9.975	399.00	.4988	5.40	.2700	.7688
Jonson	38	650	570	1.14	7.60	8.664	329.23	.5065	5.40	.3157	.8222
Stowell	40	750	600	1.25	8.00	10.000	400.00	.5333	5.40	.2880	.8213
Wiebold	40	810	600	1.35	7.72	10.422	416.88	.5147	5.40	.2667	.7814

*When the efficiency ratio is less than 1.00, no bonus is earned.

100 Percent Bonus Plan

The 100 percent bonus plan has gained in popularity because of the frequency of wage increases. The standards, stated in terms of time and output quantity, need no adjustment when wage rates change. Since the system emphasizes time rather than money, the plan lends itself to the development of controls and efficiency standards.

Group Bonus Plan. Industry uses a great variety of incentive wage plans, some of which depend upon a superior productive performance of a whole department or an entire factory. Factory operations often require employees to work in groups or crews using large machines. Although the work of each employee is essential to the machine operation, it is frequently impossible to separate the work of one member of a crew. A worker on an assembly line cannot increase output without the cooperation of the entire group. Group bonus plans have proven successful in such situations.

Group bonus plans, like those designed for individual incentive, are intended to encourage production at rates above a minimum standard. Each worker in the group receives an hourly rate for production up to the standard output. Units produced in excess of the standard are regarded as time saved by the group, and each worker is in effect paid a bonus for time saved as well as being paid for time worked. Usually, the bonus earned by the group is divided among the group members in accordance with their respective base rates.

Group plans reduce the amount of clerical work necessary to compute labor cost and payrolls and the amount of supervision necessary to operate the incentive system. Group plans may also contribute to better cooperation among workers, and good workers are likely to bring pressure upon poor workers who might jeopardize the group bonus. Group plans quite often lead to the reduction of accidents, spoilage, waste, and absenteeism. For example, a bonus may be paid to a crew or department which has not had an accident for a specified period of time, or which has a reject rate in units of output below a specified ratio.

The following table illustrates the operation of a 100 percent group bonus plan. A crew of 10 workers uses costly equipment, and each is paid $10 an hour for a regular 8-hour shift. Standard production is 50 units per hour, or 400 units per shift; overhead is $320 per 8-hour shift, or $40 per hour.

Units Produced	Standard Hours for Units Produced	Actual Hours	Regular Group Wage	Bonus (Hrs. Saved @ $10)	Total Group Earnings	Labor Cost per Unit	Over-head Cost per Unit	Conversion Cost per Unit
350	70	80	$800	$ 0	$ 800	$2.286	$.914	$3.200
400	80	80	800	0	800	2.000	.800	2.800
425	85	80	800	50	850	2.000	.753	2.753
450	90	80	800	100	900	2.000	.711	2.711
475	95	80	800	150	950	2.000	.674	2.674
500	100	80	800	200	1,000	2.000	.640	2.640

100 Percent Group Bonus Plan

Time Standards Via Learning Curve Theory

Incentive wage plans assume that monetary bonuses will motivate workers to achieve higher productivity rates. In turn, the greater the output, the lower the conversion cost per unit. Yet, the previous discussion also stresses the fact that motivation is not always based on financial rewards. Furthermore, an incentive wage plan based on fixed time standards — no matter how scientifically engineered — often does not appear to motivate workers.[1] Even with such drawbacks, many current incentive wage plans still use fixed time standards for rewarding individual performance through bonus payments; however, the deficiencies existing in such wage incentive standards have been remedied by means of the learning curve theory.

The *learning curve theory* stipulates that every time the cumulative quantity of units produced is doubled, the cumulative average time per unit is reduced by a given percentage. If it is assumed that this reduction is 20 percent, it means that the second unit requires 80 percent of the cumulative average time per unit required for the first unit; the fourth unit, 80 percent of the second; the eighth unit, 80 percent of the fourth; and so on. Based on this theory, the

---

[1] A fixed time standard is best explained by referring to the 100 percent bonus plan (page 314), in which the standard is fixed at 80 units per day (or 10 units per hour).

following table of values for an 80 percent learning curve can be computed, assuming that 10 direct labor hours are required to produce the first unit:[2]

Units	×	Cumulative Average Required Labor Hours per Unit	=	Estimated Total Hours Needed To Perform the Task
1		10.0 hours		10.0 hours
2		8.0 (10.0 × 80%)		16.0
4		6.4 (8.0 × 80%)		25.6
8		5.1 (6.4 × 80%)		40.8
16		4.1 (5.1 × 80%)		65.6
32		3.3 (4.1 × 80%)		105.6
64		2.6 (3.3 × 80%)		166.4

The results indicate that the rate is constant at each doubling of the accumulated number of times the task is performed. The figures in the third column are the cumulative average hours times the number of units. To estimate the total time needed to perform the task the first 32 times, the calculation is 32 × 3.3, or 105.6 hours.

The 80 percent learning curve is used here for illustrative purposes. The 80 percent rate is frequent among industries, and typically the percentage is no lower than 60 nor higher than 85. The actual percentage will depend on the particular situation. Generally, for more complicated tasks in terms of labor skill, there is more room for learning to occur and, therefore, a greater likelihood of a lower labor input percentage as production increases. At the extremes, the actual percentage could range from 100 percent (if no learning occurs) to 50 percent. At the latter extreme, if the average accumulated time for the first unit is 100 minutes, then the time for the second unit must equal zero (i.e., 100 minutes × 50% = 50 minutes − accumulated average time per task unit at the 2 task units level, or a total of 100 minutes for the 2 units). Thus, the 50 percent rate is an upper limit of learning—one that can never be reached. If the production period is long or the labor operations are routine, a point in production is reached when any improvement through repetition would become imperceptible, and the learning curve would level out to a steady-state condition.[3]

After the learning curve percentage has been empirically determined for a specific operation, time requirements for successive increments in output can be estimated as long as conditions remain the same. Conditions which may cause deviations from times predicted by an established learning curve include changes in product design, changes in proportions of manufactured and purchased components, and changes in equipment.[4] Of course, conditions may also change because of improvements in engineering design and in manufacturing techniques.

When production is discontinuous, with comparatively long lapses of time and changes in personnel, relearning will be required. Furthermore,

---

[2]James A. Broadston, "Learning Curve Wage Incentives," *Management Accounting,* Vol. XLIX, No. 12, pp. 15-23.
[3]For further discussion of learning curves, see Richard B. Chase and Nicholas J. Aquilano, *Production and Operations Management* (Homewood, Illinois: Richard D. Irwin, Inc., 1981), pp. 602–610.
[4]Walter B. McFarland, *Manpower Cost and Performance Measurement* (New York: National Association of Accountants, 1977), p. 43.

there may be a certain element of influence on learning curve behavior that is associated with individual worker variants over time, such as temporary productivity variations caused by health or emotional problems, or the Friday afternoon downturn of production as the weekend approaches. Worker group productivity attitudes may also have their impact.

By means of the learning curve, the time standard used for determining a worker's earnings has now changed to a variable time instead of the fixed time standard. The variable time standard meets the need of an incentive wage system more equitably.

> *The improvement phenomenon, as well as its mathematical model, the learning curve, provides an insight into human capabilities that bears directly upon the ability of workers to do work and the time required for them to learn new skills. An actual learning curve may show small irregularities; yet it will eventually follow an underlying natural characteristic of group or individual human activity.*[5]

As soon as workers have passed the learning stage and begin to produce the expected number of units (i.e., reach the standard proficiency), they will begin to draw bonus pay for doing the operation in less than standard time. They may even slow down a little and yet perform the operation in standard time or better, drawing the bonus pay but working less hard for it.

Government procurement agencies have used the learning curve as a tool for cost evaluation in negotiating prices for contracts. When a bid on a contract is entered, the unit labor cost is usually estimated. The learning curve permits the determination of lot costs for various stages of production. As production progresses, the cumulative average unit labor cost should decrease.

By comparing the budgeted cost with the experienced labor cost in the initial stages of production, the trend of the labor cost can be determined. If, for example, an average labor cost of $20 per unit is to be achieved, the following output and cost table with 80, 85, and 90 percent learning curves can be predetermined:[6]

Cumulative Quantity	Learning Curve 80%	85%	90%
25	$61.02	$45.36	$33.86
50	48.82	38.56	30.47
100	39.06	32.78	27.43
200	31.25	27.68	24.69
400	25.00	23.53	22.22
800	20.00	20.00	20.00

The learning curve allows projection of the cumulative average unit cost at any stage of production. It also predicts labor hours with accuracy and reliability, establishes work load, and allows production control to take advantage of reducing time per unit by increasing lot sizes, thereby maintaining a level work force. It also provides a basis for standard cost variance calculations (Chapter 17), allows judgment of a manager's performance relative to the

---

[5]Broadston, *op. cit.*, p. 15.
[6]William H. Boren, Some Applications of the Learning Curve to Government Contracts," *NAA Bulletin*, Vol. XLVI, No. 2, pp. 21–22.

department's target, and provides a basis for cost control through analysis of undesirable shifts of the curve.

Organization For Labor Cost Accounting and Control

Labor costing procedures involve:

1. The employment history of each worker—date hired, wage rate, initial assignment, promotions, tardiness, sickness, and vacations.
2. Adequate information for compliance with union contracts, social security laws, wage and hour legislation, income tax withholdings, and other federal, state, and local government requirements.
3. The establishment of labor time and cost standards for comparative purposes.
4. Productivity in relation to type of wage payment, creating the best system of compensation for each kind of work.
5. Each employee's time worked, wage rate, and total earnings for each payroll period.
6. The computation of deductions from gross wages for each employee.
7. The output or accomplishment of each employee.
8. The amount of direct labor cost and hours to be charged to each job, lot, process, or department, and the amount of indirect labor cost. The direct labor cost or hours information may be used as a basis for factory overhead application.
9. Total labor cost in each department for each payroll period.
10. The compilation of cumulative earnings and deductions detail for each employee.

The accounting principles, procedures, and objectives in labor costing are relatively simple, although considerable difficulty in their application may be experienced with large numbers of workers or when workers shift from one type of work to another under various factory conditions. Basically, two sets of underlying detailed records are kept, one for financial accounting and the other for cost accounting. The procedures for labor accounting are outlined as follows. The journal entries associated with these procedures, as well as those pertaining to labor-related costs, are discussed and illustrated in Chapter 13.

FINANCIAL ACCOUNTING	COST ACCOUNTING
A record is kept of the total time worked and the total amount earned by each worker.	A record is kept of the time worked on each job, process, or department by each worker and the cost thereof.
The daily or weekly amount earned by each worker is entered on the payroll book.	The direct labor hours and cost are entered on the respective job cost sheets or production reports; the indirect labor cost is entered in the proper column of the departmental expense analysis sheets.

FINANCIAL ACCOUNTING	COST ACCOUNTING
Each payroll period, the total amount of wages paid to workers results in the following entry:	The weekly or month-end entry for labor distribution is:

Payroll	xxx	Work in Process........		xxx
Employees Income		Factory Over-		
Tax Payable	xxx	head Control.........		xxx
FICA Tax Payable	xxx	Indirect Labor	xxx	
Accounts Payable or		Payroll		xxx
Cash..................	xxx			

Labor cost control begins with an adequate production planning schedule supported by labor-hour requirements and accompanying labor costs, determined well in advance of production runs. In most manufacturing plants, it is usually possible to establish a reasonably accurate ratio of direct labor hours and number of employees to dollar sales by product lines, and by relating this ratio to the sales forecast, to predict future labor requirements. The relationship between sales volume and personnel needs is perhaps more direct and predictable in wholesale, retail, financial, and service enterprises. The entire labor cost control process begins with the design of the product and continues until the product is sold. The departments that should cooperate in this process include the personnel, production planning, timekeeping, payroll, and cost departments.

Personnel Department

The chief function of a personnel department is to provide an efficient labor force. In a general way, this department is responsible for seeing that an entire organization follows good personnel policies. However, very little of the real personnel work is done by employees of the personnel department. Personnel relations are personal relations—between department heads and their subordinates, between supervisors and workers, and among all employees.

Personnel functions, dealing with the human resources of the organization, involve recruiting and employment procedures, training programs, job descriptions, job evaluations, and time and motion studies. Hiring of employees may be for replacement or for expansion. Replacement hiring starts with a labor requisition sent to the personnel department by a department head or supervisor. Expansion hiring requires authorization by executive management, in which case the authority to hire results from approval of the labor requirements of a production schedule rather than from separate requisitions to fill individual jobs. The personnel department, in conjunction with the department heads concerned, plans the expansion requirements and agrees upon promotions and transfers to be made, the number and kind of workers to be hired, and the dates at which new employees will report for work.

Employment practices must comply not only with regulations set forth at the federal level (i.e., the Equal Employment Opportunity Commission and the Department of Labor) but also with regulations of human rights commissions in several of the states.

Production Planning Department

A production planning department is responsible for the scheduling of work, the release of job orders to the producing departments, and the dispatching of work in the factory. The release of orders is generally accompanied by materials requisitions and labor time tickets that indicate the operations to be performed on the product. A specific and understandable listing of detailed operations is important if work is to be performed within the time allowed and with the materials provided. Delays caused by lack of materials, machine breakdowns, or need for additional instructions give rise to complaints by the workers and lead to additional labor costs. Production schedules prepared several weeks in advance, utilizing labor time standards for each producing department, lead to cost control through the use of departmental labor budgets similar to the following:

LABOR BUDGET

Department __Cooler Assembly__   For __October, 19--__

Prepared __September 10, 19--__

Model No.	Units Scheduled	Budgeted Assembly Hours per Unit			Total Budgeted Direct Labor Hours
		Motor	Fan	Freon	
625	2,000	1.5	.25	.5	4,500
748	1,000	1.5	.30	.6	2,400
500	3,000	1.5	.20	.4	6,300
600	1,500	1.3	.40	.5	3,300
	7,500				16,500

Variable and Fixed Costs	Total Cost	Cost per Unit	No. of Employees*
Variable costs:			
Direct labor -- 16,500 hrs. @ $6	$ 99,000	$13.200	94
Indirect labor -- 1,000 hrs. @ $4.80	4,800	.640	6
Total variable labor budget	$103,800	$13.840	
Fixed costs:			
Supervision -- 700 hrs. @ $7	$ 4,900	$ .653	4
Clerical & Packing -- 350 hrs. @ $4.60 ..	1,610	.215	2
Total fixed labor budget	$ 6,510	$ .868	
Total for October	$110,310	$14.708	106

*No. of hrs. ÷ 176 (22 days x 8 hrs.)

Timekeeping Department

Securing an accurate record of the time purchased from each employee is the first step in labor costing. To do so, it is necessary to provide a:

1. Clock card (or time card) as unquestionable evidence of the employee's presence in the plant from the time of entry to departure.
2. Time ticket (or job ticket) to secure information as to the type of work performed.

Both forms, which are illustrated as follows, are supervised, controlled, and collected by the timekeeping department. Since the earnings of the employee depend mainly upon these two forms and the timekeeper processes them in the first step toward final payment, the timekeeping department forms a most valuable link in harmonious labor-management relationships. In fact, to many workers, the timekeeper *is* management. Frequently the timekeeper's performance is the basis for a worker's first opinion of the company.

Clock Card

Time Ticket

Clock Card. A *clock card* provides space for the name and number of the employee and usually covers an entire payroll period. When completed, the clock card shows the time a worker started and stopped work each day or shift of the payroll period, with overtime and other premium hours clearly indicated.

The *time clock* (or *time recorder*) is a mechanical instrument for recording employee time in and out of the office and the factory. Under a typical procedure, each employee is assigned a clock number that identifies the department and the employee. The clock number is used for identification on the payroll and in charging labor time to departments and production orders.

Time Ticket. In accounting for materials, the receiving report and the invoice are evidence that the goods have been received and payment is in order. In accounting for labor, the clock card is evidence that time has been purchased and is comparable to the receiving report. The *time ticket* shows the specific use that has been made of the time purchased and is comparable to the materials requisition. When an individual time ticket is used, a new ticket must be made out for each job worked on during the day. Since this procedure may lead to many tickets per employee, some plants use a *daily time report* on which the worker lists jobs.

The best procedure for filling in time tickets depends upon many factors peculiar to shop operations. In some factories, the workers prepare their own time tickets, approved by the supervisor, or the supervisor prepares them. Remote computer terminals enable employees to report time distributions by direct entry to the computer. These entries are later confirmed by the supervisors, based on reports received from the computer center. In other factories, timekeepers, dispatch clerks, and supervisors have desks near the work stations. Employees report to the timekeeper when changing jobs, get a new assignment from the dispatch clerk, secure instructions at the supervisor's desk, get the required tools at the tool crib, and thus shift from one job to another.

Each day, usually after the morning shift has clocked in, the timekeeper collects all the time tickets or the daily time reports of the previous day, together with the clock cards. Before the daily time tickets are sent to the payroll department, the total time reported on each time ticket is compared with the total hours of each employee's clock card. If there is any difference, an adjustment is made. If the clock card shows more hours than the time tickets, the difference is reported as idle time. If the time tickets show more hours than the clock card, the error is corrected in consultation with the supervisor and the worker.

The degree of accuracy in reporting time varies from plant to plant, but in most situations a report to the exact minute is neither necessary nor practical. Many companies find it advantageous to use a decimal system, which is fast and which measures the hour in ten periods of six minutes each rather than the regular clock interval of five-minute periods and twelve periods per hour. On a decimal system, a job started at 9:23 a.m. and finished at 11:38 a.m. would be reported as 9.3 and 11.6, with an elapsed time of 2.3 hours.

Time tickets form the basis for calculating bonuses under a wage incentive plan. When wages are based on hours worked, the time tickets provide a means of auditing the clock cards and a source of data concerning efficient utilization of labor.

Payroll Department

Payroll data are processed in two steps: (1) computing and preparing the payroll and (2) distributing the payroll to jobs, processes, and departments. These steps may be performed by a payroll department, depending on the size and complexity of a company. Some companies require only a small payroll department staffed by one or two payroll clerks who perform the work manually; others require an elaborate payroll department with many employees and computerized procedures. In any case, the payroll department is responsible for the important task of recording the job classification, department, and wage rate for each employee. It records hours worked and wages earned, makes payroll deductions, determines the net amount due each employee, maintains a permanent earnings record for each employee, prepares the paychecks or provides the cashier's or treasurer's office with the necessary records to make the payments, and may prepare the payroll distribution.

Payroll Computation and Preparation. The company's payroll is prepared from the clock cards. The final computed payroll may be recorded in a payroll journal, payroll record, payroll report, or payroll sheet. The record may be a bound book with sheets ruled for the special needs of a company; it may be a loose-leaf book, cards, or sheets for filing; or it may be produced on sheets or rolls through the use of payroll machines or computerized methods. The record must show total wages, deductions, and the net payroll. A record of individual employee earnings and deductions must also be maintained.

In most instances, employees are paid by check. Payroll checks may be drawn against the regular checking account or a special payroll deposit. The special payroll bank account is especially advantageous with large numbers of workers. When a payroll fund is deposited in the bank, the payroll department certifies the amount required for a particular payment date, a voucher is drawn for the specified amount, and a check is drawn against the regular deposit account and is deposited in the payroll fund. By utilizing this procedure, only one check, drawn on the general bank account, appears in the cash payments journal each payroll period. For each employee, the paymaster prepares a check drawn against the special payroll account. When machine methods are used for payroll accounting, the payroll journal, the checks, the check register, and the employees' earnings records are commonly prepared in one simultaneous operation.

Payroll Distribution. The individual time ticket or daily time report shows the use made of the time purchased from each factory employee. The tickets for each employee must agree with the employee's total earnings for the week. Time tickets are sorted by jobs, departments, and types of indirect labor to permit the distribution of the total payroll to Work in Process and to the departmental expense analysis sheets controlled by Factory Overhead Control. Distribution of the payroll is speeded up when automated methods are used. If the payroll department does not prepare the distribution summary, the time tickets are sent to the cost department, which must perform this task. Labor costs distributed to jobs, processes, or departments must agree with the total amount recorded in the payroll account. The distribution summary may also show the labor hours when they are the basis for the application of factory overhead.

Cost Department

On the basis of the labor distribution summary or the time tickets, the cost department records the direct labor cost on the appropriate job cost sheets or production reports, and the indirect cost on the departmental expense analysis sheets. In some factories, cost accounting activities are decentralized, and cost work becomes largely a matter of organization and direction in carrying out a system for recording payroll information and labor costs. In such a situation, cost clerks may be stationed in producing departments to assist in accumulating and classifying labor costs, using the time tickets to compute production costs and services by job orders, units of output, departmental operations, and product types. In other factories, the cost department may be highly centralized and may not direct and control any timekeeping or payroll preparation.

Summary

The following organization chart summarizes the departmental inter-relationships required for effective labor cost control and accounting.

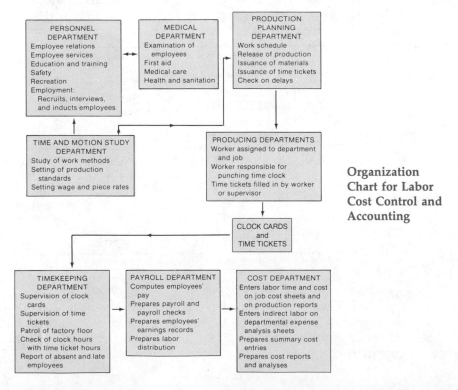

Organization Chart for Labor Cost Control and Accounting

The preceding labor costing procedures have emphasized manufacturing labor. Labor costing of nonmanufacturing labor, such as marketing and administrative employees, also requires the same detailed cost accumulation and distribution procedures.

Labor Performance Reports

Production schedules, performance standards, and labor budgets represent plans and expectations, but effective control of labor efficiency and costs depends upon meaningful and timely performance reports sent to department heads and supervisors who are directly responsible for departmental production. Labor performance reports are designed to compare budgets and standards with actual results attained, thereby pointing to variances from planned performance. The departmental direct labor cost report, the plant-wide labor cost report issued weekly or monthly, the daily performance report for labor, and daily idle time reports are the media used to provide supervisors and plant managers with information needed for effective cost control.

In the following report, the expected direct labor cost for the week is computed from the October labor budget for the Cooler Assembly Department, shown on page 321. For example, in motor assembling, the Cooler Assembly Department produced 600 units of Model No. 625 requiring 1.5 hours of budgeted labor per unit, 800 units of Model No. 500 with 1.5 hours of budgeted labor per unit, and 500 units of Model No. 600 with 1.3 hours of budgeted labor per unit, for a total of 2,750 budgeted labor hours at $6 per hour, or $16,500.

DEPARTMENTAL DIRECT LABOR COST REPORT

Department Cooler Assembly   Supervisor H. Stevenson

Production No. 625--600 units   Week Ending October 12, 19--

No. 500--800 units

No. 600--500 units

Operation	Actual Cost	Budgeted Cost	Variance*	Reasons
Motor........	$16,925.00	$16,500.00	$425 over 2.6%	Reboring hangers
Fan..........	3,000.00	3,060.00	60 under 2.0%	Good group
Freon........	5,675.00	5,220.00	455 over 8.7%	Overtime and reweld
Total...	$25,600.00	$24,780.00	$820 over	

*Expressed as a percentage of budgeted cost, e.g., $425 ÷ $16,500 = 2.6%

The following plant-wide labor cost report is sent to executive and plant management to indicate (1) the trend of direct and indirect labor cost in the three departments and (2) the actual cost compared with the estimated cost figures.

LABOR COST REPORT		Plant _Midville_ Week Ending _October 12, 19--_					
Department	Labor Class	Actual Labor Cost			Estimated Labor Cost		
		This Week	Last Week	Year to Date	This Week	Last Week	Year to Date
Cutting	Direct.... Indirect..	$28,500 2,200	$28,200 2,250	$1,174,380 81,640	$28,200 2,240	$28,000 2,200	$1,172,500 81,800
	Total..	$30,700	$30,450	$1,256,020	$30,440	$30,200	$1,254,300
Forming	Direct.... Indirect..	$13,600 1,600	$13,400 1,600	$ 430,525 65,600	$13,750 1,600	$13,450 1,620	$ 431,000 65,700
	Total..	$15,200	$15,000	$ 496,125	$15,350	$15,070	$ 496,700
Cooler Assembly	Direct.... Indirect..	$25,600 2,825	$26,100 2,800	$1,152,250 117,880	$24,780 2,750	$24,000 2,750	$1,150,000 117,000
	Total..	$28,425	$28,900	$1,270,130	$27,530	$26,750	$1,267,000

Timely reporting is required for effective cost control. While weekly reports, as illustrated above, are informative and serve a useful purpose, daily reports may be required as well. The following daily performance report and the daily idle time report[7] below combine three types of daily labor reports: (1) employee performance, (2) departmental performance, and (3) idle time. Physical factors such as hours are coupled with percentages to improve the effectiveness of these reports.

DAILY PERFORMANCE REPORT FOR LABOR							
Daily Performance Report by Employees				Daily Performance Report by Departments			
Employee No.	Actual Producing Hours	Standard Hours of Output	Percent Performance	Department	Actual Producing Hours	Standard Hours of Output	Percent Performance
105	8	10	125.0	1	110	90	81.8
110	6	7	116.7	2	280	300	107.1
112	5	4	80.0	3	150	145	96.7

DAILY IDLE TIME REPORT											
Department	Total Direct Labor Hours	Productive Direct Labor Hours		Idle Time Due To							
				Maintenance		No Materials		Other		Total	
		Amount	%	Amount	%	Amount	%	Amount	%	Amount	%
1	3,200	2,900	90.6	200	6.2	50	1.6	50	1.6	300	9.4
2	1,300	1,200	92.3	25	1.9	25	1.9	50	3.9	100	7.7
3	600	550	91.7	20	3.3	30	5.0			50	8.3
4	200	180	90.0	10	5.0			10	5.0	20	10.0
Total	5,300	4,830	91.1	255	4.8	105	2.0	110	2.1	470	8.9

[7]William L. Ferrara, "An Integrated Approach to Control of Production Costs," *NAA Bulletin*, Vol. LXI, No. 9, p. 65.

The Computer's Contribution to Labor Cost Control

Payroll procedures were among the first to be programmed for computers because most businesses had well-defined payroll accounting procedures. Computerized labor accounting begins the day an employee is hired and the data for the employee's name, number, job classification, shift, department, direct/indirect pay rate, deductions, etc., are entered in the employee's master file. From that moment on, the employee's activities and those of every other employee are inputted for payroll data, labor distribution, and a permanent employment data bank. Computerized payroll procedures are depicted in the following flowchart:

Flowchart of Computerized Payroll Procedures

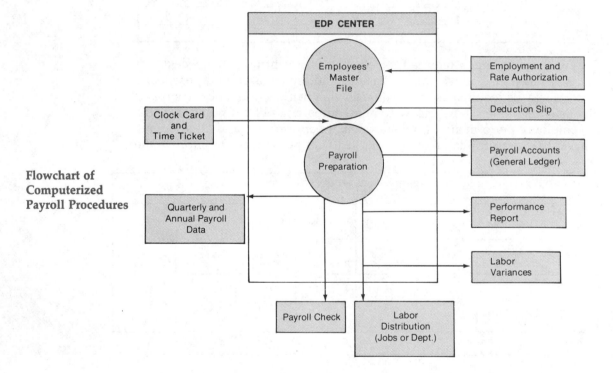

Computerized procedures can be used to produce the types of reports that have been illustrated, including use of a computer program to calculate and report each worker's daily earnings and efficiency. Because such a report is too voluminous and impractical for a plant manager or supervisor to use, one procedure is to program for significant unfavorable shifts in performance from one day to the next. This type of report provides for management by exception, whereby the supervisor can work to correct problems of a very few workers and prevent chronic difficulties. With a work force of five hundred employees, a daily report from the computer, identifying significant adverse changes, might appear as follows. This report is focused on adverse changes in performance from the workers' historical pattern. For example, Perez is a highly efficient performer, but the 81% efficiency rate seems too low for this worker, and management has an opportunity to take early corrective action if needed.

Employee	% Efficiency Last Month			% Efficiency Yesterday	Previous Five Days % Efficiency					Number of Times Reported This Month
	Low	High	Average							

EMPLOYEE PERFORMANCE REPORT
(Significant Adverse Change)   May 19, 19--

Employee	Low	High	Average	% Efficiency Yesterday	\<Previous Five Days % Efficiency\>					Number of Times Reported This Month
BOWAN, T.	72%	84%	78%	64%	76	79	83	81	78	1
DURAM, A.	75	91	83	69	71	73	85	90	90	2
GORDON, E.	70	78	74	31	76	71	75	78	74	1
HOESL, A.	62	88	75	56	80	84	76	65	87	3
PEREZ, G.	86	98	92	81	85	93	97	94	92	1

With daily efficiency performances in computer storage, management can be provided with monthly or quarterly reports on chronically inefficient workers. The following illustration indicates the information needed to increase effectiveness in labor utilization and labor cost control. Even with no knowledge of the situation, a reading of the illustration suggests that Asbury, Clarke, and probably Varney are not likely to be satisfactory workers in this department if 75% of the standard rate is considered minimal. Dettmer and Mayes seem to be improving, while Shaw appears capable of attaining the desired productivity level.

EMPLOYEE PERFORMANCE REPORT
(Chronically Low Performance)   November 30, 19--

Employee	% Efficiency Last 12 Months			% Efficiency This Month	Previous Five Months % Efficiency					Number of Times Reported This Year
	Low	High	Average		Oct	Sep	Aug	Jul	Jun	
ASBURY, M.	33%	43%	38%	40%	42	49	43	51	46	6
CLARKE, G.	42	58	50	52	56	45	51	45	51	7
DETTMER, C.	58	74	66	71	70	68	66	58	63	3
MAYES, W.	60	66	63	66	64	60	56	54	50	2
SHAW, T.	70	84	77	68	70	75	68	75	80	5
VARNEY, M.	45	73	59	64	60	65	68	66	64	4

Effective control is best achieved by careful use of comparisons between actual performance and predetermined standards of performance. Daily or weekly comparisons may be in aggregate (i.e., by department or division), or they may be made for each employee. Departmental labor cost reports can be combined to form a plant summary of operating performance, which is most useful to the plant superintendent and other production officials.

DISCUSSION QUESTIONS

1. Is it generally true that all wage payments are ultimately limited by and are usually based, directly or indirectly, on the productivity of the worker? Explain.

2. Define productivity.

3. How can labor efficiency be determined or measured?

4. What is the purpose of an incentive wage plan?

5. In most incentive wage plans, does production above standard reduce the labor cost per unit of output? Discuss.

6. Wage incentive plans are successful in plants operating near full capacity.
   (a) Discuss the desirability of using these plans during periods of curtailed production.
   (b) Is it advisable to install an incentive wage plan in a plant operating at 60% of capacity? Discuss.

7. Describe the straight piecework plan, the 100 percent bonus plan, and the group bonus plan.

8. State the basic concept underlying the relationship involved in the learning curve theory.

9. Name some situations for the application of the learning curve theory.

10. Accounting for labor has a two-fold aspect: financial accounting and cost accounting. Differentiate between the two.

11. In what way are the creation and maintenance of an efficient labor force a cooperative effort?

12. What is the purpose of determining the labor hours (a) worked by each employee; (b) worked on each job, or in each department?

13. What purpose is served by the (a) clock card; (b) time ticket?

14. If employees' clock cards show more time than their time tickets, how is the difference reconciled?

EXERCISES

1. *100 percent bonus plan.* J. Martin, employed by the Beach City Canning Company, submitted the following labor data for the first week in June:

	Units	Hours
Monday	270	8
Tuesday..........	210	8
Wednesday.......	300	8
Thursday	240	8
Friday............	260	8

Required: *Prepare a schedule showing Martin's weekly earnings, the effective hourly rate, and the labor cost per unit, assuming a 100 percent bonus plan with a base wage of $9 per hour and a standard production rate of 30 units per hour. (Round off the bonus percentage to two decimal places.)*

2. 100 percent group bonus plan. White Plains, Inc. produces printed circuits for the electronics industry. The firm has recently initiated a 100 percent group bonus plan with standard production set at 50 units per hour.

The company employs 10 workers on an 8-hour shift at $8 per hour. Depreciation on plant equipment is $9 per hour, and other overhead is applied at $7 per hour.

Production for the first week under the 100 percent group bonus plan was:

	Units
Monday	3,800
Tuesday	4,500
Wednesday	4,600
Thursday	4,500
Friday	4,400

Management is interested in appraising the results of the new incentive wage plan.

Required: Prepare a schedule showing employee earnings, unit labor cost, unit overhead cost, and conversion cost per unit. (Round off unit costs to three decimal places.)

3. Incentive wage plans. Standard production for an employee in the Assembly Department is 20 units per hour in an 8-hour day. The hourly wage rate is $7.50.

Required: Compute the employee's earnings under each of the following conditions (carrying all computations to three decimal places):

(1) If an incentive plan is used, with the worker receiving 80% of the time saved each day, and records indicate:

	Units	Hours
Monday	160	8
Tuesday	170	8.
Wednesday	175	8

(2) If the 100 percent bonus plan is used and 840 units are produced in a 40-hour week.

(3) If an incentive plan is used, providing an hourly rate increase of 5% for all hours worked each day that quota production is achieved, and records indicate:

	Units	Hours
Monday	160	8
Tuesday	168	8
Wednesday	175	8

4. Incentive wage plan evaluation. Electroscan Company, a relatively small supplier of computer-oriented parts, is currently engaged in producing a new component for the computer sensory unit. The company has been producing 150 units per week and factory overhead (all fixed) was estimated to be $1,200 per week. The following is a schedule of the pay rates of three workers assigned to the new component:

Employee	Hourly Rate
Clancy, D.	$6.00
Luken, T.	8.00
Schott, J.	7.00

Customers have been calling in for additional units, but management does not want to work more than 40 hours per week. To motivate its workers to produce more, the company decided to institute an incentive wage plan. Under the plan, each worker would be paid a base rate per hour, as shown in the following schedule, and a premium of $1 per unit for all units when the total number exceeds 150.

Employee	Base Rate
Clancy, D.	$3.50
Luken, T.	5.50
Schott, J.	4.50

The first week the plan was put into operation, production increased to 165 units. The shop superintendent studied the results and considered the plan too costly. Production had increased 10%, but the labor cost had increased by approximately 23.2%. The superintendent requested permission to redesign the plan in order to make the labor cost increase proportionate to the productivity increase.

Required:

(1) Calculate the dollar amount of the 23.2% labor cost increase.

(2) Give an opinion, supported by figures, as to whether the shop superintendent was correct in assuming that the incentive wage plan was too costly, and discuss other factors to be considered.

5. Learning curve and production cost. *A company's new process will be carried out in one department. The production process has an expected learning curve of 80%. The cost subject to the learning effect for the first batch produced by the process was $20,000.*

Required: *Compute the cumulative average cost per batch subject to the learning effect after the 16th batch has been produced, using the learning curve function.*

6. Learning curve and construction time. *A construction company has just completed a bridge over the Red River. This is the first bridge the company has built and it required 100 weeks to complete. Now, having a bridge construction crew with some experience, the company would like to continue building bridges. Because of the investment in heavy machinery needed continuously by this crew, the company believes it would have to bring the average construction time to less than one year (52 weeks) per bridge in order to earn a sufficient return on investment. The average construction time will follow an 80% learning curve.*

Required: *Compute the number of additional bridges the crew must build to bring the average construction time (over all bridges constructed) below one year per bridge.*

(CMA adapted)

7. Labor performance report. *Saxon, Inc. prepares monthly production budgets for its three departments. Budgeted and actual amounts for April for one of its products are as follows:*

Department	Budgeted Hours	Actual Labor Cost	Units Produced
Mixing.	1,100	$ 9,798	740
Processing.	3,320	28,275	615
Packaging	580	3,816	800

The following standards have been adopted for this product:

Department	Standard Hours per Unit	Standard Labor Cost per Hour
Mixing	1.5	$9.15
Processing	5.0	9.75
Packaging	0.5	9.00

Required: *Prepare a labor cost report for April, comparing actual and standard labor cost.*

PROBLEMS

12-1. Incentive wage plans. For the first week in March, the record of A. Stewart shows:

	Hours Worked	Units Produced
Monday	8	90
Tuesday	8	100
Wednesday	8	110
Thursday	8	112
Friday	8	96

Stewart's guaranteed hourly wage rate is $6 and standard production is 12 units per hour. Factory overhead per labor hour is $3.

Required:

(1) If Stewart receives 90% of the labor value of time saved during a day, prepare a schedule to show Stewart's pay, using the following headings:

Day	Premium Wage
Units Produced	Total Pay
Daily Wage	Labor Cost per Unit (to nearest 1/100¢)
Units Above Standard	Overhead per Unit (to nearest 1/100¢)
Hours Saved	Conversion Cost per Unit (to nearest 1/100¢)

(2) If the 100 percent bonus plan is used (for each week's total production), prepare a schedule to show Stewart's pay, using the following headings:

Hours Worked	Base × Efficiency Ratio
Units Produced	Week's Earnings
Standard Production	Labor Cost per Unit (to nearest 1/100¢)
Efficiency Ratio (nearest %)	Conversion Cost per Unit (to nearest 1/100¢)
Base Wage	

(3) If the daily quota is standard production of 96 units and the hourly rate increases 5% for total wages for each day of quota production and above, prepare a schedule to show Stewart's pay, using the following headings:

Day	Amount Earned
Units Produced	Labor Cost per Unit (to nearest 1/100¢)
Hourly Wage	Conversion Cost per Unit (to nearest 1/100¢)

12-2. Group bonus plans. Employees of Evans and Troup Enterprises work in groups of five, plus a group leader. Standard production for a group is 400 units for a 40-hour week. The workers are paid $6 an hour until production reaches 400 units; then a bonus of

$1.20 per unit is paid for production over 400 units, with $1 being divided equally among the five workers and the remainder passing to the group leader (who is also paid a weekly salary of $300). Factory overhead is $6 per direct labor hour and includes the group leader's earnings.

The production record of a group for one week shows:

	Hours Worked	Units Produced
Monday	40	72
Tuesday	40	81
Wednesday	40	95
Thursday	40	102
Friday	40	102

Required:

(1) Compute the week's earnings of the group (excluding the leader), the labor cost per unit, the overhead cost per unit, and the conversion cost per unit, based upon the above data and bonus plan. (Round off unit costs to four decimal places.)

(2) Prepare a schedule showing daily earnings of the group (excluding the leader), unit labor cost, unit overhead cost, and the conversion cost per unit, assuming that the company uses the group bonus plan, as described on page 315.

12-3. Quarterly bonus allotment. Rosen and Haddad, Inc., manufacturers of standard pipe fittings for water and sewage lines, pay a bonus to their employees, based upon the production recorded each calendar quarter. Normal production is set at 240,000 units per quarter. A bonus of $.50 per unit is paid for any units in excess of the normal output for each quarter. Distribution of the bonus is made on the following point basis:

Employees Participating	Points Allowed For Each Employee
1 Works manager	250
2 Production engineers	200
5 Shop supervisors	200
1 Storekeeper	100
5 Factory office clerks	10
150 Factory workers	20

The employees' earnings are not penalized for any month in which the actual output falls below the monthly average of the normal quarterly production. In such a case, the deficiency is deducted from any excess in subsequent months before any bonus is earned by and paid to the employees.

At the end of March, cumulative actual production amounted to 270,000 units.

Required:

(1) Calculate the amount of bonus payable to each group of employees. (Carry all calculations to three decimal places.)

(2) Prepare journal entries at the end of each month to record the bonus liability on the basis of the following production figures: January, 75,000 units; February, 94,000 units; March, 101,000 units. Assume that all of the bonus is charged to Factory Overhead Control.

12-4. Incentive wage plans. The company's union steward complained to the Payroll Department that several union members' wages had been miscalculated in the previous week. The following schedule indicates the wages and conditions of the earnings of the workers involved:

Worker	Incentive Wage Plan	Total Hours	Down-time Hours	Units Pro-duced	Stan-dard Units	Base Rate	Gross Wages per Books
Dodd	Straight piecework	40	5	400	—	$6.00	$284.00
Hare	Straight piecework	46	—	455*	—	6.00	277.20
Lowe	Straight piecework	44	4	420**	—	6.00	302.20
Ober	Percentage bonus plan	40	—	250	200	6.00	280.00
Rupp	Percentage bonus plan	40	—	180	200	5.00	171.00
Suggs	Emerson efficiency system	40	—	240	300	5.60	233.20
Ward	Emerson efficiency system	40	2	590	600***	5.60	280.00

*Includes 45 pieces produced during the 6 overtime hours.
**Includes 50 pieces produced during the 4 overtime hours. The overtime, brought about by the downtime, was necessary to meet a production deadline.
***Standard units for 40 hours production.

The company's union contract contains the following description of the systems for computing wages in various departments of the company. The minimum wage for a worker is the base rate, which is also paid for any downtime when the worker's machine is under repair or there is no work. Workers are paid 150% of base rates for overtime production in a standard workweek of 40 hours.

(a) Straight piecework. The worker is paid at the rate of $.66 per piece produced.

(b) Percentage bonus plan. Standard quantities of production per hour are established by the Engineering Department. The worker's average hourly production, determined from the total hours worked and the worker's production, is divided by the standard quantity of production to determine an efficiency ratio. The efficiency ratio is then applied to the base rate to determine the worker's hourly earnings for the period.

(c) Emerson efficiency system. A minimum wage is paid for total hours worked. A bonus, calculated from the following table of rates, is paid when the worker's production exceeds $66\frac{2}{3}\%$ of standard output or efficiency. The bonus rate is applied only to wages earned during productive hours.

Efficiency	Bonus
Up to $66\frac{2}{3}\%$	0
$66\frac{2}{3}$ — 79%	10%
80 — 99%	20
100 — 125%	45

Required: Prepare a schedule comparing each individual's gross wages per books with the gross wages calculated.   (AICPA adapted)

12-5. Learning curve. Tierney Company uses labor standards in manufacturing its products. Based upon past experience, the company considers the effect of an 80% learning curve when developing standards for direct labor costs.

The company is planning the production of an automatic electrical timing device requiring the assembly of purchased components. Production is planned in lots of five units each. A steady-state production phase with no further increases in labor productivity is expected after the eighth lot. The first production lot of 5 units required 90 hours of direct labor time at a standard rate of $9 per hour.

Required:
(1) Compute the standard amount the company should establish for the total direct labor cost required for the production of the first 8 lots.

(2) Discuss the factors that should be considered in establishing the direct labor standards for each unit of output produced beyond the first 8 lots.

(CMA adapted)

12-6. Planning labor costs. Ellis, Inc., a relatively new company in the environmental control industry, is experiencing tremendous growth in product demand. To meet customers' increasing demands, management is considering the addition of a nighttime production shift beginning October 1.

Production takes place in three departments: Assembly, Molding, and Finishing. Standard time in the Molding Department is 10 minutes per unit produced, while the Finishing Department averages 12½ items per hour. Employees in these two departments are paid $8 per hour. Two people are needed in the Assembly Department, each with a monthly salary of $1,500, to serve the extra shift. Five cleanup employees are needed, and one supervisor for each 19 workers (including cleanup employees) is required in the Molding and Finishing Departments. Supervisors are paid $1,900 per month, and each member of the cleanup crew is paid $5.50 per hour.

Under normal conditions, the company schedules 20 workdays per month, with a standard monthly production of 120,000 units.

Required: Prepare a monthly labor budget for the extra shift, showing the time required in each department, the labor cost for each department and service, the unit labor cost, and the number of employees required. (Round off unit costs to four decimal places.)

CASES

A. Setting productivity standards. Anvil, Inc. intends to expand its Punch Press Department with the purchase of three new presses from Presco, Inc. Mechanical studies indicate that for Anvil's intended use, the output rate for one press should be 1,000 pieces per hour. The company has similar presses now in operation that average 600 pieces per hour. This average is derived from these individual outputs:

Worker	Daily Output (In Pieces)
Allen, W.	750
Miller, G.	750
Salermo, J.	600
Velasquez, E.	500
Underwood, P.	550
Keppinger, J.	450
Total	3,600
Average daily output	600

Anvil's management also plans to institute a standard cost accounting system in the very near future. The company's engineers are supporting a standard based upon 1,000 pieces per hour; the Accounting Department, a standard based upon 750 pieces per hour; and the Punch Press Department supervisor, a standard based upon 600 pieces per hour.

Required:

(1) Specify arguments which each proponent could use.

(2) Discuss the alternative which best reconciles the needs of cost control and the motivation of improved performance, with an explanation for the choice made.

(CMA adapted)

B. Designing a compensation plan. Fabray, Inc. manufactures and sells costume jewelry and men's and women's toiletries. Sales are seasonal, with the major sales volume to retailers occurring in the months preceding Mother's Day, Father's Day, and Christmas. The company is planning to revise its methods for compensating its sales force in an attempt to encourage the salespeople to increase their sales efforts.

One compensation system under consideration is a combination salary, commission, and bonus plan. Each salesperson would receive a monthly (base) salary on the first of each month and would earn a 5% commission on all sales. The commission would be earned in two installments: half in the month of delivery and the remaining half in the month of collection. The applicable commission earned in the month would be paid on the 15th of the following month. In addition, sales personnel could earn a bonus if the sales for the month exceeded the monthly sales quota. The bonus would be equal to 2% of the commission earned for sales delivered during the month and would be paid on the 15th of the following month.

The base salary and sales quotas will be established at the beginning of the year. The base salary will be reevaluated annually for each salesperson, considering such factors as cost of living, performance, and length of service. An annual sales quota will be prepared for each sales territory, based upon management's expectations for sales in that territory. The monthly sales quota for each territory will then be determined by dividing the annual sales quota by 12.

Required:

(1) State the factors to be considered when designing a compensation plan for employees.

(2) Identify and discuss the strengths and weaknesses of the company's compensation plan in terms of:

   (a) The company's attempt to encourage its sales force to increase its sales efforts.

   (b) The behavioral and motivational factors that influence employees' actions.

(CMA adapted)

C. Payroll procedures. A team of internal auditors was assigned to review the Galena Plant's Payroll Department, including the procedures used for payroll processing. Their findings are as follows:

(a) The payroll clerk receives the clock cards from the various department supervisors at the end of each pay period, checks the employee's hourly rate against information provided by the Personnel Department, and records the regular and overtime hours for each employee.

(b) The payroll clerk sends the clock cards to the plant's Data Processing Department for compilation and processing.

(c) The Data Processing Department returns the clock cards with the printed checks and payroll journal to the payroll clerk upon completion of the processing.

(d) The payroll clerk verifies the hourly rate and hours worked for each employee by comparing the detail in the payroll journal to the clock cards.

(e) If errors are found, the payroll clerk voids the computer-generated check, prepares another check for the correct amount, and adjusts the payroll journal accordingly.

(f) The payroll clerk obtains the plant signature plate from the Accounting Department and signs the payroll checks.

(g) An employee of the Personnel Department picks up the checks and holds them until they are delivered to department supervisors for distribution to employees.

Required: Discuss the shortcomings in Payroll Department procedures and suggest corrective action.   (CMA adapted)

D. Production planning and control reports. Wilguess, Inc., a supplier of bulk metals and alloys, recently negotiated a contract to supply 3,000 sections of aluminum air-conditioning ductwork for an office building under construction. The order required fabricating, cutting, and assembly. Based on experience, the supervisor prepared the following daily budget:

Department	Sections Scheduled	Hours Budgeted
Fabricating.............................	100	50
Cutting	100	30
Assembly..............................	100	25

Realizing the need for up-to-the-minute production information, the supervisor obtained the following results for the first two days:

	Department	Sections Produced	Hours Required
First day:	Fabricating	112	48
	Cutting	81	30
	Assembly........................	77	22
Second day:	Fabricating	120	49
	Cutting	96	30
	Assembly........................	96	23

Required:

(1) Discuss the action to be taken by the supervisor, based on the first day's report.

(2) Discuss the action needed according to the results on the second day's report.

Chapter 13
Labor: Accounting for Labor-Related Costs

According to a U. S. Chamber of Commerce study, American workers have enjoyed a spectacular growth in nonwage benefits because (1) new benefits have been introduced (e.g., insurance for vision, dentistry, and legal needs), (2) benefit costs have increased, (3) the duration of benefits has increased, and (4) more employees are covered by benefits.[1] Some of the data collected by the U. S. Chamber of Commerce, for the three decades ending in 1979, are summarized in the following table:

EMPLOYEE BENEFITS 1951–1979

Cost Measure	1951	1979
Percent of payroll cost	18.7%	36.6%
Amount per hour	$.32	$2.68
Yearly amount per employee	$644	$5,560
Total benefits paid in U. S.	$26 (billion)	$390 (billion)

In addition to the basic earnings computed on hours worked or units produced, nonwage benefits are cost elements that enter into labor cost. The following possible labor-related costs that would not be included in the basic wages are expressed as a percentage of straight-time earnings:

---

[1] *Employee Benefits — Historical Data: 1951–1979* (Washington, D. C.: U. S. Chamber of Commerce, 1981).

FICA tax for employees' old-age, survivors, and disability insurance and the hospital insurance program	7.0%
Federal unemployment insurance tax (FUTA)	.8
State unemployment insurance tax (representing a typical rate, with most companies paying less than the 5.4% maximum)	4.0
State workmen's compensation insurance (rates vary with the hazards— a fraction of 1% to 3% and over)	1.0
Vacation pay and paid holidays (two weeks of vacation and 7 to 10 holidays in relation to 52 weeks of 40 hours)	8.0
Contributions to pension fund (probable average)	9.0
Recreation, health services, life insurance, medical care	4.0
Contributions to supplemental unemployment pay funds	2.0
Time off for voting, jury duty, grievance meetings	1.3
Services related to parking lots, income tax, legal advice, meal money, uniforms	1.5
Total	38.6%

In addition to the elements listed, labor cost usually includes overtime earnings; premium pay for work on holidays, Saturdays, and Sundays when overtime is not involved; shift bonuses or differentials; bonuses for attendance, length of service, no accidents, and year end; apprenticeship or trainee costs; and dismissal or severance pay. This chapter discusses the accounting procedures for many of these fringe benefits.

Overtime Earnings

The Fair Labor Standards Act of 1938, commonly referred to as the Federal Wage and Hour Law, established a minimum wage per hour with time and a half for hours worked in excess of 40 in one week. Subsequently the Act has been amended, broadening the coverage and raising the minimum wage. Some types of organizations and workers are exempt from the provisions of the Act and its amendments, or have lower minimums.

A number of payroll practices are mandatory to comply with the Federal Wage and Hour Law. For each employee, records must show:

1. Hours worked each working day and the total hours worked during each workweek.
2. Basis on which wages are paid.
3. Total daily or weekly earnings at straight time.
4. Total extra pay for overtime worked each week.
5. Total wages paid during each pay period, the date of payment, and the work period covered by the payment.

Overtime earnings consist of two elements: (1) the regular pay due for the employee's work and (2) the overtime premium pay, which is an additional amount for work done beyond the 40-hour workweek or a regular 8-hour workday (as specified in some labor union contracts). For most workers, an employer must pay as a minimum the regular rate plus one half the rate for overtime employment. For example, if an employee is paid $8 per hour for a regular workweek of 40 hours, but works 45 hours, the gross earnings are:

Regular workweek	40 hours @ $8 = $320
Overtime................................	5 hours @ 8 = 40
Overtime premium	5 hours @ 4 = 20
Gross earnings	$380

Charging overtime premium pay to a specific job or product or to factory overhead depends primarily upon the reason for the overtime work. The contract price of a particular job, taken as a rush order with the foreknowledge that overtime will be necessary, may include the premium wage factor, which should be charged to the specific job. When orders cannot be completed in the regular working hours, the overtime premium pay should be included in the predetermined factory overhead rate as factory overhead, because it cannot properly be allocated to work that happens to be in process during overtime hours.

Bonus Payments

Bonus payments may be a fixed amount per employee or job classification, a percentage of profits, a fraction of one month's wages, or some other calculated amount. The amount of bonus for each employee may be a fixed and long-established tradition of a company, or the amount may vary from year to year. Bonus payments are a production cost, a marketing expense, or an administrative expense. If a direct-labor employee's average weekly earnings are $250 and the company intends to pay two weeks' pay as a bonus at the end of the year, then earnings actually amount to $260 per week, but the additional $10 per week is paid in a lump sum of $500 ($10 × 50 weeks, assuming two weeks of vacation time) at the end of the year. To spread the bonus cost over production throughout the year via the predetermined factory overhead rate, the weekly entry would be:

	Subsidiary Record	Dr.	Cr.
Work in Process		250	
Factory Overhead Control		10	
Bonus Pay	10		
Payroll.....................................			250
Liability for Bonus			10

When the bonus is paid, the liability account is debited and Cash and the withholding accounts are credited.

In theory, this and other direct-labor-related costs are additional labor costs that should be charged to Work in Process. In practice, such a procedure usually is impractical, and these costs are generally included in the predetermined factory overhead rate.

Vacation Pay

Vacation pay presents cost problems similar to those of bonus payments. When an employee is entitled to a paid vacation of 2 weeks, the vacation pay is accrued over the 50 weeks of productive labor. For example, assume that a direct labor employee has a base wage of $300 per week and is entitled to a paid vacation of 2 weeks. The cost of labor is $300, plus $12 per week. In 50 weeks at $12 per week, the deferred payment of $600 will equal the expected vacation pay. The entry to record the weekly labor cost, including the provision for vacation pay, would be:

	Subsidiary Record	Dr.	Cr.
Work in Process		300	
Factory Overhead Control		12	
Vacation Pay	12		
Payroll			300
Liability for Vacation Pay			12

When a vacation is taken, the liability account is debited and Cash and the withholding accounts are credited. Similarly, accrual should be made for employer liability pertaining to sick leave, holidays, military training, or other personal activities for which employees receive compensation. If it becomes necessary to use temporary replacements to perform the duties of personnel who are absent, this additional expense should be charged to the department for which the replacement is made.

FASB Statement No. 43, "Accounting for Compensated Absences," requires an employer to accrue a liability for employees' rights to receive compensation for future absences when all of the following conditions are met: (1) the rights are attributable to employees' services already rendered, (2) the rights vest or accumulate, (3) payment is probable, and (4) the amount can be reasonably estimated. While the statement requires accrual of vacation benefits, it generally does not require a liability to be accrued for future sick pay benefits (unless the rights vest), holidays, and similar compensated absences until employees are actually absent.[2] In accounting for government contracts, CASB regulations require the accrual of employer obligations for labor-related costs for personal absences.[3]

Guaranteed Annual Wage Plans

While a guaranteed annual wage plan for all industrial workers is far from realization, a step in that direction has been taken in labor contracts that provide for the company to pay employees who are laid off. For example, assume that an unemployed worker is guaranteed 60 to 65 percent of normal take-home pay, beginning the second week of layoff and continuing for as long as 26 weeks. The company pay is a supplement to the state unemployment insurance. To provide funds from which payments can be made

[2]*Statement of Financial Accounting Standards, No. 43,* "Accounting for Compensated Absences" (Stamford: Financial Accounting Standards Board, 1980).
[3]*Standards, Rules and Regulations, Part 408,* "Accounting for Costs of Compensated Personal Absence" (Washington, D.C.: Cost Accounting Standards Board, 1974).

during unemployment periods, a specified amount, such as $.15 an hour for each worker, is paid into a fund by the company.

In principle, if it is assumed that layoffs will eventually occur, it is clear that the employee while working is earning $.15 an hour that is not included in the paycheck at the end of the payroll period. This amount is held in reserve by the company in order to make payments during unemployment periods. For a direct-labor employee whose base pay rate is $8 an hour, the cost effect of unemployment pay for a 40-hour week is illustrated by the following entry:

	Subsidiary Record	Dr.	Cr.
Work in Process		320	
Factory Overhead Control		6	
Unemployment Pay	6		
Payroll			320
Liability for Unemployment Pay			6

Apprenticeship and Training Programs

In many plants, new workers receive some preliminary training before they become economically productive. Of the wages paid, the portion in excess of the average or standard paid for the productive output, plus the cost of instruction, is an indirect labor cost to be charged to the total annual output through inclusion in the factory overhead rates. When unusual training programs are needed as a result of the opening of a new plant or the activating of a second or third shift, a case can be made for treating the training cost as development or starting load cost and deferring a portion of the cost over a period of time.

Human Resource Accounting

In annual reports, management often speaks in glowing terms of its employees as the company's most valuable asset. Yet management makes little effort to assess the value of this asset, and the company's accounting system does little to provide any assistance. For example, many firms invest heavily in personnel training programs without evaluating the expected payoff or the return on such investments. A firm is apt to send its managers to a variety of executive development programs whose value is essentially taken on faith and which are discontinued when profits cannot afford them.

Human resource accounting is the process of developing financial assessments of people or groups of people within organizations and society and of monitoring these assessments over time. It deals with the value of investments in human beings and with the related economic results. Managers are being asked to give more serious consideration to human resource investment decisions and to the human resource impact of all their decisions. Thus, the personnel function within an organization may serve more efficiently its role of acquisition, development, and utilization of human resource potential.

A human resource accounting system attempts to identify incurred human resource costs that are to be separated from the firm's other costs. The techniques and procedures used should distinguish between the asset and expense components of human resource costs. The resulting human resource assets would then be classified into functional categories, such as recruiting, hiring, training, development, and familiarization. Such information would purportedly enable management to make decisions based on a realistic cost/benefit analysis and cost amortization and would provide investors with an improved basis to assess the value of an enterprise.

The quantification of human resources appears to be the first stumbling block in the creation of human resource accounting. All companies have methods of measuring sales, profits, investments in plant and equipment, and investments in inventories. Similarly, incurred human resource costs, such as training programs, can be measured, although determining the time period for amortization may be difficult. But beyond the possibility of capitalizing certain incurred human resource costs, how does a company set a quantitative value for such attributes as loyalty, skills, morale, decision-making ability, and intelligence? Since it seems difficult to quantify these human factors, it seems equally difficult to assign asset status to human resources except when measured incurred costs can be identified. The justification for measuring an asset value is based on the economic concept that an asset is capable of providing future benefits to the firm. It is argued that since the employee group is important to the future success of the company, it has value that should be reported as an asset on the balance sheet. Asset determination for human resources is particularly meaningful for professional sports franchises, where a superstar is essentially the asset that creates gate receipts. As with any other asset, the professional athlete can be sold or traded, which increases the litigation involving player contracts.

In spite of the difficulties, a number of proposals have attempted to utilize human resource accounting. Some proposals focus on incurred costs only, while others encompass estimated values. These proposals are:

1. *Capitalizing salaries* — whereby a firm assumes that what the employees are doing will be of some future benefit to the firm and that appropriate rates of capitalization can be determined.
2. *Capitalizing the cost of acquiring an employee* — a plan that would require collecting the costs of acquiring, hiring, and training. (A precedent for this method exists in professional sports.)
3. *Capitalizing startup costs* — involves not only capitalizing startup costs but goes one step further by considering the synergistic components of cost and time required for members of a firm to establish effective cooperative working relationships.
4. *Behavioral variables approach* — involves periodic measurements of the key causal and intervening variables for the corporation as a whole. Statistical variation in leadership styles and technical proficiency

levels (causal variables) and the resulting changes in subordinate attitudes, motivations, and behavior (intervening variables) can establish relationships between such variables. These changes would produce changes in the end-result variables such as productivity, innovation, and human resource developments. Trends in earnings could then be predicted. These forecasts are discounted to find the present value of the human resources.

5. *Opportunity costs* — suggest that investment center managers are encouraged to bid for any scarce employee they desire. The winning manager includes the bid in the investment base. The division's benefit is the increased profit produced by the new employee.

6. *Economic value approach* — compares differences in present and future earnings of similar firms in the same industry. Ostensibly, the differences are due to human organization. Future earnings are forecast and discounted to find their present value. A portion thereof is allocated to human resources based on their contribution.

7. *Present value method* — involves determining wage payments over perhaps a five-year period, and then discounting these payments at the rate of return of owned assets in the economy for the most recent year. This calculation yields the present value of the future five-years' wage payments based on this year's return.

8. *Stochastic rewards valuation model* — involves a stochastic process defined as a natural system that changes in time in accordance with the law of probability. To measure an individual's value to an organization requires:

   (a) An estimate of the time interval during which an individual is expected to render services to the organization, and

   (b) A measure of the services expected to be derived from the individual during this interval.

   The resource's expected value is then multiplied by a discount factor to arrive at the present value of expected future services.[4]

Human resource data may be part of a large-scale accounting system or merely part of a specific project application. Although the human resource accounting movement might gain an aura of respectability from inclusion in external reports, these data seem more useful for managerial decisions, i.e., an internal reporting focus.

At present, the value of human resource accounting systems for specific purposes must be determined by designing models and methods which can be empirically tested. Further research is required to demonstrate both the feasibility and the effects of human resource accounting on management's attitude, behavior, and decisions.[5]

---

[4]Roger Jauch and Michael Skigen, "Human Resources Accounting: A Critical Evaluation," *Management Accounting*, Vol. LV, No. 11, pp. 33–36.

[5]For an example of empirical research, see Lawrence A. Tomassini, "Assessing the Impact of Human Resource Accounting: An Experimental Study of Managerial Decision Preferences," *The Accounting Review*, Vol. LII, No. 4, pp. 904–913. In this study, human resource accounting cost data caused different preferences tc be expressed between the experimental and control group subjects.

Pension Plans

A *pension plan* is an arrangement whereby a company provides retirement benefit payments for all employees in recognition of their work contribution to the company. A pension plan is probably the most important as well as the most complicated factor associated with labor and labor costs. It influences personnel relations, company financing, income determination, income tax considerations, and general economic conditions. It must also comply with governmental regulations.

Pension Cost Estimate

The ultimate cost of a company pension plan depends upon several related factors:

1. The number of employees reaching retirement age each year.
2. The average benefit to be paid to each retired employee.
3. The average period over which benefits will be paid.
4. Income from pension fund investments.
5. Income tax allowances.
6. Expense of administration.
7. Treatment of benefits to employees who leave the company before reaching the pension age.

Pension Cost Allocation

In the case of bonuses and paid vacations, part of the total earnings of an employee is withheld or accrued for a period of months and then paid in a lump sum. In the case of pension payments, the wage is earned and the labor cost is incurred many years before the payment is made. As a matter of principle, if an employee is paid a base wage for a 40-hour week and if the employer's pension cost will amount to $1.50 an hour, the pension cost incurred is $60 per week and is chargeable to factory overhead, marketing expense, or administrative expense.[6]

Employee Retirement Income Security Act of 1974

The Employee Retirement Income Security Act of 1974 (more commonly known as ERISA or the Pension Reform Act of 1974) was enacted in order to make certain that promised pensions are actually paid at retirement. This Act sets minimum government standards for vesting, participation, funding, management, and a variety of other matters. The Act also covers a wide range of employee welfare plans for health, accident, and death benefits. In ad-

---

[6]For an extensive study of accounting for pension plans, refer to: *AICPA Research Study No. 8* (1965) by E. L. Hicks; *APB Opinion No.8* (1966); *FASB Interpretation No. 3* (1974); *CAS No. 412* (1975) and *CAS No. 413* (1977); and *FASB Statement No. 35* (1980) and *Statement No. 36* (1980).

dition, it covers pension or retirement plans and establishes both labor standards (administered by the Secretary of Labor) and tax standards (administered by the Secretary of the Treasury). The labor and tax standards taken together form a common body of legislation pertaining to practically all employee benefit plans not specifically exempted from the Act.

Virtually every private pension, profit-sharing, thrift, or savings plan has been amended in recent years in order to comply with the Act. All plans must contend with increased record keeping, compliance, and reporting. Many plans have experienced increased costs and/or funding obligations.

The Pension Reform Act of 1974 is a comprehensive piece of legislation. The presentation here enumerates only a few matters relevant to labor-related costs. Among the more important requirements affecting employers and employees are:

1. New employees cannot be denied participation for more than one year unless an employee is under twenty-five years of age or benefits are fully vested at the end of a three-year waiting period. The law prohibits a plan from excluding an employee because of advanced age if employment began at least five years prior to normal retirement age.
2. An employer's minimum annual contribution generally must include the normal cost for the year plus amortization of initial past service liabilities, liabilities resulting from plan amendments, and experienced gains and losses. Amortization payments must be calculated on a level payment basis. The amortization period for initial past service costs is forty years for existing plans and thirty years for new plans. The periods for liabilities resulting from plan amendments and experienced gains and losses are thirty years and fifteen years, respectively.
3. In case the assets of a terminated or insolvent plan are not sufficient to pay the insured benefits, the Pension Benefit Guaranty Corporation (PBGC) guarantees certain specified vested benefits for each participant or beneficiary. To finance this insurance program, the PBGC collects a premium from all covered plans.
4. Descriptions of the plan and annual financial, actuarial, and other information must be provided to participants and beneficiaries, the Secretaries of Labor and the Treasury, and the PBGC.

Vesting. A participant of a pension plan is assured of receiving future benefits under a plan when rights to the benefits become vested. *Vesting* means that benefits cannot be forfeited even in the event of dismissal or discontinuance of company operations. Employees who resign will still be entitled upon reaching retirement age to receive the benefits in which their rights were vested. The Act sets minimum vesting standards that must be met by all plans subject to the participation standards.

Funding. The Act established minimum funding standards for certain defined benefit plans. The effect of these standards is to impose time limitations for accumulating sufficient assets to pay retirement benefits to participants. Generally, employers must currently contribute the normal cost of the plan for the plan year plus a level funding, including interest, of past service costs and certain other costs. The law will not permit the use of the so-called pay-as-you-go method, whereby employers would make periodic pension payments directly to retired employees.

Present Value (PV).   Basic to all funding methods is the concept of present value (PV), sometimes referred to as capitalized value. The *present value* principle permits the value at any given point of time to be expressed as the equivalent value at a different point of time under a set of future conditions. The principle is particularly useful in dealing with financial transactions involving a time series, such as periodic contributions and retirement annuities. It permits the computation of an entire series of financial transactions over a period of time to be expressed as a single value at any point of time.

The Role of the Actuary.   Computations relating to pension plan costs, contributions, and benefits are made by an *actuary,* an expert in pension, life insurance, and related matters involving life contingencies. An actuary employs mathematical, statistical, financial, and other techniques to compute costs or benefits, to equate costs with benefits, and to evaluate and project actuarial experience under a plan. Membership in the American Academy of Actuaries, or one of the other recognized actuarial organizations, identifies a person as a member of the actuarial profession.

Administrative Problems.   The Pension Reform Act of 1974 mandates sweeping changes in the structure and administration of all types of qualified employee benefit plans. In addition, the Act creates a staggering number of complicated requirements in such areas as disclosure, reporting, investments, and insurance. For example, an employer must report to four government agencies: the Department of Labor, the Pension Benefit Guaranty Corporation, the Internal Revenue Service, and the Secretary of Labor. A summary description report must also be prepared and sent to all participants and beneficiaries.

CASB Pension Cost Standards

In 1975, the Cost Accounting Standards Board promulgated CAS No. 412, "Cost Accounting Standards for Composition and Measurement of Pension Cost," establishing the components of pension cost, the bases for measuring such cost, and the criteria for assigning pension cost to cost accounting periods. This standard is to be used in accounting for government contracts to which CASB regulations apply. This standard is compatible with the requirements of the Pension Reform Act of 1974, although certain of its provisions are more restrictive than the Pension Reform Act. Furthermore, the CASB standard, while attempting to stay within the general constraints of APB Opinion No. 8, "Accounting for the Cost of Pension Plans," specifies certain features of the Opinion which are considered not appropriate for government contract costing purposes. In 1977, CAS No. 413, "Adjustment and Allocation of Pension Cost," declared that actuarial gains and losses should be calculated and gave criteria for assigning pension expense to accounting periods and to segments, as well as for valuing pension fund assets.

Additional Legislation Affecting Labor-Related Costs

Costing labor and keeping payroll records were relatively simple prior to the first social security act. This legislation made it necessary for many employers to initiate or redesign payroll procedures in order to account accurately for payroll deductions. Later, other state and federal legislation imposed additional requirements affecting the accounting for wages and salaries. For example, the Federal Insurance Contributions Act, federal and state unemployment tax laws, and workmen's compensation laws require periodic reports.[7] As a result of the multiplicity of forms and regulations, competent personnel are needed in a company's payroll department.

Federal Insurance Contributions Act (FICA)

This legislation is administered and operated entirely by the federal government. Originally enacted in August of 1935 and operative January 1, 1936, the Act provided that employers in a covered industry must withhold 1 percent of the wages paid to each employee up to $3,000 of earnings in any one year, which amounted to a maximum of $30 of FICA tax. The employer was required to contribute an equal amount. Employees in several types of work, such as agricultural workers, domestic services, federal, state, and municipal employees, nonprofit organizations, self-employed persons, and a variety of others, were specifically excluded in the 1935 Act.

The Federal Insurance Contributions Act has been amended many times since 1935, the amendments tending to bring more employees under the Act and to increase the benefits, the tax rate, and the wage base upon which the tax is levied. Under the 1965 FICA amendments, the Hospital Insurance Program (Medicare) was enacted.[8]

Records Necessitated by the FICA. The Federal Insurance Contributions Act requires that employers who are subject to its provisions keep records of:

1. The name, address, and social security account number of each employee.

---

[7]These pages summarize the major provisions. U.S. Treasury Department Internal Revenue Service Circular E, entitled "Employer's Tax Guide," is an excellent source for a more comprehensive coverage of these regulations. A free copy of the current edition can be obtained by writing to the nearest District Director, Internal Revenue Service.

[8]A rate of 7 percent for FICA tax, used in the illustrations and in the end-of-chapter material, is not the current rate. The actual rate changes from time to time. The wage base to which the tax applies, assumed in the textbook to be annual wages up to $40,000 per employee, is also subject to change.

2. The total amount and the date of each remuneration payment and the period of service covered by such payment.
3. The amount of such remuneration payment that constitutes taxable wages.
4. The amount of tax withheld or collected.

Although the legislation does not order, suggest, or recommend forms or details for securing the required information, the employer must keep records that will enable a government agency to ascertain whether the taxes for which the employer is liable are correctly computed and paid. These records must be kept for at least four years after the date the tax becomes due or the date the tax is paid, whichever is later. Employees are not required to keep records, but the Act recommends that each employee keep accurate and permanent records showing the name and address of each employer, dates for beginning and termination of employment, wages earned, and tax withheld during employment.

Collection and Payment of the FICA Tax. Employers other than those in excluded classes of employment are required to pay a tax on wages paid, equal to the amount paid by the employees. The employer is further required to collect the FICA tax from employees by deducting the current percent from the wages paid each payday up to the current annual limit or base to which the tax applies. Federal income tax withheld and employee and employer FICA taxes must be deposited with either an authorized commercial bank depository or a Federal Reserve Bank on a periodic basis, depending on the amount of taxes to be remitted.

Federal Unemployment Tax Act (FUTA)

Unemployment compensation insurance is another phase of social security legislation affecting labor costs and payroll records. Unlike FICA, which is strictly a federal program, FUTA provides for cooperation between state and federal governments in the establishment and administration of unemployment insurance. When the initial legislation was enacted by the federal government in August, 1935, provisions of FUTA forced various states to pass adequate unemployment laws.

Under the provisions of the Federal Unemployment Tax Act, an employer in covered employment pays an unemployment insurance tax of 6.2 percent. The annual earnings base is $7,000 of each employee's wages paid, with .8 percent payable to the federal government and 5.4 percent to the state.[9] States generally provide an experience rating plan under which an employer who stabilizes employment may pay less than 5.4 percent to the state agency, with zero as a possible payment. While the federal act requires no employee contribution, some states also levy an unemployment insurance tax on the employee.

---

[9] The 5.4 percent state tax rate is effective as of January 1, 1985. Prior to this date, the state tax rate is 2.7 percent.

Records Necessitated by the FUTA. Every employer subject to unemployment taxes must keep records of:

1. The total amount of remuneration paid to each employee during the calendar year.
2. The total amount of such remuneration that constitutes taxable wages.
3. The amount of contributions paid into each state unemployment compensation fund, showing separately (a) payments made and not deducted from the remuneration of employees and (b) payments made and deducted from the remuneration of employees.
4. All information required to be shown on the prescribed tax return.

As with the FICA tax, the Federal Unemployment Tax Act does not prescribe or recommend forms or procedures for securing the required information. Each employer is expected to use accounting procedures and to maintain records that will enable the Internal Revenue Service to determine whether the tax is correctly computed and paid.

Payment of the FUTA Tax. The federal portion of the unemployment tax is payable quarterly. However, if the employer's tax liability (plus any accumulated tax liability for previous quarters) is $100 or less for the fiscal year, only one payment is required by January 31 of the following year. The related tax return is due annually on January 31.

State Unemployment Reports and Payments. The various state unemployment compensation laws require reports from employers to determine their liability to make contributions, the amount of taxes to be paid, and the amount of benefit to which each employee is entitled if unemployment occurs. While the reports and report forms vary from state to state, the more important requirements are:

1. *Status Report.* The status report determines whether an employer is required to make contributions to the state unemployment insurance fund.
2. *Contribution and Wage Report.* All employers covered by the state unemployment compensation laws are required to file a quarterly contribution and wage report. This report provides a summary of wages paid during the quarter, a computation of the tax, names of employees, and wages paid to each during the quarter.
3. *Separation Report.* When it becomes necessary to lay off workers, printed materials prepared by the state employment commission are provided, informing employees how to secure new employment and how to make an application for unemployment benefits. An employee who quits without good cause or before working a certain number of weeks, is discharged for ample reason, or has been unemployed for a short period may be ineligible for unemployment payments. In these cases, an employer files a separation notice with the state employment commission. Since any unemployment benefits paid to a former employee may increase the employer's state rate, the

separation notice is filed in order to prevent the charge-back that the state employment commission would otherwise make.

Workmen's Compensation Insurance

Workmen's compensation insurance laws provide insurance benefits for workers or their survivors for losses caused by accidents and occupational diseases suffered in the course of employment. In most states, these laws have been in effect for many years. While the benefits, premium costs, and various other details vary from state to state, the total insurance cost is borne by the employer. The employer may have the option of insuring with an approved insurance company or through a state insurance fund. In some cases, if the size and the financial resources are sufficient, the enterprise may carry its own risk.

Withholding of Federal Income Tax, State Income Tax, and City Wage Tax

The employer is required to withhold federal income tax—and state income and city wage taxes if applicable—from salary and wage payments to employees and to furnish information to the Internal Revenue Service and to state and city taxing authorities, showing the amount of remuneration paid each employee and the amount of income taxes withheld. The collection of income taxes from employees and the remittance of these taxes affect payroll accounting. Before new employees begin work, they are required to fill out a withholding exemption certificate (W-4 form).

Income taxes are withheld from each wage payment in accordance with the amount of the employee's earnings and the exemptions claimed on the W-4 form. Employers are required to furnish a written statement or receipt to each employee from whom taxes have been withheld, showing the total wages earned and the amount of taxes withheld (income taxes and FICA) during a calendar year. This withholding statement (W-2 form) must be delivered to the employee on or before January 31 of the following year. If employment is terminated before December 31, the W-2 form, if requested by the employee, must be furnished within 30 days (1) from the date requested or (2) from the last payment of wages, whichever is later. If it is not requested by the employee, the normal January 31 deadline applies.

As mentioned previously, each employer must periodically deposit federal income tax withheld and FICA taxes. Also, a reconciliation of the periodic returns with duplicate copies of the W-2 forms furnished employees must be filed annually. Therefore, payroll records must show the names of persons employed during the year, the periods of employment, the amounts and dates of payment, and the taxes withheld each payroll date.

The state may also levy an income tax that must be withheld from employees' wages. The tax withheld must be remitted to the taxing authorities along with the required reports. Information must also be supplied to the employee.

A city or municipality may levy a wage earnings tax on an employee working within its boundaries even though the employee is not a resident. Here, too, not only must reports and payments be made to the local taxing authority, but information must also be supplied to the employee.

Labor-Related Deductions

In addition to compulsory payroll deductions, a variety of other deductions may be withheld from take-home pay, with the consent of the employee.

Insurance

Many companies provide various benefits for their employees, such as health, accident, hospital, and life insurance. It is common for the company and the employees to share the cost, with the employees' share being deducted from wages each payroll period or at regular intervals. If the company has paid insurance premiums in advance, including the employees' share, an asset account, such as Prepaid Health and Accident Insurance, will be debited at the time that the payments are made. The employer's share will subsequently be credited to the asset account and debited to expenses, and the asset account will be credited for the employees' share of the premiums when the payroll deductions are made. In this payroll deduction, as in all similar cases, a subsidiary ledger showing the contributions of each employee is necessary, and one or more general ledger accounts are maintained.

Union Dues

Many enterprises employing union labor agree to a union shop and to a deduction of initiation fees and regular membership dues from the wages of each employee. To account for these deductions, a column is provided in the payroll journal, and a general ledger account entitled Union Dues Payable shows the liability for amounts withheld from the employees. At regular intervals, the company prepares a report and remits the dues collected to the union treasurer.

U.S. Savings Bonds

To cooperate with the federal government, an employer and an employee frequently agree to some systematic plan of withholding from wages a fixed amount for the purpose of purchasing U.S. Savings Bonds. A deduction column is provided in the payroll journal, and a general ledger account entitled U.S. Savings Bonds Payable is set up to show the liability for wages withheld for this purpose. When the accumulated amount withheld from a given employee is sufficient to purchase a bond, an entry is made debiting

U.S. Savings Bonds Payable and crediting Cash. Similar procedures may be used for other employee savings and investment plans.

Payroll Advances

For a variety of reasons, payroll advances may be made to officers, sales representatives, and factory workers. The advances may be in the form of cash, materials, or finished goods. To provide control, an advance authorization form should be executed by a responsible official and should be sent to the payroll department. The asset account debited for all advances represents a receivable to the company and may be entitled Salary and Wage Advances.

When the advances take the form of merchandise, Materials or Finished Goods is credited. If the merchandise is charged to the employee at a figure above cost, Sales may be credited. When the price is above cost but substantially less than the regular sales price, an account entitled Sales to Employees might be maintained. At the regular payroll date, the employee's earnings are entered in the payroll journal as usual, and the advance is deducted from wages to be paid. The amount of the advance being deducted is credited to Salary and Wage Advances.

Recording Labor Costs

The basic principle of labor costing is simple and straightforward. A record of the labor time "purchased" is made through use of the clock card; a record of the performance received is made through the use of time tickets or the daily time report. The accounting entries required are:

1. To record wage payments due employees and the liability for all amounts withheld from wages.
2. To charge the total labor cost to appropriate jobs, processes, and departments.

Weekly, semimonthly, monthly, or as often as a payroll is met, the total amount earned by workers is debited to Payroll, with credits to Accrued Payroll and to the withholding accounts. The cost of labor purchased is summarized and recorded as debits to Work in Process, Factory Overhead Control, Marketing Expenses Control, and Administrative Expenses Control and as a credit to Payroll. Employer payroll taxes and other labor-related costs are recorded, and at appropriate times, payments are made to discharge payroll-related liabilities.

The accounting for labor costs and payroll liabilities is illustrated in general journal form on pages 356 and 357, based upon these assumptions:

1. The payroll period is for January, 19B.
2. The payroll is paid on January 9, 19B, and on January 23, 19B, covering wages earned through the preceding Saturday. Note that

the wages of the last week of December, 19A, would be paid on January 9 and that the payment of January 23 would cover work done through January 19. Refer to the following calendar.

JANUARY, 19B

Sun	Mon	Tue	Wed	Thu	Fri	Sat
		1	2	3	4	5
6	7	8	9	10	11	12
13	14	15	16	17	18	19
20	21	22	23	24	25	26
27	28	29	30	31		

3. Payroll figures for wages earned during January are:

Direct factory labor	$38,500
Indirect factory labor	18,000
Sales salaries	20,000
Office and administrative salaries	12,000
Total payroll	$88,500

4. Wages paid during January, 19B: $50,000 on January 9, and $40,000 on January 23. Of the federal income tax withheld, $6,000 is on the payroll of January 9 and $5,500 on that of January 23.
5. Wages earned and unpaid on December 31, 19A, total $26,000. On January 31, the amount is $24,500.
6. The cost of the employer's payroll taxes is recorded when the month-end labor cost distribution entry is made, with separate liability accounts for federal and state agencies. Employees' FICA taxes are recorded when they are withheld at the payroll date, in compliance with the regulations.

Added assumptions:

FICA tax, 7%.
Workmen's compensation, 1% of payroll.
Unemployment insurance: .8% federal, 5.4% state.
Pension cost estimated to be $4,000 per month, divided as follows: direct labor, $1,540; indirect labor, $900; sales salaries, $1,000; office and administrative salaries, $560.
Payroll advances, $2,200 deducted on January 9 payroll.
Union dues collected, $1,000 each payroll period.
Savings bonds deductions, $1,200 on January 9 and $900 on January 23.
Health and accident insurance, 2% of payroll, shared equally — employees' share as wages paid, employer's share as wages earned.
Cost for supplemental unemployment benefits, 2% of factory labor earned.

This illustration records the employer's payroll taxes as a liability when the wages are earned, which follows the accrual concept of accounting. As a practical matter, many employers do not accrue payroll taxes at the end of each fiscal period because the legal liability does not occur until the next period when the wages are paid. This latter practice may be considered acceptable if it is consistently applied or if the amounts are not material. It is, however, required for income tax purposes.

	Subsidiary Record	Dr.	Cr.
Reversing entry for wages payable as of December 31:			
Jan. 2 Accrued Payroll...		26,000	
Payroll..			26,000
9 Payroll..		50,000	
Accrued Payroll.......................................			35,600
Employees' Income Tax Payable........................			6,000
FICA Tax Payable.....................................			3,500
Salary and Wage Advances............................			2,200
Union Dues Payable...................................			1,000
U.S. Savings Bonds Payable...........................			1,200
Prepaid Health and Accident Insurance................			500
9 Accrued Payroll.......................................		35,600	
Cash...			35,600
23 Payroll...		40,000	
Accrued Payroll.......................................			29,400
Employees Income Tax Payable.........................			5,500
FICA Tax Payable.....................................			2,800
Union Dues Payable...................................			1,000
U.S. Savings Bonds Payable...........................			900
Prepaid Health and Accident Insurance................			400
23 Accrued Payroll.......................................		29,400	
Cash...			29,400
31 Payroll...		24,500	
Accrued Payroll.......................................			24,500
31 Work in Process..		38,500	
Factory Overhead Control.............................		8,162	
FICA Tax..	2,695		
Unemployment Insurance Taxes....................	2,387		
Workmen's Compensation.........................	385		
Pension Expense................................	1,540		
Health and Accident Insurance...................	385		
Estimated Unemployment Expense.................	770		
Payroll..			38,500
FICA Tax Payable.....................................			2,695
Federal Unemployment Tax Payable....................			308
State Unemployment Tax Payable......................			2,079
Prepaid Workmen's Compensation.....................			385
Liability for Pensions.................................			1,540
Prepaid Health and Accident Insurance................			385
Liability for Unemployment Pay........................			770

	Subsidiary Record	Dr.	Cr.
31 Factory Overhead Control..		21,996	
Indirect Labor..	18,000		
FICA Tax	1,260		
Unemployment Insurance Taxes..................................	1,116		
Workmen's Compensation	180		
Pension Expense	900		
Health and Accident Insurance	180		
Estimated Unemployment Expense	360		
Payroll..			18,000
FICA Tax Payable..			1,260
Federal Unemployment Tax Payable			144
State Unemployment Tax Payable			972
Prepaid Workmen's Compensation...............................			180
Liability for Pensions			900
Prepaid Health and Accident Insurance..........................			180
Liability for Unemployment Pay			360
31 Marketing Expenses Control...		24,040	
Sales Salaries	20,000		
FICA Tax	1,400		
Unemployment Insurance Taxes..................................	1,240		
Workmen's Compensation	200		
Pension Expense	1,000		
Health and Accident Insurance	200		
Payroll..			20,000
FICA Tax Payable..			1,400
Federal Unemployment Tax Payable			160
State Unemployment Tax Payable................................			1,080
Prepaid Workmen's Compensation...............................			200
Liability for Pensions..			1,000
Prepaid Health and Accident Insurance..........................			200
31 Administrative Expenses Control.....................................		14,384	
Office and Administrative Salaries	12,000		
FICA Tax	840		
Unemployment Insurance Taxes..................................	744		
Workmen's Compensation	120		
Pension Expense	560		
Health and Accident Insurance	120		
Payroll..			12,000
FICA Tax Payable..			840
Federal Unemployment Tax Payable			96
State Unemployment Tax Payable................................			648
Prepaid Workmen's Compensation			120
Liability for Pensions			560
Prepaid Health and Accident Insurance..........................			120

DISCUSSION QUESTIONS

1. The hourly wage of an employee is $9, but the labor cost of the employee is considerably more than $9 an hour. Explain.

2. Discuss the accounting treatment of fringe benefits to factory employees.

3. Give two costing methods of accounting for the premium costs of overtime direct labor. State circumstances under which each method would be appropriate.   (AICPA adapted)

4. For many years, a company has paid all employees one week's wages as a year-end bonus. It is also company policy to give 2-week paid vacations. What accounting procedures should be followed with respect to the bonus and vacation pay?

5. The productive efficiency of a company depends upon superior group leaders. The company management suggests that group leaders and selected workers organize a class in personnel administration and group leadership. The class is set up at a nearby university, with one of the regular professors in charge. The employees attend the class at night on their own time, but the company pays the tuition charges. How should the company account for this cost?

6. (a) Define human resource accounting.
   (b) What are the objectives of the concept?
   (c) State the theoretical proposals that have been made in favor of human resource accounting.
   (d) What are some of the more serious drawbacks of this concept?

7. The total cost of contributions that must be paid ultimately to provide pensions for the present participants in a plan cannot be determined precisely in advance; however, reasonably accurate estimates can be made by the use of actuarial techniques. List the factors entering into the determination of the ultimate cost of a funded pension plan.   (AICPA adapted)

8. The term "pension plan" has been referred to as a formal arrangement for employee retirement benefits, whether established unilaterally or through negotiation, by which specific or implied commitments have been made and used as the basis for estimating costs. Explain the preferable procedure for computing and accruing the costs under a pension plan.
     (AICPA adapted)

9. What is meant by the experience-rating provisions of the unemployment compensation laws of various states?

Unless otherwise directed, use the following rates in the exercises and problems: FICA tax, 7%; FUTA tax, .8%; state unemployment insurance tax, 5.4%. Round all monetary amounts to the nearest cent.

EXERCISES

1. *Recording overtime premium.* A direct-labor employee in the Mixing Department is paid $8.40 per hour for a regular week of 40 hours. During the week ended April 30, the employee worked 52 hours and earned time and a half for overtime hours.

Required:
(1) Prepare the journal entry to distribute the labor cost if the overtime premium is not charged to production worked on during the overtime hours.
(2) Prepare the journal entry to distribute the labor cost if the overtime premium is charged to production worked on during the overtime hours.

2. Bonus and vacation pay liability. A production worker earns $1,150 per month and the company pays the worker a year-end bonus equal to one month's wages. The worker is also entitled to a half-month paid vacation per year. Company policy dictates that bonus and vacation benefits be treated as indirect costs and accrued during the 11½ months the employee is at work.

Required: Prepare the journal entry to record and distribute (simultaneously) the labor cost of the production worker for a month. Assume that there are no deductions from gross wages.

3. Bonus and vacation pay liability. Four factory workers and a supervisor comprise a team in the Machining Department. The supervisor earns $10 per hour and the combined hourly direct wages of the four workers is $32. Each employee is entitled to a two-week paid vacation and a bonus equal to four weeks' wages each year. Vacation pay and bonuses are treated as an indirect cost and are accrued over the 50-week work year. A provision in the union contract does not allow these employees to work in excess of 40 hours per week.

Required: Prepare the journal entry to record the bonus and vacation pay liability applicable to one week's production.

4. Fringe benefits. A production worker earns $1,656 a month, and the company pays one month's salary as a bonus at the end of the year. The worker is also entitled to a half-month paid vacation, and the company pays $1,840 a year into a pension fund for the worker. Bonus, vacation pay, and pension costs are charged to production during the 11½ months the employee is at work. The federal and state unemployment insurance tax rates are .8% and 3.6%, respectively. The employer's share of FICA tax is 7%. All labor-related fringe benefits for production workers are treated as factory overhead.

Required: Prepare the journal entries to record the March payroll distribution and the cost of fringe benefits.

5. Employer's labor-related expenses. Digby Company has employees engaged in manufacturing, marketing, and administrative functions. The February payroll was:

Direct labor	$25,000
Indirect labor	10,000
Marketing	8,000
Administrative	7,000
	$50,000

The company incurs the following labor-related expenses:

Pension plan	7.8%
FICA tax	7.0
Federal unemployment insurance	.8
State unemployment insurance	4.6
Workmen's compensation	4.0
Medical insurance	1.0

Required: Present the journal entry to record the employer's labor-related expenses.
(CGAA adapted)

6. Payroll entries. For the first payroll in November, the records of Nans Company show: direct labor, $20,000; indirect labor, $4,000; sales salaries, $5,000; and office salaries,

$3,600. FICA tax is applicable to 75% of the payroll in each department, while unemployment insurance tax applies to only 25%. Federal income tax to be withheld totals $3,000, and employees pay a city income tax of 1% on gross earnings.

Required: Prepare the journal entries to record the payroll liability, distribute the payroll, and record the employer's payroll taxes, treated as an indirect cost. The state unemployment tax rate is 3%.

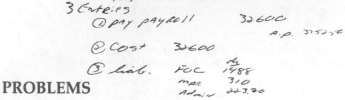

PROBLEMS

13-1. Entries for payroll and payroll taxes. For the December 1–15 payroll, which totaled $28,000, employees' FICA deductions amounted to only $1,230, since some of the employees had already earned the maximum applicable during the year. For the same period, income tax withheld totaled $2,872.

The company apportions employer FICA taxes as follows: 60% to factory overhead, 30% to marketing expense, and 10% to general office expense. The state unemployment insurance tax rate is 4%, and only $5,000 of the payroll (all factory employees) is subject to this tax, since all other employees had earned more than $7,000 by December 1. The company closed for the year on December 15 and had no more payroll expenses.

Required: Prepare the entry to record the payroll for the period December 1–15, the entry to pay the payroll of December 1–15, and the entry to record the employer's payroll taxes for the period December 1–15.

13-2. Payroll, tax deductions, and payroll distribution. The following information, taken from the daily time tickets of a producing department, summarizes time and piecework for the week ended April 30:

Employee	Clock No.	Job No.	Hours Worked	Production Pieces	Hourly Rate	Piece Rate
Belcastro, V.	90	641	40	960	—	$.30
Cherpack, C.	91	—	46	—	$7.00	—
Meadows, A.	92	638	40	—	5.80	—
Smeltzer, S.	93	—	40	—	7.20	—

The company operates on a 40-hour week and pays time and a half for overtime. Additional information:

(a) A FICA tax deduction should be made for each employee.
(b) An advance of $20 was made to Belcastro on April 26.
(c) A 2% deduction is to be made from each employee's wage for the company's employee health and hospital benefit plan.
(d) Cherpack works in the storeroom issuing materials; Smeltzer is the supervisor; the others work directly on special orders as noted.
(e) Use 10% in computing income tax withheld. The state unemployment tax rate is 4%.

Required:
(1) Compute each employee's gross pay, deductions, and net pay.

(2) Prepare journal entries to (a) set up the accrued payroll and other liabilities, (b) pay the payroll, and (c) distribute the payroll and record the employer's payroll taxes. Include subsidiary record detail.

13-3. Payroll taxes, vacation pay, and payroll. The normal workweek at Starks Publishing, Inc. is Monday through Friday, with payday being the following Tuesday. On November 1, after the reversing entry was posted, the payroll account showed a $2,230 credit balance, representing labor purchased during the last two days of October. (See the following calendar.)

NOVEMBER

Sun	Mon	Tue	Wed	Thu	Fri	Sat
			1	2	3	4
5	6	7	8	9	10	11
12	13	14	15	16	17	18
19	20	21	22	23	24	25
26	27	28	29	30		

Deductions for FICA tax and 10% for income tax are withheld from each payroll check. The labor summary for November shows $16,400 of direct labor and $5,600 of indirect labor. Vacation pay is charged to current production at a rate of 8% of total payroll. Payrolls were:

November 7	$5,890
14	4,920
21	5,900
28	4,880

Required:
(1) Prepare entries to record each payroll.
(2) Prepare the entry on November 30 to distribute the payroll and to record the employer's payroll taxes, treating the employer's payroll taxes and vacation pay as factory overhead. The state unemployment tax rate is 4%. Include subsidiary record detail.
(3) Prepare T-accounts for Payroll and Accrued Payroll and the entry to record accrued wages at the end of November.

13-4. Payroll cycle. The payroll department of the Banderillo Company, Inc. prepares its monthly and biweekly payroll using the following payroll data:

(a) The payroll period deals with August and September; the last payment was made on August 25. Refer to the following calendars:

AUGUST						
Sun	Mon	Tue	Wed	Thu	Fri	Sat
		1	2	3	4	5
6	7	8	9	10	11	12
13	14	15	16	17	18	19
20	21	22	23	24	25	26
27	28	29	30	31		

SEPTEMBER						
Sun	Mon	Tue	Wed	Thu	Fri	Sat
					1	2
3	4	5	6	7	8	9
10	11	12	13	14	15	16
17	18	19	20	21	22	23
24	25	26	27	28	29	30

(b) The company pays its factory, marketing, and office and administrative personnel on a biweekly basis. The workweek is Monday through Friday; paychecks are distributed on the Friday following the close of the two weeks. Executives, superintendents, and department heads are paid on a monthly basis on the first Friday following the last day of the month. The 4th of September is Labor Day; all employees will be paid, but the direct labor cost is charged to factory overhead.

(c) The payroll is based on these data:

Monthly salaries:
     2 executives: $3,000 each per month
     3 superintendents: $2,500 each per month
     2 department heads: $2,000 each per month

Hourly workers:
     Direct factory labor: 200 employees; 40 hours per week; average pay, $6 per hour
     Indirect factory labor: 30 employees; 40 hours per week; average pay, $4 per hour

Weekly rates:
     Marketing personnel: 12 employees; average pay, $350 per week
     Office and administrative personnel: 9 employees; average pay, $305 per week

(d) Additional information:

Federal income tax withheld: 15% on monthly salaries; 10% on all others
FICA tax: 7% (Maximum $40,000 earnings per year)
Federal unemployment tax: .8% up to $7,000 per employee
State unemployment tax: 5.4% up to $7,000 per employee
     The FICA tax is recorded as a liability when it is withheld at the payroll date, in compliance with regulations. The employer's payroll taxes are recorded when the cost distribution entry is made; separate liability accounts are kept for federal and state agencies; month-end payroll accrual entries are made only at the end of the calendar year.
Workmen's compensation insurance: 1% of total payroll.
Pension cost: 5% for monthly salaries, with equal contributions by these employees deducted from their paychecks; 3% for all other employees, with no contributions by them.
Union dues: $.50 deducted each payday from each hourly worker.
Health insurance: 1% of earnings, shared equally between employees and employer.

Required: Prepare journal entries, including subsidiary record detail, to record:
(1) The monthly salaries to be paid in September, with all applicable deductions. Distribution is to be made as follows: 2 executives to administration; 3 superintendents to factory; 1 department head to marketing; 1 department head to administration (office).
(2) Factory, marketing, and office employees' earnings to be paid in September on a biweekly basis, with all applicable deductions. Distribution is to be made on the basis of the four categories.
(3) The earnings of one direct factory laborer for the first of the two-week payroll periods, in order to illustrate the procedure required for an individual employee.

13-5. Payroll entries—general and factory offices. Bonaire, Inc., a manufacturer of air pollution control devices, maintains factory records at each plant location. At the Lansdale factory, where there are four producing departments, a payroll journal is maintained as a book of original entry for the factory employees, even though salaries of personnel in the Shipping Department and Finished Goods Stockroom are charged to marketing expense. Payroll checks are prepared at the home office and sent to the factory for delivery to the factory employees. Overtime premium wages are treated as factory overhead. The liability for payroll taxes is kept on the general office books. Factory payroll taxes are charged to factory overhead.

For the week ended May 30, the following factory payroll summary was prepared:

Department	Labor Hours	Payroll (Earned Hours)	Overtime Premium	Federal Income Tax Withheld (10%)	FICA Tax (7%)	Net Pay
Casting..................	240	$ 1,620	$108	$ 172.80	$120.96	$1,434.24
Forging..................	410	2,542	160	270.20	189.14	2,242.66
Machining...............	560	3,976	120	409.60	286.72	3,399.68
Assembly................	160	960	—	96.00	67.20	796.80
Toolroom................	84	428	16	44.40	31.08	368.52
Storeroom	82	410	8	41.80	29.26	346.94
Stockroom..............	40	180	—	18.00	12.60	149.40
Shipping	40	192	—	19.20	13.44	159.36
Total..................	1,616	$10,308	$412	$1,072.00	$750.40	$8,897.60
Sales Office.............	—	$ 2,200	—	$ 220.00	$154.00	$1,826.00
General Office	—	1,550	$150	170.00	119.00	1,411.00

Required: Prepare journal entries for the general office and factory office books, including subsidiary record detail, to record:
(1) Preparation of the payroll.
(2) Payment of the payroll.
(3) Distribution of the payroll.
(4) Recording of the employer's payroll taxes. (The state unemployment tax rate is 3.2%.)

CASES

A. Cost principles and cost determination. As a subcontractor under a prime contract with a governmental agency, a company operating a machine shop undertook to produce certain parts on a cost-plus-fixed-fee basis. The hours of operation were about evenly divided between the above contract and the regular business of the company.

Each day, the work required for the regular company business was completed first. The remainder of the day, with whatever overtime was necessary, was given over to production under the contract. During the contract period, overtime hours represented a substantial portion of the total hours worked. Under an agreement with the employees, time and a half was paid for all hours over eight worked each day.

Job sheets recorded the actual costs of materials and direct labor, including any overtime premium paid. Factory overhead was applied on the basis of the labor cost so recorded, and the job sheets were adjusted each month to eliminate any balance in the overhead variance account.

Required: State objections to the cost accounting priciples applied, reasons for any incorrectness of the client's statements, and the procedure for making a revised cost determination.   (AICPA adapted)

B. Human resource accounting. The Consumer Products Division of Liberty Manufacturing Company experienced reduced sales in the first quarter of 19B and has forecasted that the decline in sales will continue through the remainder of the year.

Liberty's executive management believes in a decentralized organization, and division managers have considerable managerial latitude, receiving bonuses of a specified percentage of division profits, in addition to their annual salaries. At the end of the first quarter of 19B, J. Spassen, the Consumer Products Division manager, felt that drastic action was needed to reduce costs and improve the division's performance. Consequently 20 highly-trained, skilled employees were dismissed as one cost-reduction step. Five of these employees are expected to be available for reemployment when business is projected to return to normal in 19C.

Executive management, upon reviewing the steps taken by Spassen, was concerned about the consequences of dismissing the 20 skilled employees. The company officials had recently attended a seminar on human resource accounting and wondered if Spassen would have taken that particular action if a cost-based human resource accounting system had been in operation.

Required:
  (1) Explain what is accounted for in a cost-based human resource accounting system.
  (2) Explain how information generated by such a system might apply to the decision to dismiss the 20 skilled employees.   (CMA adapted)

Part Five
Planning and Control
of Sales and Costs

Chapter 14
Budgeting:
Profits, Sales, Costs, and
Expenses

Effective planning and control of operations depend upon cost accounting, which provides management with detailed statements of the actual cost of materials, labor, factory overhead, marketing expenses, and administrative expenses. Comparisons and analyses of these actual costs with estimates and standards prepared in advance of production and sales enable management to identify the reasons for any differences. Management can then formulate intelligent production plans and sales policies for achieving the organization's objectives.

Profit Planning

The terms "profit planning" and "budgeting" can be viewed as synonymous. *Profit planning* is a well thought-out operational plan with its financial implications expressed in the form of long- and short-range income statements, balance sheets, and cash and working capital projections. A budget is simply a plan expressed in financial and other quantitative terms. Profit planning is directed to the ultimate objectives of the organization and serves as a guide to maintaining a definite course of activity.

Sound and intelligent planning of profits is a difficult task, because technology changes rapidly, and economic, social, and political factors exert strong influences on business. To accomplish this task, managers must be motivated to strive for attainment of their personal objectives in congruence with the organization's objectives.

Setting Profit Objectives

Fundamentally, three different procedures can be followed in setting profit objectives:

1. The *a priori* method, in which the profit objectives take precedence over the planning process. At the outset, management specifies a given rate of return, which it seeks to realize in the long run by means of planning toward that end.
2. The *a posteriori* method, in which the determination of profit objectives is subordinated to the planning, and the objectives emerge as the product of the planning itself.
3. The *pragmatic* method, in which management uses a profit standard that has been tested empirically and sanctioned by experience. By using a target rate of profit derived from experience, expectations, or comparisons, management establishes a relative profit standard which is considered satisfactory for the company.[1]

In setting profit objectives, management needs to consider the following factors:

1. Profit or loss resulting from a given volume of sales.
2. Sales volume required to recover all consumed costs, to produce a profit adequate to pay dividends on preferred and common stock, and to retain sufficient earnings in the business for future needs.
3. Break-even point.
4. Sales volume that the present operating capacity can produce.
5. Operating capacity necessary to attain the profit objectives.
6. Return on capital employed.

Public expectations with regard to social responsibilities compel companies to also consider the social consequences of profit objectives. Increasingly, important actions must be evaluated in a context that includes social as well as economic impacts. Potential social impacts specifically pertain to "... environmental pollution, the consumption of nonrenewable resources, and other ecological factors; the rights of individuals and groups; the maintenance of public service; public safety; health and education; and many other social concerns."[2]

---

[1]*Research Report No. 42*, "Long-Range Profit Planning" (New York: National Association of Accountants, 1964), pp. 60–65.

[2]Robert K. Elliott, "Social Accounting and Corporate Decision-Making," *Management Controls*, Vol. XXI, No. 1, p. 2.

Long-Range Profit Planning

Business has become increasingly aware of a need to develop long-range profit plans or forecasts. Long-range planning has been defined as "the continuous process of making present decisions systematically and, with the best possible knowledge of their futurity, organizing systematically the efforts needed to carry out these decisions, and measuring the results of these decisions against the expectations through organized, systematic feedback."[3] Long-range plans are not stated in precise terms, nor are they expected to be completely coordinated future plans. They deal rather with specific areas such as sales, capital expenditures, extensive research and development activities, and financial requirements.

In long-range profit planning, management attempts to find the most probable course of events. Long-range planning does not eliminate risk, for risk-taking is the essence of economic activity. An end result of successful long-range profit planning is a capacity to take a greater risk, which is a fundamental way to improve entrepreneurial performance.

Market trends and economic factors, inflation, growth of population, personal consumption expenditures, and indexes of industrial production form the background for long-range planning. Quantitative and dollar sales estimates for a three- to five-year forecast may be developed from this information. A prospective income statement can then be prepared, showing anticipated sales, fixed and variable costs (factory, marketing, and administrative), contribution margin, and operating income by years. A balance sheet by years should indicate anticipated cash balances, inventory levels, accounts receivable balances, and liabilities. This financial long-range plan might also be supported by a cash flow statement.

The rate of return on capital (total assets) employed is an important statistic in long-range profit planning and in setting profit objectives. To measure the effectiveness with which management is likely to use the assets, rates of return are computed for each individual year covered in the long-range plan. These figures show whether planned increases in total net income will keep pace with increases in assets at the corporate as well as divisional or operating levels. Though return on capital employed is the basic measure of profit performance (discussed in detail in Chapter 22), companies typically use several other measures, such as the ratio of net income to sales, the ratio of sales to shareholders' capital, and earnings per common share.[4]

Short-Range Plans or Budgets

Management's long-range plans can only be achieved through successful long-run profit performance, which requires growth and a reasonably high and stable level of profit. Long-range plans with their future expectancy

[3]Peter F. Drucker, "Long-Range Planning," *Management Science*, Vol. 5, No. 3, p. 240.
[4]*Research Report No. 42, loc. cit.*

of profits and growth must, however, be incorporated into a shorter-range budget for both planning and control of the contemplated course of action. Although one year is the usual planning period, the short-range budget may cover periods of three, six, or twelve months, depending upon the nature of the business. For efficient planning, the annual budget should be expanded into an eighteen-month budget, allowing for a three-month period at the end of the old year, twelve months for the regular budget period, and an additional three months into the third year. These overlapping months are needed in order to allow transition from year to year and to make adjustments based on prior months' experience. The budget period should:

1. Be divided into months.
2. Be long enough to complete production of the various products.
3. Cover at least one entire seasonal cycle for a business of a seasonal nature.
4. Be long enough to allow for the financing of production well in advance of actual needs.
5. Coincide with the financial accounting period to compare actual results with budget estimates.

Some organizations use a continuous budget, by which a month or quarter in the future is added as the month or quarter just ended is dropped, and the budget for the entire period is revised and updated as needed. This procedure forces management to think continuously about its short-range plans.

Advantages of Profit Planning

Profit planning, or budgeting, has the advantages of:

1. Providing a disciplined approach to the solution of problems.
2. Obliging management to make an early study of its problems and instilling into an organization the habit of careful study before making decisions.
3. Developing throughout the organization an atmosphere of profit-mindedness, and encouraging an attitude of cost-consciousness and maximum resource utilization.
4. Enlisting the aid and coordinating the operating plans of the diverse segments of the entire management organization so that the final decisions and contingency plans represent the total organization in the form of an integrated, comprehensive plan.
5. Affording the opportunity of appraising systematically every facet of the organization as well as examining and restating periodically its basic policies and guiding principles.
6. Coordinating and correlating all efforts, since no management activity reveals weaknesses in organization as quickly as the orderly procedure necessary for systematic budgeting.
7. Aiding in directing capital and effort into the most profitable channels.

8. Encouraging a high standard of performance by stimulating competition, providing a sense of purpose, and serving as an incentive to perform more effectively.
9. Providing yardsticks or standards for measuring performance and gauging the managerial judgment and ability of the individual executive.

Limitations of Profit Planning

While the advantages of profit planning are unquestionably impressive and far reaching, certain limitations and pitfalls need to be mentioned:

1. Forecasting is not an exact science; a certain amount of judgment is present in any budget. A revision or modification of estimates should be made when variations from the estimates warrant a change of plans.
2. The budget could focus a manager's attention on goals (e.g., high production, high credit sales, etc.) which are not necessarily in harmony with the organization's overall objectives. Thus, care must be used to properly channel the managers' efforts.
3. A profit planning program needs the cooperation and participation of all members of management. The basis for success is executive management's sustained adherence to and enthusiasm for the profit plan. Too often a profit plan has failed because executive management has paid only lip service to its execution. Also, involvement at all levels is needed to avoid the feeling at lower management levels that the budget is being imposed on them without their participation.
4. Profit planning does not eliminate nor take over the role of administration. Executives should not feel restricted by the budget. Rather, the profit plan is designed to provide detailed information that allows the executives to operate with strength and vision toward achievement of the organization's objectives.
5. Installation takes time. Management often becomes impatient and loses interest because it expects too much too soon. The budget must first be sold to the responsible people; and they, in turn, must then be guided, trained, and educated in the fundamental steps, methods, and purposes of a budgetary system.

Principles of Budgeting

A company's organization chart and its chart of accounts form the basic framework on which to build a coordinated and efficient system of managerial planning and budgetary control. The organization chart defines the functional responsibilities of executives and thereby justifies their budgets. Although final responsibility for the budget rests with executive management, all managers are responsible for the preparation and execution of their departmental budgets. If a budgetary control system is to be successful, these managers must fully cooperate and must understand their role in making the budget system successful.

The Budget Committee

The budgeting process is usually directed by a budget committee, which is composed of the sales manager, the production manager, the chief engineer, the treasurer, and the controller. The principal functions of the budget committee are to:

1. Decide on general policies.
2. Request, receive, and review individual budget estimates.
3. Suggest revisions in individual budget estimates.
4. Approve budgets and later revisions.
5. Receive and analyze budget reports.
6. Recommend actions designed to improve efficiency where necessary.

In performing these functions, the budget committee becomes a management committee. It is a powerful force in coordinating the various activities of the business and in controlling operations.

Budget Development and Implementation

The procedure used in developing a budget may be as important as its content and should include these fundamental principles:

1. Provide adequate guidance so that all management levels are working on the same assumptions, targeted objectives, and agenda. All managers should understand the limitations and constraints of their participation and the bounds of their decision making. Participants should be told, prior to the time the budget is established, how their activities will fit into the entire organization and what constraints will be placed upon them and their activities by upper-level administrative decisions.
2. Encourage participation in the budgeting process at each level within the organization. Structure the activity of developing the budget to involve the people who will be responsible for implementing the budget and who will be rewarded according to its accomplishments.
3. Structure the climate of budget preparation to eliminate anxiety and defensiveness. Individuals should have the freedom and authority to influence and accept their own performance levels, and should assume the responsibility for accomplishment. Budget preparation should be oriented to the problems and opportunities of the participants.

4. Structure the preparation of the budget so that there is a reasonably high probability of successful attainment of objectives. When challenging but attainable objectives are achieved, feelings of success, confidence, and satisfaction are produced and aspiration levels are raised. If objectives are not accomplished, the reasons for this failure should be clear. A careful distinction should be made between controllable factors for which individuals should be responsible and for uncontrollable factors for which they are not.[5]

If the proper procedure for developing a budget has been followed, implementation difficulties are minimized. Proper budget implementation requires adherence to the following principles:

1. Establish rewards and reward contingencies that will lead to achieving the organizational objectives. Too often, the budgeting process does not provide sufficient rewards to induce employees to accomplish organizational objectives.
2. The organization should focus on rewarding achievement rather than punishing failure. Feelings of success or failure largely determine attitudes toward the budget and the level of performance to which employees will aspire.
3. Provide rapid feedback on the performance of each work team or individual. This principle necessitates the use of reports and reporting procedures that are understandable to workers and supervisors at the department level, so that they can analyze their results and initiate corrective action.[6]

The Complete Periodic Budget

A complete set of budgets generally consists of:

1. A sales budget.
2. Estimates of inventory and production requirements.
3. Budgets of materials, labor, and factory overhead, combined into a cost of goods manufactured and sold schedule.
4. Budgets for marketing and administrative expenses.
5. Estimates of other income and expense items and income tax.
6. A budgeted income statement.
7. A budget of capital expenditures and of research and development expenditures.
8. A cash receipts and disbursements budget.
9. A budgeted balance sheet showing the estimated financial position of the company at the end of the budget period.

---

[5]J. Owen Cherrington and David J. Cherrington, "Budget Games for Fun and Frustration," *Management Accounting*, Vol. LVII, No. 7, p. 32.
[6]*Ibid.*

Items 1 through 6 form the basis for preparing the budgeted income statement. They are discussed and illustrated in the remainder of this chapter, while items 7 through 9 are covered in the first portion of Chapter 15.

The following data are used to illustrate the budget components that comprise the income statement. As each budget component is discussed, the relevant data are used to illustrate the preparation of the related budget schedule. Subsequent schedules are cross-referenced to show the linkage between the various budget parts, building to the budgeted income statement. Assume that Franklin Company manufactures three products, A, B, and C, which are marketed in two territories, the Midwest and the Southwest. The production departments are designated Cutting, Assembling, and Finishing. The management and the department heads have made the following estimates for the coming year ending December 31:

1. Sales forecast:

Product	Midwest	Southwest	Sales Price
A..................	4,000 units	3,000 units	$200 per unit
B..................	6,000	5,000	150
C..................	9,000	6,000	100

2. Inventories:
   Materials:

Material	Beginning Inventory Units	Ending Inventory Units	Unit Cost
X...............	30,000	40,000	$ 1.00
Y...............	10,000	12,000	14.00
Z...............	2,000	2,500	2.50

Work in process: None at the beginning or end of the period.
Finished goods (fifo):

Product	Beginning Inventory Units	Beginning Inventory Unit Cost	Ending Inventory Units
A	200	$125.70	250
B	400	82.50	200
C	500	64.00	400

3. Materials requirements and unit cost:

	Material X	Material Y	Material Z
Product A	12	5	2
Product B	8	3	1
Product C	6	2	1
Materials unit cost........	$1.00	$14.00	$2.50

4. Labor time requirements and rate per hour:

	Cutting	Assembling	Finishing
Product A	.500 hour	2.500 hours	.800 hour
Product B	.375	2.000	.500
Product C	.375	1.750	.500
Rate per hour.	$8.00	$10.00	$9.00

5. Unit overhead rates:

Product	Cutting	Assembling	Finishing	Total
A.	$3.00	$7.50	$4.80	$15.30
B.	2.25	6.00	3.00	11.25
C.	2.25	5.25	3.00	10.50

6. Marketing expenses: $450,000.
   Administrative expenses: $270,000.
   Other income: $70,000.
   Other expenses: $105,000.
   Income tax rate: 40%.

To achieve a concise yet comprehensive illustration, only annual data are shown. As previously noted, however, monthly budget details are often desirable and necessary. Also, customer group classifications for sales are omitted, and factory overhead, marketing and administrative expenses, and other income and expense items are not shown in detail.

Sales Budget

One of the most important elements in a budgetary control system is a realistic sales forecast that is based on analyses of past sales and the present market. The task of preparing the sales budget is usually approached from two different angles: (1) judging and evaluating external influences and (2) considering internal influences. These two influences are brought together in a workable sales budget. External influences include the general trend of industrial activity, governmental policies, cyclical phases of the nation's economy, price-level expectations, purchasing power of the population, population shift, and changes in buying habits and modes of living. Internal influences are sales trends, factory capacities, new products, plant expansion, seasonal products, sales estimates, and establishment of quotas for sales-people and sales territories. The profit desired by the company is a highly significant consideration.

The annual sales budget for Franklin Company on page 374, detailed by product and by territory, is prepared from the data on page 372.

Forecasting Sales. The preparation of sales estimates is usually the responsibility of the marketing manager, assisted by individual salespeople and market research personnel. Because of the many dissimilarities in the marketing of products, actual methods used to forecast sales vary widely. One

Schedule 1

Franklin Company
Sales Budget
For the Year Ending December 31, 19--

| | Territories | | |
	Midwest	Southwest	Total
Product A			
Units	4,000	3,000	7,000
Unit price	$200	$200	$200
Total	$ 800,000	$ 600,000	$1,400,000
Product B			
Units	6,000	5,000	11,000
Unit price	$150	$150	$150
Total	$ 900,000	$ 750,000	$1,650,000
Product C			
Units	9,000	6,000	15,000
Unit price	$100	$100	$100
Total	$ 900,000	$ 600,000	$1,500,000
Total	$2,600,000	$1,950,000	$4,550,000

method used by many companies is the preparation of sales estimates by individual salespeople. All salespeople supply their district managers with estimates of probable sales in their territories. These estimates are consolidated and adjusted by the district marketing manager. They are then forwarded to the general marketing manager, who makes further adjustments. These adjustments include allowances for expected economic conditions and competitive conditions of which salespeople are unaware, as well as allowances for expected canceled orders and sales returns that salespeople would likely disregard because their estimates are based on the orders they expect to procure.

In estimating sales as well as expenditures, the tendency to over- or underestimate plans must be recognized. Individuals tend to be overly pessimistic or optimistic in setting goals and in making plans. Therefore, the budgeting system should be designed to monitor this tendency in order to keep goals and plans within reasonable bounds.

In most large organizations, the forecasting procedure usually starts with known factors; namely, (1) the company's sales of past years broken down by product groups and profit margins, (2) industry or trade sales volume and perhaps profits, and (3) unusual factors influencing sales in the past. The company's past sales figures often require a restudy or reclassification due to changes in products, profit margins, competition, sales areas, distribution methods, or changes within the industry. Industry or trade sales and profits are secured from trade associations, trade publications, and various business magazines. For some industries, the U. S. Department of Commerce publishes information that is useful as background data. Unusual factors influencing past sales are inventory conditions, public economic sentiment, competition, and customer relations. Charting a company's volume in units of various products for a three- to five-year period and comparing it with the industry's volume will disclose the company's sales trend and will pinpoint factors that affected past sales.

Although the feeling frequently exists that the sales forecast is a crystal-ball area, a sound basis for determining future sales may be established by applying probability analysis techniques to the consideration of general business conditions, the industry's prospects, the company's potential share of the total industry market, and the plans of competitive companies.

Seasonal Variations. When the annual sales forecast has been approved, it must be placed on an operating period basis, which is usually a month. The monthly sales budget should show seasonal sales patterns for each product manufactured. These patterns are evident from the company's experience and from records of a product's trend during past years. Any fluctuations in a trend should be considered, as well as the causes of fluctuations, such as customs or habits based on local or national traits, climate, holidays, or even the influences of companies in the firm's own industry.

The seasonal or operating sales budget is of great help in judging the records of individual salespeople. Averaging sales over a budget period is not sufficient to assure success of a sales program. Too many times, low sales in one month have been excused with the optimistic statement that sales in the following month will make up the difference. When this does not happen, the sales budget and the entire budget plan suffer.

Sales Budget on a Territory and Customer Basis. A sales budget should not only be placed on a monthly basis for each product, but should also be classified by territories or districts and by types of customers. The customer classification should show sales to jobbers, wholesalers, retailers, institutions, governmental agencies, schools and colleges, foreign businesses, etc. Such a breakdown indicates the contribution of each territory and customer class to total sales and profits. An analysis of this type often reveals that certain territories or classes of customers are not given sufficient attention by sales managers and sales representatives. A detailed sales budget can be a strong means for analyzing possible new trade outlets. It also assists in identifying reasons for a drop in sales, in investigating such a decrease, and in taking remedial steps.

Estimating Production and Inventory Requirements. Prior to the final acceptance of a sales budget, the factory's capacity to produce the estimated quantities must be determined. The production level should maintain inventories that are sufficient to fulfill periodic sales requirements.

If factory capacity is available, production should be planned at a level that will keep workers and equipment operating all year. Serious fluctuations in employment are expensive and do not promote good labor relations. If the sales budget indicates that factory employment in certain months would fall below a desirable level, it would be necessary to attempt to increase sales volume or increase inventories. At the same time, the investment in inventories should be held to a level consistent with sound financial policy. If estimated sales are higher than available capacity, the purchase or rental of new machinery and factory space must be considered as a means of increasing plant capacity.

Sales Forecast Follow-Up. Follow-up review should occur at intervals influenced by the frequency of change in the company, its industry, and general economic conditions. The review should determine (1) the accuracy of past forecasts, (2) location of the major forecast errors, (3) the best method by which to update forecasts, and (4) the steps needed for improvement of the making and monitoring of future forecasts.

Past errors indicate the reliance that can be placed on sales forecasts and provide insight into the company and the personal bias built into the forecast. When forecasts are monitored, comparison with actual results should extend beyond financial results to include consideration of the underlying factors and key assumptions. Such comparisons might require the monitoring of unit sales volumes, prices, production rates, backlogs of sales orders, changes in capacity, and economic indicators.

Production Budget

The production budget deals with the scheduling of operations, the determination of volume, and the establishment of maximum and minimum quantities of finished goods inventories. It provides the basis for preparing the budgets of materials, labor, and factory overhead.

A production budget is stated in physical units. As shown in the following illustration, this budget is frequently the sales budget adjusted for any inventory changes.

Schedule 2	Franklin Company Production Budget For the Year Ending December 31, 19--		
		Products	
	A	B	C
Units required to meet sales budget (Schedule 1)........	7,000	11,000	15,000
Add desired ending inventory...........................	250	200	400
Total units required..................................	7,250	11,200	15,400
Less beginning inventory.............................	200	400	500
Planned production for the year.......................	7,050	10,800	14,900

If there is work in process inventory, the equivalent number of such units in the ending inventory would be added to, and units in the beginning inventory would be subtracted from, the above calculations in order to determine the units to be produced.

The production budget, like other budgets, may be detailed by months or quarters as well as annually. For comparison with actual production, the detailed budget should be broken down by work stations. The nature of this division will be determined by plant layout, type of production, and other factors.

For a company that does not manufacture standard products but produces only on orders, a detailed production budget may not be possible. In special-order work, the primary problem is to be prepared for production when orders are received. Work must be routed and scheduled through the factory, so that delays are prevented and production facilities are fully utilized.

No division of a manufacturing business has made so much progress in scientific management as the production department. Constant effort is directed toward devising new ways and shortcuts that will lead to more efficient production and cost savings which will be reflected in earnings.

Manufacturing Budgets

With the forecast sales translated into physical units in the production budget, the estimated manufacturing costs essential to the sales and production program can be computed. Detailed budgets are prepared for direct materials and direct labor in order to identify these costs with products and responsible managers. The factory overhead is budgeted in detail by responsibility centers or departments. This budget information becomes part of the master budget to be used as a standard or target against which the performance of the individual department is judged and evaluated.

Direct Materials Budget. The budgeting of direct materials specifies the quantity and cost of materials required to produce the predetermined units of finished goods. It (1) leads to the determination of quantities of materials that must be on hand, (2) permits the purchasing department to set up a purchasing schedule that assures delivery of materials when needed, and (3) establishes a means by which the treasurer can include in the cash budget the necessary funds for periodic purchases as well as for all other cash payments. Although the materials budget usually deals only with direct materials, these budgeting procedures are also applicable to supplies and indirect materials that are included in the factory overhead budget and the commercial expenses budget.

The schedules for Franklin Company on pages 378 and 379 consist of (1) the direct materials budget expressed in units required for production (Schedule 3), (2) the purchases budget, specifying inventory levels and units as well as the cost of purchases (Schedule 4), and (3) the calculation of the cost of materials required for production (Schedule 5).

The production planning department determines the quantity and type of materials required for the various products manufactured by a company. Most companies have standard parts lists and bills of materials which detail all materials requirements. These requirements are given to the purchasing department, which sets up a buying schedule. This schedule is based on the objective of providing sufficient materials without overstocking. In preparing

Schedule 3

Franklin Company
Direct Materials Budget in Units
For the Year Ending December 31, 19--

	Units To Be Manufactured	Materials		
		X	Y	Z
Product A				
Units to be manufactured (Schedule 2)	7,050			
Materials rate............................		12	5	2
Units of materials required		84,600	35,250	14,100
Product B				
Units to be manufactured (Schedule 2)	10,800			
Materials rate............................		8	3	1
Units of materials required		86,400	32,400	10,800
Product C				
Units to be manufactured (Schedule 2)	14,900			
Materials rate............................		6	2	1
Units of materials required		89,400	29,800	14,900
Total units of materials required............		260,400	97,450	39,800

Schedule 4

Franklin Company
Purchases Budget
For the Year Ending December 31, 19--

	Materials			Total
	X	Y	Z	
Units required for production (Schedule 3)...............	260,400	97,450	39,800	
Add desired ending inventory..	40,000	12,000	2,500	
	300,400	109,450	42,300	
Less beginning inventory......	30,000	10,000	2,000	
Units to be purchased	270,400	99,450	40,300	
Unit cost	$1.00	$14.00	$2.50	
Total cost of purchases	$270,400	$1,392,300	$100,750	$1,763,450

a buying schedule, the purchasing department must consider changes in possible delivery promises by the supplier and changes in the rate of materials consumption because of unforeseen circumstances.

The materials ledger cards of many companies include a section which shows the minimum and maximum quantities to be stored. When quantities are greater than the maximum or less than the minimum, the stock record clerk should inform the purchasing department or the production planning department. The coordination of materials records with purchasing department data acts as a check on both the overstocking of materials and the danger of a possible shortage.

Schedule 5

Franklin Company
Cost of Materials Required for Production
For the Year Ending December 31, 19--

	Materials			
	X	Y	Z	Total
Product A				
Units of materials required for production (Schedule 3)...	84,600	35,250	14,100	
Unit cost	$1.00	$14.00	$2.50	
Total.................	$ 84,600	$ 493,500	$35,250	$ 613,350
Product B				
Units of materials required for production (Schedule 3)...	86,400	32,400	10,800	
Unit cost	$1.00	$14.00	$2.50	
Total.................	$ 86,400	$ 453,600	$27,000	$ 567,000
Product C				
Units of materials required for production (Schedule 3)...	89,400	29,800	14,900	
Unit cost	$1.00	$14.00	$2.50	
Total.................	$ 89,400	$ 417,200	$37,250	$ 543,850
Total	$260,400	$1,364,300	$99,500	$1,724,200

Direct Labor Budget. The annual budget is the principal tool for the overall planning for human resources. When the budget is completed and approved, it should include a human resources plan that is coordinated with planned sales and production activities as well as the profit goal.

The direct labor budget, based on specifications drawn up by product engineers, guides the personnel department in determining the number and type of workers needed. If the labor force has been with the firm for several years and if the production schedule does not call for additional workers, the task of the personnel department is rather easy. If an increase or decrease in the labor force is required, the personnel department must make plans in advance to assure the availability of workers. Frequently, the personnel department must provide a training program which provides workers to the production department at the proper time. When workers are to be laid off, the personnel department must prepare a list of those affected, giving due recognition to skill and seniority rights. In many companies, this schedule is prepared in collaboration with union representatives in order to protect employees from any injustice or hardship.

For each type of labor, the hours or the number of workers must be translated into dollar values. Established labor rates as agreed upon in union contracts are generally used. If conditions indicate that labor rates might change, the new rates should be used, so that the financial budget reflects the most recent figures available. The following direct labor budget for Franklin Company is prepared from the data on page 373:

Schedule 6	Franklin Company Direct Labor Budget For the Year Ending December 31, 19--			
	Cutting	Assembling	Finishing	Total
Product A				
Hours per unit	.500	2.500	.800	
Units to be manufactured				
(Schedule 2).....................	7,050	7,050	7,050	
Hours of labor required	3,525	17,625	5,640	
Labor cost per hour	$8	$10	$9	
Total labor cost	$ 28,200	$176,250	$ 50,760	$255,210
Product B				
Hours per unit	.375	2.000	.500	
Units to be manufactured				
(Schedule 2).....................	10,800	10,800	10,800	
Hours of labor required	4,050	21,600	5,400	
Labor cost per hour	$8	$10	$9	
Total labor cost	$ 32,400	$216,000	$ 48,600	$297,000
Product C				
Hours per unit	.375	1.750	.500	
Units to be manufactured				
(Schedule 2).....................	14,900	14,900	14,900	
Hours of labor required	5,587.5	26,075	7,450	
Labor cost per hour	$8	$10	$9	
Total labor cost	$ 44,700	$260,750	$ 67,050	$372,500
	$105,300	$653,000	$166,410	$924,710

Indirect labor is included in the factory overhead budget and consists of such employees as helpers in producing departments, maintenance workers, crane operators, materials clerks, and receiving clerks. Labor requirements for marketing and administrative activities must be budgeted as part of the commercial expenses budget.

Factory Overhead Budget. The detailed factory overhead budget is prepared on the basis of the chart of accounts, which properly classifies expense accounts and details the various cost centers for planning and control and assignment of factory overhead to product cost. As discussed and illustrated in Chapter 8, expenses are grouped according to:

1. Natural expense classification, such as indirect materials and supplies, indirect labor, freight, light, and power.
2. Departmental or functional classification according to the producing or service department or cost center in which the expense originated.
3. Division of expenses according to variability, i.e., variable and fixed.

The natural expense classification alone is not useful for budget purposes, since expenses are usually incurred by various departments. By classifying expenses according to individual departments, the value and importance of budgetary control for expenses becomes significant.

Preparation of any expense budget should be guided by the principle that every expense is chargeable to a department, and that an executive, department head, or supervisor should be held accountable and responsible for expenses incurred. Those expenses for which the department supervisor is directly responsible should be identified in the supervisor's budget. Allocated expenses for which the supervisor has little or no responsibility should also be identified.

If department supervisors accept the budget, they are more likely to cooperate in its execution. Therefore, supervisors should be asked to prepare their own estimates of departmental expenses, based on the department's projected activity for the budget period. These estimates and any revisions should be reviewed and coordinated with other budgets before they are incorporated into the overall budget.

The detailed expense estimates lead to calculation of departmental factory overhead rates (as illustrated in Chapter 8), which are then used to estimate factory overhead for units to be manufactured. For Franklin Company, these costs are shown in the following budget:

Schedule 7	Franklin Company Factory Overhead Budget For the Year Ending December 31, 19--			
	Cutting	Assembling	Finishing	Total
Product A				
Units to be manufactured (Schedule 2).................	7,050	7,050	7,050	
Estimated departmental factory overhead per unit.........	$3.00	$7.50	$4.80	
Total cost	$21,150	$ 52,875	$ 33,840	$107,865
Product B				
Units to be manufactured (Schedule 2).................	10,800	10,800	10,800	
Estimated departmental factory overhead per unit.........	$2.25	$6.00	$3.00	
Total cost	$24,300	$ 64,800	$ 32,400	$121,500
Product C				
Units to be manufactured (Schedule 2).................	14,900	14,900	14,900	
Estimated departmental factory overhead per unit.........	$2.25	$5.25	$3.00	
Total cost	$33,525	$ 78,225	$ 44,700	$156,450
Total factory overhead	$78,975	$195,900	$110,940	$385,815

Beginning and Ending Inventories. Not only must inventory quantities be determined for materials, work in process, and finished goods, but the inventories must be costed in order to make available the necessary information leading to preparation of a budgeted cost of goods manufactured and sold statement and ultimately to an income statement and a balance sheet. For Franklin Company, beginning and ending inventory quantities and costs are summarized in the following schedule. Observe that the ending inventory unit costs for finished goods are the summation of estimates for direct materials, direct labor, and factory overhead.

Schedule 8							
	Franklin Company Beginning and Ending Inventories For the Year Ending December 31, 19--						
	Beginning Inventory			Ending Inventory			
	Units	Cost	Total	Units	Cost	Total	
Materials:							
X......................	30,000	$ 1.00	$ 30,000	40,000	$ 1.00	$ 40,000	
Y......................	10,000	14.00	140,000	12,000	14.00	168,000	
Z......................	2,000	2.50	5,000	2,500	2.50	6,250	
Total................			$175,000			$214,250	
Work in process: None							
Finished goods:							
Product A.............	200	$125.70	$ 25,140	250	$138.50*	$ 34,625	
Product B.............	400	82.50	33,000	200	91.25	18,250	
Product C.............	500	64.00	32,000	400	72.00	28,800	
Total................			$ 90,140			$ 81,675	
Total....................			$265,140			$295,925	

*Ending inventory unit costs for finished goods:

	Product A	Product B	Product C
Materials:			
X: 12 × $ 1.00	$ 12.00		
8 × 1.00		$ 8.00	
6 × 1.00			$ 6.00
Y: 5 × $14.00	70.00		
3 × 14.00		42.00	
2 × 14.00			28.00
Z: 2 × $ 2.50	5.00		
1 × 2.50		2.50	
1 × 2.50			2.50
Direct labor:			
Cutting: .500 × $ 8	4.00		
.375 × 8		3.00	
.375 × 8			3.00
Assembling: 2.500 × $10	25.00		
2.000 × 10		20.00	
1.750 × 10			17.50
Finishing: .800 × $ 9	7.20		
.500 × 9		4.50	
.500 × 9			4.50
Factory overhead	15.30	11.25	10.50
Total.............................	$138.50	$91.25	$72.00

Budgeted Cost of Goods Manufactured and Sold Statement. This statement requires no new estimates. Figures taken from various manufacturing schedules are arranged in the form of a cost of goods manufactured and sold statement, illustrated as follows. Source schedules are referenced to indicate the linkage with the budget components previously discussed and illustrated.

Schedule 9	Franklin Company	
	Budgeted Cost of Goods Manufactured and Sold Statement	
	For the Year Ending December 31, 19--	
Materials:		
Beginning inventory (Schedule 8)	$ 175,000	
Add purchases (Schedule 4)	1,763,450	
Total goods available for use	$1,938,450	
Less ending inventory (Schedule 8)	214,250	
Cost of materials used (Schedule 5)		$1,724,200
Direct labor (Schedule 6)		924,710
Factory overhead (Schedule 7)		385,815
Total manufacturing cost		$3,034,725
Add beginning inventory of finished goods (Schedule 8)		90,140
Cost of goods available for sale		$3,124,865
Less ending inventory of finished goods (Schedule 8)		81,675
Cost of goods sold		$3,043,190

Budgeting Commercial Expenses

The company's chart of accounts is also the basis for budgetary control of commercial expenses, which include both marketing (selling or distribution) and administrative expenses. These expenses may be classified by primary accounts and by functions.

Budgeting and analyzing commercial expenses by primary accounts is the simplest method of classification. This method stresses the nature or the type of expenditure, such as salaries, commissions, repairs, light and heat, rent, telephone and telegraph, postage, advertising, travel expenses, sales promotion, entertainment, delivery expense, freight out, insurance, donations, depreciation, taxes, and interest. As expenses are incurred, they are recorded in primary expense accounts, posted to ledger accounts, and then taken directly to the income statement. No further allocation is made. At the end of an accounting period, actual expenses are compared with either budgeted expenses or expenses of the previous month or year.

To control commercial expenses effectively, it is necessary to group them by functional activities or operating units. Classification by function emphasizes departmental activities, such as selling, advertising, warehousing, billing, credit and collection, transportation, accounting, purchasing, engineering, and financing. Such a classification is consistent with the concept of responsibility accounting and may be compared to collecting factory overhead by departments or cost centers. A departmental classification adds to rather than replaces the process of classifying expenses by primary accounts, because primary account classifications are maintained within each department.

When a departmental classification system is used, it is important that each expense be charged to a department, and that the classification conforms to the company's organization chart at the corporate level as well as each marketing territory level. However, it is impossible to suggest exact classifications, since organizational structures vary so much in business organizations. Departments known by the same name may perform widely differing functions.

Commercial expenses grouped by department may be subclassified as direct and indirect expenses. Direct expenses, such as salaries and supplies, are charged directly to a department. Indirect expenses are general or service department expenses that are prorated to benefiting departments. Expenses such as rent, insurance, and utilities, when shared by several departments, constitute this type of expense. Control responsibility should be highlighted.

To identify an outlay of cash or the incurrence of a liability with a function requires considerably more work than is required by the primary account method. However, the chart of accounts will normally provide the initial breakdown of expenses. Usually the allocation of expenses to departments and the identification of the primary account classification within each department can be made when the voucher is prepared. This procedure requires coding the expenditure when it is requisitioned for purchase. Any increase in expenses caused by the use of this functional method is more than offset by the advantages of improved cost control.

Commercial expenses are not detailed in the Franklin Company illustration, but rather are shown only in summary form in the budgeted income statement. Budget detail for primary accounts as well as for functional activities is shown in Chapter 21, using marketing expenses as the basis for illustration.

Marketing Expenses Budget. A company's marketing activities can be divided into two broad categories:

1. Obtaining the order—involves the functions of selling and advertising.
2. Filling the order—involves the functions of warehousing, packing and shipping, credit and collection, and general accounting (for marketing).

The supervisors of functions connected with marketing activities should prepare budget estimates of these costs. Some estimates are based on individual judgment, while others are based on the costs experienced in previous years, modified by expected sales volume. Expenses such as depreciation and insurance depend upon the policy established by management.

Administrative Expenses Budget. Administrative expenses include some costs which are peculiar to the administrative function, such as directors' fees, franchise taxes, capital stock taxes, and professional services of accountants, lawyers, and engineers. Other expenses, such as purchasing, engineering, personnel, and research, are shared by the production and marketing as well as the administrative functions.

As a result of the problem of classifying certain expenses, the budgeting and control of administrative expenses is often quite difficult. The difficulty is increased because the persons responsible for the control of certain of these expenses may not be identifiable. However, an attempt should be made to place every item of expense under the jurisdiction and control of an executive, such as the chief executive, treasurer, controller, general accounting supervisor, or office manager. This person should be responsible for estimating the administrative expenses of a specific section or division, and should have authority to control the incurrence of the division's expenses. For example, the office manager should supervise filing clerks, mail clerks, librarians, stenographers, secretaries, and receptionists. This arrangement permits better control and more intense utilization of personnel in clerical jobs, where overlapping and overexpansion are common.

Budgeted Income Statement

A budgeted income statement contains summaries of the sales, manufacturing, and expense budgets. It projects net income, the goal toward which all efforts are directed, and it offers management the opportunity to judge the accuracy of the budget work and to investigate causes for variances. The budgeted income statement for Franklin Company is as follows:

Schedule 10	Franklin Company Budgeted Income Statement For the Year Ending December 31, 19--		
		Amount	% of Sales
Sales (Schedule 1)		$4,550,000	100.0%
Cost of goods sold (Schedule 9)		3,043,190	66.9
Gross profit		$1,506,810	33.1%
Commercial expenses:			
Marketing expenses	$450,000 (9.9%)		
Administrative expenses	270,000 (5.9%)	720,000	15.8
Income from operations		$ 786,810	17.3%
Other (income) expense		35,000	.8
Income before income tax		$ 751,810	16.5%
Less provision for income tax		300,724	6.6
Net income		$ 451,086	9.9%

The sales budget gives expected sales revenue, from which the budgeted cost of goods sold is deducted to give the estimated gross profit. Budgeted marketing and administrative expenses are subtracted from estimated gross profit to arrive at income from operations, which is then adjusted for other income and expense to determine income before income tax. Finally, the provision for income tax is deducted to determine net income. The inclusion of percentages of sales may aid in determining whether various income statement components are in line with expectations.

The budgeted income statement and related supporting budgets may be shown by months or quarters. Furthermore, the income statement may be segmented by individual products or product groups and by individual marketing territories.

DISCUSSION QUESTIONS

1. Profit planning includes a complete financial and operational plan for all phases and facets of the business. Discuss.

2. Discuss the three different procedures that a company's management might follow to set profit objectives.

3. Differentiate between long-range profit planning and short-range budgeting.

4. What is a budget and how is it related to the control function?

5. The development of a budgetary control program requires specific systems and procedures needed in carrying out management's functions of planning, organizing, and controlling. Enumerate these steps.

6. The human factors in budget preparation are more important than its technical intricacies. Explain.

7. Commercial expenses are generally identified as marketing and administrative expenses. How should these expenses be grouped for budgetary purposes?

8. The budgeted income statement may be viewed as the apex of budgeting. Explain this statement.

EXERCISES

1. *Sales budget.* Bosque Brothers is a wholesaler for three chemical compounds, Barb, Shir, and Bett, for which the following information relates to the year 19A:

Product	Sales (In Pounds)	Average Sales Price per Pound	Gross Profit per Pound
Barb	10,000	$24	$3
Shir	7,500	18	2
Bett	7,500	23	2

Barb has greatly increased in popularity, and demand is expected to double in 19B. Shir will probably experience a 40% increase in demand, while demand for Bett is expected to remain constant. In line with the overall economy, sales prices will increase by 4%, except for Barb, whose market value will increase to $37. Unit costs of goods sold are expected to increase by the following multiples: Barb, 1/3; Shir, 1/8; Bett, 1/10.

Required: Prepare a schedule presenting budgeted sales revenue and gross profit, by product, for 19B.

2. Sales and production forecasts. *Robar Company produces and sells commercial printing presses. Accounting records from the past four years reveal the following:*

Press Model Number	Sales in Units			
	Year 1	Year 2	Year 3	Year 4
222	100	110	120	130
333	100	120	160	240
444	100	95	85	70

The trends over the past four years are expected to extend to Year 5.
    Inventory estimates for Year 5 are:

Press Model Number	Beginning Inventory	Ending Inventory
222	2	3
333	5	4
444	4	4

Required: *Prepare sales and production forecasts for Year 5, in units and by product.*

3. Production budget. *Schwankenfelder Company's sales forecast for the next quarter, ending June 30, indicates the following:*

Product	Expected Sales
Ceno.......................................	21,000 units
Nepo.......................................	37,500
Teno.......................................	54,300

Inventories at the beginning and desired quantities at the end of the quarter are as follows:

Product	March 31	June 30
Ceno...........................	5,800 units	6,200 units
Nepo...........................	10,600	10,500
Teno...........................	13,000	12,200

Required: *Prepare a production budget for the second quarter.*

4. Production budget. *Bass Enterprises produces three perfumes. The sales department prepared the following tentative sales budget for the first quarter of the coming year:*

Perfume	Units
Moon Glow	250,000
Enchanting.........................	175,000
Day Dream	325,000

The following inventory levels have been established:

Perfume	Work in Process				Finished Goods	
	Beginning		Ending		Beginning	Ending
	Units	% Processed	Units	% Processed	Units	Units
Moon Glow	4,000	50%	7,000	60%	16,000	15,000
Enchanting..........	6,000	30	5,000	40	12,000	10,000
Day Dream	8,000	80	8,000	75	25,000	20,000

Required: *Prepare a production budget, by product.*

5. *Production budget and raw materials purchases requirements.* Crawford Industries produces television antennas and has estimated sales for the next six-month period as follows:

Model Number	Units
1001	200
1002	150
1003	425
2001	175
2002	325
2003	215

Raw materials requirements for each model are:

	Raw Material in Pounds	
Model Number	X	Y
1001	5	1
1002	7	2
1003	10	3
2001	4	1.5
2002	6	2
2003	8	2.5

Estimated inventories are:

	Beginning Inventory	Ending Inventory
Raw Materials:		
X	5,000 lbs.	7,000 lbs.
Y	2,000	1,500
Finished Goods:		
1001	50 units	40 units
1002	25	25
1003	75	60
2001	15	20
2002	35	35
2003	20	20

Required:
(1) Prepare a production budget, by product.
(2) Compute the raw materials purchases requirements, by raw material.

6. *Production budget, purchase requirements, and manufacturing costs.* Groningen Company prepared the following figures as a basis for its annual budget:

			Required Materials per Unit	
Product	Expected Sales	Estimated per Unit Sales Price	A	B
Tribolite	80,000 units	$1.50	1 kg	2 kg
Polycal	40,000	2.00	2	—
Powder X	100,000	.80	—	1

Estimated inventories at the beginning and desired quantities at the end of the year are:

Material	Beginning	Ending	Purchase Price per Kilogram
A	10 000 kg	12 000 kg	$.20
B	12 000	15 000	.10

Product	Beginning	Ending	Direct Labor Hours per 1,000 Units
Tribolite	5,000 units	6,000 units	50.0
Polycal	4,000	2,000	125.0
Powder X...................	10,000	8,000	12.5

The direct labor cost is budgeted at $8 per hour and variable factory overhead at $6 per hour of direct labor. Fixed factory overhead, estimated to be $40,000, is a joint cost and is not allocated to specific products in developing the manufacturing budget for internal management use.

Required:

(1) Prepare a production budget.
(2) Prepare a purchases budget for each material.
(3) Prepare a budget of manufacturing costs, by product and in total.

7. Budgeted cost of goods sold statement. Hennepin, Inc., with $20,000,000 of par stock outstanding, plans to budget earnings of 6%, before income tax, on this stock.

The Marketing Department budgets sales at $12,000,000. The budget director approves the sales budget and expenses as follows:

Marketing.................................	15% of sales
Administrative	5%
Financial..................................	1%

Labor is expected to be 50% of the total manufacturing cost; materials issued for the budgeted production will cost $2,500,000; therefore, any savings in manufacturing cost will have to be in factory overhead.

Inventories are to be as follows:

	Beginning of Year	End of Year
Finished goods................................	$800,000	$1,000,000
Work in Process..............................	100,000	300,000
Materials	500,000	400,000

Required: Prepare the budgeted cost of goods manufactured and sold statement, showing the budgeted purchases of materials and the adjustments for inventories of materials, work in process, and finished goods.

8. Budgeted income statement. Schwarzstein Company has just received a franchise to distribute air conditioners. The company began business on January 1 with the following assets:

Cash..	$ 45,000
Inventory	94,000
Warehouse, office, and delivery facilities and equipment	800,000

All facilities and equipment have a useful life of 20 years and no residual value. First quarter sales are expected to be $360,000 and should be doubled in the second quarter. Third quarter sales are expected to be $1,080,000. One percent of sales are considered *to be uncollectible. The gross profit margin should be 30%. Variable marketing expenses (except uncollectible accounts) are budgeted at 12% of sales and fixed marketing expenses at $48,000 per quarter, exclusive of depreciation. Variable administrative expenses are expected to be 3% of sales and fixed administrative expenses should total $34,200 per quarter, exclusive of depreciation.*

Required: *Prepare a budgeted income statement for the second quarter.*

(CGAA adapted)

PROBLEMS

14-1. Sales and manufacturing budgets. Scarborough Corporation manufactures and sells two products, Thingone and Thingtwo. In July, 19A, Scarborough's Budget Department gathered the following data in order to project sales and budget requirements for 19B:

19B projected sales:

Product	Units	Price
Thingone.........	60,000	$ 70
Thingtwo.........	40,000	$100

19B inventories (in units):

Product	Expected— January 1, 19B	Desired— December 31, 19B
Thingone....................	20,000	25,000
Thingtwo....................	8,000	9,000

To produce one unit of Thingone and Thingtwo, the following raw materials are used:

Raw Material	Amount Used per Unit	
	Thingone	Thingtwo
A................................	4 lbs.	5 lbs.
B................................	2 lbs.	3 lbs.
C................................	—	1 unit

Projected data for 19B with respect to raw materials are as follows:

Raw Material	Anticipated Purchase Price	Expected Inventories January 1, 19B	Desired Inventories December 31, 19B
A......................	$8	32,000 lbs.	36,000 lbs.
B......................	$5	29,000 lbs.	32,000 lbs.
C......................	$3	6,000 units	7,000 units

Projected direct labor requirements and rates for 19B are as follows:

Product	Hours per Unit	Rate per Hour
Thingone....................	2	$6
Thingtwo....................	3	$8

Factory overhead is applied at the rate of $2 per direct labor hour.

Required: Based on the above projections and budget requirements for 19B for Thingone and Thingtwo, prepare the following 19B budgets:

(1) Sales budget.
(2) Production budget.
(3) Raw materials purchases budget.
(4) Direct labor budget.
(5) Budgeted finished goods inventory at December 31, 19B.   (AICPA adapted)

14-2. Production and manufacturing budgets. The following data are provided for Reid Corporation:

Sales:

Sales through June 30, 19A, the first six months of the current year, are 24,000 units. Expected sales for the full year are 60,000 units. Actual sales in units for May and June and estimated unit sales for the next four months are as follows:

May....................	4,000 units
June	4,000
July..................	5,000
August...............	6,000
September............	7,000
October	7,000

Direct materials:

At each month end, Reid desires to have sufficient materials on hand to produce the next month's estimated sales. Data regarding materials are as follows:

Direct Material	Units of Material Required	Cost per Unit	Inventory Units, June 30, 19A
101	6	$2.40	35,000
211	4	3.60	30,000
242	2	1.20	14,000

Direct labor:

Process	Hours per Unit	Hourly Labor Rate
Forming................	.80	$8.00
Assembly..............	2.00	5.50
Finishing	.25	6.00

Factory overhead:

The company produced 27,000 units during the six-month period through June 30, 19A, and expects to produce 60,000 units during the year. The actual variable factory overhead costs incurred during this six-month period are as follows. The controller believes that these costs will be incurred at the same rate during the remainder of 19A.

Supplies......................................	$ 59,400
Electricity....................................	27,000
Indirect labor	54,000
Other	8,100
Total variable factory overhead	$148,500

The fixed factory overhead costs incurred during the first six months of 19A amounted to $93,000. Fixed overhead costs are budgeted for the full year as follows:

Supervision	$ 60,000
Property tax	7,200
Depreciation	86,400
Other	32,400
Total fixed factory overhead	$186,000

Finished goods inventory:

The desired monthly ending finished goods inventory in units is 80% of the next month's estimated sales. There are 5,600 finished units in the June 30, 19A inventory.

Required:
(1) Prepare the production budget for the third quarter ending September 30, 19A.
(2) Prepare the direct materials purchases budget for the third quarter.
(3) Prepare the direct labor budget for the third quarter.
(4) Prepare the factory overhead budget for the six months ending December 31, 19A, presenting two figures, i.e., for total variable and fixed overhead.

(CMA adapted)

14-3. Sales budget; purchases and materials requirements. The management of Consumer Food Products decided to install a budgetary control system under the supervision of a budget director and a committee. Among its products, the company manufactures a patented breakfast food that is sold in packages of two sizes—1 lb. and 2 lb. The cereal is made from two types of grain, called R (rye) and S (soy) for this purpose. There are two operations: (a) processing and blending and (b) packaging. The grains are purchased by the bushel measure, a bushel of R containing 70 lbs. and a bushel of S containing 80 lbs. Three bushels of grain mixed in the proportion of 2R:1S produce 198 lbs. of finished product. The entire loss occurs in the first department.

To prepare estimated sales figures for the first six months of the coming year, the budget committee first asked the salespeople to prepare sales estimates in units. The following data were submitted:

	Territories				
	I	II	III	Other	6-Month Total
1-lb. package	10,000	15,000	12,000	613,000	650,000
2-lb. package	12,000	18,000	12,000	783,000	825,000
Total	22,000	33,000	24,000	1,396,000	1,475,000

The figures submitted are analyzed by the budget committee in the light of general business conditions. The company uses the Federal Reserve Board Index together with its own trade index to prepare a trend percentage that exists in the business. The trend percentage indicates that a .90 general index figure should be applied to the estimates in order to arrive at the final sales figures. The finished goods inventory is to be kept at zero if possible. The work in process inventory is to be kept near the present level, which is about 160,000 lbs. of blended material.

Factory facilities permit processing sales requirements as stated in the sales budget. The production manager decided to accept the monthly sales figures for the production budget.

Purchases of grains in bushels have been arranged as follows:

	Type R		Type S	
	Quantity	Price	Quantity	Price
January.........................	5,000 bu.	$1.30	2,000 bu.	$1.20
February	2,000	1.40	1,000	1.20
March...........................	–0–	–0–	3,000	1.25
April...........................	8,000	1.50	3,000	1.00
May............................	3,000	1.50	–0–	–0–
June	4,000	1.60	4,000	1.00
Beginning inventory, January 1....	10,000	1.20	3,000	1.00

Materials are charged into production on the fifo basis.

Required:
(1) Prepare a revised sales budget in units for the six-month period, based on the index.
(2) Prepare a sales budget in dollars, assuming that the 1-lb. package sells for $.25 and the 2-lb. package for $.50.
(3) Prepare a schedule of materials purchases.
(4) Prepare a computation of materials requirements for production. (Round off to the nearest whole amount.)
(5) Prepare a schedule of the materials account (fifo basis), in units and dollars, indicating beginning inventory, purchases, usage, and ending inventory for the six-month period taken as a whole.

14-4. Budgeted income statement. The president of a hardware manufacturing company has asked the controller to prepare an income forecast for the next year, by quarters, with sales reported for each of the two major segments—commercial and government.

The Marketing Department provided the following sales estimates:

	1st Quarter	2d Quarter	3d Quarter	4th Quarter
Commercial sales...........	$250,000	$266,000	$275,000	$300,000
Government sales	100,000	120,000	110,000	115,000

The controller's office assembled these figures:

(a) Cost of goods sold: 46% of total sales.
(b) Advertising expenditures: $4,000 each quarter.
(c) Selling expenses: 10% of total sales.
(d) Administrative expenses: 16.8% of gross profit.
(e) General office expenses: 12% of gross profit.
(f) Other income: $8,000 per quarter.
(g) Corporate income tax rate: 40%.

Required:
(1) Prepare a budgeted income statement, by quarters and in total. All figures should be shown in thousands of dollars and rounded to the nearest thousand, adding four quarters across to obtain total figures.
(2) Prepare an analysis of the effect of a 5% increase in commercial sales revenue, using the same income statement format as for (1).

14-5. Preliminary profit plan. Barr Food Manufacturing Company is a medium-size publicly held corporation, producing a variety of consumer food and specialty products. Current-year data were prepared as follows for the salad dressing product line, using five months of actual expenses and a seven-month projection:

Projected Income Statement
For the Year Ending December 31, 19A
(5 months actual; 7 months projected)
(000s omitted)

Volume in gallons..	5,000
Gross sales	$30,000
Freight, allowances, and discounts....................................	3,000
Net sales	$27,000
Less manufacturing costs:	
Variable..	$13,500
Fixed...	2,100
Depreciation...	700
Total manufacturing cost.....................................	$16,300
Gross profit..	$10,700
Less expenses:	
Marketing	$ 4,000
Brokerage	1,650
General and administrative....................................	2,100
Research and development....................................	500
Total expenses	$ 8,250
Income before income tax..	$ 2,450

The current-year projection was accepted as being accurate, but it was agreed that the projected income was not at a satisfactory level. The president stated that he wanted, at a minimum, a 15% increase in gross sales dollars and not less than 10% before-tax profit on gross sales for 19B. He also stated that he would be responsible for a $200,000 reduction in the general and administrative expenses to help achieve the profit goal.

Both the vice-president–marketing and the vice-president–production felt that the president's objectives would be difficult to achieve; however, they offered the following suggestions to reach the objectives:

(a) Sales volume — Barr's current share of the salad dressing market is 15% and the total salad dressing market is expected to increase by 5% for 19B. Barr's current market share can be maintained by a marketing expenditure of $4,200,000. The two vice-presidents estimated that the market share could be increased by additional expenditures for advertising and sales promotion. For an additional expenditure of $525,000, the market share can be raised by one percentage point until the market share reaches 17%. To achieve further market penetration, an additional $875,000 must be spent for each percentage point until the market share reaches 20%. Any advertising and promotion expenditures beyond this level are not likely to increase the market share to more than 20%.

(b) Sales price — The sales price, which will remain at $6 per gallon, is very closely related to the cost of the ingredients, which is not expected to change in 19B from that experienced in 19A.

(c) Variable manufacturing cost — Variable manufacturing cost is projected at 50% of the net sales dollar (gross sales less freight, allowances, and discounts.)

(d) Fixed manufacturing cost — An increase of $100,000 is projected for 19B.

(e) Depreciation — A projected increase in equipment will increase depreciation by $25,000 over the 19A projection.

(f) Freight, allowances, and discounts — The current rate of 10% of gross sales dollars is expected to continue in 19B.

(g) Brokerage expense — A rate of 5% of gross sales dollars is projected for 19B.

(h) General and administrative expense—A $200,000 decrease in general and administrative expense from the 19A forecast is projected, an amount consistent with the president's commitment.

(i) Research and development expense—A 5% increase from the absolute dollars in the 19A forecast will be necessary to meet divisional research targets.

Required: Prepare a profit plan (budgeted income statements) for 15% through 20% market shares, at 1% increments, indicating the market share percentage most in harmony with the president's objectives. (CMA adapted)

14-6. Budgeted income statement and related schedules. A1 Sound Systems manufactures speakers for component stereo systems. Three models are produced: Model 150, Model 100, and Model 50. The speakers are marketed in two regions, the South and Southwest. The production departments are designated Cutting, Assembling, and Finishing. Lumber, speakers, and a finishing compound are the materials used in producing the speakers.

The following estimates have been made for the coming year:

(a) Sales forecast:

Model	South	Southwest	Sales Price
150	3,000 units	4,000 units	$175 per unit
100	5,000	7,000	120
50	7,000	8,000	90

(b) Inventories:

Materials:

	Beginning Inventory Units	Ending Inventory Units	Unit Cost
Lumber (board feet)...	40,000	30,000	$ .75
Speakers............	10,000	8,000	15.00
Finish (pints)........	1,500	2,000	2.00

Work in process: None at the beginning or end of the period.

Finished goods (fifo):

	Beginning Inventory		Ending Inventory	
Model	Units	Unit Cost	Units	Unit Cost
150	200	$98.00	200	$105.50
100	300	62.00	400	66.75
50	400	47.00	300	50.25

(c) Materials requirements:

Model	Lumber (Board Feet)	Speakers	Finish (Pints)
150	12	5	2
100	8	3	1
50	6	2	1

(d) Estimated materials cost:
Lumber, $.75 per board foot.
Speakers, $15 per speaker.
Finish, $2 per pint.

(e) Estimated labor cost:

	Cutting	Assembling	Finishing
Rate per hour	$6.00	$5.00	$4.00

Estimated labor time requirements:

Model	Cutting	Assembling	Finishing
150............................	.375 hour	2.0 hours	.375 hour
100............................	.375	1.5	.250
50............................	.375	1.5	.250

(f) Factory overhead budgets show the following unit overhead rates:

Model	Cutting	Assembling	Finishing
150............................	$1.00	$2.00	$.75
100............................	1.00	1.50	.50
50............................	1.00	1.50	.50

(g) Marketing expenses: $500,000.
Administrative expenses: $300,000.
Income tax rate: 50%.

Required: Prepare annual budget schedules utilizing the budget estimates provided. The schedules should be designed to provide essential data in an easily understood form. Titles and schedule numbers to be used are as follows. Cross-references should be made using schedule numbers.

Schedule	Title
(1)	Sales budget—by models and by sales regions
(2)	Production budget—by models and by units
(3)	Direct materials budget in units—by materials and by models
(4)	Purchases budget—by materials and by cost
(5)	Cost of materials required for production—by materials and by models
(6)	Direct labor budget—by models and by departments
(7)	Factory overhead budget (applied overhead)—by models and by departments
(8)	Beginning and ending inventories—by materials and by models
(9)	Budgeted cost of goods manufactured and sold statement
(10)	Budgeted income statement—with each item shown as a percentage of sales (round off percentages to the nearest tenth of a percent)

CASES

A. Evaluation of budget procedures. Schaffer Company, a large multidivision firm with several plants in each division, uses a comprehensive budgeting system for planning operations and measuring performance. The annual budgeting process begins in August, five months prior to the beginning of the fiscal year. At this time, the division managers submit proposed budgets for sales, production and inventory levels, and expenses. Capital expenditure requests also are formalized at this time. The expense budgets include direct labor and all factory overhead items, separated into fixed and variable components. Direct materials are budgeted separately in developing the production and inventory schedules.

The expense budgets for each division are developed from each plant's results, as measured by the percent variation from an adjusted budget in the first six months of the current year, and a target expense reduction percentage established by the corporation.

To determine plant percentages, the plant budget for the just completed half-year period is revised to recognize changes in operating procedures and costs outside the control of plant management (e.g., labor wage rate changes and product style changes). The difference between this revised budget and the actual expenses is the controllable variance, expressed as a percentage of the actual expenses. If unfavorable, this percentage is added to the corporate target expense reduction percentage. A favorable plant variance percentage is subtracted from the corporate target. If a plant had a 2% unfavorable controllable variance and the corporate target reduction was 4%, the plant's budget for next year should reflect costs approximately 6% below this year's actual costs.

Next year's final budgets for the corporation, its divisions, and plants are adopted after corporate analysis of the proposed budgets and a careful review with each division manager of the changes made by corporate management.

Division profit budgets include allocated corporate costs, and plant profit budgets include allocated division and corporate costs.

Required: Evaluate the budget procedures of Schaffer Company with respect to its effectiveness for planning and controlling operations.   (CMA adapted)

B. Budget evaluation. Executive management receives the following budget information for 19B from a subsidiary, the Papion Men's Clothing Company:

The Papion Men's Clothing Company expects the operating results for 19B to be better than for 19A, because several actions have been taken which will improve sales and solve operating problems. Sales should increase substantially due to the introduction of a new line of women's sportswear to be distributed through company-owned stores. Progress was also made last year in attracting other retailers to handle Papion's lines. Additional sales increases can be expected this year if negotiations to induce a major chain to distribute Papion lines are successful. The budget that follows includes the sales expected to be made through this large chain retailer.

Original Budget for 19A
Forecast of Actual Operations for 19A
Proposed Budget for 19B
(000s omitted)

	19A Budget	19A Forecast of Actual Operations	19B Budget
Sales.........................	$10,000	$8,500	$12,000
Cost of goods sold:			
Materials	$ 1,050	$ 975	$ 1,260
Labor	1,400	1,400	1,680
Factory overhead	1,750	1,600	1,800
Marketing expenses:			
Sales force	500	425	600
Advertising and promotion	600	500	950
Company stores	1,000	950	1,100
General administration	750	755	825
Total expenses.............	$ 7,050	$6,605	$ 8,215
Income before income tax	$ 2,950	$1,895	$ 3,785

Prepared and submitted: October, 19A.

Operating costs should be lower this year. A new production facility should be completed in February to replace an older plant. This older plant has caused production shortages due to frequent equipment breakdowns. Also, labor problems which existed at the Midwest Plant have been resolved, thus correcting the lower output and higher costs of that plant.

Required:
(1) Evaluate the report's usefulness to executive management in exercising control over the subsidiary.
(2) Identify the report changes needed to improve its effectiveness in communicating Papion's 19B plans.   (CMA adapted)

Chapter 15
Budgeting: Capital Expenditures, Research and Development Expenditures, and Cash; PERT/Cost

Budgeting is usually an iterative process. Budgets are prepared, reviewed, and revised until executive management is satisfied that the result represents the best plans that can be devised under existing circumstances. Furthermore, management may develop contingency plans for dealing with various eventualities. As the planning period unfolds, budget revisions may be required, and such revisions will be facilitated if management has anticipated alterations called for by changing circumstances and conditions.

This chapter discusses specific budgets, such as capital expenditures and research and development budgets, which play a significant part in the long- and short-range plans of any management. Closely related thereto is the cash budget, which reveals excesses or shortages of funds. The budgeted income statement (Chapter 14) and balance sheet serve as a master budget and final check on the ultimate results expected from the combined sales-cost-profit plan. Computerized budgeting, financial forecasts for external users, budgeting for nonmanufacturing businesses and nonprofit organizations, zero-base budgeting, PERT and PERT/cost, and probabilistic budgets conclude the presentation.

Capital Expenditures Budget

Capital expenditures are long-term commitments of resources to realize future benefits. Budgeting capital expenditures is one of the most important areas of managerial decision. Facility improvements and plant expansion programs must be geared to a limited supply of funds from internal operations and external sources. The magnitude of funds involved in each expenditure and the length of time required to recover the investment call for penetrating analysis and capable judgment. Decisions regarding current manufacturing operations can always be changed, but because the benefits of a capital expenditure will be reaped over a fairly extended length of time, managerial errors could be quite costly.

Evaluating Capital Expenditures

To minimize the number of capital expenditure errors, many firms have established definite procedures for evaluating the merits of a project before funds are released. True control of capital expenditures is exercised in advance by requiring that each request be based on evaluation analyses, described and illustrated in Chapter 26. Managerial control requires facts regarding engineering estimates, expected sales volumes, production costs, and marketing costs. Management usually has a firm conviction as to what is consistent with the long-range objectives of the business. It is fundamentally interested in making certain that the project will contribute to the earnings position of the company.

Short- and Long-Range Capital Expenditures

Capital expenditure programs involve both short- and long-range projects. Provisions must be made in the current budget for short-range capital expenditures. These short-range projects must be examined in the light of their economic worth as compared with other projects seeking final approval. The process of budgeting provides the only opportunity to examine projects side by side and to evaluate their contribution to future periods.

Long-range projects which will not be implemented in the current budget period need only be stated in general terms, since the exchange and addition of capital assets are only significant in the current budget period. In the main, long-range capital expenditure plans are a management responsibility and are translated into budget commitments only as the opportune time for their implementation approaches. Timing is most important to the achievement of the most profitable results in planning and budgeting capital expenditures.

Research and Development Budget

Research and development activities have been defined as follows:

1. *Research* is planned search or critical investigation aimed at discovery of new knowledge with the hope that such knowledge will be useful in developing a new product or service (hereinafter "product") or a new process or technique (hereinafter "process") or in bringing about a significant improvement to an existing product or process.
2. *Development* is the translation of research findings or other knowledge into a plan or design for a new product or process or for a significant improvement to an existing product or process whether intended for sale or use. It includes the conceptual formulation, design, and testing of product alternatives, construction of prototypes, and operation of pilot plants. It does not include routine or periodic alterations to existing products, production lines, manufacturing processes, and other ongoing operations even though those alterations may represent improvements and it does not include market research or market testing activities.[1]

The managements of many firms are acutely aware of the increased necessity for and rapid growth of research and development activities and of the need to consider their costs from both the long- and short-range points of view. From the long-range viewpoint, management must assure itself that a program is in line with future market trends and demands and that the future cost of a program is not at odds with forecast economic and financial conditions. From the short-range viewpoint, management must be assured that experimental efforts are being expended on programs which promise a satisfactory rate of return on the dollars invested.

Research and development projects compete with other projects for available financial resources. The value of the research and development program must be shown as clearly as possible, so that management can compare it with similar programs and other investment opportunities. Therefore, the motivation and intent of experimental activities must be carefully identified.

The research and development budget involves identifying program components and estimating their costs. Other planning devices are used at times, but the budget is considered best for (1) balancing the research and development program, (2) coordinating the program with the company's other projects, and (3) checking certain phases of nonfinancial planning. The budget forces management to think in advance about planned expenditures, both in total amounts and in sphere of effort. It helps achieve coordination, because it presents an overall picture of proposed research and development activities which can be reviewed and criticized by other operating managers. Exchange of opinions and information at planning meetings is management's best control over the program.

---

[1] *Statement of Financial Accounting Standards, No. 2,* "Accounting for Research and Development Costs" (Stamford: Financial Accounting Standards Board, 1974), par. 8.

Another important purpose of research and development budgeting is to coordinate these plans with the immediate and long-term financial plans of the company. The budget also forces the research and development director and staff to think in advance about major aspects of the program: personnel requirements, individual or group work loads, equipment requirements, special materials, and necessary facilities. These phases of the research and development program are often overlooked or duplicated.

Forms of a Research and Development Budget

Management expects the research and development staff to present ideas along with a complete and detailed budget which can be evaluated as part of the entire planning program. The controller's staff may assist in the preparation of budgets with clearly defined goals and properly evaluated cost data.

Submission of data takes many forms. Information regarding segmentation and allocation of time and effort to various phases of the program is of particular interest to executive management as well as to divisional managers. The following example of a research and development budget has been proposed:[2]

RESEARCH AND DEVELOPMENT BUDGET
PROGRAM PLANNED FOR 19--

(Percentages of Total Effort by Area of Inquiry and by Phase)

Phase	Cost Reduction			Improved Products			New Products			Total
	A*	B	C	A	B	C	A	B	C	
Basic research	4%	3%	3%	2%	4%	4%	1%	1%	3%	25%
Applied research	5	12	3	4	1		2		3	30
Development.........	7	6	2	5			10		15	45
Total by product lines	16%	21%	8%	11%	5%	4%	13%	1%	21%	100%
Total by area of inquiry............		45%			20%			35%		

*A, B, and C refer to product lines.

The overall research and development program should be supported by a specific budget request which indicates the jobs or steps within each project, the necessary labor hours, the service department time required, and required direct departmental funds. Each active project should be reviewed monthly, comparing projected plans with results attained.

The Franklin Company illustration from the preceding chapter did not include budgeted research and development expenditures. Such a budget could be detailed in dollars, using a format similar to the budget shown above. The dollar amount would be included in the budgeted income state-

[2]J. B. Quinn, "Study of the Usefulness of Research and Development Budgets," *NAA Bulletin*, Vol. XL, No. 1, pp. 79–90.

ment, consistent with the accounting procedures described in the following paragraph.

Accounting for Research and Development Costs

Research and development costs generally should be expensed in the period incurred because of the uncertainty of the extent or length of future benefit to the company. An exception to the expensing requirement applies to costs of research and development expenditures that are (1) conducted for others, (2) unique to extractive industries, or (3) incurred by a government-regulated enterprise, such as a public utility, which often defers research and development costs because of the rate-regulated aspects of its business. Equipment and purchased intangibles having alternative future uses should be recorded as assets and expensed through depreciation or amortization. Research and development costs, when expensed, should be reported as one item in the operating expense section of the income statement.[3]

For government contract costing, the Cost Accounting Standards Board promulgated a standard dealing with accounting for independent research and development costs and bid and proposal costs. It provides criteria for (1) accumulation of such costs, (2) their allocation among contractor divisions, and (3) allocation of these costs to contracts.[4]

Cash Budget

A *cash budget* involves detailed estimates of anticipated cash receipts and disbursements for the budget period or some other specific period. It has generally been recognized as an extremely useful and essential management tool. Planning and controlling cash is basic to good management. Even if a company does not prepare extensive budgets for sales and production, it should set up a budget or estimate of cash receipts and disbursements as an aid to cash management.

Purpose and Nature of a Cash Budget

A cash budget:

1. Indicates cash requirements needed for current operating activities.
2. Aids in focusing on cash usage priorities currently unavoidable and required versus postponable or permanently avoidable.
3. Indicates the effect on the cash position of seasonal requirements, large inventories, unusual receipts, and slowness in collecting receivables.

---

[3]*Statement of Financial Accounting Standards, No. 2, op. cit.,* pars. 2, 3, and 11–14.
[4]For specifics, see *Standards, Rules and Regulations, Part 420,* "Accounting for Independent Research and Development Costs and Bid and Proposal Costs" (Washington, D.C.: Cost Accounting Standards Board, 1980).

4. Indicates the availability of cash for taking advantage of discounts.
5. Indicates the cash requirements for a plant or equipment expansion program.
6. Assists in planning the financial requirements of bond retirements, income tax installments, and payments to pension and retirement funds.
7. Shows the availability of excess funds for short-term or long-term investments.
8. Shows the need for additional funds from sources such as bank loans or sales of securities and the time factors involved. In this connection, it might also exert a cautionary influence on plans for plant expansion, leading to a modification of capital expenditure decisions.
9. Serves as a basis for evaluating the actual cash management performance of responsible individuals, using measurement criteria such as the target average daily balance as compared with the actual average daily balance in each cash account.

The period of time covered by a cash budget varies with each type of business. A cash budget is generally quite accurate when it covers a short period, but it requires constant attention. A yearly cash budget should usually be prepared by months, with changes made at the end of each month in order to (1) incorporate deviations from the previous forecast and (2) add a month to replace the month just passed, so that a *rolling cash budget* covering the next twelve months is always available. As the coming month or week moves closer, weekly or even daily cash receipts and disbursements schedules are necessary for prudent and efficient cash management.

Preparation of a Cash Budget

Preparation of a cash budget involves estimating cash receipts and disbursements by time periods. All anticipated cash receipts, such as cash sales, cash collections on accounts receivable, dividends, interest on notes and bonds, proceeds from sales of assets, royalties, bank loans, and stock sales, are carefully estimated. Likewise, cash requirements for materials purchases, supplies, payroll, repayment of loans, dividends, taxes, and purchases of plant or equipment must be determined.

The primary sources of cash receipts are cash sales and collections of accounts receivable. Estimates of collections of accounts receivable are based on the sales budget and on the company's collection experience. A study is made of a representative period to determine how customers pay their accounts, how many take the discount offered, and how many pay within 10 days, 30 days, and so forth. These experiences are set up in a schedule of anticipated collections from credit sales. Collections during a month will be the result of (1) this month's sales and (2) accounts receivable of prior months' sales. Seasonal variations should also be considered if they affect the collections pattern. To illustrate, assume that during each month, collections on accounts receivable show the following pattern:

From this month's sales..	10.8%
From prior months' accounts receivable:	
Last month's sales	77.4
2 months old	6.3
3 months old	2.1
4 months old	1.2
Cash discounts taken...	1.2
Doubtful accounts...	1.0
	100.0%

On the basis of these percentages, collections for January are computed as follows:

Month	Credit Sales	%	Collections
January.....................................	$400,000	10.8	$ 43,200
December...................................	385,000	77.4	297,990
November...................................	420,000	6.3	26,460
October.....................................	360,000	2.1	7,560
September	340,000	1.2	4,080
Total collections for January....................................			$379,290

Estimated cash disbursements are computed from the:

1. Purchases budget, which shows planned purchases of materials and supplies.
2. Direct labor budget, which indicates direct labor wages to be paid.
3. Various types of expense budgets, both manufacturing and commercial, which indicate expenses expected to be incurred. Noncash expenses such as depreciation are excluded.
4. Plant and equipment budget, which details cash needed for the purchase of new equipment or replacements.
5. Treasurer's budget, which indicates requirements for items such as dividends, interest and payments on loans and bonds, donations, and income tax.

For each item, the estimated timing of the cash disbursements is required. A cash budget includes no accrual items. For example, assume that direct labor payroll accrued at the beginning and the end of January is $14,800 and $13,300, respectively, and the budget shows that $90,000 will be earned by direct labor employees. The treasurer computes the monthly cash requirement for the direct labor payroll as follows:

Accrued payroll at beginning of January	$ 14,800
Add payroll earned as per budget..................................	90,000
	$104,800
Deduct accrued payroll at end of January...........................	13,300
Amount of cash to be paid out during January.......................	$ 91,500

A similar approach can be used to estimate the timing of other cash disbursements as well. Alternatively, a cash payment may be estimated in the following manner. Assume that direct materials purchases and other items such as factory overhead and commercial expenses occur fairly uniformly throughout each month and that approximately ten days (1/3 month) normally elapse between the recording of an indebtedness and its payment. Assume further that cash discounts are always taken and that they average 2 percent. Using data that would be obtained from the direct materials budget, the January cash disbursement for direct materials purchased is:

December purchases [($200,000 − 2% cash discount)	
× 1/3 paid in January]	$ 65,333
January purchases [($130,000 − 2% cash discount)	
× 2/3 paid in January]	84,933
January cash disbursement for direct materials purchased	$150,266

If indebtedness does not occur uniformly, variations in the pattern should be considered in estimating the timing of cash disbursements.

After all the cash receipts and cash disbursements have been estimated for each month of the budget year, the year-end cash balance for inclusion in the budgeted balance sheet can be determined. This amount is the beginning of the budget year's cash balance, plus the estimated total annual cash receipts from all sources, less the estimated total annual disbursements necessary to satisfy all cash demands.

Electronic Cash Management

The basic premise of cash management is that dollars in transit are not earning assets. They cannot be utilized until they are available as deposits. Similarly, cash lying idle in checking accounts contributes nothing to corporate profitability.

Organizations with multiple, geographically dispersed units, or firms with a widespread customer base making individual payments to dispersed collecting units can especially benefit from electronic cash management systems. The system involves cash concentration by means of nationwide electronic transfers which accelerate the collection of deposits from local banks into a central account on a same-day basis. By drawing checks on its centrally located account, the firm has the additional advantage of *float* for the time it takes the check to be cleared back to the central bank account. Such procedures enhance efficient and effective cash management.

Another and broader electronic cash management application is found in *electronic funds transfer systems* (EFTS). These systems are designed to reduce the number of paper documents and to increase the use of electronic data in carrying out banking cash transfer functions, thus reducing bank transaction costs and expediting cash transfers. These developing cash payment systems include unstaffed customer banking facilities, automated clearinghouses for interbank cash transfers, point-of-sale facilities, pay-by-phone service, and corporate funds transfers.[5] For the manager, the potential for virtually

---

[5]Howard C. Johnson and Edward C. Arnold, "The Emerging Revolution in Electronic Payments," *Price Water-house Review*, Vol. 22, No. 3, pp. 26–31.

instantaneous receipts and payments of cash requires consideration in the management of cash resources.

Budgeted Balance Sheet

A balance sheet for the beginning of the budget period is the starting point in preparing a budgeted balance sheet for the end of the budget period. The following budgeted balance sheet for Franklin Company incorporates all changes in assets, liabilities, and capital in the budgets sumitted by the various departments, functions, or segments.

Franklin Company Budgeted Balance Sheet At December 31, 19--		
Assets		
Cash		$ 245,750
Accounts receivable	$ 370,265	
Less allowance for doubtful accounts	7,400	362,865
Inventories:		
Finished goods		81,675
Materials		214,250
Plant and equipment	$1,604,740	
Less accumulated depreciation	418,610	1,186,130
Other assets		143,834
Total assets		$2,234,504
Liabilities and Capital		
Current liabilities		$ 327,942
Long-term debt		450,000
Common stock		800,000
Retained earnings		656,562
Total liabilities and capital		$2,234,504

The finished goods and materials inventory balances agree with those shown in the company's budgeted cost of goods manufactured and sold statement on page 383. While these inventory account changes are directly related to income statement transactions, other accounts may be affected in part by non-income statement transactions. For example, in the case of cash, proceeds from a bank loan or the payment of a cash dividend to stockholders are of the latter type of transaction.

Numerous advantages result from the preparation of a budgeted balance sheet. One advantage is that it discloses unfavorable ratios which management may wish to change for various reasons. Unfavorable ratios can lower credit ratings or cause a drop in the value of the corporation's securities. A second advantage is that it serves as a check on the accuracy of all other budgets. Still another advantage is that a return-on-investment ratio can be computed by relating net income to capital employed. An inadequate return on investment would suggest a need for budget changes.

Computerized Budgeting[6]

The time required to assemble the periodic budget and to achieve a consensus of the managers involved is so great that the budgeting process is often inhibited. Time constraints may be handled more effectively, however, by converting the elements of the conventional budgeting process into a functional planning tool through the use of computer modeling techniques. Tedious arithmetic can be eliminated by converting budgeting procedures into a computerized set of straightforward algebraic formulas. The resulting computerized model entails the following primary components:

1. A line-by-line outline which describes the format of the desired output of budget schedules and statements.
2. A structure of algebraic logic or procedures which demonstrates the computational processes in simple formulas.
3. Elements of data which, when passed through the computational process, will generate the desired output.

The development of a computerized budgeting process can result in substantial benefits. These benefits include:

1. Shortening the planning cycle time. By reducing computational effort, it is frequently possible to delay the start of budget preparation until more accurate inputs are available. Thus the quality of sales forecasts and cost estimates may be improved.
2. Reconsidering planning assumptions. Time savings make it feasible to reconsider planning assumptions early in the budgeting process. Cost and profit implications of various assumptions can be estimated before any commitment is made.
3. Continuous budgeting. Plans can be updated continuously throughout the budget period and, in some cases, planning horizons can be extended beyond the current budget period.
4. Operating analysis capability. If procedures and data are maintained in current form, the computerized model is available to produce instant answers to "what if" questions. More alternatives can be evaluated when such a model is used.
5. Discipline. Development of a model requires precise understanding and definition of the organization and its accounting system. Therefore, the discipline of developing the relationships inherent in a computerized budgeting model is of itself a valuable learning experience.

Financial Forecasts for External Users

Recent years have seen increasing recognition of the importance of financial forecasts for external users, because investors and potential inves-

---

[6]This discussion adapted from Richard C. Murphy, "A Computerized Model Approach to Budgeting," *Management Accounting*, Vol. LVI, No. 12, pp. 34–36, 38.

tors seek to enhance the process of predicting the future. What has happened in the past, as reported in the financial statements, may be viewed as an indicator of the future. Often, however, past results may not be indicative of future expectations and may need to be tempered accordingly.

The question of whether forecasts should be included in external financial statements is controversial. Opponents point out that the uncertainty of forecasts and the potential dangers of undue reliance upon them could result in added legal liability, a drop in credibility, or both. These concerns and potentially advantageous disclosures to competitors have been cited as causes of widespread opposition by management.

On the positive side, it has been argued that the inclusion of forecasts in external financial statements "should be provided when they will enhance the reliability of users' predictions."[7] Furthermore, the assertion has been made that:

1. *Forecasts..should be presented with their significant underlying assumptions, so that each user can evaluate them in the context of his own needs. The underlying assumptions supporting forecasts, however, should not be presented in such detail that they affect adversely the enterprise's competitive position.*
2. *The use of ranges to supplement single numbers may be appropriate...The limits of the range would indicate the uncertainty inherent in the forecast.*
3. *Forecasts...should be updated periodically and ultimately compared with actual accomplishments....The preparer should explain...significant differences between the original and revised forecasts and between forecasts and actual results.*[8]

In 1975, the American Institute of Certified Public Accountants issued a statement setting forth guidelines for published financial forecasts which are "an estimate of the most probable financial positions, results of operations, and changes in financial position for one or more future periods." The AICPA excludes projections defined as estimates of financial results which are based on "what-would-happen-if" assumptions. Primarily, the AICPA recommends that:

1. Financial forecasts be presented in the same format as historical financial statements.
2. Accounting principles used in the forecast be consistent with those expected to be used in the historical statements for the forecast period.
3. Forecast amounts should represent the single most probable forecast result, but supplementary ranges or probability statements for key items are encouraged.
4. Crucial assumptions in the forecast and key factors in the financial results be disclosed.[9]

---

[7]Report of the Study Group on the Objectives of Financial Statements, *Objectives of Financial Statements* (New York: American Institute of Certified Public Accountants, 1973), p. 46.

[8]*Ibid.*, p. 47.

[9]*Statement of Position, No. 75-4*, "Presentation and Disclosure of Financial Forecasts" (New York: American Institute of Certified Public Accountants, August, 1975), pp. 3–5.

Securities and Exchange Commission regulations presently encourage but do not require inclusion of financial forecasts in external financial reports. Furthermore, a safe harbor rule gives SEC-regulated companies and their auditors protection from legal liability should public forecasts fail to materialize. For the rule to apply, forecasts must be made on a reasonable basis, in good faith, with assumptions disclosed. The Commission requires that materially incorrect predictions be corrected in subsequent financial reports. SEC guidelines are in harmony with AICPA recommendations.

Planning and Budgeting for Nonmanufacturing Businesses and Nonprofit Organizations

Many industrial concerns still pay only lip service to the suggested steps, methods, and procedures of budgeting. To an even greater extent, nonmanufacturing businesses—and especially nonprofit organizations—generally lack effective planning and control mechanisms. However, examples of effective budgeting do exist.

Nonmanufacturing Businesses

Under the guidance of the National Retail Merchants Association, department stores have followed merchandise budget procedures that have a long and quite successful history. A budget for a retail store is a necessity, since the profit per dollar of sales is generally low—usually from 1 to 3 percent. Planning, budgeting, and control administration is strongly oriented toward profit control on the total store as well as on a departmental basis. The merchandise budget shows predetermined sales and profits, generally on a six-month basis following the two merchandising seasons: spring-summer and fall-winter. The merchandise budget includes sales, purchases, expenses, capital expenditures, cash, and annual statements.

Although it is logical for a department store or a wholesaler to plan and budget its activities, banks, savings and loan associations, and insurance companies should also create a long-range profit plan coordinating long-term goals and objectives of the institution. In these businesses, forecasting would deal with deposit size and mix, number of insured and mix of policies, capital requirements, types of earning assets, physical facilities, personnel requirements, operational changes, and new, additional, or changed depositor or client services. The long-range goal should be translated into short-range budgets, starting at the lowest level of responsibility, building and combining the various organizational units into a whole.

Nonprofit Organizations

Annual budgets for government at all levels in the United States now exceed one trillion dollars—an enormous sum of money. Yet, in spite of the many decades in which governmental budgeting has been practiced, the general public is increasingly critical of services received for money spent. While the federal government might be under more obvious attack, state, county, and municipal governments are equally criticized not only for the lack of a satisfactory control system, but also for the ill-conceived procedure for planning the costs and revenues needed to govern. Therefore, a budget based on a managerial approach would go a long way toward responsibly meeting these criticisms.

The difficulty of planning and budgeting in governments and nonprofit organizations is measuring the benefits or outputs of programs. A private enterprise measures its benefits in terms of increased revenue or decreased cost. In the public sector, however, social problems complicate the measurement of benefits. Consequently, such endeavors have often resulted in relatively meaningless monetary outcome data. For governmental as well as other nonprofit organizations, program performance evaluation is needed. Problems encountered in monetary output measurements suggest that monetary inputs (costs) might be more meaningfully related to nonmonetary outcomes for specific programs.[10]

The concept of a planning, programming, budgeting system, commonly referred to as PPBS, had its origin in the Defense Department's attempt to quantify huge expenditures in terms of benefits derived from activities and programs of the public sector. *PPBS* might be defined as an analytical tool to assist management (1) in the analysis of alternatives as the basis for rational decision making and (2) in allocating resources to accomplish stated goals and objectives over a designated time period. The analysis technique is closely related to cost-benefit analysis, focusing upon the outputs or final results, rather than the inputs or the initial dollars expended. The outputs are directly relatable to the planned objectives through the use of performance budgets.

The idea that governmental programs should be undertaken in the light of final benefits has caused agencies in the field of health, education, and welfare services as well as other nonprofit organizations to apply PPBS to their activities and programs. However, PPBS has been criticized because its required specification of objectives cannot be transformed readily into operational outcome quantities or statistics. PPBS, if effective, needs a great deal of refinement and innovation, an understanding of its aims and methods, and active participation of executive and middle management.

In the same way that governmental units have become budget and cost conscious, nonprofit organizations, such as hospitals, churches, school districts, colleges, universities, fraternal orders, libraries, and labor unions, are adopting strong measures of budgetary control. In the past, efforts to control costs were generally exercised through pressure to reduce budget increases rather than through method improvements or program changes. Long-range planning was seldom practiced.

Basically, the objectives of nonprofit organizations are directed toward the economic, social, educational, or spiritual benefit of individuals or groups

---

[10]For additional discussion and illustration, see James E. Sorensen and Hugh D. Grove, "Cost-Outcome and Cost-Effectiveness Analysis: Emerging Nonprofit Performance Evaluation Techniques," *The Accounting Review*, Vol. LII, No. 3, pp. 658–675.

who have no vested interest in such organizations in the form of ownership or investment. The presidents, boards of directors, trustees, or administrative officers, like their counterparts in profit-seeking enterprises, are charged with the stewardship of economic resources, except that their job is primarily to use or spend these resources instead of trying to derive monetary gain. It is expressly for this nonprofit objective that these organizations should install adequate and effective methods and procedures in planning, budgeting, and cost control. Personnel practices, such as programs to train and improve the performance of the administrative personnel, should also be made effective within these institutions.[11]

Zero-Base Budgeting

Customarily, those in charge of an established budgetary program are required to justify only the increase sought above last year's appropriation. What they are already spending is usually accepted as necessary, with little or no examination. *Zero-base budgeting*, however, is a budget-planning procedure for the reevaluation of an organization's program and expenditures. It requires each manager to justify the entire budget request in detail and places the burden of proof on the manager to justify why authorization to spend any money at all should be granted. It starts with the assumption that zero will be spent on each activity — thus, the term "zero-base." What a manager is already spending is not accepted as a starting point.

Managers are asked to prepare for each activity or operation under their control a *decision package* that includes an analysis of cost, purpose, alternative courses of action, measures of performance, consequences of not performing the activity, and benefits. The zero-base budgeting approach asserts that in building the budget from zero, two types of alternatives should be considered by managers: (1) different ways of performing the same activity and (2) different levels of effort in performing the activity.

A decision package identifies an activity in a definitive manner for evaluation and comparison with other activities. Devising these decision packages, ranking them, and making funding decisions according to the rank order comprise the heart of the zero-base budgeting process.

Success in implementing zero-base budgeting requires:

1. Linkage of zero-base budgeting to the short- and long-range planning process.
2. Sustained support and commitment from executive management.
3. Innovation among the managers who make up the budget decision packages.
4. Sale of the procedure to the people who must perform the work necessary to keep the concept vigorous.

---

[11]Budgeting for nonprofit organizations other than governmental, health care, and higher education is discussed in considerable detail in *Financial Planning and Evaluation for the Nonprofit Organization*, by Anthony J. Gambino and Thomas J. Reardon (New York: National Association of Accountants, 1981).

PERT and PERT/Cost — Systems for Planning and Control

The accountant's involvement in management planning and control has led to the use of network analysis systems for planning, measuring progress to schedule, evaluating changes to schedule, forecasting future progress, and predicting and controlling costs. These systems are variously referred to as PERT (Program Evaluation and Review Technique) or CPM (Critical Path Method). The origin of PERT is military; it was introduced in connection with the Navy Polaris program. CPM's origin is industrial.

Many companies have been using these methods in planning, scheduling, and costing such diverse projects as constructing buildings, installing equipment, and research and development. There is also an opportunity for using PERT in business administration tasks, such as scheduling the closing of books, revising standard cost data, scheduling the time elements for the preparation of departmental budgets, cash flows, and preparing the annual profit plan, as well as for audit planning and control. In conjunction with PERT and critical path techniques, computer systems are providing executive management with far better means for directing large-scale, complex projects. Management can now measure cost, time, and technical performance on an integrated basis. Actual results can be compared with the network plan and revisions made as needed.

The PERT System

PERT is a probabilistic diagram of the interrelationships of a complex series of activities. Whether a military, industrial, or business administration task, time is the fundamental element of any of these activities. The major burden of PERT is the determination of the longest time duration for the completion of the entire project. This calculation is based on the length of time required for the longest sequence of activities.

All of the individual tasks to complete a given job or program must be visualized in a *network* of events and activities. An *event* represents a specified accomplishment at a particular instant in time, such as B or E in the network on page 414. An *activity* represents the time and resources necessary to move from one event to another, e.g., B → E in the chart. Some of the activities may be in series; e.g., market research cannot be performed before the research design is planned. Other activities may be parallel; e.g., the engines for a ship can be built at the same time the hull is being constructed.

Time estimates for PERT are made for each activity on a three-way basis, i.e., optimistic (t_o), most likely (t_m), and pessimistic (t_p). In the network illustrated, the three time estimates, expressed in units of one week, are indicated under each activity line. From these estimates, an expected time (t_e) is calculated for each activity. The expected time represents the average time an activity would require if it were repeated a large number of times. The calculation is generally based on the assumption that the distribution of activity

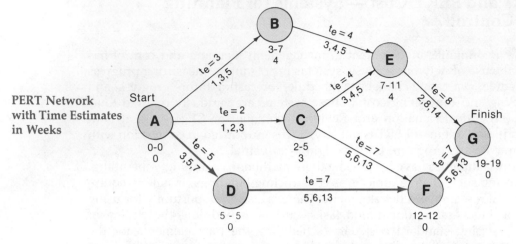

PERT Network
with Time Estimates
in Weeks

times closely approximates a Beta probability distribution. Such distributions may be symmetrical or skewed. The following formula is used to compute the mean of the Beta probability distribution, which is the expected time:

$$t_e = \frac{t_o + 4t_m + t_p}{6}$$

For example, the activity D-F has a value of $t_e = 7$, determined as follows:

$$\text{If: } t_o = 5$$
$$t_m = 6$$
$$t_p = 13$$

$$\text{Then: } t_e = \frac{5 + 4(6) + 13}{6} = \frac{42}{6} = 7$$

Below each event in the network are noted the earliest expected and latest allowable times, and below these two numbers, the slack time is shown. The *earliest expected time* is the earliest time that an activity can be expected to start, because of its relationship to pending activities. The *latest allowable time* is the latest time that an activity may begin and not delay completion of the project.

The Critical Path. The longest path through the network is known as the *critical path* and is denoted on the flowchart by the arrows connecting A-D-F-G. Shortening of total time can be accomplished only by shortening the critical path. However, if the critical path A-D-F-G is shortened from nineteen weeks to fifteen weeks, A-C-F-G (assuming F-G remains unchanged) would then become the critical path because it would be the longest.

Slack Time. Activities along the critical path (A-D-F-G) have a slack of zero. All noncritical activities have positive slack. The less the amount of slack time, the more critical an activity or path, and vice versa.

Slack is computed by subtracting the earliest expected time from the latest allowable time. It is determinable only in relation to an entire path through the network. When multiple activities lead to an event, the event's earliest expected starting time is always the largest sum of expected times of the preceding activities. When multiple activities lead from an event, the latest allowable time at that event is always the smallest figure found by subtracting from total project time the sum of expected times of subsequent network activities. For example, path A-C-E-G at event C has an earliest expected time of two weeks and a latest allowable time of five weeks $[19 - (7 + 7)]$, for a slack time of three weeks. At event E, the earliest expected time is seven weeks $(3 + 4)$ and the latest allowable time is eleven weeks $(19 - 8)$, for a slack time of four weeks. However, if any slack time is used up, that is, if a noncritical activity utilizes more than the expected time, the slack times for subsequent activities must be recomputed. Recomputation would also be necessary when less than the expected times are required.

Slack allows management some flexibility. If available slack time is not exceeded, noncritical activities can be delayed without delaying the project's completion date. Slack time information provides useful data for initial planning and continuous project monitoring when the project's status is compared with the plan.

The PERT/Cost System

PERT/cost is an integrated management information system designed to furnish management with timely information for planning and controlling schedules and costs of projects. The PERT/cost system is really an expansion of PERT. It assigns cost to time and activities, thereby providing total financial planning and control by functional responsibility.

The predetermination of cost is in harmony with the accountant's budgeting task and follows the organizational and procedural steps used in responsibility accounting. The PERT/cost estimates are activity- or project-oriented, and the addition of the cost component permits analyses involving time/cost tradeoffs. Each activity is defined at a level of detail necessary for individual job assignments and supervisory control. Control is on scheduled tasks, with time and cost as the common control factors. Cost accumulation methods must be devised to be compatible with PERT/cost control concepts.

In the network on page 416, the activities noted by the dark green circles, A, B, C, and D, represent completed events. The dollar figures in the white blocks represent estimated costs, e.g., $30,000 for activity F-G. Figures in the light green blocks to the right of the estimates are actual costs. Estimated times (t_e) and actual times (t_a) are shown below the activity lines.

Activities A-B, A-C, and A-D have been completed. A-B required one-half week more time than planned; however, it is not on the critical path and will not affect total project duration. If excess time were such that another path became long enough to be the critical path, then total time would be involved.

The actual activity cost of $10,000 for A-B compared to a budget of $12,000 indicates an underrun of $2,000. Activity A-C budget and actual figures coincide for time and cost. A-D had an overrun of $5,000 and a two-week slippage.

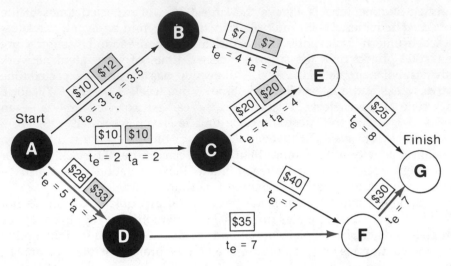

PERT/Cost Network and Time (in Weeks) and Cost (in Thousands of Dollars)

The slippage requires immediate attention because A-D is on the critical path. Immediate investigation and corrective action seem needed for B-E and C-E. According to the present status report, both activities have consumed the budgeted time and cost and are not yet completed.

While comparison of actual versus planned time and cost figures is essential, comparison alone is not enough to evaluate a project. Evaluation of performance is needed to complete the process. For example, a project is not necessarily in financial trouble when actual expenditures exceed budgeted. Progress may be correspondingly ahead of schedule. Nor is a project necessarily meeting performance standards when it is within the budget. To evaluate the true status, management needs to study performance, cost, and timing.[12]

Probabilistic Budgets

The budget may be developed based on one set of assumptions as to the most likely performance in the forthcoming period. However, there is increasing evidence that several sets of assumptions are evaluated by management before the budget is finalized. One possibility is the PERT-like three-level estimates — optimistic, most likely, and pessimistic. This involves estimating each budget component assuming each of the three conditions. Probability trees can be used in which several variables can be considered in the analysis, e.g., number of units sold, sales price, and variable manufacturing and marketing costs.

To each discrete set of assumptions, a probability can be assigned, based on past experience and management's best judgment about the future, thus

[12]For additional discussion of PERT/cost as a control tool, see Fara Elikai and Shane Moriarity, "Variance Analysis with PERT/Cost," *The Accounting Review,* Vol. LVII, No. 1, pp. 161–170.

revealing to management not only a range of possible outcomes but also a probability associated with each. Further statistical techniques can then be applied, including an expected (weighted, composite) value, the range, and the standard deviation for the various budget elements, such as sales, manufacturing cost, and marketing cost. For example, the expected value for sales may be $960,000, with a range from a low of $780,000 to a high of $1,200,000 and a standard deviation of $114,600.

The computational capability of the computer facilitates the consideration of complex sets of assumptions and permits the use of simulation programs, making it possible to develop more objectively determined probabilities.[13]

DISCUSSION QUESTIONS

1. What is meant by a capital expenditure? How does it differ from a revenue expenditure?

2. Name some purposes of and some reasons for a research and development program.

3. Companies should establish budgetary procedures to provide control and accounting systems for research and development expenditures. What are such procedures specifically designed to achieve?

4. Managers consider a cash budget an extremely useful management tool. Why?

5. The budgeted balance sheet may indicate an unsatisfactory financial condition. Discuss.

6. What governing criterion has been suggested for determining whether to include forecasts in external financial statements?

7. Discuss the need for planning and budgeting in (a) nonmanufacturing businesses and (b) non-profit organizations.

8. What is the objective of the control concept generally referred to as PPBS?

9. (a) Describe zero-base budgeting. (b) Explain how zero-base budgeting differs from traditional budgeting. (c) Identify the advantages and disadvantages of zero-base budgeting.
(CMA adapted)

10. Discuss the role of PERT as it might apply to project development.

11. Discuss the conditions determining when PERT is appropriate.

12. Explain the computation of slack in the PERT network.

13. State the relationship between PERT and PERT/cost systems.

14. Contrast the probabilistic budget and the traditional budget in terms of information provided to management.

---

[13]An exhaustive treatment of these techniques is beyond the scope of this discussion. For expanded discussion and illustrations, see:

William L. Ferrara and Jack C. Hayya, "Toward Probabilistic Profit Budgets," *Management Accounting*, Vol. LII, No. 3, pp. 23–28.

Belverd E. Neddles, Jr., "Budgeting Techniques: Subjective to Probabilistic," *Management Accounting*, Vol. LIII, No. 6, pp. 39–45.

Edmund J. Hall and Richard J. Kolkmann, "A Vote for the Probabilistic Pro Forma Income Statement," *Management Accounting*, Vol. LVII, No. 7, pp. 45–48.

Davis L. S. Chang and Shu S. Liao, "Measuring and Disclosing Forecast Reliability," *The Journal of Accountancy*, Vol. 143, No. 5, pp. 76–87, (Monte Carlo simulation).

EXERCISES

1. *Cash budget — accounts receivable collections.* Varsity Co. is preparing its cash budget for May. The following information on accounts receivable collections is available from Varsity's past collection experience:

Current month's sales	12%
Prior month's sales	75
Sales two months prior to current month	6
Sales three months prior to current month	4
Doubtful accounts	3

Credit sales are as follows:

May — estimated	$100,000
April	90,000
March	80,000
February	95,000

Required: Compute estimated accounts receivable collections for May.

(AICPA adapted)

2. *Budgeted cash receipts.* Lodge Company produces trailers for sale to the public, and missile transports under government contract. Nongovernment credit sales data are:

19A actual:	November	$210,000
	December	190,000
19B estimated:	January	$230,000
	February	200,000
	March	260,000

The collection pattern for these credit sales is:

Month of sale	60%
Month after sale	30
Second month after sale	7
Loss on doubtful accounts	3

The company has contracted to deliver 120 missile transports in the first three months of 19B, at the monthly rate of 40 units and $44,000 total monthly production costs. General and administrative expenses of 10% of the sales price are allocated to government contracts. The contract states that monthly payments (the sales price) shall be made by the government at 120% of the previous month's applicable costs and expenses.

Required: Compute monthly cash receipts, January through March.

3. *Estimated cash disbursements.* Serven Corporation has estimated its activity for June, as follows:

(a)	Sales	$700,000
	Gross profit (based on sales)	30%
	Increase in trade accounts receivable during month	$ 20,000
	Change in accounts payable during month	$ -0-
	Increase in inventory during month	$ 10,000

(b) Variable selling, general, and administrative expenses (S, G, & A) include a charge for uncollectible accounts of 1% of sales.

(c) Total S, G, & A is $71,000 monthly plus 15% of sales.

(d) Monthly depreciation expense of $40,000 is included in fixed S, G, & A.

Required: Determine the estimated June cash disbursements. *$629,000*

4. Cash budget for inventory purchases. The following information has been obtained by Ellis Company during its budgeting process:

(a) Inventory policy is to have in stock at the end of each month an amount equal to 25% of next month's requirements, provided this quantity does not exceed 4,000 units.

(b) Purchases are spread evenly throughout the month. All suppliers offer a discount of 2/10, n/30. Ellis Company takes advantage of all cash discounts.

(c) The average sales price per unit is $50 and the average markup is 40% of sales.

(d) Sales in units:

April	20,000
May	18,000
June	14,000
July	8,000
August	9,000

Required: Calculate the cash required for payments on account in June.   *$416,500*

(CGAA adapted)

5. Cash budget. Brando Furniture Company is preparing a cash budget for September and October. The following estimates were made:

	September	October		September	October
Sales on account	$68,000	$97,150	Purchases discounts	$ 4,000	$ 2,000
Cash sales	50,000	48,000	Accounts payable — beginning	13,000	15,000
Purchases on account	80,000	70,000	Accounts payable — ending	15,000	13,000
Cash purchases	15,000	20,000	Cash operating expenses	56,500	50,500

No change is expected in beginning or ending inventories for either month. Sales on account are collected in the following manner: 50% in the month of sale, 30% in the month following, and 20% in the second following month. Sales on account in July and August were $80,000 and $100,000, respectively. Brando Furniture Company has a well-established line of credit at its bank and prefers to negotiate short-term loans (at 8% interest) rather than face overdrafts in its account. No loan payments are to be made in September or October. Brando's policy is to begin each month with a minimum cash balance of $20,000, which was the September 1 cash balance.

Required: Prepare a cash budget for each month.

6. PERT critical path and expected time. Dryfus Company specializes in large construction projects and regularly employs PERT for project planning, coordination, and control. The schedule of separable activities and their expected completion times on page 420 has been developed for an office building which Dryfus is to construct.

Required:

(1) Prepare a PERT network.

(2) Identify the critical path.

(3) Explain the calculation and meaning of expected time, using the Beta probability distribution.

(CMA adapted)

Activity Code	Activity Description	Expected Activity Completion Time (in weeks)
0-1	Excavation	2
1-2	Foundation	3
1-7	Underground utilities	7
2-5	Rough plumbing	4
2-3	Framing	5
3-4	Roofing	3
4-5	Electrical work	3
5-6	Interior walls	4
6-7	Finish plumbing	2
4-7	Exterior finishing	6
7-8	Landscaping	2

7. PERT network. Wittimer Construction Company has decided that a PERT network will help in planning a new job. The network for the new project is as follows, with optimistic, most likely, and pessimistic time estimates, in days, shown on the connecting lines between events:

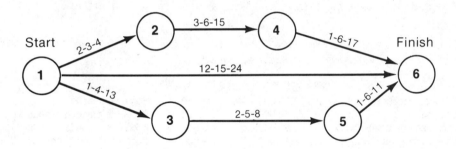

Required: Determine the critical path. (CGAA adapted)

8. PERT network. Fess Company wishes to complete a project having the following PERT network diagram, with optimistic, most likely, and pessimistic completion times, respectively, in days:

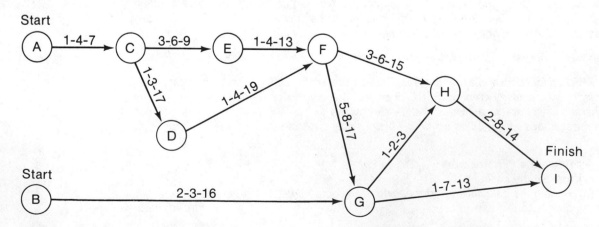

Required:

(1) Compute the expected completion time (t_e) for each activity.
(2) Identify the critical path(s).
(3) Determine the slack time at event B.

9. PERT network for auditing liabilities. *All audits have a critical path, but auditors seldom recognize it as such without the aid of network analysis. In the auditing of liabilities, the following activities and expected times have been identified:*

Activity Code	Activity Description	Expected Time (Hours)
6.10–6.11	Obtain schedule of liabilities	2
6.11–6.12	Mail confirmations	12
6.12–6.16	Process confirmations	39
6.16–6.17	Investigate debit balances	5
6.11–6.13	Vouch selected liabilities	64
6.13–6.14	Test accruals and amortization	4
6.11–6.14	Test pension plan	4
6.14–6.15	Reconcile interest expense to debt	8
6.15–6.17	Verify debt restriction compliance	5
6.17–6.18	Review subsequent payments	10

Required: Construct the PERT network, identifying the critical path and including slack times.

PROBLEMS

15-1. Cash and purchases budget for a manufacturer. Eselein Company seeks assistance in developing cash and other budget information for May, June, and July. On April 30, the company had cash of $5,500, accounts receivable of $437,000, inventories of $309,400, and accounts payable of $133,055. The budget is to be based on the following assumptions:

Sales:

(a) Each month's sales are billed on the last day of the month.
(b) Customers are allowed a 3% discount if payment is made within 10 days after the billing date. Receivables are recorded at the gross sales price.
(c) Sixty percent of the billings are collected within the discount period; 25% by the end of the month; 9% by the end of the second month; and 6% prove uncollectible.

Purchases:

(a) Fifty-four percent of all purchases of materials and a like percentage of marketing, general, and administrative expenses are paid in the month purchased, with the remainder paid in the following month.
(b) Each month's units of ending materials inventory are equal to 130% of next month's production requirement.
(c) The cost of each unit of inventory is $20.
(d) Wages and salaries earned each month by employees total $38,000.
(e) Marketing, general, and administrative expenses (of which $2,000 is depreciation) are equal to 15% of the current month's sales.

Actual and projected sales are as follows:

March	$354,000	June	$342,000
April	363,000	July	360,000
May	357,000	August	366,000

Actual and projected materials needed for production:

March	11,800 units	June	11,400 units
April	12,100	July	12,000
May	11,900	August	12,200

Accrued payroll at the end of each month is as follows:

March	$3,100	June	$3,400
April	2,900	July	3,000
May	3,300	August	2,800

Required: Compute the following:
(1) Budgeted cash disbursements during June.
(2) Budgeted cash collections during May.
(3) Budgeted units of inventory to be purchased during July.   (AICPA adapted)

15-2. Cash and purchases budgets. Russon Corporation is a retailer whose sales are all made on credit. Sales are billed twice monthly, on the 10th of the month for the last half of the prior month's sales and on the 20th of the month for the first half of the current month's sales. The terms of all sales are 2/10, net 30, from the billing date. Based upon past experience, the collection experience of accounts receivable is as follows:

Within the discount period	80%
On the 30th day	18
Uncollectible	2

Sales for May and forecast sales for the next four months are:

May (actual)	$500,000
June	600,000
July	700,000
August	700,000
September	400,000

Russon's average markup on its products is 20% of the sales price.

Russon purchases merchandise for resale to meet the current month's sales demand and to maintain a desired monthly ending inventory of 25% of the next month's sales. All purchases are on credit, with terms of net 30. Russon pays for one half of a month's purchases in the month of purchase and the other half in the month following the purchase.

All sales and purchases occur uniformly throughout the month.

Required: Compute the following:
(1) Russon's budgeted cash collections in July.
(2) Russon's budgeted cash collections in September from August sales.
(3) Desired August 31 inventory.
(4) Budgeted June purchases.   (CMA adapted)

15-3. Cash budget. Reynard Furniture Company has the following forecast data available:

	September	October
Cash sales	$ 40,000	$60,000
Sales on account	77,500	95,000
Cash purchases	20,000	20,000
Purchases on account	100,000	80,000
Purchases discounts	6,000	3,000
Accounts payable — beginning	10,000 ·	12,000
Accounts payable — ending	12,000	9,000
Cash operating expenses	46,500	10,000

Net sales on account are collected 50% in the month of sale, 40% in the month following, and 10% in the second following month. Such sales in July and August were $100,000 and $120,000, respectively. The estimated September 1 cash balance is $13,000.

Required: Prepare a cash budget for September and October.

15-4. Revenue projection for a school system. The Beaver County School Board bases its revenues budget for the fiscal year ending July 31, 19B, on projections of receipts for the fiscal year ending July 31, 19A. The actual revenues received as of April 30, 19A, are summarized by type and source as follows:

Type and Source	Sales Tax	State Grants	Federal Grants	Allocation Of Federal Revenue Sharing
City A	$ 300,000			$ 250,000
City B	450,000			300,000
All other cities	210,000			200,000
Unincorporated areas	150,000			
Federal government			$750,000	
State government	300,000	$200,000		1,000,000
Total	$1,410,000	$200,000	$750,000	$1,750,000

Projected receipts for the remainder of the fiscal year ending July 31, 19A, are: (a) sales tax collections should continue at the same rate; (b) additional state grants are expected to total $50,000; (c) no more federal funds of any kind are forthcoming until after July 31, 19A.

Revenues for 19B are expected to change as follows: (a) sales tax collections are projected to increase by 10%; (b) state grants will remain the same; (c) federal grants will be cut by two thirds; (d) federal revenue-sharing allocations should increase by 10%.

Required:
   (1) Prepare a schedule of actual and projected revenues (by type and source) for the fiscal year ending July 31, 19A.
   (2) Prepare a schedule of projected revenues (by type and source) for the fiscal year ending July 31, 19B.

15-5. Projected financial statements. CL Corporation appears to be experiencing a good year, with sales in the first quarter of 19B one third ahead of last year and the Sales Department predicting continuation of this rate throughout the year. The controller has been asked to prepare a new forecast for the year and to analyze the differences from 19A results. The forecast is to be based on actual results obtained in the first quarter plus the expected costs of programs to be carried out in the remainder of the year. Various department heads (production, sales, etc.) have provided the necessary information and the results are as follows:

CL Corporation
Projected Trial Balance
For December 31, 19B
(000s omitted)

Cash	1,200	
Accounts Receivable	80,000	
Inventory (1/1/19A, 40,000 units)	48,000	
Plant and Equipment	130,000	
Accumulated Depreciation		41,000
Accounts Payable		45,000
Accrued Payables		23,250
Notes Payable (due within one year)		50,000
Common Stock		70,000
Retained Earnings		108,200
Sales		600,000
Other Income		9,000
Cost of Goods Sold		—
Manufacturing Costs:		
Materials	213,000	
Direct Labor	218,000	
Variable Factory Overhead	130,000	
Depreciation	5,000	
Other Fixed Factory Overhead	7,750	
Marketing:		
Salaries	16,000	
Commissions	20,000	
Promotion and Advertising	45,000	
General and Administrative:		
Salaries	16,000	
Travel	2,500	
Office Costs	9,000	
Income Tax	—	
Dividends	5,000	
	946,450	946,450

Adjustments for the change in inventory and for income tax have not been made. The scheduled production for 19B is 450 million units, while the sales volume will reach 400 million units. Sales and production volume in 19A was 300 million units. A full-cost, first-in, first-out inventory system is used. The company is subject to a 40% income tax rate. The actual financial statements for 19A follow:

CL Corporation
Balance Sheet
As of December 31, 19A
(000s omitted)
Assets

Current assets:		
Cash	$ 23,000	
Accounts receivable	50,000	
Inventory	48,000	$121,000
Plant and equipment	$130,000	
Less accumulated depreciation	36,000	94,000
Total assets		$215,000

Liabilities and Shareholders' Equity

Current liabilities:

Accounts payable	$ 13,000	
Accrued payables	12,800	
Notes payable	11,000	$ 36,800

Shareholders' equity:

Common stock	$ 70,000	
Retained earnings	108,200	178,200
Total liabilities and shareholders' equity		$215,000

CL Corporation
Statement of Income and Retained Earnings
For Year Ended December 31, 19A
(000s omitted)

Revenue:

Sales		$450,000	
Other income		15,000	$465,000

Expenses:

Cost of goods manufactured and sold:

Materials	$132,000		
Direct labor	135,000		
Variable factory overhead	81,000		
Fixed factory overhead	12,000		
	$360,000		
Beginning inventory	48,000		
	$408,000		
Ending inventory	48,000	$360,000	

Marketing:

Salaries	$ 13,500		
Commissions	15,000		
Promotion and advertising	31,500	60,000	

General and administrative:

Salaries	$ 14,000		
Travel	2,000		
Office costs	8,000	24,000	
Income tax		8,400	452,400
Net income			$ 12,600
Beginning retained earnings			100,600
			$113,200
Less dividends			5,000
Ending retained earnings			$108,200

Required:

(1) Prepare projected financial statements (statement of income and retained earnings, and balance sheet) for 19B.

(2) Using the 19A information provided for comparison:

    (a) Evaluate the 19B projected profit performance.

    (b) Specify areas of 19B operating performance to be investigated.

    (c) Recommend programs for improved management performance.

(CMA adapted)

15-6. Budgeted statement of financial position. Breckenridge Institute is a nonprofit foundation that undertakes scientific research on a contract basis for federal, state, and local governments as well as for business firms. The objectives of the institute as established by the board of trustees are to operate a financially sound organization and to provide quality research service at reasonable cost for the government and business community. The board is also committed to operate with a minimum amount of debt.

Pursuant to these objectives, management is endeavoring to serve its clients without using outside consultants or subcontracting work to other laboratories. The institute has gained an excellent reputation for its research capabilities and for the economical manner in which it is operated.

The statement of financial position for the institute at April 30, 19A, is shown below. The statement of revenues and expenses showing the actual results for the year ended April 30, 19A, and the budgeted amount for the coming year ending April 30, 19B, appears on page 427. The statement of cash receipts and disbursements, presenting actual results and budgeted figures for the years ending April 30, 19A and 19B, respectively, also appears on page 427.

During the construction of the budget, the following additional information was developed:

(a) Purchases of materials and supplies were budgeted at $610,000.
(b) Write-offs of specific accounts receivable are estimated as follows:
    (1) $8,000 of the accounts receivable balance at April 30, 19A.
    (2) Uncollectible accounts of $12,000 from fiscal 19B sales to be written off in fiscal 19B.
(c) The unusually large budgeted expenditure for capital equipment is part of a three-year program begun in 19A to enable the institute to enter new areas of scientific research. Similar amounts will be spent in the next two years for additional equipment. Increased revenues from the new capabilities will not be significant until 19D.
(d) The increased level of consultant fees is expected to continue until the capital expansion program is complete.

Breckenridge Institute
Statement of Financial Position
April 30, 19A
(000s omitted)

Assets				Liabilities and Equities			
Current assets:				Current liabilities:			
Cash			$ 110	Accounts payable			$ 120
Marketable securities			80	Accrued payroll, payroll taxes,			
Accounts receivable:				and benefits			46
Government contracts		$230		Due to outside consultants			20
Private contracts	$150			Interest payable			16
Less allowance for				Current portion of long-term			
doubtful accounts	10	140	370	debt			60
Materials and supplies			64	Total current liabilities			$ 262
Prepaid insurance			6	Long-term debt			240
Total current assets			$ 630	Total liabilities			$ 502
Plant and equipment (net of				Original capital		$1,000	
depreciation)			1,200	Accumulated excess of revenues			
Total assets			$1,830	over expenditures		328	1,328
				Total liabilities and equities			$1,830

Breckenridge Institute
Statement of Revenues and Expenses (000s omitted)

	Actual Results For The Year Ended 4/30/A	Budget For The Year Ending 4/30/B
Revenues from operations:		
Federal government	$1,500	$1,650
State and local government	224	250
Private (less allowance for doubtful accounts of $19 and $25)	1,216	1,335
Interest	4	2
Total revenues	$2,944	$3,237
Operating expenses:		
Personnel:		
Salaries	$1,390	$1,300
Wages	175	200
Employee benefits and payroll taxes	273	300
Consultants	35	250
Employee training	20	35
Materials and supplies	548	600
Utilities	60	60
Insurance	20	20
Depreciation	160	165
Other expenses	117	123
Interest charges	16	14
Total operating expenses	$2,814	$3,067
Excess of revenues over expenses	$ 130	$ 170

Breckenridge Institute
Cash Receipts and Disbursements (000s omitted)

	Actual Results For The Year Ended 4/30/A	Budget For The Year Ending 4/30/B
Receipts:		
Contracts:		
Federal, state, and local governments	$1,700	$1,820
Private	1,200	1,300
	$2,900	$3,120
Interest	4	2
Sales of marketable securities (no gain or loss on sale)	—	50
Total receipts	$2,904	$3,172
Disbursements:		
Salaries and wages	$1,560	$1,510
Employee benefits	260	300
Consultant fees	15	230
Employee training programs	20	35
Materials and supplies	540	575
Utilities	55	65
Insurance	20	22
Other expenses	117	123
Interest	18	16
Retirement of debt	60	60
Purchases of capital equipment	80	315
Total disbursements	$2,745	$3,251
Increase (decrease) in cash	$ 159	$ (79)

Required:
  (1) Prepare a budgeted statement of financial position (in thousands of dollars) as of April 30, 19B, for presentation to the board of trustees.
  (2) Identify the financial difficulties the institute's management will face in the next several years in fulfilling the objectives established by the board of trustees.

(CMA adapted)

15-7. PERT/cost network. The following network has been prepared for a project:

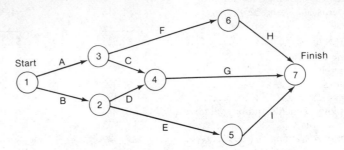

Expected time and cost estimates are:

Activity	Time	Cost
A	5 days	$ 4,000
B	5	4,000
C	10	15,000
D	7	3,500
E	5	10,000
F	7	14,000
G	5	5,000
H	10	20,000
I	10	30,000

Costs for each activity occur uniformly; e.g., activity A requires $800 each day.

Required:
  (1) Identify the critical path.
  (2) Prepare a daily activity and cost schedule.   (CGAA adapted)

15-8. PERT/cost network for planning. Niswonger Construction Company is faced with the following PERT/cost network situation:

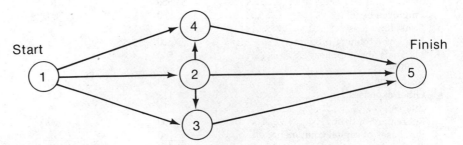

Time/Cost Table

Activity	Expected Time (t_e) Days	Activity Cost	Possible Reduced Time Days	Activity Cost
1–4	2	$ 800	1	$1,300
1–2	3	700	1	1,900
1–3	6	1,100	5	1,350
2–4	4	600	3	800
2–3	2	900	1	1,000
2–5	7	850	6	1,050
4–5	4	1,050	3	1,450
3–5	3	500	2	700
		$6,500		$9,550

Required:
(1) Identify the critical path and determine the slack time.
(2) Determine the cheapest way to reduce the critical path by one day and by two days and the cost in each case.
(3) State management's best decision if a $1,000 bonus will be paid if the project is finished two days early.

15-9. PERT network and project planning. The following diagram and accompanying schedule have been prepared for a proposed retail store opening. The schedule describes the activities, the expected time (in weeks), the expected cost of each activity, and the possible reduced time (in weeks) and related incremental cost for those activities which can be accomplished in a shorter time period. It is estimated that the store should produce a contribution of about $2,000 per week to operating income.

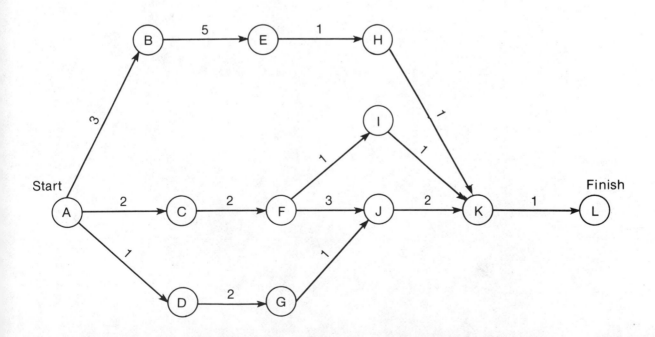

Activity	Description of Activity	Expected Time	Possible Reduced Time	Expected Cost	Incremental Cost To Achieve Reduced Time
A–B	Design exterior	3 weeks	1 week	$ 5,000	$4,500
A–C	Determine inventory needs	2	NC	500	0
A–D	Develop staffing plan	1	NC	500	0
B–E	Do exterior structural work	5	3	27,000	3,500
E–H	Paint exterior	1	NC	4,000	0
H–K	Install exterior signs	1	NC	15,000	0
C–F	Order inventory	2	NC	1,500	0
F–I	Develop special prices for opening	1	NC	2,000	0
I–K	Advertise opening and special prices	1	NC	8,000	0
F–J	Receive inventory	3	2	4,000	2,000
D–G	Acquire staff	2	1	3,000	1,000
G–J	Train staff	1	NC	5,000	0
J–K	Stock shelves	2	1	3,500	1,500
K–L	Final preparations for grand opening	1	NC	6,000	0

NC denotes no change in time is possible.

Required:

(1) Determine the normal critical path, its length in weeks, and the normal cost to be incurred in opening the store.

(2) Compute the minimum time in which the store could be opened and the costs incurred to achieve the earlier opening.

(3) Explain whether the store should be opened following the normal schedule or the reduced program. (CMA adapted)

Chapter 16
Budgeting:
The Flexible Budget;
Cost Behavior Analysis

Budgets are based on certain definite assumed conditions and results. The budgets discussed and illustrated in Chapters 14 and 15 are known as fixed or forecast budgets, while the budgets discussed in this chapter are known as flexible budgets. The term "fixed" is misleading, however, since a fixed budget is subject to revision. *Fixed* merely denotes that the budget is not adjusted to actual volume attained. It represents a prefixed point of sales and cost estimates with which actual results are compared. A *flexible budget*, however, is adjusted to actual volume.

Both fixed and flexible budgets provide management with information necessary to attain the major objectives of budgetary control, which include:

1. An organized procedure for planning.
2. A means for coordinating the activities of the various divisions of a business.
3. A basis for cost control.

Planning is one of the primary functions of management. The fixed budget provides an organized method of planning and a procedure for measuring the nature and the extent of deviations from the preconceived plan. It is the organized means for formalizing and coordinating plans of the many individuals whose decisions influence the conduct of a business.

A budget plan requires the coordination of all management levels of a business. Production must be planned in relation to expected sales; materials must be acquired in line with expected production requirements; facilities must be expanded as foreseeable future needs justify; and finances must be planned in relation to the funds needed for the expected volume of sales and production.

Cost control is predicated on the idea that actual costs will be compared with budgeted costs, relating what did happen with what should have happened. To accomplish this, an acceptable measure of what costs should be under any given set of conditions must be available.

The Flexible Budget

When a company's activities can be estimated within close limits, the fixed budget is satisfactory. However, completely predictable situations exist in only a few cases. If actual volume differs from that planned, a comparison of actual results with a fixed budget may be misleading. For example, suppose that 1,000 units of product were planned at a budgeted cost of $10,000, but that 1,100 units are actually produced at a cost of $10,500. A simple comparison of budgeted costs with actual costs indicates an unfavorable variance of $500; however, further examination reveals that actual production exceeds that planned by 100 units. Since budgeted and actual costs contain both fixed and variable costs, it is not clear whether the variance is favorable or unfavorable. To make such a determination, actual costs must be compared with a budget based on the actual volume. This is the purpose of a flexible budget, i.e., to provide a budget adjusted to actual volume.

To prepare a flexible budget, a formula must be developed for each account within each department or cost center. Each formula indicates the fixed cost and/or the variable cost rate for the account. The variable portion of the formula is a rate of cost in relation to some measure of activity such as direct labor hours, machine hours, or units of production. The fixed amount and the variable rate remain constant within prescribed ranges of activity.

The application of these formulas to the level of activity actually experienced produces allowable budget expenditures for the volume of activity actually attained. These budget figures are compared with actual costs in order to measure the performance of each department or cost center.

Originally, the flexible budget was applied principally to the control of departmental factory overhead. Now, however, the idea is applied to the entire budget, so that marketing and administrative budgets as well as manufacturing budgets are prepared on a flexible budget basis. The flexible budget is also a useful planning tool because it can be used to evaluate the effects of different volumes of activity on profits and on the cash position.

Capacity and Volume

The discussion of the actual preparation of a flexible budget must be preceded by a basic understanding of the term "capacity." The terms "capacity" and "volume" (or activity) are used in connection with the construction and use of both fixed and flexible budgets. *Capacity* is that fixed amount of plant and machinery and number of personnel for which management has committed itself and with which it expects to conduct the business. *Volume* is a measure of business activity. It is related to capacity, in that management seeks to attain a volume that makes the best use of existing capacity.

Capacity Levels

The following terms are used to describe different levels of capacity: theoretical, practical, expected actual, and normal. Current federal income tax regulations[1] permit the use of practical, expected actual, or normal capacity in assigning factory overhead costs to inventories.

Theoretical Capacity. The theoretical capacity of a department is its capacity to produce at full speed without interruptions. It is achieved if the plant or department produces at 100 percent of its rated capacity.

Practical Capacity. It is highly improbable that any company can operate at theoretical capacity. Allowances must be made for unavoidable interruptions, such as time lost for repairs, inefficiencies, breakdowns, setups, failures, unsatisfactory materials, delays in delivery of materials or supplies, labor shortages and absences, Sundays, holidays, vacations, inventory taking, and pattern and model changes. The number of work shifts must also be considered. These allowances reduce theoretical capacity to the practical capacity level. This reduction is caused by internal influences and does not consider the chief external cause, lack of customers' orders. Reduction from theoretical to practical capacity typically ranges from 15 percent to 25 percent, which results in a practical capacity level of 75 percent to 85 percent of theoretical capacity.

Expected Actual Capacity. Expected actual capacity is based on a short-range outlook. The use of expected actual capacity is feasible with firms whose products are of a seasonal nature, and market and style changes allow price adjustments according to competitive conditions and customer demands.

Normal Capacity. Firms may modify the above capacity levels by considering the utilization of the plant or various departments in the light of meeting average sales demands over a period long enough to level out the peaks and valleys which come with seasonal and cyclical variations. Finding a satisfactory and logical balance between plant capacity and sales volume is one of the important problems of business management.

---

[1]*Regulations*, Section 1.471-11.

Purposes of Establishing Normal Capacity. Although there may be some differences between a normal long-run volume and the sales volume expected in the next period, normal capacity is useful in establishing sales prices and controlling costs. It is the basis for the entire budget system, and it can be used for the following purposes and aims:

1. Preparation of departmental flexible budgets and computation of pre-determined factory overhead rates.
2. Compilation of the standard cost of each product.
3. Scheduling production.
4. Assigning cost to inventories.
5. Measurement of the effects of changing volumes of production.
6. Determination of the break-even point.

Although other capacity assumptions are sometimes used due to existing circumstances, normal capacity fulfills both long- and short-term purposes. The long-term utilization of the normal capacity level relates the marketing phase and therewith the pricing policy of the business to the production phase over a long period of time, leveling out fluctuations that are of short duration and of comparatively minor significance. The short-term utilization relates to management's analysis of changes or fluctuations that occur during an operating year. This short-term utilization measures temporary idleness and aids in an analysis of its causes.

Factors Involved in Determining Normal Capacity. In determining the normal capacity of a plant, both its physical capacity and average sales expectancy must be considered. Neither plant capacity nor sales potential alone is sufficient. As previously mentioned, sales expectancy should be determined for a period long enough to level out cyclical variations rather than on the sales expectancy for a short period of time. It should also be noted that outmoded machinery and machinery bought for future use must be excluded from the considerations which lead to the determination of the normal capacity level.

Calculation of the normal capacity of a plant requires many different judgment factors. Normal capacity should be determined first for the business as a whole and then broken down by plants and departments. Determination of a departmental capacity figure might indicate that for a certain department the planned program is an overload, while in another it will result in excess capacity. The capacities of several departments will seldom be in such perfect balance as to produce an unhampered flow of production. For the department with the overload, often termed the "bottleneck" department, actions such as the following might have to be taken:

1. Working overtime.
2. Introducing an additional shift.
3. Temporarily transferring operations to another department where spare capacity is available.
4. Subcontracting the excess load.
5. Purchasing additional equipment.

On the other hand, the excess facilities of other departments might have to be reduced. Or the sales department might be asked to search for additional orders to utilize the spare capacity in these departments.

Effect of Capacity on Overhead Rates

The effect of the various capacity levels on predetermined factory overhead rates is illustrated as follows. If the 75 percent capacity level is considered to be the normal operating level, the overhead rate is $2.40 per direct labor hour.

**EFFECT OF VARIOUS CAPACITY LEVELS ON
PREDETERMINED FACTORY OVERHEAD RATES**

Item	Normal Capacity	Practical Capacity	Theoretical Capacity
Percentage of production capacity	75%	85%	100%
Direct labor hours.	7,500 hrs.	8,500 hrs.	10,000 hrs.
Budgeted factory overhead:			
Fixed.	$12,000	$12,000	$12,000
Variable	6,000	6,800	8,000
Total	$18,000	$18,800	$20,000
Fixed factory overhead rate per direct labor hour	$1.60	$1.41	$1.20
Variable factory overhead rate per direct labor hour	.80	.80	.80
Total factory overhead rate per direct labor hour	$2.40	$2.21	$2.00

At higher capacity levels, the rate is lower, because the fixed overhead is spread over more hours.

Idle Capacity vs. Excess Capacity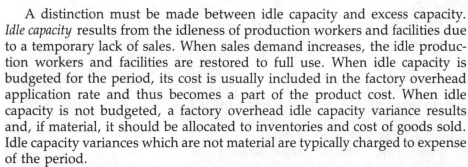

A distinction must be made between idle capacity and excess capacity. *Idle capacity* results from the idleness of production workers and facilities due to a temporary lack of sales. When sales demand increases, the idle production workers and facilities are restored to full use. When idle capacity is budgeted for the period, its cost is usually included in the factory overhead application rate and thus becomes a part of the product cost. When idle capacity is not budgeted, a factory overhead idle capacity variance results and, if material, it should be allocated to inventories and cost of goods sold. Idle capacity variances which are not material are typically charged to expense of the period.

Excess capacity, conversely, results either from greater productive capacity than the company could ever hope to use, or from an imbalance in equipment or machinery. This imbalance involves the excess capacity of one machine in contrast with the output of other machines with which it must be synchronized. Any expense arising from excess capacity should be excluded from the factory overhead rate and from the product cost. The expense should be treated as a deduction in the income statement. In many instances, it may be wise to dispose of excess plant and equipment.

Analysis of Cost Behavior

The success of a flexible budget depends upon careful study and analysis of the relationship of expenses to volume of activity or production and results in classifying expenses as fixed, variable, and semivariable.

Fixed Expenses

A *fixed expense* remains the same in total as activity increases or decreases. Fixed factory overhead includes conventional items such as straight-line depreciation, property insurance, and real estate taxes. Other expenses not inherently fixed acquire the fixed characteristic through the dictates of management policy.

The classification of an expense as fixed is valid only on the assumption that the underlying conditions remain unchanged. Thus, there is really nothing irrevocably fixed with respect to any expense classified as fixed. In the long run, all expenses are variable. In the short run, some fixed expenses, sometimes called *programmed fixed expenses*, will change because of changes in the volume of activity or for such reasons as changes in the number and salaries of the management groups. Other fixed expenses (e.g., depreciation or a long-term lease agreement) may commit management for a much longer period of time; therefore, they have been labeled *committed fixed expenses*.

Variable Expenses

A *variable expense* is expected to increase proportionately with an increase in activity and decrease proportionately with a decrease in activity. Variable expenses include the cost of supplies, indirect factory labor, receiving, storing, rework, perishable tools, and maintenance of machinery and tools. A measure of activity — such as direct labor hours or dollars, or machine hours — must be selected as an independent variable for use in estimating the variable expense, the dependent variable, at specified levels of activity. A rate of variability per unit of activity is thus determined.

Variable expenses are subject to certain fundamental assumptions if they are to remain so classified. For instance, it is assumed that prices of supplies or indirect labor do not change, that manufacturing methods and procedures do not vary, and that efficiencies do not fluctuate. If conditions change, the need for and use of variable expense items also change. For these reasons, variable expenses require constant attention so that revisions can be instigated from time to time.

Semivariable Expenses

A *semivariable expense* displays both fixed and variable characteristics. Examples of such expenses are the salaries of supervisors, accountants, buyers, typists, clerks, and janitors; employees' insurance and pension plans; maintenance of buildings and grounds; and power, water, gas, telephone and telegraph, office machine rentals, coal, fuel oil, some supplies, and even membership dues in trade, professional, and recreational organizations and clubs.

Three reasons for this semivariable characteristic of some expenses are:

1. A minimum of organization may be needed, or a minimum quantity of supplies or services may need to be consumed, in order to maintain readiness to operate. Beyond this minimum cost, which is fixed, additional cost varies with volume.
2. Accounting classifications, based upon the object of expenditure or function, commonly group fixed and variable items together. As an example, the cost of steam may be charged to one account, although the cost of steam used for heating is dependent upon weather, while the cost of steam used in the manufacturing process varies closely with volume of production in the factory.
3. Production factors are divisible into infinitely small units. When such costs are charted against their volume, their movements appear as a series of steps rather than as a continuous straight line. This situation is quite noticeable in moving from a one-shift to a two-shift or from a two-shift to a three-shift operation. Such moves result in definite steps in the cost line because a complete set of workers must be added at one point.[2]

The cost line of a semivariable expense is depicted graphically as follows. The graph illustrates that the fixed portion of this expense is at $380 (Line A).

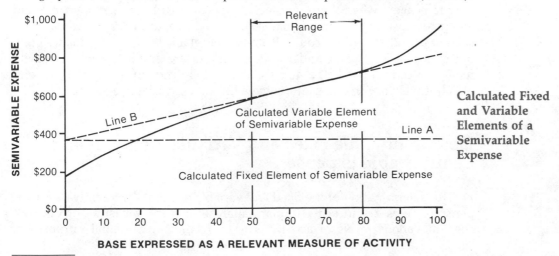

Calculated Fixed and Variable Elements of a Semivariable Expense

The variable portion increases in a straight line (Line B), indicating that for each increase in volume (the independent variable), there is a corresponding increase in the variable portion of the expense (the dependent variable).

The cost line of a semivariable expense is often stated as being in linear or proportional relationship to the base. Linearity is assumed and used in most cost studies, even though it may not be applicable over the entire range of possible activity. In most cases, linearity is a reasonable approximation of the relationship between a cost and a related activity within a limited range, referred to as the relevant range. The *relevant range* is the range of activity over which the calculated amount of fixed expense and the variable expense rate remain unchanged.

The solid line in the graph represents actual costs at all levels of activity. In this illustration, the actual cost line is nonlinear. This could occur because of the use of different production techniques or equipment and/or because of different degrees of capacity utilization at different levels of activity. The dash lines are linear and represent the calculated fixed and variable costs (Line A and Line B, respectively) at all levels of activity as determined from observations within the relevant range. Where Line B and the solid line coincide, the linear assumption closely approximates the actual relationship. This area of coincidence is the relevant range. The calculated fixed expense and the variable expense rate are inaccurate and must be recomputed for activity outside of the relevant range.

Analysis of Direct Materials and Direct Labor

The analysis of cost behavior discussed in this chapter focuses on factory overhead costs. However, the flexible budget for a producing department may include direct materials and direct labor, which also have cost behavior characteristics. Direct materials are viewed as varying directly with changes in the level of production. Although direct labor costs are similarly viewed, they tend to be fixed when there is a stable labor force with no overtime work and when the cost of idle time is likely to be charged to factory overhead or a current period variance account. If a relatively stable labor force is maintained, but overtime is worked and/or extra workers are employed when activity reaches a certain level, the direct labor cost is fixed up to a point, beyond which it will vary in steps and behave like a semivariable expense.

Determining the Fixed and Variable Elements of a Semivariable Expense

The determination of the fixed and variable elements of a semivariable expense is necessary in order to plan, analyze, control, measure, or evaluate costs at various levels of activity. These are the fundamental purposes of the flexible budget. As discussed in later chapters, the fixed and variable components of semivariable costs must also be segregated for the following purposes:

1. Direct costing and contribution margin analysis.
2. Marketing profitability analysis by territories, products, and customers.
3. Break-even and cost-volume-profit analysis.
4. Differential and comparative cost analysis.
5. Short-run profit maximization and cost minimization decisions.
6. Capital budgeting decisions.

The following methods are used in determining the fixed and variable elements of a semivariable expense: (1) high and low points method, (2) statistical scattergraph method, and (3) method of least squares. These methods are also used to determine the rate of variability of expenses that are entirely variable. Since these methods deal primarily with past costs, the values determined thereby might not fit the situation expected to exist in the coming month or year. Therefore, findings should be adjusted when future conditions point to a change, and unusual conditions should be eliminated from the computation in order to assure reliability and comparability of data.

To illustrate the three methods of determining the fixed and variable elements of a semivariable expense, assume that the following data are taken from Barker Company's records for the preceding year:

Month	Direct Labor Hours	Electricity Expense
January	34,000	$ 640
February	30,000	620
March	34,000	620
April	39,000	590
May	42,000	500
June.	32,000	530
July	26,000	500
August.	26,000	500
September	31,000	530
October.	35,000	550
November.	43,000	580
December.	48,000	680
Total.	420,000	$6,840
Monthly average	35,000	$ 570

High and Low Points Method

In the high and low points method, the fixed and variable elements of a semivariable expense are computed from two data points. The data points (periods) selected from the historical data being analyzed are the high and low periods as to activity level. These periods are usually, but not necessarily, also the highest and lowest figures for the expense being analyzed. If the periods having the highest or lowest activity levels are not the same as those having the highest or lowest expense being analyzed, the activity level should govern in making the selection. The high and low periods are selected because they represent conditions for the two activity levels which are the farthest apart. However, care must be taken not to select data points distorted by abnormal conditions.

Using the data for Barker Company, the fixed and variable elements are determined as follows:

	Activity Level	Expense
High	48,000 hours	$680
Low	26,000 hours	500
Difference	22,000 hours	$180

Variable rate: $180 ÷ 22,000 hours = $.00818 per direct labor hour

	High	Low
Total expense	$680	$500
Variable expense (rounded)	393	213
Fixed expense	$287	$287

The high and low activity levels differ by 22,000 direct labor hours, with a cost variation of $180. The assumption is that the difference in the costs at the two levels of activity occurred because of the activity being measured and is therefore pure variable cost. The variable rate is determined by dividing the difference in expense ($180) by the difference in activity (22,000 direct labor hours). In this example, the variable rate is determined to be $.00818 per direct labor hour. The total variable expense at either the high or low level of activity can be determined by multiplying the variable rate times the activity level. This results in a total variable cost at the high level of $393 ($.00818 × 48,000 hours) and at the low level, $213 ($.00818 × 26,000 hours). The difference between the total expense and the total variable expense is the fixed expense, which in this example is determined to be $287. The fixed expense is the same, whether computed from the high or low data.[3]

With variable and fixed elements established, the expense totals for various levels of activity can be calculated. This factor is important in the construction of the flexible budget and in the determination of the budget allowance in standard cost accounting.

---

[3]The high and low points method is equivalent to solving two simultaneous equations, based on the assumption that both points fall on the locus of the true variable cost line. Using the above figures, equations could be set up and solved as follows:

$$\begin{array}{rcl} F + 48{,}000V & = & \$\ \ 680 \\ -F - 26{,}000V & = & -500 \\ \hline 22{,}000V & = & \$\ \ 180 \end{array}$$

$$V = \frac{\$180}{22{,}000} = \$.00818 \text{ per direct labor hour}$$

The high and low points method is simple, but it has the disadvantage of using only two data points to determine cost behavior, and it is based on the assumption that the other data points lie on a straight line between the high and low points. Because it uses only two data points, it may not yield answers that are as accurate as those derived by other methods that consider a larger number of points.

Statistical Scattergraph Method

The statistical scattergraph method can be used for analyzing semivariable expenses. In this method, various costs (the dependent variable) are plotted on a vertical line — the *y-axis* — and measurement figures (the independent variable, e.g., direct labor dollars, direct labor hours, units of output, or percentage of capacity) are plotted along a horizontal line — the *x-axis*.

The data from the electricity expense illustration on page 439 are plotted on the following graph. Each point on the graph represents the electricity expense for a particular month. For instance, the point labeled "Nov." represents the electricity expense for November, when 43,000 direct labor hours were worked. The x-axis shows the direct labor hours, and the y-axis shows the electricity expense. Line B is plotted by visual inspection. This line represents the trend shown by the majority of data points. Generally, there should be as many data points above as below the line. Another line (Line A) is drawn parallel to the base line from the point of intersection on the y-axis, which is read from the scattergraph as approximately $440. This line represents the fixed element of the electricity expense for all activity levels within the relevant range.

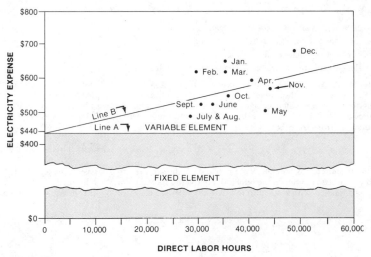

Statistical Scattergraph Representing the Fixed and Variable Elements for Electricity Expense

The triangle formed by Lines A and B shows the increase in electricity expense as direct labor hours increase. This increase, based on direct labor hours, is computed as follows:

$$\begin{array}{ccc}
\text{Average monthly} & - & \text{Fixed} & = & \text{Average monthly variable} \\
\text{expense} & & \text{element} & & \text{element of expense} \\
\$570 & - & \$440 & = & \$130
\end{array}$$

$$\frac{\text{Average monthly variable element of expense}}{\text{Average monthly direct labor hours}} = \frac{\text{Variable cost per}}{\text{direct labor hour}}$$

$$\frac{\$130}{35,000 \text{ hours}} = \$.0037 \text{ per direct labor hour}$$

Thus, the electricity expense consists of $440 fixed expense per month and of a variable factor of $.0037 per direct labor hour.

Method of Least Squares

In the preceding graph, Line B is drawn as a straight line, even though the points do not follow a perfect linear pattern. In most analyses, a straight line is adequate, because it is a reasonable approximation of cost behavior within the relevant range. However, the method of least squares may be used to compute a more exact straight line, called a *regression line*.

The *method of least squares* (sometimes called *simple regression analysis*) determines mathematically a line of best fit or a linear regression line drawn through a set of plotted points, so that the sum of the squared deviations of each actual plotted point from the point directly above or below it on the regression line is at a minimum.[4]

---

[4]The formula for a straight line is

$$y_i = a + bx_i$$

where y_i = dependent variable (expense) at period i

x_i = independent variable (activity) at period i

a = intercept (estimate of fixed expense)

b = slope (estimate of variable expense per unit of activity)

The difference between y_i (an actual observation) and $a + bx_i$ (an estimate of y_i) is often referred to as prediction error, e_i. Since the regression line exactly splits the plotted sample y_is, so that the sum of the values of the e_is above the line will exactly equal the sum of the values of the e_is below the line, the e_is will equal zero if they are totaled. To have a value to work with, the e_is are squared before being summed. This sum of the squared error terms, SSE, is expressed as follows:

$$SSE = \sum(y_i - a - bx_i)^2 = \sum y_i^2 - 2b\sum x_i y_i + 2ab\sum x_i + b^2\sum x_i^2 + na^2 - 2a\sum y_i$$

where y, a, b, and x are as previously defined and n is the sample size. For ease of presentation, the subscripts for x and y have been omitted in the remainder of the footnote. To find the minimum value of SSE, first partial derivatives are taken with respect to the two unknowns, i.e., a and b, and set equal to zero as follows:

$$\frac{\partial SSE}{\partial a} = 2b\sum x + 2na - 2\sum y = 0$$

$$\frac{\partial SSE}{\partial b} = -2\sum xy + 2a\sum x + 2b\sum x^2 = 0$$

Rearranging terms and dividing through by 2 yields the so-called normal equations:

To illustrate this method, the data from page 439 are used in completing the following table:

	(1) x_i Direct Labor Hours	(2) $(x_i - \bar{x})$ Difference from Average of 35,000 Hours	(3) y_i Electricity Expense	(4) $(y_i - \bar{y})$ Difference from Average of $570 Electricity Expense	(5) $(x_i - \bar{x})^2$ (2) Squared	(6) $(x_i - \bar{x})(y_i - \bar{y})$ (2) × (4)	(7) $(y_i - \bar{y})^2$ (4) Squared
Month							
January.....	34,000	(1,000)	$ 640	$ 70	1,000,000	$ (70,000)	$ 4,900
February....	30,000	(5,000)	620	50	25,000,000	(250,000)	2,500
March......	34,000	(1,000)	620	50	1,000,000	(50,000)	2,500
April.......	39,000	4,000	590	20	16,000,000	80,000	400
May........	42,000	7,000	500	(70)	49,000,000	(490,000)	4,900
June	32,000	(3,000)	530	(40)	9,000,000	120,000	1,600
July........	26,000	(9,000)	500	(70)	81,000,000	630,000	4,900
August	26,000	(9,000)	500	(70)	81,000,000	630,000	4,900
September..	31,000	(4,000)	530	(40)	16,000,000	160,000	1,600
October	35,000	0	550	(20)	0	0	400
November ..	43,000	8,000	580	10	64,000,000	80,000	100
December ..	48,000	13,000	680	110	169,000,000	1,430,000	12,100
Total	420,000	0*	$6,840	0*	512,000,000	$2,270,000	$40,800

*The sum of these columns is always zero, except for rounding differences.

$$\Sigma y = na + b\Sigma x$$
$$\Sigma xy = a\Sigma x + b\Sigma x^2$$

The normal equations each contain two unknowns. However, since the two equations are not linear transformations of one another, they can be solved. One way would be to multiply both sides of the first equation by $\Sigma x/n$ and then to subtract the first equation from the second in order to eliminate one of the unknowns (a in this case):

$$\Sigma xy = a\Sigma x + b\Sigma x^2$$

$$-\frac{\Sigma x\Sigma y}{n} = -a\Sigma x - \frac{b\Sigma x\Sigma x}{n}$$

$$\Sigma xy - \frac{\Sigma x\Sigma y}{n} = b\Sigma x^2 - \frac{b\Sigma x\Sigma x}{n} \quad \text{or} \quad n\Sigma xy - \Sigma x\Sigma y = nb\Sigma x^2 - b\Sigma x\Sigma x$$

Solving for b yields:

$$b = \frac{n\Sigma xy - \Sigma x\Sigma y}{n\Sigma x^2 - \Sigma x\Sigma x} = \frac{\Sigma xy - \dfrac{\Sigma x\Sigma y}{n}}{\Sigma x^2 - \dfrac{\Sigma x\Sigma x}{n}} = \frac{\Sigma xy - \bar{x}\bar{y}}{\Sigma x^2 - \bar{x}^2} = \frac{\Sigma(x - \bar{x})(y - \bar{y})}{\Sigma(x - \bar{x})^2}$$

where $\bar{x} = \Sigma x/n$

and $\bar{y} = \Sigma y/n$

Since $y = a + bx$, then the remaining unknown, a, is computed as follows:

$$a = \bar{y} - b\bar{x}$$

To prepare this table, the following steps are required:

1. First, determine the average direct labor hours, $\bar{x}$, and the average electricity expense, $\bar{y}$. The total direct labor hours are 420,000. When this amount is divided by the sample size, 12, the average of 35,000 hours per month results. The total electricity expense is $6,840, or an average of $570 per month ($6,840 ÷ 12).
2. Compute the differences between actual monthly figures for direct labor hours, x_i, and electricity expense, y_i, and their respective monthly averages, $\bar{x}$ and $\bar{y}$ computed in Step 1. These differences are entered in Columns 2 and 4.
3. Next, two multiplications must be made. First, square each of the differences entered in Column 2, $(x_i - \bar{x})$, and enter in Column 5, $(x_i - \bar{x})^2$. Second, multiply each of the differences in Column 2, $(x_i - \bar{x})$, by the corresponding differences in Column 4, $(y_i - \bar{y})$, and enter the products in Column 6, $(x_i - \bar{x})(y_i - \bar{y})$. [The differences entered in Column 4, $(y_i - \bar{y})$, are also squared and entered in Column 7, $(y_i - \bar{y})^2$. This column will be used on page 448 in computing the coefficient of determination.]

The variable rate for electricity expense, b, is computed as follows:

$$b = \frac{\text{Column 6 total}}{\text{Column 5 total}} = \frac{\Sigma(x_i - \bar{x})(y_i - \bar{y})}{\Sigma(x_i - \bar{x})^2} = \frac{\$2,270,000}{512,000,000} = \$.0044 \text{ per direct labor hour}$$

The fixed expense a can then be computed, using the formula for a straight line as follows:

$$\bar{y} = a + b\bar{x}$$

$$\$570 = a + (\$.0044)(35,000)$$

$$\$570 = a + \$154$$

$$a = \$416 \text{ fixed element of electricity expense per month}$$

The answer above differs somewhat from the figure determined by the scattergraph method, because visual inspection is not as accurate as the mathematical procedure. This preciseness injects a higher degree of objectivity and lack of bias into the figures. Many accountants and industrial engineers responsible for budget preparations prefer this more scientific technique. However, it is still useful to plot the data first in order to verify visually the existence of a reasonable degree of correlation. Whatever method is used, abnormal data should be excluded, and a sufficient number of data points should be included in order to represent a full range of usual operating conditions. In this illustration, the sample size was small in order to simplify the computations.

Standard Error of the Estimate. The purpose of the flexible budget is to provide a budget adjusted to the actual level of activity attained. The regression equation, which in the Barker Company illustration is $y_i' = \$416 + \$.0044x_i$, can be used to predict expense at a given level of activity. However, since the regression equation is determined from a limited sample and since variables which are not included in the regression equation may have some influence on the expense being predicted, the calculated expense will usually be different from the actual expense at the same level of activity. The visual scatter around the regression line portrayed in the graph on page 441 illustrates that the actual electricity expense will likely vary from what might be estimated using the calculated fixed expense and the variable expense rate. Because some variation can be expected, management should determine an acceptable range of tolerance for use in exercising control over expenses. Expenses within the limits of variation can be accepted. Expenses beyond the limits should be investigated, and any necessary corrective action should be taken.

The *standard error of the estimate* is defined as the standard deviation about the regression line. Management can use this concept to develop a confidence interval which, in turn, can be used to decide whether a given level of expense indicates a need for management action. To illustrate, the following table can be prepared from the data on page 439:

Month	(1) x_i Direct Labor Hours	(2) y_i Actual Electricity Expense	(3) $(y_i' = a + bx_i)$ Predicted Electricity Expense*	(4) $(y_i - y_i')$ Prediction Error [(2) − (3)]	(5) $(y_i - y_i')^2$ Prediction Error Squared [(4) Squared]
January	34,000	$ 640	$ 566	$ 74	$ 5,476
February	30,000	620	548	72	5,184
March	34,000	620	566	54	2,916
April	39,000	590	588	2	4
May	42,000	500	601	(101)	10,201
June	32,000	530	557	(27)	729
July	26,000	500	530	(30)	900
August	26,000	500	530	(30)	900
September	31,000	530	552	(22)	484
October	35,000	550	570	(20)	400
November	43,000	580	605	(25)	625
December	48,000	680	627	53	2,809
Total	420,000	$6,840	$6,840	0 **	$30,628

*Calculated regression line, y_i', values, (direct labor hours × $.0044) + $416, are rounded to the nearest dollar.
**The sum of this column is always zero, except for rounding differences.

The standard error of the estimate is then calculated as follows:

$$s' = \sqrt{\frac{\Sigma(y_i - y_i')^2}{n - 2}} = \sqrt{\frac{\text{Col. 5 total}}{12 - 2}} = \sqrt{\frac{\$30,628}{10}} = \sqrt{\$3,062.80} = \$55.34$$

The prediction errors are usually assumed to follow a standard normal distribution. However, for small samples, the Student's t distribution is a more appropriate assumption. A table of selected t values (based on the assumption that two tails of the distribution are of concern, i.e., that managers are concerned about both favorable and unfavorable variances) follows:

Degrees of Freedom	Desired Confidence Level			
	90%	95%	99%	99.8%
1	6.314	12.706	63.657	318.310
2	2.920	4.303	9.925	22.326
3	2.353	3.182	5.841	10.213
4	2.132	2.776	4.604	7.173
5	2.015	2.571	4.032	5.893
6	1.943	2.447	3.707	5.208
7	1.895	2.365	3.499	4.785
8	1.860	2.306	3.355	4.501
9	1.833	2.262	3.250	4.297
10	1.812	2.228	3.169	4.144
11	1.796	2.201	3.106	4.025
12	1.782	2.179	3.055	3.930
13	1.771	2.160	3.012	3.852
14	1.761	2.145	2.977	3.787
15	1.753	2.131	2.947	3.733
20	1.725	2.086	2.845	3.552
25	1.708	2.060	2.787	3.450
30	1.697	2.042	2.750	3.385
40	1.684	2.021	2.704	3.307
60	1.671	2.000	2.660	3.232
120	1.658	1.980	2.617	3.160
∞	1.645	1.960	2.576	3.090

The acceptable range of actual expense around the predicted expense would be computed for a sample of size n by multiplying the standard error of the estimate by the t value for n − 2 degrees of freedom[5] at the desired confidence level, t_p, and by a correction factor for small samples as follows:

$$y_i' \pm t_p s' \sqrt{1 + \frac{1}{n} + \frac{(x_i - \bar{x})^2}{\Sigma(x_i - \bar{x})^2}}$$

where all variables above are as previously defined.

To illustrate the computation and use of the confidence interval, assume that the actual level of activity for a period is 40,000 direct labor hours. The electricity expense computed for the flexible budget from the regression equation determined in the previous example is $592 [$416 + $.0044 (40,000)]. Assume further that management wants to be 95 percent confident that the actual electricity expense is within acceptable tolerance limits. Based on the table factor of 2.228 for t at the 95 percent confidence level, with df = 12 − 2, and on the standard error of the estimate computed above (s' = $55.34), the confidence interval would be:

---

[5]Degrees of freedom (df) refers to the number of values which are free to vary after certain restrictions have been placed on the data. In general, if a regression equation involves p unknown parameters, then df = n − p. In linear bivariate regression, there are two unknown parameters, a and b; thus, df = n − 2.

$$y'_i \pm t_{95\%} s' \sqrt{1 + \frac{1}{n} + \frac{(x_i - \bar{x})^2}{\Sigma(x_i - \bar{x})^2}}$$

$$\$592.00 \pm (2.228)(\$55.34) \sqrt{1 + \frac{1}{12} + \frac{(40,000 - 35,000)^2}{512,000,000}}$$

$$\$592.00 \pm (2.228)(\$55.34)(1.064)$$

$$\$592.00 \pm \$131.19$$

Management can expect the actual electricity expense to be between \$460.81 (\$592.00 − \$131.19) and \$723.19 (\$592.00 + \$131.19) about 95 percent of the time. Electricity expense outside of these limits will occur because of random chance only 5 percent of the time. If the actual electricity expense is less than \$460.81 or greater than \$723.19, management should investigate the cause and take any necessary corrective action.

For large samples, the Student's t distribution approaches the standard normal distribution and the correction factor for small samples (the square root term) approaches one. For large samples, therefore, the computation of the acceptable range of actual expense around the predicted expense may be simplified by omitting the correction factor and using the appropriate z value for the standard normal distribution.[6] If the sample size used in computing the regression equation and the standard error of the estimate in the illustration were large, the 95 percent confidence interval for electricity expense at 40,000 direct labor hours would be:

$$\$592.00 \pm (1.960)(\$55.34)$$
$$\$592.00 \pm \$108.47$$

Correlation Analysis. The application of the statistical scattergraph method accomplishes visual verification of a reasonable degree of correlation. *Correlation* is the relationship between the values of two attributes — the independent variable (*x*, or direct labor hours in the illustration) and the dependent variable (*y*, or electricity expense in the illustration) — before arriving at the fixed cost and the variable rate for semivariable expenses, or the variable rate for entirely variable expenses. If all plotted points fell on the regression line, perfect correlation would exist.

Mathematical measurements may be used to quantify correlation. In statistical theory, the *coefficient of correlation*, denoted *r*, is a measure of the extent to which two variables are related linearly. When r = 0, there is no correlation; and when r = ±1, the correlation is perfect. As r approaches +1, the correlation is positive, which means that the dependent variable, y, increases as the independent variable, x, increases, and the regression line slopes upward to the right. As r approaches −1, the correlation is negative or inverse, which means that the dependent variable, y, decreases as the independent variable, x, increases, and the regression line slopes downward to the right.

---

[6]The t values presented in the table on page 446 for df = ∞ are equal to the z values for the standard normal distribution at the probability levels indicated at the head of each column.

The *coefficient of determination, r^2,* is found by squaring the coefficient of correlation. The coefficient of determination is considered easier to interpret than the coefficient of correlation, r, because it represents the percentage of explained variance in the dependent variable. The larger the coefficient of determination, the closer it comes to the coefficient of correlation until both coefficients equal 1. The word "explained" means that the variations in the dependent variable are related to, but not necessarily caused by, the variations in the independent variable.

The formula for calculating the coefficient of correlation is:

$$r = \frac{\Sigma(x_i - \bar{x})(y_i - \bar{y})}{\sqrt{\Sigma(x_i - \bar{x})^2 \Sigma(y_i - \bar{y})^2}}$$

where $x_i - \bar{x}$ is the difference between each independent variable (direct labor hours in the Barker Company illustration) and the average of the independent variables; and $y_i - \bar{y}$ is the difference between each dependent variable (electricity expense) and the average of the dependent variables. The coefficient of correlation, r, and the coefficient of determination, r^2, for the data on page 443 are calculated as follows:

$$r = \frac{\Sigma(x_i - \bar{x})(y_i - \bar{y})}{\sqrt{\Sigma(x_i - \bar{x})^2 \Sigma(y_i - \bar{y})^2}} = \frac{\text{Column 6}}{\sqrt{(\text{Column 5})(\text{Column 7})}}$$

$$= \frac{2,270,000}{\sqrt{(512,000,000)(40,800)}} = \frac{2,270,000}{\sqrt{20,889,600,000,000}}$$

$$= \frac{2,270,000}{4,570,514.2} = +.49666$$

$$r^2 = .24667$$

The coefficient of determination of less than .25 means that less than 25 percent of the change in electricity expense is related to the change in direct labor hours. The conclusion is that the cost is related not only to direct labor hours but to other factors as well, such as the time of day for production or the season of the year. Furthermore, some other independent variable, such as machine hours, may afford a better correlation.

To illustrate a case in which a high degree of correlation exists, the cost of electricity from the previous example is slightly altered, with direct labor hours remaining on the same level. The solution on page 449 indicates an almost perfect correlation between the two attributes, which means that this relationship could be accepted as the basis for calculating the factory overhead rate and constructing the flexible budget.

Method of Least Squares for Multiple Independent Variables. Typically, cost behavior is shown as dependent on a single measure of volume or on some other independent variable. In the discussion above, for example, the behavior of the dependent variable, electricity expense, was described by the independent variable, direct labor hours. However, a cost may vary because of more than one factor.

Multiple regression analysis is a further application and expansion of the method of least squares, permitting consideration of more than one indepen-

Month	(1) x_i Direct Labor Hours	(2) $(x_i - \bar{x})$ Difference from Average of 35,000 Hours	(3) y_i Electricity Expense	(4) $(y_i - \bar{y})$ Difference from Average of $655 Electricity Expense	(5) $(x_i - \bar{x})^2$ (2) Squared	(6) $(x_i - \bar{x})(y_i - \bar{y})$ (2) × (4)	(7) $(y_i - \bar{y})^2$ (4) Squared
January.....	34,000	(1,000)	$ 660	$ 5	1,000,000	$ (5,000)	$ 25
February....	30,000	(5,000)	590	(65)	25,000,000	325,000	4,225
March......	34,000	(1,000)	660	5	1,000,000	(5,000)	25
April........	39,000	4,000	680	25	16,000,000	100,000	625
May........	42,000	7,000	740	85	49,000,000	595,000	7,225
June	32,000	(3,000)	610	(45)	9,000,000	135,000	2,025
July........	26,000	(9,000)	580	(75)	81,000,000	675,000	5,625
August	26,000	(9,000)	550	(105)	81,000,000	945,000	11,025
September..	31,000	(4,000)	630	(25)	16,000,000	100,000	625
October	35,000	0	640	(15)	0	0	225
November ..	43,000	8,000	750	95	64,000,000	760,000	9,025
December ..	48,000	13,000	770	115	169,000,000	1,495,000	13,225
	420,000	0	$7,860	0	512,000,000	$5,120,000	$53,900

$$r = \frac{\Sigma(x_i - \bar{x})(y_i - \bar{y})}{\sqrt{\Sigma(x_i - \bar{x})^2 \, \Sigma(y_i - \bar{y})^2}} = \frac{\text{Column 6 total}}{\sqrt{(\text{Column 5 total})(\text{Column 7 total})}}$$

$$= \frac{5,120,000}{\sqrt{(512,000,000)(53,900)}} = \frac{5,120,000}{\sqrt{27,596,800,000,000}}$$

$$= \frac{5,120,000}{5,253,265.7} = +.97463$$

$$r^2 = .94991$$

dent variable. In multiple regression analysis, the simple least-squares equation for a straight line, $y = a + bx$, is expanded to include more than one independent variable. For example, in the equation $y = a + bx + cz$, c is the degree of variability for an additional independent variable z.

The least-squares concept is fundamentally the same for several independent variables as it is for only one. Although the cost relationship can no longer be shown on a two-dimensional graph and the arithmetical computations become more complex, the widespread availability of computer programs makes the use of multiple regression analysis more feasible.

If the cost behavior of a group of expenses in one or more expense accounts is being described, an alternate to multiple variables (and hence to the considerations necessitated by multiple variables when applying the least squares method) may be possible. That is, expenses may be grouped and classified in sufficient detail so that expenses in a particular group are all largely related to only one independent variable. This would allow the use of the method of least squares as earlier illustrated, i.e., simple regression analysis. If this approach is not feasible, i.e., if more than one independent variable is still required to describe the cost behavior, then multiple regression analysis should be employed.[7]

---

[7]For a comprehensive treatment, see Chapter 13, "Regression and Correlation—Curvilinear and Multivariate Analysis," Charles T. Clark and Lawrence L. Schkade, *Statistical Analysis for Administrative Decisions* (Cincinnati: South-Western Publishing Co., 1983).

Preparing a Flexible Budget

Considerable discussion has been devoted to the development of the underlying details necessary for the preparation of a flexible budget. It is not intended to convey the idea, however, that the factory overhead budget outranks the budgets for other functions of the business, because these other functions can also utilize the flexible budget concept. Any increase or decrease in business activity must be reflected throughout the enterprise. In some activities or departments, changes will be greater or smaller than in others. Certain departments have the ability to produce more without much additional cost. In others, costs increase or decrease in more or less direct proportion to production increases or decreases. The flexible budget attempts to deal with this problem.

When the fixed dollar amount and the variable rate of an expense have been determined, budget allowances for any level within a relevant range of activity can be computed without difficulty. For example, a budget allowances schedule, based on normal capacity, for the Machining Department of a manufacturing company, is as follows:

BUDGET ALLOWANCES FOR MACHINING DEPARTMENT

Activity Base: Normal capacity, 4,000 direct labor hours per month = 80% of rated capacity

Expense	Fixed Expense	Variable Rate per Direct Labor Hour
Indirect labor	$ 600	$ .175
Clerical help	100	.050
Setup crew	800	.070
Rework operations	100	
Supervision	1,200	
Factory supplies	200	.055
Total controllable by department head	$ 3,000	$ .350
Insurance—fire, etc.	$ 80	
Taxes—state and local	50	
Depreciation	500	
Total noncontrollable	$ 630	
Maintenance	$ 600	$ .20
Building occupancy	780	.10
Gas, water, steam, and air	540	.30
General expenses	450	.05
Total service departments (apportioned)	$ 2,370	$ .65
Total	$ 6,000	$1.00

Summary:

Fixed expense	$ 6,000
Variable expense, 4,000 direct labor hours @ $1 per hour	4,000
Total cost at normal capacity	$10,000
Factory overhead rate of Machining Department at normal capacity ($10,000 ÷ 4,000 hours)	$2.50 per direct labor hour

The schedule of budget allowances is the basis for the following flexible budget. In this budget, the factory overhead rate declines steadily as production moves to the 90 percent operating level. As production approaches theoretical capacity, the overhead rate increases, because items such as rework operations and supervision increase faster than at lower levels and overtime premiums and night premiums are introduced. While such cost increases are revealed through the flexible budget, the situation indicates a possible departure from the use of the equation for a straight line, $y = a + bx$, or $6,000 fixed expense $+ 1.00(x)$ for all levels of activity. However, it must be emphasized that one definite level must be agreed upon and used for setting the predetermined factory overhead rate for applying overhead cost to production. Costs, the base selected, and the resulting rate will lead to spending and idle capacity variances that might warrant a rate change in the next period for the sake of more meaningful cost control and pricing procedures. In any case, the effective use of cost data for planning, control, and decision-making purposes requires reasonably accurate knowledge of cost behavior.

FLEXIBLE BUDGET FOR MACHINING DEPARTMENT

Operating level:				
Based on direct labor hours..................	3,500	4,000*	4,500	5,000
Percentage of rated capacity.................	70%	80%	90%	100%
Monthly allowances for expenses:				
Indirect labor...............................	$1,212.50	$ 1,300.00	$ 1,387.50	$ 1,475.00
Clerical help	275.00	300.00	325.00	350.00
Setup crew	1,045.00	1,080.00	1,115.00	1,150.00
Rework operations..........................	100.00	100.00	100.00	135.00
Supervision................................	1,200.00	1,200.00	1,200.00	1,400.00
Factory supplies...........................	392.50	420.00	447.50	475.00
Overtime premium..........................	—	—	—	500.00
Night premium	—	—	—	100.00
Total controllable by department head........	$4,225.00	$ 4,400.00	$ 4,575.00	$ 5,585.00
Insurance—fire, etc.........................	$ 80.00	$ 80.00	$ 80.00	$ 80.00
Taxes—state and local	50.00	50.00	50.00	50.00
Depreciation	500.00	500.00	500.00	500.00
Total noncontrollable......................	$ 630.00	$ 630.00	$ 630.00	$ 630.00
Maintenance	$1,300.00	$ 1,400.00	$ 1,500.00	$ 1,600.00
Building occupancy	1,130.00	1,180.00	1,230.00	1,280.00
Gas, water, steam, and air...................	1,590.00	1,740.00	1,890.00	2,040.00
General expenses	625.00	650.00	675.00	700.00
Total service departments	$4,645.00	$ 4,970.00	$ 5,295.00	$ 5,620.00
Total factory overhead.....................	$9,500.00	$10,000.00	$10,500.00	$11,835.00
Factory overhead rate per direct labor hour.....	$2.714	$2.500	$2.333	$2.367

*Normal capacity.

In the flexible budget for the Machining Department, the factory overhead rate based on direct labor hours means that all variable expenses are related to this activity base. In many instances, however, the activity base is not uniform for all overhead items. Certain departments within a firm may have different bases, and a single department may require different bases and rates for different groups of expenses. Within a department, only a low correlation or none at all may exist between some of the expenses and the activity base selected. It is therefore essential to study the correlation of volume in physical terms, such as units produced, labor hours worked, or machine hours used, with the dollar cost for each item or group of items. Such studies quite often indicate that a new base must be chosen for some or all of the expenses to arrive at the most acceptable separation of fixed and variable expenses. The use of statistical correlation analysis is suggested to discover the correct volume base to be used before attempting to separate the fixed and variable elements of the many expense items that are semivariable in nature and before describing the rate of variability of entirely variable expenses.

Flexible Budgeting Through Electronic Data Processing and Step Charts

The determination of the fixed and variable elements in each departmental expense is a time-consuming task, particularly when computations, calculations, and analyses are performed either manually or by a desk calculator. The application of data processing techniques can eliminate this tedious chore and at the same time provide the necessary tools for budgetary control and responsibility reporting throughout the year.

Predetermined rates are usually used. However, when increases or decreases in certain expenses are anticipated due to a change in the product or a change in processing, the projected overhead amounts are adjusted accordingly. Some expenses are budgeted on a step-chart basis which is in harmony with the relevant range idea mentioned previously.[8]

The step chart on page 453 indicates the allowance for nonproduction personnel at various levels of production activity. Each bisected square is an indication as to the number of nonproduction personnel (upper left-hand corner) and salary levels allowable (lower right-hand corner) at each step. The levels are based on the number of production workers.

In a step chart for a service department, the levels might be based on the total number of production hours in all producing departments. Such detailed data enhance the development of monthly departmental budgets by subexpense classifications.

Flexible Budget for a Service Department

Flexible budgets for service departments permit (1) comparison of actual expenses with allowed expenses at the prevailing level of operations and (2) establishment of a fairer use rate or sold-hour rate by charging operating departments with fixed expenses regardless of activity and with a variable cost

---

[8]Eugene J. McNaboe, "Flexible Budgeting Through Electronic Data Processing," *Management Accounting*, Section 1, Vol. XLVII, No. 7, pp. 9–17.

Department _____

MONTHLY DEPARTMENTAL ALLOWANCE FOR NONPRODUCTION PERSONNEL

NUMBER OF PRODUCTION PERSONNEL		DEPARTMENT HEAD	SUPERVISOR	ASSISTANT SUPERVISOR	MFG. QUALITY ANALYST					
From	To									
0	10	1 1674								
11	20	1 1674	1 1000		1 1050					
21	30	1 1674	2 2000		1 1050					
31	40	1 1674	4 4000		2 2100					
41	50	1 1674	5 5000	1 1200	2 2100					
51	60	1 1674	5 5000	1 1200	3 3150					
61	70	1 1674	6 6000	1 1200	3 3150					
71	80	1 1674	6 6000	1 1200	4 4200					
81	90	1 1674	7 7000	1 1200	4 4200					
91	100									

Step Chart for a Producing Department

based on departmental activity. In the following flexible budget for the Maintenance Department of a company, the expenses of the department are estimated at a fixed amount of $4,200. At 80 percent capacity, the total expense is $27,000. Assuming that the company has two producing departments and two service departments to which a fixed cost of $1,200, $2,000, $600, and $400, respectively, is charged as the readiness-to-serve cost of the Maintenance Department, the remaining balance of $22,800 is divided by the total number of maintenance hours, 2,400, to arrive at a variable rate of $9.50 per hour.

FLEXIBLE BUDGET FOR MAINTENANCE DEPARTMENT

Operating level:				
Maintenance hours	2,100	2,400	2,700	3,000
Percentage of plant capacity	70%	80%	90%	100%
Monthly allowances for expenses:				
Artisans	$12,600	$14,400	$16,200	$18,000
Supervision	2,000	2,000	2,000	2,000
Factory supplies	5,950	6,800	7,650	8,500
Tools	1,400	1,600	1,800	2,000
Depreciation	1,400	1,400	1,400	1,400
Building occupancy	800	800	800	800
Total expense	$24,150	$27,000	$29,850	$32,700
Fixed expense	$ 4,200	$ 4,200	$ 4,200	$ 4,200
Variable expense	19,950	22,800	25,650	28,500
Variable charging rate per maintenance hour	$9.50	$9.50	$9.50	$9.50

Flexible Marketing and Administrative Budgets

In contrast to the factory overhead budget, which bases its expense levels in most cases on direct labor hours, machine hours, or direct labor dollars, the budget for commercial expenses is often based on net sales, as shown in the following illustration. This practice has been criticized, and other methods are suggested in Chapter 21.

FLEXIBLE MARKETING AND ADMINISTRATIVE BUDGET						
Net sales		$600,000	$700,000	$800,000	$900,000	$1,000,000
Monthly allowances for marketing expenses:	Based on Sales					
Sales salaries	5%	$30,000	$35,000	$40,000	$45,000	$50,000
Advertising.	1%	6,000	7,000	8,000	9,000	10,000
Sales expenses	2%	12,000	14,000	16,000	18,000	20,000
Misc. expenses.	.5%	3,000	3,500	4,000	4,500	5,000
Depreciation	Fixed	10,000	10,000	10,000	10,000	10,000
Total marketing.		$61,000	$69,500	$78,000	$86,500	$95,000
Monthly allowances for administrative expenses:	Based on Sales					
Executives' salaries	Fixed	$20,000	$20,000	$20,000	$30,000	$50,000
General expenses	3%	18,000	21,000	24,000	27,000	30,000
Depreciation	Fixed	5,000	5,000	5,000	5,000	5,000
Insurance.	Fixed	3,000	3,000	3,000	3,000	3,000
Taxes	Fixed	4,000	4,000	4,000	4,000	4,000
Total administrative		$50,000	$53,000	$56,000	$69,000	$92,000

DISCUSSION QUESTIONS

1. Name some relative advantages in the use of a flexible budget over a fixed budget.

2. What is the underlying principle of a flexible budget?

3. A company has been operating a budget system for a number of years. Production volume fluctuates widely, reaching its peak in the fall, but is quite low during the rest of the year. Manufacturing for stock during the dull period as a means of smoothing out the volume fluctuations is impractical because of frequent and sudden changes in specifications prescribed by the customers. Actual annual volume has been substantially below normal. The budget produces large unfavorable capacity variances since overhead rates are computed from normal volume and are inadequate to absorb the overhead which should be charged into production during the low-volume periods. This fixed type of budget based on an unrealistic normal production volume fails to serve its planning and control purpose. As a consultant, diagnose the situation and offer advice.

4. Differentiate between (a) theoretical capacity, (b) practical capacity, (c) expected actual capacity, and (d) normal capacity.

5. (a) What situations give rise to idle capacity costs? (b) How and why should such costs be accounted for? (c) What is excess capacity cost?

6. Explain the difference between variable, fixed, and semivariable factory overhead.

7. Why should semivariable expenses be separated into their fixed and variable elements?

8. What methods are available for separating semivariable expenses?

9. Define and discuss the method of least squares with reference to assumptions, accounting data used, and single and multiple independent variables.   (AICPA adapted)

10. The least-squares relationship between electric power consumed, y, and production, x, was computed to be: $y = 10,000 + 50x$. Determine the predicted electric power demands for the coming week if the planned production is 500 units.   (CGAA adapted)

11. Explain the meaning of $200 and $4 in the regression equation, $S = \$200 + \$4H$, where S denotes total monthly costs of indirect supplies and H is machine hours per month.   (CMA adapted)

12. Using the equation from Question 11 and assuming a coefficient of correlation of $r = .87$, explain the meaning of the r measure and evaluate the r value, .87.   (CMA adapted)

13. Define the standard error of the estimate and explain its use in setting tolerance limits.

14. Can service departments' expenses be set up using flexible budget procedures? What makes the situation difficult? Suggest how the expenses can be allocated meaningfully to producing departments.

EXERCISES

1. *Critique of performance report.* Jewett Company uses a fixed or forecast budget to measure its performance against the objectives set by the forecast and to help in controlling costs. At the end of a month, management received the following report, which compares actual performance with budgeted figures:

Items of Cost	Budget	Actual
Units produced	75,000	73,500
VAR Direct materials	$39,000	$37,020
VAR Direct labor	6,000	5,950
VAR Factory supplies	1,500	1,550
VAR Indirect labor	726	710
VAR Repairs and maintenance	2,250	2,300
Insurance and property tax	355	350
FIND Rent	2,000	2,000
COST Depreciation	2,200	2,200
Total	$54,031	$52,080

Required: What conclusions can be drawn from this report? Indicate weaknesses, if any, of this type of budget.

2. *Flexible budget for performance evaluation.* The University of Boyne offers an extensive continuing education program in many cities throughout the state. For the convenience of its faculty and administrative staff and to save costs, the university employs a supervisor to operate a motor pool. The motor pool operated with 20 vehicles until February, when an additional automobile was acquired. The motor pool furnishes gasoline, oil, and other supplies for its automobiles. A mechanic does routine maintenance and minor repairs. Major repairs are done at a nearby commercial garage.

Each year, the supervisor prepares an operating budget, which informs the university administration of the funds needed for operating the pool. Depreciation (straight-line) on *the automobiles is recorded in the budget in order to determine the cost per mile.*

The following schedule presents the annual budget approved by the university, with March's actual costs compared to one twelfth of the annual budget:

University Motor Pool
Budget Report for March

	Annual Budget	One-Month Budget	March Actual	(Over) Under
Gasoline...................................	$ 52,500	$ 4,375	$ 5,323	$(948)
Oil, minor repairs, parts, and supplies...........	3,600	300	380	(80)
Outside repairs...............................	2,700	225	50	175
Insurance....................................	6,000	500	525	(25)
Salaries and benefits.........................	30,000	2,500	2,500	—
Depreciation	26,400	2,200	2,310	(110)
	$121,200	$10,100	$11,088	$(988)
Total miles..................................	600,000	50,000	63,000	
Cost per mile................................	$ .2020	$ .2020	$ .1760	
Number of automobiles.......................	20	20	21	

The annual budget was constructed upon these assumptions:

(a) 20 automobiles in the pool.
(b) 30,000 miles per year per automobile.
(c) 16 miles per gallon per automobile.
(d) $1.40 per gallon of gasoline.
(e) $.006 per mile for oil, minor repairs, parts, and supplies.
(f) $135 per automobile for outside repairs.

The supervisor is unhappy with the monthly report comparing budget and actual costs for March, claiming it presents an unfair picture of performance. A previous employer used flexible budgeting to compare actual costs to budgeted amounts.

Required:
    (1) Prepare a report showing budgeted amounts, actual costs, and monthly variations for March, using flexible budget techniques. (Round off computations to four decimal places.)
    (2) Explain the basis of the budget figure for outside repairs.   *(CMA adapted)*

3. Flexible budget. *Operating at normal capacity, Bertha Company employs 20 production workers in the Assembly Department, working 8 hours per day, 20 days per month at a wage rate of $9 per hour. Normal capacity is 3,800 units of production per month. Supplies average $.23 per direct labor hour, indirect labor cost is ⅛ of direct labor cost, and other charges are $.18 per direct labor hour. The flexible budget at the normal capacity activity level follows:*

Direct materials..............................	$ 4,760
Direct labor	28,800
Fixed factory overhead	670
Supplies.....................................	736
Indirect labor...............................	3,600
Other charges...............................	576
Total	$39,142
Cost per unit................................	$10.30

Required: *Prepare the flexible budget for one month at 60% and 75% capacity.*

4. Flexible budget. *Aspen Inc. employs 10 production workers, working 8 hours a day, 20 days per month, at a normal capacity of 2,400 units. The direct labor wage rate is $6.30 per hour; direct materials are budgeted at $2 per unit produced. Fixed factory overhead is $960; supplies average $.25 per direct labor hour; indirect labor is ⅙ of direct labor cost; and other charges are $.45 per direct labor hour.*

Required: *Prepare the flexible budget for one month at 60%, 80%, and 100% of normal capacity, showing itemized manufacturing costs, total manufacturing cost, and total manufacturing cost per unit.*

5. Flexible budget and overapplied fixed factory overhead. *Panda Corporation uses a flexible budgeting system. The following flexible budget is provided for 80% and 100% of normal capacity:*

	80% Capacity	100% Capacity
Units of production..	2,000	2,500
Direct labor	$ 4,000	$ 5,000
Direct materials..	6,000	7,500
Total prime cost	$10,000	$12,500
Factory overhead:		
Utilities	$ 900	$ 1,000
Supplies...	800	1,000
Indirect labor......................................	1,000	1,250
Depreciation of plant and equipment....................	3,000	3,000
Miscellaneous indirect factory expenses................	1,000	1,200
Total factory overhead.............................	$ 6,700	$ 7,450
Total budgeted manufacturing cost.....................	$16,700	$19,950

$20,600

Required:
(1) *Prepare the allowable flexible budget on the assumption that 2,600 units are actually produced in the current period.*
(2) *If the factory overhead application rate were based on 100% of actual capacity and actual production costs were equal to the allowable budget for 2,600 units, what would be the amount of over- or underapplied factory overhead?*

6. Determining variable and fixed factory overhead budget allowances. *The following information has been used by the Tolgate Company in preparing its budgets for January and February:*

	January	February
Units to be sold	9,000	11,000
Units to be produced..................................	12,000	10,000
Direct labor hours....................................	24,000	20,000
Insurance on factory	$ 2,000	$ 2,000
Sales salaries......................................	13,000	15,000
Depreciation (factory building and machinery).............	10,000	10,000
Light and heat (factory)..............................	340	300
Advertising...	15,000	15,000
Indirect factory labor	3,800	3,300
Factory supplies.....................................	3,000	2,500
Direct materials used.................................	60,000	50,000
Lubricants for factory machinery.......................	1,800	1,500

Required:

(1) *Compute the variable budget allowance per direct labor hour for each factory overhead expense. (Carry computations to three decimal places.)*

(2) *Compute the fixed budget allowance for each factory overhead expense.*

(CGAA adapted)

7. Cost behavior and correlation analysis. *Stocks Company is developing a flexible budget. The company's total maintenance expense for the past 10 months is $48,000. Some of the maintenance activity appears related to the operation of machinery, and the accountant desires to determine whether machine hours should be used as a basis upon which to estimate maintenance expense at various levels of capacity. Machine hours for the same period totaled 80,000 hours. The machine hour differences from average multiplied by the maintenance expense differences from its average and summed $[\Sigma(x_i - \bar{x})(y_i - \bar{y})]$ is 1,800. The machine hour differences from average squared and summed $[\Sigma(x_i - \bar{x})^2]$ is 4,000, and the maintenance expense differences from average squared and summed $[\Sigma(y_i - \bar{y})^2]$ is 1,000.*

Required:

(1) *Compute the coefficient of correlation, r, and the coefficient of determination, r^2, for maintenance expense and machine hours.*

(2) *Compute the variable maintenance expense per machine hour, using the method of least squares.*

(3) *Compute the fixed maintenance expense, using the method of least squares.*

8. Choosing appropriate activity measure and separating fixed and variable costs. *Hansen Company is developing a flexible budget. The company's total electricity expense for the past 20 months is $42,000. An activity measure upon which to base estimates of electricity expense is needed. The two activity measures being considered are direct labor hours and machine hours. Direct labor hours for the period totaled 180,000, and machine hours totaled 120,000. The direct labor hour differences from average multiplied by the electricity expense differences from its average and summed $[\Sigma(x_i - \bar{x})(y_i - \bar{y})]$ is 5,700. The direct labor hour differences from average squared and summed $[\Sigma(x_i - \bar{x})^2]$ is 28,500. The electricity expense differences from average squared and summed $[\Sigma(y_i - \bar{y})^2]$ is 1,264. The machine hour differences from average multiplied by the electricity expense differences from its average and summed $[\Sigma(x_i - \bar{x})(y_i - \bar{y})]$ is 7,000. The machine hour differences from average squared and summed $[\Sigma(x_i - \bar{x})^2]$ is 50,000.*

Required:

(1) *Compute the coefficient of correlation, r, and the coefficient of determination, r^2, for direct labor hours and electricity expense.*

(2) *Compute the coefficient of correlation, r, and the coefficient of determination, r^2, for machine hours and electricity expense.*

(3) *Which activity measure should be used for the estimation of fixed and variable electricity expense for the Hansen Company? Explain.*

(4) *Compute the variable electricity expense rate and the fixed expense, using the method of least squares.*

PROBLEMS

16-1. Flexible vs fixed budget. Pearsons Inc. is a regional chain of restaurants, each with a carryout delicatessen department. Company management has prepared the following budget for a typical unit:

Typical Pearsons Restaurant—Deli
Budgeted Income Statement for the Year

	Restaurant	Delicatessen	Total
Sales...	$2,500,000	$1,000,000	$3,500,000
Purchases	$1,000,000	$ 600,000	$1,600,000
Hourly wages (variable)...................	875,000	50,000	925,000
Franchise fee.............................	75,000	30,000	105,000
Advertising (fixed)	200,000	100,000	300,000
Utilities (variable)	125,000	70,000	195,000
Depreciation.............................	75,000	50,000	125,000
Lease expense	50,000	30,000	80,000
Salaries (fixed)	50,000	30,000	80,000
Total	$2,450,000	$ 960,000	$3,410,000
Income before income tax.................	$ 50,000	$ 40,000	$ 90,000

All units are approximately the same size, with a uniform style of building and facilities. The corporation charges a franchise fee, which is a percentage of sales, for use of the company name, the building and facilities design, and advertising advice.

The Akron, Ohio unit was selected to test the budget program. Its performance for the year just ended, compared to the typical budget, is as follows:

Pearsons Restaurant—Deli, Akron, Ohio
Income Statement for the Year Ended December 31, 19--

	Actual Restaurant	Actual Delicatessen	Total	Budget	Over (Under) Budget
Sales........................	$2,000,000	$1,200,000	$3,200,000	$3,500,000	$(300,000)
Purchases	$ 800,000	$ 780,000	$1,580,000	$1,600,000	$ (20,000)
Hourly wages................	700,000	60,000	760,000	925,000	(165,000)
Franchise fee.................	60,000	36,000	96,000	105,000	(9,000)
Advertising..................	200,000	100,000	300,000	300,000	—
Utilities......................	100,000	76,000	176,000	195,000	(19,000)
Depreciation	75,000	50,000	125,000	125,000	—
Lease expense	50,000	30,000	80,000	80,000	—
Salaries......................	50,000	30,000	80,000	80,000	—
Total	$2,035,000	$1,162,000	$3,197,000	$3,410,000	$(213,000)
Income before income tax	$ (35,000)	$ 38,000	$ 3,000	$ 90,000	$ (87,000)

A review of the report and a discussion of its meaning by Pearsons' management led to the conclusion that a more meaningful comparison would result if a flexible budget analysis for each of the two lines were performed.

Required:
(1) Prepare an income statement for the Akron unit's deli line, comparing actual performance to a flexible budget.
(2) Discuss whether or not a complete report, comparing the performance of each of the two lines to its flexible budget, would make Akron's operating problems easier to identify.
(3) What are the advantages of comparing actual performance to a flexible budget as a part of the regular annual as well as monthly reporting system? (CMA adapted)

16-2. **Flexible budget; overhead rate.** The controller of Oakhill Corporation decided to prepare a flexible factory overhead budget ranging from 80% to 100% of capacity for the next year, with 50,000 hours as the 100% level. The data available are based on either past experiences, shop supervisors' figures, or management's decisions. For expenses of a semivariable nature, the fixed amount and the variable rate are determined via the high and low points method. The direct labor rate is $7.50 per hour. Additional data for factory overhead are:

Annual fixed expenses:

Depreciation	$ 9,000
Insurance	1,500
Maintenance cost (including pay-roll taxes and fringe benefits)	24,000
Property tax	1,500
Supervisory staff (including pay-roll taxes and fringe benefits)	36,000

Variable expenses:

Shop supplies	$.10 per direct labor hour
Indirect labor (excluding inspection)	$.45 per direct labor hour
Payroll taxes and fringe benefits	18% of labor cost, direct and indirect

Semivariable expenses (from previous five years):

Year	Direct Labor Hours	Power and Light	Inspection (Including Payroll Taxes and Fringe Benefits)	Other Semi-Variable Expenses
19A	44,000	$1,500	$ 9,200	$8,000
19B	40,000	1,400	9,000	7,400
19C	45,000	1,600	9,200	8,200
19D	49,000	1,650	10,000	8,800
19E	50,000	1,700	10,200	8,900

Required

(1) Prepare a flexible factory overhead budget ranging from 80% to 100% of capacity, with 10% intervals.
(2) Compute the total factory overhead rate, variable cost rate, and fixed cost rate for 100% of capacity. (Round off to two decimal places.)

16-3. Flexible budget. Department A, one of 15 departments in the manufacturing plant, is involved in the production of all of the six products manufactured by Augustin Products Inc. Because Department A is highly mechanized, its output is measured in direct machine hours. Flexible budgets are utilized throughout the plant in planning and controlling costs, but this problem's focus is upon the application of flexible budgets in Department A only.

On March 15, 19A, the following flexible budget was approved for Department A to be used throughout the fiscal year 19A–B, beginning on July 1, 19A. This flexible budget was developed through the cooperative efforts of Department A's manager, the supervisor, and members of the Budget Department.

Flexible Budget for Department A
For Fiscal Year 19A–B

Controllable Costs	Fixed Amount per Month	Variable Rate per Direct Machine Hour
Employees' salaries	$ 9,000	
Indirect wages	18,000	$.07
Indirect materials		.09
Other costs	6,000	.03
Total	$33,000	$.19

On May 5, 19A, the annual sales plan and the production budget were completed. To continue preparation of the annual profit plan, which was detailed by month, the production budget was translated to planned activity for each of the 15 departments. The planned activity for Department A was:

	July	August	September	October–June	For Twelve Months Ending June 30, 19B
Planned output in direct machine hours...........	22,000	25,000	29,000	249,000	325,000

On August 31, 19A, Department A's manager was informed that the planned September output had been revised to 34,000 direct machine hours. On September 30, 19A, Department A's accounting records showed the following actual data for September:

Actual output in direct machine hours	33,000
Actual controllable costs incurred:	
Employees' salaries.......................................	$ 9,300
Indirect wages	20,500
Indirect materials...	2,850
Other costs	7,510
Total	$40,160

The following requirements relate primarily to the potential uses of the flexible budget for the period March through September, 19A.

Required:
(1) Explain how the range of the activity base to which the variable rates per direct machine hour are relevant should be determined.
(2) Illustrate the application of the high and low points method of determining the fixed and variable components of indirect wage costs for Department A. Assume that the high and low values for indirect wages are $19,400 at 20,000 direct machine hours and $20,100 at 30,000 direct machine hours.
(3) Explain and illustrate the use of the flexible budget in:
   (a) Budgeting costs when the annual sales plan and production budget are completed (about May 5, 19A, or shortly thereafter).
   (b) Budgeting a cost revision based upon a revised production budget (about August 31, 19A, or shortly thereafter).
   (c) Preparing a cost performance report for September, 19A.   (AICPA adapted)

16-4. Cost behavior analysis; standard error of the estimate; correlation analysis. The following data have been collected by the controller of Wilson Corporation over the past 10 months:

Month	Maintenance Expense	Machine Hours
January.......................	$ 2,200	25,000
February	2,150	23,500
March........................	2,000	20,000
April.........................	2,150	24,000
May..........................	2,050	21,000
June	2,200	26,000
July..........................	2,150	24,500
August.......................	2,250	25,500
September....................	2,300	27,000
October	2,150	24,500
Total	$21,600	241,000

Required:

(1) Using the high and low points method, determine the average amount of fixed maintenance expense per month and the variable maintenance rate per machine hour.
(2) Determine the fixed expense and the variable expense rate, using the method of least squares.
(3) Determine the 95% confidence interval for maintenance expense at the 25,000 machine hour level of activity.
(4) Compute the coefficient of correlation, r, and the coefficient of determination, r^2, between the machine hours and the maintenance expense.

16-5. Cost behavior analysis; standard error of the estimate; correlation analysis. The management of the Roberts Hotel is interested in an analysis of the fixed and variable costs in the electricity used relative to hotel occupancy. The following data have been gathered from records for the year:

	Guest Days	Electricity Cost
January...............	1,000	$ 400
February	1,500	500
March................	2,500	500
April.................	3,000	700
May..................	2,500	600
June	4,500	800
July..................	6,500	1,000
August...............	6,000	900
September............	5,500	900
October	3,000	700
November............	2,500	600
December	3,500	800
Year total...........	42,000	$8,400

Required:

(1) Determine the fixed and variable elements of the electricity cost, using (a) the method of least squares, (b) the high and low points method, and (c) a scattergraph with trend line fitted by inspection. (Round off the variable rate to four decimal places.)
(2) What other elements, besides occupancy, might affect the amount of electricity used in any one month?
(3) Compute the standard error of the estimate.
(4) Compute the 90% confidence interval for electricity expense at the 2,000 guest days capacity.
(5) Compute the coefficient of correlation, r, and the coefficient of determination, r^2, for guest days and electricity expense.

16-6. Cost behavior analysis; standard error of the estimate; correlation analysis. A company making tubing from aluminum billets uses a process in which the billets are heated by induction to a very high temperature before being put through an extruding machine that shapes the tubing from the billets. The inducer, a very large coil into which the billet is placed, must sustain a great flow of current to heat the billets to the desired temperature. Regardless of the number of billets to be processed, the coil is kept on during the entire operating day because of the time involved in starting it up. The Cost Department wants to charge the variable electricity cost to each billet and the fixed electricity cost to factory overhead. The following data have been assembled:

Month	Number of Billets	Cost of Electricity	Month	Number of Billets	Cost of Electricity
January.............	2,000	$400	July	1,400	$340
February	1,800	380	August	1,900	390
March..............	1,900	390	September	1,800	380
April................	2,200	420	October..............	2,400	440
May................	2,100	410	November	2,300	430
June	2,000	400	December............	2,200	420

Required:
(1) Provide a fixed-variable expense analysis using the method of least squares.
(2) Prepare a graph indicating the results calculated.
(3) Compute the standard error of the estimate and the 95% confidence interval for electricity expense at the 2,200 billets level of activity.
(4) Compute the coefficient of correlation, r, and the coefficient of determination, r^2.

16-7. Cost behavior analysis; standard error of the estimate; correlation analysis. Randal Company manufactures a wide range of electrical products at several different plant locations. Due to fluctuations, its Franklin plant has been experiencing difficulties in estimating the level of monthly overhead.

Management needs more accurate estimates to plan its operational and financial needs. A trade association publication indicates that for companies like Randal, overhead tends to vary with direct labor hours. Based on this information, one member of the accounting staff proposes that the overhead cost behavior pattern be determined in order to calculate the overhead cost in relation to budgeted direct labor hours. Another member of the accounting staff suggests that a good starting place for determining the cost behavior pattern of the overhead cost would be an analysis of historical data to provide a basis for estimating future overhead costs.

Direct labor hours and the respective factory overhead costs for the past three years are as follows:

	19A Direct Labor Hours	19A Factory Overhead Costs	19B Direct Labor Hours	19B Factory Overhead Costs	19C Direct Labor Hours	19C Factory Overhead Costs
January...................	2,000	$8,500	2,100	$8,700	2,000	$8,600
February	2,400	9,900	2,300	9,300	2,300	9,300
March...................	2,200	8,950	2,200	9,300	2,300	9,400
April....................	2,300	9,000	2,200	8,700	2,200	8,700
May.....................	2,000	8,150	2,000	8,000	2,000	8,100
June	1,900	7,550	1,800	7,650	1,800	7,600
July	1,400	7,050	1,200	6,750	1,300	7,000
August..................	1,000	6,450	1,300	7,100	1,200	6,900
September...............	1,200	6,900	1,500	7,350	1,300	7,100
October	1,700	7,500	1,700	7,250	1,800	7,500
November...............	1,600	7,150	1,500	7,100	1,500	7,000
December	1,900	7,800	1,800	7,500	1,900	7,600

Required:
(1) Compute the amount of fixed factory overhead and the variable cost rate, using the method of least squares. (Round fixed factory overhead to the nearest dollar and the variable cost rate to the nearest cent.)
(2) Compute the standard error of the estimate. (Round to the nearest dollar.)

(continued)

(3) Compute the 95% confidence interval for factory overhead costs at the 2,200 direct labor hour level of activity. (Assume that the sample size is sufficiently large that the standard normal probability distribution can be assumed and that the correction factor for small samples can be omitted. Round to the nearest dollar.)
(4) Compute the coefficient of correlation, r, and the coefficient of determination, r^2, for factory overhead costs and direct labor hours. (Round to four decimal places.)

16-8. Choosing appropriate activity measure; cost behavior analysis. The controller of Quality Products Corporation has asked for help in the selection of the appropriate activity measure to be used in estimating variable supplies expense for the company's flexible budget. The following information about past expenses and two potential activity measures has been supplied:

Month	Supplies Expense	Direct Labor Hours	Machine Hours
January	$ 1,500	3,900	2,100
February	1,400	4,200	2,000
March	1,600	4,200	2,100
April	1,550	3,950	2,000
May	1,450	3,800	1,950
June	1,450	3,900	2,000
July	1,500	4,200	2,050
August	1,550	4,300	2,100
September	1,650	4,250	2,400
October	1,550	4,300	2,300
Total	$15,200	41,000	21,000

Required:
(1) Compute the coefficient of correlation, r, and the coefficient of determination, r^2, between supplies expense and each of the two activity measures.
(2) Which of the two activity measures above should be used as a basis upon which to estimate the allowable supplies expense?
(3) Using the activity measure selected in requirement (2) above, determine the fixed expense and the variable expense rate by the method of least squares.

16-9. Correlation analysis. The Cost Department of Honska Supply Company attempts to establish a flexible budget to assist in the control of marketing expenses. An examination of individual expenses shows:

Item	Fixed Portion	Variable Portion
Sales staff:		
Salaries	$1,200	none
Retainers	2,000	none
Commissions	none	4% on sales values
Advertising	5,000	none
Travel expense	?	?

Statistical analysis is needed to split the travel expense satisfactorily into its fixed and variable portions. Before beginning such an analysis, it is thought that the variable portion of the travel expense might vary in accordance either with the number of calls made on customers each month or the value of orders received each month. Records reveal the following details over the past twelve months:

Month	Calls Made	Orders Received	Travel Expense
January..............	410	$53,000	$3,000
February	420	65,000	3,200
March..............	380	48,000	2,800
April...............	460	73,000	3,400
May................	430	62,000	3,100
June	450	67,000	3,200
July	390	60,000	2,900
August..............	470	76,000	3,300
September...........	480	82,000	3,500
October	490	62,000	3,400
November...........	440	64,000	3,200
December	460	80,000	3,400

Required:
(1) Compute the coefficient of correlation, r, and coefficient of determination, r^2, between (a) the travel expense and the number of calls made and (b) the travel expense and orders received. (Round off to four decimal places.)
(2) Compare the answers obtained in (1a) and (1b).

CASES

A. Cost behavior analysis using method of least squares. Alma Company's plant management wishes to develop a flexible budget formula to use in estimating factory overhead which can be expected to be incurred at various activity levels. The formula is to be developed using the method of least squares. Sufficient evidence is available to conclude that factory overhead varies with direct labor hours, and monthly data for the last three years were provided from plant records.

The three-year period contained various occurrences not uncommon to many businesses. During the first year, production was severely curtailed for two months because of wildcat strikes. In the second year, production was reduced in one month because of material shortages and materially increased (overtime scheduled) during two months to meet the units required for a one-time sales order. At the end of the second year, employee benefits were raised significantly as the result of a labor agreement. Production during the third year was not affected by any special circumstances.

Various members of Alma's staff raised some issues regarding the historical data collected for the cost behavior analysis.

(a) Some believed that the use of data from all 36 months would provide a more accurate portrayal of cost behavior. While they recognized that any of the monthly data could include efficiencies and inefficiencies, they believed these efficiencies and inefficiencies would tend to balance out over a longer period of time.
(b) Others suggested that only those months which were considered normal should be used, so that the analysis would not be distorted.
(c) Still others felt that only the most recent 12 months should be used, because they were the most relevant.

(d) Some questioned whether historical data should be used at all to form the basis for a flexible budget formula.

The Accounting Department ran two methods of least squares analyses of the data—one using the data from all 36 months and the other using only the data from the last 12 months. The following information was derived:

	Data from All 36 Months	Data from Most Recent 12 Months
Coefficients:		
Fixed cost	$123,810	$109,020
Variable rate	$ 1.6003	$ 4.1977
Coefficient of correlation	.4710	.6891
Standard error of the estimate	$ 13,003	$ 7,473

Required:
(1) From the analysis that used data from all 36 months, determine:
    (a) The flexible budget formula to use in estimating monthly factory overhead.
    (b) The factory overhead estimate when 25,000 direct labor hours are worked.
(2) Select the analysis results (36 months vs. 12 months) to be preferred as a basis for cost behavior estimation.
(3) Comment on the four specific issues raised by members of Alma's staff.

(CMA adapted)

B. Regression and correlation analysis—utility and implementation. Naomi McCarty, controller of Arkansas Distribution Company, is responsible for development and administration of the company's internal information system as well as the coordination of the company's budget preparation.

At a meeting with Don Tuma, the vice-president, McCarty proposed that the company employ regression analysis (the least-squares method) and correlation analysis as a standard part of its internal information system relating to sales and expenses. She felt that such analyses, including projections, would be significant decision-making aids.

Tuma admitted that he had forgotten the exact mechanics of regression and correlation analysis. However, he did comment that:

(a) Regression and correlation calculations for weekly or monthly amounts would involve enormous numbers of calculations because the company's budget and control system uses weekly amounts for sales and some expenses and monthly amounts for other expenses.

(b) A great deal of caution must be exercised when relying on predictions calculated by regression analysis techniques.

McCarty agreed that a large number of calculations would be required, but felt that this problem might be overcome by computerizing the analysis. The computerized analysis would have to suit the company's budget and control system and cover all significant sales and expense accounts, of which there are about 100.

The company's computer is not large and operates only with card and magnetic tape input/output. No standard computer programs are available for this kind of analysis. Therefore, a program must be specially written, its accompanying data gathered, and the processing problems solved.

To pursue her idea, McCarty decided to obtain sample data regarding sales and related selling expenses for the past five years. Using regression analysis, she predicted sales of $30,500,000 for the coming year and calculated a coefficient of correlation of .4 between sales and the selling expenses.

Required:
   (1) What are the advantages and limitations of using regression and correlation analysis according to McCarty?
   (2) Identify those matters that should be considered before the regression analysis is made, based on the sample data collected.
   (3) Provide an outline of the programming and operating problems that might be encountered if the analysis is computerized using the available computer.

(CICA adapted)

C. Cost behavior analysis; standard error of the estimate; correlation analysis. A company's cost department has compiled weekly records of production volume (in units), electric power used, and direct labor hours employed. The range of output for which the following statistics were computed is from 500 to 2,000 units per week:

Electric power:
   $y = 1,000 + .4x$, where y is electric power and x is units of production
   Standard error of the estimate: 100
   Coefficient of correlation: .45

Direct labor:
   $y = 100 + 1.2x$, where y is direct labor hours and x is units of production
   Standard error of the estimate: 300
   Coefficient of correlation: .70

Required:
   (1) Compute the best estimate of the additional number of required direct labor hours, if production for the next period should be 500 units greater than production in this period.
   (2) Comment on the reliability of the above equations for estimating electric power and direct labor requirements, together with the necessary assumptions if the estimating equations are to be used to predict future requirements. An interpretation of the standard error of the estimate and the coefficient of correlation should be included.

(CGAA adapted)

Chapter 17
Standard Costing:
Setting of Standards and
Analysis of Variances

A *standard cost* is the predetermined cost of manufacturing a single unit or a number of product units during a specific period in the immediate future. It is the planned cost of a product under current and/or anticipated operating conditions.

A standard cost has two components: a standard and a cost. A standard is like a norm and whatever is considered normal can generally be accepted as standard. For example, if a score of 72 is the standard for a golf course, a golfer's score is judged on the basis of this standard. In industry, the standards for making a desk, assembling a radio, refining crude oil, or manufacturing railway cars are based on carefully determined quantitative and qualitative measurements and engineering methods. A standard must be thought of as a norm in terms of specific items, such as pounds of materials, hours of labor required, and percentage of plant capacity to be used. In many firms, a standard can be operative for a long time. A change is needed only when production methods or the products themselves have become obsolete or undesirable.

Purposes of Standard Costs

Standard cost systems aid in planning and controlling operations and in gaining insights into the probable impact of managerial decisions on cost levels and profits. Standard costs are used for:

1. Establishing budgets.
2. Controlling costs and motivating and measuring efficiencies.
3. Promoting possible cost reduction.
4. Simplifying costing procedures and expediting cost reports.
5. Assigning costs to materials, work in process, and finished goods inventories.
6. Forming the basis for establishing bids and contracts and for setting sales prices.

The effectiveness of controlling costs depends greatly upon a knowledge of expected costs. Standards serve as measurements which call attention to cost variations. Executives and supervisors become cost-conscious as they become aware of results. This cost-consciousness tends to reduce costs and encourages economies in all phases of the business.

The use of standard costs for accounting purposes simplifies costing procedures through the reduction of clerical labor and expense. A complete standard cost system is usually accompanied by standardization of productive operations. Standard production or manufacturing orders, calling for standard quantities of product and specific labor operations, can be prepared in advance of actual production. Materials requisitions, labor time tickets, and operation cards can be prepared in advance of production, and standard costs can be compiled. As orders for a part are placed in the shop, previously established requirements, processes, and costs will apply. The more standardized the production, the simpler the clerical effort. Reports can be systematized to present complete information regarding standards, actual costs, and variances. Reports that are integrated and tied in with the financial accounts through journal entries are discussed in Chapter 18.

A complete standard cost file by parts and operations simplifies assigning costs to materials, work in process, and finished goods inventories. The use of standard costs stabilizes the influence of materials costs. Placing bids, securing contracts, and establishing sales prices are greatly enhanced by the availability of reliable standards and the continuous review of standard costs.

The standard cost system may be used in connection with either the process or job order cost accumulation method. However, it is more often used in process costing because it is more practical to set standards for a continuous flow of like units than for unique job orders.

Comparison of Budgets and Standards

The budget is one method of securing reliable and prompt information regarding the operation and control of an enterprise. When manufacturing budgets are based on standards for materials, labor, and factory overhead, a strong team for possible control and reduction of costs is created.

Standards are almost indispensable in establishing a budget. Because both standards and budgets aim at the same objective — managerial control — it is often felt that the two are the same and cannot function independently. This opinion is supported by the fact that both use predetermined costs for the coming period. Both budgets and standard costs make it possible to prepare reports which compare actual costs and predetermined costs for management.

Building budgets without the use of standard cost figures can never lead to a real budgetary control system. The figures used in the illustrations in the budget chapters are only fair estimates, even though they have been set with great care and the cooperation of those responsible. Under such conditions, the budget can hardly be considered the basis against which actual results are to be measured. This shortcoming is recognized by adding the flexible budget as a refinement. With the use of standard costs, the preparation of budgets for any volume and mixture of products is more reliably and speedily accomplished, and a budget becomes a summary of standards for items of cost, because a budget refers to total dollars while a standard is set on a unit basis.

The principal difference between budgets and standard costs lies in their scope. The budget, as a statement of expected costs, acts as a guidepost which keeps the business on a charted course. Standards, on the other hand, do not tell what costs are expected to be, but rather what they will be if certain performances are achieved. A budget emphasizes the volume of business and the cost level which should be maintained if the firm is to operate as desired. Standards stress the level to which costs should be reduced. If costs reach this level, profits will be increased.

Standard Costs and Variances

Calculation of a standard cost is based on physical standards, two types of which are often discussed: basic and current. A *basic standard* is a yardstick against which both expected and actual performances are compared. It is similar to an index number against which all later results are measured. *Current standards* are of three types:

1. The *expected actual standard* is a standard set for an expected level of operation and efficiency. It is a reasonably close estimate of actual results.
2. The *normal standard* is a standard set for a normal level of operation and efficiency, intended to represent challenging yet attainable results.
3. The *theoretical standard* is a standard set for an ideal or maximum level of operation and efficiency. Such standards constitute goals to be aimed for rather than performances that can be currently achieved.

Materials and labor costs are generally based on normal, current conditions, allowing for alterations of prices and rates and tempered by the desired efficiency level. Factory overhead is based on normal conditions of efficiency and volume.

Standards must be established for a definite period of time to be effective in the control and analysis of costs. Standards are usually computed for a six- or twelve-month period, although a longer period is sometimes used.

The success of a standard cost system depends on the reliability, accuracy, and acceptance of the standards. Extreme care must be taken to be sure that all factors are considered in the establishment of standards. In certain cases, samplings of averages derived from the records of previous periods are used as standards. However, the most effective standards are set by the industrial engineering department on the basis of careful studies of products and operations, using appropriate sampling techniques and including participation by those individuals whose performance is to be measured by the standards.

Standards must be set, and the system implemented, in an atmosphere that gives full consideration to behavior characteristics of managers and workers. In the long run, workers and plant management will tend to react negatively if they feel threatened by imposed standards. If they participate in setting standards, they can more readily identify with the standard costing procedure and the standards could become their personal goals.

Standards which are too loose or too tight will generally have a negative impact on worker motivation. If standards are too loose, workers will tend to set their goals at this low rate, thus reducing productivity below what is obtainable. If the standard is too tight, workers realize the impossibility of attaining the standard, become frustrated, and will not attempt to meet the standard. A reasonable standard which can be attained under normal working conditions is likely to contribute to the worker's motivation to achieve the designated level of activity or productivity.

Once standards are set, it is important to provide the proper standard cost cards, on which the itemized cost of each materials part, labor operation, and overhead cost is shown. A master standard cost card, illustrated as follows, gives the standard unit cost of a product.

Date of Standard July 1, 19--			STANDARD COST CARD FOR PRODUCT Alpac						
DIRECT MATERIALS	ITEM CODE	QUAN-TITY	STANDARD UNIT PRICE	DEPARTMENT					TOTALS
				1	2	3	4	5	
	2–234	4	$6.00/pc.		$24.00				
	3–671	24	3.00/doz.			$6.00			
	5–489	2	2.50/pc.					$ 5.00	
	5–361	8	6.50/pc.					52.00	
			TOTAL DIRECT MATERIALS COST						$ 87.00
DIRECT LABOR	OPERA-TION NUMBER	STANDARD HOURS	STANDARD RATE PER HOUR	DEPARTMENT					
				1	2	3	4	5	
	2–476	3	$9.00		$27.00				
	2–581	11½	9.40		108.10				
	3–218	4	9.30			$37.20			
	5–420	2½	9.20					$23.00	
			TOTAL DIRECT LABOR COST						195.30
FACTORY OVERHEAD	STANDARD HOURS	RATE PER DIRECT LABOR HOUR		DEPARTMENT					
				1	2	3	4	5	
	14½	$4.80			$69.60				
	4	2.00				$8.00			
	2½	3.50						$8.75	
		TOTAL FACTORY OVERHEAD							86.35
		TOTAL MANUFACTURING COST PER UNIT							$368.65

Standard Cost Card

The master standard cost card is supported by individual cards that indicate how the standard cost was compiled and computed. Each subcost card represents a form of standard cost card.

For each direct material, labor operation, and for departmentalized factory overhead, actual costs are measured against standard costs, resulting in differences. These differences are analyzed and identified as specific types of variances.

If actual cost exceeds standard cost, the cost variance is labeled "unfavorable" because the excess has an unfavorable effect on income. Conversely, if standard cost exceeds actual cost, the cost variance is labeled "favorable" because it has a favorable effect on income. But the analysis does not end with such labeling. The variance is the question, not the answer. The reasons for the variances must be determined and appropriate management action taken, if the desired cost control is to occur.

Materials Cost Standards

Two standards must be developed for direct materials costs:

1. A materials price standard.
2. A materials quantity (or usage) standard.

Materials Price Standard and Variance

Price standards permit (1) checking the performance of the purchasing department and the influence of various internal and external factors and (2) measuring the effect of price increases or decreases on the company's profits. Determining the price or cost to be used as the standard cost is often difficult, because the prices used are controlled more by external factors than by a company's management. Prices selected should reflect current market prices and are generally used throughout the forthcoming fiscal period.

If the actual price paid is more or less than the standard price, a price variance occurs. Price increases or decreases occurring during the fiscal period are recorded in the materials price variance account(s). Price standards are revised at inventory dates or whenever there is a major change in the market price of any of the principal materials or parts.

To illustrate the computation of a price variance, assume that 5,000 pieces of Item 5-489 on the standard cost card for Alpac (page 471) are purchased at a unit price of $2.47. The *materials purchase price variance* is computed as follows:

	Pieces	×	Unit Cost	=	Amount
Actual quantity purchased	5,000		$2.47 actual		$12,350
Actual quantity purchased	5,000		2.50 standard		12,500
Materials purchase price variance	5,000		$ (.03)		$ (150) fav.

The $150 materials purchase price variance is favorable because the actual price is less than the standard price, and $.03 expresses the unit cost difference. As an alternative, the materials purchase price variance can be recognized when the materials are used rather than when they are purchased and is then called the *materials price usage variance* (Chapter 18).

Materials Quantity Standard and Variance

Quantity or usage standards are generally developed from materials specifications prepared by the departments of engineering (mechanical, electrical, or chemical) or product design. In a small or medium-size company, the superintendent or even the foremen will provide basic specifications regarding type, quantity, and quality of materials needed and operations to be performed.

Quantity standards should be set after the most economical size, shape, and quality of the product and the results expected from the use of various kinds and grades of materials have been analyzed. The standard quantity should be increased to include allowances for acceptable levels of waste, spoilage, shrinkage, seepage, evaporation, and leakage. The determination of the percentage of spoilage or waste should be based on figures that prevail after the experimental and developmental stages of the product have been passed.

The *materials quantity variance* is computed by comparing the actual quantity of materials used with the standard quantity allowed, both priced at standard cost. The standard quantity allowed is determined by multiplying the quantity of materials that should be required to produce one unit (the standard quantity per unit) times the actual number of units produced during the period. The units produced are the equivalent units of production for the materials cost being analyzed.

The materials quantity (or usage) variance for Item 5-489, of which 3,550 pieces are used in producing 1,750 equivalent units of Alpac, is computed as follows:

	Pieces	×	Unit Cost	=	Amount
Actual quantity used	3,550		$2.50 standard		$8,875
Standard quantity allowed	3,500		2.50 standard		8,750
Materials quantity variance.	50		2.50 standard		$ 125 unfav.

The standard quantity allowed is the result of multiplying 1,750 units of Alpac by the standard quantity of two pieces per unit. The $125 materials quantity (or usage) variance is unfavorable because the actual quantity used exceeded the standard quantity by 50 units.

Labor Cost Standards

Two standards must also be developed for direct labor costs:

1. A rate (wage or cost) standard.
2. An efficiency (time or usage) standard.

Labor Rate Standard and Variance

In many plants, the standard is based on rates established in collective bargaining agreements that define hourly wages, piece rates, and bonus differentials. Without a union contract, rates are based on the earnings rate as determined by agreement between the employee and the personnel department. Since rates are generally based on definite agreements, labor rate variances are not too frequent. If they occur, they are generally due to unusual short-term conditions existing in the factory.

To assure fairness in rates paid for each operation performed, job rating has become a recognized procedure in industry. When a rate is revised or a change is authorized temporarily, it must be reported promptly to the payroll department to avoid delays, incorrect pay, and faulty reporting. Any difference between the standard and actual rates results in a *labor rate* (wage or cost) *variance*.

To illustrate the computation of the labor rate variance for Operation 2-476 on the standard cost card for Alpac (page 471), assume that 1,880 hours are worked at a rate of $9.50 per hour to produce 530 equivalent units of Alpac. The labor rate variance is computed as follows:

	Time	×	Rate	=	Amount
Actual hours worked	1,880		$9.50 actual		$17,860
Actual hours worked	1,880		9.00 standard		16,920
Labor rate variance	1,880		$ .50		$ 940 unfav.

The labor rate variance of $940 is unfavorable. The difference in terms of the rate is $.50 per hour.

Labor Efficiency Standard and Variance

Determination of labor efficiency standards is a specialized function. Therefore, they are usually established by industrial engineers, using time and motion studies. Standards are set in accordance with scientific methods and accepted practices. They are based on actual performance of a worker or group of workers possessing average skill and using average effort while performing manual operations or working on machines operating under normal conditions. Time factors for acceptable levels of fatigue, personal needs, and delays beyond the control of the worker are studied and included in the standard. Such allowances are an integral part of the labor standard, but time required for setting up machines, waiting, or a breakdown is included in the factory overhead standard.

The establishment of time standards requires a detailed study of manufacturing operations. Standards based on operations should be understood by supervisors and used to enhance labor efficiency. However, time standards are of limited use "where operating times are strongly influenced by factors which cannot be standardized and controlled by management or where output from highly mechanized work is a function of machine time and speed rather than of labor hours worked."[1]

When a new product or process is started, the labor efficiency standard for costing and budget development should be based on the learning curve phenomenon (Chapter 12). The learning curve may well be, at least in part, an explanation of the labor efficiency variance associated with employees assigned to existing tasks that are new to them. Labor-related factory overhead costs and perhaps materials usage might also be affected.

The *labor efficiency variance* is computed at the end of any reporting period (day, week, or month) by comparing actual hours worked with standard hours allowed, both at the standard labor rate. The standard hours allowed figure is determined by multiplying the number of direct labor hours established or predetermined to produce one unit (the standard labor hours per unit) times the actual number of units produced during the period for which the variances are being computed. The units produced are the equivalent units of production for the labor cost being analyzed.

The labor efficiency variance for Operation 2-476 is computed as follows:

	Time	×	Rate	=	Amount
Actual hours worked	1,880		$9.00 standard		$16,920
Standard hours allowed	1,590		9.00 standard		14,310
Labor efficiency variance	290		9.00 standard		$ 2,610 unfav.

The standard hours allowed is the result of multiplying 530 units of Alpac by three standard hours per unit. The unfavorable labor efficiency variance of $2,610 is due to the use of 290 hours in excess of standard hours allowed.

Factory Overhead Cost Standards

Procedures for establishing and using standard factory overhead rates are similar to the methods discussed in Chapters 7 and 8, dealing with the estimated direct and indirect factory overhead and its application to jobs and products. An overhead budget for rate calculation provides a budget allowance for a specific, predetermined level of activity, while a flexible budget provides allowances for various levels of activity. Both types of budgets aim for the control of factory overhead. Control is achieved by keeping actual expenses within ranges established by the budget. The maximum limit of a range is the amount set up in the flexible budget. However, for costing jobs or products it is necessary to establish a normal overhead rate based on total estimated factory overhead at normal capacity volume.

The effect of volume on overhead cost per unit is illustrated as follows:

[1]Walter B. McFarland, *Manpower Cost and Performance Measurement* (New York: National Association of Accountants, 1977), p. 60.

Production volume (units)	80,000	90,000	100,000	110,000
Factory overhead:				
Variable	$112,000	$126,000	$140,000	$154,000
Fixed	60,000	60,000	60,000	60,000
Total	$172,000	$186,000	$200,000	$214,000
Factory overhead per unit:				
Variable	$1.40	$1.400	$1.40	$1.400
Fixed	.75	.667	.60	.545
Total unit overhead cost	$2.15	$2.067	$2.00	$1.945

The illustration indicates the basic pattern of overhead behavior. Fixed expenses remain fixed, within the relevant range of activity, as volume (output) changes, but they vary per unit. The greater the number of units, the smaller the amount of fixed overhead expense per unit. Variable expenses, on the other hand, increase proportionately with each increase of volume (output) and remain fixed per unit within the relevant range.

This characteristic of overhead behavior is important in establishing a standard factory overhead rate. Overhead absorption is accomplished by selecting a plant capacity as the base for charging variable and fixed overhead to jobs or products.

With the aid of a flexible budget, the supervisors should measure and control variable expenses at any volume. The variable expenses in the flexible budget correspond to applied variable overhead, and *variable overhead variances* result from a comparison of actual variable costs with the flexible budget (applied) variable factory overhead.

Fixed expenses can be absorbed fully only by operating at the volume on which the rate is based. If the base set for overhead absorption is reached, budgeted and absorbed cost figures will be identical. Since this is highly improbable, a difference occurs between budgeted fixed expenses and absorbed fixed overhead, and *fixed overhead variances* result from an analysis of this difference. For purposes of analysis, budgeted fixed overhead is used. Any difference that might occur between budgeted and actual fixed overhead becomes a part of the variable overhead variances (i.e., the spending or controllable variance) in the methods of analysis presented in this chapter. Alternatively, this difference can be identified as a separate variance, called the *fixed spending variance*.

The variances associated with variable and fixed factory overhead permit management to measure the success or failure of its control of overhead and utilization of facilities.

The Standard Factory Overhead Rate

The *standard factory overhead rate* is a predetermined rate that is usually based on direct labor hours. Other bases may also be used, e.g., direct labor dollars or machine hours. The use of direct labor dollars, however, may cause some distortion in the variances computed, because the actual direct labor dollar figure includes any labor rate variations from the standard labor rate.

The data from the following flexible budget for Department 3, which is involved in producing Alpac, are used to illustrate the computation of the standard overhead rate and the overhead variances.

DEPARTMENT 3
MONTHLY FLEXIBLE BUDGET

	80%	90%	100%	
Capacity..........................	80%	90%	100%	
Standard production	800	1,000	1,200	
Direct labor hours.................	3,200	4,000	4,800	
Variable factory overhead:				
Indirect labor....................	$1,600	$2,000	$2,400	$ .50 per dlh
Indirect materials	960	1,200	1,440	.30
Supplies........................	640	800	960	.20
Repairs.........................	480	600	720	.15
Power and light.................	160	200	240	.05
Total variable factory overhead	$3,840	$4,800	$5,760	$1.20 per dlh
Fixed factory overhead:				
Supervisor......................	$1,200	$1,200	$1,200	
Depreciation of machinery	700	700	700	
Insurance.......................	250	250	250	
Property tax.....................	250	250	250	
Power and light.................	400	400	400	
Maintenance	400	400	400	
Total fixed factory overhead.......	$3,200	$3,200	$3,200	
Total factory overhead.............	$7,040	$8,000	$8,960	$3,200 per month + $1.20 per dlh

Assuming that the 90% column represents normal capacity, the standard factory overhead rate is computed as follows:

$$\frac{\text{Total factory overhead}}{\text{Direct labor hours}} = \frac{\$8,000}{4,000} = \$2 \text{ per standard direct labor hour}$$

At the 90% capacity level, the rate consists of:

$$\frac{\text{Total variable factory overhead}}{\text{Direct labor hours}} = \frac{\$4,800}{4,000} = \$1.20 \text{ variable factory overhead rate}$$

$$\frac{\text{Total fixed factory overhead}}{\text{Direct labor hours}} = \frac{\$3,200}{4,000} = \underline{\quad .80} \text{ fixed factory overhead rate}$$

Total factory overhead rate at normal
  capacity........................... $2.00 per standard direct labor hour

Factory Overhead Variances

Jobs or processes are charged with costs on the basis of standard hours allowed multiplied by the standard factory overhead rate. The standard hours allowed figure is determined by multiplying the labor hours required to produce one unit (the standard labor hours per unit) times the actual number of units produced during the period. The units produced are the equivalent units of production for the departmental factory overhead cost being analyzed. At the end of each month, overhead actually incurred is compared with the expenses charged into process using the standard factory overhead rate. The difference between these two figures is called the *overall* (or *net*) *factory overhead variance*.

At the end of a month, the data for Department 3 are as follows:

```
Actual overhead ..............................................    $7,384
Standard hours allowed for actual production....................   3,400 hours*
Actual hours used ............................................    3,475 hours
```

*850 equivalent units produced × 4 standard direct labor hours per unit of production.

The overall factory overhead variance is computed as follows:

```
Actual departmental overhead ..................................    $7,384
Overhead charged to production (3,400 standard hours allowed
   × $2 standard overhead rate) ...............................     6,800
Overall (or net) overhead variance.............................    $  584  unfav.
```

This unfavorable overall overhead variance needs further analysis to reveal detailed causes for the variance and to guide management toward remedial action. This analysis may be made by using (1) the two-variance method, (2) the three-variance method, or (3) the four-variance method.

Two-Variance Method. The two variances are the (1) controllable variance and (2) volume variance. The *controllable variance* is the difference between actual overhead incurred and the budget allowance based on standard hours allowed for work performed. The *volume variance* represents the difference between the budget allowance and the standard overhead charged to work in process (standard hours allowed × standard overhead rate).

Controllable Variance. The controllable variance is the responsibility of the department managers to the extent that they can exercise control over the costs to which the variances relate. Part of the controllable variance consists of variable overhead, and part consists of any difference between budgeted and actual fixed overhead. The controllable variance is usually computed as follows:

```
Actual factory overhead ...............................              $7,384
Budget allowance based on standard hours allowed:
   Fixed overhead budgeted...........................    $3,200
   Variable overhead (3,400 standard hours allowed ×
      $1.20 variable overhead rate) ..................     4,080     7,280
Controllable variance..................................              $  104  unfav.
```

Volume Variance. The volume variance indicates the cost of capacity available but not utilized or not utilized efficiently and is considered the responsibility of executive and departmental management. It is computed as follows:

```
Budget allowance based on standard hours allowed .................   $7,280
Overhead charged to production..................................     6,800
Volume variance.................................................    $  480  unfav.
```

This variance consists of fixed overhead only and can also be computed as follows:

Normal capacity hours	4,000
Standard hours allowed for actual production	3,400
Capacity hours not utilized, or not utilized efficiently	600
Volume variance (600 hours × $.80*)	$ 480 unfav.

*Fixed overhead rate at normal capacity.

Three-Variance Method. The three variances are the (1) spending variance, (2) idle capacity variance, and (3) efficiency variance. The *spending variance* is the difference between actual overhead incurred and the budget allowance based on actual hours worked. The *idle capacity variance* is the difference between the budget allowance based on actual hours and actual hours worked multiplied by the standard overhead rate. These two variances are identical with the spending and idle capacity variances discussed in Chapters 7 and 8. The *efficiency variance* is the difference between actual hours worked multiplied by the standard overhead rate and the standard hours allowed times the standard overhead rate.

Spending Variance. The spending variance is the responsibility of the department manager, who is expected to keep actual expenses within the budget. Part of the spending variance consists of variable overhead and part consists of any difference between budgeted and actual fixed overhead. The spending variance is usually computed as follows:

Actual factory overhead		$7,384
Budget allowance based on actual hours worked:		
Fixed overhead budgeted	$3,200	
Variable overhead (3,475 actual hours × $1.20 variable overhead rate)	4,170	7,370
Spending variance		$ 14 unfav.

By basing the budget allowance on actual hours instead of on standard hours allowed, as shown in the controllable variance, the department manager receives a more favorable allowance, which reduces the variance from $104 to $14. This reduction is caused by the influence of efficiency (or, in this case, inefficiency), which is identified separately as the variable expense portion of the efficiency variance.

Idle Capacity Variance. The idle capacity variance is the responsibility of executive management, and is computed as follows:

Budget allowance based on actual hours worked	$7,370
Actual hours (3,475) × standard overhead rate ($2)	6,950
Idle capacity variance	$ 420 unfav.

This variance consists of fixed overhead only and can also be computed as follows: (4,000 normal capacity hours − 3,475 actual hours) × $.80 fixed overhead rate = $420. It indicates the amount of overhead that is either under-

or overabsorbed because actual hours are either less or more than the hours on which the overhead rate was based. Department 3 operated at 86.875% of normal capacity based on actual hours.

Efficiency Variance. The efficiency variance is the responsibility of department management and is caused by inefficiencies, inexperienced labor, changes in operations, new tools, and different types of materials. It is computed as follows:

Actual hours (3,475) × standard overhead rate ($2)	$6,950
Overhead charged to production..................................	6,800
Efficiency variance..	$ 150 unfav.

This variance can also be computed as follows: (3,475 actual hours − 3,400 standard hours allowed) × $2 = $150. It consists of both fixed and variable overhead and results when actual hours used are more or less than standard hours allowed. When labor hours are the basis for applying factory overhead, this variance and its cause reflect the effect of the labor efficiency variance on factory overhead. When machine hours are the basis, the variance relates to efficiency of machine usage.

Four-Variance Method. The four variances — (1) spending variance, (2) variable efficiency variance, (3) fixed efficiency variance, and (4) idle capacity variance — add to the three-variance method an analysis which divides the efficiency variance into its fixed and variable components.

Spending Variance. The spending variance is identical with that of the three-variance method and is computed as follows:

Actual factory overhead	$7,384
Budget allowance based on actual hours worked....................	7,370
Spending variance..	$ 14 unfav.

Variable Efficiency Variance. The variable efficiency variance is computed as follows:

Budget allowance based on actual hours worked....................	$7,370
Budget allowance based on standard hours allowed	7,280
Variable efficiency variance	$ 90 unfav.

This variance recognizes the difference between the 3,475 actual hours worked and the 3,400 standard (or allowed) hours for the work performed. Multiplying the difference of 75 hours times $1.20 (variable overhead rate) results in $90. The sum of the spending and variable efficiency variances equals the controllable variance, $104, of the two-variance method.

Fixed Efficiency Variance. The fixed efficiency variance is computed as follows:

Actual hours (3,475) × fixed overhead rate ($.80)	$2,780
Standard hours allowed (3,400) × fixed overhead rate ($.80)	2,720
Fixed efficiency variance (75 hours × $.80)........................	$ 60 unfav.

When the variable efficiency variance and the fixed efficiency variance are combined, they equal the efficiency variance of the three-variance method.

Idle Capacity Variance. This variance is identical with the idle capacity variance of the three-variance method and represents the idle or unused capacity, i.e., the difference between budgeted (normal) capacity and actual capacity. It is computed as follows:

Normal capacity hours (4,000) × fixed overhead rate ($.80)	$3,200
Actual hours worked (3,475) × fixed overhead rate ($.80)	2,780
Idle capacity variance (525 hours × $.80)	$ 420 unfav.

The fixed efficiency variance and the idle capacity variance are split-offs of the $480 unfavorable volume variance of the two-variance method, which was computed by multiplying the 600 hours not utilized by the $.80 fixed overhead rate. The fixed efficiency variance indicates how effectively or ineffectively available capacity was used, while the idle capacity variance informs management that 525 hours otherwise available and expected to be used, costing $420 in terms of fixed expense, remained idle during the month.

Summary. Although all methods of factory overhead variance analysis are commonly used, the two-variance method seems to be favored. It should be noted that at times the methods are intermingled, are given different titles, and involve additional analyses. A summary of the three methods described in this chapter is given on pages 482 and 483.

Reconciling from the four-variance method, the spending and variable efficiency variances combine to equal the controllable variance, and the fixed efficiency and idle capacity variances combine to equal the volume variance of the two-variance method. The spending and idle capacity variances are the same as for the three-variance method, with the variable and fixed efficiency variances combined to equal the efficiency variance of the three-variance method. There are other ways that the four variances might be combined to equal either two or three variances. For example, some companies use a three-variance method that combines the fixed efficiency and idle capacity variances to equal the volume variance and show the spending and variable efficiency variances separately. Furthermore, as earlier noted, any portion of the spending or controllable variance representing a difference in budgeted and actual fixed factory overhead may be isolated separately and labeled as the fixed spending variance.

Mix and Yield Variances

Basically, the establishment of a standard product cost requires the determination of price and quantity standards. In many industries, particularly of the process type, materials mix and materials yield play significant parts in the final product cost, in cost reduction, and in profit improvement.

| | | | SUMMARY OF FACTORY OVERHEAD | |
Method	(1) Actual Factory Overhead	(2) Budget Allowance for Factory Overhead (Actual Hours Worked)	(3) Budget Allowance for Factory Overhead (Standard Hours Allowed)	(4) Actual Hours × Standard Overhead Rate*
Two- Variance Method	$7,384		$7,280	
Three- Variance Method	$7,384	$7,370		$6,950
Four- Variance Method	$7,384	$7,370	$7,280	$6,950

*3,475 actual hours worked × $2 standard factory overhead rate.

Materials specification standards are generally set up for various grades of materials and types of secondary materials. In most cases, specifications are based on laboratory or engineering tests. Comparative costs of various grades of materials are used to arrive at a satisfactory materials mix, and changes are often made when it seems possible to use less costly grades of materials or substitute materials. In addition, a substantial cost reduction might be achieved through the improvement of the yield of good product units in the factory. At times, trade offs may occur; e.g., a cost saving resulting from use of a less costly grade of materials may result in a poorer yield, or vice versa. A variance analysis program identifying and evaluating the nature, magnitude, and causes of mix and yield variances is an aid to operating management.

Mix Variance

After the standard specification has been established, a variance representing the difference between the standard cost of formula materials and the standard cost of the materials actually used can be calculated. This variance is generally recognized as a *mix* (or *blend*) *variance*, which is the result of mixing basic materials in a ratio different from standard materials specifications. In a woolen mill, for instance, the standard proportions of the grades of wool for each yarn number are reflected in the standard blend cost. Any difference

VARIANCE ANALYSIS METHODS

(5) Factory Overhead Charged to Production**	Variances for Each Method		Overall (or Net) Factory Overhead Variance (Unfavorable)
$6,800	Controllable variance (Col. 1–Col. 3.)	$104 ⎫	$584
	Volume variance (Col. 3–Col. 5)	$480 ⎭	
$6,800	Spending variance (Col. 1–Col. 2)	$ 14 ⎫	$584
	Idle capacity variance (Col. 2–Col. 4)	$420 ⎬	
	Efficiency variance (Col. 4–Col. 5)	$150 ⎭	
$6,800	Spending variance (Col. 1–Col. 2)	$ 14 ⎫	$584
	Variable efficiency variance (Col. 2–Col. 3) . .	$ 90 ⎪	
	Fixed efficiency variance***	$ 60 ⎬	
	Idle capacity variance****	$420 ⎭	

**3,400 standard hours allowed × $2 standard factory overhead rate.
***(3,475 actual hours worked − 3,400 standard hours allowed) × $.80 fixed factory overhead rate.
****(4,000 normal capacity hours − 3,475 actual hours worked) × $.80 fixed factory overhead rate. This variance can also be computed by subtracting Column 4 from Column 2.

between the actual wool used and the standard blend results in a blend or mix variance.

Industries like textiles, rubber, and chemicals, whose products must possess certain chemical or physical qualities, find it quite feasible and economical to apply different combinations of basic materials and still achieve a perfect product. In cotton fabrics, it is common to mix cotton from many parts of the world with the hope that the new mix and its cost will contribute to improved profits. In many cases, the new mix is accompanied by either a favorable or unfavorable yield of the final product. Such a situation may make it difficult to judge correctly the origin of the variances. A favorable mix variance, for instance, may be offset by an unfavorable yield variance, or vice versa. Thus, any apparent advantage created by one may be canceled out by the other.

Yield Variance

Yield can be defined as the amount of prime product manufactured from a given amount of materials. The *yield variance* is the result of obtaining a yield different from the one expected on the basis of input.

In sugar refining, a normal loss of yield develops because, on the average, it takes approximately 102.5 pounds of sucrose in raw sugar form to produce 100 pounds of sucrose in refined sugars. Part of this sucrose emerges as black-strap molasses, but a small percentage is completely lost.

In the canning industry, it is customary to estimate the expected yield of grades per ton of fruit purchases or delivered to the plant. The actual yield should be compared to the one expected and should be evaluated in terms of cost. If the actual yield deviates from predetermined percentages, cost and profit will differ.

Since the final product cost contains not only materials but also labor and factory overhead, a yield variance for labor and factory overhead should be determined when the product is finished. The actual quantities resulting from the processes are multiplied by the standard cost, which includes all three cost elements. A labor yield variance must be looked upon as the result of the quality and/or quantity of the materials handled, while the factory overhead yield variance is due to the greater or smaller number of hours worked. It should be noted that the overhead yield variance may have a significant effect on the amount of over- or underabsorbed factory overhead.

Illustration of Variances

To illustrate the calculation of mix and yield variances, assume that the Springmint Company, a manufacturer of chewing gum, uses a standard cost system. Standard product and cost specifications for 1,000 lbs. of chewing gum are as follows:

Material	Quantity	×	Unit Cost	=	Amount
A	800		$.25 per lb.		$200
B	200		.40		80
C	200		.10		20
Input	1,200 lbs.				$300; $300 ÷ 1,200 lbs. = $.25 per lb.*
Output. . . .	1,000 lbs.				$300; $300 ÷ 1,000 lbs. = $.30 per lb.*

*Weighted averages.

The production of 1,000 lbs. of chewing gum requires 1,200 lbs. of raw materials. Hence, the expected yield is 1,000 lbs. ÷ 1,200 lbs., or ⅚ of input. Materials records indicate:

Material	Beginning Inventory	Purchases in January	Ending Inventory
A.	10,000 lbs.	162,000 lbs. @ $.24	15,000 lbs.
B.	12,000	30,000 @ .42	4,000
C.	15,000	32,000 @ .11	11,000

To convert 1,200 lbs. of raw materials into 1,000 lbs. of finished product requires 20 direct labor hours at $9 per hour, or $.18 per lb. of finished product. Actual direct labor hours and cost for January are 3,800 hours at $34,656.

Factory overhead is applied on a direct labor hour basis at a rate of $5 per hour ($3 fixed, $2 variable), or $.10 per lb. of finished product. Normal overhead is $20,000, with 4,000 direct labor hours. Actual overhead for the month is $22,000. Actual finished production for January is 200,000 lbs.

The standard cost per pound of finished chewing gum is:

Materials..............................	$.30 per lb.	
Labor....................................	.18	
Factory overhead	.10	
	$.58 per lb.	

Materials Variances. The materials variances for January consist of (1) price variances, (2) a mix variance, (3) a yield variance, and (4) quantity variances. The company computes the materials price variances as follows, using the procedure illustrated on page 472, and recognizes these variances when the materials are purchased.

Material	Quantity	Actual Cost	Standard Cost	Unit Cost Variation	Price Variance
A...............	162,000	$.24	$.25	$(.01)	$(1,620)
B...............	30,000	.42	.40	.02	600
C...............	32,000	.11	.10	.01	320
Net materials purchase price variance.............................					$ (700) fav.

The materials mix variance results from combining materials in a ratio different from the standard materials specifications. It is computed as follows:

Actual quantities at individual standard materials costs:

A............	157,000 lbs. @ $.25		$39,250	
B............	38,000	@ $.40	15,200	
C............	36,000	@ $.10	3,600	$58,050
	231,000 lbs.			

Actual quantity at weighted average of standard materials cost input (231,000 lbs. × $.25)		57,750*
Materials mix variance		$ 300 unfav.

*This figure can also be determined by multiplying the standard (expected) output from actual input (192,500 lbs., or ⅚ of 231,000 lbs.) by $.30 weighted average of standard materials cost output.

The influence of individual raw materials on the total materials mix variance can be computed in the following manner:

Material	Actual Quantity	Standard Formula	×	Total Actual Quantity	=	Actual Quantity Using Standard Formula	Quantity Variation	×	Standard Unit Cost	=	Materials Mix Variance
A.............	157,000 lbs.	$\frac{800}{1,200}$		231,000 lbs.		154,000 lbs.	3,000 lbs.		$.25		$750
B.............	38,000	$\frac{200}{1,200}$		231,000		38,500	(500)		.40		(200)
C.............	36,000	$\frac{200}{1,200}$		231,000		38,500	(2,500)		.10		(250)
	231,000 lbs.					231,000 lbs.	-0-				$300

The yield variance is computed as follows:

Actual quantity at weighted average of standard materials cost................		$57,750
Actual output quantity at weighted average of standard materials cost (200,000 lbs. × $.30)		60,000*
Materials yield variance		$ (2,250) fav.

*This figure can also be determined by multiplying the input needed to produce 200,000 lbs. (240,000 lbs.) by $.25.

The yield variance occurred because the actual production of 200,000 lbs. exceeded the expected output of 192,500 lbs. (⅚ of 231,000 lbs.) by 7,500 lbs. The yield difference multiplied by the standard weighted materials cost of $.30 per output pound equals the favorable yield variance of $2,250.

The materials quantity variance can be computed for each item as follows, using the procedure illustrated on page 473:

Material	Unit	×	Standard Unit Cost	=	Amount	Materials Quantity Variance
A: Actual quantity used	157,000 lbs.		$.25		$39,250	
Standard quantity allowed	160,000 lbs.*		.25		40,000	$ (750) fav.
B: Actual quantity used	38,000 lbs.		$.40		$15,200	
Standard quantity allowed	40,000 lbs.**		.40		16,000	(800) fav.
C: Actual quantity used	36,000 lbs.		$.10		$ 3,600	
Standard quantity allowed	40,000 lbs.***		.10		4,000	(400) fav.
Total materials quantity variance						$(1,950) fav.

*An output of 200,000 lbs. should require an input of 240,000 lbs., with a standard yield of 1,000 lbs. output for each 1,200 lbs. input. Then the 240,000 lbs. × (800 lbs. ÷ 1,200 lbs.) Material A portion of the formula = 160,000 lbs.
**The 240,000 lbs. × (200 lbs. ÷ 1,200 lbs.) Material B portion of the formula = 40,000 lbs.
***The 240,000 lbs. × (200 lbs. ÷ 1,200 lbs.) Material C portion of the formula = 40,000 lbs.

The total materials quantity variance can also be determined by comparing actual quantities at standard prices, $58,050 ($39,250 + $15,200 + $3,600), to actual output quantity at the weighted average of standard materials cost, $60,000 (200,000 lbs. × $.30) for a total favorable variance of $1,950. The mix and yield variances separate the materials quantity variance into two parts:

Materials mix variance	$ 300 unfav.
Materials yield variance	(2,250) fav.
Materials quantity variance	$(1,950) fav.

Labor Variances. The expected output of 192,500 lbs. of chewing gum should require 3,850 standard labor hours (20 hours per thousand pounds of chewing gum produced). Similarly, the actual output of 200,000 lbs. of chewing gum should require 4,000 standard labor hours.

The labor variances are the (1) rate variance, (2) efficiency variance, and (3) yield variance. The computation of these variances for January is as follows:

Actual payroll	$34,656
Actual hours (3,800) × standard labor rate ($9)	34,200
Labor rate variance	$ 456 unfav.

Actual hours × standard labor rate	$34,200
Standard hours allowed for expected output (3,850) × standard labor rate ($9)	34,650
Labor efficiency variance	$ (450) fav.

Standard hours allowed for expected output × standard labor rate	$34,650
Standard hours allowed for actual output (4,000) × standard labor rate ($9)	36,000
Labor yield variance	$ (1,350) fav.

The labor rate variance is computed as shown on page 474. The traditional labor efficiency variance, as illustrated on page 475, is computed as follows:

	Time ×	Standard Rate =	Amount
Actual hours worked......................	3,800	$9	$34,200
Standard hours allowed....................	4,000	9	36,000
Labor efficiency variance..................	(200)	9	$(1,800) fav.

The labor yield variance identifies the portion of the labor efficiency variance attributable to obtaining an unfavorable or, as in this illustration, a favorable yield [(3,850 standard hours allowed for expected output − 4,000 standard hours allowed for actual output) × $9 standard labor rate = $1,350]. The favorable labor efficiency variance of $450 is the portion of the traditional labor efficiency variance that is attributable to factors other than yield. The sum of the two variances, $1,350 plus $450, equals the $1,800 traditional labor efficiency variance. When a standard mix of labor skills or classes is called for, mix and yield variances patterned after those computed for materials can be isolated.

Factory Overhead Variances. A yield variance can also be computed for factory overhead. When the three-variance method is used, the overhead variances consist of the (1) spending variance, (2) idle capacity variance, (3) efficiency variance, and (4) yield variance. These variances are computed as follows:

THREE-VARIANCE METHOD ADAPTED TO COMPUTE A YIELD VARIANCE

Actual factory overhead		$22,000
Budget allowance (based on actual hours):		
Fixed overhead budgeted.................................	$12,000	
Variable overhead (3,800 hours × $2)	7,600	19,600
Spending variance...		$ 2,400 unfav.
Budget allowance (based on actual hours)...............................		$19,600
Actual hours (3,800) × standard overhead rate ($5)		19,000
Idle capacity variance		$ 600 unfav.
Actual hours × standard overhead rate		$19,000
Standard hours allowed for expected output (3,850) × standard overhead rate ($5)...		19,250
Overhead efficiency variance		$ (250) fav.
Standard hours allowed for expected output × standard overhead rate		$19,250
Standard hours allowed for actual output (4,000) × standard overhead rate ($5)...		20,000
Overhead yield variance...		$ (750) fav.

The spending and idle capacity variances are computed in the same manner as discussed on page 479. The overhead efficiency variance and the overhead yield variance, when combined, equal the efficiency variance discussed earlier in this chapter. The overhead yield variance measures that portion of the total overhead variance resulting from a favorable yield [(3,850 hours − 4,000 hours) × $5 = $750].

When the two-variance method is used, the overhead variances are the (1) controllable variance, (2) volume variance, and (3) yield variance. These variances are computed as follows:

TWO-VARIANCE METHOD ADAPTED TO COMPUTE A YIELD VARIANCE

Actual factory overhead		$22,000
Budget allowance (based on standard hours allowed for expected output):		
Fixed overhead budgeted.	$12,000	
Variable overhead (3,850 hours × $2)	7,700	19,700
Controllable variance.		$ 2,300 unfav.
Budget allowance (based on standard hours allowed for expected output). . . .		$19,700
Standard hours allowed for expected output (3,850) × standard overhead		
rate ($5).		19,250
Overhead volume variance		$ 450 unfav.
Standard hours allowed for expected output × standard overhead rate		$19,250
Standard hours allowed for actual output (4,000) × standard overhead		
rate ($5).		20,000
Overhead yield variance.		$ (750) fav.

The $2,300 unfavorable controllable variance equals the unfavorable spending variance, $2,400, combined with the $100 variable part of the favorable overhead efficiency variance [(3,800 hours − 3,850 hours) × $2]. The $450 unfavorable overhead volume variance equals the unfavorable idle capacity variance, $600, combined with the $150 fixed part of the favorable overhead efficiency variance [(3,800 hours − 3,850 hours) × $3].

The favorable overhead yield variance is the same as for the three-variance method and can be viewed as consisting of $300 variable cost [(3,850 standard hours allowed for expected output − 4,000 standard hours allowed for actual output) × $2], and $450 fixed cost [(3,850 − 4,000) × $3].

Managerial Usefulness of Variance Analysis

Costs of production are affected by internal factors over which management has a large degree of control. An important job of executive management is to help the members of various management levels understand that all of them are part of the management team. Standard costs and their variances are an aid to keeping management informed of the effectiveness of production effort as well as that of the supervisory personnel.

Supervisors who often handle two thirds to three fourths of the dollar cost of the product are made directly responsible for the variances which, as the chapter discussion indicates, show up as materials variances (price, quantity, mix, and yield) or as direct labor variances (rate and efficiency). Materials and labor variances can be computed for each materials item, for each labor operation, and for each worker. Factory overhead variances (spending, controllable, idle capacity, volume, and efficiency) indicate the failures or successes of the control of variable and fixed overhead expenses in each department.

Variances are not ends in themselves but springboards for further analysis, investigation, and action. Variances also permit the supervisory personnel to defend themselves and their employees against failures that were not their fault. A variance provides the yardstick to measure the fairness of the standard, allowing management to redirect its effort and to make reasonable adjustments. Action to eliminate the causes of undesirable variances and to encourage and reward desired performance lies in the field of management, but supervisory and operating personnel rely on the accounting information system for facts which facilitate intelligent action toward the control of costs.

DISCUSSION QUESTIONS

1. (a) Define standard costs.
   (b) Name some advantages of a standard cost system.

2. A team of management consultants and company executives concluded that a standard cost installation was a desirable vehicle for accomplishing the objectives of a progressive management. State some uses of standard costs that can be associated with the above decision.

3. Does a standard cost system increase or decrease the amount of accounting and clerical effort and expense required to prepare cost reports and financial statements?

4. Explain how standards relate to job order and process cost accumulation procedures.

5. A conference speaker discussing budgeted and standard costs made the following statement: "Budgets and standards are not the same thing. They have different purposes and are set up and used in different ways; yet a specific relationship exists between them."
   (a) Identify distinctions or differences between budgets and standards.
   (b) Identify similarities between budgets and standards.

6. The use of standard costs in pricing and budgeting is quite valuable, since decisions in the fields of pricing and budgetary planning are made before the costs under consideration are incurred. Discuss.

7. Explain how materials, labor, and factory overhead standards are set, including the types of people involved and the methods used.

8. Standards are used by many concerns to generate data relevant to acquisition and utilization of component cost elements in a manufacturing process. Discuss.   (AICPA adapted)

9. Describe the two standards that must be developed for materials cost and how the variances (both favorable and unfavorable) from these standards are calculated. (Disregard mix and yield variances.)   (AICPA adapted)

10. Describe the two standards that must be developed for labor cost and how the two primary variances (both favorable and unfavorable) from these standards are calculated.
     (AICPA adapted)

11. In a paper mill, materials specification standards are set up for various grades of pulp and secondary furnish (waste paper) for each grade and kind of paper produced. Yet at regular intervals the cost accountant is able to determine a materials mix variance. Why does a mix variance occur?

12. How does the calculation of a mix variance differ from that of a quantity variance?

13. A cost standard in a process industry is often based on an assumed yield rate. Any difference in actual yield from standard yield will produce a yield variance. Express this variance in formula form.

EXERCISES

Whenever variances are required in the following exercises, indicate whether they are favorable or unfavorable.

1. **Materials variance analysis.** The standard price for Material 3-291 is $3.65 per liter. During November, 2 000 liters were purchased at $3.60 per liter. The quantity of Material 3-291 issued during the month was 1 775 liters and the quantity allowed for November production was 1 825 liters.

Required: Compute the materials price variance, assuming that:
(1) It is recorded at the time of purchase.
(2) It is recorded at the time of issue.

2. **Materials and labor variance analysis.** The following data pertain to the first week of June:

Materials:	Actual usage..................	1 100 meters at a cost of $1,320
	Standard usage	1 000 meters at a cost of $750
	Materials purchased	1 500 meters at a cost of $1,800
Direct labor:	Actual hours	600 hours at a cost of $5,700
	Standard hours.......................	500 hours at $9 per hour

Required:
(1) Compute the materials variances — price (when recognized at time of purchase and when recognized at time of usage) and quantity.
(2) Compute the labor variances — rate and efficiency.

3. **Factory overhead variance analysis.** The normal capacity of the Assembly Department is 16,000 machine hours per month. At normal capacity, the standard factory overhead rate is $2.25 per machine hour, consisting of $20,000 fixed expense and variable expense of $1 per machine hour. During April, the department operated at 15,000 machine hours, with actual factory overhead of $35,000. Standard machine hours allowed for the production attained is 14,800.

Required: Prepare an analysis of factory overhead by (a) the two-variance method and (b) the three-variance method.

4. **Factory overhead variance analysis.** Standard direct labor hours allowed for actual July production were 2,000, with factory overhead at that level budgeted at $10,000, of which $3,000 is variable.

Actual labor hours were 100 less than the normal capacity hours. Standard hours allowed for actual July production were 150 more than actual hours. The controllable variance was $350 favorable.

Required: Compute factory overhead variances using the four-variance method.

5. Factory overhead variance analysis. Charlottesville Company has developed the following standard factory overhead costs, based on a capacity of 180,000 direct labor hours:

Standard cost per unit:

Variable portion......................	2 hours @ $3 = $ 6
Fixed portion..........................	2 hours @ $5 = 10
	$16

During April, 85,000 units were scheduled for production; however, only 80,000 units were actually produced. The following data relate to April:

(a) Actual direct labor cost incurred was $644,000 for 165,000 actual hours of work.
(b) Actual factory overhead incurred totaled $1,378,000—$518,000 variable and $860,000 fixed.
(c) All inventories are carried at standard cost.

Required: Prepare a factory overhead variance analysis using the three-variance method.
(CMA adapted)

6. Variance analysis: materials, labor, and factory overhead. Teltrob Company uses a standard cost system. Standard costs on a per unit basis for the company's main product, Jarnol, were set as follows:

Materials, 2 lbs. @ $3.33 per lb.	$ 6.66
Labor, 1½ hrs. @ $6 per hour....................................	9.00
Factory overhead (based on normal capacity of 5,000 units, 7,500 direct labor hours):	
Variable portion @ $.20 per hour............................ $ .30	
Fixed portion @ $.40 per hour .... .60	.90
Total standard cost per unit....................................	$16.56

Actual data for the month:

Materials purchases, 14,000 lbs. @ $3.30 per lb.
Production, 6,000 completed units requiring 12,500 lbs. of material
Actual labor hours, 8,950 hrs. @ $6 per hr.
Actual factory overhead, $5,120

Required: Prepare a variance analysis of (a) direct materials, (b) direct labor, and (c) factory overhead (two- and three-variance methods). The materials price variance is computed at the time that materials are purchased.

7. Equivalent production and standard costing variance analysis. Marshall Company uses a standard process costing system in accounting for costs in its one production department. Material A is added at the beginning of the process, and Material B when the units are 90% complete. Conversion costs are incurred uniformly throughout the process. Inspection takes place at the end of the process and spoilage is expected to be 5% of good output. The standard cost of abnormal spoilage is charged to a current period expense account. Normal capacity is 7,800 direct labor hours per month.

Standard cost per unit:

Material A: 4 gallons @ $1.20	$ 4.80
Material B: 2 square feet @ $.70..	1.40
Direct labor: 1 hour @ $11.50...	11.50
Variable factory overhead: 1 hour @ $1.80	1.80
Fixed factory overhead: 1 hour @ $5.00.................................	5.00
Total	$24.50

Actual data for January:

(a) *Beginning work in process inventory—3,000 units (33⅓% converted).*
(b) *Started in process during the month—11,000 units.*
(c) *Finished during the month—8,000 units.*
(d) *Ending work in process inventory—5,000 units (40% converted).*
(e) *Actual costs incurred:*

Material A used	50,000 gallons @ $1.00
Material B used	18,000 sq. ft. @ $.75
Direct labor	10,200 hours @ $12.00
Factory overhead....................................	$60,100

Required:

(1) *Compute the January equivalent production for Material A, Material B, and for conversion costs.*
(2) *Compute two variances each for Material A, Material B, and direct labor, and three for factory overhead.* (CGAA adapted)

8. Price, mix, and yield variances. *The standard mix for producing 8,000 bottles of Product X is:*

Material A: 1 000 liters @ $.10
Material B: 2 000   @ $.40

During May, 10,000 bottles of Product X were produced from an input of:

Material A: 1 500 liters @ $.11
Material B: 3 300   @ $.37

Required: *Compute the materials price, mix, and yield variances for May.*

9. Price, mix, and yield variances. *Malmuta Company uses a standard cost system. The standard cost card for one of its products shows the following materials standards:*

Material	Pounds	×	Standard Cost per Pound	=	Amount
A	20		.70		$14
B	5		.40		2
C	25		.20		5
Total materials cost per unit................					$21

The standard 50 lb. mix cost per lb. is $.42 ($21 ÷ 50 lbs.). The standard mix should produce 40 lbs. of finished product, and the standard cost of finished product per lb. is $.525 ($21 ÷ 40 lbs.).

Materials of 500,000 lbs. were used as follows:

Material A	230,000 lbs. @ $.80
Material B	50,000 @ $.35
Material C	220,000 @ $.25

The output of the finished product was 390,000 lbs.

Required: *Prepare a product analysis showing materials price, mix, and yield variances.*

10. Price, mix, and yield variances. *The standard product mix for making 12,500 tubes of liquid solder is:*

Material A: 1 500 kilograms @ $.06	$ 90	
Material B: 625 @ .40	250	
Material C: 1 000 @ .25	250	

During April, 77,500 tubes of solder were produced from an input of:

Material A: 8 750 kilograms @ $.056	$ 490	
Material B: 3 750 @ .380	1,425	
Material C: 6 250 @ .280	1,750	

Required: *Compute the materials price, mix, and yield variances, including an analysis of the portion of the mix variance attributable to each material.*

PROBLEMS

Whenever variances are required in the following problems, indicate whether they are favorable or unfavorable.

17-1. Variance analysis: materials, labor, and factory overhead. Zeta Company has developed the following standard unit cost for its only product, Zay:

Direct materials	4 lbs. @ $3	$12
Direct labor	2 hrs. @ 9	18
Variable factory overhead	2 hrs. @ 2	4
Fixed factory overhead	2 hrs. @ 5	10
		$44

The company recognizes the materials price variance at the point of purchase. Fixed factory overhead budgeted is $120,000.

Actual activity for January included:

50,000 lbs. of direct materials were purchased for $149,000.
10,000 units of Zay were produced.
41,500 lbs. of direct materials were put into process.
The direct labor payroll was $196,560 (21,000 hrs. @ $9.36).
Actual factory overhead costs were $41,000 variable and $117,000 fixed.

Required: Compute two variances for each cost element.   (CGAA adapted)

17-2. Equivalent production and standard costing variance analysis. Melody Corporation produces a single product known as Jupiter. Melody uses the first-in, first-out process costing method for both financial statement and internal management reporting.

In analyzing production results, standard costs are used, whereas actual costs are used for financial statement reporting. The standards, which are based upon equivalent units of production, are as follows:

Raw materials per unit	1 pound at $10 per pound
Direct labor per unit	2 hours at $4 per hour
Factory overhead per unit	2 hours at $1.25 per hour

Budgeted factory overhead for standard hours allowed for April production is $30,000. Data for April are as follows:

(a) The beginning inventory consisted of 2,500 units which were 100% complete as to raw materials and 40% complete as to direct labor and factory overhead.

(b) An additional 10,000 units were started during the month.

(c) The ending inventory consisted of 2,000 units which were 100% complete as to raw materials and 40% complete as to direct labor and factory overhead.

(d) Costs applicable to April production are as follows:

	Actual Cost	Standard Cost
Raw materials used (11,000 pounds).....................	$121,000	$100,000
Direct labor (25,000 hours actually worked)..............	105,575	82,400
Factory overhead.....................................	31,930	25,750

Required:

(1) For each element of production for April (raw materials, direct labor, and factory overhead) compute the following:
   (a) Equivalent units of production
   (b) Cost per equivalent unit of production at actual and at standard.

(2) Prepare a schedule analyzing two variances for each cost element for April production. (AICPA adapted)

17-3. Equivalent production and standard costing variance analysis. The standard cost card for Torno Company's product is:

Materials: 7 liters @ $.50..	$3.50
Labor: ½ hr. @ $6.00	3.00
Variable factory overhead: ½ hr. @ $2.00..............................	1.00
Fixed factory overhead: ½ hr. @ $4.00	2.00
Standard product cost per unit	$9.50

Data for November:

(a) 1,000 units (40% converted) were in process at the beginning of the month.
   5,050 units were started during the month.
   5,000 units were transferred to finished goods.
   800 units (25% converted) were in process at the end of the month.

(b) Materials are all added at the beginning of the process. Conversion costs are incurred evenly throughout the process. Inspection takes place when the units are 80% converted. Under normal conditions, no spoilage should occur.

(c) 40 000 liters of materials were purchased for $19,200 and were charged to inventory at standard cost.

(d) 37 000 liters of materials were issued to production.

(e) Direct labor payroll was $15,600 for 2,400 hours.

(f) Actual factory overhead costs were:

Indirect labor (variable)		$ 4,000
Supervision...		4,000
Depreciation (based on time)		2,500
Supplies..		1,000
Heat, light, and power (variable)	$ 300	
(fixed)	1,200	1,500
Property tax		200
Insurance..		500
		$13,700

(g) Marketing and administrative expenses were: variable, $1 per unit sold; fixed, $13,500.

(h) Normal output for a month is 4,000 units.

Required:

(1) Compute the November equivalent production for materials and for conversion costs.

(2) Determine the standard cost of:
    (a) Units transferred to finished goods.
    (b) Abnormal spoilage, to be charged directly to a current period expense account.
    (c) Ending inventory of work in process.

(3) Compute the (a) materials price and quantity variances, (b) labor rate and efficiency variances, and (c) factory overhead variances, using the four-variance method.

(CGAA adapted)

17-4. Standard process costing: cost of production report at standard; variance analysis. Weissritter Company uses a standard process costing system in accounting for its one product, which is produced in one department. All materials are added at the beginning of the process. Inspection takes place at the end of the process. Any spoiled units revealed by inspection are considered abnormal and completed as to all cost elements, and the related standard cost is charged to a current period expense account.

Standard cost per unit:	
Materials: 3 square meters @ $.60	$1.80
Direct labor: ¼ hour @ $10.00	2.50
Variable factory overhead: ¼ hour @ $2.00	.50
Fixed factory overhead: ¼ hour @ $2.80	.70
Total	$5.50

Normal capacity is 8,750 direct labor hours per month.

Actual data for November:

(a) Beginning work in process inventory—5,000 units (40% converted).

(b) Started in process during the month—30,000 units.

(c) Spoiled during November—1,000 units.

(d) Ending work in process inventory—2,000 units (80% converted).

(e) Actual costs incurred:

Materials purchased	100 000 square meters @ $.64, recorded at standard cost
Materials used	92 000 square meters
Direct labor	8,000 hours @ $10.60
Variable factory overhead	$17,000
Fixed factory overhead	$25,000

Required:

(1) Prepare a cost of production report, at standard, for November.

(2) Compute two variances each for materials and direct labor and three for factory overhead.

(CGAA adapted)

17-5. Variance analysis: materials, labor, and factory overhead; job order costing. Vogue Fashions Inc. manufactures ladies' blouses of one quality, produced in lots to fill each special order from its customers, comprised of department stores located in various cities.

Vogue sews the particular stores' labels on the blouses. The standard costs for a dozen blouses are:

Direct materials	24 yards @ $1.10	$26.40
Direct labor.......................................	3 hours @ $4.90	14.70
Factory overhead..................................	3 hours @ $4.00	12.00
Standard cost per dozen		$53.10

During June, Vogue worked on three orders, for which the month's job cost records disclose the following:

Lot No.	Units in Lot (dozens)	Material Used (yards)	Hours Worked
22..................................	1,000	24,100	2,980
23..................................	1,700	40,440	5,130
24..................................	1,200	28,825	2,890

The following information is also available:

(a) Vogue purchased 95,000 yards of material during June at a cost of $106,400. The materials price variance is recorded when goods are purchased. All inventories are carried at standard cost.

(b) Direct labor during June amounted to $55,000. According to payroll records, production employees were paid $5 per hour.

(c) Factory overhead during June amounted to $45,600.

(d) A total of $576,000 was budgeted for factory overhead for 19A, based on estimated production at the plant's normal capacity of 48,000 dozen blouses annually. Factory overhead at this level of production is 40% fixed and 60% variable. Factory overhead is applied on the basis of direct labor hours.

(e) There was no work in process at June 1. During June, Lots 22 and 23 were completed. All material was issued for Lot 24, which was 80% completed as to direct labor.

Required:

(1) Prepare a schedule showing the computation of standard cost of Lots 22, 23, and 24 for June.

(2) Prepare a schedule showing the computation of the materials price variance for June.

(3) Prepare a schedule showing, for each lot produced during June, computations of the
   (a) Materials quantity variance.
   (b) Labor efficiency variance.
   (c) Labor rate variance.

(4) Prepare a schedule showing computations of the total controllable and volume factory overhead variances for June.   (AICPA adapted)

17-6. Price, mix, and yield variances. Chocolate manufacturing operations require close control of daily production and cost data. The computer printout for a batch of one ton of cocoa powder indicates the following materials standards:

Ingredients	Quantities (Pounds)	Unit Cost	Mix Cost
Cocoa beans	800	$.45	$ 360
Milk	3,700	.50	1,850
Sugar	500	.25	125
Total batch..................	5,000	$.467 (weighted average)	$2,335

On December 7, the company's Commodity Accounting and Analysis Section reported the following production and cost data for the December 6 operations:

Ingredients put in process:

Cocoa beans:	225,000 lbs. @ $.425	$ 95,625
Milk:	1,400,000 lbs. @ $.533	746,200
Sugar:	250,000 lbs. @ $.240	60,000
	1,875,000 lbs.	$901,825

Transferred to cocoa powder inventory: 387 tons. There was no work in process inventory.

Required: Compute the materials price, mix, and yield variances.

17-7. Mix and yield variances for direct labor. When a standard mix of labor skills or classes is called for, mix and yield variances patterned after those computed for materials can be isolated, as demonstrated by Landeau Company, which has a process cost accumulation system utilizing standard costs.

The standard direct labor rates in effect for the current year and the standard hours allowed for the output for April are shown in the following schedule:

	Standard Direct Labor Rate per Hour	Standard Direct Labor Hours Allowed for Output
Labor Class III	$8.00	500
Labor Class II	7.00	500
Labor Class I	5.00	500

The actual direct labor hours (DLH) worked and the actual direct labor rates per hour experienced for April were as follows:

	Actual Direct Labor Rate per Hour	Actual Direct Labor Hours
Labor Class III	$8.50	550
Labor Class II	7.50	650
Labor Class I	5.40	375

Required:

(1) Compute the rate and efficiency variances for each labor class.
(2) Compute the direct labor mix and yield variances. (Compute the weighted average standard DLH rate to five decimal places and round computed variances to nearest dollar.)   (CMA adapted)

17-8. Materials, labor, and overhead variances; mix and yield variances. Century Cement Company uses a standard cost system. Cement is produced by mixing two major components, A (lime) and B (clay), with water and by adding a third component, C, quantitatively insignificant.

Materials standards and costs for the production of 100 tons of output are:

	Tons	Cost	Percent of Input Quantity	Amount	
Material A	55	$43.00	50%	$2,365	
Material B	44	35.00	40	1,540	
Material C	11	25.00	10	275	
Input	110		100%	$4,180	= $38.00 per ton
Output	100			$4,180	= $41.80 per ton

The monthly factory overhead budget for a normal capacity level of 16,500 direct labor hours is as follows:

	Fixed Overhead	Variable Overhead
Plant manager	$ 2,000	
Supervisors............................	1,800	
Indirect labor	2,220	$ 810
Indirect supplies	850	2,040
Power and light.......................	300	2,200
Water	480	2,000
Repairs and maintenance	500	1,200
Insurance.............................	450	
Depreciation—production facilities	3,775	
Total	$12,375	$8,250

To convert 110 tons of materials into 100 tons of finished cement requires 500 direct labor hours at $7.50 per hour or $37.50 per ton. Factory overhead is applied on a direct labor hour basis.

In producing 3,234 tons of finished cement in April, the following costs were incurred:

Direct labor......................................	15,800 hrs. @ $7.95
Fixed factory overhead...........................	$11,075
Variable factory overhead	$ 8,490

	Materials Purchased		Materials Requisitioned
	Quantity	Cost per Ton	Quantity
Material A.................	2,000 tons	$44	1,870 tons
Material B	1,200	37	1,100
Material C................	500	24	440

There were no inventories of materials or work in process at the beginning of April. The materials price variance is recognized at the time of purchase.

Required:
(1) Compute the materials price, mix, and yield variances.
(2) Compute the direct labor rate, efficiency, and yield variances.
(3) Compute the factory overhead spending, idle capacity, efficiency, and yield variances.

17-9. Materials, labor, and overhead variances; mix and yield variances. Bowman Crunchies Inc. manufactures breakfast cereal, using the following proportion of ingredients:

	Quantity	Unit Cost	Amount
Wheat germ	25 lbs.	$2.00	$ 50
Barley..........................	100	1.00	100
Oats	125	.80	100
Input.........................	250 lbs.		$250 = $1.00 per lb.
Output........................	200 lbs.		$250 = $1.25 per lb.

Materials records for October indicate:

	Beginning Inventory	Purchases	Unit Cost	Ending Inventory
Wheat germ	2,000 lbs.	8,000 lbs.	$2.05 per lb.	1,200 lbs.
Barley....................	5,000	35,000	1.10	5,300
Oats	4,000	45,000	.75	7,000

The materials price variance is recognized when the materials are purchased.

The conversion of 250 pounds of materials into 200 pounds of finished product requires 25 direct labor hours at $8 per hour. The actual direct labor for the month was 8,000 hours and cost $64,800.

Factory overhead is applied on a direct labor hour basis at a rate of $3 per hour ($1 fixed, $2 variable). Normal capacity overhead is $30,000 with 10,000 direct labor hours. Actual overhead for October was $28,000. Actual finished production for the month was 70,000 pounds.

Required:
   (1) Compute the materials purchase price, mix, and yield variances and the materials quantity variance for each material.
   (2) Compute the labor rate, efficiency, and yield variances.
   (3) Compute the factory overhead (a) spending, idle capacity, efficiency, and yield variances, and (b) controllable, volume, and yield variances.

CASES

A. Motivation via standard costing. Kelly Company manufactures and sells pottery items. All manufacturing takes place in one plant, having four departments, with each department producing only one product. The four products are plaques, cups, vases, and plates. Sam Kelly, the president and founder, credits the company's success to well-designed, quality products and to an effective cost control system which was installed early in the firm's existence to improve cost control and to serve as a basis for planning.

With the participation of plant management, the company establishes standard costs for materials and labor. Each year, the plant manager, the department heads, and the time-study engineers are invited by executive management to recommend changes in the standards for the next year. Executive management reviews these recommendations and the records of actual performance for the current year before setting the new standards. As a general rule, tight standards representing very efficient performance are established, so that no inefficiency or slack will be included in cost goals. The plant manager and department heads are charged with cost control responsibility and the variances from standard costs are used to measure their performance in carrying out this charge.

No standards are set for factory overhead because management believes it is too difficult to predict and relate overhead to output. The actual factory overhead for the departments and the plant is accumulated in one "pool." The actual overhead is then allocated to the departments on the basis of departmental output.

The company's executives are convinced that more effective cost control can be obtained than is currently being realized from the standard cost system. A review of cost performance for recent years disclosed several factors that led them to this conclusion:
   (a) Unfavorable variances were the norm rather than the exception, although the size of the variances was quite uniform.
   (b) Employee motivation, especially among firstline supervisors, appeared to be low.

Required:
   (1) Identify the probable effects on motivation of plant managers and department heads resulting from:
      (a) The participative standard cost system.
      (b) The use of tight standards.   (continued)

(2) State the effect on the motivation of department heads to control overhead costs when actual factory overhead costs are applied on the basis of actual units.

(CMA adapted)

B. Factory overhead variance analysis. Stringfellow Company uses a standard cost system and budgets the following sales and costs for 19--:

Unit sales...	20,000
Sales...	$200,000
Total production cost at standard...................................	130,000
Gross profit...	70,000
Beginning inventories...	None
Ending inventories..	None

The 19-- budgeted sales level was the normal capacity level used in calculating the factory overhead predetermined standard cost rate per direct labor hour.

At the end of 19--, Stringfellow Company reported production and sales of 19,200 units. Total factory overhead incurred was exactly equal to budgeted factory overhead for the year and there was underapplied total factory overhead of $2,000 at December 31. Factory overhead is applied to the work in process inventory on the basis of standard direct labor hours allowed for units produced. Although there was a favorable labor efficiency variance, there was neither a labor rate variance nor materials variances for the year.

Required: Write an explanation of the underapplied factory overhead of $2,000, being as specific as the data permit and indicating the overhead variances affected. Stringfellow uses a three-variance method to analyze the total factory overhead.   (AICPA adapted)

Chapter 18
Standard Costing: Accumulating and Evaluating Costs and Variances

Some companies prefer to keep standard costs for statistical purposes only. However, the incorporation of standard costs into the regular accounting system permits the most efficient use of a standard cost system and leads to savings and increased accuracy in clerical work. In either case, variances can be analyzed for cost control, and standard costs can be used in developing budgets, bidding on contracts, and setting prices.

Standard Costing Methods

Standard costs should be viewed as costs which pass through the data processing system into financial statements. However, variations exist in the methods of accumulating these costs. Some systems employ the partial plan, others the single plan. Both plans center around the entries to the work in process account. Under either plan, the work in process account can be broken down by individual cost elements (materials, labor, and factory overhead) and/or by departments. The plans are summarized as follows:

Partial Plan		Single Plan	
Work in Process		*Work in Process*	
Actual cost	Standard cost	Standard cost	Standard cost

The Partial Plan

In the partial plan, the work in process account is debited for the actual cost of materials, labor, and factory overhead and is credited at standard cost when goods are completed and transferred to finished goods inventory. Any balance remaining in the work in process account consists of two elements: (1) the standard cost of work still in process and (2) the variances between actual and standard costs. To isolate these variances, additional analysis is needed.

The Single Plan

Since timely identification and reporting are major control features of standard cost accounting, prompt communication for very short time frames may be required. The single plan debits and credits the work in process account at standard costs only, and variances are recorded in separate variance accounts. These entries are periodic (often monthly) summaries of standard costs, actual costs, and resulting variances. They are discussed in detail in the following pages and are used in the exercises and problems of this chapter.

Standard Cost Accounting Procedures for Materials

The recording of materials purchased can be handled by three different methods:

1. *Record the price variance when materials are received and placed in stores.* The general ledger control account, Materials, is debited at standard cost and the materials ledger cards are kept in quantities only. A standard price is noted on the card when the standards are set. As purchases are made, no prices are recorded on these cards. This procedure results in clerical savings and speedier postings.
2. *Record the materials at actual cost when received, and determine the price variance when the materials are requisitioned for production.* The general ledger control account, Materials, is debited at actual cost and the materials ledger cards show quantities and dollar values as in a historical cost system.
3. *Use a combination of methods (1) and (2).* Calculate price variances when the materials are received, but defer charging them to production until the materials are actually placed in process. At that time, only the price variance applicable to the quantity used will appear as a current charge, the balance remaining as a part of the materials inventory. This method results in two types of materials price variances: (1) a materials purchase price variance originating when materials purchases are first recorded, and (2) a materials price usage variance when materials are used. The occurrence of the materials price usage variance is a reduction of the materials purchase price variance.

For control purposes, the price variance should be determined when the materials are received. If it is not computed and reported until the materials are requisitioned for production, then remedial action is difficult because the time of computation is so far removed from the time of purchase. Also, the problem of deciding which actual cost is applicable is again present.

These methods for recording materials purchased are illustrated below, using the following data for Item 5-489 (page 473):

Standard unit price as per standard cost card	$2.50
Purchases.	5,000 pieces @ $2.47
Requisitioned	3,550 pieces
Standard quantity allowed for actual production	3,500 pieces

Method 1

The journal entry when materials are received is:

Materials	12,500	
Accounts Payable		12,350
Materials Purchase Price Variance		150

When materials issued to the factory are recorded, the entry is:

Work in Process	8,750	
Materials Quantity Variance	125	
Materials		8,875

Method 2

When materials are received, no variance is computed and the entry is:

Materials	12,350	
Accounts Payable		12,350

When materials issued are recorded, the entry is:

Work in Process	8,750.00	
Materials Quantity Variance	125.00	
Materials		8,768.50
Materials Price Usage Variance		106.50

Computations for this entry are:

	Pieces	×	Unit Cost	=	Amount
Actual quantity used	3,550		$2.47 actual		$8,768.50
Actual quantity used	3,550		2.50 standard		8,875.00
Materials price usage variance	3,550		$ (.03)		$ (106.50) fav.

	Pieces	×	Unit Cost	=	Amount
Actual quantity used	3,550		$2.50 standard		$8,875.00
Standard quantity allowed	3,500		2.50 standard		8,750.00
Materials quantity variance.	50		2.50 standard		$ 125.00 unfav.

For this computation, the cost used is $2.47 per piece, since no other actual cost is available and no other purchases were made. In practice, the actual cost used would depend upon the type of inventory costing method employed, such as fifo, lifo, or average costing.

In this method, the materials price usage variance account appears on the books after the materials are issued, and then only for the quantity issued — not for the entire purchase. The price variance occurred because the materials were purchased at $.03 less than the standard price; the quantity variance, because 50 pieces were used in excess of the standard quantity allowed.

Method 3

The following entry, identical with the first entry in Method 1, would be made when the materials are received:

Materials	12,500	
Accounts Payable		12,350
Materials Purchase Price Variance		150

When the materials issued are recorded, two entries are made. The following entry, identical with the second entry in Method 1, recognizes the 50 pieces used beyond the standard quantity:

Work in Process	8,750	
Materials Quantity Variance	125	
Materials		8,875

The next entry transfers $106.50 from the purchase price variance account to the price usage variance account.

Materials Purchase Price Variance	106.50	
Materials Price Usage Variance		106.50

In Method 3, any balance remaining in the materials purchase price variance account at the end of the accounting period is used to adjust the inventory to actual cost. This balance is shown in the balance sheet as follows:

Materials (at standard cost)	$3,625.00
Less materials purchase price variance	43.50
Materials (adjusted to actual)	$3,581.50

Standard Cost Accounting Procedures for Labor

The payroll is computed on the basis of clock cards, job tickets, and other labor time information furnished to the payroll department. In a standard cost system, these basic records supply the data for the computation of labor variances.

The necessary journal entries are illustrated with the following data for Operation 2-476 (page 474):

Actual hours worked	1,880
Actual rate paid per hour	$9.50
Standard hours allowed for actual production	1,590
Standard rate per hour	$9.00

The following journal entry records the total actual direct labor payroll, assuming that there were no payroll deductions:

Payroll	17,860	
Accrued Payroll		17,860

To distribute the payroll and to set up the variance accounts, the journal entry is:

Work in Process	14,310	
Labor Rate Variance	940	
Labor Efficiency Variance	2,610	
Payroll		17,860

Standard Cost Accounting Procedures for Factory Overhead

The close relationship between standard costs and budgetary control methods is particularly important for the analysis of factory overhead. Actual factory overhead is measured not only against the applied overhead cost, but also against a budget based on actual and standard activity allowed for actual production.

The following data for Department 3 (page 478) are used to illustrate the journal entries for the two-variance, three-variance, and four-variance methods.

Normal capacity (in direct labor hours)		4,000 hours
Total factory overhead at normal capacity:		
Fixed	$3,200	
Variable	4,800	$8,000
Factory overhead rate per direct labor hour:		
Fixed	$ .80	
Variable	1.20	$2.00
Actual factory overhead		$7,384
Actual direct labor hours		3,475 hours
Standard hours allowed for actual production		3,400 hours

Two-Variance Method

The entry to record the actual factory overhead is:

Factory Overhead Control	7,384	
Various Credits		7,384

When overhead is applied to work in process:

Work in Process	6,800	
Factory Overhead Control		6,800

(If the applied factory overhead account is used, it is subsequently transferred to the factory overhead control account.)

The factory overhead control account now has a debit balance of $584, which can be analyzed and closed out as follows:

Factory Overhead Controllable Variance	104	
Factory Overhead Volume Variance	480	
Factory Overhead Control		584

Three-Variance Method

The entry to record the actual factory overhead is:

Factory Overhead Control	7,384	
Various Credits		7,384

When overhead is applied to work in process:

Work in Process	6,800	
Factory Overhead Efficiency Variance	150	
Factory Overhead Control		6,950

The factory overhead control account now has a debit balance of $434, which can be analyzed as to spending and idle capacity variances and closed as follows:

Factory Overhead Spending Variance	14	
Factory Overhead Idle Capacity Variance	420	
Factory Overhead Control		434

As an alternative, the second entry may be recorded as a debit to Work in Process and a credit to Factory Overhead Control for $6,800. The balance of $584 in Factory Overhead Control would then be closed as follows:

Factory Overhead Spending Variance	14	
Factory Overhead Efficiency Variance	150	
Factory Overhead Idle Capacity Variance	420	
Factory Overhead Control		584

Four-Variance Method

The entry to record the actual factory overhead is:

Factory Overhead Control	7,384	
Various Credits		7,384

When overhead is applied to work in process:

Work in Process	6,800	
Factory Overhead Variable Efficiency Variance	90	
Factory Overhead Fixed Efficiency Variance	60	
Factory Overhead Control		6,950

The factory overhead control account has a debit balance of $434, which can be analyzed as to spending and idle capacity variances and closed as follows:

Factory Overhead Spending Variance	14	
Factory Overhead Idle Capacity Variance	420	
Factory Overhead Control		434

As an alternative, the second entry may be recorded as a debit to Work in Process and a credit to Factory Overhead Control for $6,800. The balance of $584 in Factory Overhead Control would then be closed as follows:

Factory Overhead Spending Variance	14	
Factory Overhead Variable Efficiency Variance	90	
Factory Overhead Fixed Efficiency Variance	60	
Factory Overhead Idle Capacity Variance	420	
Factory Overhead Control		584

Standard Cost Accounting Procedures for Completed Products

The completion of production requires the transfer of cost from the work in process account of one department to the work in process account of another department, or, in the case of the last department, to the finished goods account. The cost transferred is the standard cost.

The journal entry for the transfer of finished products is as follows:

Finished Goods (at standard cost)	xxxx	
Work in Process (at standard cost)		xxxx

The finished goods ledger card will show quantities only, because the standard cost of the units remains the same during a period unless severe cost changes occur. When goods are shipped to customers, the entry is:

Cost of Goods Sold (at standard cost)	xxxx	
Finished Goods (at standard cost)		xxxx

Journal Entries for Mix and Yield Variances

The journal entries for the mix and yield variances computed in Chapter 17 are:

Materials

To record materials purchases:

Materials	55,700	
Accounts Payable		55,000
Materials Purchase Price Variance		700

To charge materials into production:

Work in Process	57,750	
Materials Mix Variance	300	
Materials		58,050

To transfer materials cost to finished goods:

Finished Goods	60,000	
Materials Yield Variance		2,250
Work in Process		57,750

Labor

To set up payroll liability:

Payroll	34,656	
Accrued Payroll		34,656

To transfer payroll to work in process and to isolate variances:

Work in Process	34,650	
Labor Rate Variance	456	
Labor Efficiency Variance		450
Payroll		34,656

To transfer labor cost to finished goods:

Finished Goods	36,000	
Labor Yield Variance		1,350
Work in Process		34,650

Factory Overhead (Two-Variance Method)

To record actual overhead:

Factory Overhead Control	22,000	
Various Credits		22,000

To apply factory overhead to products:

Work in Process	19,250	
Factory Overhead Control		19,250

To set up controllable and volume variances:

Factory Overhead Controllable Variance	2,300	
Factory Overhead Volume Variance	450	
Factory Overhead Control		2,750

To transfer factory overhead to finished goods:

Finished Goods	20,000	
Factory Overhead Yield Variance		750
Work in Process		19,250

It should be noted that Work in Process is debited for the standard production that should be attained from the input into the system and not for the standard for the amount of actual production. The resulting difference is the yield variance for each cost element.

When the transfer of the finished products to the warehouse or stockroom is reported to the cost department, one compound journal entry could be made, as follows, in place of the three individual entries for each element.

Finished Goods (200,000 lbs. × $.58)	116,000	
Work in Process (192,500 lbs. expected yield × $.58)		111,650
Yield Variance (7,500 lbs. gain × $.58)		4,350

The $4,350 favorable yield variance is comprised of:

Materials yield variance	$2,250 fav.
Labor yield variance	1,350 fav.
Factory overhead yield variance	750 fav.

Expressed as a percentage, the yield gain is 3.90 percent:

$$\frac{7,500 \text{ lbs.}}{192,500 \text{ lbs.}} \times 100 = 3.90\%$$

Responsibility and Control of Variances

Management scrutinizes variances in an attempt to determine why they occur, what corrective action can be taken, and how efficient and effective performance should be rewarded. There is no substitute for competent supervision, but variance reporting should be an aid to the supervisor in carrying out control responsibilities. However, management should recognize that explanations of the reasons for variances have limited usefulness in improving future control of costs, because the explanations seldom suggest corrective action. Consequently, the results of implemented corrective action must be measured and reported if cost control is to be effective.

The extent of variance investigation should be based on the estimated cost of making the investigation versus the value of the anticipated benefits. To be of greatest value, variances should be identified quickly and reported as frequently as possible (in some instances, daily), since the closer the reporting to the point of incurrence, the greater the chance for control and remedial action. Also, variances should be reported in physical units as well as dollars.

Causes of Variances

A variance is a symptom. Every significant variance, whether favorable or unfavorable, should be investigated and critically analyzed, either because performance has deviated from the standard or the standard itself is wrong. Perhaps standards are out-of-date. For example, the manufacturing process may change, thus changing physical standards, or rapidly rising materials prices may cause monetary standards to be out-of-date. Perhaps a favorable variance is more than offset by a related unfavorable variance (e.g., low-cost materials of poor quality), or necessary activities such as maintenance of equipment are being neglected, causing lower expenditures and a favorable variance. Furthermore, there may be a causal linkage; e.g., faulty material or equipment may cause labor inefficiency.

The purchasing department carries the primary responsibility for materials price variances, and control is obtained by getting several quotations, buying in economical lots, taking advantage of cash discounts, and selecting the most economical means of delivery. However, economic conditions and unexpected price changes by suppliers may be outside the limits of the department's control, and may be caused by inflation, an excess or shortage of the quantity available in the market, or a fortunate buy. Thus, this variance may be more a measure of forecasting ability than a failure to buy at predetermined prices. Internal factors, such as costly rush orders requiring materials at special prices, would not be the fault of the purchasing department.

Materials quantity variances may result from many causes, which must be identified if the variances are to have any meaning. If the materials are of poor quality, the fault may be with the individual who prepared the purchase requisition informing the purchasing department about the quality of materials to be purchased. If the materials purchased varied from the purchase requisition specifications, the fault may lie with the purchasing department. Or perhaps the faulty materials went unnoticed during inspection when received. Other causes include inexperienced or inefficient workers, poor equipment, pilferage, changes in production or quality control methods, or faulty blueprints.

Labor rate variances tend to be fairly minor because labor rates are usually based on union agreements. Rate variances may occur, however, because of the use of a single average rate for a department, operation, or craft, while several different rates exist for the individual workers. Then, too, a worker may be assigned to a task that normally pays a different rate. In this case, the planning or scheduling of work assignments would be the cause of the variance, and may pertain to isolated workers or to a broader change in the worker mix.

Labor efficiency variances may occur for a multitude of reasons. These reasons include a lack of materials or faulty materials, inexperienced workers and the related learning curve phenomenon (pages 156–157), poor equipment and breakdowns, changes in production methods, poor or incorrect production planning and scheduling, faulty blueprints or instructions, worker dissatisfaction, or work interruptions.

Factory overhead variances relate to the variable and the fixed factory overhead. The portion of the spending variance attributable to each expense category can be determined as discussed on pages 488–489. The spending or controllable variance is basically the responsibility of the department head, but differences between the actual cost and the allowed budget figure may be caused by higher prices or different labor rates. The idle capacity or volume variance is generally ascribed to executive management levels. The decision with regard to the utilization of plant capacity and the setting of the predetermined overhead rate's volume base rests with the planning group. Within the range of fixed costs, however, changes occur due to changes in depreciation rates, increases in insurance premiums, or increases in salaries of top-level managers. The responsibility for overhead efficiency variances, including both the fixed and variable components, is generally attributed to the department manager.

Tolerance Limits for Variance Control

The control of standard cost variances is the responsibility of a designated manager. However, some variance in cost measurements can be expected, due to the factors employed in creating the basic physical and economic standards and due to the nature of the variance. With an expected variance in mind, the question must be asked, "How large a variance from standard should be tolerated before it is considered abnormal?" In other words, some tolerance limit or range should be established, so that if the cost variance falls within this range, it can be considered acceptable. If the variance is outside the range, an investigation should be made if the cost of doing so is reasonable. In this manner, the notion of management by exception can be employed effectively and efficiently.

Each variance should be highlighted in a manner indicating whether the variance is within the control limit. Such information enables the responsible manager or supervisor to accept deviations from the standard as a valuable tool for the control of costs and lessens the dangers of their being more averse to risk than upper-level managers prefer. A manager who is unduly concerned about the penalty for even small variances may perform in a manner that hampers rather than enhances efficient operations.

Past data on established operations, tempered by estimated changes in the future, usually furnish reliable bases for estimating expected costs and calculating control limits that serve to indicate good as well as poor operation and that aid in the decision to investigate a variance. The limits may be expressed as minimum dollar amounts or as percentage differences. Their determination may be based on subjective judgments, hunches, guesses, and biases, or on careful analysis and estimates, including the possible use of statistical procedures such as the standard error of the estimate (pages 444–447). In setting and applying tolerance limits, it is important to recognize that the relative magnitude of a variance is more significant than its absolute value.

To illustrate the use of tolerance limits, assume that $10,000 appears in a factory overhead budget for maintenance expense. Based on past experience and future expectations, assume that the significant range should be ±$2,000. At the end of the month, the actual maintenance expense is $14,000, indicating a variance of $4,000 ($14,000 − $10,000). Such a result would call for further investigation into the causes of the variance. If the actual expense is only $10,900 and the variance is $900, the deviation is acceptable and requires no further investigation, at least at this time. If the unfavorable variance persists in subsequent report periods, however, the causes should be examined, because they may be significant in the long run.

In this example, maintenance expense is classified as a fixed cost, since no deviation from the basic amount is expected as a result of a change in the level of activity. However, this cost is generally classified as a semivariable expense, i.e., a fixed amount plus a variable rate which depends, in this case, on direct labor hours as the source of activity or volume. Thus, a relationship between the variance and volume must be established for the maintenance expense.

To modify the previous example, assume a tolerance limit of $3,000 when activity is 10,000 direct labor hours. When direct labor hours increase or decrease, the tolerance limit is $3,000 ± $.05 per hour for any difference between the 10,000 direct labor hours and the standard hours allowed for actual production. Assuming that $10,000 is the budget allowance for 12,700 direct labor hours and the actual cost of $14,000 was incurred when standard direct labor hours allowed were 12,700, the tolerance limit would be $3,135 [$3,000 + ($.05 × 2,700)]. This amount would be used to evaluate the $4,000 variance.

Disposition of Variances

Variances may be disposed of in either of the following ways: they may be (1) closed to Income Summary or (2) treated as adjustments to Cost of Goods Sold and to inventories.

Variances Closed to Income Summary

Stating the work in process and finished goods inventories and the cost of goods sold at standard costs allows comparison of sales revenue and standard cost by product class. At the end of the month or year, the procedure for handling cost variances is to consider them as profit or loss items. Unfavorable (or debit) manufacturing cost variances are deducted from the gross profit calculated at standard cost. Favorable (or credit) variances are added to the gross profit computed at standard cost. The treatment of manufacturing cost variances using this method is depicted in the following income statement, which should be supported by a variance analysis report:

Income Statement For Year Ended December 31, 19--		
Sales..		$52,000
Cost of goods sold (at standard) — Schedule 1..................		24,000
Gross profit (at standard).....................................		$28,000
Adjustments for standard cost variances:		
Unfavorable variances:		
Materials purchase price variance	$ 1,200	
Labor efficiency variance	600	
Factory overhead controllable variance....................	720	
Factory overhead volume variance........................	1,200	
Total unfavorable variances..............................		3,720
Gross profit (adjusted)..		$24,280
Less: Marketing expenses	$12,000	
Administrative expenses	6,000	18,000
Operating income...		$ 6,280

```
                              Schedule 1
                           Cost of Goods Sold
                      For Year Ended December 31, 19--

Materials purchased.......................................    $20,000
Less ending inventory .....................................     4,000
Materials used............................................              $16,000
Direct labor..............................................               10,000
Factory overhead .........................................               20,000
                                                                        $46,000
Less ending work in process inventory......................              16,000
Cost of goods manufactured.................................              $30,000
Less ending finished goods inventory.......................               6,000
Cost of goods sold ........................................              $24,000
```

At the end of the period, variance accounts are closed to the income summary account, as follows:

```
Income Summary ...........................................    3,720
    Materials Purchase Price Variance ...........................    1,200
    Labor Efficiency Variance .......................................      600
    Factory Overhead Controllable Variance ........................      720
    Factory Overhead Volume Variance ............................    1,200
```

As an alternative, if variances are considered a manufacturing function responsibility, they are closed to the cost of goods sold account, rather than directly to the income summary account. The total amount in Cost of Goods Sold (the standard cost of units sold plus the variance) would then be closed to Income Summary. Variances closed to the cost of goods sold account will appear in the cost of goods sold statement. Variances closed to the income summary account will appear in the income statement.

Accountants who use these procedures believe that only the standard costs should be considered the true costs. Variances are treated not as increases or decreases in manufacturing costs but as deviations from contemplated costs, due to abnormal inactivity, extravagance, inefficiencies or efficiencies, or other changes of business conditions. This viewpoint leads to the closing of all variances to the income summary account, which is an acceptable procedure as long as standards are reasonably representative of what costs ought to be. However, some proponents of this procedure suggest that the unused portion of the materials purchase price variance should be linked with materials still on hand and shown on the balance sheet as part of the cost of the ending materials inventory.

If an adjustment is made for the materials purchace price variance, whereby a part of the variance is attached to the materials inventory, the following computation would be made in this example:

> Balance in materials inventory: $4,000 or 20% of purchases made
> Materials purchase price variance: $1,200
> Variance transferred to the materials account: $240 (20% of $1,200)

The materials account would be increased and the amount closed to Income Summary would be decreased, thereby increasing the operating income from $6,280 to $6,520. The journal entry to close the variance accounts would be:

Income Summary	3,480	
Materials	240	
Materials Purchase Price Variance		1,200
Labor Efficiency Variance		600
Factory Overhead Controllable Variance		720
Factory Overhead Volume Variance		1,200

Variances Allocated to Cost of Goods Sold and Inventories

With respect to the cost of inventories, *Accounting Research Bulletin No. 43* implies that significant variances are to be allocated between cost of goods sold and inventories:

> *Standard costs are acceptable if adjusted at reasonable intervals to reflect current conditions so that at the balance-sheet date standard costs reasonably approximate costs computed under one of the recognized bases. In such cases descriptive language should be used which will express this relationship, as, for instance, "approximate costs determined on the first-in, first-out basis," or, if it is desired to mention standard costs, "at standard costs, approximating average costs."*[1]

CASB regulations require that significant standard cost variances be included in inventories. Current Internal Revenue Service regulations also require the inclusion of a portion of significant variances in inventories. When the amount involved is not significant in relation to total actual factory overhead for the year, an allocation is not required by the IRS unless such allocation is made for financial reporting purposes. Also, the taxpayer must treat both favorable and unfavorable variances consistently. Regulations, however, do permit expensing of the idle capacity variance.[2]

To illustrate the allocation of variances, the percentage of cost elements in the inventories and cost of goods sold of the previous example are:

Account	Materials Amount	%	Labor Amount	%	Factory Overhead Amount	%
Work in Process	$ 6,000	37.5	$ 2,000	20	$ 8,000	40
Finished Goods	2,000	12.5	2,000	20	2,000	10
Cost of Goods Sold	8,000	50.0	6,000	60	10,000	50
Total	$16,000	100.0	$10,000	100	$20,000	100

only for units that were produced + sold during that period.

The allocation of the variances shown on page 512 is summarized in the following table. The materials purchase price variance of $960 ($1,200 − $240 allocated to Materials) is multiplied by the respective percentage of materials

---

[1]*Accounting Research Bulletin*, No. 43, "Inventory Pricing" (New York: American Institute of Certified Public Accountants, 1953), Chapter 4, par. 6.
[2]*Regulations*, Section 1.471-11(d)(3).

in the inventories and cost of goods sold accounts (37.5%, 12.5%, and 50.0%). The labor and factory overhead variances are allocated in a similar manner.

Account	Total Amount	Work in Process	Finished Goods	Cost of Goods Sold
Materials Purchase Price Variance...........	$ 960	$ 360	$120	$ 480
Labor Efficiency Variance....................	600	120	120	360
Factory Overhead Controllable Variance......	720	288	72	360
Factory Overhead Volume Variance..........	1,200	480	120	600
Total	$3,480	$1,248	$432	$1,800

The proration of these variances to work in process, finished goods, and cost of goods sold results in the following income statement:

Income Statement
For Year Ended December 31, 19--

Sales		$52,000
Cost of goods sold (standard adjusted to actual) — Schedule 1		25,800
Gross profit (actual)		$26,200
Less: Marketing expenses.......................................	$12,000	
Administrative expenses.......................................	6,000	18,000
Operating income		$ 8,200

Schedule 1
Cost of Goods Sold
For Year Ended December 31, 19--

	Standard	Variance	Actual
Materials available......................................	$20,000		$21,200
Materials purchase price variance		$1,200	
Less materials inventory (ending)........................	4,000		4,240
Materials purchase price variance		240	
Materials used	$16,000		$16,960
Materials purchase price variance		$ 960	
Direct labor	10,000		10,600
Efficiency variance......................................		600	
Factory overhead.......................................	20,000		21,920
Controllable variance....................................		720	
Volume variance..		1,200	
Total manufacturing cost................................	$46,000	$3,480	$49,480
Less ending work in process inventory	16,000	1,248	17,248
Cost of goods manufactured	$30,000	$2,232	$32,232
Less ending finished goods inventory	6,000	432	6,432
Cost of goods sold......................................	$24,000	$1,800	$25,800

The $1,920 difference between the adjusted operating income of $8,200 and the operating income of $6,280 shown in the income statement on page 512 is summarized as follows:

Cost added to: Materials...	$ 240
Work in process	1,248
Finished goods	432
Total..	$1,920

Entries transfer the prorated amounts to the respective accounts in the general ledger only. Subsidiary inventory accounts and records are not adjusted. The various adjustment accounts could be shown on the balance sheet as valuation or contra accounts against standard inventory values, or combined with them to form one amount. At the beginning of the next period, the portion of these proration entries that affects inventory accounts is reversed in order to return beginning inventories to standard costs. At the end of that period, the amount reversed plus new variances are allocated in the same manner as before, based on ending inventory and cost of goods sold account balances.

In connection with closing variances, a problem arises in the allocation of variances to product or commodity groups. Preferably, standard cost variances are shown as deductions in total and are not allocated to major commodity groups to determine the profit and loss per commodity. Experience has shown that it is almost impossible to do otherwise. The basic idea of variance analysis is misconstrued when such prorations are attempted. The isolation of variances is for the purpose of controlling costs and determining what the variances are, where they occurred, and what caused them.

The Logic of Disposition of Variances

The treatment of variances depends upon the (1) type of variance (materials, labor, or factory overhead), (2) size of variance, (3) experience with standard costs, (4) cause of variance (e.g., incorrect standards), and (5) timing of variance (e.g., a variance caused by seasonal fluctuations). Therefore, determining the most acceptable treatment requires consideration of more than the argument that only actual costs should be shown in the financial statements. The determination of an actual cost may be impossible, and to argue that charging off variances in the period in which they arise might distort the operating income reveals a misunderstanding of standard costs.

One view of the disposition of variances has been expressed as follows:

1. Where the standards are current and attainable, companies would "state their inventories at standard cost and charge the variances against the income of the period in which the variances arise. They justify this practice on the grounds that variances represent inefficiencies, avoidable waste not recoverable in the selling price, and random fluctuations in actual cost."

2. Where standards are not current, "the general practice is to divide the variances between inventories and cost of goods sold or profit and loss thereby converting both inventories and cost of sales to approximate actual costs."[3]

---

[3]NAA Research Report, Nos. 11–15, "How Standard Costs Are Being Used Currently" (New York: National Association of Accountants, 1948), pp. 65–66.

Another view asserts that:

1. Any variances which are caused by inactivity, waste, or extravagance (outside acceptable tolerance limits) should be written off, since they represent losses. They should not be deferred by capitalizing them in the inventory accounts. This would include quantity variances on materials and labor as well as idle time (capacity) and efficiency variances on overhead. To assign a portion of such costs to inventory may cloud the product pricing decision. For example, "the inclusion of idle capacity costs in product costs has the effect of raising [inventory] costs when it is most difficult to raise prices [low volume periods] and lowering [inventory] costs when it is easiest to ask for higher prices [high volume periods]."[4]

2. An inventory reserve account should be established and charged with part of the price (spending and rate) variances (and quantity, capacity, and efficiency variances within acceptable tolerance limits) to an extent which would bring the materials, work in process, and finished goods inventories up to, but not in excess of, current market values. The rest of the price (spending and rate) variance amounts (as well as those variances described in (1) above) should be written off, since they represent excess costs. In this way, the inventory accounts themselves will be stated at standard cost while the inventories on the balance sheet will, as a whole, be shown at reasonable costs through the use of the inventory reserve account. In addition, losses caused by excessive costs and inefficiencies will be shown in the operating statement for the period in which they occur.[5]

Disposition of Variances for Interim Financial Reporting

The AICPA takes the following position concerning variance disposition for interim financial reporting in published financial statements:

Companies that use standard cost accounting systems for determining inventory and product costs should generally follow the same procedures in reporting purchase price, wage rate, usage or efficiency variances from standard cost at the end of an interim period as followed at the end of a fiscal year. Purchase price variances or volume or capacity cost variances that are planned and expected to be absorbed by the end of the annual period, should ordinarily be deferred at interim reporting dates. The effect of unplanned or unanticipated purchase price or volume variances, however, should be reported at the end of an interim period following the same procedures used at the end of a fiscal year.[6]

---

[4]Edwin Bartenstein, "Different Costs for Different Purposes," *Management Accounting*, Vol. LX, No. 2, p. 46.
[5]W. Wesley Miller, "Standard Costs and Their Relation to Cost Control," *NA(C)A Bulletin*, Vol. XXVII, No. 15, p. 692.
[6]*Opinions of the Accounting Principles Board, No. 28*, "Interim Financial Reporting" (New York: American Institute of Certified Public Accountants, 1973), par. 14.

Revision of Standard Costs

Standards should be changed only when underlying conditions change or when they no longer reflect the original concept. The idea that standards should be changed more than once a year weakens their effectiveness and increases operational details. However, standard costs require continuous review and, at times, frequent change.

Events, rather than time, determine whether standard costs should be revised. These events may be classified as internal or external. Technological advances, design revisions, method changes, labor rate adjustments, and changes in physical facilities are among the internal conditions. External events include price changes (including inflation's impact), market trends, specific customer requirements, and changes in the competitive situation.

When standard costs are changed, any adjustment to inventory should be made with care so that inventories are not written up or down arbitrarily. The National Association of Accountants has made the following comments concerning whether the ending inventory should be adjusted for such changes:

1. *If the new standard costs reflect conditions which affected the actual cost of the goods in the ending inventory, most firms adjust inventory to the new standard cost and carry the contra side of the adjusting entry to cost of sales by way of the variance accounts. In effect, this procedure assumes that the standard costs used to cost goods in the inventory have been incorrect and that restatement of inventory cost is needed to bring inventories to a correct figure on the books. Since the use of incorrect standards has affected the variance accounts as well as the inventory, the adjustment is carried to the variance accounts.*

2. *If the standard costs represent conditions which are expected to prevail in the coming period but which have not affected costs in the past period, ending inventories are costed at the old standards. It appears to be common practice to adjust the detailed inventory records to new standard costs.*

   In order to maintain the control relationship which the inventory accounts have over subsidiary records, the same adjustment is entered in the inventory control accounts; and the contra entry is carried to an inventory valuation account. Thus, the net effect is to state the inventory in the closing balance sheet at old standard costs. In the next period the inventory valuation account is closed to cost of sales when the goods to which the reserve relates move out of inventories. By use of this technique, the detailed records can be adjusted to new standards before the beginning of the year while at the same time the net charge to cost of sales in the new period is for old standard cost since the latter cost was correct at the time the goods were acquired.[7]

Broad Applicability of Standard Costing

The use of standard costing is not limited to manufacturing situations. This powerful working tool for planning and control can be used in other aspects of business organizations. For example, standards can be used for marketing activities, as discussed in Chapter 21, and for maintenance work.[8] The

---

[7]*NAA Research Report, Nos. 11–15, op. cit.* p. 64.

[8]See James H. Bullock, *Maintenance Planning and Control* (New York: National Association of Accountants, 1979), Chapter 6, "Maintenance Standards and Performance Measurement," pp. 99–111.

nonprofit organization sector (hospitals, governmental agencies, etc.) also affords many opportunities to utilize standard costing concepts and techniques. Though standard costs may not be formally recorded in the accounts, many relatively small organizations, such as automotive repair shops and construction contractors, can utilize the comparison of actual to standard quantities, times, and costs for bidding, pricing of jobs or projects, and the planning and control of routine operating activities.

DISCUSSION QUESTIONS

1. Some firms incorporate standard costs into their accounts; others maintain them only for statistical comparisons. Discuss these different uses of standard costs.

2. Compare the use of actual cost methods to standard costing systems for inventory costing.

3. Differences between actual costs and standard costs may be recorded in variance accounts. What considerations might determine the number of variance accounts?

4. In a standard cost system, the computation of variances is a first step. What steps should follow?

5. Name several advantages of using standard costs for finished goods and goods sold.

6. Discuss the meaning of variance control and responsibility by various levels of management.

7. (a) Describe the features of tolerance limits.
   (b) Discuss potential benefits of tolerance limits to an organization.
   (c) Identify and discuss potential behavioral problems which can occur in using tolerance limits.   (CMA adapted)

8. The determination of periodic income depends greatly upon the cost assigned to materials, work in process, and finished goods inventories. What considerations determine the costing of inventories at standard or approximate actual costs by companies using standard costs?

9. Present arguments in support of each of the following three methods of treating standard cost variances for purposes of financial reporting:
   (a) As deferred charges or credits on the balance sheet.
   (b) As charges or credits on the income statement.
   (c) Allocated between inventories and cost of goods sold.   (AICPA adapted)

EXERCISES

Whenever variances are required in the following exercises, indicate whether they are favorable or unfavorable.

1. *Journal entries for materials; variance analysis.* Lipton Corporation uses a standard costing system. The standard for one of its products, Lipco, is 2 units of raw material LEQ at a cost of $1 per unit. During April, 17,600 Lipcos were manufactured. Inventory of raw material LEQ on April 1 was 8,000 units, costing $8,400; purchases were 32,000 units @ $1.04 per unit; and ending inventory was 6,000 units, costing $1.04 each.

Required: *Prepare the journal entries for the purchase and issue of LEQ, using the three methods for recording materials purchased.*

2. *Journal entries for labor; variance analysis.* The processing of one unit of Product X requires a standard of 1.75 hours at $9.08 per hour to perform Operation A86. During the month, 1,500 units were manufactured, requiring 2,590 hours at $9.28 per hour for this operation.

Required: Prepare the journal entries for labor operation A86, including variances.

3. *Factory overhead variance analysis and journal entries.* The theoretical capacity of Lawrence Products is 3,600 units or 9,000 direct labor hours. At the normal capacity level (80% of theoretical), the following factory overhead amounts have been budgeted:

$$
\begin{array}{ll}
\text{Fixed}................ & \$4,392 \\
\text{Variable}............ & 5,904
\end{array}
$$

Standards were set as follows:

Direct labor, 2.5 hours per unit
Factory overhead, $1.43 per direct labor hour

Actual data for May were:

Production, 2,870 units
Labor, 7,150 hours
Factory overhead, $10,236

Required:
(1) Compute the variances resulting when the two-, three-, and four-variance methods are used.
(2) For each method, prepare the journal entries to record actual factory overhead, applied factory overhead, and variances.

4. *Factory overhead variance analysis; budget report.* The Cost Department of Dalton Products Inc. prepared the following flexible budget for November:

	9,938 units	11,180 units	12,422 units
Production based on standard............	9,938 units	11,180 units	12,422 units
Labor hours...........................	4,000 hours	4,500 hours	5,000 hours
Capacity percentage....................	80%	90%	100%*
*Normal capacity			
Fixed factory overhead:			
Superintendence.....................	$ 6,510	$ 6,510	$ 6,510
Indirect labor.......................	5,750	5,750	5,750
Manufacturing supplies...............	3,490	3,490	3,490
Maintenance........................	1,680	1,680	1,680
Heat, power, and light...............	110	110	110
Depreciation.......................	675	675	675
Insurance..........................	352	352	352
Total fixed overhead...............	$18,567	$18,567	$18,567
Variable factory overhead:			
Indirect labor.......................	$ 1,928	$ 2,169	$ 2,410
Manufacturing supplies...............	1,720	1,935	2,150
Maintenance........................	628	707	785
Heat, power, and light...............	61	68	76
Total variable overhead.............	$ 4,337	$ 4,879	$ 5,421
Total factory overhead.............	$22,904	$23,446	$23,988

At the end of November, cost accounting tabulation showed 9,689 items manufactured, 4,150 labor hours worked, and actual factory overhead as follows:

Superintendence	$ 6,605
Indirect labor	7,512
Manufacturing supplies	5,450
Maintenance	2,317
Heat, power, and light	195
Depreciation	675
Insurance	352
Total factory overhead	$23,106

Required:

(1) Compute factory overhead variances, using (a) the three-variance and (b) the two-variance methods. (Round off overhead rates to four decimal places; round off variances to the nearest dollar.)

(2) Prepare an itemized budget report for the spending variance, including actual factory overhead, budgeted factory overhead, and variances.

5. Journal entries; variance analysis. Irvine Company manufactures a product having the following standard costs:

Materials	3 sq. ft. @ $2	$ 6.00
Labor	½ hr. @ 8	4.00
Variable factory overhead	½ hr. @ 3	1.50
Fixed factory overhead (normal capacity is 4,000 labor hours)	½ hr. @ 2	1.00
		$12.50

The following information pertains to actual activity for March:

(a) 9,000 units were produced.

(b) 30,000 sq. ft. of materials were purchased at $2.07. The materials price variance is recorded when the purchase is made.

(c) 28,000 sq. ft. of materials were used.

(d) Direct labor was $36,080 for 4,400 hours. The liability has been recorded, but the payroll account has not been distributed.

(e) Factory overhead was $22,500.

(f) 8,200 units were sold at $16.

(g) Marketing and administrative expenses were $20,000.

Required: Prepare the journal entries to record the above information, including two variances for each cost element.   (CGAA adapted)

6. Journal entries; variance analysis. Newport Manufacturing Inc. produces custom-made, tie-dyed sweat shirts for distribution on college campuses. The following standards have been established:

Materials:	
Cotton cloth: 2 yards @ $1	$2.00
Dyes: 1 pint @ $.50	.50
Labor: ½ hour @ $6	3.00
Factory overhead: ½ hour @ $1	.50
	$6.00

The yearly production budget is based upon normal plant operations of 20,000 hours, with fixed factory overhead of $6,000.

Inventories at January 1 were:

Cotton cloth (2,000 yards @ $1).................................	$2,000
Dye (1,000 prints @ $.50)	500
Work in process (1,000 units; ¼ finished as to conversion; all materials issued)...	3,375
Finished goods (500 @ $6)	3,000

Production for January:

3,000 units completed
750 units ⅓ converted, all materials added

Transactions for January:

Cotton cloth purchased..........................	5,000 yds. @ $1.10
Dyes purchased.................................	2,500 pints @ $.49
Cotton cloth issued to factory	5,600 yards
Dyes issued to factory..........................	2,700 pints
Direct labor payroll..............................	1,550 hours @ $5.90
Actual factory overhead	$1,620
Sales on account	3,100 sweat shirts @ $9

Required: *Prepare the journal entries to record the January transactions, accounting for work in process at standard cost and recognizing variances in the proper accounts. Use the two-variance method in computing materials, labor, and factory overhead variances; recognize the materials price variance at the time of purchase. Use separate inventory and variance accounts for each material. Close all variances into Cost of Goods Sold.*

7. Price, mix, and yield variances; journal entries. *Medicope Inc. produces an antiseptic powder which is sold in bulk to institutions such as schools and hospitals. The product's mixture is tested at intervals during the production process. Materials are added as needed to give the mixture the desired drying and medicating properties. The standard mixture with standard prices for a 100-lb. batch is as follows:*

10 lbs. of Hexachlorophene @ $.45
10 lbs. of Para-chlor-meta-xylenol @ $.30
30 lbs. of Bentonite @ $.08
20 lbs. of Kaolin @ $.10
50 lbs. of Talc @ $.05

During January, the following materials were purchased:

1,500 lbs. of Hexachlorophene @ $.47
1,100 lbs. of Para-chlor-meta-xylenol @ $.33
4,000 lbs. of Bentonite @ $.07
2,500 lbs. of Kaolin @ $.11
6,000 lbs. of Talc @ $.04

The materials price variance is recorded when materials are purchased. Production for the month consisted of 10,700 lbs. of finished product. There were no beginning or ending inventories of work in process. The following actual materials quantities were put into production:

1,050 lbs. of Hexachlorophene
1,125 lbs. of Para-chlor-meta-xylenol
3,080 lbs. of Bentonite
2,200 lbs. of Kaolin
5,300 lbs. of Talc

Required:

  (1) Calculate materials variances (price, mix, and yield).

  (2) Prepare the journal entries for (a) purchase, (b) usage, (c) completion of materials, and (d) disposition of variances, assuming all completed units were sold.

8. Disposition of variances. Atlas Corporation uses standard costing in accounting for the manufacturing costs of its only product, Xerco. Variances are allocated to the cost of goods sold and ending inventories. The following information was extracted from the corporation's books for January:

	Debit	Credit
Materials purchase price variance	$1,500	
Materials quantity variance	660	
Labor rate variance	250	
Labor efficiency variance	290	
Controllable variance		$300
Volume variance	120	

The following inventories were on hand on January 31:

Finished goods	900 units
Work in process	1,200 units
Raw materials	none

The work in process inventory was 100% complete as to materials and 50% complete as to direct labor and factory overhead. During January, 1,500 units were sold.

Required: Allocate the variances. Round distribution percentages to the nearest percent and allocations to the nearest dollar.

9. Standard cost card; income statement. Madison Inc. manufactures a product based on standard specifications and costs. The following information is available for April:

	Quantities	Standard Cost
Inventories, April 1:		
Finished goods	4,000 units	$112,000
Materials	6,000	12,000

Actual and standard quantities and costs for the month are summarized as follows:

	Quantities		Costs	
	Actual	Standard	Actual	Standard
Materials purchases (units)	100,000		$195,500	$200,000
Materials requisitions (units)	95,000	94,000		
Direct labor (hours)	46,800	47,000	329,940	329,000
Factory overhead—actual			143,800	

The company's standard factory overhead rate is based on a variable factory overhead rate of $2 per direct labor hour, and fixed factory overhead of $50,000 for 50,000 direct labor hours, which is considered normal capacity. During the month, the company planned 24,000 units, but only 23,500 units were produced and placed into finished goods inventory. There was no work in process at the beginning or the end of the period; 21,000 units were sold for $40 per unit. Marketing and administrative expenses were $185,000.

Required:

  (1) Prepare the standard manufacturing cost card for the product.

(2) *Prepare an income statement for the month. Variances for materials, labor, and factory overhead are closed to Cost of Goods Sold. Use the two-variance method for factory overhead.*

10. *Revision of standard costs.* One of Morgantown Company's products has a standard labor cost of $58 per 100 units. Beginning in January, the cost is to be increased to $62.50, and because of the use of a greater percentage of less skilled workers, only 90 units are expected to be produced in the same time period previously required for producing 100 units.

In addition, Morgantown was notified by its material supplier that a lower quality material would be supplied after January 1, with an estimated 5% of the units manufactured being rejected upon final inspection because of defective material. In the past, no units were lost for this reason.

In January, the company plans to produce 42,750 units of this product.

Required: *Compute the amount of expected labor costs under the previous and the revised standards, indicating the amount of the change associated with the material change and with the labor change.* *(CMA adapted)*

PROBLEMS

Whenever variances are required in the following problems, indicate whether they are favorable or unfavorable.

18-1. Conversion to standard cost; factory ledger journal entries; variance analysis. On May 1, 19--, the trial balance of the factory ledger accounts of Murphy Company appeared as follows:

Materials (1 000 kilograms)	620	
Finished Goods (100 units)	5,600	
General Ledger Control................................		6,220
	6,220	6,220

The company desires to install and maintain a system of standard costs, with inventories carried at standard cost. It has made the necessary materials and labor studies which reveal the following standards for its product:

Direct materials: 20 kg should be used for each unit of finished product and should cost $.60 per kg.

Direct labor: Time studies indicate an allowance of 5 hours of direct labor at an hourly rate of $7.50 for each unit of finished product.

The only data the company has concerning factory overhead are the following for the first four months of 19--:

	Direct Labor Hours	Total Factory Overhead
January...................	5,000	$ 8,100
February	9,500	9,990
March....................	13,000	11,460
April....................	8,000	9,360

The plant had been constructed to provide a normal productive capacity for 2,500 units of finished product per month. The controller suggested that a standard overhead rate be calculated at normal capacity, using a flexible budget based on the data for the first four months of 19--, as determined by the high and low points method.

Operating data for May:

Materials purchased: 60 000 kg @ $.58

Materials used: 48 000 kg

Payroll:

Direct labor: 12,000 hours at $7.20 per hour

Indirect labor: 1,000 hours at $6 per hour

Factory overhead charges transferred from the home office: $5,500

Units produced: 2,300

Units sold: 2,200

No work in process inventory at the beginning or end of May.

Required:

(1) Prepare a standard cost card for the product.

(2) Prepare journal entries to record the operating data for May, using two materials variances, two labor variances, and two factory overhead variances, including an entry to adjust all beginning inventories to standard cost. Liability accounts and the cost of goods sold account are not a part of the factory ledger. An applied factory overhead account is used.

18-2. Journal entries; variance analysis; income statement. Halifax Company uses the following standard costs in accounting for its only product:

Material, 3 liters × $4.............................	$12.00
Direct labor, ½ hour × $7	3.50
Variable factory overhead, ½ hour × $6	3.00
Fixed factory overhead, ½ hour × $9.................	4.50
	$23.00

Fixed factory overhead budgeted was $49,500 per month.

Actual activity for November was:

(a) 40 000 liters of material were purchased for $159,200. The related price variance is recorded at the time of purchase.

(b) 10,000 units were produced.

(c) There was no work in process at the beginning or end of November.

(d) 31 000 liters of material were issued to production.

(e) The direct labor payroll to be distributed (credit the payroll account) is $35,616 for 4,800 hours.

(f) Actual factory overhead cost of $81,500 was incurred.

(g) 8,000 units were sold on account at $40 each.

(h) Marketing and administrative expenses of $60,000 were incurred.

Required:

(1) Prepare journal entries to record the November activity. (Ignore overhead variances.)

(2) Prepare a three-variance analysis of under- or overapplied factory overhead.

(3) Prepare an income statement, assuming that all variances are to be closed to Cost of Goods Sold.   (CGAA adapted)

18-3. Journal entries; variance analysis. The following information pertains to production operations of Leon Company for April:

Inventories:

Work in process: Beginning, 2,000 units, all materials, ½ converted; ending, 3,000 units, all materials, ⅓ converted; no spoilage.

Finished goods: No beginning or ending inventory.

Standard and actual costs:

Materials: Standard quantity, 5 square feet per unit; 50,000 square feet were purchased @ $.52; the unfavorable materials purchase price variance was $1,000; 29,500 square feet of materials were requisitioned from the storeroom.

Labor: Standard per unit, ½ hour at $9 per hour; actual labor rate was $9.05 per hour for 2,600 hours.

Factory overhead: Normal capacity, 2,000 labor hours; fixed factory overhead standard, $2 per unit or $4 per labor hour; actual factory overhead was $5,500 variable and $8,200 fixed; efficiency variance, $700 unfavorable; spending variance, $400 unfavorable.

Five thousand units were sold for cash at $15 each.

Required: Prepare the journal entries to record the cost accounting cycle transactions, using standard costing. Variances will not be disposed of until June, the end of the fiscal year.   (CGAA adapted)

18-4. Variance analysis: materials, labor, factory overhead; income statement. The following information concerns Pierpont Company, which manufactures one product and uses a standard costing system:

Standard cost per unit:

Materials: 3 liters @ $2	$ 6
Direct labor: 2 hours @ $8	16
Variable factory overhead: 2 hours @ $3	6
Fixed factory overhead: 2 hours @ $2	4
	$32

Actual production — 11,000 units

Materials purchased — 50 000 liters @ $1.90; purchases are recorded at standard cost

Direct labor (23,000 hours) — $193,200

Depreciation of factory building and equipment — $10,000

Sales salaries — $12,000

Insurance: factory — $2,000; office — $200

Sales — 9,000 units @ $45

Indirect labor (includes $25,000 fixed) — $60,000

Normal capacity — 10,000 units or 20,000 direct labor hours

Heat and light — office — $800

Heat, light, and power — factory — $11,000 (includes $4,000 fixed)

Advertising — $8,000

Materials used — 35 000 liters

Office supplies used — $500

Administrative salaries — $14,000

Depreciation of office building — $1,000

Indirect factory materials used (variable) — $20,000

Delivery expense — $4,000

Required:
  (1) Prepare an analysis of the materials, direct labor, and factory overhead variances, using the three-variance method for factory overhead.
  (2) Prepare an income statement, supported by a schedule of variances and treating all variances as period costs.   (CGAA adapted)

18-5. Income statement; variance analysis. Fenton Corporation manufactures Product G, which sells for $25 per unit. Material M is added before processing starts, and labor and overhead are added evenly during the manufacturing process. Production capacity is budgeted at 110,000 units of G annually. The standard costs per unit of G are:

Direct materials:		
M: 2 pounds @ $1.50..............................		$ 3.00
Direct labor: 1.5 hours at $8 per hour.....................		12.00
Factory overhead:		
Variable	$1.50	
Fixed...	1.10	2.60
Total standard cost per unit		$17.60

A process cost system is used. Inventories are valued at standard cost. All variances from standard costs are charged or credited to Cost of Goods Sold in the year incurred.

Inventory data for 19--:

	January 1	December 31
Material M..................................	50,000 pounds	60,000 pounds
Work in process:		
All materials, ⅔ processed	10,000 units	
All materials, ⅓ processed		15,000 units
Inventory, finished goods	20,000 units	12,000 units

During 19--, 250,000 pounds of M were purchased at an average cost of $1.485 per pound; and 240,000 pounds were transferred to work in process inventory. Direct labor costs amounted to $1,313,760 at an average hourly labor rate of $8.16.

Actual factory overhead for 19--:

Variable	$181,500
Fixed...	114,000

A total of 110,000 units of G were completed and transferred to finished goods inventory.

Marketing and administrative expenses were $681,000.

Required: Prepare an income statement for 19--, including all manufacturing cost variances and using the two-variance method for factory overhead.   (AICPA adapted)

18-6. Standard production costs; materials variance analysis (price, quantity, mix, and yield). Panacea Pharmaceutical Company processes a single product, Mudexin, and uses a standard cost accounting system. The process requires preparation and blending of three materials in large batches, with a variation from the standard mixture sometimes necessary to maintain quality. The information that follows is available for the Blending Department.

During October, 410 batches of 500 pounds each of the finished compound were completed and transferred to the Packaging Department.

Blending Department inventories totaled 6,000 pounds at the beginning of the month and 9,000 pounds at the end of the month. These inventories consisted of materials in their standard proportions and were completely processed but not transferred. Inventories are carried in the accounts at standard cost prices.

The standard cost card for a 500-pound batch shows the following standard costs:

	Quantity	Unit Cost	Total Cost
Materials:			
Mucilloid	250 pounds	$ .14	$35
Dextrose	200	.09	18
Other ingredients	50	.08	4
Total per batch	500 pounds		$ 57
Labor:			
Blending	10 hours	$6.00	60
Factory overhead:			
Variable	10 hours	$1.00	$10
Fixed	10	.30	3	13
Total standard cost per 500-pound batch			$130

During October, the following materials were purchased and put into production:

	Pounds	Unit Cost	Total Cost
Mucilloid	114,400	$.17	$19,448
Dextrose	85,800	.11	9,438
Other ingredients	19,800	.10	1,980
Total	220,000		$30,866

Required:
(1) Prepare a schedule presenting the equivalent production computation for the Blending Department for October production, in both pounds and batches, and the standard cost of October production, itemized by components of materials, labor, and factory overhead.
(2) Prepare schedules computing the differences between actual and standard materials costs, and analyzing the differences as materials variances (for each material) caused by (a) price differences and (b) quantity differences. No labor or overhead variances are to be calculated.
(3) Explain how materials variances arising from quantity differences could be further analyzed, with schedules presenting such an analysis. (Carry computations to three decimal places.) (AICPA adapted)

18-7. Allocating variances. Hamm Corporation commenced doing business on December 1. The corporation uses a standard cost system for the manufacturing costs of its only product, Hamex. The standard costs for a unit of Hamex are:

Materials: 10 kilograms @ .70	$ 7
Direct labor: 1 hour @ $8	8
Factory overhead (applied on the basis of $2 per direct labor hour)	2
Total	$17

The following data were extracted from the corporation's books for December:

	Units	Debit	Credit
Budgeted production	3,000		
Units sold	1,500		
Sales...			$45,000
Sales discounts.................................		$ 500	
Materials price usage variance....................		1,500	
Materials quantity variance.......................		660	
Direct labor rate variance........................		250	
Factory overhead spending variance			300
Discounts lost..................................		120	

The company records purchases of materials net of discounts. The amounts shown for discounts lost and materials price usage variance are applicable to materials used in manufacturing operations during December.

Inventory data at December 31 indicate the following inventories were on hand:

Finished goods...........................	900 units
Work in process.........................	1,200 units
Materials	None

The work in process inventory was 100% complete as to materials and 50% as to direct labor and factory overhead. The corporation's policy is to allocate variances to the cost of goods sold and ending inventories, i.e., work in process and finished goods.

Required: Prepare the following schedules:
(1) Allocating the variances and discounts lost on purchases to the ending inventories and to cost of goods sold.
(2) Computing the cost of goods manufactured at standard cost and at actual cost for December. Amounts for materials, labor, and factory overhead should be shown separately.
(3) Computing the actual cost of materials, labor, and factory overhead included in the work in process inventory and in the finished goods inventory at December 31.
(AICPA adapted)

18-8. Revision of standard costs. The standard cost of Product MSY-2, manufactured by New Boston Company, is as follows:

	Prime Cost	Factory Overhead (50%)	Total
Material A.....................................	$10.00		$10.00
Material B.....................................	5.00		5.00
Material C.....................................	2.00		2.00
Direct labor—cutting.........................	8.00	$4.00	12.00
Direct labor—shaping.........................	4.00	2.00	6.00
Direct labor—assembling	2.00	1.00	3.00
Direct labor—boxing	1.00	.50	1.50
Total	$32.00	$7.50	$39.50

The company manufactured 10,000 units of Product MSY-2 during the period under review. Materials A, B, and C are issued in the Cutting Department.

The following variances relating to this product appear on the books for the period:

	Unfavorable	Favorable
Materials price variance:		
Due to a favorable purchase of total requirements of Material A		$19,500
Materials usage variance:		
Excessive waste during period..................................	$ 6,000	
Labor rate variance:		
5% wage increase to direct workers	7,500	
Labor efficiency variance:		
Due to shutdown caused by strike	17,000	
Factory overhead variance—fixed overhead:		
Due to shutdown caused by strike	8,000	
Factory overhead variance—variable overhead:		
Due to permanent savings in costs of certain services..............		18,000

Required: Prepare a schedule of revised standard costs, which will clearly indicate the cumulative standard for each successive operation.　　　　　　　　(AICPA adapted)

CASES

A. Variance analysis; variance control responsibility. Capitol Corporation manufactures and sells a single product, using a standard cost system. The standard cost per unit of product is:

Materials: 1 pound of plastic @ $2......................................	$ 2.00
Direct labor: 1.6 hours @ $4...	6.40
Variable factory overhead cost per unit.................................	3.00
Fixed factory overhead cost per unit	1.45
	$12.85

The factory overhead cost per unit was calculated from the following annual overhead cost budget for a 60,000-unit volume:

Variable factory overhead cost:	
Indirect labor (30,000 hours @ $4)................................	$120,000
Supplies (oil—60,000 gallons @ $.50).............................	30,000
Allocated variable service department cost.........................	30,000
Total variable factory overhead cost...................................	$180,000
Fixed factory overhead cost:	
Supervision	$ 27,000
Depreciation	45,000
Other fixed costs	15,000
Total fixed factory overhead cost	$ 87,000
Total budgeted annual factory overhead cost for 60,000 units	$267,000

The charges to the Manufacturing Department for November, when 5,000 units were produced, were:

Materials (5,300 pounds @ $2).....................................	$10,600
Direct labor (8,200 hours @ $4.10)	33,620
Indirect labor (2,400 hours @ $4.10)...............................	9,840
Supplies (oil—6,000 gallons @ $.55)...............................	3,300
Allocated variable service department cost..........................	3,200
Supervision	2,475
Depreciation	3,750
Other fixed costs	1,250
Total	$68,035

The Purchasing Department normally buys about the same quantity of plastic as is used in production during a month. In November, 5,200 pounds were purchased at a price of $2.10 per pound.

The company has divided its responsibilities so that the Purchasing Department is responsible for the price at which materials and supplies are purchased, while the Manufacturing Department is responsible for the quantities of materials used.

The Manufacturing Department manager performs the timekeeping function and, at various times, an analysis of factory overhead and direct labor variances has shown that the manager has deliberately misclassified labor hours (e.g., direct labor hours might be classified as indirect labor hours and vice versa), so that only one of the two labor variances is unfavorable. It is not economically feasible to hire a separate timekeeper.

Required:
(1) Calculate these variances from standard costs for the data given: (a) materials purchase price variance; (b) materials quantity variance; (c) direct labor rate variance; (d) direct labor efficiency variance; (e) factory overhead controllable variance, analyzed for each expense classification.
(2) Explain whether the division of responsibilities should solve the conflict between price and quantity variances.
(3) Prepare a report which details the factory overhead budget variance. The report, which will be given to the Manufacturing Department manager, should display only that part of the variance that is the manager's responsibility and should highlight information useful to that manager in evaluating departmental performance and in considering corrective action.
(4) Suggest a solution to the company's problem involving the classification of labor hours.   (CMA adapted)

B. In-depth analysis of labor variances. Technowave Company manufactures a complete line of radios. Because a large number of models have plastic cases, the company has its own molding department for producing them. The month of April was devoted to the production of the plastic case for one of the portable radios—Model SX76.

The Molding Department has two operations—molding and trimming; there usually is no interaction of labor in these two operations. The standard labor cost for producing 10 plastic cases for Model SX76 is as follows:

Molding: ½ hour @ $6.....................................	$3
Trimming: ¼ hour @ $4	1
	$4

During April, 70,000 plastic cases were produced in the Molding Department; however, 10% of these cases had to be discarded because they were found to be defective at final inspection. The Purchasing Department had changed to a new plastic supplier to take advantage of a lower price for comparable plastic. The new plastic turned out to be of a lower quality, resulting in the rejection of the 7,000 cases.

Direct labor hours worked and direct labor costs charged to the Molding Department are as follows:

Molding: 3,800 hours @ $6.25	....	$23,750
Trimming: 1,600 hours @ $4.15	....	6,640
Total labor charges	....	$30,390

As a result of poor scheduling by the Production Scheduling Department, the supervisor of the Molding Department had to shift molders to the trimming operation for 200 hours during April. The company paid the molding workers their regular hourly rate, even though they were performing a lower-rated task. There was no significant loss of efficiency caused by the shift. In addition, as a result of unexpected machinery repairs required during the month, 75 hours and 35 hours of idle time occurred in the molding and trimming operations, respectively.

The monthly report which compares actual costs with standard cost of output for April shows the following labor variance for the Molding Department:

Actual labor cost for April	....	$30,390
Standard labor cost of output [63,000 × ($4 ÷ 10)]	....	25,200
Unfavorable labor variance	....	$ 5,190

This variance is significantly higher than normal.

Required:
(1) Prepare a detailed analysis of the unfavorable labor variance for the Molding Department, showing the variance resulting from (a) labor rates; (b) labor substitution; (c) material substitution; (d) operating efficiency; and (e) idle time.
(2) Evaluate the Molding Department supervisor's argument that the variances due to labor substitution and change in raw materials should not be charged to the department.   (CMA adapted)

C. Standard costs in inventory and variance disposition. Many advocates of standard costing take the position that these costs are a proper basis for inventory costing for external reporting purposes. Accounting Research Bulletin No. 43, however, reflects the widespread view that standard costs are not acceptable unless "adjusted at reasonable intervals to reflect current conditions so that at the balance-sheet date standard costs reasonably approximate costs computed under one of the recognized bases."

Required:
(1) Discuss the conceptual merits of using standard costs as the basis for inventory costing for external reporting purposes.
(2) Prepare general journal entries for three alternative dispositions of a $1,500 unfavorable variance, when all goods manufactured during the period are included in the ending finished goods inventory. Assume that a formal standard cost system is in operation, that $500 of the variance resulted from actual costs exceeding normal (attainable) standard cost, and that $1,000 of the variance resulted from the difference between the theoretical (ideal) standard and a normal standard.
(3) Discuss the conceptual merits of each of the three alternative methods of disposition requested in (2) above.   (AICPA adapted)

Part Six
Analysis of Costs and Profits

Chapter 19
Gross Profit Analysis

Gross profit is the difference between the cost of goods sold and sales. Since the adherence of the actual to the budgeted or standard gross profit figure is highly desirable, a careful analysis of unexpected changes in gross profit is useful to a company's management. These changes are the result of one or a combination of the following:

1. Changes in sales prices of products.
2. Changes in volume sold.
   a. Changes in the number of physical units sold.
   b. Changes in the types of products sold, often called the *product mix* or *sales mix*.
3. Changes in cost elements, i.e., materials, labor, and overhead costs.

The determination of the various causes for an increase or decrease in gross profit is similar to the computation of standard cost variances, although gross profit analysis is often possible without the use of standard costs or budgets. In such a case, prices and costs of the previous period, or any period selected as the basis for the comparison, serve as the basis for the computation of the variances. When standard costs and budgetary methods are employed, however, a greater degree of accuracy and more effective results are achieved. Both methods are illustrated on the following pages.

Gross Profit Analysis Based on the Previous Period's Figures

As the basis for illustrating the analysis of gross profit using the previous period's figures, the following gross profit sections of the Jefferson Company's operating statements for the year 19A and 19B are presented:

	19A *Base*	19B *Actual*	Changes
Sales (net).............................	$120,000	$140,000	+$20,000
Cost of goods sold......................	100,000	110,000	+ 10,000
Gross profit	$ 20,000	$ 30,000	+$10,000 net increase

In comparison with 19A, sales in 19B increased $20,000 and costs increased $10,000, resulting in an increase in gross profit of $10,000.

Additional data taken from various records indicate that the sales and the cost of goods sold figures can be broken down as follows:

Product	Quantity	19A Sales Unit Price	19A Sales Amount	19A Cost of Goods Sold Unit Cost	19A Cost of Goods Sold Amount
X................	8,000 units	$5.00	$ 40,000	$4.000	$ 32,000
Y................	7,000	4.00	28,000	3.500	24,500
Z................	20,000	2.60	52,000	2.175	43,500
		Total sales	$120,000	Total cost	$100,000

Product	Quantity	19B Sales Unit Price	19B Sales Amount	19B Cost of Goods Sold Unit Cost	19B Cost of Goods Sold Amount
X................	10,000 units	$6.60	$ 66,000	$4.00	$ 40,000
Y................	4,000	3.50	14,000	3.50	14,000
Z................	20,000	3.00	60,000	2.80	56,000
		Total sales	$140,000	Total cost	$110,000

In analyzing the change in the gross profit of Jefferson Company, the sales and costs of 19A are accepted as the basis (or standard) for all comparisons. A sales price variance and a sales volume variance are computed first, followed by the computation of a cost price variance and a cost volume variance. The sales volume variance and the cost volume variance are analyzed further as a third step, which results in the computation of a sales mix variance and a final sales volume variance.

Computation of the Sales Price and Sales Volume Variances

The sales price and sales volume variances of Jefferson Company are computed as follows:

Actual 19B sales...		$140,000
Actual 19B sales at 19A prices:		
X: 10,000 units @ $5.00	$50,000	
Y: 4,000 @ 4.00	16,000	
Z: 20,000 @ 2.60	52,000	118,000
Sales price variance		$ 22,000 fav.
Actual 19B sales at 19A prices		$118,000
Total 19A sales (used as standard)		120,000
Sales volume variance.......................................		$ 2,000 unfav.

Computation of the Cost Price and Cost Volume Variances

The cost price and cost volume variances are computed as follows:

Actual 19B cost of goods sold.................................		$110,000
Actual 19B sales at 19A costs:		
X: 10,000 units @ $4.000	$40,000	
Y: 4,000 @ 3.500	14,000	
Z: 20,000 @ 2.175	43,500	97,500
Cost price variance..		$ 12,500 unfav.
Actual 19B sales at 19A costs.................................		$ 97,500
Cost of goods sold in 19A (used as standard)...................		100,000
Cost volume variance..		$ 2,500 fav.

Computation of the Sales Mix and Final Sales Volume Variances

The results of the preceding computations explain the reason for the $10,000 increase in gross profit:

Sales price variance		$22,000 fav.
Volume variances (net) consisting of:		
Cost volume variance	$2,500 fav.	
Less sales volume variance.........................	2,000 unfav.	
Net volume variance		500 fav.
		$22,500
Less cost price variance...		12,500 unfav.
Net increase in gross profit		$10,000

The net $500 favorable volume variance is a composite of the sales volume and cost volume variances. It should be further analyzed to determine the more significant sales mix and final sales volume variances. To accomplish this analysis, one additional figure must be determined — the average gross profit realized on the units sold in the base (or standard) period. The computation is:

$$\frac{\text{Total gross profit of 19A sales}}{\text{Total number of units sold in 19A}} = \frac{\$20,000}{35,000} = \$.5714 \text{ per unit}$$

The $.5714 average gross profit per unit sold in 19A is multiplied by the total number of units sold in 19B (34,000 units). The resulting $19,428 is the total gross profit that would have been achieved in 19B if all units had been sold at 19A's average gross profit per unit.

The sales mix and the final sales volume variances can now be calculated:

19B sales at 19A prices	$118,000
19B sales at 19A costs	97,500
Difference	$ 20,500
19B sales at 19A average gross profit	19,428
Sales mix variance	$ 1,072 fav.
19B sales at 19A average gross profit	$ 19,428
Total 19A sales (used as standard)	$120,000
Cost of goods sold in 19A (used as standard)	100,000
Difference	20,000
Final sales volume variance	$ 572 unfav.
Check: Sales mix variance	$ 1,072 fav.
Final sales volume variance	572 unfav.
Net volume variance	$ 500 fav.

The sales mix variance can be viewed in the following manner:

Product	(1) 19B Sales in Units	19A Sales Units	%	(2) 19B Sales (In 19A Proportions)	(3) (1) − (2)	(4) 19A Unit Gross Profit	Sales Mix Variance (3) × (4)
X	10,000	8,000	22.86	7,772[1]	2,228	$1.000[2]	$2,228
Y	4,000	7,000	20.00	6,800	(2,800)	.500	(1,400)
Z	20,000	20,000	57.14	19,428	572	.425	243
Total	34,000	35,000	100.00	34,000	−0−		
Rounding difference							1
Net sales mix variance							$1,072 fav.

[1]34,000 × 22.86% = 7,772
[2]$5 sales price − $4 cost of goods sold = $1

The final sales volume variance is the difference in the number of units sold for the two years, multiplied by the 19A average gross profit per unit:

19B sales in units	34,000
19A sales in units	35,000
Unit sales difference	1,000
Average gross profit per unit	×$.5714
	$571.40
Rounding difference	.60
Final sales volume variance	$572.00 unfav.

Combining two or more products or product types having different cost or sales prices into a single product category should be avoided. Such aggregation will result in the price variances including a portion of what is actually the mix variance as the mix within such a combination changes.[1]

Recapitulation of Variances

The variances identified in the preceding computations are summarized as follows:

	Gains	Losses
Gain due to increased sales price.........................	$22,000	
Loss due to increased cost...............................		$12,500
Gain due to shift in sales mix...........................	1,072	
Loss due to decrease in units sold		572
Total...	$23,072	$13,072
	13,072	
Net increase in gross profit.............................	$10,000	

Gross Profit Analysis Based on Budgets and Standard Costs

As the basis for illustrating the analysis of gross profit using budgets and standard costs, three financial statements for Collier Inc. are presented:

1. The budgeted income statement prepared at the beginning of the period.
2. The actual income statement prepared at the end of the period.
3. An income statement prepared at the end of the period on the basis of actual sales units at budgeted sales prices and at standard costs.

Statement 1

Collier Inc.
Income Statement (Budgeted)

Product	Units	Sales		Cost		Gross Profit	
		Unit Price	Amount	Unit Cost	Amount	Per Unit	Amount
A	6,000	$15.00	$ 90,000	$12.00	$ 72,000	$3.00	$18,000
B	3,500	12.00	42,000	10.00	35,000	2.00	7,000
C	1,000	10.00	10,000	8.75	8,750	1.25	1,250
	10,500	$13.52*	$142,000	$11.02*	$115,750	$2.50*	$26,250

*Weighted average.

---

[1]Robert E. Malcolm, "The Effect of Product Aggregation in Determining Sales Variances," *The Accounting Review*, Vol. LIII, No. 1, pp. 162–169. Problem 19-6 is adapted from this article.

Statement 2

Collier Inc.
Income Statement (Actual)

Product	Units	Sales		Cost		Gross Profit	
		Unit Price	Amount	Unit Cost	Amount	Per Unit	Amount
A	5,112	$16.00	$ 81,792	$13.98	$ 71,466	$2.02	$10,326
B	4,208	12.00	50,496	9.72	40,902	2.28	9,594
C	1,105	9.00	9,945	8.83	9,757	.17	188
	10,425	$13.64*	$142,233	$11.71*	$122,125	$1.93*	$20,108

*Weighted average.

Statement 3

Collier Inc.
Income Statement (Actual Units At Budgeted Prices and Costs)

Product	Units	Sales		Cost		Gross Profit	
		Unit Price	Amount	Unit Cost	Amount	Per Unit	Amount
A	5,112	$15.00	$ 76,680	$12.00	$ 61,344	$3.00	$15,336
B	4,208	12.00	50,496	10.00	42,080	2.00	8,416
C	1,105	10.00	11,050	8.75	9,669	1.25	1,381
	10,425	$13.26*	$138,226	$10.85*	$113,093	$2.41*	$25,133

*Weighted average.

According to Statement 1, Collier Inc. expected a gross profit of $26,250, based on an estimated production of 10,500 units and an average gross profit of $2.50 per unit. As shown in Statement 2, the company actually made a gross profit of only $20,108, or $1.93 per unit. Statement 3 indicates that the average gross profit for the actual units sold would have been $2.41 per unit if the budgeted sales prices and costs per unit had been achieved.

The $6,142 difference between the budgeted gross profit and the actual gross profit is the result of changes in sales prices, sales volume, sales mix, and costs. For example, on the basis of the budget, A is the most profitable product while C is the least profitable per unit. Due to variations in sales price and cost, B is actually the most profitable while C is the least profitable per unit. The dollar effect of such changes is shown by the calculation of the sales price, sales volume, cost price, cost volume, sales mix, and final sales volume variances.

Computation of the Sales Price and Sales Volume Variances

Using the figures from the statements on pages 537 and 538, the sales price and sales volume variances for Collier Inc. are computed as follows:

Actual sales..	$142,233
Actual sales at budgeted prices	138,226
Sales price variance	$ 4,007 fav.
Actual sales at budgeted prices	$138,226
Budgeted sales..	142,000
Sales volume variance	$ 3,774 unfav.

Computation of the Cost Price and Cost Volume Variances

The cost price and cost volume variances are computed as follows:

Cost of goods sold — actual...	$122,125
Budgeted cost of actual units sold	113,093
Cost price variance	$ 9,032 unfav.
Budgeted cost of actual units sold	$113,093
Budgeted cost of budgeted units sold	115,750
Cost volume variance	$ 2,657 fav.

Computation of the Sales Mix and Final Sales Volume Variances

In the above calculations, two volume variances appear:

Sales volume variance	$3,774 unfav.
Cost volume variance	2,657 fav.
Net volume variance	$1,117 unfav.

The net volume variance should be further analyzed to determine the sales mix and the final sales volume variances. These variances are computed as follows:

Actual sales at budgeted prices		$138,226.00
Budgeted cost of actual units sold		113,093.00
Difference		$ 25,133.00
Budgeted gross profit of actual units sold (10,425 actual units × $2.50 budgeted gross profit per unit).............		26,062.50
Sales mix variance......................................		$ 929.50 unfav.
Budgeted gross profit of actual units sold.................		$ 26,062.50
Budgeted sales...	$142,000	
Budgeted cost of budgeted units sold	115,750	
Budgeted gross profit		26,250.00
Final sales volume variance.............................		$ 187.50 unfav.
Check: Sales mix variance...............................		$ 929.50 unfav.
Final sales volume variance......................		187.50 unfav.
Net volume variance		$ 1,117.00 unfav.

Again, the sales mix variance can be viewed in the following manner:

Product	(1) Actual Sales in Units	Budgeted Sales Units	Budgeted Sales %	(2) Actual Sales (in Budgeted Proportions)	(3) (1) − (2)	(4) Budgeted Unit Gross Profit	Sales Mix Variance (3) × (4)
A	5,112	6,000	57.14	5,957*	(845)	$3.00	$(2,535.00)
B	4,208	3,500	33.33	3,475	733	2.00	1,466.00
C	1,105	1,000	9.53	993	112	1.25	140.00
Total	10,425	10,500	100.00	10,425	–0–		
Rounding difference							(.50)
Net sales mix variance							$ (929.50) unfav.

*10,425 × 57.14% = 5,957.

The final sales volume variance is the difference in the number of actual and budgeted units sold, multiplied by the budgeted average gross profit per unit:

Actual sales units	10,425
Budgeted sales units	10,500
Unit sales difference	75
Budgeted average gross profit per unit	×$2.50
Final sales volume variance	$187.50 unfav.

Recapitulation of Variances

The variances identified in the preceding computations are summarized as follows:

	Gains	Losses
Gain due to increased sales prices	$4,007	
Loss due to increased cost		$ 9,032.00
Loss due to shift in sales mix		929.50
Loss due to decrease in units sold		187.50
Total	$4,007	$10,149.00
		4,007.00
Net decrease in gross profit		$ 6,142.00

Refinement of Sales Volume Analysis

In the above computation, the sales mix and final sales volume variances were determined with the aid of an average gross profit figure and total figures only. However, it is often necessary to trace the causes for a change to the individual products. Using the figures from the income statements of Collier Inc., an analysis by product can be made as follows:

COLLIER INC.
ANALYSIS BY PRODUCT

Amounts Based On	Product A Sales	Cost	Product B Sales	Cost	Product C Sales	Cost
Statement 3..........	$76,680	$61,344	$50,496	$42,080	$11,050	$9,669
Statement 1..........	90,000	72,000	42,000	35,000	10,000	8,750
Difference	−$13,320	+$10,656	+$ 8,496	−$ 7,080	+$ 1,050	−$ 919
Net	−$2,664		+$1,416		+$131	

Recapitulation:

	Sales Volume Gains	Losses
On Product A		$2,664
On Product B	$1,416	
On Product C	131	
Total	$1,547	$2,664
		1,547
Net loss due to sales mix variance and final sales volume variance		$1,117

Uses of Gross Profit Analysis

The gross profit analysis based on budgets and standard costs depicts the weak spots in the period's performance. Management is now able to outline the remedies that should correct the situation. For Collier Inc., the gain due to higher prices is more than offset by the increase in cost, the shift to less profitable products, and the decrease in units sold. As the planned gross profit is the responsibility of the marketing as well as the manufacturing functions, the gross profit analysis brings together these two major functional areas of the firm and points to the need for further study by both of them. The marketing function must explain the changes in sales prices, the shift in the sales mix, and the decrease in units sold, while the production function must account for the increase in cost. To be of real value, the cost price variance should be further analyzed to determine variances for materials, labor, and factory overhead.

DISCUSSION QUESTIONS

1. Why is the gross profit figure significant?

2. What causes changes in the gross profit?

3. Explain product mix or sales mix.

4. By what methods can a change in the gross profit figure be analyzed?

5. Describe how the sales price variance is determined. If the sales price variance were journalized in the books, how would such an entry vary from the entry for the materials purchase price variance?

6. How are the sales mix and the final sales volume variances computed?

7. What is the significance of the average gross profit figure of the base or standard period?

8. The gross profit analysis based on budgets and standards makes use of three basic statements. Name them.

9. What important information is revealed by a gross profit analysis on a product basis?

10. Whose task is it to see that the planned gross profit is met?

EXERCISES

1. *Gross profit analysis.* Nashville Company presents the following data for two retail inventory items:

	19A			19B		
	Units	Per Unit	Amount	Units	Per Unit	Amount
Sales:						
X	11,000	$2.50	$27,500	13,000	$2.55	$33,150
Y	5,000	2.00	10,000	8,000	1.95	15,600
			$37,500			$48,750
Cost of goods sold:						
X	11,000	$2.00	$22,000	13,000	$2.02	$26,260
Y	5,000	1.40	7,000	8,000	1.45	11,600
			$29,000			$37,860
Gross profit	16,000	$.53125	$ 8,500	21,000	$.51857	$10,890

Required: Compute the price and volume variances for sales and cost, and the sales mix and final sales volume variances.

2. *Gross profit analysis.* A cost analyst has prepared a monthly gross profit analysis for Alboc Company, comparing actual to budget for two products, Alco and Bacco. June budget and actual data follow:

	Sales			Cost of Goods Sold		Gross Profit	
	Units	Unit Price	Amount	Unit Cost	Amount	Per Unit	Amount
Budget:							
Alco	8,000	$20.00	$160,000	$16.00	$128,000	$4.00	$32,000
Bacco	4,200	14.00	58,800	12.00	50,400	2.00	8,400
Total budget	12,200	$17.9344*	$218,800	$14.6229*	$178,400	$3.3115*	$40,400
Actual:							
Alco	7,500	$21.00	$157,500	$16.50	$123,750	$4.50	$33,750
Bacco	4,500	13.50	60,750	11.50	51,750	2.00	9,000
Total actual	12,000	$18.1875*	$218,250	$14.625*	$175,500	$3.5625*	$42,750

*Weighted average

Required: Compute the price and volume variances for sales and cost, and the sales mix and final sales volume variances.

3. Gross profit analysis. MCF Industries requests an analysis of changes in gross profit. The following data have been extracted from the company's books:

19A

Product	Units Sold	Unit Price	Total Sales	Cost of Goods Sold Unit	Cost of Goods Sold Total	Gross Profit
Dee.................	20,000	$5.10	$102,000	$4.00	$ 80,000	$22,000
Zee	10,000	3.90	39,000	2.80	28,000	11,000
Total	30,000		$141,000		$108,000	$33,000

19B

Product	Units Sold	Unit Price	Total Sales	Cost of Goods Sold Unit	Cost of Goods Sold Total	Gross Profit
Dee.................	25,000	$5.15	$128,750	$4.01	$100,250	$28,500
Zee	16,000	4.00	64,000	2.93	46,880	17,120
Total	41,000		$192,750		$147,130	$45,620

Required: Compute the price and volume variances for sales and cost, and the sales mix and final sales volume variances.

4. Gross profit analysis. Young Sporting Goods Shop presents the following data for two types of racquetball gloves, leather and fabric, for 19A and 19B:

	19A Units	19A Per Unit	19A Amount	19B Units	19B Per Unit	19B Amount
Sales:						
Leather racquetball gloves..............	8,000	$8.00	$64,000	12,000	$10.00	$120,000
Fabric racquetball gloves	8,000	4.00	32,000	20,000	6.00	120,000
			$96,000			$240,000
Cost of goods sold:						
Leather racquetball gloves..............	8,000	$6.00	$48,000	12,000	$ 9.00	$108,000
Fabric racquetball gloves	8,000	3.00	24,000	20,000	5.00	$100,000
			$72,000			$208,000
Gross profit	16,000	$1.50	$24,000	32,000	$ 1.00	$ 32,000

Required: Compute the price and volume variances for sales and cost, and the sales mix and final sales volume variances.

5. Gross profit analysis. Young Men's Shop handles two lines of men's suits — Bostonian and Varsity. On these suits, the store realized a gross profit of $159,300 in 19A and $159,570 in 19B. The store manager was puzzled because the dollar sales volume and the number of suits sold were higher for 19B than for 19A, yet the gross profit remained about the same.

The firm's accounting records provided the following detailed information:

Year	Bostonian Suits	Bostonian Cost	Bostonian Sales Price	Varsity Suits	Varsity Cost	Varsity Sales Price
19A...............	1,650	$105	$175	1,460	$70	$100
19B...............	1,320	114	190	1,975	80	110

Required: Compute the price and volume variances for sales and cost, and the sales mix and final sales volume variances. (Round off the 19A average gross profit per unit to three decimal places.)

6. Gross profit analysis for one product. *The president of Gladewater Wholesale Company, which markets a single product, requests an explanation for the gross profit decline for August. The following information is available:*

	July			August		
	Units	Per Unit	Total	Units	Per Unit	Total
Sales......................	25,000	$3.00	$75,000	24,000	$2.75	$66,000
Cost of goods sold..........	25,000	$2.38	59,500	24,000	$2.40	57,600
Gross profit			$15,500			$ 8,400

Required: *Prepare a gross profit analysis.*

7. Gross profit analysis based on inpatient service days. *The controller of Brentwood Hospital prepared the following statement of operations, comparing 19B to 19A:*

	19B	19A
Inpatient service days	82,500	75,000
Patient service revenues	$13,860,00	$12,000,000
Cost of services rendered:		
Medicines, linens, and other supplies	$ 1,400,000	$ 1,000,000
Salaries—nurses, interns, residents, staff	9,000,000	7,500,000
Patient service overhead	1,500,000	1,500,000
Total cost of services rendered	$11,900,000	$10,000,000
Gross profit	$ 1,960,000	$ 2,000,000
Administrative expenses..........................	2,013,000	1,800,000
Excess of revenues over expenditures	$ (53,000)	$ 200,000

Required: *Prepare an analysis of the gross profit, including the revenue rate (price), revenue volume, cost price, and cost volume variances. (Round off computations to the nearest thousand.)*

8. Gross profit analysis. *Duo Company's gross profit data for the last year follow (000s omitted):*

	Product AR-10		Product ZR-7		Total	
	Budget	Actual	Budget	Actual	Budget	Actual
Unit sales..............	2,000	2,800	6,000	5,600	8,000	8,400
Sales..................	$6,000	$7,560	$12,000	$11,760	$18,000	$19,320
Cost of goods sold.......	$2,400	$2,800	$ 6,000	$ 5,880	$ 8,400	$ 8,680

Required: *Compute the following:*
(1) Effect on gross profit of Product AR-10's volume variance.
(2) Product ZR-7's sales price variance.
(3) Net gross profit effect from the change in Product ZR-7's unit cost of goods sold.
(4) Sales mix variance.
(5) Final sales volume variance.   *(CMA adapted)*

PROBLEMS

19-1. Gross profit analysis. Kleinfuss Shoe Company manufactures a wide line of ladies' footwear. Sales volume had been increasing rapidly for seven years. However, after a change in executive management, the new president believed that sales volume should increase at an even faster rate. The plan was to increase volume, with the price level remaining the same or declining. After lengthy discussions with the plant manager and the sales manager, a mutually agreeable plan was formulated, whereby the volume was expected to increase with a decrease in the sales price. At the time of this proposal, both the plant manager and the sales manager believed that the existing level of gross profit could be maintained.

In 19A, the last year before adoption of the new plan, the following company data had been recorded with respect to two lines of ladies' footwear–Loafers and Sandals.

	Loafers	Sandals
Shoes sold	10,000	5,000
Revenue	$200,000	$150,000
Gross profit	70,000	60,000

The proposed plan did have the desired effect on 19B gross profit. The president was quite enthusiastic over the success of the plan, but wanted to know if the increased gross profit was attributable to increased sales or reduced costs.

Data for 19B:

	Loafers	Sandals
Shoes sold	12,000	6,000
Revenue	$208,000	$144,000
Cost of goods sold	124,000	86,000
Gross profit	$ 84,000	$ 58,000

Required: Prepare an analysis to indicate the underlying reasons for the change in gross profit.

19-2. Gross profit analysis. The marketing vice-president for Boston Products Company requests an analysis to explain why the gross profit for 19B is smaller than for 19A. The following information is available:

		19A Sales		19A Cost of Goods Sold		19A
Product	Quantity	Unit Price	Amount	Unit Cost	Amount	Gross Profit
A	30,000 units	$3.62	$108,600	$2.70	$ 81,000	$27,600
B	25,000	3.00	75,000	2.38	59,500	15,500
C	75,000	2.50	187,500	2.00	150,000	37,500
Total			$371,100		$290,500	$80,600

		19B Sales		19B Cost of Goods Sold		19B
Product	Quantity	Unit Price	Amount	Unit Cost	Amount	Gross Profit
A	40,000 units	$4.00	$160,000	$3.00	$120,000	$40,000
B	24,000	2.75	66,000	2.40	57,600	8,400
C	70,000	2.50	175,000	2.10	147,000	28,000
Total			$401,000		$324,600	$76,400

Required: Prepare the requested analysis for the marketing vice-president.

19-3. Gross profit analysis. Management of Fargo Wholesale Products Company requested an analysis of changes in gross profit, comparing the year 19B to 19A. The following data have been extracted from the company's books:

19A

Product	Units Sold	Unit Price	Total Sales	Unit Cost	Total	Gross Profit
				Cost of Goods Sold		
X	30,000	$2.13	$63,900	$1.44	$43,200	$20,700
Y	16,000	4.65	74,400	3.81	60,960	13,440
Z	22,000	2.58	56,760	2.13	46,860	9,900
Total	68,000		$195,060		$151,020	$44,040

19B

Product	Units Sold	Unit Price	Total Sales	Unit Cost	Total	Gross Profit
				Cost of Goods Sold		
X	32,000	$2.17	$69,440	$1.84	$58,880	$10,560
Y	18,000	4.95	89,100	4.23	76,140	12,960
Z	24,000	2.72	65,280	2.312	55,488	9,792
Total	74,000		$223,820		$190,508	$33,312

Required:

(1) Compute the price and volume variances for sales and cost.
(2) Prepare an analysis of the total volume variance into the sales mix and final sales volume variances.

19-4. Gross profit analysis. Tribal Products Inc. was organized ten years ago by James Littlebear for the purpose of making and selling souvenirs to tourists in Southwestern Arizona. After much experimentation, the product line has been limited to five products: moccasins, strings of beads, rawhide vests, leather belts, and feathered headdresses. All transactions take place in two small buildings located on tribal land.

In 19B, despite an increase in the total number of units sold, the gross profit of the firm dropped. As a result, Littlebear tentatively blamed the drop in profit on a change in the sales mix.

The accountant has been given the task of analyzing the gross profit of the past two years, shown as follows, in an attempt to pin down the cause of the loss in profits.

19A

	Quantity	Unit Cost	Total Cost	Unit Price	Total Sales	Gross Profit
Moccasins	1,000	$2.50	$ 2,500	$5.00	$ 5,000	$ 2,500
Beads	6,000	.20	1,200	.50	3,000	1,800
Vests	1,500	1.75	2,625	3.50	5,250	2,625
Belts	4,000	.45	1,800	1.00	4,000	2,200
Headdresses	500	4.00	2,000	7.50	3,750	1,750
Total	13,000		$10,125		$21,000	$10,875

19B

	Quantity	Unit Cost	Total Cost	Unit Price	Total Sales	Gross Profit
Moccasins	1,100	$2.60	$2,860	$5.00	$ 5,500	$ 2,640
Beads	6,800	.20	1,360	.50	3,400	2,040
Vests	1,200	1.80	2,160	3.50	4,200	2,040
Belts	4,200	.50	2,100	1.00	4,200	2,100
Headdresses	350	3.80	1,330	7.50	2,625	1,295
Total	13,650		$9,810		$19,925	$10,115

Required: Prepare an analysis of the gross profit decline from 19A to 19B. (Round off the 19A average gross profit per unit to four decimal places.)

19-5. Gross profit analysis and the effect of product aggregation. Cambridge Appliance Company markets irons for home use, classified as nonsteam and steam. For 19A, budgeted and actual sales, cost and gross profit follow:

19A Budget:

Item	Units	Sales Per Unit	Sales Total	Cost Per Unit	Cost Total	Gross Profit Per Unit	Gross Profit Total
Nonsteam	4,000	$22.500	$ 90,000	$20.000	$ 80,000	$2.50	$10,000
Steam	8,000	31.875	255,000	28.625	229,000	3.25	26,000
	12,000	$28.75*	$345,000	$25.75*	$309,000	$3.00*	$36,000

*Weighted average

19A Actual:

Item	Units	Sales Per Unit	Sales Total	Cost Per Unit	Cost Total	Gross Profit Per Unit	Gross Profit Total
Nonsteam	4,000	$21.75	$ 87,000	$19.40	$ 77,600	$2.35	$ 9,400
Steam	10,000	32.50	325,000	29.10	291,000	3.40	34,000
	14,000	$29.43*	$412,000	$26.33*	$368,600	$3.10*	$43,400

*Rounded weighted average

Each iron is of two types—noncoated and coated. The above data, further segmented into four categories, rather than two, follow:

19A Budget:

Item	Units	Sales Per Unit	Sales Total	Cost Per Unit	Cost Total	Gross Profit Per Unit	Gross Profit Total
Nonsteam-Noncoated.....	2,000	$20.00	$ 40,000	$18.00	$ 36,000	$2.00	$ 4,000
Nonsteam-Coated	2,000	25.00	50,000	22.00	44,000	3.00	6,000
Steam-Noncoated	5,000	30.00	150,000	27.20	136,000	2.80	14,000
Steam-Coated	3,000	35.00	105,000	31.00	93,000	4.00	12,000
	12,000	$28.75*	$345,000	$25.75*	$309,000	$3.00*	$36,000

*Weighted average

19A Actual:

Item	Units	Sales Per Unit	Sales Total	Cost Per Unit	Cost Total	Gross Profit Per Unit	Gross Profit Total
Nonsteam-Noncoated.....	2,600	$20.00	$ 52,000	$18.00	$ 46,800	$2.00	$ 5,200
Nonsteam-Coated	1,400	25.00	35,000	22.00	30,800	3.00	4,200
Steam-Noncoated	5,000	30.00	150,000	27.20	136,000	2.80	14,000
Steam-Coated	5,000	35.00	175,000	31.00	155,000	4.00	20,000
	14,000	$29.43*	$412,000	$26.33*	$368,600	$3.10*	$43,400

*Rounded weighted average

Required:

   (1) Prepare a gross profit analysis of irons segmented into two categories: nonsteam and steam.

   (2) Prepare a gross profit analysis of irons segmented into four categories: nonsteam—noncoated and coated, and steam—noncoated and coated.

   (3) Explain the differences in the answers to (1) and (2).

(Based on an article in The Accounting Review)

19-6. Final sales volume and sales mix variances using contribution margin. Morocco Co. makes three grades of indoor-outdoor carpets. The sales volume for the annual budget is determined by estimating the total market volume for indoor-outdoor carpet and then applying the company's prior year's market share, adjusted for planned changes due to company programs for the coming year. The volume is apportioned between the three grades, based upon the prior year's product mix, again adjusted for planned changes due to company programs for the coming year.

   The company's budgeted income statement and the results of operations for the current year are as follows:

Income Statement (Budgeted)
(in thousands of dollars)

	Grade 1	Grade 2	Grade 3	Total
Sales in units.................	1,000 rolls	1,000 rolls	2,000 rolls	4,000 rolls
Sales in dollars................	$1,000	$2,000	$3,000	$6,000
Variable expense	700	1,600	2,300	4,600
Contribution margin...........	$ 300	$ 400	$ 700	$1,400
Traceable fixed expense........	200	200	300	700
Traceable margin..............	$ 100	$ 200	$ 400	$ 700
Marketing and administrative expenses				250
Operating income				$ 450

Income Statement (Actual)
(in thousands of dollars)

	Grade 1	Grade 2	Grade 3	Total
Sales in units	800 rolls	1,000 rolls	2,100 rolls	3,900 rolls
Sales in dollars................	$810	$2,000	$3,000	$5,810
Variable expense	560	1,610	2,320	4,490
Contribution margin...........	$250	$ 390	$ 680	$1,320
Traceable fixed expense........	210	220	315	745
Traceable margin..............	$ 40	$ 170	$ 365	$ 575
Marketing and administrative expenses.............................				275
Operating income				$ 300

   Industry volume was estimated at 40,000 rolls. Actual industry volume for the year was 38,000 rolls.

Required:

   (1) Compute the final sales volume variance, using budgeted contribution margins.

   (2) Explain the effect of the present condition of the carpet industry on the final sales volume variance.

   (3) Compute the dollar impact on profits (using budgeted contribution margins) of the shift in product mix from the budgeted mix.

(CMA adapted)

Chapter 20
Direct Costing and the Contribution Margin

The factory overhead chapters presented the use of the factory overhead rate for product costing. All factory overhead costs were combined into a composite, predetermined rate. When this rate is constructed, a capacity, volume, or activity level must be selected, so that all costs and expenses can be expected to be recovered over a certain period of time. This type of costing, known as *absorption, full,* or *conventional costing,* assigns direct materials and direct labor costs and a share of both fixed and variable factory overhead to units of production.

In responsibility accounting, the division of factory overhead into fixed and variable elements aids management in placing cost accountability on those individuals responsible for the incurrence of these costs. The factory overhead rate used for product costing, however, still includes both variable and fixed elements.

When costs are assigned to production on the basis of a short-run volume, but the predetermined rate is based on the long-run average or normal capacity, the difference is a fixed-cost-oriented variance. If it could be expected that such favorable or unfavorable variances would balance out in the long run, they could be deferred, and the fixed costs included in the periodic cost of goods sold would vary directly and proportionately with sales volume. In such cases, the fixed overhead would behave like the unit variable cost.

However, if the fixed overhead variance is expensed each period or if an actual rather than a predetermined overhead rate is used, fluctuations in the unit product cost occur.

Information accumulated in NAA research studies over a period of years indicates that the concept of long-range normal or standard unit cost for costing production, sales, and inventory is often not applied in practice. The reasons for this failure are:

1. *Long-range normal or standard volume cannot be reliably determined. First, this is a consequence of the fact that long-range volume for a growing company with indefinite future life cannot be defined in concrete terms capable of being implemented by measurement techniques. Second, long-range forecasts of future volume have, at best, a wide and unknown margin of error.*

2. *The services of manufacturing facilities and organizations tend to expire with the passage of time whether or not utilized to produce salable goods. Consequently, the period costs of these services also expire with time. To carry such costs forward to future periods results in mismatching of costs with revenues because no benefits from such costs will be received in the future and nothing is contributed by the cost toward production of future revenues. Thus, the practice of charging unabsorbed period cost against revenues of the current period has been justified by reasoning that this charge measures cost of idle capacity and not cost of production. Similarly, apportionment of large overabsorbed balances reflects the opinion that unit product costs based on standard volume have been overstated.* [1]

The NAA study concludes that "the concept of long-run unit cost of production is unsatisfactory in measuring short period income. The fault in this case is that the wrong cost concept was chosen for the purpose—i.e., the long-run concept of cost was used to measure short-run operations." [2]

The normal capacity concept used for establishing overhead rates is long-range in nature; however, management wants monthly and even weekly earnings reports. It wants to know what was earned last month. It does not ask for a profit figure covering the firm's entire production and sales cycle. Although the usefulness of costing methods for managerial purposes has been aided immeasurably through the use of factory overhead rates and flexible budgets, management always asks for more direct and understandable answers. Direct costing seeks to satisfy these demands.

Direct Costing Defined

Direct costing, also referred to as *variable costing* or *marginal costing*, charges products with only those manufacturing costs that vary directly with volume. Only prime costs (direct materials and direct labor) plus variable factory over-

---

[1] *NAA Research Report, No. 37*, "Applications of Direct Costing" (New York: National Association of Accountants, 1961), pp. 72–73.
[2] *Ibid.*, p. 73.

head expenses are assigned to inventories, both work in process and finished goods, and to the cost of goods sold. Thus, these variable costs are charged to the product, while fixed manufacturing costs are totally expensed in the current period. Manufacturing costs, such as depreciation, insurance, and taxes that are a function of time rather than of production, are excluded from the cost of the product. Also excluded are salaries of factory supervisors and office employees as well as wages of certain factory employees, such as maintenance crews and guards. Because the incurrence of fixed costs is more closely associated with the passage of time than with production activity, such costs are often referred to as *period costs*. In contrast, variable costs are often referred to as *product costs* because they are more closely associated with production activity than with the passage of time.

Facets of Direct Costing

Direct costing focuses attention on the product and its costs. This interest moves in two directions: (1) to internal uses of the fixed-variable cost relationship and the contribution margin concept, and (2) to external uses involving the costing of inventories, income determination, and financial reporting. The internal uses deal with the application of direct costing in profit planning, product pricing, other phases of decision making, and in cost control. These facets of direct costing can be presented as follows:

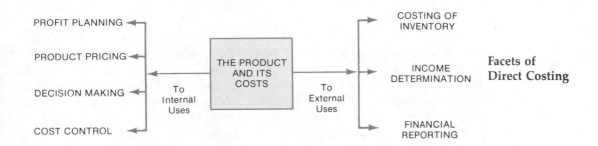

Facets of
Direct Costing

Internal Uses of Direct Costing

Executive management, including marketing executives, production managers, and cost analysts, has generally praised the planning, control, and analytical potentialities of direct costing. Fixed costs calculated on a unit cost basis tend to vary. On the other hand, direct unit costs and the contribution margin per unit tend to remain constant for various volumes of production and sales.

The *contribution margin* or *marginal income* is the result of subtracting all variable costs, both manufacturing and nonmanufacturing, from sales revenue. In direct costing, an income per unit is not calculated. Only total income is determined by subtracting the total fixed cost from the contribution margin, as shown in the following illustration. In this illustration, the figures are based on the assumption that the total variable cost is perfectly variable, with the unit variable cost remaining at $42, and that the fixed cost is perfectly fixed in total.

	Per Unit	Total	Percentage of Sales
Sales (10,000 units)	$70	$700,000	100
Less variable cost	42	420,000	60
Contribution margin	$28	$280,000	40
Less fixed cost		175,000	25
Operating income		$105,000	15

Direct Costing as a Profit-Planning Tool. A *profit plan*, often called a *budget* or *plan of operations*, covers all phases of future operations to attain a stated profit goal. Although such a plan includes both long- and short-range operations, direct costing is quite useful in planning for short periods, in pricing special orders, or in making current operating decisions.

The variable cost and the contribution margin allow quick and fairly reliable profit approximations for making decisions in the short run. In such situations, it is assumed that the change or shift of a small segment within the total volume does not require major changes in capacity, which would change fixed or period costs. Period costs that are specific or relevant to a product, a product line, or any segment of the business should be isolated and attached to the product in order to increase the usefulness of these costs for decision-making purposes.

With its separation of variable and fixed costs and its calculation of the contribution margin, direct costing facilitates analysis of the cost-volume-profit relationship. Direct costing aids in identifying the relevant analytical data for determining the break-even point, the rate of return on investment, the contribution margin by a segment of total sales, and the total profit from all operations based on a given volume. Direct costing also aids management in planning and evaluating the profit resulting from a change of volume, a change in the sales mix, make-or-buy situations, and the acquisition of new equipment. A knowledge of the variable or out-of-pocket costs, fixed costs, and contribution margin provides guidelines for the selection of the most profitable products, customers, territories, and other segments of the entire business. These uses are discussed in later chapters.

Direct Costing as a Guide to Product Pricing. The economist uses the term "monopolistic competition," a hybrid of pure competition and monopoly, to describe a market that has certain characteristics: (1) many firms sell the same or similar products, differentiated only by name, by real or alleged quality, or by service, rather than by price; (2) a firm cannot change the price without considering the reactions of its competitors; and (3) a firm has little difficulty entering or leaving the market. These characteristics are typical for most company situations. How do these features of monopolistic competition affect pricing?

The best or optimum price is that which will yield the maximum excess of total revenue over total cost. The volume at which the increase in total cost due to the addition of one more unit of volume is just equal to the increase in total revenue, or a zero increase in total profit, is the optimum volume. The price at which this volume can be obtained is the optimum price. A higher price will lower the quantity demanded and decrease total profit. A lower price will increase the quantity sold but decrease total profit.

In a highly competitive market, prices are determined through supply and demand interaction. Management regulates supply and attempts to stimulate demand. The primary influence on demand, however, is the consumer. These aspects of pricing and pricing methods are discussed in Chapter 22.

In multiproduct pricing, management needs to know whether each product can be priced competitively in the industry and still contribute sufficiently to the contribution margin for fixed cost recovery and profit. In making pricing decisions, the useful part of a unit cost is the direct cost segment, since it consists of those cost elements that are comparable among firms in the same industry. A long-run pricing policy should, however, make use of a full product cost, i.e., a product cost which includes that portion of fixed (capacity) cost instrumental in the manufacturing process, as well as including a full share of nonmanufacturing costs.

Direct Costing for Managerial Decision Making. Installation of a direct costing system requires a study of cost trends and a segregation of fixed and variable costs. The classification of costs as either fixed or variable, with semivariable expenses properly subdivided into their fixed and variable components, provides a framework for the accumulation and analysis of costs. This also provides a basis for the study of contemplated changes in production levels or proposed actions concerning new markets, plant expansion or contraction, or special promotional activities. Of course, it is important to recognize that a study of cost behavior that identifies fixed and variable costs can be accomplished without the use of a formal direct costing system.

In NAA Research Report No. 37, findings on this phase of direct costing are summarized as follows:

> Companies participating in this study generally feel that direct costing's major field of usefulness is in forecasting and reporting income for internal management purposes. The distinctive feature of direct costing which makes it useful for this purpose is the manner in which costs are matched with revenues.
>
> The marginal income [contribution margin] figure which results from the first step in matching costs and revenues in the direct costing income statement is reported to be a particularly useful figure to management because it can be readily projected to measure increments in net income which accompany increments in sales. The theory underlying this observed usefulness of the marginal income figure in decision making rests upon the fact that, within a limited volume range, period costs tend to remain constant in total when volume changes occur. Under such conditions, only the direct costs are relevant in costing increments in volume.

The tendency of net income to fluctuate directly with sales volume was reported to be an important practical advantage possessed by the direct costing approach to income determination because it enables management to trace changes in sales to their consequence in net income. Another advantage attributed to the direct costing income statement was that management has a better understanding of the impact that period costs have on profits when such costs are brought together in a single group.[3]

Direct Costing as a Control Tool.   The direct costing procedure is said to be the product of an allegedly incomprehensible income statement prepared for management. The possible inverse fluctuations of production costs and sales figures due to fixed manufacturing cost allocations between inventories and cost of goods sold require a different type of costing procedure. By adopting direct costing, management and marketing management in particular believe that a more meaningful and understandable income statement can be furnished by the accountant. However, reports issued should serve not only the marketing department but all divisions of an enterprise. It seems appropriate, therefore, to prepare reports for all departments or responsibility centers based on standard costs, flexible budgets, and a division of all costs into their fixed and variable components.

The marketing manager should receive a statement placing sales and production costs in direct relationship to one another. Differences between intended sales and actual sales caused by changes in sales price, sales volume, or sales mix, which are the direct responsibility of the marketing manager, are detailed for analysis as discussed in Chapter 19. Control of marketing costs is also vital to the total cost control framework (Chapter 21).

Other managers can examine and interpret their reports with respect to the production cost variances originating in their respective areas of responsibility. The production manager is able to study the materials quantity variance, the labor efficiency variance, and the controllable overhead variance. Variable expenses actually incurred can be analyzed by comparing them with the allowable budget figure for work performed. The purchasing agent or manager evaluates the purchase price variance. The personnel manager can be held accountable for labor rate variances. General management, which originally authorized and approved plant capacity in the form of labor and machines, is primarily responsible for utilization of existing facilities. In direct costing, however, no variances result with respect to fixed expenses, since all fixed costs are charged currently against revenue instead of to the product.

Reports constructed on the direct costing basis and augmented by the additional information described become valuable control tools. A profit-responsible management group is continually reminded of the original profit objective for the period. Subsequent approved deviations from the objective are reappraised in light of the current performance. Accounting by organizational lines makes it possible to direct attention to the appropriate

---

[3]*Ibid.*, pp. 84–85.

responsibility. Performance is no longer evaluated on the basis of last month or last year, since each period now has its own standard.

External Uses of Direct Costing

The proponents of direct costing believe that the separation of fixed and variable expenses, and the accounting for each according to some direct costing plan, simplifies both the understanding of the income statement and the assignment of costs to inventories.

To keep fixed overhead out of the reported product costs, variable and fixed expenses should be recorded in separate accounts. Therefore, the chart of accounts should be expanded so that each natural classification has two accounts, as needed—one for the variable and one for the fixed portion of the expense. Also, instead of one overhead control account, two should be used: Factory Overhead Control—Variable Expenses and Factory Overhead Control—Fixed Expenses. When a predetermined overhead rate is used to charge variable expenses to work in process, an applied overhead account labeled Applied Variable Factory Overhead is credited. Differences between actual and applied variable overhead constitute controllable or spending and variable efficiency variances when a standard cost system is used and a spending variance when standard costing is not used. Because fixed expenses are not charged to work in process, they are excluded from the predetermined overhead rate. The total fixed expense accumulated in the account, Factory Overhead Control—Fixed Expenses, is charged directly to Income Summary.

To illustrate the effects of direct costing for external uses, assume that the normal capacity of a plant is 20,000 units per month, or 240,000 units a year. Variable standard costs per unit are: direct materials, $3; direct labor, $2.25; and variable factory overhead, $.75—a total of $6. Fixed factory overhead is $300,000 per year, $25,000 per month, or $1.25 per unit at normal capacity, with any over- or underapplied fixed factory overhead closed to Cost of Goods Sold. The units of production basis is used for applying overhead. Fixed marketing and administrative expenses are $5,000 per month, or $60,000 a year; and variable marketing and administrative expenses are $3,400, $3,600, $4,000, and $3,000 for the first, second, third, and fourth months, respectively.

Actual variable factory overhead is not given. Actual and applied variable overhead are assumed to be the same; otherwise, variable overhead variances could be computed. Likewise, no materials or labor variances are assumed. These variances would not differ and would be presented in the financial statements in the same way, regardless of whether absorption costing or direct costing is used.

In this illustration, there is no work in process inventory; standard costs are assigned to finished goods only. If work in process inventories were present, they would also be assigned standard costs. If standard costs are not used, then an assumption as to flow of costs must be followed in costing inventories, e.g., average, fifo, or lifo.

The sales price per unit is $10, and actual production, sales, and finished goods inventories in units are:

	First Month	Second Month	Third Month	Fourth Month
Units in beginning inventory			3,000	1,000
Units produced	17,500	21,000	19,000	20,000
Units sold	17,500	18,000	21,000	16,500
Units in ending inventory.		3,000	1,000	4,500

From this information, income statements can be prepared. The following income statement — based on absorption costing — includes the fixed factory overhead in the unit cost and also in the costs assigned to inventory. The income statement on page 557 — based on direct costing — excludes the fixed factory overhead from the unit cost and from the costs assigned to inventory.

Income Statement— Absorption Costing

	First Month	Second Month	Third Month	Fourth Month
Sales.	$175,000	$180,000	$210,000	$165,000
Direct materials.	$ 52,500	$ 63,000	$ 57,000	$ 60,000
Direct labor	39,375	47,250	42,750	45,000
Variable factory overhead.	13,125	15,750	14,250	15,000
Fixed factory overhead	21,875	26,250	23,750	25,000
Cost of goods manufactured	$126,875	$152,250	$137,750	$145,000
Beginning inventory			21,750	7,250
Cost of goods available for sale	$126,875	$152,250	$159,500	$152,250
Ending inventory.		21,750	7,250	32,625
Cost of goods sold.	$126,875	$130,500	$152,250	$119,625
Fixed (over-) or underapplied factory overhead. . .	3,125	(1,250)	1,250	
Cost of goods sold at actual	$130,000	$129,250	$153,500	$119,625
Gross profit	$ 45,000	$ 50,750	$ 56,500	$ 45,375
Marketing and administrative expenses.	8,400	8,600	9,000	8,000
Operating income for the month	$ 36,600	$ 42,150	$ 47,500	$ 37,375

Costs Assigned to Inventory. The illustrations show the following ending inventories.

	First Month	Second Month	Third Month	Fourth Month
Absorption costing	−0−	$21,750	$7,250	$32,625
Direct costing.	−0−	18,000	6,000	27,000
Differences.	−0−	$ 3,750	$1,250	$ 5,625

The differences are caused by the elimination of fixed manufacturing expenses from inventories in direct costing. In absorption costing, these fixed expenses form part of the predetermined factory overhead rate and are included in inventories. The exclusion of this overhead from inventories and its offsetting effect on periodic income determination has been particularly criticized by opponents of direct costing.

It has been observed that the amount of fixed cost charged to inventory is affected not only by the quantities produced but also by the inventory costing method employed—a fact which is largely overlooked. It is often correct but not universally valid to say that when production exceeds sales, absorption costing shows a higher profit than does direct costing; or when sales exceed production, absorption costing shows a lower profit than does direct costing. In relation to four methods of inventory costing—average costing, fifo, lifo, and standard costing—an analysis of the differences in operating income under absorption costing and direct costing has shown that the usual generalizations about full and direct costing hold only under the lifo and the standard costing methods. However, under the fifo and the average costing methods, the results are more complex than those considered by the usual generalizations, which therefore do not apply.[4]

	First Month	Second Month	Third Month	Fourth Month
Sales.....................................	$175,000	$180,000	$210,000	$165,000
Direct materials..........................	$ 52,500	$ 63,000	$ 57,000	$ 60,000
Direct labor	39,375	47,250	42,750	45,000
Variable factory overhead..................	13,125	15,750	14,250	15,000
Variable cost of goods manufactured.........	$105,000	$126,000	$114,000	$120,000
Beginning inventory........................			18,000	6,000
Variable cost of goods available for sale......	$105,000	$126,000	$132,000	$126,000
Ending inventory...........................		18,000	6,000	27,000
Variable cost of goods sold	$105,000	$108,000	$126,000	$ 99,000
Gross contribution margin	$ 70,000	$ 72,000	$ 84,000	$ 66,000
Variable marketing and administrative expenses...............................	3,400	3,600	4,000	3,000
Contribution margin........................	$ 66,600	$ 68,400	$ 80,000	$ 63,000
Less fixed expenses:				
Factory overhead........................	$ 25,000	$ 25,000	$ 25,000	$ 25,000
Marketing and administrative..............	5,000	5,000	5,000	5,000
Total fixed expense	$ 30,000	$ 30,000	$ 30,000	$ 30,000
Operating income for the month	$ 36,600	$ 38,400	$ 50,000	$ 33,000

Income Statement— Direct Costing

As explained previously, managers favor direct costing because sales figures guide cost figures. The variable cost of goods sold varies directly with sales volume, and the influence of production on profit is eliminated. The idea of "selling overhead to inventories" might sound plausible and appear pleasing at first; but when the prior month's inventories become this month's beginning inventories, the apparent advantages cancel out. The results of the second month with absorption costing offer a good example of the effects of large production with cost being deferred in inventories into the next period. The absorption costing income statement also demonstrates the effect of expensing the fixed over- or underapplied factory overhead resulting from production fluctuations.

Operating Profits. The inclusion or exclusion of fixed expenses from inventories and cost of goods sold causes the gross profit to vary considerably from the gross contribution margin. The gross contribution margin (sales revenue −

[4]Yuji Ijiri, Robert K. Jaedicke, and John L. Livingstone, "The Effect of Inventory Costing Methods on Full and Direct Costing," *Journal of Accounting Research*, Vol. 3, No. 1, pp. 63–74.

variable manufacturing cost) in direct costing is greater than the gross profit in absorption costing. This difference has also resulted in some criticism of direct costing. It is argued that a greater gross contribution margin might mislead the marketing function into asking for lower prices or demanding higher bonuses or benefits. In most cases, however, sales prices and bonuses are based not on gross profit but on operating income.

The income statements on pages 556 and 557 also show differences in operating income. These differences are attributable to the fixed cost charged to inventory, as follows:

	First Month	Second Month	Third Month	Fourth Month
Absorption costing:				
Operating income for the month	$36,600	$42,150	$ 47,500	$37,375
Direct costing:				
Operating income for the month	36,600	38,400	50,000	33,000
Difference	–0–	$ 3,750	$ (2,500)	$ 4,375
Absorption costing:				
Inventory change (ending less beginning inventory), increase (decrease).............	–0–	$21,750	$(14,500)	$25,375
Direct costing:				
Inventory change (ending less beginning inventory), increase (decrease).............	–0–	18,000	(12,000)	21,000
Difference (inventory change in units × $1.25 fixed portion of overhead rate)	–0–	$ 3,750	$ (2,500)	$ 4,375

The inventory change in this illustration is for finished goods only. If there were work in process inventories, however, they too would be included in the inventory change in order to reconcile the difference in operating income. Also, any over- or underapplied fixed factory overhead deferred on the balance sheet rather than being currently expensed would be a reconciling item in explaining the difference in operating income.

The operating income will be the same in each method when no inventories exist or when no change in the total cost assigned to inventory occurs from the beginning to the end of the period. Although the two illustrations are on a monthly basis, they could just as well be quarterly or annual. The shorter period is chosen to indicate more forcefully the effects of each method.

Financial Reporting. The use of direct costing for financial reporting is not accepted by the American Institute of Certified Public Accountants, the Internal Revenue Service, or the Securities and Exchange Commission, nor has it been endorsed by the Financial Accounting Standards Board. The position of these groups is generally based on their opposition to excluding fixed costs from inventories.

The Position of the AICPA. The basis for the AICPA's position on direct costing is Accounting Research Bulletin No. 43. Its "Inventory Pricing" chapter begins by stressing that "a major objective of accounting for inventories is the proper determination of income through the process of matching appropriate costs against revenues."

The bulletin continues by stating that "the primary basis of accounting for inventories is cost, which has been defined generally as the price paid or consideration given to acquire an asset. As applied to inventories, cost means in principle the sum of the applicable expenditures and charges directly or indirectly incurred in bringing an article to its existing condition and location." In discussing the second point, the bulletin states quite emphatically that "it should also be recognized that the exclusion of all overheads from inventory costs does not constitute an accepted accounting procedure." This last statement seems to apply to direct costing. Proponents of direct costing might argue, however, that while the exclusion of all overhead is not acceptable, by inference the exclusion of some is acceptable. This argument might sound true, but it does not seem to have any bearing on the AICPA's acceptance of direct costing, since in an earlier discussion of cost, the bulletin states that "under some circumstances, items such as idle facility expense, excessive spoilage, double freight, and rehandling costs may be so abnormal as to require treatment as current period charges rather than as a portion of the inventory cost." This appears to be the type of overhead that the AICPA recognizes as excludable from inventories.

The Position of the IRS.   The Internal Revenue Service position is directed by Section 1.471-3(c) of the Regulations, which defines inventory cost in the case of merchandise produced to be: "(1) the cost of raw materials and supplies entering into or consumed in connection with the product, (2) expenditures for direct labor, and (3) indirect production costs incident to and necessary for the production of the particular article, including in such indirect production costs an appropriate portion of management expenses. . . ." Furthermore, Section 1.471-11(a) of the Regulations specifically requires the use of the full absorption method of inventory costing.

The Position of the SEC.   The SEC's refusal to accept annual financial reports prepared on the basis of direct costing is generally the result of (1) its policy to favor consistency among reporting companies as far as possible and (2) its attitude that direct costing is not generally accepted accounting procedure. In filing reports with the SEC, a firm that uses direct costing must adjust its inventories and reported income to what they would have been had absorption costing been used.

Adjustment of Direct Costing Figures for External Reporting.   Companies using direct costing internally make adjustments in preparing income tax returns and external reports. Company practice indicates that comparatively simple procedures are used to determine the amount of periodic adjustment. According to NAA Research Report No. 37, one company reported that period manufacturing costs are divided by actual production to create a costing rate which is applied to the units on hand. Another company expresses these period expenses as a rate per dollar of direct expenses at normal volume. The dollar amount of variable expenses in inventory is then multiplied by the foregoing rate to arrive at the period manufacturing expense component.[5]

---

[5]*NAA Research Report, No. 37, op. cit.*, pp. 94–95.

DISCUSSION QUESTIONS

1. Differentiate between direct costs and direct costing.

2. Distinguish between product and period costs and relate this distinction to direct costing.

3. Describe the difference between direct costing and the current generally accepted method of costing inventory for external reporting.

4. Why does the direct costing theorist exclude fixed manufacturing costs from inventories?

5. Why is it said that an income statement prepared by the direct costing procedure is more helpful to management than an income statement prepared by the absorption costing method?

6. In the process of determining a proper sales price, what kind of cost figures are likely to be most helpful?

7. Describe how direct costing facilitates calculation of the contribution margin and the break-even point.   (AICPA adapted)

8. Why must the chart of accounts be expanded when direct costing is used?

9. List the arguments for and against the use of direct costing.

EXERCISES

1. *Direct and absorption costing.* During the past year, Morgan Company produced 150,000 units (100% of normal capacity) of a product and sold 120,000 of these units. Production costs consisted of $300,000 direct materials, $375,000 direct labor, $150,000 variable factory overhead, and $187,500 fixed factory overhead.

Required:
    (1) Using direct costing, compute (a) the per unit cost of production and (b) the year-end inventory cost.
    (2) Using absorption costing, compute (a) the per unit cost of production and (b) the year-end inventory cost.

2. *Absorption and direct costing.* JV Company began its operations on January 1, 19A, and produces one product that sells for $7. Normal capacity is 100,000 units per year, with 100,000 units produced and 80,000 units sold in 19A.

    Manufacturing costs and marketing and administrative expenses were as follows:

	Fixed Costs	Variable Costs
Materials	—	$1.50 per unit produced
Direct labor	—	1.00 per unit produced
Factory overhead...................	$150,000	.50 per unit produced
Marketing and administrative expenses ..	80,000	.50 per unit sold

There were no variances from the standard variable costs. Any under- or overapplied overhead is written off directly at year end as an adjustment to the cost of goods sold.

Required:
  (1) In presenting inventory on the December 31, 19A balance sheet, compute the unit cost under absorption costing.
  (2) Determine the 19A operating income, using direct costing.

3. Direct and absorption costing. Nebbish Company is comparing its present absorption costing practices with direct costing methods. An examination of its records produced the following information:

Maximum plant capacity...	40,000 units
Normal capacity...	36,000
Fixed factory overhead..	$54,000
Fixed marketing and administrative expenses............................	20,000
Sales price per unit..	10
Standard variable manufacturing cost per unit............................	4
Variable marketing expense per unit sold..............................	1

For the year, the following data are available:

Budgeted production...	36,000 units
Actual production...	30,000
Sales..	28,000
Finished goods inventory, January 1.................................	1,000
Unfavorable variances from standard variable manufacturing costs.........	$ 5,000

All variances are written off directly at year end as an adjustment to the cost of goods sold.

Required:
  (1) Prepare a direct costing income statement.
  (2) Determine operating income if absorption costing had been used, with the standard factory overhead per unit based on normal capacity.   (CGAA adapted)

4. Income statements—absorption costing vs. direct costing. The following data pertain to April:

Beginning inventory...	-0-
Units sold...	5,000
Units produced...	8,000
Sales price per unit...	$ 24
var Direct manufacturing cost per unit................................	10
Fixed factory overhead—total......................................	28,000
Fixed factory overhead—per unit....................................	3.50
Commercial expense (all fixed).....................................	10,000

Required:
  (1) Prepare an income statement using absorption costing. *$42500 Inc*
  (2) Prepare an income statement using direct costing.   *$ 38000 Inc*
  (3) Provide computations explaining the difference in operating income between the two methods.   *Reconciliation*

5. Direct costing gross profit statements and comparison with absorption costing. In one of its divisions, Snapcraft Inc. produces a patented connector sold primarily to commercial fertilizer distributors at a unit price of $12. Normal monthly production is 6,000 units, and at this level the variable manufacturing cost is $5 per unit and the fixed manufacturing cost is $18,000 per month.

Gross profit statements for the first three months of the year, using absorption costing, show:

	January	February	March
Sales.	$48,000	$36,000	$96,000
Beginning inventory.	-0-	$16,000	$40,000
Cost of goods manufactured	$48,000	48,000	48,000
Cost of goods available for sale	$48,000	$64,000	$88,000
Ending inventory.	16,000	40,000	24,000
Cost of goods sold.	$32,000	$24,000	$64,000
Gross profit	$16,000	$12,000	$32,000

Required:

(1) Prepare gross profit statements for each month, using direct costing.
(2) Provide computations explaining the differences in gross profit for each month.

6. Inventory costs—absorption vs. direct costing. Olson Company produces a product having the following standard cost per unit:

Direct materials.	$6
Direct labor	8
Variable factory overhead.	5
Fixed factory overhead	2

Normal capacity is 80,000 units. During 19A, 75,000 units were produced and 60,000 were sold. There was no finished goods beginning inventory and no beginning or ending work in process inventory.

Actual 19A costs incurred were:

Direct materials.	$ 460,000
Direct labor	625,000
Variable factory overhead.	370,000
Fixed factory overhead	148,500
Total	$1,603,500

Required: Determine the cost assigned to finished goods ending inventory under each of the following methods:

(1) Direct costing, using standard cost, with variable cost variances prorated.
(2) Absorption costing, using actual cost.
(3) Absorption costing, using actual prime cost and applied factory overhead, based on normal capacity and assuming factory overhead variances are not prorated.

(CGAA adapted)

7. Comparison of direct costing to absorption costing. Huber Corporation's November income statement, based on direct costing, is as follows:

Sales (100,000 units @ $24).		$2,400,000
Variable cost of goods sold (100,000 units @ $12).		1,200,000
Contribution margin		$1,200,000
Less fixed expenses:		
Factory overhead.	$600,000	
Marketing and administrative.	400,000	1,000,000
Operating income.		$ 200,000

Normal capacity for November is 150,000 units, with 145,000 units produced in November.

Required:

(1) *Prepare the November income statement on an absorption costing basis, with applied factory overhead based on normal capacity and any over- or underapplied factory overhead closed to Cost of Goods Sold.*

(2) *Reconcile and explain the difference between the direct costing and the absorption costing operating income figures.*

(3) *Explain the features associated with direct costing income measurement that should be useful to management.* (CMA adapted)

8. *Income statements — absorption costing vs. direct costing. The following annual flexible budget has been prepared by Strohaus Inc. for use in making decisions relating to its Product X:*

	100,000 Units	150,000 Units	200,000 Units
Sales.	$800,000	$1,200,000	$1,600,000
Manufacturing costs:			
Variable	$300,000	$ 450,000	$ 600,000
Fixed.	200,000	200,000	200,000
Total manufacturing cost.	$500,000	$ 650,000	$ 800,000
Marketing and other expenses:			
Variable	$200,000	$ 300,000	$ 400,000
Fixed.	160,000	160,000	160,000
Total marketing and other expenses	$360,000	$ 460,000	$ 560,000
Operating income (loss)	$ (60,000)	$ 90,000	$ 240,000

The 200,000-unit budget has been adopted and will be used for allocating the fixed manufacturing cost to units of Product X. At the end of the first six months, the following information is available:

> Production completed . . . .   120,000 units
> Sales @ $8 per unit. . . . .   60,000 units

All fixed costs are budgeted and incurred uniformly throughout the year, and all costs incurred coincide with the budget. The over- and underapplied fixed manufacturing cost is deferred on the balance sheet until the end of the year.

Required:

(1) *Compute the amount of fixed manufacturing cost applied to production during the first six months under absorption costing.*

(2) *In income statement format (including ending inventory), show (a) the operating income (loss) for the first six months under absorption costing; (b) the operating income (loss) for the first six months under direct costing.*

(3) *Prepare computations explaining the difference in operating income (loss).*

(AICPA adapted)

PROBLEMS

20-1. Income statements — absorption costing vs. direct costing. Sales and operating profits of Cregg Company for the first two quarters of the year were as follows:

	First Quarter	Second Quarter
Sales..................	$300,000	$450,000
Operating profit........	55,000	57,000

The directors were concerned that a 50% increase in sales resulted in only a small increase in operating profit. Using the following data, the chief accountant explained that unabsorbed factory overhead was charged to second-quarter operations.

	First Quarter	Second Quarter
Sales in units	20,000	30,000
Production in units......................................	30,000	24,000
Ending inventory in units...............................	10,000	4,000
Sales price per unit.....................................	$ 15	$ 15
Variable manufacturing cost per unit.....................	5	5
Fixed manufacturing cost	180,000	180,000
Fixed factory overhead rate per unit.....................	6	6
Marketing and administrative expenses ($25,000 fixed).....	25,000	27,000

All over- and underapplied factory overhead is closed to the cost of goods sold account at the end of each quarter.

Required:

(1) Prepare an income statement for the second quarter, using the method now employed by Cregg Company.
(2) Prepare a direct costing income statement for the second quarter.
(3) Explain the difference in the requirement (1) and (2) answers.
(4) Compute operating profit for the second quarter under each method, if production in that period had been 30,000 units. Explain the difference, if any.

(CGAA adapted)

20-2. Direct costing statements; explanation of profit differences. In one of its divisions, Connects Inc. produces a connector sold primarily to commercial fertilizer distributors at $8 each. Normal production is 6,000 units per month, and at this level the variable manufacturing cost is $2.50 per unit and the fixed manufacturing cost is $9,000 per month. Gross profit statements for this product for the first three months of the year, using absorption costing, show:

	January		February		March	
Sales..............................		$36,000		$32,000		$48,000
Beginning inventory.................	-0-		$ 6,000		$14,000	
Cost of goods manufactured..........	$24,000		24,000		24,000	
Cost of goods available for sale.......	$24,000		$30,000		$38,000	
Ending inventory....................	6,000		14,000		14,000	
Cost of goods sold		18,000		16,000		24,000
Gross profit.........................		$18,000		$16,000		$24,000

Required:

(1) Prepare statements for each of the three months, using direct costing.
(2) Explain the statement differences for each month under absorption costing and direct costing.

20-3. Income statements — absorption costing vs. direct costing. On January 2, Commerce Reel Company began production of a new model. First quarter sales were 20,000 units and second quarter sales were 26,000 units at a unit price of $10. Unit production costs each quarter were: direct materials, $1; direct labor, $2; and variable factory overhead, $1.50. Fixed factory overhead was $62,400 each quarter and, for absorption costing, is assigned to inventory based on actual units produced.

Marketing and administrative expenses consisted of a $15,000 fixed portion each quarter and a variable portion which was 5% of sales. Units produced in the first quarter and the second quarter totaled 30,000 and 20,000, respectively. The fifo inventory costing method is used.

Required: Prepare comparative income statements for the first and second quarters, using (a) absorption costing and (b) direct costing.

20-4. Direct costing income statement. Crawford Company uses a standard cost system in accounting for its only product, Craw, which it sells for $22 per unit. The standard cost per unit is:

Direct materials	$ 4
Direct labor	6
Variable factory overhead	2
Fixed factory overhead (based on normal capacity of 60,000 units)	3
	$15

All variances are closed to Cost of Goods Sold.

On October 1, there were 10,000 units of Craw on hand. During October, 50,000 units were produced and 45,000 were sold. Costs incurred during October were:

Direct materials	$198,000
Direct labor	305,000
Variable factory overhead	103,000
Fixed factory overhead	186,000
Variable marketing and administrative	50,000
Fixed marketing and administrative	74,000

Required:
(1) Explain whether Crawford uses direct or absorption costing.
(2) Prepare an income statement for October, using direct costing.
(3) Compute the operating income for October if absorption costing is used.

(CGAA adapted)

20-5. Income statements — absorption costing vs. direct costing. Vanderstraat Company is a specialty glass company that makes glass equipment for scientific research. Its main product is Dewar flasks used for storing liquid nitrogen and helium, which evaporate rapidly at warmer temperatures. The Dewar flask is a continuous tube of glass forming a U-shape, with a short stand on the bottom, and it functions much like a thermos bottle.

Vanderstraat Company uses highly skilled glassblowers to make the flasks by hand. A tube of glass is heated and bent into the U-shape. While the bottom of the U is still hot, the foot or stand is blown. The inside of the tube is then silvered, the air evacuated, and the ends sealed off. The silvering and the vacuum serve to reduce heat transfer and deflect light, so that when a liquid gas is poured into the container and the lid (purchased elsewhere by the user) is sealed in place, the element will remain liquid for several hours.

This small company accounts for production costs on an absorption costing basis. Vanderstraat, however, the president and a glassblower by trade, has difficulty understanding how the cost of tools, lights, protective glasses, and other fixed factory overhead items can become inventory, and feels that the business could be managed better if only direct materials and labor and variable factory overhead were to be assigned to inventory and all fixed factory overhead charged to expense as it occurs. The standard cost of one Dewar flask, as used in the firm's standard costing system, is:

Glass..	$ 2.00
Silver (.5 ounce @ $6.00)................................	3.00
Direct labor (3 hours @ $8.00)...........................	24.00
Variable factory overhead ($.50 per dlh)	1.50
Fixed factory overhead ($1.00 per dlh)...................	3.00
	$33.50

Other data for April are:

Sales price, $50.00.

Sales, 175 units.

Production, 184 units, which equals the normal capacity activity level.

April 30 inventory of Dewar flasks, 20 units.

Favorable materials variance (glass), $18.40.

Silver prices have been going up and the average price of all silver used last month was $6.45 per ounce. But, in an effort to save on the increase in price, only 98% of the standard quantity was used, which can be done without making the flask unsafe.

Actual factory overhead was $950.

Administrative expenses have been running about 5% of sales revenue.

Required: Prepare income statements for April, using absorption costing and direct costing, with a reconciliation of any profit difference. The firm closes all standard cost variances to the cost of goods sold account.

20-6. Absorption costing vs. direct costing. Reep Corporation is considering changing its method of inventory costing from absorption to direct costing and wants to determine the effect of the proposed change on its financial statements. The firm manufactures Gink, which is sold for $20 per unit. A raw material, Marsh, is added before processing starts; labor and factory overhead are added evenly during the manufacturing process. Production capacity is budgeted at 110,000 units of Gink annually. The standard costs per unit of Gink are:

Marsh (2 lbs. @ $1.50).....................................	$ 3.00
Labor	6.00
Variable factory overhead	1.00
Fixed factory overhead.....................................	1.10
Total unit cost...	$11.10

Process costing is used with standard costs. Variances from standard costs are now debited or credited to Cost of Goods Sold. If direct costing were adopted, only variances resulting from variable costs would be debited or credited to Cost of Goods Sold.

Inventory data for the year are as follows:

	January 1	December 31
Marsh..	50,000 lbs.	40,000 lbs.
Work in process:		
⅔ processed	10,000 units	
⅓ processed		15,000 units
Finished goods.............................	20,000	12,000

During the year, 220,000 lbs. of Marsh were purchased, and 230,000 lbs. were transferred to work in process inventory. Also, 110,000 units of Gink were transferred to finished goods inventory. Annual fixed factory overhead, budgeted and actual, was $121,000. There were no variances between standard and actual variable costs during the year.

Required:

(1) Compute (a) equivalent units of production for materials, labor, and factory overhead for the year; (b) number of units sold during the year; (c) standard unit costs under direct costing and absorption costing; (d) over- or underapplied fixed factory overhead, if any, for the year.

(2) Prepare a comparative cost of goods sold statement for the year, using standard direct costing and standard absorption costing. (AICPA adapted)

20-7. Income statements — direct costing vs. absorption costing. Hogg Company uses direct costing for its internal management purposes and absorption costing for external reporting. Thus, at the end of each·year, financial data must be converted from direct costing to absorption costing in order to satisfy external requirements.

At the end of 19A, the company anticipated that sales would increase 20% next year. Therefore, production was increased from 20,000 units to 24,000 units to meet this expected demand. However, economic conditions kept the sales level at 20,000 units for each year.

The following data pertain to 19A and 19B:

	19A	19B
Sales price per unit	$30	$30
Sales (units)	20,000	20,000
Beginning inventory (units)	2,000	2,000
Production (units)	20,000	24,000
Ending inventory (units)	2,000	6,000
Total unfavorable materials, labor, and variable factory overhead variances	$5,000	$4,000

Standard variable costs per unit for 19A and 19B are:

Materials	$ 4.50
Labor	7.50
Variable factory overhead	3.00
Total	$15.00

Annual fixed costs for 19A and 19B (budgeted and actual) are:

Production	$ 90,000
Marketing and administrative	100,000
Total	$190,000

The factory overhead rate under absorption costing is based on practical plant capacity, which is 30,000 units per year. All variances and over- or underabsorbed factory overhead are closed to Cost of Goods Sold.

Required:

(1) Prepare income statements for 19B, based on (a) direct costing and (b) absorption costing. (The beginning and ending inventories need not be shown on the income statements, i.e., show cost of goods as one figure.)

(2) Explain the difference, if any, in the operating income figures and make the entry, if necessary, to adjust the book figures to the financial statement figures.

(CMA adapted)

CASE

Sales and production volume effects—absorption costing vs. direct costing.
Star Company, a wholly-owned subsidiary of Orbit Inc., produces and sells three main product lines. The company employs a standard cost accounting system for record-keeping purposes.

At the beginning of the year, the president of Star Company presented the budget to the parent company and accepted a commitment to contribute $15,800 to Orbit's consolidated profit in 19--. The president has been confident that the year's profit would exceed the budget target, since the monthly sales reports have shown that sales for the year will exceed the budget by 10%. The president is both disturbed and confused when the controller presents an adjusted forecast as of November 30, indicating that profit will be 11% under budget. The two forecasts are as follows:

	Forecasts as of	
	January 1	November 30
Sales..	$268,000	$294,800
Cost of goods sold at standard......................	212,000*	233,200
Gross profit at standard	$ 56,000	$ 61,600
Less underapplied factory overhead	—	6,000
Gross profit at actual..............................	$ 56,000	$ 55,600
Marketing expense.................................	$ 13,400	$ 14,740
Administrative expense.............................	26,800	26,800
Total commercial expense	$ 40,200	$ 41,540
Income from operations	$ 15,800	$ 14,060

*Includes fixed factory overhead of $30,000.

There have been no sales price changes or product mix shifts since the January 1 forecast. The only cost variance on the income statement is the underapplied factory overhead. This arose because the company used only 16,000 standard machine hours (budgeted machine hours were 20,000) during the year as a result of a shortage of raw materials. Fortunately, Star Company's finished goods inventory was large enough to fill all sales orders received.

Required:
(1) Analyze and explain the forecast profit decline, in spite of increased sales and good cost control.
(2) Explain and illustrate an alternative internal cost reporting procedure which would avoid the confusing effect of the present procedure.   (CMA adapted)

Chapter 21
Marketing Cost and Profitability Analysis

Marketing is the matching of a company's products with markets for the satisfaction of customers at a reasonable profit for the firm. Marketing managers must decide the (1) product selection, design, color, size, and packaging, (2) prices to be charged, (3) advertising and promotion needed, and (4) physical distribution to be followed. These numerous decisions require organization, planning, and control. Marketing is usually organized by product or brand lines or by territories or districts. The planning and control phases should be based on a well-structured marketing cost and profitability analysis system.

The preparation of budgets and the need for budgeting in planning and controlling the marketing effort of a firm are discussed in Chapter 14. At the end of each month, budget reports that indicate the success or failure of the budgetary boundaries are issued. However, the problems associated with marketing costs do not end with these budgetary procedures. Cost control at the departmental level is the important feature of any cost improvement program. Yet, in marketing, the emphasis ordinarily rests on selling rather than on costs. To limit marketing costs unreasonably might lead to a curtailment of sales activities, which in turn could mean the gradual deterioration or elimination of certain types of sales. Conversely, indiscriminate and wasteful spending should not be sanctioned.

It is important to note that general and administrative expenses and research and development costs should also be planned, analyzed, and controlled. Department stores and other merchandising businesses recognized the functional cost control concept many years ago. The financial success of these firms is in no small measure due to the control and reduction of costs on a departmental-functional line basis. In fact, the same concepts and techniques are applicable to costs experienced in local, state, and federal governmental units and in other nonbusiness organizations where functional cost control and analysis are not only possible but necessary. For example, municipal functions such as trash collection or street cleaning should be placed on a departmental budget basis, with a supervisor responsible for the efficient operation of the function and accountable for the cost control within the limits of the budget.

Scope of Marketing Costs

Control and analysis of marketing costs complement each other and involve the assignment of marketing expenses to various costing groups such as territories, customers, and products. However, assigned costs must be controlled through analysis within the jurisdictional function as well, in order to hold each marketing activity to the budgeted level.

This phase of cost accounting also calls for the determination of marketing costs for managerial decisions, thereby making it an integral part of business planning and policy formulation. Management requires meaningful marketing cost information in order to determine and analyze the profitability of (1) a territory or territories; (2) certain classes of customers, such as wholesalers, retailers, institutions, and governmental units; (3) products, product lines, or brands; and (4) promotional efforts by salespersons, telephone, mail, television, or radio.

The scope of today's marketing activities includes not only the fulfilling of existing demands, but also the creation and discovery of new demands for a company's products and services. Industry must concentrate on satisfying customers rather than on merely producing products. This outlook requires the best available working tools for management's use. In many organizations, the marketing activity has always received management's attention, and in some cases even more attention than that rendered to other business operations. In today's economy, the strategic importance and magnitude of marketing costs merit still greater attention.

Comparison of Marketing and Manufacturing Costs

The control and analysis of marketing costs present certain complexities. First of all, logistic systems are many and varied. Manufacturers of certain products use basically the same materials and machinery. However, these companies may use vastly different channels of distribution, ranging from a simple, direct distribution to a complex marketing system, with promotional efforts directed to narrow or broad customer groups. Therefore, a meaningful comparison of the marketing costs of one company with another is almost impossible.

Not only do distribution methods vary, but they are also extremely flexible. A company may find that a change in market conditions necessitates a change in its channels of distribution. Distribution standards must be revised with every change in the method of distribution, so tactics may change several times before the best method is found. Such changes would be disastrous in production, however. Once a factory is set up, management is not likely to change its manufacturing techniques to any great extent. Therefore, standards set for a particular machine do not require much revision.

The psychological factors present in selling a product are perhaps the main reasons for differences between manufacturing and marketing costing. Management can control the cost of labor, hours of operation, and number of machines operated; but management cannot control what the customer will do. Various salespersons may have different effects on a customer, who responds to varying appeals. Customer resistance is the enigma in marketing cost analysis. The customer is a controlling rather than a controllable factor, whose wishes and peculiarities govern the method of doing business.

The attitudes of marketing and manufacturing management also differ. Although factory managers are eager to measure their accomplishments in terms of reduced cost per unit, most sales managers consider sales the yardstick for measuring their efficiency, although increased sales do not always mean greater profits.

Cause and effect, generally obvious in the factory, are not so readily discernible in the marketing processes. For example, many promotional costs are incurred for future results, creating a time lag between cause and effect. Conversely, the effects of manufacturing changes are usually felt quickly, and matching between effort and result can usually be achieved. Furthermore, manufacturing results are more readily quantified than are marketing costs. For marketing costs, it is often not easy to identify quantities or units of activity with the cost incurred and results achieved.

Generally accepted accounting practice does not charge Cost of Goods Sold and ending inventories with marketing and administrative expenses. These and other nonmanufacturing expenses usually fall into the category of period costs, even if variable, and as such are charged off in total at the end of the accounting period. Thus, marketing costs are generally charged against the operations of the accounting period in which they are incurred, while production costs are held in inventory until the units are sold. This practice is followed because too much uncertainty exists as to the probable results in future periods arising from incurred marketing expenses. Depreciable marketing assets (such as delivery trucks) should, of course, be expensed over their useful lives, not when acquired.

In the field of marketing costs, it is more common to speak of marketing cost analysis rather than of marketing cost accounting. A tie-in of marketing costing with the general accounts, although desirable, is often not necessary.

Marketing cost control and analysis deals primarily with historical or past costs, evaluating past performances as related to standards and budgets. In connection with future policies, forecast or predetermined figures are employed. In either case, whether judging past performances or deciding on future activities, the possibility of reducing costs and increasing profits through modern methods applied to the marketing area presents a real challenge to management and the accountant.

The control and analysis of marketing costs should follow methods that are similar to those used for manufacturing costs. The control of marketing costs is aided by the following procedures:

1. Departmentalization of activities or functions.
2. Assignment of responsibility for operations.
3. Recognition of direct and indirect departmental expenses.
4. Separation of fixed and variable expenses.
5. Determination and establishment of bases for applying indirect expenses to territories, customers, or products.
6. Comparison of actual with budgeted expenses for continuous control by responsible department supervisors.
7. Use of flexible budgets and standard costs.

Marketing Studies for Profit Planning and Control

Marketing studies deal with the collection, organization, and analysis of data to solve a wide variety of problems. Some of these problems are identified in the following chart:[1]

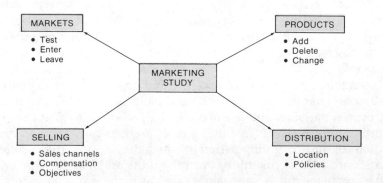

[1]Adapted from Neil Doppelt, "Marketing Studies," *Arthur Andersen Chronicle* (Chicago: Arthur Andersen & Co.), Vol. XXXVII, No. 1, pp. 31–39.

Marketing studies support strategic planning decisions and their control. The skills required for these studies are comparable to those normally needed for the planning, design, and implementation of business information systems in general and include (1) project definition, (2) technical skills, including accounting, (3) analytical and interpretive ability, (4) industry knowledge, and (5) project management—all in the context of relevant data provided by the accounting information system.

Marketing Cost Control

The first step in the control of marketing costs is the classification of natural expenses according to functions or activities. It is essential that each function and its associated expenses be made the responsibility of an individual department head.

Marketing functions are of many types, depending on the nature of the business and its organization, size, and method of operation. Each function should be a homogeneous unit, whose activity can be related to specific items of cost. A function might follow a particular pattern of natural expenses, but most functions will have similar expenses, such as salaries, insurance, property taxes, heat, light, power, and supplies.

The chart of accounts should be so designed that each function receives directly as many of its charges as possible instead of through allocations. In the chart of accounts illustrated in Chapter 2, marketing expenses have been coded in the 500 series (500–599). However, a three-digit number is ordinarily not sufficient to permit the proper assignment of an expense. For this reason, the original number might be expanded as follows:

Digits	Code	Classification
First two digits	05	Marketing expenses
Third and fourth digits	-01-	Primary or natural expense (e.g., Salaries—Sales Supervision)
Fifth and sixth digits	-10-	Function or department
Seventh and eighth digits	-20-	Territory or district
Ninth and tenth digits	-30-	Product or product line

The use of a ten-digit code number indicates the great amount of detail required for a meaningful analysis. Electronic data processing equipment permits the use of these and additional code numbers and classifications.

Functional classifications of marketing costs might be structured in the following manner:

1. Selling.
2. Advertising.
3. Warehousing.
4. Packing and shipping.
5. Credit and collection.
6. General accounting (for marketing).

These functional classifications can be grouped into two broad categories: order-getting costs and order-filling costs. Order-getting costs are the costs of activities carried on to bring in the sales orders and include selling and advertising. Order-filling costs are the costs of warehousing, packing and shipping, credit and collection, and general accounting.

A broad category of marketing administration costs may also be identified. This category includes the costs of marketing planning and organization, market research and forecasting, product design and development, and product-line planning.

Direct and Indirect Expenses

Direct expenses are those expenses that can be identified directly with a function or department, such as the salary of a department manager or the depreciation of a delivery truck. Expenses which can be identified with a territory, customer, product, or definite type of sales outlet may also be considered direct costs. Conversely, indirect expenses are incurred for more than one function or other classification and hence must be allocated. A direct expense may also be allocated when direct identification requires excessive clerical expense.

Marketing expenses may be directly identifiable with functional classifications although indirectly with respect to other classifications such as territories or products, or vice versa, or the expense may be indirect both as to function as well as to other classifications. Thus, the functional classifications may themselves include indirect costs. Expenses of this type include items such as heat, light, maintenance, and the marketing manager's salary. Because these expenses cannot be assigned directly, they are recorded in total and then allocated by appropriate bases to various functions.

Functionally classified marketing costs which are indirect with respect to other classifications may be allocated to such classifications as territories and products by (1) using a percentage based on actual sales, manufacturing cost, or some other basis, or (2) creating a standard unit cost for each activity—similar to factory costs. Expenses that are directly identified with one of these other classifications must be excluded from the allocation; otherwise, double counting would result.

The assignment of functional marketing expenses as percentages of actual sales or manufacturing costs, or on some other basis, does not offer reliable results. The procedure has been used in the past for want of more satisfactory methods. The determination of a functional standard unit costing rate is a more dependable solution. The charging of marketing expense activities on the basis of a costing rate is a logical extension of widely adopted factory standard costing procedures. Furthermore, the availability of such a rate permits quick and decisive analysis. Actual expenses would be collected in the customary manner and charged to their departmental and natural expense classifications in a subsidiary ledger controlled by a marketing expenses control account in the general ledger.

Selection of Bases for the Allocation of Functional Costs. The apportionment process poses two basic questions: (1) what bases should be used for the allocation and (2) how far should the allocations be carried out? As a solution to the first, the bases used should be fair and equitable. They should be an ideal combination of efforts expended and benefits reaped. The second question occurs because of doubts raised as to the advantages of full allocation of all indirect expenses. Suggestions have been made that certain expenses should be omitted from the allocation procedure when they are not measurable in relation to the function or activity. This is especially true when benefits are so widely dispersed that any allocation is a mere guess.

Factory overhead rates use a base which most definitely expresses the effort connected with the work of the department, such as labor hours, machine hours, or labor cost. A similar procedure for allocating marketing expenses is to divide the total cost of each marketing function by the units of functional service (the base) to obtain the cost per unit. Either an actual rate or a predetermined standard rate may be used, but the latter is preferable.

The selection of bases or units of measurement requires careful analysis, because the degree to which the final rates represent acceptable costs is greatly dependent upon the adequacy of the bases selected. Each function must be examined with respect to that factor which most influences the volume of its work. Because of the varied services rendered by the numerous functions, different bases are used. It is possible, however, to use one basis for two or more functions. Some of the bases for each function are as follows:

Function	Cost Allocation Bases
Selling	Gross sales dollar value of products sold or number of salespersons' calls on customers (based on salespersons' time reports)
Advertising	Quantity of product units sold, relative media circulation, or cost of space directly assignable
Warehousing	Size, weight, or number of products shipped or handled
Packing and shipping	Number of shipping units, weight, or size of units
Credit and collection	Number of customers' orders, transactions, or invoice lines
General accounting	Number of customers' orders, transactions, or invoice lines

CAS 418, "Allocation of Direct and Indirect Costs," calls for the allocation of indirect costs to be based on one of the following, listed in order of preference: (1) a resource consumption measure, (2) an output measure, or (3) a surrogate that is representative of resources consumed.[2] These bases pertain to the subject of indirect costs assigned to government contracts. However, for

---

[2]*Standards, Rules and Regulations, Part 418*, "Allocation of Direct and Indirect Costs" (Washington, D.C.: Cost Accounting Standards Board, 1980).

broader cost accounting system uses, they afford useful instruction in determining appropriate bases for allocating costs of various marketing as well as manufacturing functions, resulting in more equitable allocations and more meaningful functional unit costs.

Determination of Functional Unit Cost. The unit cost of an activity is calculated by dividing the total cost of the function by the measurement unit or base selected. A vast amount of information must be collected in order to establish a functional unit costing rate. The tedious assembly of such underlying information is often the reason for the lack of a marketing cost system. When the system is based on standards, the initial work might be more elaborate. However, once the procedure is established, its actual operation should not only be less expensive, but the value derived should far outweigh any previous expenses incurred in establishing the system.

Fixed and Variable Expenses

Recognition of the fixed-variable cost classification is valuable in controlling marketing costs and in making decisions dealing with the possible opening or closing of a territory, new methods of packaging goods, servicing different types of outlets, or adding or dropping a product line. Fixed marketing expenses include salaries of executive and administrative sales staffs; salaries of warehousing, advertising, shipping, billing, and collection departments; and rent and depreciation of associated permanent facilities. These fixed costs have also been called *capacity costs*.

Variable marketing costs include the expenses of handling, warehousing, and shipping that tend to vary with sales volume. They have been referred to as *volume costs* or as expenses connected with the filling of an order. Another type of variable marketing cost originates in connection with promotional expenses such as salespersons' salaries, travel, and entertainment and some advertising expenses. Management must examine these costs carefully in the planning stage, since sales volume may have little influence upon their behavior. These expenses are variable because of management decisions. In fact, once agreed to by management, these expenses may be fixed, at least for the budget period under consideration.

Flexible Budget and Standards for Marketing Functions

Sales estimates are basically the most important figures in any budget. The accuracy and usefulness of most other estimates depend on them. Methods used in determining sales budget estimates are discussed in Chapter 14. Total sales are ordinarily broken down into the various kinds of products to be sold, into monthly or weekly sales, and into sales by salespersons, territories, classes of customers, and methods of distribution. In each division, quotas may be useful for determining the desirability of cultivating various outlets and for judging the efficiency of sales methods and policies.

Budgets are set up to anticipate the amount of functional expenses for the coming period and to compare them with the actual expenses. Because of the influence of volume and capacity, a comparison of actual costs with predetermined fixed budget figures does not always give a fair evaluation of the activities of a function. Therefore, the use of flexible budgets for the control of marketing costs should be considered.

The flexible budget for a distributive function such as billing might take the following form:

FLEXIBLE BUDGET FOR BILLING DEPARTMENT

Expenses	Functional Unit — Invoice Line			
	50,000	55,000	60,000	65,000
Clerical salaries	$ 4,000	$ 4,000	$ 4,000	$ 4,000
Supervision	3,000	3,000	3,000	3,000
Depreciation — building.....................	750	750	750	750
Depreciation — equipment	1,250	1,250	1,250	1,250
Supplies...................................	2,500	2,750	3,000	3,250
Total	$11,500	$11,750	$12,000	$12,250

A standard functional unit cost is then established for each activity or function on the basis of normal capacity. These standard unit costs will furnish bases for comparisons with actual costs, and spending and idle capacity variances can be isolated. Using the Billing Department as an example and assuming that 60,000 invoice lines represent normal capacity, the following standard billing rate per invoice line would be computed:

$$\frac{\$12,000}{60,000 \text{ invoice lines}} = \$.20 \text{ per invoice line}$$

Assuming $9,000 fixed expense and $3,000 variable expense, the variable portion of the rate is:

$$\frac{\$3,000}{60,000 \text{ invoice lines}} = \$.05 \text{ per invoice line}$$

The cost variances for billing expenses can be computed in a manner similar to that discussed in connection with factory overhead (Chapter 7) and consistent with the basic idea of flexible budgeting. If actual sales required 63,000 invoice lines for a month at a total of $12,500, the variances for the Billing Department would be determined as follows:

Actual expense		$12,500
Spending variance		
Budget allowance:		
Fixed expense budgeted.............	$9,000	
Variable expense ($.05 × 63,000		
invoice lines)	3,150	12,150
Idle capacity variance..............		
Standard cost charged in ($.20 ×		
63,000 invoice lines)................		12,600

$350 unfav.

(450) fav.

The increased volume leads to a favorable idle capacity variance due to overabsorption of fixed expenses. On the other hand, the supervisor overspent the $12,150 budget allowance by $350.

Accountants usually do not favor carrying this type of variance analysis through ledger accounts. The analysis is usually statistical and is presented to management in report form. However, the following journal entries similar to those for factory overhead could be made:

Billing Expense Charged In	12,600	
Applied Billing Expense		12,600
Actual Billing Expense	12,500	
Sundry Credits		12,500
Applied Billing Expense	12,600	
Billing Expense—Spending Variance	350	
Billing Expense—Idle Capacity Variance		450
Actual Billing Expense		12,500

Marketing Profitability Analysis

The functional unit costs are used to analyze costs and determine the profitability of territories, customers, products, and salespersons. In most cases, a continuous reshuffling or rearranging of expense items is needed to find the required costs and profits. The possibility of improving marketing cost and profitability analysis has been enhanced by the availability of electronic data processing equipment capable of processing the great amount of quantitative detail so characteristic of these analyses.

Analysis by Territories

Perhaps the simplest analysis of marketing profitability is by territories. When marketing activities are organized on a territorial basis, each identifiable geographical unit can be charged directly with the expenses incurred within its area, thereby minimizing the proration of expenses. Expenses that can be assigned directly to a territory are: salespersons' salaries, commissions, and traveling expenses; transportation cost within the delivery area; packing and shipping costs; and advertising specifically identified with the territory. Expenses that must be prorated to the territory are: general management, general office, general sales manager, credit and collection, and general accounting.

When expenses are identified by territories, a comparative income statement can be prepared. This statement, illustrated as follows, permits control and analysis of expenses as well as the computation of profit margins. When sales or expenses seem to be out of line, management can take corrective action.

INCOME STATEMENT BY TERRITORIES

	Territory No. 1	Territory No. 2	Territory No. 3
Net sales	$210,000	$80,000	$175,000
Cost of goods sold	160,000	60,000	140,000
Gross profit	$ 50,000	$20,000	$ 35,000
Marketing expenses:			
Selling	$ 15,000	$ 8,600	$ 23,900
Warehousing	3,600	1,400	3,100
Packing and shipping	1,500	400	1,900
Advertising	2,000	1,000	500
Credit and collection	800	250	1,200
General accounting	1,200	1,400	1,800
Total marketing expense	$ 24,100	$13,050	$ 32,400
Administrative expenses (equally)	5,000	5,000	5,000
Total marketing and administrative expenses	$ 29,100	$18,050	$ 37,400
Operating income (loss) per territory	$ 20,900	$ 1,950	$ (2,400)

Analysis by Customers

Although most marketing costs can be assigned directly to territories, relatively few of these costs can be traced directly to customers. Perhaps transportation expenses and sales discounts can be considered direct, but all other expenses are allocated on the basis of functional unit costing rates.

The large number of customers makes the allocation and analysis of marketing costs by customers rather cumbersome if not impossible. For this reason, customers are grouped according to certain characteristics to make the analysis meaningful. The grouping may be by (1) territories, (2) amount of average order, (3) customer-volume groups, or (4) kinds of customers.

Analysis of Customers by Territories. This type of analysis reflects territorial cost differences due to the customer's proximity to warehouses, volume of purchases, service requirements, and the kinds of merchandise bought. These factors can make some sales profitable or unprofitable. The analysis proceeds in the same manner outlined for territories, except that the costs would be broken down by customers or kinds of customers within each territory.

Analysis of Customers by Amount of Average Order. The amount of a customer's order is closely related to profitability. An analysis might indicate that a considerable portion of orders comes from customers who cost the company more in selling to them than the orders are worth in terms of gross profit. Companies have therefore resorted to setting minimum dollar values or minimum quantities for orders as well as price differentials, thereby reducing the number of transactions and increasing profits. Although selective selling has found much favor among many executives, it requires changes in habits and routines.

To present management with a quick view of the situation regarding the amount of the average order in relation to the number of customers, time spent, and total dollar sales, the following chart might be helpful:

Analysis of Customers by Amount of Average Order

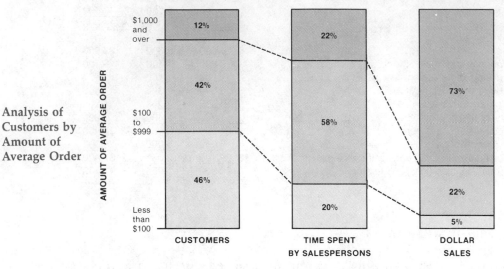

Analysis by Customer-Volume Groups. An analysis of customers by customer-volume groups is similar to that of the amount-of-average-order analysis. Instead of classifying customers by an order's dollar value, however, the customer-volume group analysis is based on quantity or volume. This type of analysis yields information concerning (1) the profitability of various customer-volume groups and (2) the establishment of minimum orders and price differentials.

The following analysis indicates that only sales to customers who buy more than 150 units during a week result in a positive contribution margin:

Customer-Volume Group (Number of Units Purchased During Week)	Customers (% of Total)	Volume (% of Total)	Gross Contribution Margin per 100 Units	Variable Commercial Expenses per 100 Units	Contribution Margin per 100 Units
ANALYSIS BY CUSTOMER-VOLUME GROUPS					
Customers unsuccessfully solicited	17.1%	....	....	....	....
1–25	7.6	0.2%	$1.66	$4.01	$(2.35)
26–50	8.3	0.7	1.38	2.55	(1.17)
51–100	12.0	1.9	1.25	1.78	(.53)
101–150	9.3	2.4	1.26	1.32	(.06)
151–200	7.8	2.9	1.14	1.13	.01
201–250	6.4	3.0	1.12	.95	.17
251–500	17.1	13.2	1.06	.75	.31
501–1,000	12.7	18.6	1.02	.49	.53
1,001–10,000	1.7	57.1	.81	.24	.57
Total	100.0%	100.0%			

The variable cost of goods sold is subtracted from sales to compute the gross contribution margin, from which the variable commercial (marketing and administrative) expenses are subtracted to compute the contribution margin. Although the customers buying more than 150 units weekly represent only about 46 percent of the customers, they purchase approximately 95 percent of the units sold and thus provide the profits.

In spite of the higher gross contribution margin received from orders by customers who buy less than 150 units, it is not sufficient to cover variable commercial expenses. As a result, the sales to this group provide nothing for fixed expenses and profit.

Analysis by Kinds of Customers. This type of analysis makes a distinction between manufacturers, wholesalers, retailers, government (local, state, and federal), schools, colleges and universities, and hospitals. Prices might be uniform within each customer group but might vary between groups. Different salespersons are often employed for each category; hence their salaries and related expenses can be assigned directly to the group. Delivery to such groups might be different, with one delivery contracted with outside truckers and another made by the firm's own trucks. For analytical purposes, revenue and costs should be related to each kind of customer.

Analysis by Products

Just as customers are grouped for purposes of analysis, products sold can be grouped according to product lines or brands possessing common characteristics. With the aid of functional costing rates, a product-line (or brand-line) income statement can be prepared for the evaluation of profitable and unprofitable product lines. The statement on page 582 relates the actual contribution of each product line to total profits and to the recovery of common costs for the year.

Analysis by Salespersons

The selling function includes costs such as salaries, travel, and other expenses connected with the work of sales representatives. In many instances, salespersons' expenses form a substantial part of the total expense incurred in selling. The control and analysis of these expenses should, therefore, receive management's closest attention. To achieve this control, performance standards and standard costs should be established. These standards are used not only for the control of costs but also for determining the profitability of sales made by salespersons.

Cost Control. The allocation table on page 575 indicates that selling expenses may be allocated on the basis of the number of calls made. A call or visit by a salesperson is usually made for two reasons: to sell and to promote the merchandise or products. The problem is to determine the cost of doing each

PRODUCT-LINE INCOME STATEMENT
(CONTRIBUTION MARGIN APPROACH)

	Total	Product Line 1	Product Line 2	Product Line 3
Net sales	$3,100,000	$1,540,000	$1,070,000	$490,000
Less variable cost of goods sold.	1,927,000	925,000	590,000	412,000
Gross contribution margin	$1,173,000	$ 615,000	$ 480,000	$ 78,000
Less variable marketing expenses:				
Selling.	$ 243,300	$ 112,300	$ 89,000	$ 42,000
Warehousing.	87,100	48,000	27,500	11,600
Packing and Shipping	66,000	39,000	17,800	9,200
Advertising.	38,000	20,000	12,000	6,000
Credit and collection	19,700	12,300	4,200	3,200
General accounting	52,200	23,000	16,800	12,400
Total variable marketing expense*	$ 506,300	$ 254,600	$ 167,300	$ 84,400
Margin available for fixed expenses and operating income (contribution margin)	$ 666,700	$ 360,400	$ 312,700	$ (6,400)
Less fixed expenses (manufacturing and nonmanufacturing) directly related to individual product lines	120,000	40,000	60,000	20,000
Margin available for common fixed expenses and operating income	$ 546,700	$ 320,400	$ 252,700	$ (26,400)
Less common fixed expenses (manufacturing and non-manufacturing)	230,000		Not allocated	
Operating income.	$ 316,700			

*In this illustration, all administrative expenses are fixed.

of these types of work and to compare the actual cost with the standard cost allowed for a call.

A salesperson's call often involves several kinds of work: not only calling on the customer, but also helping the merchant with the display in the store. This practice is common in cosmetic, pharmaceutical, and fast-food businesses. Because the salesperson's time is consumed by such activities, a standard time allowed per call is often very difficult to establish. To obtain the necessary statistics for establishing such standards and to make comparisons, the sales representative might be asked to prepare a report providing information regarding the type of calls made as well as the quantity, type, and dollar values of products sold. This information is the basis for much of the analysis discussed previously.

Profitability Analysis. It is also possible to analyze sales in relation to profitability. Sales volume alone does not tell the complete story. High volume does not always insure high profit, and the sales mix plays an important part in the final profit. Although a sales representative might wish to follow the line of least resistance, management must strive to sell the merchandise of all product groups, particularly those with the highest profit margins. Since sales territories are often planned for sales according to product groups, it is necessary that anticipated sales be followed up by analyzing the salespersons' efforts. The following table indicates how such an analysis can be made:

SALES, COSTS, AND PROFITS BY INDIVIDUAL SALESPERSONS FOR APRIL, 19--

(1) Sales-person	(2) Ship-ments	(3) % of Quota	(4) Salary and Commis-sion	(5) Travel Expense	(6) Cost of Handling	(7) Total Cost (4) + (5) + (6)	(8) Gross Profit	(9) Profit (8) − (7)	(10) Profit, % of Sales (9) ÷ (2)	(11) Ship-ments, % of Total*	(12) Potential, % of Total*
A	$26,000	80%	$2,000	$3,000	$2,340	$ 7,340	$ 7,540	$ 200	.8%	6.7%	9.0%
B	26,000	122	1,900	1,800	2,340	6,040	7,800	1,760	6.8	6.7	5.5
C	39,000	100	2,800	2,100	3,500	8,400	11,700	3,300	8.5	10.1	10.5
D	22,000	108	1,800	2,000	1,980	5,780	7,050	1,270	5.8	5.8	5.5
E	21,000	110	1,700	1,700	1,890	5,290	6,720	1,430	6.8	5.4	5.0
F	54,000	125	3,500	3,100	5,700	12,300	14,600	2,300	4.3	14.0	10.0
G	21,000	98	1,600	1,200	1,700	4,500	6,720	2,220	10.6	5.5	5.5
H	46,000	101	3,400	1,000	4,100	8,500	13,800	5,300	11.5	12.0	12.0

*For 8 salespersons out of a total of 15 salespersons.

The Contribution Margin Approach

Generally, the income statement shows a profit figure after all marketing and administrative expenses have been deducted. The total cost and profit approach assigns all the expenses, direct or indirect, fixed or variable, to each segment analyzed. This procedure is commonly used, since management is familiar with it and believes that no profit is realized until all manufacturing and nonmanufacturing expenses have been recovered.

Marketing cost analysis attempts to allocate marketing expenses to territories, customers, products, or salespersons. However, because these marketing costs contain direct, indirect, fixed, and variable amounts, allocations are extremely difficult and the end results may be misleading. It has been suggested that only the variable manufacturing cost be subtracted from each segment's sales, thus arriving at a figure described as "gross contribution margin." (The conventional income statement deducts all manufacturing costs in arriving at a figure described as "gross profit.") Furthermore, only the variable nonmanufacturing expense would be subtracted from the gross contribution margin of a territory, customer class, product, or salesperson, resulting in the contribution margin for each segment. Fixed expenses would be shown separately and not allocated unless specifically attributable to a segment. When a territory, customer class, or product group contributes nothing to the recovery of fixed expenses, the situation should be examined and remedial steps taken. The product-line income statement on page 582 illustrates this approach. Moreover, in the case of joint costs, variable as well as fixed costs should be viewed as they relate to the contribution made by the group of products or territories rather than based on arbitrary allocations, e.g., to individual products or territories (pages 131–132). The arbitrary nature of joint cost allocations is also a fundamental reason for criticism of requirements to report segment or product-line revenue, costs, and profits in published financial statements.

Although sales volume is the ultimate goal of most sales managers, the trend has been toward a greater recognition of contribution margin as the basis for judging the success and profitability of marketing activities. The increased use of standard production costs has aided the analysis of gross profit, as discussed in Chapter 19. Even though a manufacturer might know the production costs, the question remains: "How much can the company afford for marketing costs?" The problem of determining allowable marketing expenses is intensified because once a sales program gets under way, the majority of expenses become fixed costs, at least in the short run.

The analysis discussed here combines the fixed and variable costs of each functional group to arrive at a functional unit costing rate per activity. But the allocation of joint expense in any type of analysis is often difficult and uncertain. Proponents of the contribution margin approach point out that only specific and direct costs, whether variable or fixed, should be assigned to territories, customers, product groups, or salespersons, with a clear distinction as to their fixed and variable characteristics. Moreover, for the purpose of identifying costs with responsible managers, it is desirable to identify each reported cost with its controllability by the manager in charge of the reported activity.

The contribution margin approach has influened the thinking of the volume-minded sales manager or salesperson who must recognize that profit is more beneficial than volume. The contribution margin is a better indicator than sales as to the amount available for recovery of fixed manufacturing cost, fixed marketing and administrative expenses, and a profit.

Effect of the Robinson-Patman Act on Marketing Cost Analysis

The Robinson-Patman Act of June, 1936, amended Section 2 of the Clayton Act, which was enacted to prevent large buyers from securing excessive advantages over their smaller competitors by virtue of their size and purchasing power. Since the Clayton Act prohibited discrimination only where it had a serious effect on competition in general, and since it contained no other provisions for the control of price discrimination, the Act was amended in order to insure competitive equality of the individual enterprise. The following clause of the Robinson-Patman Act is of special interest in connection with marketing costs:

> *To make it unlawful for any person engaged in commerce to discriminate in price or terms of sale between purchasers of commodities of like grades and quality; to prohibit the payment of brokerage or commissions under certain conditions; to suppress*

pseudo-advertising allowances; to provide a presumptive measure of damages in certain cases; and to protect the independent merchant, the public whom he serves, and the manufacturer who sells him his goods from exploitation by unfair competitors.

The Robinson-Patman Act intends to preclude price discrimination that decreases competition. The seller has three acceptable defenses for price cuts:

1. They resulted from changing conditions in the market place (discontinued products, distress sales, perishable goods, etc.),
2. They temporarily changed in a good-faith attempt to meet an equally low and lawful price of a competitor, or
3. They reflect lower costs that resulted from different methods or quantities of sale or delivery.

The amendment does not imply that price discriminations in the sense of price differentials are entirely prohibited or that a seller is compelled or required to grant any price differential whatever. A vendor may sell to all customers at the same price regardless of differences in the cost of serving them. At the core of the amendment are the provisions that deal with charging different prices to different customers. To meet the third of the defenses for price cuts, differentials granted must not exceed differences in the cost of serving different customers. The cost of serving includes the cost of manufacturing, selling, and delivering, which may differ according to methods of selling and quantities sold. The burden of proof is on both the buyer and the seller and requires a definite justification for the discounts granted and received. It is necessary to prove that no discrimination took place with respect to (1) price differences, (2) discounts, (3) delivery service, (4) allowances for service, (5) advertising appropriations, (6) brokerage or commissions, or (7) consignment policies.

These possibilities for discrimination fall chiefly into the field of marketing costs. Many interesting problems have arisen because of the nature of these costs and the numerous variations and combinations in the manner of sale and delivery. As indicated, it is difficult to apply many marketing costs to particular products. Therefore, it is important for concerns performing distribution functions to accumulate costs statistics regarding their marketing costs, because the Act makes allowances for differences in costs. The Act increases the interest in marketing cost analysis and its part in the determination of prices. The following cost justification study illustrates this point:

COST JUSTIFICATION STUDY

A producer of a heavy bulk chemical, which sells FOB point of manufacture at $25 a ton in minimum quantities of a full rail carload (approximately 40 tons), is offered a contract for 500 to 1,000 carloads a year if it will reduce its FOB shipping point price by 6 percent. The producer does not want to reduce the selling price to other customers, to whom annual shipments range from 10 to 200 carloads. The only source of cost differences is sales solicitation and service expense.

The sales manager estimates (since exact records are not available) that salespersons typically pursue the following call schedule:

Customer Size (in Carloads)	Annual Number of Sales Calls
10–40	12
41–80	24
81–150	36
151 and up	50

The sales manager further estimates that each sales call costs approximately $50–$70 regardless of customer size. After questioning, the manager agrees that study would probably show that calls on large customers (more than 100 carloads) are longer in duration than calls on smaller customers. For study and testing purposes, it was assumed that a call on a small customer costs $60 and a call on a large customer costs $90. The following cost-sales relationship can now be developed:

**DIFFERENTIAL COST
LARGE VS. SMALL CUSTOMERS**

	Annual Carloads per Customer				
	25	*50*	*100*	*200*	*500*
Sales value	$25,000	$50,000	$100,000	$200,000	$500,000
Number of sales calls	12	24	36	50	50
Assumed cost per call........	$ 60	$ 60	$ 90	$ 90	$ 90
Assumed cost of call per customer	720	1,440	3,240	4,500	4,500
Assumed cost of call as a percent of sales	2.9%	2.9%	3.2%	2.25%	0.9%

Since the assumed differential costs are less than the 6 percent proposed discount, it appears obvious that a discount of that magnitude is not susceptible to cost justification. Indeed, it is possible that even a one percent discount to a 500-carload customer might be hard to justify since it is probable that more exact costing would narrow the spread in the percentages among the various classes.

Adapted from "Cost Justification of Price Differences" by Herbert G. Whiting, *Management Services*, Vol. 3, No. 4, pp. 31–32. Copyright 1966 by the American Institute of Certified Public Accountants.

A competitor who believes that discrimination exists must file a complaint substantiated by evidence acquired from published price lists or from other persuasive evidence of this kind. The complaint is valid if all of the following violations have been committed:

1. Price discrimination.
2. Discrimination between competitors.
3. Discrimination on products of like grades and quality.
4. Discrimination in interstate commerce.
5. Injurious effect on competition.

The most effective method for a firm to answer any such complaint is to have a functional unit cost system for marketing costs. In fact, no firm should be placed in a situation of having to make a cost study after being cited. Experience has proven that such belated cost justification studies seldom are successful. Therefore, the firm should (1) establish records that show that price differentials are extended only to the extent justified by maximum allowable cost savings and (2) maintain the cost data currently through spot checks conducted periodically to insure that the price differentials are in conformance with current cost conditions.

In justifying price differentials, marginal costing cannot be utilized; i.e., a plant operating at 80 percent capacity and wishing to add an order to increase its capacity to 90 percent cannot restrict its cost considerations to that incremental element of variable cost due to the volume change. The reduced cost per unit resulting from the greater volume must be spread over all units. Thus, the government, in consistently rejecting the marginal approach, endorses instead a method which is often called fully distributed cost analysis and only these fully distributed or average total costs are acceptable for a cost justification defense under the Robinson-Patman Act. The government has held that only identifiable savings, whether manufacturing or marketing, resulting from specific methods or quantities connected with given orders can be properly passed in their entirety to specific customers. For example, if the price difference is related to special manufacturing runs, then cost factors that can be considered include the differences between customer runs, which can cause a difference in unit costs. Typical of such costs are setup costs, skill and number of direct laborers, tool-wear costs, machine downtime, scrap rates, order scheduling, and inspection.

In general, the Robinson-Patman Act seems to be working toward greater equity between prices, since pricing schedules appear to be more carefully attuned to differences in costs than they were before the enactment of this particular type of control. The accountant must be prepared to study the subject actively and continuously to help management avoid unintentional price discriminations that might be in violation of the law. The marketing manager must also follow the effect of any pricing policy to determine whether it is profitable and produces the kind of business necessary for the wholesome operation of the enterprise.

Illustrative Problem in Marketing Cost and Profitability Analysis

Ambler Company manufactures and sells a variety of small power tools, dies, drills, files, milling cutters, saws, and other miscellaneous hardware. The company's catalog lists the merchandise under sixteen major classifications. Customers fall into five categories: retail hardware stores, manufacturers, public school systems, municipalities, and public utilities. Territories included New Jersey and Pennsylvania. The company's president believes that in certain areas the cost of marketing the products is too high, that certain customers' orders do not contribute enough to cover fixed costs and earn a profit, and that certain products are being sold to customers and in territories on an unprofitable basis. Therefore, the president has instructed the controller to review the firm's marketing costs and to study the steps, methods, and procedures necessary to provide more accurate information about the profitability of territories, products, and customers.

The controller has designed and operated a standard marketing cost system which gives management the desired information for the control and analysis of marketing and administrative expenses. The preparation and assembling of statistical and cost data were carried out in the following sequence:

1. Total marketing expenses were estimated (or budgeted).
2. Six marketing functions (selling, warehousing, packing and shipping, advertising, credit and collection, general accounting) were established.
3. Direct costs were assigned directly to functions; indirect expenses were allocated to functions via a measurement unit, such as kilowatt-hour, footage, or number of employees.
4. Fixed and variable expenses were determined for each function.
5. Functional unit measurement bases were selected for the purpose of assigning costs to the segments to be analyzed, i.e., territory or product.
6. Functional unit measurements or bases applicable to a territory or a product were determined.
7. Unit standard manufacturing costs and standard product sales prices were established.
8. Data regarding the types and number of units sold in the territories were prepared.
9. Income statements by (a) territories and (b) product lines in one territory were prepared for management.

Exhibit 1 on page 589 summarizes the results of the study prepared by the controller. Column 1 shows the total budgeted expense per function. Each total is supported by a budget showing the amount for each individual expense of the function. Columns 2 and 3 place total expenses in a variable and fixed expense classification. Column 4 indicates the functional unit measurement selected as being reliably applicable to that function. Column 5 lists the quantity or value of the measurement unit used to determine the functional unit costing rate. Columns 6, 7, and 8 indicate the variable, fixed, and total functional unit costing rates.

Exhibits 2 and 3 list the details necessary for the preparation of Exhibits 1, 4, and 5. To simplify the illustration, nonmanufacturing costs other than marketing costs have been excluded.

The product-line income statement for the territory of Pennsylvania (Exhibit 5) indicates that the volume and/or price of Product 1 is not sufficient to result in a profit. In Exhibit 6, this analysis is carried further with the aid of a fixed-variable analysis of manufacturing costs and marketing expenses to determine the contribution made by the product line to the total fixed cost and profit. This exhibit assumes the nonexistence of unallocated cost, fixed or variable. The product-line income statement on page 582 illustrates a presentation with unallocated costs.

Next, the steps required to bring about an improvement in the profitability of this product line should be determined. Functional marketing cost analysis permits this type of analysis, which should eventually lead to a selective selling program supported by product break-even analyses and by cost-volume-profit and differential cost analyses (Chapters 23 and 24).

Exhibit 1
DETERMINATION OF FUNCTIONAL UNIT COSTING RATES

Function	Budgeted Expenses Total (1)	Variable (2)	Fixed (3)	Functional Unit Measurement Base (4)	Quantity (5)	Functional Unit Costing Rates Variable (6)	Fixed (7)	Total (8)
Selling...................	$ 95,500	$ 38,200	$ 57,300	Gross sales dollar value of product sold	$1,910,000	2%	3%	5%
Warehousing.............	75,000	45,000	30,000	Weight of units shipped	375 000	$ .12	$ .08	$ .20
Packing and shipping	63,000	37,500	25,500	Quantity of product units sold	150,000	.25	.17	.42
Advertising...............	54,000		54,000	Quantity of product units sold	150,000		.36	.36
Credit and collection	28,800	18,720	10,080	Number of customers' orders	7,200	2.60	1.40	4.00
General accounting	49,200	21,300	27,900	Number of times product items appear on customers' invoices	15,000	1.42	1.86	3.28
Total functional distribution expense.............	$365,500	$160,720	$204,780					

Exhibit 2
DATA CONCERNING PRICE, COST, QUANTITY, WEIGHT, AND TRANSACTIONS OF PRODUCTS

Product Class	Product 1	Product 2	Product 3
Standard product sales price.......................	$10.00	$15.00	$18.00
Unit standard manufacturing cost...................	8.00	11.00	12.00
Quantity of product units sold	80,000	50,000	20,000
Weight of units shipped (kilograms)	2.25 kg	2.5 kg	3.5 kg
Number of times product items appear on customers' invoices.............................	6,400	5,700	2,900
Number of customers' orders	2,400	3,000	1,800

Exhibit 3

DATA CONCERNING TRANSACTIONS IN TERRITORIES

Territory	Quantity of Products Sold			Number of Times Product Items Appear on Customers' Invoices			Number of Customers' Orders		
	Product 1	Product 2	Product 3	Product 1	Product 2	Product 3	Product 1	Product 2	Product 3
Pennsylvania.........	55,000	30,000	16,000	4,000	2,900	1,000	1,000	1,900	900
New Jersey...........	25,000	20,000	4,000	2,400	2,800	1,900	1,400	1,100	900

Exhibit 4

INCOME STATEMENT FOR ALL PRODUCT CLASSES IN THE TWO TERRITORIES

		Territory	
	Total	Pennsylvania	New Jersey
Gross sales.......................................	$1,910,000	$1,288,000	$622,000
Less cost of goods sold	1,430,000	962,000	468,000
Gross profit	$ 480,000	$ 326,000	$154,000
Less marketing expenses:			
Selling..	$ 95,500	$ 64,400	$ 31,100
Warehousing..................................	75,000	50,950	24,050
Packing and shipping	63,000	42,420	20,580
Advertising...................................	54,000	36,360	17,640
Credit and collection	28,800	15,200	13,600
General accounting	49,200	25,912	23,288
Total	$ 365,500	$ 235,242	$130,258
Operating income.................................	$ 114,500	$ 90,758	$ 23,742

Exhibit 5

INCOME STATEMENT BY PRODUCT CLASSES IN THE PENNSYLVANIA TERRITORY

		Product Class		
	Total	Product 1	Product 2	Product 3
Gross sales...............................	$1,288,000	$550,000	$450,000	$288,000
Less cost of goods sold	962,000	440,000	330,000	192,000
Gross profit	$ 326,000	$110,000	$120,000	$ 96,000
Less marketing expenses:				
Selling.................................	$ 64,600	$ 27,500	$ 22,500	$ 14,400
Warehousing..........................	50,950	24,750	15,000	11,200
Packing and shipping	42,420	23,100	12,600	6,720
Advertising............................	36,360	19,800	10,800	5,760
Credit and collection	15,200	4,000	7,600	3,600
General accounting	25,912	13,120	9,512	3,280
Total	$ 235,242	$112,270	$ 78,012	$ 44,960
Operating income (loss)	$ 90,758	$(2,270)	$ 41,988	$ 51,040

Exhibit 6

INCOME STATEMENT OF PRODUCT CLASS WITH FIXED-VARIABLE ANALYSIS OF MANUFACTURING AND MARKETING COSTS IN THE PENNSYLVANIA TERRITORY

		Product 1
Gross sales..........		$550,000
Less cost of goods sold (variable unit cost = 60% of $8).......		264,000
Gross contribution margin.........		$286,000
Less variable marketing expenses:		
Selling......	$ 11,000	
Warehousing......	14,850	
Packing and shipping	13,750	
Credit and collection	2,600	
General accounting	5,680	47,880
Contribution margin.......		$238,120
Less fixed costs and expenses:		
Manufacturing cost—fixed......	$176,000	
Marketing expenses—fixed:		
Selling......	$ 16,500	
Warehousing......	9,900	
Packing and shipping	9,350	
Advertising......	19,800	
Credit and collection	1,400	
General accounting	7,440	240,390
Operating loss—Product Class 1—Pennsylvania......		$ (2,270)

DISCUSSION QUESTIONS

1. What general principles should be observed in planning a system of control for marketing expenses?

2. How should marketing expenses be classified in order to find the cost of selling jobs or products?

3. A method still commonly used today in analyzing marketing expenses is to relate them to either the total factory cost or the total sales value. This method is merely a relationship and not a scientific basis. Discuss.

4. A firm employing its own transport service delivers its products up to a distance of 130 miles from home in quantities varying from 1 to 20 cwt. On the return trip, empty containers are collected from certain customers and a quantity of materials are picked up from suppliers. How should the cost incurred for these services be distributed?

5. The advertising policy of a company includes exhibition of the plant to customers. Visitors are received and guides are supplied from the production staff.
   (a) How should this cost be treated in the records?
   (b) What adequate control of this expenditure can be provided from the point of view of production and sales promotion?

6. Outline a procedure for determining the marketing costs for a concern manufacturing two products. This organization uses national advertising and assigns salespersons to definite territories for contact with established dealers and also to secure additional retail outlets.

7. What are the objectives of profit analysis by sales territories?

8. A company with a national sales force divides the country into sales territories, which are subdivided into districts. The products are nationally advertised and are sold to retail shops. Assuming 1,000 orders per day with an average of four items per order, what marketing cost system should be installed to accumulate:
   (a) The necessary sales statistics to control sales by territories and lines?
   (b) The expenses of such a sales force?
   (c) Records and statistical analyses for use in the preparation of sales budgets and profit margins?

9. What difficulties may arise if an attempt is made to set standards for marketing expenses?

10. Explain briefly the difference between the profit approach and the contribution margin approach in marketing cost analysis.

11. Why did the Robinson-Patman Act lead to the establishment of marketing cost procedures in business?

EXERCISES

1. *Marketing cost control using flexible budget and standards.* Kasrail Company sells various imported products through selected retail outlets. Data relative to standard selling costs for one of the company's salespersons show:

Standard sales for the year	$180,000
Standard selling cost for the year	21,600
Sales for October	14,000
Selling costs for October:	
Actual cost	1,725
Budgeted cost for $14,000 sales	1,650

Required:
   (1) Compute the standard selling cost to be charged if the salesperson reported $5,500 sales the first week of October.
   (2) Compute the spending variance and the idle capacity variance for the salesperson's October selling costs.

2. *Marketing cost control using flexible budget and standards.* The monthly flexible budget for the General Accounting Department is as follows:

	Functional Unit — Number of Transactions			
Expense	10,000	15,000	20,000	25,000
Supervision	$ 3,000	$ 3,000	$ 3,000	$ 3,000
Clerical salaries	11,500	11,500	11,500	11,500
Utilities	500	500	500	500
Depreciation — building	750	750	750	750
Depreciation — equipment	1,250	1,250	1,250	1,250
Supplies	2,500	3,000	3,500	4,000
Total	$19,500	$20,000	$20,500	$21,000
Cost per transaction	$1.9500	$1.3333	$1.0250	$ .8400

During June, the General Accounting Department handled 23,500 transactions; actual costs were $20,930. Normal capacity calls for the handling of 20,000 transactions.

Required: Compute the budget allowance for 23,500 transactions, the spending variance, and the idle capacity variance.

3. Marketing cost analysis by territories. *Smith Air Freshener Company of Waco, Texas, markets a single product in Waco and Dallas. Marketing expenses for the past year were:*

Sales salaries	$ 86,000
Salespersons' expenses	16,200
Advertising	24,000
Delivery expense	25,200
Credit investigation expense	6,800
Collection expense	11,400
Total	$169,600

Additional information:

(a) *The company has five salespersons, three in Dallas and two in Waco, and each is paid the same salary.*

(b) *The salespersons receive equal allowances for expenses, except that the Dallas salespersons each receive $400 per year extra for turnpike toll fees.*

(c) *All advertising is placed according to the number of subscribers to the Waco and Dallas daily newspapers, 150,000 and 750,000 respectively.*

(d) *Delivery is made by an outside agency which charges a flat annual fee. The agency made 4,800 deliveries (3,000 in Dallas, 1,800 in Waco) from a centrally located warehouse.*

(e) *680 new customers were obtained (400 from Dallas, 280 from Waco).*

(f) *6,000 customers' remittances were received (4,500 from Dallas, 1,500 from Waco).*

Required: *Prepare a marketing cost analysis for the two territories.*

4. Marketing cost analysis by territories. *Alpron Corporation sells hardware items in California, Colorado, and Nevada. Marketing expenses for last month were as follows:*

Sales salaries	$60,000
Sales commissions	6,960
Travel expense	3,650
Advertising expense	20,000
Warehousing expense	2,160
Delivery expense	1,500
Collection expense	1,675

Additional information:

(a) *Ten salespersons are employed, five in Colorado, three in California, and two in Nevada. All are paid the same base salary. Sales were as follows:*

				Salesperson		
State	Total	#1	#2	#3	#4	#5
Colorado	$138,000	$56,000	$28,000	$25,000	$4,000	$25,000
California	85,000	17,000	20,000	48,000		
Nevada	97,000	50,000	47,000			

(b) *The following commission schedule has been established:*

Sales	Commission (% of Sales)
First $10,000	0%
Next $40,000	3
Over $50,000	6

(c) *Travel expense is allocated 5:3:2 among Colorado, California, and Nevada, respectively.*

(d) *Advertising is allocated on the basis of dollar sales volume.*

(e) *Warehousing expense is allocated in a fixed and variable manner. The fixed portion is distributed as follows: Colorado, $250; Nevada, $100; and California, $100. The variable portion is distributed in the same ratio as travel expense.*

(f) *Delivery expense is allocated 40% to Colorado, 30% to California, and 30% to Nevada.*

(g) *Collection expense is allocated on the basis of the volume of remittances. A total of 20,000 remittances were received from customers: Nevada, 6,000; California, 4,000; Colorado, 10,000.*

Required: *Prepare a marketing cost analysis by state.*

5. *Income statement by customer classes. Southern Illinois Company assembles a washing machine that is sold to three classes of customers. The data with respect to these customers are as follows:*

Customer Class	Sales	Gross Profit	Number of Sales Calls	Number of Orders	Number of Invoice Lines
Department stores.......	$180,000	$ 26,000	240	120	2,100
Retail appliance stores ...	240,000	80,000	360	580	4,600
Wholesalers............	300,000	71,000	400	300	3,300
Total................	$720,000	$177,000	1,000	1,000	10,000

Actual marketing costs for the year are:

Function	Costs	Measure of Activity
Selling...........................	$65,000	Salespersons' calls
Packing and shipping	12,000	Customers' orders
Advertising.......................	20,000	Dollar sales
Credit and collection	15,000	Invoice lines
General accounting	18,000	Customers' orders

Required: *Prepare an income statement by customer classes, with functional distribution of marketing expenses. (When allocating the advertising expense, round to the nearest $100.)*

6. *Salesperson's performance reports. A corporate budget director designed a control scheme in order to compare and evaluate the efforts of the company's three salespersons and the results attained. Specifically, each salesperson is to make five calls per day; the budget provides for $40 per day per salesperson for travel and entertainment expenses; each salesperson was assigned a sales quota of $400 a day. The Budget Department collects the data on actual performance from the daily sales reports and the weekly expense vouchers and then prepares a monthly report. This report includes variances from standard and performance indexes. For the performance index, standard performance equals 100.*

The records for November, with 20 working days, show:

Salesperson	Sales Calls	Travel Expenses	Sales
Palmer, K.	70	$1,000	$14,000
Thompson, J.	100	800	8,400
Miller, O.	120	720	6,000

Required: *Prepare a monthly report comparing the standard and actual performances of the salespersons, including the performance indexes for (1) sales calls, (2) travel expenses, (3) sales, and (4) sales revenue per call.*

PROBLEMS

21-1. Standard cost variance analysis; revision of sales prices. Dover Corporation's actual and standard (for budgeted hours) marketing costs for January are:

	Budget at Standard Cost	Actual
Sales	$750,000	$750,000
Direct marketing costs:		
Selling	$ 12,000	$ 15,000
Shipping salaries	21,000	28,350
Indirect marketing costs:		
Order filling	17,250	21,500
Other costs	2,100	2,500
Total cost	$ 52,350	$ 67,350

Additional data:

(a) The company sells one product at $10 per unit.
(b) The other indirect marketing costs and shipping salaries are allocated on the basis of shipping hours. January shipping hours are:

Budgeted hours	3,500
Standard hours (at January operating level)	4,400
Actual hours	4,500

(c) Order-filling costs are allocated on the basis of sales and are comprised of freight, packing, and warehousing costs. An analysis of the amount of these standard costs by unit order size follows:

Unit-Volume Classification	1–15	16–50	Over 50	Total
Freight	$ 1,200	$ 1,440	$ 2,250	$ 4,890
Packing	2,400	3,240	4,500	10,140
Warehousing	600	720	900	2,220
Total	$ 4,200	$ 5,400	$ 7,650	$17,250
Units sold	12,000	18,000	45,000	75,000

Management realizes that the marketing cost per unit decreases with an increase in the size of the order and, hence, wants to revise its unit sales prices upward or downward on the basis of the quantity ordered in proportion to the allocated freight, packing, and warehousing standard costs. Management assumes that the revised unit prices will require no changes in standards for sales volume, the number of units sold in each order-size classification, and the profit per unit sold.

Required:

(1) Compute and analyze variances from standard cost for (a) other indirect marketing costs and (b) shipping salaries. The analysis should compare actual and standard costs at the January standard operating level.

(2) Prepare a schedule computing the standard cost per unit for each order-filling cost in each unit-volume classification. Use the same format as in item (c).

(3) Prepare a schedule computing the revised unit sales prices for each unit-volume classification.   (AICPA adapted)

21-2. Marketing cost analysis by territories. Scott Company sells toiletries to retail stores throughout the United States. For planning and control purposes, the company is organized into twelve geographic regions, with two to six territories within each region. One salesperson is assigned to each territory and has exclusive rights to all sales made in that territory. Merchandise is shipped from the manufacturing plant to the twelve regional warehouses, from which the sales in each territory are shipped. National headquarters allocates a specific amount at the beginning of the year for regional advertising.

The net sales for Scott Company for the six months ended September 30 total $10 million. Costs incurred by national headquarters are:

National administration	$250,000
National advertising	125,000
National warehousing	175,000
	$550,000

The results of operations for the South Atlantic Region for the six months ended September 30 are:

Scott Company
Statement of Operations for South Atlantic Region
For the Six Months Ended September 30, 19--

Sales		$900,000
Costs and expenses:		
Advertising fees	$ 54,700	
Uncollectible accounts expense	3,600	
Cost of goods sold	460,000	
Freight out	22,600	
Insurance	10,000	
Salaries and employee benefits	81,600	
Sales commissions	36,000	
Supplies	12,000	
Travel and entertainment	14,100	
Wages and employee benefits	36,000	
Warehouse depreciation	8,000	
Warehouse operating cost	15,000	
Total cost and expense		753,600
Territory contribution		$146,400

The South Atlantic Region consists of two territories—Green and Purple. The salaries and employee benefits consist of the following items:

Regional vice-president	$24,000
Regional marketing manager	15,000
Regional warehouse manager	13,400
Salespersons (one for each territory, with both receiving the same salary base)	15,600
Employee benefits (20%)	13,600
	$81,600

The salespersons receive a base salary plus a 4% commission on all items sold in their territory. Uncollectible accounts expense has averaged .4% of sales in the past. Travel and entertainment costs are incurred by the salespersons in calling upon their customers and are based on a fixed authorized amount. Freight out is a function of the quantity of goods shipped and the distance shipped. Thirty percent of the insurance is expended for protection of the inventory while it is in the regional warehouse, and the remainder is incurred for the protection of the warehouse. Supplies are used in the warehouse for packing the merchandise to be shipped. Wages (a variable cost) relate to the hourly employees who fill orders in the warehouse. The warehouse operating cost account contains such costs as heat, light, and maintenance.

The following cost analyses and statistics by territory for the current period are representative of past experience and of expected future operations:

	Green	Purple	Total
Sales	$300,000	$600,000	$900,000
Cost of goods sold*	184,000	276,000	460,000
Advertising fees	21,800	32,900	54,700
Travel and entertainment	6,300	7,800	14,100
Freight out	9,000	13,600	22,600
Units sold	150,000	350,000	500,000
Pounds shipped**	210,000	390,000	600,000
Sales travel (miles)	21,600	38,400	60,000

*Use to allocate inventory insurance to territories.
**Use to allocate supplies and wages and employee benefits to territories.

The executive management of Scott Company wants the regional vice-presidents to present their operating data in a more meaningful manner. Therefore, management has requested that the regions separate their operating costs into the fixed and variable components of order-getting, order-filling, and administrative. The data are to be presented in the following format:

	Territory Cost		Regional	Total
	Green	Purple	Cost	Cost
Order-getting				
Order-filling				
Administrative				

Required:
(1) Prepare a statement which presents the cost for the region by territory, with the costs separated into variable and fixed categories and using management's suggested format.
(2) Identify the data presented that are relevant to a decision (either for or against) to split the Purple Territory into two separate territories (Red and Blue), and specify other data needed to aid management in its decision.
(3) Explain the use of standards and flexible budgets for planning and controlling marketing costs, assuming that Scott Company keeps its records in accordance with the classification required in (1). (CMA adapted)

21-3. Income statements by products and amount-of-order classes. The feasibility of allocating marketing and administrative expenses to products or amount-of-order classes for managerial purposes has been considered by Brentwood Company. It is apparent that some costs can be assigned equitably to these classifications, while others cannot. The company's cost analyst proposed the following bases for apportionment:

Expense	Type of Analysis	
	By Products	By Amount of Order
Sales salaries.............................	Not allocated	Sales dollars times number of customers in class
Sales travel	Not allocated	Number of customers in class
Sales office	Not allocated	Number of customers in class
Sales commissions........................	Direct	Direct
Credit management	Volume of sales in dollars	Number of customers in class
Packing and shipping	Weight times number of units	Weight times number of units
Warehousing	Weight times number of units	Weight times number of units
Advertising..............................	Not allocated	Not allocated
Bookkeeping and billing	Volume of sales in dollars	Number of orders
General marketing and administrative........	Not allocated	Not allocated

From books, records, and other sources, the following data have been compiled:

Amount of Order	Number of Customers	Number of Orders	Cost of Goods Sold	Total Sales	Product Sales		
					X	Y	Z
Under $25	1,000	6,000	$ 59,000	$ 100,000	$ 35,000	$ 40,000	$ 25,000
$26–$100	250	4,000	177,000	300,000	105,000	120,000	75,000
$101–$200	100	4,000	354,000	600,000	210,000	240,000	150,000
Over $200	50	1,000	236,000	400,000	140,000	160,000	100,000
Total	1,400	15,000	$826,000	$1,400,000	$490,000	$560,000	$350,000

Other data:

Product	Weight	Cost of Goods Sold	Units Sold
X	1 kg	$252,000	98,000
Y	3 kg	294,000	70,000
Z	2 kg	280,000	175,000

Marketing and administrative expenses for the year:

Sales salaries...	$ 38,250
Sales travel	28,000
Sales office (variable)	15,400
Sales commissions (5%).......................................	70,000
Credit management	14,000
Packing and shipping...	32,900
Warehousing..	16,450
Advertising...	150,000
Bookkeeping and billing	42,000
General marketing and administrative..........................	90,000
Total...	$497,000

Required:

(1) Prepare a product income statement showing the allocation of marketing and administrative expenses to each product.

(2) Prepare an income statement showing the allocation of marketing and administrative expenses to each order class.

(For both requirements, round off all base computations to five decimal places and all allocated amounts to the nearest dollar.)

21-4. Product-line income statement—contribution margin approach. Pralina Products Company has three major product lines—cereals, breakfast bars, and dog food. The following income statement for the year ended April 30 was prepared by product line, using full cost allocation:

Pralina Products Company
Income Statement
For the Year Ended April 30, 19--
(000s omitted)

	Cereals	Breakfast Bars	Dog Food	Total
Sales (in pounds)...................	2,000	500	500	3,000
Revenue from sales.................	$1,000	$400	$200	$1,600
Cost of goods sold:				
Materials	$ 330	$160	$100	$ 590
Direct labor.....................	90	40	20	150
Factory overhead.................	108	48	24	180
Total cost of goods sold...........	$ 528	$248	$144	$ 920
Gross profit......................	$ 472	$152	$ 56	$ 680
Commercial expenses:				
Marketing expenses:				
Advertising....................	$ 50	$ 30	$ 20	$ 100
Commissions	50	40	20	110
Sales salaries and related benefits ..	30	20	10	60
Total marketing expense.........	$ 130	$ 90	$ 50	$ 270
General and administrative expenses:				
Licenses.......................	$ 50	$ 20	$ 15	$ 85
Salaries and related benefits......	60	25	15	100
Total general and administrative expenses	$ 110	$ 45	$ 30	$ 185
Total commercial expense...........	$ 240	$135	$ 80	$ 455
Operating income	$ 232	$ 17	$(24)	$ 225

Explanatory data:

(a) Cost of goods sold. The company's inventories of materials and finished products do not vary significantly from year to year. Factory overhead was applied to products at 120% of direct labor dollars. The factory overhead costs for the year were as follows:

Variable indirect labor and supplies	$ 15,000
Variable employee benefits on factory labor.......................	30,000
Supervisory salaries and related benefits.........................	35,000
Plant occupancy cost	100,000
	$180,000

There was no over- or underapplied factory overhead at year end.

(b) Advertising. The company has been unable to determine any direct causal relationship between the level of sales volume and the level of advertising expenditures. However, because management believes advertising is necessary, an annual advertising program has been implemented for each product line, independent of the others.

(c) Commissions. Sales commissions are paid to the sales force at the rate of 5% on the cereals and 10% on the breakfast bars and dog food.

(d) Licenses. Various licenses are required for each product line, renewed annually for each product line at a fixed amount.

(e) Salaries and related benefits. Sales and general and administrative personnel devote time and effort to all product lines. Their salaries and wages are allocated on the basis of management's estimates of time spent on each product line.

(f) Fixed factory overhead and the salaries and related benefits for sales and general and administrative personnel are not traceable to individual product lines on any objective basis.

Required: Prepare a product-line income statement, using the contribution margin approach.   (CMA adapted)

21-5. Cost allocations to individual stores; sales expansion decision. McNamara Foods Inc., a grocery chain consisting of three stores, operates in a state that permits each of its municipalities to levy an income tax on corporations operating within their respective city limits. This legislation establishes a uniform tax rate that may be levied by the municipality. Regulations also provide that the tax is to be computed on income derived within the taxing municipality after a reasonable and consistent allocation of general overhead expenses, which include warehouse, central office, advertising, and delivery expenses. General overhead expenses have not been allocated previously to McNamara's stores.

Each municipality in which McNamara operates a store has levied the corporate income tax as provided by state legislation, and management is considering two plans for allocating general overhead expenses to each store.

General overhead expenses for the year were as follows:

Delivery and warehousing expenses:		
Delivery expense	$40,000	
Warehouse operations	30,000	
Warehouse depreciation	20,000	$ 90,000
Central office expenses:		
Advertising	18,000	
Central office salaries	37,000	
Other central office expense	28,000	83,000
Total general overhead expense		$173,000

Additional information:

(a) One fifth of the warehouse space is used to house the central office, and depreciation of this space is included in the other central office expense. Warehouse operating expenses vary with the quantity of merchandise sold.

(b) All advertising is prepared by the central office and is distributed in the areas in which stores are located.

(c) As each store was opened, the fixed portion of central office salaries increased by $7,000, while other central office expense increased by $2,500. Basic fixed central office salaries were $10,000 and the basic fixed other central office expense was $12,000. The remainder of central office salaries and the remainder of other central office expense vary with sales.

(d) The delivery expense varies with the distance and the number of deliveries. The distances from the warehouse to each store and the number of deliveries made during the year were:

Store	Miles	Number of Deliveries
Ashville	120	140
Burns	200	64
Clinton.	100	104

The year's operating results, before deducting general overhead expense and the tax for each store, were:

| | Store | | | |
	Ashville	Burns	Clinton	Total
Net sales	$416,000	$353,600	$270,400	$1,040,000
Less cost of goods sold	215,700	183,300	140,200	539,200
Gross profit.	$200,300	$170,300	$130,200	$ 500,800
Less other local operating expenses:				
Fixed.	$ 60,800	$ 48,750	$ 50,200	$ 159,750
Variable	54,700	64,220	27,448	146,368
Total	$115,500	$112,970	$ 77,648	$ 306,118
Operating income before general overhead				
and income tax.	$ 84,800	$ 57,330	$ 52,552	$ 194,682

Required:

(1) Under each of the following allocation plans, compute the operating income for each store that would be subject to the municipal tax levy on corporation income:

Plan 1: Allocate all general overhead expenses on the basis of sales volume.

Plan 2: First, allocate central office salaries and the other central office expense equally to warehouse operations and to each store.

Second, allocate the resulting warehouse operations expense, warehouse depreciation, and advertising to each store on the basis of sales volume.

Third, allocate delivery expense to each store on the basis of delivery miles multiplied by number of deliveries.

(2) Formulate a management decision to determine which store should be selected for expansion in order to maximize corporate profits. This expansion will increase McNamara's sales by $60,000 and its local fixed operating expense by $7,500, and it will require ten additional deliveries from the warehouse.   (AICPA adapted)

CASES

A. Account number coding system. Baker Company's executive committee consists of the president and four vice-presidents—marketing, manufacturing, finance, and systems. The company has ordered a new computer for use in processing its financial information. Because this acquisition requires a substantial investment, the president wants to make certain of its effective use.

The new computer will enable Baker to revise its financial information system so that the several departments will get more useful information. This should be especially helpful in marketing because its personnel are distributed widely throughout the country. The Marketing Department is organized into nine territories and 25 sales offices. The vice-president of marketing wants monthly reports to (a) reflect those items for which the department is responsible and can control, (b) identify the most profitable products, and (c) show performance by territory and sales office.

The vice-president of finance has recommended that the accounting system be revised so that reports would be prepared on a contribution margin basis. Further, only those cost items which are controlled by the respective departments would appear on their reports. The monthly report for the Manufacturing Department would compare actual production costs with a budget containing the standard costs for the actual volume of production. The Marketing Department would be provided with the standard variable manufacturing cost for each product, so that it could calculate the variable contribution margin of each product. The monthly reports to the Marketing Department would reflect the variable contribution approach. The reports would present the net contribution of the department, calculated by deducting standard variable manufacturing costs and marketing expenses (both variable and fixed) from sales.

A portion of Baker Company's chart of accounts follows:

Account Number	Description
2000	Sales
2500	Cost of goods sold
3000	Manufacturing expenses
4000	Engineering expenses
5000	Marketing expenses
6000	Administrative expenses

The company wants to retain the basic structure of the chart of accounts to minimize the number of changes. However, the numbering system will have to be expanded in order to provide desired additional information.

Required: Using marketing as the example, design an account number coding system for preparation of the contribution reports for the Marketing Department. The account number coding system should (a) add additional accounts to the chart of accounts as needed, (b) provide flexibility in the coding structure so that it would not have to be revised completely should the company expand or restructure its sales area, and (c) explain and justify the coding structure presented.   (CMA adapted)

B. Use of standard rates and selection of cost allocation bases. Columbia Company is a regional office supply chain with 26 independent stores. Each store has been responsible for its own credit and collections. The assistant manager in each store has been assigned the responsibility for credit activities, including the collection of delinquent accounts, because the stores do not need a full-time employee assigned to credit activities. The company has experienced a sharp rise in uncollectibles the last two years. Therefore, corporate management has decided to establish a Collections Department in the home office to be responsible for the collection function company-wide. The home office will hire the necessary full-time personnel. The size of this department will be based upon the historical credit activity of all of the stores.

The new centralized Collections Department was discussed at a recent management meeting. A method to assign the costs of the new department to the stores has been difficult to determine because this type of home office service is somewhat unique. Alternative methods are being reviewed by executive management. The controller favors using a standard rate for charging the costs to the stores. The standard rate would be based on budgeted costs. The vice-president of sales has a strong preference for an actual cost charging system.

In addition, the basis for the collection charges to the stores was discussed. The controller identified the following measures of services (allocation bases) which could be used:

(a) Total dollar sales.
(b) Average number of past-due accounts.
(c) Number of uncollectible accounts written off.
(d) One twenty-sixth of the cost to each of the stores.

The executive vice-president stated that he would like the Accounting Department to prepare a detailed analysis of the two charging methods and the four allocation bases.

Required:
(1) Evaluate the two methods identified — standard rate versus actual cost — in terms of:
  (a) Practicality and ease of use.
  (b) Cost control.
(2) For each allocation base, discuss whether or not it is appropriate to use in this situation, and identify possible behavioral problems.   (CMA adapted)

C. Sales force motivation and performance. The XYZ Recreational Products Company, in an attempt to increase its sales and profits, has decided to change from a straight salary system to a commission-plus-bonus arrangement for compensating its salespersons. The XYZ Company manufactures and sells a line of fiberglass canoes and water skis. The company's sales are highly seasonal, with more than 75% of its business occurring between May and September.

The compensation plan under consideration calls for the salespersons to receive monthly a 10% commission on all sales that exceed the monthly sales quotas. If sales do not exceed the monthly quota, the salespersons will receive a 5% commission on the amount sold. The commission would be earned in two installments, one half in the month the order is shipped and one half in the month the customer pays for the product. Sales personnel can earn an additional 2% bonus on all their sales for the year if the quota is attained each month for a 12-month period.

At the beginning of each year, the yearly sales quota for each salesperson is determined by joint agreement between the salesperson and his or her supervisor. The monthly sales quota for each territory is then determined by dividing the annual sales quota by 12.

Required:
(1) List aspects of the new compensation plan that are likely to have a positive effect on employee motivation and performance.
(2) List aspects of the new compensation plan that are likely to have a negative effect on employee motivation and performance.   (CIA adapted)

D. Compensation program for salespersons. Betterbuilt Corporation manufactures a full line of windows and doors, including casement windows, bow windows, and patio doors. The bow windows and patio doors have a significantly higher profit margin per unit than casement windows, as shown in the following schedule:

	Casement Windows	Bow Windows	Patio Doors
Sales price	$130	$250	$260
Manufacturing costs:			
Direct materials	$ 25	$ 40	$ 50
Direct labor	20	35	30
Variable overhead	16	28	24
Fixed overhead	24	42	36
Total manufacturing cost	$ 85	$145	$140
Gross profit	$ 45	$105	$120

The company sells almost entirely to general contractors of residential housing. Most of these contractors complete and sell 15 to 50 houses per year. Each contractor builds tract houses that are similar, with some variations in exteriors and rooflines.

When contractors contact Betterbuilt, they are likely to seek bids for all the windows in the houses they plan to build in the next year. At this point, the Betterbuilt salespersons have an opportunity to influence the window configuration of these houses by suggesting patio doors or bow windows as variations for one or more casement windows for each of the several exteriors and rooflines built by the contractor.

The bow windows and patio doors are approximately twice as wide as the casement windows. A bow window or a patio door usually is substituted for two casement windows. Casement windows are usually ordered in pairs and placed side-by-side in those houses which could be modified to accept bow windows and patio doors.

Joseph Hite, president of Betterbuilt Corporation, is perplexed with the company's profit performance. In a conversation with his sales manager, he declared, "Our total dollar sales volume is growing, but our net income has not increased as it should. Our unit sales of casement windows have increased proportionately more than the sale of bow windows or patio doors. Why aren't our sales representatives pushing our more profitable products?" The sales manager responded with a sense of frustration, "I don't know what else can be done. They have been told which type of windows we want sold, due to the greater profit margin. Furthermore, they have the best compensation plan in the industry, with a $1,000 base monthly salary and commissions of 5% on sales dollars."

Required:
   (1) Identify the needs of the salespersons that are being met by the current compensation program.
   (2) Explain why Betterbuilt's present compensation program for its salespersons does not support the president's objectives to sell the more profitable units.
   (3) Specify alternative compensation programs which may be more appropriate for motivating the salespersons to sell the more profitable units.   (CMA adapted)

Chapter 22
Profit Performance Measurements; Intracompany Transfer Pricing; Product Pricing Methods

The establishment of a profit goal based on marketing and manufacturing plans expressed as budgets and standards, the delegation of authority and the assignment of responsibility to middle and lower management levels, and finally the creation of decentralized, autonomous divisions of a company lead to the need for measuring the operating and profit performance of top as well as subordinate executives. This chapter discusses the return-on-capital-employed concept, which assists management in appraising company-wide as well as divisional operating performance, and intracompany transfer pricing, which plays a significant role in measuring divisional results. The chapter also deals with different methods by which management can establish the product prices needed to cover costs and return a profit.

The Rate of Return on Capital Employed

The term "return on capital employed" used here refers to an internal measure of operating mangement. The term "return on investment" is sometimes used to refer to this notion, but such usage may be confusing because the term also refers to the average annual return on investment method (discussed in Chapter 26), which is a capital expenditure evaluation technique, and to a return or yield on equity capital, which is primarily an investor's guide. The return on equity capital also has some value as an internal measure, but for financial, not operating, management.

The rate of return on capital employed may be expressed as the product of two factors: the percentage of profit to sales and the capital-employed turnover rate. In equation form, the rate of return is developed as follows:

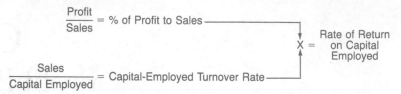

If sales were canceled out in the two fractions, the end result would still be the same. However, the shortened formula does not express the real objective of the concept, which deals with two independent variables — profit on sales and turnover of capital employed. Using the full formula gives management a better comprehension of the elements leading to the final result. The profit percentage reflects a cost-price relationship affected by the level and mix of sales, the price of products sold, and the success or lack of success in maintaining satisfactory control of costs. The turnover rate reflects the rapidity with which committed assets are employed in the operations.

Because the rate of return on capital employed is the product of two factors, numerous combinations can lead to the same result, illustrated as follows for a 20 percent rate of return:

Percentage of Profit to Sales	Capital-Employed Turnover Rate	Rate of Return on Capital Employed
10%	2.000	20%
8	2.500	20
6	3.333	20
4	5.000	20
2	10.000	20

There is no rate of return on capital employed that is satisfactory for all companies. Manufacturing companies in various industries will have different rates, as will utilities, banking institutions, merchandising firms, and service companies. Management can establish an objective rate by using judgment and experience supported by comparisons with other companies. Every industry has companies with high, medium, and low rates of return. Structure and size of the firm influence the rate considerably. A company with diversified divisions might have only a fair return rate when all of them are pooled in the analysis. In such cases, it seems advisable to establish separate objectives for each division as well as for the total company. Methods for divisional analyses are discussed in a later section of this chapter.

The Formula's Underlying Data

None of the factors or elements that produce the final rate can be disregarded, minimized, or overemphasized without impairing the quality of managerial decisions. Complete details of the relationships of the capital-employed ratio to the underlying ratios — percentage of profit to sales and capital-employed turnover rate — are portrayed in the following chart:

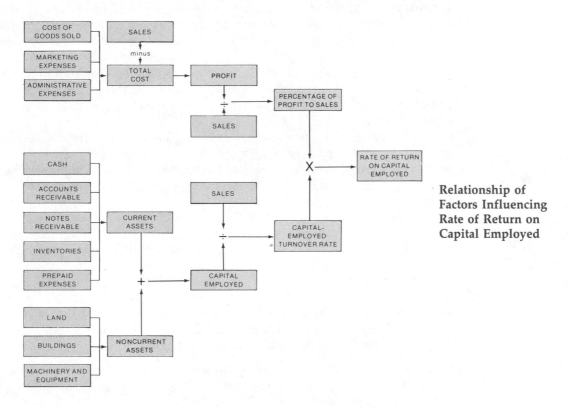

Relationship of Factors Influencing Rate of Return on Capital Employed

A rate of return on capital employed is computed by using figures from the balance sheet and income statement. Probability estimates can also be incorporated as a part of the computation.[1] The sales figure commonly used is net sales — gross sales less sales returns, allowances, and discounts. No general agreement exists with respect to the profit and capital-employed figures used in computing the rate. Consistency and uniformity are primary requisites, however, since the return on capital employed generally deals with a complexity of operations and/or a great diversity of divisions. Under such circumstances, it seems wise to avoid additional complexity and to seek clarity in the presentation of operating results without sacrifice of substance.

---

[1]William L. Ferrara, "Probabilistic Approaches to Return on Investment and Residual Income," *The Accounting Review,* Vol. LII, No. 3, pp. 597–604.

The income statement generally reports several profits, such as (1) operating income, which includes cost of goods sold and marketing and administrative expenses but excludes nonoperating income and expenses; (2) income before income tax, which would include the nonoperating income and expense items, and (3) the net income, which is the amount that is transferred to retained earnings. Using operating income means that only transactions of an operating nature should be considered. This profit figure is preferred for divisional analyses, since nonoperating items are usually the responsibility of the entire company. The use of income before or after income tax is significant when judging the enterprise as a whole. Net income is more defensible because tax money is not available to management, and managerial efficiency should be judged only by the ultimate result. If capital employed is restated to give recognition to inflation accounting, as discussed later in this chapter, then comparability calls for a similar restatement of the effect of inflation accounting on profit.

Capital employed refers to total assets or the sum of current assets and noncurrent assets. In describing capital employed, the word "investment" is intentionally avoided because it is used in connection with capital investment (noncurrent assets) and owner's investment (net worth or equity capital), and its meaning would be confusing.

Many accountants suggest that the amount of capital employed should be averaged over the fiscal period, if possible. Such a procedure tends to equalize unusually high or low year-end asset values or seasonal influences, particularly in divisional comparisons. Also, the sources of funds are not considered in determining the amount of capital employed. Therefore, current and long-term liabilities, which provided the money used in the purchase of assets, are not deducted from the assets. However, some accountants believe that current liabilities should be deducted from current assets to obtain a working capital figure to be used in place of the current assets figure.

Current Assets.   The three most significant items classified as current assets are cash, receivables, and inventories. Problems of valuation are connected with each of these assets.

Cash.   Ordinarily, the cash shown on the balance sheet is the amount required for total business operations. Cash funds set aside for pensions, taxes, or future expansion or development programs should be excluded. However, some companies believe that if such items are treated uniformly in relation to total cash or assets, no change of the cash balance sheet figure is warranted. On the other hand, certain managers do not accept the stated cash figure but consider a predetermined percentage based on the cost of goods sold or the annual operating expenses.

Receivables.   Values used for receivables should be either the gross amount or the net amount after deducting the allowance for doubtful accounts. The procedure should be uniform for all receivables allowances.

Inventories.   Different inventory costing methods, such as fifo, average, or lifo, give rise to some balance sheet and income statement differences. When return ratios of companies in the same industry are compared, an allowance for such differences should be made. Again, if an allowance account is used for lower of cost or market adjustments, the question arises as to whether the inventory figure used should be net of the allowance. Here, too, uniformity plays a significant role.

Some companies' inventories are costed on a standard cost or direct costing basis. Use of these two bases will, as in the case of lifo, generally depress inventory values on a company's balance sheet. For internal comparison, however, the use of either method on a uniform basis should not influence results. The same reasoning applies to other deviations from normal procedures.

Noncurrent Assets. In dealing with noncurrent assets, three possible valuation methods have been favored: (1) original cost (original book value), (2) depreciated cost (original cost less the depreciation allowance, i.e., net book value), and (3) inflation accounting.

Original Cost. Those accountants favoring the original cost basis argue that:

1. Assets of manufacturing companies, unlike those of mining companies, are on a continuing rather than on a depleted and abandoned basis.
2. Gross assets of one plant can be compared better with those of another plant, where depreciation practices or the age of the assets may be different.
3. Accumulated depreciation should not be deducted from the gross asset value of property, since it represents retention of the funds required to keep the stockholders' original investment intact. Actually, noncurrent assets are used to produce a profit during their entire life. Therefore, full cost is considered an investment until the assets are retired from use.

Depreciated Cost. Those accountants who favor the use of the depreciated cost for noncurrent assets state that:

1. While noncurrent assets are conventionally understated at the present time, the wrong method of increasing the original cost cannot be relied on to furnish the correct results. The attempt can only add to the existing confusion in accounting thinking.
2. An investment is something separate and distinct from the media through which it is made. The purchase price of a machine should be regarded as the prepaid cost for the number of years of production expected. Each year this number will decline. The function of depreciation accounting is to maintain the aggregate capital by currently providing substitute assets to replace the aggregate asset consumption (depreciation) of the year.

The several acceptable depreciation methods, such as straight-line or the various accelerated methods, result in the balance sheet and income statement differences. When return ratios of companies in the same industry are compared, such differences should be considered.

Inflation Accounting.   Those accountants who maintain that noncurrent assets should be included at current cost or at historical cost adjusted to constant dollars argue that such values are more realistic. They believe that a company receiving a certain and apparently satisfactory return based on book values should recognize the situation as being out-of-step with actual conditions. They further assert that some equalization of facility values of different divisions or companies should be provided, especially between those with old plants that were built at relatively low cost and those with new plants that were built at high cost. This method, of course, poses the serious problem of finding proper values.

Closely allied to any discussion of appropriate noncurrent asset values in an inflation accounting context are considerations as to the effect on profits, sales, and capital employed. Sales, costs currently incurred, and current assets might be measured in current dollar values, while the noncurrent assets and their expired cost might lag years behind. When the noncurrent asset effects are translated into current costs or constant dollars, the rate of return on capital employed is more realistic.

Divisional Rates of Return

The determination of divisonal (segment) return on capital is a matter of relating performance to assets placed at the disposal of divisional management.[2] This involves certain allocation difficulties. Some analysts believe that only a segment's sales, costs, and capital employed should be included in calculating a divisional rate of return, because only these figures are under the control of the divisional manager. Others argue that if certain expenses or capital employed are not allocated, the segments will show a higher return in the aggregate than that of the company. Such a result might create a psychological dilemma which would make it difficult to obtain additional effort from the unit supervisory staff that shows a higher or better return than the company average. Perhaps the best alternative is to calculate a rate of return based on sales, costs, and capital employed specific to the segment, followed by a rate of return calculation that includes a full allocation of total company sales, costs, and capital employed, so that both rates of return are clearly presented.

Sales figures usually can be identified directly with specific divisions. The allocation of costs, however, involves the same rationale as the allocation of overhead; i.e., direct departmental expenses are charged to the departments, followed by allocations of general and service department expenses.

The allocation of capital employed that is not directly identified with segments might be achieved as follows:

---

[2]Although this discussion refers to divisions as segments, the rate of return on capital employed may be computed for other segments, such as products, following the procedures described for divisions.

Cash might be allocated to segments on the basis of (1) gross sales billed, (2) cost of goods sold, (3) a ratio to total product cost, (4) a standard percentage of sales or cost of goods sold, or (5) manufacturing cost less any noncash items.

Accounts Receivable might be allocated to segments or products based on gross sales billed, or allocated on the basis of gross sales for the average number of days reflected in the receivables.

Materials might be allocated on the basis of (1) materials consumed, (2) annual consumption figures, or (3) a ratio to actual or normal usage or standard direct materials cost.

Finished Goods would be directly assigned.

Noncurrent Assets might be allocated on the basis of use of facilities at either normal, standard, or actual volume.

Divisional return-on-capital-employed measures have been criticized as a motivational tool because a division may seek to maximize relative profits rather than absolute profits. Assume that a division which is presently earning 30 percent on capital employed is considering a project whose return would be only 25 percent. The divisional management might decline the project because the return on total divisional capital would decrease. Yet, if the acceptance of the project would make the best use of these divisional resources from a total company point of view, then even with a lower rate of return for the segment or for the total company, the project should be accepted.

This suboptimum behavior might be overcome by calculating a *residual income figure* — a division's income less an amount representing the company's cost of capital employed by the division. This additional calculation would emphasize marginal profit dollars above the cost of capital, rather than the rate of return on capital employed.

Residual income is a counterpart to the return-on-capital-employed computation and is a dollar measure of profitability. The concept is analogous to the net present value obtained when discounting cash flows (Chapter 26). A positive residual income indicates earnings in excess of the desired return, while a negative residual income indicates earnings less than the desired return.[3]

Using the Rate of Return on Capital Employed

The return on capital employed is a measure of profitability for the total company as well as for divisions and individual plants and products. While a company's total analysis and comparison with the industry's ratios are significant for executive management, the real purpose of the return-on-capital-employed ratio is for internal profit measurement and control, with trends more meaningful than single ratios. It is not a guide for shareholders or investors who measure profitability or earning power by relating profit to equity capital.

---

[3]*Ibid.*, p. 599.

Executive management of many companies has shown a growing acceptance of the rate-of-return-on-capital-employed concept as a tool in planning, in establishing sales prices, and in measuring operational profitability. Return-on-capital-employed information is useful to executives, plant managers, plant engineers, and salespersons. It provides executives with a brief yet comprehensive picture of overall operations, of operations in each division, and of operations for plants and products. The plant manager receives a statement which measures the plant's operating results in a single figure. The product engineer's responsibility is to create products which can be manufactured at minimum cost and sold in profitable quantities without abnormal increases in asset investment. The sales staff realizes that price changes, justified as they may seem, are effective only if they contain a profit increment which yields an adequate return.

The return on capital employed not only acts as a measurement of the cooperative efforts of a company's segments but also shows the extent to which profitable coordination exists. A company's interlocking efforts are most effectively demonstrated by this rate. An appreciation of this concept by all employees will build an organization interested in achieving fair profits and an adequate rate of return.

Budgeting is the principal planning and control technique employed by most companies. Among the multiple phases of budgeting, sales forecasting is still considered the most difficult profit-planning task. Assuming that an acceptable sales budget has been established and that production, manufacturing, and commercial expense budgets have been prepared, return-on-capital-employed ratios are useful in evaluating the entire planning procedure.

Management's objectives with respect to the long-range return, as well as the immediate returns for each division, plant, or product, influence and guide budget-building procedures. As sales, costs, and assets employed are placed in the perspective of the rate of return on capital employed as envisioned by management, there is a marked change in the attitude of the people responsible for assembling the figures. Segment budgets are compared with predetermined goals. If too low, examination and revision can perhaps achieve the desired result. If an unusually excellent return is calculated, the reasons for it can be investigated. Mangement can either accept the situation as is or decide on a temporary modification of its planning goal. At any rate, the return on capital employed offers a satisfactory foundation for the construction of both annual and long-range planning budgets. When considering long-range plans regarding addition of new products, dropping of old products, expansion of production facilities, or investing additional capital in research and development, application of the return on capital employed on any future projects has a sobering effect if these projects have been conceived haphazardly or overoptimistically.

A successful technique in planning for profit improvement is to (1) define quantitatively (for sales, profits, and capital employed) the gap which exists between performance at present and that represented by long-term objectives, (2) fix the problems precisely by examining the details of each factor, (3) formulate a specific scheduled program of action for each factor, and (4) translate the planned results of each program in terms of its effect upon income and asset accounts. The application of this technique is shown in the following example:

EFFECT OF PLANNED PROGRAMS FOR PROFIT IMPROVEMENT

	Present		Change by Volume	Change by Cost Reduction	Asset Curtailment	Future	
Assets:							
Inventory	$ 500,000				−$100,000	$ 400,000	
Other current assets	200,000		+$ 20,000			220,000	
Noncurrent assets	300,000			+$80,000		380,000	
Total assets.	$1,000,000		+$ 20,000	+$80,000	−$100,000	$1,000,000	
Profit:							
Sales billed	$1,000,000	100.0%	+$200,000			$1,200,000	100.0%
Manufacturing cost.	$ 770,000	77.0%	+$140,000	−$88,000		$ 822,000	68.5%
Marketing and administrative							
expenses	130,000	13.0	+ 10,000	− 2,000		138,000	11.5
Total cost and expense.	$ 900,000	90.0%	$150,000			$ 960,000	80.0%
Operating profit.	$ 100,000	10.0%	+$ 50,000	+$90,000		$ 240,000	20.0%
Return on capital employed:							
% of profit to sales.		10.0%					20.0%
Capital-employed							
turnover rate (times)		1.0					1.2
Return on capital employed (%) . .		10.0%					24.0%

Advantages of the Use of the Return on Capital Employed. In general, the advantages of the use of the rate of return on capital employed are its tendency to:

1. Focus management's attention upon earning the best profit possible on the capital (total assets) available.
2. Serve as a yardstick in measuring management's efficiency and effectiveness for the company as a whole and its divisions.
3. Tie together the many phases of financial planning, sales objectives, cost control, and the profit goal.
4. Afford comparison of managerial results, both internally and externally.
5. Develop a keener sense of responsibility and team effort in divisional managers by enabling them to measure and evaluate their own activities in the light of the results achieved by other managers.
6. Aid in detecting weakness with respect to the use or nonuse of individual assets, particularly in connection with inventories.

Limitations of the Use of the Return on Capital Employed. The use of the return-on-capital-employed ratio may be subject to some of the following limitations:

1. Lack of agreement on the optimum rate of return might discourage managers who believe the rate is set at an unfair level.
2. Proper allocation requires certain data regarding sales, costs, and assets. The accounting and cost system might not give such needed details.
3. Valuations of assets, particularly with regard to jointly used assets, might give rise to difficulties and misunderstandings.
4. For the sake of making the current period rate of return on capital employed "look good," managers may be influenced to make decisions that are not the best for the long-run interests of the firm. This problem is especially likely if managers are presumed to be in positions for only a short time before being reassigned, thus personally avoiding responsibility for long-run consequences.
5. A single measure of performance, such as return on capital employed, may result in a fixation on improving the components of the one measure to the neglect of needed attention to other desirable activities. Product research and development, managerial development, progressive personnel policies, good employee morale, and good customer and public relations are just as important in earning a greater profit and assuring continuous growth.

Multiple Performance Measurements. Many well-managed companies use multiple performance measurements in order to overcome limitations of a single measure. One company that uses multiple measurements for rating divisional performance describes its method as a quantification of progress against agreed-upon standards. Each year, common standards are adopted by agreement of divisional managers and corporate management. Points are assigned to standards, reflecting those areas which require special attention in each division, as determined by management. Performance is measured as follows:

1. Profits for the current year are compared with the profits for the preceding year in absolute dollars, margins, and return on capital employed.
2. Profits are compared with the budget.
3. Cash and capital management measures are employed. Here, the emphasis is on effective management of inventory and receivables.

The claimed advantages of this method are that:

1. Performances of division managers are measured more fairly than would result from using solely a return-on-capital-employed figure.
2. Management can readily see those divisions which are performing well and those which are not.
3. Lost points serve as "red flags" by directing management to areas requiring attention and to the reasons and the corrective actions taken or needed.
4. The system has flexibility as to timely, needed shifting of management emphasis.

In this company, management concludes that it is not enough to tabulate performance statistics. The results must be effectively communicated, corrective action taken, and good performance rewarded. The system must also have the interest and support of division and corporate management.[4]

Graphs as Operating Guides.   Sound planning and successful operation must point toward the optimum combination of profits, sales, and capital employed. As stated earlier, the combination will necessarily vary, depending upon the characteristics of the operation. An industry with products tailor-made to customers' specifications will not have the same profit margins and turnover ratios as industries that mass produce highly competitive consumer goods.

In multiproduct companies, the three basic factors cannot be uniform, due to different types of operations. However, a special type of graph can be of assistance in judging the performance of segments or products in their relationship to a desired overall return on capital employed. Such a graph has the advantage of flexibility in appraising profit performance and offers an approach by which performance can be analyzed for improvement.

The following graph shows possible combinations of percentage of profit to sales and capital-employed turnover rate which yield a 20 percent return. When individual divisions or products are plotted on the graph, the segment's data might appear to the left or right of the basic curve. If on the left, the unit has a capital-employed-return performance below that expected for the company as a whole. A segment whose ratios appear to the right of the basic curve has a return in excess of that expected for the entire company. The same interpretation applies when the company's total return is plotted.

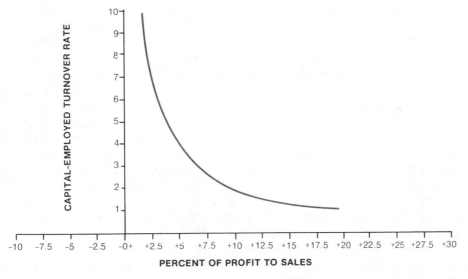

Relationship Between Percent of Profit to Sales and Capital-Employed Turnover Rate

[4]Frank J. Tanzola, "Performance Rating for Divisional Control," *Financial Executive*, Vol. XLIII, No. 3, pp. 20–24.

Intracompany Transfer Pricing

The effectiveness of the return on capital employed as a device for measuring the performance of divisional segments of a company depends considerably on the accuracy of allocating the costs and assets associated with the segment. In a decentralized multiplant or multiproduct organization, the unit managers are expected to run portions of the enterprise as a semiautonomous business. Thus, a shift to the return-on-capital-employed concept for measuring operational performance requires some rather fundamental policy changes.

As long as a segment is not entirely independent and separable, goods and services are generally transferred from one unit to another, a situation common to integrated corporations. The finished or semifinished product of one or more divisions or subsidiaries frequently becomes the raw material of one or more other divisions. In addition, some service functions are centralized and might conceivably deal with a number of profit centers. When transfers of goods or services are made, a portion of the revenue of one segment becomes a portion of cost of another, and the price at which transfers are made influences the earnings reported by each profit center. The value of these earnings as a measure of performance depends not only upon the manager's executive abilities but also upon the transfer prices used. Whatever pricing system is used can distort any reported profit and make it a poor guide for operating decisions. In the end, the cost or price used for the transfer will be used in the calculation of the return on capital employed, due to the very nature of the formula.

Years ago, transfer pricing played only a minor role in cost control. Today, the technique of transfer pricing has expanded into a complex set of procedures in the administration of the decentralized segments of an enterprise. This complexity and the arbitrary nature of intracompany transfer pricing is one reason for criticism of proposals to report segment or product-line revenues and profits in published financial statements. A steel company may operate a coal mine and sell some of its output on the open market but use the remainder in its own steel mills. The coal's transfer price can control whether the mining division shows a large, small, or zero profit.

External factors may influence the transfer price determination. A company with an overseas plant, where tax rates are low, may keep the transfer price high for materials sent to the domestic facility in order to retain profits abroad. Or a company with warehouses in a state with an inventory tax may keep transfer prices low on goods brought into the state in order to reduce its tax bill.

The existence of multiple management objectives makes it extremely difficult for a company to establish logical and sound intracompany transfer prices. A pricing method can be chosen only after the primary purposes for the use of the information from transfers have been identified. Therefore, a transfer pricing system must satisfy these three fundamental criteria: (1) allow central management to judge as accurately as possible the performance of the divisional profit center in terms of its separate contribution to the total corporate profit, (2) motivate the divisional manager to pursue the division's own profit goal in a manner conducive to the success of the company as a whole, and (3) stimulate the manager's efficiency without losing the division's autonomy as a profit center.[5] The system should also be easy to apply, meet legal and external reporting requirements, and permit each unit of a company to earn a profit commensurate with the functions it performs. As a practical matter, these criteria may be difficult to satisfy, because behavioral considerations are of paramount importance. Accordingly, a transfer price should be a just price to both the selling and buying parties. An advantage gained by one will be a disadvantage to the other and, in the end, may be detrimental to the corporate profit goal.

A profit center manager's interest must remain congruent with the firm's interest. For example, assume that Division X offers its Product A to Division Y at a transfer price of $14, which includes a $2 profit, a $9 variable cost, and a $3 fixed cost that presumably will remain unchanged in total as activity fluctuates. The same product is also available from an outside supplier at $11. Division Y, acting to minimize its costs, will prefer to purchase Product A at the lower external price of $11. However, such a decision would not be congruent with the best interests of the total firm, since the $11 external price is greater than the $9 variable cost which, in this example, is the differential cost, i.e., the incremental cost incurred to produce additional units. This analysis assumes that from the total firm point of view, no more profitable use could be made of the Division X facilities used in supplying Product A to Division Y.

Four basic methods of pricing intracompany transfers are available: (1) transfer pricing based on cost, (2) market-based transfer pricing, (3) negotiated transfer pricing, and (4) arbitrary transfer pricing. No one method of transfer pricing can effectively satisfy all of the requirements, so the best transfer price can be defined only as it is best for a particular purpose. Regardless of what transfer price is used, the differential cost of goods transferred from division to division should be known and used for decision-making purposes.[6]

Transfer Pricing Based on Cost

In a totally centralized firm, executive management basically makes all decisions with respect to the operations of the divisions. This responsibility makes cost control the basis for measuring a manager's performance. A cost-based transfer price is usually sufficient in this situation. A company without

---

[5]Joshua Ronen and George McKinney III, "Transfer Pricing for Divisional Autonomy," *Journal of Accounting Research*, Vol. 8, No. 1, pp. 99–112.
[6]For further study, the nature and scope of several major transfer pricing models categorized as to (1) the economic theory of the firm, (2) mathematical programming approaches, and (3) other analytical approaches, are covered in "Transfer Pricing—A Synthesis," by A. Rashad Abdel-khalik and Edward J. Lusk, *The Accounting Review*, Vol. XLIX, No. 1, pp. 8–23.

any integrated operations might have so little volume of intracompany transfers that it would be too time consuming and costly to price the transfer at other than cost.

The cost figure may be the total actual or standard cost or based on direct costing, and the company's cost system should permit the computation of a product's unit cost, even at various stages of production. When service departments are involved in a company's operations, a service charging rate similar to the one described on page 210 should be established in advance of the work performed, so that servicing and benefiting departments or plants know in advance the costs connected with services.

The cost method's primary advantage is simplicity, in that it avoids the elimination of intracompany profits from inventories in consolidated financial statements and income tax returns. Also, the transferred cost can readily be used to measure production efficiency by comparing actual with budgeted costs. Finally, the method allows simple and adequate end-product costing for profit analysis by product lines.

Considering the disadvantages, a transfer price based on cost is not suited to decentralized companies that need to measure the profitability of autonomous units. Also, producing segments may not be sufficiently conscientious in controlling costs that are to be transferred, although the use of standard costs for transfer pricing may alleviate this problem. A transfer price based on cost lacks not only utility for divisional planning, motivating, and evaluating, but also the objectivity required of a good performance standard.

In an analysis of a study of interdivisional transfer pricing, made by the National Industrial Conference Board, Sharav observes that in most cases of vertical transfers (meaning transfers between divisions at different stages of the manufacturing and marketing processes), transfers are priced at cost if the transferring division is viewed as a cost center (where the manager is responsible for cost only). However, if the transferee is a profit center (where the manager is responsible for cost and revenue), the transfer price may include a profit factor, thus approximating outside market prices. In horizontal transfers (meaning that transferer and transferee are situated at the same stage of the production and marketing processes), the transfers are usually executed at cost, which may include freight and handling charges. In many cases, companies using cost-based transfer prices choose actual costs which are derived from divisional operating statements and underlying cost records. Standard or budgeted costs are employed when available. Variable costs are used by only a few companies. A modified version of cost is the so-called cost-plus transfer price. It is comprised of cost plus a markup that is meant to provide a return on investment in divisional assets. Much less frequently used, this transfer price may be applied in lieu of the market price.[7]

Another cost-based transfer price that has been advocated is standard variable cost plus the per unit contribution margin given up on the outside

[7]Itzhak Sharav, "Transfer Pricing—Diversity of Goals and Practices," *The Journal of Accountancy,* Vol. 137, No. 4, p. 59.

sale by the company when a segment sells internally. For profit centers, the result generally approximates market price, while for cost centers, the transfer price is standard variable cost plus the possibility of an assigned portion of fixed cost.[8]

Market-Based Transfer Pricing

The market-based transfer price is usually identical with the one charged to outside customers, although some companies apply a discount to the market price to reflect the economies of intracompany trading. This method is the best profitability and performance measurement because it is objective. It reflects product profitability and division management performance, with divisions operating on a competitive basis. It also aids in planning and is generally required by foreign tariff laws and income tax regulations.

The most serious drawback to this method is the requirement for a well-developed outside competitive market. Unfortunately, a market price is not always determinable for intermediate products. Also, the market-based price adds an element of profit or loss with each transfer of product. Thus, the determination of the actual cost of the final product is difficult when the product has passed through numerous manufacturing stages.

Statement of Financial Accounting Standards No. 14, "Financial Reporting for Segments of a Business Enterprise," does not specify the transfer pricing method to be used in segment reporting, but it does require disclosure of the method used. A review of 250 annual reports for 1977 indicated that of the surveyed companies which were required to make such a disclosure, 75% used a market-based transfer price.[9] The SEC, however, requires disclosure of:

1. *When and where intersegment transfers are made at prices substantially higher or lower than the prevailing market price or the price charged to unaffiliated parties for similar products or services, and*
2. *The estimated or approximate amounts (or the percentage of increase or decrease in the amounts) of the revenue and operating profit or loss that the particular segments would have had if the intersegment transfers had been made at the prevailing market price.*[10]

Negotiated Transfer Pricing

Setting the transfer price by negotiation between buying and selling divisions allows unit managers the greatest degree of authority and control over the profit of their units. The managers should consider costs and mar-

---

[8]Ralph L. Benke, Jr. and James Don Edwards, *Transfer Pricing: Techniques and Issues* (New York: National Association of Accountants, 1980).

[9]Robert Mednick, "Companies Slice and Serve Up Their Financial Results Under FASB 14," *Financial Executive*, Vol. XLVII, No. 3, p. 54.

[10]*Ibid.*, p. 55.

ket conditions and neither negotiating party should have an unfair bargaining position.

A serious problem encountered with this method is that negotiation can not only become time-consuming but can also require frequent reexamination and revision of prices. Often the negotiated price diverts the efforts of the manager from activities promoting company welfare to those affecting divisional results only.

Arbitrary Transfer Pricing

Arbitrary transfer prices have been used quite frequently in the past and may be employed even when market-based prices are available. A price is established by interaction between buying and selling divisions and is at a level considered best for overall company interests, with neither the buying nor selling units having any control over the final decision. The method's disadvantages, however, far outweigh any advantage. It can defeat the most important purpose of decentralizing profit responsibility, i.e., making divisional personnel profit-conscious, and it severely hampers the profit incentive of unit managers.

Dual Transfer Pricing

The consuming (buying) and producing (selling) divisions may differ in the purpose a transfer price is to serve. For example, a consuming division may rely on a transfer price in make-or-buy decisions or in determining a final product's sales price based on an awareness of total differential cost. A producing division may use a transfer price to measure its divisional performance and, accordingly, would argue against any price that would not provide a divisional profit. In such circumstances, a company may find it useful to adopt a dual transfer pricing approach in which the:

1. Producing division uses a market-based, negotiated, or arbitrary transfer price in computing its revenue from intracompany sales.
2. Variable costs of the producing division are transferred to the purchasing division, together with an equitable portion of the fixed cost.
3. Total of the divisional profits will be greater than for the company as a whole, and the profit assigned to the producing division would be eliminated in preparing company-wide financial statements.

Under this system, a producing division would have a profit inducement to expand sales and production, both externally and internally. Yet, the consuming divisions would not be misled. Their costs would be the firm's actual costs and would not include an artificial profit. Variable costs, as well as fixed costs, should be associated with the purchase to ensure that the consuming division is aware of the total cost implications. Of course, the benefits from a dual transfer pricing approach can be achieved only if the underlying cost data are accurate and reliable.

Product Pricing Methods

Product pricing is a complex subject and is neither a one-person nor a one-activity job. Theorists and practitioners differ on various pricing theories. In practice, the solution to a pricing problem becomes a research job that requires the cooperation and coordination of the economist, statistician, market specialist, industrial engineer, and accountant. Since the determination of a sales price requires consideration of many factors, some of which defy measurement or control, prudent and practical judgment is necessary. Accountants can provide executive management and marketing managers with mileposts to be used as guides when traveling the relatively uncharted road toward successful pricing.

Costs are generally considered to be the starting point in a pricing situation, even though a rigid relationship is not expected to exist. Prices and pricing policy vary in relation to costs and market conditions as well as to the selection of a long- or short-range view. The long-run approach allows changes in products, manufacturing methods, plant capacity, and marketing and distribution methods. It aims to obtain prices which will return all costs and provide an adequate return on the capital invested. A normal or average product cost is the basis used for long-range pricing. A short-range pricing policy looks toward the recovery of at least part of the total cost in order to meet changing needs resulting from fluctuating sales volume, sales mix, and prices. In such cases, the differential cost of a product may serve as a guide for the determination of prices. Variable costs are the principal source of cost differentials which must be computed in such pricing problems (Chapters 20 and 24). In any case, the figures used should be current, which may require adjusting historical costs to reflect inflation accounting.

The relationship between costs and prices is one of the most difficult for a manager to determine. Price setting is that field of business in which management truly becomes an art. A sales price, generally thought of as the rate of exchange between two commodities, is determined in many industries in a manner that gives individual companies some degree of control over the price. Even companies that experience a great deal of competition have some measure of control, since products, quality, and/or the services rendered may differ. Although a firm may exercise some control over sales prices, the costs incurred in order to do business are usually more within its control.

Prices may be influenced not only by competition but also by what customers are willing to pay and by governmental regulations and controls. The Robinson-Patman Act must be complied with to avoid alleged price discrimination. Even if a company has little or no control over a sales price, it faces the question of whether it can operate profitably at the price that can be charged. Costs must be known and used as building blocks for determining the minimum price required to justify entering or continuing in a given market.

The accountant's assistance to management in the highly important field of pricing products requires knowledge and recognition of inventory costing methods as well as all cost items as they flow through the cost accounting cycle. The development of an appreciation for and an understanding of economic, social, and legal considerations is also required. The accountant must be not only an economist but also an investment analyst and must be able to see problems through management's eyes. By doing so, the accountant becomes a vital part of management, with cost accounting as a necessary tool.

Even though price-setting procedures are difficult, several cost-oriented methods are available that will assist in their computation and determination. These methods include (1) profit maximization—relating total revenue to total cost, (2) pricing based on a return on capital employed, (3) conversion cost pricing, (4) the contribution margin and the differential cost approach to pricing, and (5) standard costs for pricing.

Profit Maximization

A key objective of most business enterprises is to obtain a price that contributes the largest amount of profit. Economic theorists describe this as *profit maximization*. The profit return on each unit sold is not so important as the total profit realized from all units sold. The price that yields the largest profit at a certain volume is the price to be charged to a consumer.

The following schedule shows the variable cost at $7 per unit, with fixed cost at $300,000 for all ranges of output. The most profitable sales price is $14 per unit, with a contribution margin of $560,000 and a profit of $260,000, after deducting the fixed cost.

Sales Price per Unit	Number of Units To Be Sold	Total Sales Volume	Variable Cost ($7 per Unit)	Fixed Cost	Profit (Loss)
$20	20,000	$ 400,000	$140,000	$300,000	$ (40,000)
18	40,000	720,000	280,000	300,000	140,000
16	60,000	960,000	420,000	300,000	240,000
14	80,000	1,120,000	560,000	300,000	260,000
12	100,000	1,200,000	700,000	300,000	200,000
10	120,000	1,200,000	840,000	300,000	60,000
8	140,000	1,120,000	980,000	300,000	(160,000)

In other situations, the unit variable cost and the total fixed cost may vary according to the total number of units to be sold, thus influencing the most profitable sales price.

Profit maximization is not to be looked upon as the immediate return expected, but rather as a goal to be realized over several months or years. However, during these months and years, sales policies, competition, customer practices, cost changes, and other economic influences might radically alter all previous assumptions. Profit maximization is not necessarily the single objective or even the dominant objective of firms. A recent study found that firms pursue multiple objectives in setting their prices. These include major objectives—profits, return on investment, market share, and total sales—and lesser objectives—price-earnings ratio, liquidity, employee job security, and industrial relations. While each firm surveyed gave weight to many of these objectives, certain patterns of dominance were found:

...for firms selling standard products, market share was the dominant pricing policy objective. In contrast, firms handling custom-made products were more concerned with return on investment and [employee] job security.... Where firms seemed to be competing on the basis of price and service, sales maximization was the principal pricing objective. Where product innovation was the major source of competition, profits seemed to dominate....[11]

Pricing Based on a Return on Capital Employed

Some companies attempt to develop prices that will yield a predetermined or desired rate of return on capital employed. To illustrate, assume that a single-product company's total cost is $210,000, total capital employed is $200,000, the sales volume is 50,000 units, and the desired rate of return on capital employed is 20%. The formula used and the determination of the product's sales price would be:

$$\text{Price} = \frac{\text{Total cost} + (\text{Desired rate of return} \times \text{Total capital employed})}{\text{Sales volume in units}}$$

$$\text{Price} = \frac{\$210,000 + (20\% \times \$200,000)}{50,000 \text{ units}} = \frac{\$250,000}{50,000 \text{ units}} = \$5$$

Proof: Sales (50,000 units × $5) $250,000
       Less total cost 210,000
       Profit (20% × $200,000) .... $ 40,000

Pricing procedures using capital employed as part of the pricing formula may be complex, however. The illustrations assume no change in capital employed. Actually, as prices and costs change, capital employed may be expected to change. With an increase in capital employed, more cash will be required to serve the business. With higher prices, accounts receivable will be higher, and inventory costs will increase in proportion to increases in factory costs. Decreases would have the reverse effect.

If it is assumed that a firm is in business to maximize its value to the shareholders, then its pricing policy should be based largely on a target rate of return on capital employed. To be effective in its control and analysis, management's pricing decisions should be made after this rate, the standard costs, and the estimated plant capacity have been considered.

Conversion Cost Pricing

Conversion cost pricing attempts to direct management's attention to the amount of labor and factory overhead that products require. To illustrate, assume that a company manufactures two products, each selling for $10. The

[11]Lawrence A. Gordon, Robert Cooper, Haim Falk, and Danny Miller, *The Pricing Decision* (New York: National Association of Accountants, 1981; and Hamilton, Ontario: The Society of Management Accountants of Canada, 1980), pp. 9, 15–17.

manufacturing cost for each is $9, resulting in a gross profit of $1 per unit, indicating that from a profit point of view it does not matter which product is promoted. However, a breakdown of the costs reveals the following:

Item of Cost	Product A	Product B
Direct materials............................	$ 6	$ 3
Direct labor.................................	2	4
Factory overhead	1	2
Total manufacturing cost....................	$ 9	$ 9
Sales price.................................	10	10
Gross profit................................	$ 1	$ 1

The cost breakdown indicates that Product A requires only half the labor and factory overhead that is required for Product B. If it were possible to shift all efforts to A, a greater number of units could be produced and sold with the same gross profit per unit. Marketing costs of A versus B must also be considered. Of course, any volume increase might disturb market equilibrium and even cause a decrease in the price because of increased supply. These difficulties are discussed in Chapter 23.

Contribution Margin Approach to Pricing

In direct costing, the contribution margin figure indicates a product's contribution to the recovery of fixed costs and to profit. The fixed and variable cost classifications permit an evaluation of each product by a comparison of specific contribution margins. While this contribution margin approach might be used for a firm's entire business, it is of even greater value in the analysis of its divisions, plants, products, product lines, customers, and territories. Care must be taken, however, not to confuse contribution with profit, since profit is realized only after all fixed costs are covered.

The differential cost of an order is the variable cost necessary to produce the additional units, plus additional fixed costs (if any) at the new production level. If the cost of additional units is accepted as a basis for pricing them, any price over and above total differential cost would be acceptable. This procedure is, of course, applicable only to the additional units.

To base sales prices on differential cost requires careful scrutiny of all related factors. For example, long-term sales promotion should not be used for a product priced on the basis of differential costs when total cost recovery and a reasonable profit will not result.

Standard Costs for Pricing

If cost estimates used for pricing purposes are prepared on the basis of the standard costs for materials, labor, and factory overhead, the tasks of preparing the estimate and using the data to set the price will be considerably easier. The use of standard costs for pricing purposes makes cost figures more quickly available and reduces clerical detail. Since a standard cost represents the cost that should be attained in an efficiently operated plant at normal capacity, it is essential, once the sales price has been established, that the cost department furnish up-to-the-minute information to all parties to make certain that the cost stays within the rate set by the estimate. Any significant deviation between actual and standard costs should come to light for quick action through the accounting system.

The National Association of Accountants has stated that companies can be divided into four groups with respect to the type of cost figures which they supply to pricing executives. These groups are composed of:

1. Companies which supply executives with standard costs without the application of any adjustments to the standards.
2. Companies in which the standard costs are adjusted by the ratio of actual costs to standard costs as shown by the variance accounts.
3. Companies which use current market prices for materials, and in a few cases for labor, with standard costs for other elements of product cost.
4. Companies which adjust standard costs to reflect the actual costs anticipated during the period for which the prices are to be in effect, including inflation's impact on costs.[12]

When standard costs are used for bid prices, they might be based on estimates previously submitted. However, while some materials parts or labor operations might be identical with those used for another product, executives need the most up-to-date information on all cost components in order to set a profitable price. Companies that must present bids adjust the costs developed from the detailed standards to approximate actual costs expected.

DISCUSSION QUESTIONS

1. How is the return on capital employed computed?

2. What management activities are measured by each of the factors involved in determining the rate of return on capital employed?

3. What items are generally included in the term "capital employed"?

4. State two major objectives that management may have in mind when setting up a system for measuring the return on divisional capital employed.

5. Identify the basic methods used in pricing intracompany transfers.

---

[12]Research Series, No. 14, "Standard Manufacturing Costs for Pricing and Budgeting," *NAA Bulletin*, Vol. XXX, No. 3, pp. 165–166.

6. From an organizational point of view, two approaches to transfer pricing are (a) to let the managers of profit centers bargain with one another and arrive at their own transfer prices (negotiated transfer pricing) and (b) to have the firm's executive management set transfer prices for transactions between the profit centers (arbitrary transfer pricing). State the fundamental advantage and disadvantage of each approach.
(CGAA adapted)

7. Explain the dual transfer pricing approach in intracompany transfer pricing.

8. Discuss the statement, "Price setting is truly an art."

9. What accounting-based methods are available that might assist and permit the computation and determination of a sales price?

10. Discuss the profit-maximization method of pricing.

11. Why are standard costs helpful in setting prices?

EXERCISES

1. Rate of return on capital employed. During the past year, Kaw Waterworks Company had a net income of $160,000. Net sales were $800,000 and total capital employed was $1,600,000.

Required: Compute (1) the capital-employed turnover rate, (2) the percentage of profit to sales, and (3) the rate of return on capital employed.

2. Rate of return on capital employed; minimum price. Provence Corporation manufactures a highly specialized alloy used in missile skins. Rising materials costs led the company to adopt the lifo method for inventory costing. In 19A, the company produced 702 000 kilograms of alloy. New government contracts and other new business should increase volume by about 30%. In spite of increased costs, management felt that it could reduce the sales price from $12.30 per kilogram in 19A to $11.40 in 19B and still maintain the same rate of return on capital employed. However, prices of basic raw materials climbed higher than expected and the desired return and profit did not materialize. The following data are available (000s omitted):

	19A	19B
Sales.	$8,450	$8,550
Cost of goods sold and commercial expenses.	7,370	7,931
Net income	901	896
Cash.	1,200	500
Accounts receivable.	1,000	1,000
Inventories.	1,750	2,300
Noncurrent assets	6,650	7,400

Required: Compute (1) the actual rate of return on capital employed for the past two years, and (2) the minimum price that the company should have charged.

3. Rate of return on capital employed for regions. Hutton Sales Company has three regions: Eastern, Central, and Western. The cost of assets employed is determined by averaging the December 31, 19A balance of $1,446,000 and the December 31, 19B balance of $1,632,000. The assets are distributed among the Eastern, Central, and Western *regions in a ratio of 3:1:2, respectively. The 19B condensed income statement is as follows:*

Hutton Sales Company
Income Statement
For the Year Ended December 31, 19B

	Eastern	Central	Western	Total
Sales..........................	$3,078,000	$513,000	$2,308,500	$5,899,500
Cost of goods sold...............	2,016,000	383,000	1,818,500	4,217,500
Gross profit.....................	$1,062,000	$130,000	$ 490,000	$1,682,000
Commercial expenses............	908,100	88,960	443,830	1,440,890
Operating income................	$ 153,900	$ 41,040	$ 46,170	$ 241,110

Required: *For each region and in total, compute:*
(1) The capital-employed turnover rate. (Compute answers to one decimal place.)
(2) The percentage of profit to sales. (Compute answers to ¹⁄₁₀ of 1%)
(3) The rate of return on capital employed. (Compute answers to ¹⁄₁₀ of 1%.)

4. *Rate of return on capital employed for product lines. Electro Products Company has three lines of products, Mechanical, Household, and Commercial. Each year, new models are developed; hence, there are no year-end inventories of finished goods. Sales results and production costs for each product line are shown in the following income statement:*

	Mechanical	Household	Commercial	Total
Sales.....................................	$1,500,000	$800,000	$700,000	$3,000,000
Cost of goods sold:				
Materials	$ 160,000	$200,000	$150,000	$ 510,000
Labor	330,000	220,000	125,000	675,000
Factory overhead.......................	410,000	160,000	140,000	710,000
Total	$ 900,000	$580,000	$415,000	$1,895,000
Gross profit.............................	$ 600,000	$220,000	$285,000	$1,105,000
Marketing and administrative.............	133,950	71,440	62,510	267,900
Operating income........................	$ 466,050	$148,560	$222,490	$ 837,100
Provision for income tax.................	223,704	71,309	106,795	401,808
Net income	$ 242,346	$ 77,251	$115,695	$ 435,292

Average assets employed by the company during the year totaled $2,943,000. This amount is allocated to the product lines, Mechanical, Household, and Commercial, in a ratio of 5:2½:1½, respectively.

Required: *For each product line and for the three product lines combined, compute the (1) capital-employed turnover rate, (2) percentage of profit to sales, and (3) return-on-capital-employed rate. Round answers to three decimal places or ¹⁄₁₀ of one percent.*

5. *Transfer pricing. Wallach Iron Mill produces high-grade pig iron in its single blast furnace in Bedford, Pennsylvania. Coal from nearby mines is converted into coke in company-owned ovens, and 80% of the coke produced is used in the blast furnace. The management of the mill is experimenting with divisional profit reporting and control and has established the blast furnace as well as the coke-producing activity as profit centers. Coke used by the blast furnace is charged to that profit center at $6 per ton, which approximates the current market price less costs of marketing (including substantial freight costs). The remaining 20% of the coke produced at a normal annual volume output of 80,000 tons is sold to other mills in the area at $7.50 per ton.*

The cost of coal and other variable costs of coke production amount to $4.50 per ton. Fixed costs of the coke division amount to $40,000 a year.

The blast furnace manager, with authority to purchase outside, has found a reliable, independent coke producer who has offered to sell coke at a delivered price of $5 per ton on a long-term contract. The manager of Wallach Iron Mill's coke division claims it cannot match that price and maintain profitable operations.

The manager of the coke division indicates that with an expenditure of $60,000 annually for fixed productive and delivery equipment, the division's entire annual normal output could be sold to outside firms at $6 per ton, FOB the Wallach Iron Mill plant. Other marketing expenses will be $.50 per ton. The increased fixed costs would reduce variable production costs by $1.50 per ton.

Required:
(1) Prepare calculations to guide the coke division manager in deciding whether to accept the offer, assuming that Wallach Iron Mill cannot increase its sales of coke to outsiders above the 20% of normal production.
(2) Prepare calculations to aid executive management in deciding whether to make the additional investment and sell the entire coke division's output to outsiders.

6. Product pricing. Warren Company is considering changing its sales price of Salien, which is presently $15. Increases and decreases of both 10% and 25%, as well as increases in advertising and promotion expenditures, are being considered, with the following estimated results for 19A and 19B:

	Estimated Unit Sales		Estimated Advertising and Promotion Expenditures	
Price	19A	19B	19A	19B
−25%	190,000	200,000	$200,000	$210,000
−10%	180,000	190,000	250,000	250,000
No change	160,000	170,000	300,000	300,000
+10%	140,000	150,000	400,000	450,000
+25%	130,000	140,000	450,000	550,000

The company has the necessary flexibility in its production capacity to meet these volume levels. The variable manufacturing cost per unit of Salien is estimated to be $7.25 in 19A and $7.80 in 19B.

Required: Determine the recommended sales price. (CMA adapted)

7. Contribution margin approach to pricing. The Gelotech Company is a large manufacturer of refrigeration units. The firm's product line includes refrigerators for homes, industry, and ships. The firm is composed of three divisions. The Motor Division is responsible for manufacturing the motors for all of the various refrigeration units. In the Shell Division, the refrigerator shells are produced and the motors transferred from the Motor Division are installed. The Marketing Division is responsible for the sale and distribution of the final product.

While a market exists outside the firm for both the motors and shells, the transfer price between divisions is set by executive management. This is done to avoid unnecessary friction, which management feels might impair efficiency and prove wasteful.

Recently the company was asked to submit a bid for 100 refrigeration units for a local shipbuilding firm. The following unit cost estimate has been prepared:

	Motor	Shell	Marketing
Manufacturing materials	$195	$ 180	—
Receiving and handling (60% fixed).	10	25	$ 20
Motor	—	600	—
Refrigeration units	—	—	1,240
Shipping materials	—	—	30
Direct labor	190	220	35
Factory overhead:			
Fixed.	55	45	15
Variable	100	80	10
General administrative cost	28	57	67
Transfer price	600	1,240	—

Prior to submitting its bid, Gelotech has learned that its principal competitor has sub-mitted a bid of $1,200 per unit.

Required: *Prepare an analysis as to whether or not Gelotech can match the competitor's bid.*

PROBLEMS

22-1. Rate of return on capital employed. Venice Corporation's management is concerned over its current financial position and return on capital employed. In a request for assistance in analyzing these financial conditions, the controller provides the following statements:

Venice Corporation
Statement of Working Capital Deficit
December 31, 19A

Current liabilities		$198,625
Less current assets:		
Cash.	$ 5,973	
Accounts receivable (net)	70,952	
Inventory	90,200	167,125
Working capital deficit		$ 31,500

Venice Corporation
Income Statement
For the Year Ended December 31, 19A

Sales (90,500 units)	$751,150
Cost of goods sold	451,000
Gross profit	$300,150
Marketing and general expenses, including $22,980 depreciation	149,920
Income before income tax.	$150,230
Less income tax (50%)	75,115
Net income	$ 75,115

Noncurrent assets consist of land, a building, and equipment, with a book value of $350,000 on December 31, 19A.

Sales of 100,000 units are forecast for 19B. Within this relevant range of activity, costs are estimated as follows (excluding income tax):

	Fixed Cost	Variable Cost per Unit
Cost of goods sold		$4.90
Marketing and general expenses, including		
$15,450 depreciation	$125,750	1.10
Total	$125,750	$6.00

The income tax rate is expected to be 50%. Past experience indicates that current assets vary in direct proportion to sales dollars. Management feels that in 19B the market will support a sales price of $8.40 at a sales volume of 100,000 units.

Required:
    (1) Compute the 19A return-on-capital-employed ratio (after income tax), to 1/10 of one percent.
    (2) Compute the 19B rate of return (after income tax) on book value of total assets, to 1/10 of one percent.   (AICPA adapted)

22-2. Profit and rate of return on capital employed using various proposals. Lauren Toy Company manufactures two specialty children's toys marketed under the trade names of Springy and Leapy. During the year, the following costs, revenue, and capital employed by the company in the production of these two items were:

	Springy	Leapy
Sales price per unit...............................	$ 1.50	$ 1.95
Sales in units	280,000	150,000
Materials cost per unit............................	$ .20	$ .30
Labor cost per unit	.50	.75
Variable factory overhead per unit	.15	.20
Variable marketing cost per unit	.05	.10
Fixed factory overhead	100,000	30,000
Fixed marketing cost	30,000	15,000
Variable capital employed........................	10% of sales	20% of sales
Fixed capital employed	$148,000	$ 91,500

Fixed administrative and other nonallocable fixed costs amounted to $28,000, and nonallocable capital employed was $25,000.

Management, dissatisfied with the return on total capital employed, is considering a number of alternatives to improve this return.

The market for Springy appears to be underdeveloped, and the consensus is that sales can be increased to 325,000 units at the same price with an increase of $9,500 in the fixed advertising cost. An increase in the production of Springy will require use of some equipment previously utilized in the production of Leapy and a transfer of $10,000 of fixed capital and $5,000 of fixed factory overhead to the production of Springy.

For Leapy, it would mean limiting its production to 100,000 units, which could be marketed with the current sales effort at (a) an increase in price of $.15 per unit; (b) without a price increase and with a reduction in current fixed advertising cost of

$9,000; or (c) with a $.05 per unit increase in price and a $7,500 reduction in the current fixed advertising cost.

Required:
   (1) Compute the income before income tax and the return on capital employed for each product and in total for the year, to $\frac{1}{10}$ of one percent.
   (2) Compute the income before income tax and the return on capital employed for each product and in total under each alternative, to $\frac{1}{10}$ of one percent.

22-3. Product pricing and transfer pricing. National Industries is a diversified corporation with separate and distinct operating divisions. Each division's performance is evaluated on the basis of total dollar profits and return on division investment.

The WindAir Division manufactures and sells air conditioner units. The coming year's budgeted income statement, based on a sales volume of 15,000 units, is as follows:

WindAir Division
Budgeted Income Statement
For 19A

	Per Unit	Total
Sales revenue	$400	$6,000,000
Manufacturing costs:		
Compressor	$ 70	$1,050,000
Other raw materials	37	555,000
Direct labor	30	450,000
Variable factory overhead	45	675,000
Fixed factory overhead	32	480,000
Total manufacturing cost	$214	$3,210,000
Gross profit	$186	$2,790,000
Commercial expenses:		
Variable marketing	$ 18	$ 270,000
Fixed marketing	19	285,000
Fixed administrative	38	570,000
Total commercial expense	$ 75	$1,125,000
Income before income tax	$111	$1,665,000

WindAir's division manager believes sales can be increased if the unit sales price is reduced. A market research study conducted by an independent firm at the request of the manager indicates that a 5% reduction in the sales price ($20) would increase sales volume 16%, or 2,400 units. WindAir has sufficient production capacity to manage this increased volume with no increase in fixed cost.

At the present time, WindAir uses a compressor in its units, which it purchases from an outside supplier at a cost of $70 each. The division manager of WindAir has approached the manager of the Compressor Division regarding the sale of compressor units to WindAir. The Compressor Division currently manufactures and sells a unit exclusively to outside firms which is similar to the unit used by WindAir. Specifications for the WindAir compressor are slightly different, which would reduce the Compressor Division's raw materials cost by $1.50 per unit. In addition, the Compressor Division would not incur any variable marketing cost for the units sold to WindAir. The manager of WindAir wants all of the compressors it uses to come from one supplier and has offered to pay the Compressor Division $50 for each unit.

The Compressor Division has the capacity to produce 75,000 units. The coming year's budgeted income statement for the Compressor Division, shown as follows, is based on a sales volume of 64,000 units, without considering WindAir's proposal:

Compressor Division
Budgeted Income Statement
For 19A

	Per Unit	Total
Sales revenue	$100	$6,400,000
Manufacturing costs:		
Raw materials	$ 12	$ 768,000
Direct labor	8	512,000
Variable factory overhead	10	640,000
Fixed factory overhead	11	704,000
Total manufacturing cost	$ 41	$2,624,000
Gross profit	$ 59	$3,776,000
Commercial expenses:		
Variable marketing	$ 6	$ 384,000
Fixed marketing	4	256,000
Fixed administrative	7	448,000
Total commercial expense	$ 17	$1,088,000
Income before income tax	$ 42	$2,688,000

Required:
   (1) Compute the estimated result if the WindAir Division reduces its sales price by 5%, even if it cannot acquire the compressors internally at $50 each.
   (2) Compute the estimated effect on the Compressor Division, from its own viewpoint, if the 17,400 units are supplied to WindAir at $50 each.
   (3) Determine whether it would be in the best interests of National Industries for the Compressor Division to supply the 17,400 units at $50 each.

(CMA adapted)

22-4. Transfer pricing. Martin Corporation, a diversified company, recently implemented a decentralization policy under which divisional managers are expected to make their own operating decisions, including whether to do business with other divisions. The performances and year-end bonuses of divisional managers are measured by the return on capital employed of their divisions. Because most divisions have operated at full capacity, it is company policy that all transfers between divisions are to be priced at 120% of standard manufacturing cost (to allow for a "normal" divisional profit margin). This transfer price is not negotiable.

    The president of the company is currently faced with a dispute between the general managers of two divisions: the Consumer Products Division and the Engineering Division. The Consumer Products Division makes and sells several household articles, including a home appliance that has, until recently, been one of the company's steadiest sellers. Recently, this division has had marketing difficulties and has reduced its production of the appliance to 56,000 a year from its usual production at capacity. The unused capacity cannot be utilized for other products. The Engineering Division makes a wide variety of items, including a specialized part (Part TX) that is sold to the Consumer Products Division and to a few small outside companies. The latter buy a steady 12% of the Engineering Division's annual production capacity for the part.

    The Consumer Products Division uses four of these parts in each home appliance unit and maintains no significant inventory of unused parts but acquires them from the Engineering Division as needed to meet its production requirements. The parts are not available from any other source.

    Because the Consumer Products Division has recently reduced its requirement for Part TX, the Engineering Division has been seeking new customers and has received an offer to buy 100,000 units of the part annually, at a price of $5 each, which is less than the $5.40 each paid by the small outside companies but more than the transfer price paid by the Consumer Products Division. The company making the offer is in a market unrelated to that of either the Consumer Products Division or the small outside companies.

Following are data with respect to Part TX and the home appliance involved in the dispute between the two managers:

	Part TX (Engineering Division)	Home Appliance (Consumer Products Division)
Annual production capacity	300,000 units	66,000 units
Unit sales price to outside customers	$5.40	$80.00
Standard manufacturing cost per unit (based on production at full capacity):		
Division's own costs:		
Variable	$2.00	$37.00
Fixed	1.75	13.00
Transfers from the Engineering Division.......	—	18.00
Standard manufacturing cost per unit	$3.75	$68.00

The manager of the Consumer Products Division has requested that the president instruct the manager of the Engineering Division to refuse the offer received, since (1) no other source for Part TX can be found, (2) the marketing problems with the home appliance are expected to be temporary, and (3) the Engineering Division cannot expand its production capacity for Part TX.

Required:

(1) Determine the action that the manager of the Engineering Division should take as a result of the offer, in order to maximize the results of that division. Include calculations of the offer's effect on the Engineering Division.

(2) Determine the overall effect on the company, under existing circumstances, if the Engineering Division's manager accepts the offer.

(3) Identify the factors that the president should consider in deciding whether to intervene in the dispute.

(4) Revise the transfer pricing policy to assist the divisional managers in making optimal decisions for the company.   (CICA adapted)

22-5. Product pricing. Delaware Valley Corporation produces an electronic component. Product demand is highly elastic, within a specified range. At present, 100,000 units are sold at $10 each, and the additional demand expected with price reductions is:

Unit Price	Units of Estimated Demand
$9.75	120,000
9.50	150,000
9.25	190,000
9.00	240,000
8.75	300,000

Present capacity is 125,000 units. Further estimates are that the first capacity increase will require a $500,000 capital expenditure and, including depreciation, will increase annual fixed costs by $100,000 from the present $250,000 level. Each subsequent addition of 75,000 units will require further capital investment of $450,000 and will increase annual fixed costs by $75,000. Commercial expenses included in the present $250,000 figure will not change at the higher volumes. Other unit costs are estimated as follows:

	Less Than 150,000	150,000 to 200,000*	More Than 200,000*
Direct materials	$4.00	$3.80	$3.60
Direct labor.................	1.00	1.00	1.10
Variable factory overhead and commercial expenses	1.00	1.00	1.00

*Average costs for total production.

The board of directors will not approve additional capital expenditures unless a minimum pretax return of 20% is anticipated.

Required: Prepare a profitability statement at the various operating volumes, including the required 20% return on additional investment.

22-6. Public utility rate based on capital employed. Yantis Water Company is a public utility providing water service to 3,000 customers. As a privately owned public utility, its rates are subject to government regulation. Its rate structure is designed to provide a reasonable rate of return, calculated by expressing net income as a percentage of the company's rate base. The rate base, in turn, is the depreciated cost of the utility plant, averaged between the beginning and end of the year. Operating results for the year were as follows:

Water revenue		$90,000
Expenses:		
Fixed..	$38,668	
Variable	12,852	
Depreciation on utility plant.............................	17,000	68,520
Income before income tax		$21,480
Income tax...		4,510
Net income		$16,970

Yantis's directors feel that the present net income is inadequate and are considering applying for higher rates. At present, each customer is charged a flat rate of $30 per annum.

An analysis of metered water consumption data indicates the following ranges of average monthly usage:

Range	Consumption	Number of Customers
A	0–100 cu. ft. (average: 50 cu. ft.)	900
B	101–500 cu. ft. (average: 300 cu. ft.)	1,800
C	over 500 cu. ft. (average: 700 cu. ft.)	300
		3,000

Other data:

Utility plant in service, January 1	$800,000
Less accumulated depreciation....................................	200,000
Depreciated cost of utility plant, January 1..........................	$600,000
Utility plant addition during the year	$ 81,000

The income tax rate on earnings up to $80,000 is unchanged.

Required:

(1) Calculate the rate base and rate of return for the year, to 1/10 of one percent.

(2) Based on the information:
   (a) Compute the flat rate annual customer charge necessary to provide a 10% rate of return.
   (b) For each of the three consumption ranges, compute the charge per cubic foot of water necessary to provide a 10% rate of return, with the charge for consumption within Range B being double that within Range C, and two thirds of that within Range A; i.e., a customer consuming 150 cu. ft. of water would be billed at the Range A rate for the first 100 cu. ft. and at the lower Range B rate for the additional 50 cu. ft. (Compute answers to nearest $\frac{1}{10}$ of a cent.)

(CGAA adapted)

22-7. Contribution margin approach to pricing. J. Schifflein manufactures custom-made pleasure boats ranging in price from $10,000 to $250,000. For the past thirty years, Schifflein has determined each boat's sales price by estimating the costs of materials, labor, and a prorated portion of overhead and by adding 20% to these estimated costs. For example, a recent price quotation was determined as follows:

Direct materials	$ 5,000
Direct labor	8,000
Overhead	2,000
	$15,000
Plus 20%	3,000
Sales price	$18,000

The overhead figure was determined by estimating the total overhead cost for the year and allocating it at 25% of direct labor.

If a customer rejects the price and business is slack, Schifflein is often willing to reduce the markup to as little as 5% over estimated costs. Thus, average markup for the year is estimated at 15%.

Schifflein has just completed a pricing course and believes that the company could use some of the modern techniques taught in the course. The course emphasized the contribution margin approach to pricing, and Schifflein feels that such an approach would be helpful in determining the sales prices of custom-made pleasure boats.

Total overhead (including marketing and administrative expenses for the year) has been estimated at $150,000, of which $90,000 is fixed and the remainder is variable in direct proportion to direct labor.

Required:
(1) (a) Compute the difference in profit for the year if a customer's offer of $15,000 instead of the $18,000 price quotation shown above is accepted.
   (b) Determine the minimum sales price Schifflein could have quoted without reducing or increasing profit.
(2) State the advantages that the contribution margin approach to pricing has over the approach used by Schifflein.
(3) Identify the pitfalls, if any, to contribution margin pricing.   (CMA adapted)

CASES

A. Divisional rates of return. Notewon Corporation is a highly diversified company which grants its divisional executives a significant amount of operating authority. Each division is responsible for its own sales, pricing, production, costs of operations, and management of accounts receivable, inventories, accounts payable, and use of existing facilities. Cash is managed by corporate headquarters. All cash in excess of normal operating needs of the divisions is transferred periodically to corporate headquarters for redistribution or investment.

Divisional executives are responsible for presenting investment project requests to corporate management, which has authority for decisions to commit funds.

Corporate management evaluates the performance of division executives by the return-on-capital-employed (RCE) measure, with an asset base composed of fixed assets employed plus working capital exclusive of cash.

RCE is the most important appraisal factor for divisional executives in salary adjustments. Additionally, RCE affects the annual bonus, with increases in RCE being especially important. The company adopted the RCE performance measure and related compensation procedures about ten years ago to increase divisional management awareness of the importance of the asset-profit relationship and to provide additional incentive to divisional executives in seeking investment opportunities.

Although the RCE has continued to grow in each division, the corporate RCE has declined in recent years, and during the past three years the corporation has accumulated a sizeable amount of cash and short-term marketable securities.

Required:
  (1) Specify actions division managers might have taken to cause RCE to grow in each division but decline for the corporation.
  (2) Explain how Notewon's emphasis on the use of RCE might have resulted in the recent decline in the corporation's return on capital employed and the increase in cash and short-term marketable securities.
  (3) Suggest changes in the compensation policy to avoid this problem.(CMA adapted)

B. Transfer pricing. MBR Inc. consists of three divisions which formerly were three independent manufacturing companies. Bader Corporation and Roach Company merged in 19A and the merged corporation acquired Mitchell Company in 19B. The name of the corporation was subsequently changed to MBR Inc., and each company became a separate division, retaining the name of the original company.

The three divisions have operated as independent entities, each having its own sales force and production facilities. Each division manager is responsible for sales, cost of operations, acquisition and financing of divisional assets, and working capital management. The corporate management of MBR evaluates the performance of the divisions and division managers on the basis of rate of return on capital employed.

Mitchell Division has just been awarded a contract for a product which uses a component manufactured by the Roach Division as well as by outside suppliers. Mitchell used a cost figure of $3.80 for the component manufactured by Roach in preparing its bid for the new product, a figure supplied by Roach in response to Mitchell's request for the average variable cost of the component. It represents the standard variable manufacturing cost and variable marketing expense.

Roach has an active sales force that is continually soliciting new prospects, and its sales price for the component Mitchell needs is $6.50. Sales of this component are expected to increase; however, the Roach management has indicated that it could supply Mitchell with the required quantities at the regular sales price less variable marketing expense. Mitchell's management has responded by offering to pay standard variable manufacturing cost plus 20%.

The two divisions have been unable to agree on a transfer price. Corporate management has never established a transfer price policy because interdivisional transactions have never occurred. As a compromise, the corporate vice-president of finance has suggested a price equal to the standard full manufacturing cost (i.e., no marketing expense) plus a 15% markup. This price has also been rejected by the two division managers, because each considered it grossly unfair.

The unit cost structure for the Roach component and the three suggested prices are as follows:

Regular sales price	$6.50
Standard variable manufacturing cost	$3.20
Standard fixed manufacturing cost	1.20
Variable marketing expense	.60
	$5.00
Regular sales price less variable marketing expense ($6.50 − $.60)	$5.90
Variable manufacturing cost plus 20% ($3.20 × 1.20)	$3.84
Standard full manufacturing cost plus 15% ($4.40 × 1.15)	$5.06

Required:
(1) State the effect of the three proposed prices on the Roach Division's attitude toward intracompany business.
(2) Evaluate the negotiation method for setting the transfer price.
(3) Specify the extent of desired MBR corporate management involvement in setting the transfer price.   (CMA adapted)

C. Transfer pricing. Defco Division of Gunnco Corporation requests of Ajax Division, operating at capacity, a supply of Electrical Fitting #1726 that is not available from any other source. Ajax Division sells this part to its regular customers for $7.50 each. Defco, operating at 50% capacity, is willing to pay $5 each for this fitting. Defco will put the fitting into a brake unit which it manufactures on essentially a cost basis for a commercial jet plane manufacturer.

Ajax Division produces Electrical Fitting #1726 at a variable cost of $4.25. The cost (and sales price) of the brake unit as it is being built by the Defco Division is:

Purchased parts (outside vendors)	$22.50
Ajax Electrical Fitting #1726	5.00
Other variable costs	14.00
Fixed factory overhead and administrative expenses	8.00
Total	$49.50

Defco believes that the price concession is necessary to obtain the job.

Gunnco uses return on investment and dollar profits in measuring division and division manager performance.

Required:
(1) Recommend whether or not the Ajax Division should supply Electrical Fitting #1726 to the Defco Division. (Ignore income tax.)
(2) Discuss whether or not it would be to the short-run economic advantage of the Gunnco Corporation for the Ajax Division to supply the Defco Division with Electrical Fitting #1726 at $5 each. (Ignore income tax.)
(3) Discuss the organizational and managerial behavior difficulties inherent in this situation and recommend to Gunnco's president how the problem should be handled.   (CMA adapted)

Chapter 23
Break-Even and Cost-Volume-Profit Analysis

Break-even analysis, the construction of break-even charts, and the related cost-volume-profit analysis constitute another area of cost accounting that provides management with cost-and-profit data for profit planning, policy formulating, and decision making. *Break-even analysis* indicates the point at which the company neither makes a profit nor suffers a loss. *Cost-volume-profit analysis*, integrally related to break-even analysis, is concerned with determining the optimal level and mix of output to be produced with available resources. These analyses focus on the firm's short-run output decisions, as does much of the subject matter presented in Chapters 24 and 25.

The Nature of Break-Even Analysis

Break-even analysis determines at what level cost and revenue are in equilibrium. The *break-even point*, determined directly by mathematical computation, is usually presented in graphic form because it not only shows management the point at which neither a profit nor a loss occurs, but also indicates the possibilities associated with changes in costs or sales. Thus, a *break-even chart* can be defined as a graphic analysis of the relationship of costs and sales to profit. Break-even analysis is generally accomplished with the aid of a break-even chart because it is a compact, readable reporting device.

Determining the Break-Even Point

Data for break-even analysis cannot be taken directly from the conventional or full-costing income statement. The form of the statement and the manner in which the data are presented do not permit a convenient and practical analysis for planning, policy making, and profit determination. Therefore, each expense shown in the conventional income statement must be analyzed to determine its fixed and variable portions. Of the three classes of expenses—fixed, semivariable, and variable—the semivariable expenses must be separated into their fixed and variable components. The fixed portion is stated as a total figure, and the variable portion as a rate or a percentage. This procedure is demonstrated beginning on page 438.

Break-even analysis may be based on historical data, past operations, or future sales and costs. In the latter case, the starting point of the analysis is the determination of estimated or standard costs for various levels of output, with the help of the flexible budget. The analysis then resolves itself into three major elements: (1) defining volume and sales price, (2) determining fixed and variable costs, and (3) relating cost to volume. The anticipated sales revenue based on market conditions and tempered by plant capacity is determined. Existing flexible budgets are reviewed and revised to incorporate expected changes in prices and operating conditions. Forecast production (in units of product or hours) becomes the basis for establishing standard costs for materials, labor, and factory overhead. Values so determined are then incorporated in the budget. Where possible, standards for marketing and administrative activities are also used in constructing the budget, which becomes a summary of standards.

The data in the flexible budget can be used directly and without refinement for break-even analysis or can be converted into a break-even chart. Standard costs, which are a current, accurate, and readily obtainable source of data for various types of cost reports and analyses, form a most valuable tool for the preparation of an analysis designed to indicate future profit possibilities.

To illustrate the calculation of the break-even point, assume that the following costs and expenses have been determined by Webb Company:

	Total	Variable	Fixed
Materials	$1,000,000	$1,000,000	
Labor	1,400,000	1,400,000	
Factory overhead	1,600,000	400,000	$1,200,000
Marketing expense	350,000	150,000	200,000
Administrative expense	250,000	50,000	200,000
	$4,600,000	$3,000,000	$1,600,000

Webb Company has used direct costing in preparing the following income statement, which emphasizes the margin available for fixed costs and profit:

Sales	$5,000,000
Less variable cost	3,000,000
Contribution margin	$2,000,000
Less fixed cost	1,600,000
Profit[1]	$ 400,000

---

[1] The term "profit" in this discussion denotes operating income before income tax.

In this illustration, $.60 of every sales dollar, or 60 percent, is required to pay variable cost. Each dollar of sales contributes $.40, or 40 percent, toward covering fixed cost and making a profit. The 40 percent, referred to as the *contribution margin ratio (C/M),* is determined by dividing the contribution margin (sales minus variable cost) by sales revenue. The total sales dollars required to recover the fixed cost is calculated as follows:

$$\frac{\text{Break-even sales}}{\text{volume in dollars}} = \frac{\text{Fixed cost}}{\text{Contribution margin ratio (C/M)}} = \frac{\$1,600,000}{.40} = \$4,000,000$$

(or)

$$\frac{\text{Break-even sales}}{\text{volume in dollars}} = \frac{\text{Fixed cost}}{1 - \dfrac{\text{Variable cost}}{\text{Sales}}} = \frac{\$1,600,000}{1 - \dfrac{\$3,000,000}{\$5,000,000}}$$

$$= \frac{\$1,600,000}{1 - .60}$$

$$= \frac{\$1,600,000}{.40}$$

$$= \$4,000,000$$

The resulting $4,000,000 is the break-even point, at which neither a profit nor a loss is incurred. This break-even figure can be verified as follows:

Sales	$4,000,000
Less variable cost (60% of sales)	2,400,000
Contribution margin	$1,600,000
Less fixed cost	1,600,000
Profit	—0—

If a sales volume of $5,000,000 can be regarded as normal, the percentage of normal at which the company must operate in order to break even is computed as follows:

$$\frac{\text{Break-even sales volume in dollars}}{\text{Normal sales volume in dollars}} = \frac{\$4,000,000}{\$5,000,000} = 80\% \text{ break-even capacity percentage}$$

Sales and cost figures used in break-even analysis should be current. For fixed costs, which include figures for depreciation and amortization, consideration should be given to adjusting for inflation's impact on older historical cost dollars in order to more clearly identify sales required to truly break even. This adjustment may involve a restatement at current cost or at historical cost adjusted to constant dollars.

If a profit is desired, an activity level higher than the break-even capacity percentage must be reached. For this reason, a manager should not set the break-even point as a goal. Break-even analysis is not an easy mechanical substitute for the complex art of managing an enterprise. Analysis is a means to an end—not an end in itself.

The break-even point can also be computed in units. With a unit sales price of $4 and variable cost at 60 percent of sales, or $2.40 (60% of $4) per unit, the contribution margin per unit is $1.60 ($4 − $2.40). Dividing the total fixed cost by the contribution margin per unit, the break-even point in units is obtained:

$$\frac{\text{Break-even sales}}{\text{volume in units}} = \frac{\text{Fixed cost}}{\text{Contribution margin per unit}} = \frac{\$1,600,000}{\$1.60} = 1,000,000 \text{ units}$$

If the break-even sales volume in dollars is determined first, break-even units can be found by dividing dollar sales by the unit sales price:

$$\frac{\text{Break-even sales volume in dollars}}{\text{Unit sales price}} = \frac{\$4,000,000}{\$4} = 1,000,000 \text{ units}$$

Conversely, if break-even units are computed first, break-even sales dollars can be determined by multiplying break-even units by the unit sales price:

$$\text{Break-even sales volume in units} \times \text{Unit sales price} = 1,000,000 \text{ units} \times \$4 = \$4,000,000$$

Constructing a Break-Even Chart

Break-even computations can be presented in a break-even chart, in which the cost line and the sales line intersect at the break-even point. The information needed to construct this chart is forecast sales and fixed and variable costs.

A conventional break-even chart for Webb Company is illustrated as follows:

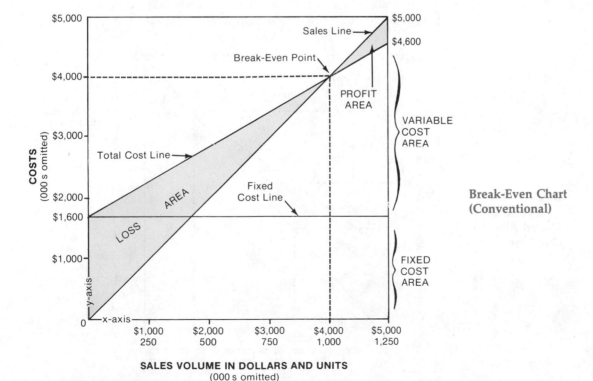

Break-Even Chart
(Conventional)

The conventional break-even chart is constructed as follows:

1. A horizontal base line, the x-axis, is drawn and spaced into equal distances to represent the sales volume in dollars or in number of units, or as a percentage of some specified volume.
2. A vertical line, the y-axis, is drawn at the extreme left and right sides of the chart. The y-axis at the left is spaced into equal parts and represents sales and costs in dollars.
3. A fixed cost line is drawn parallel to the x-axis at the $1,600,000 point of the y-axis.
4. A total cost line is drawn from the $1,600,000 fixed cost point on the y-axis to the $4,600,000 cost point on the right side of the y-axis.
5. The sales line is drawn from the 0 point at the left (the intersection of the x-axis and y-axis) to the $5,000,000 point on the right y-axis.
6. The total cost line intersects the sales line at the break-even point, representing $4,000,000 sales or 1,000,000 units of sales.
7. The shaded area to the left of the break-even point is the loss area, while the shaded area to the right is the profit area.

In the conventional break-even chart, the fixed cost line is parallel to the x-axis and variable cost is plotted above the fixed cost. Such a chart emphasizes fixed cost at a definite amount for various levels of activity. Many analysts, however, prefer an alternative form of chart, in which the variable cost is drawn first and fixed cost is plotted above the variable cost line. An example of this type of chart is as follows, using Webb Company data:

Break-Even Chart with Fixed Cost Plotted Above Variable Cost

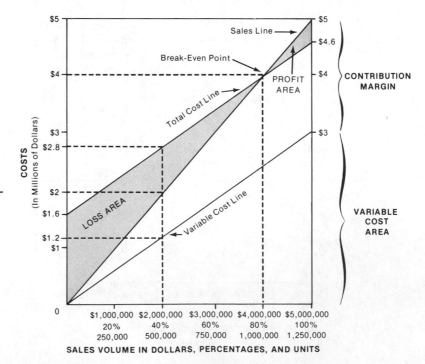

The space between the variable cost line and the sales line represents the contribution margin. Where the total cost line intersects the sales line, the break-even point has been reached. The space between the sales line and the total cost line beyond the break-even point represents the profit for the period at any volume. The space between the total cost line and the sales line to the left of the break-even point indicates the fixed costs not yet recovered by the contribution margin and is the loss for the period at any volume below the break-even point.

This alternative break-even chart indicates the recovery of fixed costs at various levels of percentage capacity and at dollar sales or unit sales. If sales, for example, drop to $2,000,000, variable costs would be $1,200,000 (60 percent of $2,000,000) while fixed costs remain at $1,600,000. The loss at this point would be $800,000 [$2,000,000 − ($1,200,000 + $1,600,000)]. The chart shows $2,000,000 on the sales line to be $800,000 below the total cost line. In columnar form, the analysis can be illustrated as follows:

(1) Number of Units	(2) Sales	(3) Variable Cost	(4) Contribution Margin (2)−(3)	(5) Fixed Cost	(6) Profit (Loss) (4)−(5)
250,000	$1,000,000	$ 600,000	$ 400,000	$1,600,000	$(1,200,000)
500,000	2,000,000	1,200,000	800,000	1,600,000	(800,000)
750,000	3,000,000	1,800,000	1,200,000	1,600,000	(400,000)
1,000,000	4,000,000	2,400,000	1,600,000	1,600,000	None
1,250,000	5,000,000	3,000,000	2,000,000	1,600,000	400,000

A break-even chart can be constructed in even greater detail by breaking down fixed and variable costs into subclassifications. Variable expenses, for example, may be classified as direct materials, direct labor, variable factory overhead, and variable marketing and administrative expenses. Fixed expenses may be divided in a similar manner, showing fixed factory overhead and fixed marketing and administrative expenses separately. Even the profit wedge might be subdivided to indicate application of the profit to income tax, interest and dividend payments, and retained earnings. Such a chart is illustrated on page 644.

Break-Even Analysis for Decision Making

The accounting data involved, the assumptions made, the manner in which the information is obtained, and the way the data are expressed are limitations that must be considered in connection with the results of break-even analysis. The break-even chart is fundamentally a static analysis. In most cases, changes can only be shown by drawing a new chart or a series of charts. The notion of relevant range as stated in the flexible budget discussion (page 438) is applicable. That is, the amount of fixed and variable costs, as well as the slope of the sales line, is meaningful only in a defined range of activity and must be redefined for activity outside the relevant range. Furthermore,

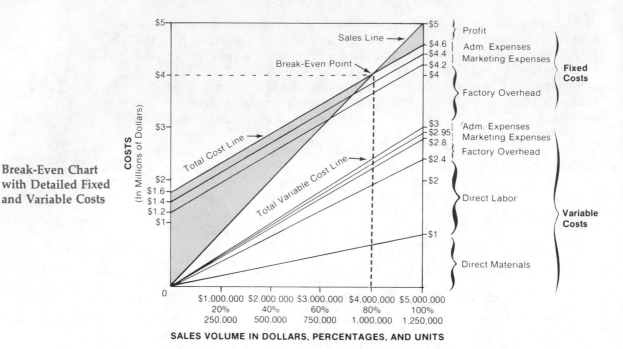

Break-Even Chart with Detailed Fixed and Variable Costs

linear cost and sales behavior is assumed and has general acceptance within the relevant range of activity.[2]

Despite its limitations, break-even analysis offers wide application for testing proposed actions, for considering alternatives, or for other decision-making purposes. For example, the technique permits determination of the effect on profit of a shift in fixed and/or variable expenses when old machinery is replaced by new equipment. Firms with multiple plants, products, and sales territories may prepare charts which show the effects of the shift in sales quantities, sales prices, and sales efforts. With such information, management is able to direct the firm's operations into the most profitable channels. For a company with numerous divisions, the analysis is particularly valuable in determining the influence on profits of an increase in divisional fixed cost. If, for example, a company's overall contribution margin ratio is 25 percent, a division manager must realize that for every $1 of proposed increase in fixed cost, sales revenue must increase by no less than $4 if the existing profit position is to be maintained ($1 ÷ 25% = $4).

The break-even analysis formula is also useful in projecting sales necessary to realize a projected profit or to minimize a calculated loss. To illustrate, the sales figure necessary to realize a profit objective of $400,000 for Webb Company is:

$$\frac{\text{Fixed cost} + \text{Profit objective}}{\text{Contribution margin ratio (C/M)}} = \frac{\$1,600,000 + \$400,000}{.40} = \$5,000,000$$

---

[2]Calculus can be employed in dealing with curvilinear functions. See Travis P. Goggans, "Break-Even Analysis with Curvilinear Functions," *The Accounting Review*, Vol. XL, No. 4, pp. 867–871.

If management wants to determine the sales level when an operating loss of $200,000 is predicted, then:

$$\frac{\text{Fixed cost} - \text{Estimated loss}}{\text{Contribution margin ratio (C/M)}} = \frac{\$1,600,000 - \$200,000}{.40} = \$3,500,000$$

These projections can also be read from the break-even charts on pages 641 and 642.

In using break-even analysis, management should understand that:

1. A change in per unit variable cost changes the contribution margin ratio and the break-even point.
2. A change in sales price changes the contribution margin ratio and the break-even point.
3. A change in fixed cost changes the break-even point but not the contribution margin figure.
4. A combined change in fixed and variable costs in the same direction causes an extremely sharp change in the break-even point.

Effect of Changes in Fixed Cost. If Webb Company management were able to reduce fixed expense to $1,450,000, the break-even point would be $3,625,000 ($1,450,000 ÷ .40). If sales remained at the $5,000,000 figure, the profit would increase from $400,000 to $550,000, and the break-even point would be 72.5 percent of sales instead of 80 percent. The change in the break-even point resulting from a reduction in fixed cost is shown by the broken lines in the following chart:

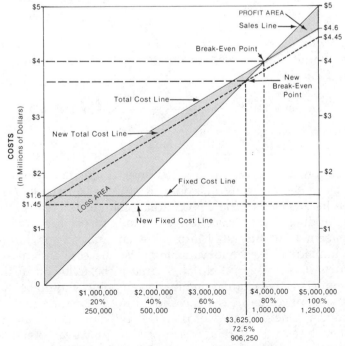

Break-Even Chart with a Reduction in Fixed Cost

SALES VOLUME IN DOLLARS, PERCENTAGES, AND UNITS

The effects of changes in the per unit variable cost or in the unit sales price could also be charted. Thus, a dynamic dimension could be added to the analysis.

Effect of Changes in Sales Mix. When a shift in product sales mix occurs, a change in profit can also be expected, unless the same contribution margin ratio is realized on all products. To illustrate, assume that the sales of a high-margin item are reduced for a company that has the following budget:

Sales		$1,500,000
Variable cost	$900,000	
Fixed cost	400,000	1,300,000
Profit		$ 200,000

The break-even sales would be computed as follows:

$$\text{Break-even sales} = \frac{\$400,000}{1 - \dfrac{\$\ 900,000}{\$1,500,000}} = \frac{\$400,000}{1 - .60} = \$1,000,000$$

At the end of the fiscal period (assuming no change occurred in the total fixed cost or in the per unit sales price or variable cost of individual products), the company's income statement shows:

Sales		$1,420,000
Variable cost	$908,800	
Fixed cost	400,000	1,308,800
Profit		$ 111,200

The break-even sales is now $1,111,111, indicating that the decrease in sales of the high-margin item caused an unfavorable increase of $111,111 in the break-even point:

$$\text{Break-even sales} = \frac{\$400,000}{1 - \dfrac{\$\ 908,800}{\$1,420,000}} = \frac{\$400,000}{1 - .64} = \$1,111,111$$

This situation can happen in any business. It illustrates the necessity of taking various sales mixes into account in any break-even analysis. It also stresses the inadequacy of the conventional composite break-even chart in which one product or a consistent average mix of products is considered. When management is interested in break-even analyses for different products, with individual fixed and variable costs, the conventional composite break-even chart is not very helpful. A rule to be followed in the case of multiple products is that changes in break-even points should be the result of changes in sales prices and costs and should not be distorted by an internal mix of products. One way to overcome this difficulty is to have individual break-even analyses and charts for each product; however, if arbitrarily allocated joint costs are included, the results are of limited value.

The Unit Profit Graph. A break-even chart is generally prepared on the basis of total revenue and expense. These dollar sales and expense figures can be translated into a profit-per-unit graph in order to show more vividly the influence of fixed cost on the product unit cost. Assume, for example, the following: normal capacity, 100 percent; total sales, $50,000 (500 units @ $100); variable cost, $30,000; fixed cost, $15,000; profit, $5,000. The break-even point is $37,500 ($15,000 ÷ .40) or 75 percent of normal capacity ($37,500 ÷ $50,000). The variable cost is $60 per unit, and the fixed cost is $30 per unit if 500 units are made and sold. As volume decreases, the fixed cost per unit increases. This relationship is illustrated in the following graph:

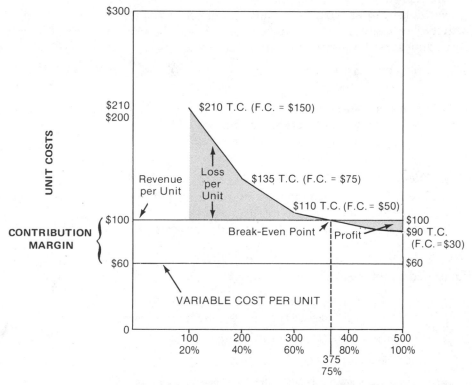

Unit Profit Graph
Showing the
Influence of Fixed
and Variable Costs
on Unit Cost

UNITS OF PRODUCT AND PERCENTAGE OF NORMAL CAPACITY

The effect of varying volume on the fixed cost per unit can also be expressed as follows:

	\multicolumn{6}{c}{Units}					
	100	*200*	*300*	*375*	*400*	*500*
Variable unit cost..........................	$ 60	$ 60	$ 60	$ 60	$ 60.00	$ 60
Fixed unit cost	150	75	50	40	37.50	30
Total unit cost..........................	$ 210	$ 135	$ 110	$ 100	$ 97.50	$ 90
Unit sales price..........................	100	100	100	100	100.00	100
Profit (loss) per unit.....................	$(110)	$ (35)	$ (10)	Break even	$ 2.50	$ 10

The analysis illustrated in the unit profit graph and in the tabular presentation, together with a break-even analysis, are important tools in determining which unit cost(s) should be used in setting sales prices. A break-even chart will help in understanding the effect on total profits when sales prices and fixed and variable costs are related to sales volume.

Unit Cost Formulas. The unit profit graph and the tabular presentation show a total unit cost that varies from a high of $210 per unit to a low of $90 per unit. To obtain a true comparison, unit costs must be computed at all levels of activity. When unit costs of various products are compared, the analyst must observe the production rates of each product, each of which may be at a different level.

Formulas can aid in determining the effect of changing costs or level of activity. For example, the following formula can be used to determine unit costs under conditions of fluctuating activity levels:

$$\text{Unit cost} = \frac{a + bx}{cx}$$

Where: a = fixed cost

b = variable cost at normal capacity

c = units of production at normal capacity

x = level of activity, expressed as a percentage of normal capacity

Using figures from the example introduced on page 647, the total cost of $45,000 ($15,000 + $30,000) divided by total units (500) gives a unit cost of $90 at the 100 percent level of activity.

To illustrate the utility of the formula, assume that the fixed expense increases to $17,000 and that the variable expense decreases to $27,000 at the 100-percent level of activity. Using these facts, the new break-even point is computed as follows:

New profit = (sx − bx) − a, where a, b, and x are as previously defined and s = total sales at normal capacity

New profit = ($50,000x − $27,000x) − $17,000

New profit = $23,000x − $17,000

Let new profit equal 0 (the break-even point) and solve for x:

0 = $23,000x − $17,000

$$x = \frac{\$17,000}{\$23,000}$$

x = .739 × 100, or 74% capacity (approximate)

(or)

Fixed cost = $17,000

Variable cost = $27,000, or $54 per unit, or 54% of sales

$$\frac{\$17,000}{1 - .54} = \frac{\$17,000}{.46} = \$37,000, \text{ or 74\% capacity, or 370 units}$$

The unit cost at the new break-even point can then be computed as follows:

$$\text{Unit cost} = \frac{a + bx}{cx}$$

$$= \frac{\$17,000 + \$27,000(.74)}{500(.74)}$$

$$= \frac{\$17,000 + \$19,980}{370}$$

$$= \$100 \text{ (approximate)}$$

Assuming the same changes in the fixed and variable expenses, the unit cost at 90 percent of capacity would be determined as follows:

$$\text{Unit cost} = \frac{\$17,000 + \$27,000(.90)}{500(.90)}$$

$$= \frac{\$17,000 + \$24,300}{450}$$

$$= \$92 \text{ (approximate)}$$

The above equations permit the development of unit costs, using data included in the budget. They further permit quick and easy computations in connection with problems raised by changing conditions. Budget data expressed in equation form permit quicker analysis of the effects of a variety of changes on unit costs.

Margin of Safety.   Information developed from a break-even analysis offers additional useful control data such as the *margin of safety,* which indicates how much sales may decrease from a selected sales figure before the company will break even, i.e., before the company will begin to suffer a loss. From the Webb Company data on page 639, where sales are $5,000,000, the margin of safety is $1,000,000 ($5,000,000 − $4,000,000). The margin of safety expressed as a percentage of sales is called the *margin of safety ratio (M/S)* and is computed as follows:

$$\text{Margin of safety ratio (M/S)} = \frac{\text{Selected sales figure} - \text{Break-even sales}}{\text{Selected sales figure}}$$

$$= \frac{\$5,000,000 - \$4,000,000}{\$5,000,000}$$

$$= 20\%$$

The margin of safety is directly related to profit. Using the same data from page 639, with a contribution margin ratio of 40 percent and a margin of safety ratio of 20 percent, then:

$$\text{Profit percentage} = \text{Contribution margin ratio} \times \text{Margin of safety ratio}$$

$$P = C/M \times M/S$$

$$P = 40\% \times 20\%$$

$$P = 8\%$$

This computation indicates that of the margin of safety dollars, i.e., the sales above the break-even point, the contribution margin ratio portion is available for profit. Thus, 8 percent (40 percent of 20 percent) is the percentage of the total selected sales figure that is profit.

Proof: Profit = Margin of safety dollars × Contribution margin ratio

P = $1,000,000 × 40%

P = $400,000

and

Profit = Selected sales figure × Margin of safety ratio

P = $5,000,000 × 8%

P = $400,000

If the contribution margin ratio and the profit percentage are known, the margin of safety ratio is:

$$M/S = \frac{P}{C/M} = \frac{8\%}{40\%} = 20\%$$

Uses of Break-Even Analysis Summarized

There are many specific uses of break-even analysis which management can make. Among these, some of the more significant ones are summarized as follows:

1. Aiding budgetary control. Helps indicate what changes, if any, are needed to bring expenses into line with revenue.
2. Improving and balancing sales. Acts as a warning signal to alert management to potential trouble in the sales program. If sales relative to costs are not as high as they should be, this fact will show up. Then it may be time to reevaluate (a) sales techniques, (b) training of sales staff, and (c) lines carried in relation to customers.
3. Analyzing volume change impact. Provides answers to specific questions such as the following: (a) How much of the present sales volume can the company lose before profit disappears? (b) How much will profit increase with an increase in volume?
4. Analyzing sales price and cost change impact. Indicates the probable effects on profit of sales price changes in combination with other changes. For example: (a) What changes may be expected in profit with changes in price, assuming all other factors remain constant? (b) If prices are reduced, what is the most practical combination of volume and cost changes to expect and what is the net effect of the combination of changes on profit? (c) Similarly, if prices are increased, what combination of changes and what effect on profit may reasonably be expected?

5. Negotiating wages. Assists management by: (a) quickly reflecting the probable influence on profit of proposed wage changes (assuming no change in employee efficiency) and (b) providing aid in determining possible economies and efficiencies that might protect the profit position of the company.
6. Analyzing product mix. Enables critical examination of the product mix. Break-even analysis for each product line is a valuable aid in determining which products should be pushed and which should possibly be eliminated.
7. Assessing further capitalization and expansion decisions. Provides a means of appraising in advance proposed capital expenditures which may change the cost structure of the business.
8. Analyzing margin of safety. Serves as a reminder of the margin of safety and of how changes may affect it.

Applying Cost-Volume-Profit Analysis

A cost-volume-profit analysis is generally prepared from annual budget figures, but figures from monthly statements can also be used. Furthermore, the analysis can be applied to a specific product class, to distribution outlets, to methods of sale, and for profit determination. The following illustration shows an analysis based on data from two representative months:

	Sales	Total Cost	Profit
June........................	$50,000	$40,000	$10,000
May	40,000	36,000	4,000
Difference..................	$10,000	$ 4,000	$ 6,000

An increase in sales of $10,000 resulted in an increase in costs of $4,000 and an increase in profit of $6,000. This indicates that each dollar increase in sales covered its variable cost of $.40 and contributed $.60 to profit or fixed expense and profit.

The variable cost factor is found by subtracting the C/M ratio from 100 percent. Since $6,000 ÷ $10,000 = 60 percent (the C/M ratio), the variable cost ratio is 40 percent (100 percent − 60 percent) or, more directly, $4,000 ÷ $10,000 = 40 percent. Knowing the variable cost ratio, the fixed cost in the total cost for June may be determined as follows:

Total cost	$40,000
Variable cost ($50,000 × .40)	20,000
Fixed cost..	$20,000

For May, the fixed cost is also $20,000, computed as follows: $36,000 − $16,000 ($40,000 sales × .40) = $20,000. This fact is in accordance with the generally accepted validity of the linear relationship of the cost-output figures.

The correctness of this assumption can be tested by assuming the following data for October:

Sales	$60,000
Total cost	45,000
Profit	$15,000

Previously, the variable cost ratio was 40 percent, and the fixed cost was $20,000. However, a check shows:

Total actual cost		$45,000
Expected: Variable cost ($60,000 × .40)	$24,000	
Fixed cost	20,000	44,000
Difference		$ 1,000

This difference should be investigated. Fixed and variable costs must be checked to discover any shift of these elements. However, the cause may be a shift of the product mix or numerous other factors.

The C/M ratio permits a profit computation without the necessity of detailed calculations of variable costs. The formula is:

$$\text{Profit} = (\text{Sales} \times \text{C/M}) - \text{Fixed cost}$$

Again using the figures from Webb Company's income statement on page 639, the profit could be computed as follows:

$$P = (S \times C/M) - FC$$

$$P = (\$5,000,000 \times .40) - \$1,600,000$$

$$P = \$2,000,000 - \$1,600,000$$

$$P = \$400,000$$

The same formula permits the computation of additional figures. If, for example, a company has a fixed cost of $90,000 with sales at $300,000 and a profit of $60,000, the C/M ratio is:

$$P = (S \times C/M) - FC$$

$$\$60,000 = (\$300,000 \times C/M) - \$90,000$$

$$\$60,000 + \$90,000 = \$300,000 \times C/M$$

$$\frac{\$150,000}{\$300,000} = C/M$$

$$50\% = C/M$$

If the same company with a C/M ratio of 50 percent suffers a $30,000 loss, the volume of sales is:

$$P = (S \times C/M) - FC$$

$$-\$30,000 = (S \times .50) - \$90,000$$

$$-\$30,000 + \$90,000 = S \times .50$$

$$\frac{\$60,000}{.50} = S$$

$$\$120,000 = S$$

The answer can be verified as follows:

Sales..		$ 120,000
Variable cost (50% of sales).............................	$60,000	
Fixed cost..	90,000	150,000
Loss..		$ (30,000)

While such quick computations are indeed possible and undoubtedly help-ful in many circumstances, the fact still remains that the reasonably accurate separation of expenses into their fixed and variable elements must precede any subsequent use of such figures, if the figures are to be meaningful.

Price Decreases and Volume Increases

In an analysis of the effect of a sales price decrease on volume, it is often argued that the price decrease will in most instances be offset by an increase in volume, and, therefore, profit will not be reduced and might even be increased. Such an argument seems quite plausible at first. Many companies, however, have found that price reduction does not necessarily lead to the desired increase in volume. If the increase in volume does occur, it is often not large enough to overcome the effect of the price reduction on total profit.

This problem of a possible price reduction being offset by a volume in-crease was studied by the U. S. Steel Corporation. The purpose of the study was to ascertain the increase in volume that would have to take place to offset various decreases in steel prices by the company's subsidiaries, taking into consideration the effect of increased volume on cost, and to estimate the financial gain or loss which would result from price reductions. The study concluded that, because of the low elasticity of demand for steel, the increase in volume resulting from a reduction in price would be less than the increase needed to offset the adverse effects of the lower price on profit. While off-setting volume increases may be more favorable in other types of businesses and industries, they are, in general, hardly enough to overcome reduced prices. In most cases, a price reduction must be accompanied not only by increased volume but also by a reduction in the cost of the product.

The Profit-Volume Analysis Graph

Break-even analysis and cost-volume-profit analysis also employ the *profit-volume (P/V) analysis graph,* which relates profit to volume. Using the figures from the income statement on page 639, a P/V analysis graph is illustrated as follows:

Profit-Volume Analysis Graph

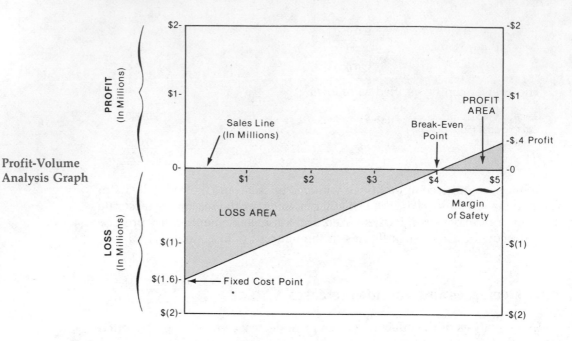

The P/V analysis graph is constructed as follows:

1. The graph is divided into two parts by the sales line.
2. The total fixed cost is marked off below the sales line on the left-hand vertical line. The computed profit or loss figure is located by moving horizontally to the point representing assumed sales dollars, then moving vertically to the point representing the computed profit or loss.
3. Fixed cost and profit points are joined by a diagonal line which crosses the sales line at the break-even point.

When management is considering various courses of action, a tabular report can present the possible results. For example, the effect of possible sales price increases and decreases for a product are shown in the following report:

	Decrease		Normal Volume	Increase	
	20%	10%		10%	20%
Units	200,000	200,000	200,000	200,000	200,000
Sales	$320,000	$360,000	$400,000	$440,000	$480,000
Variable cost	200,000	200,000	200,000	200,000	200,000
Contribution margin	$120,000	$160,000	$200,000	$240,000	$280,000
Fixed cost	160,000	160,000	160,000	160,000	160,000
Profit	—	0	$ 40,000	$ 80,000	$120,000
Loss	$ 40,000	0	—	—	—
Profit per unit	—	—	$.20	$.40	$.60
Loss per unit	$.20	—	—	—	—
% change in profit	−200%	−100%	—	+100%	+200%
Return on investment of $200,000	− 20%	0%	20%	40%	60%
Break-even point	$426,667	$360,000	$320,000	$293,333	$274,286

In this illustration, a 10 percent drop in price reduces the profit to the break-even point, and a 20 percent drop in price causes a $40,000 loss. However, the 10 percent and 20 percent price increases cause profit to increase $40,000 and $80,000, respectively. These effects are indicated more effectively, however, in a P/V analysis graph, as follows:

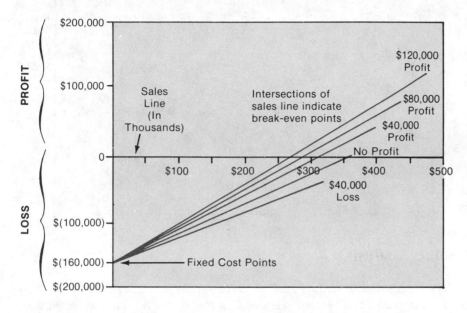

P/V Analysis Graph Illustrating the Effect of Possible Sales Price Changes on Profit

As another example of the use of a P/V analysis graph, assume that a company's management has the following plans regarding sales, costs, volume, and profit:

Plan 1		Plan 2	
Decrease in price..............	10%	Increase in price..............	10%
Increase in volume.............	12%	Decrease in volume............	12%
Variable cost increase..........	4%	Variable cost decrease.........	4%
Fixed cost increase	5%	Fixed cost decrease	5%

The effect of these plans is summarized as follows:

	Plan 1	Normal Volume	Plan 2
Units...	224,000	200,000	176,000
Sales...	$403,200	$400,000	$387,200
Variable cost.....................................	232,960	200,000	168,960
Contribution margin...............................	$170,240	$200,000	$218,240
Fixed cost.......................................	168,000	160,000	152,000
Profit...	$ 2,240	$ 40,000	$ 66,240
Profit per unit	$.01	$.20	$.3763
% change in profit	−94.4%	....	+65.6%
Return on investment of $200,000....................	1.12%	20%	33.1%
Break-even point	$397,895	$320,000	$269,677

The following graph, based on the summary data, is a composite, highly informative P/V analysis graph:

P/V Analysis Graph Illustrating the Effect of All Profit-Volume Factors

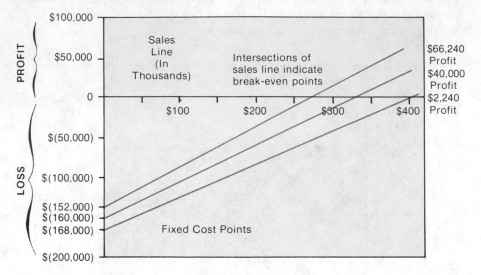

Product Analysis

The discussion so far has dealt with cost-volume-profit relationships based on total cost and total sales revenue. It is much more desirable, however, to investigate these relationships for individual products. A breakdown of costs and sales by products might appear impractical, especially when hundreds of small items are manufactured. In such instances, it is advisable to reduce the large number of products to several major lines. To determine a better product cost for purposes of planning and control, many firms have departmentalized their sprawling factory output. With such departmentalization, the contribution that each product or product group makes to the total contribution margin can be gauged more satisfactorily.

Variable costs used in previous illustrations are a composite of the variable costs of the several manufacturing cost centers, the marketing departments, and administrative divisions. However, it is possible to determine the variable cost of each product line because:

1. Direct materials and direct labor costs can be based on standard costs.
2. Variable factory overhead can be based on normal production hours, labor cost, or machine hours established for the cost centers of the plant. The flexible budget for each cost center serves as an excellent basis for the determination of product factory overhead.
3. Variable marketing and administrative expenses can be charged directly to products or allocated on the basis of the sales value of each product or gross profit return or other bases discussed in Chapter 21. Of course, allocations of either nonmanufacturing or manufacturing costs are arbitrary, a limitation that should not be overlooked.

Once the sales value and the variable cost of each product have been determined, it will be apparent that each product has a different contribution margin and a C/M ratio. To illustrate cost-volume-profit analysis by products, the figures of the Normal Volume column of the summary on page 655 are divided between four products, resulting in the following data:

Product	Sales Value of Production	Variable Cost	% of Variable Cost to Sales	Contribution Margin	C/M Ratio
A	$120,000	$100,000	83%	$ 20,000	17%
B	140,000	60,000	43	80,000	57
C	90,000	30,000	33	60,000	67
D	50,000	10,000	20	40,000	80
Total	$400,000	$200,000	50	$200,000	50
			Less fixed cost...	160,000	
			Profit...........	$ 40,000	

$$\text{Break-even point} = \frac{\$160,000}{.50} = \$320,000$$

The contribution margin and C/M ratio are shown for each product and in total. The C/M ratio varies from 17 percent for Product A to 80 percent for Product D. If the present sales mix can be altered or if sales can be expanded, products with higher C/M ratios afford greater relative contributions to profit per dollar of sales. But the product's C/M ratio, sales dollars, and contribution margin must be related to facility utilization. The product offering the higher C/M ratio is desirable only if the resulting contribution margin (C/M ratio × sales dollars) is greater than could be achieved by some alternative use of the same limited facilities. If unused or idle facilities are available, perhaps both alternatives can be pursued profitably.

The following P/V analysis graph indicates the profit path for each product, A, B, C, and D:

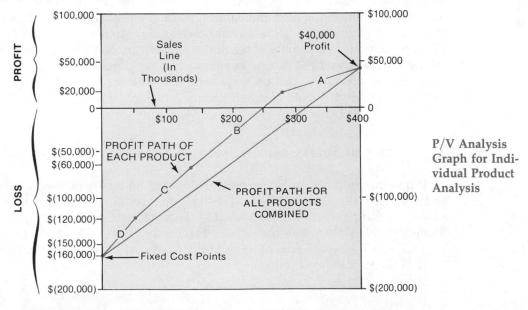

P/V Analysis Graph for Individual Product Analysis

This P/V analysis graph is constructed as follows:

1. The horizontal line 00 represents sales and is marked off from zero to $400,000.
2. The profit path for all products combined is then drawn, starting at the $(160,000) fixed cost point in the loss area and ending at the $40,000 profit point in the profit area. The break-even point is at the point of crossover from the loss to the profit area.
3. The profit path of each product is plotted next. It starts with the product with the highest C/M ratio, Product D. The line begins at the total fixed cost point and is drawn to the $(120,000) point in the loss area directly below the $50,000 sales volume point. The plotting indicates that $40,000 of the $160,000 fixed cost has been recovered.
4. The profit path of Product C starts at the point where D's path ended. The line for Product C ends opposite the loss figure of $(60,000) and below the sales volume figure of $140,000. The $(60,000) figure shows that $60,000 additional fixed cost was recovered. The $140,000 point on the sales line is the accumulated sales total of Products D and C ($50,000 + $90,000).
5. The profit path for Product B begins at the end of C's path and leads across the sales line into the profit area to the $20,000 profit point immediately above the sales volume figure of $280,000.
6. Product A with the lowest C/M ratio is charted last. It adds $20,000 to the profit, and its path ends at the $40,000 profit figure.

The plotting of the profit path of each product provides management with an interesting pictorial report—the steeper the slope, the higher the C/M ratio. If any product did not have a contribution margin, its path or slope would be downward. Also, the dollar amount of each product's contribution margin can be read from the graph by measuring the vertical distance from one plotted point to the next. Similar graphs can be prepared for the analysis of sales by territories, salespersons, and classes of customers. It is then possible to portray the profitability of territories, the effectiveness of salespersons' selling activities, and the type of customers whose purchases mean greatest profit to the company. In this way, sales effort is measured by marginal contributions toward fixed cost and profit—and not by sales volume.

The Fallacy of Total Cost Analysis

When the profitability of a product is determined by distributing all fixed and variable costs to all products, it is likely that certain products will show a loss, depending on the methods used to allocate fixed cost. For example, the following illustration uses the figures for Products A, B, C, and D, from page 657, and shows the distribution of the fixed cost to each product on the basis of the variable cost ratios:

FIXED COST DISTRIBUTION TO EACH PRODUCT
BASED ON VARIABLE COST RATIOS

Product	Sales Value of Production	Total Cost*	Profit	Percentage of Profit to Sales
A	$120,000	$180,000	−$60,000	−50%
B	140,000	108,000	32,000	22.8
C	90,000	54,000	36,000	40
D	50,000	18,000	32,000	64
Total	$400,000	$360,000	$40,000	10

*Computation of total cost:

Product	Variable Cost	Variable Cost Ratio		Fixed Cost		Fixed Cost Distribution	Total Cost
A	$100,000	$\dfrac{\$100,000}{\$200,000}$	×	$160,000	=	$80,000	$180,000
B	60,000	$\dfrac{60,000}{200,000}$	×	160,000	=	48,000	108,000
C	30,000	$\dfrac{30,000}{200,000}$	×	160,000	=	24,000	54,000
D	10,000	$\dfrac{10,000}{200,000}$	×	160,000	=	8,000	18,000
Total	$200,000						

The analysis indicates that Product A is a loss item. Because it also contributes a lower contribution margin and C/M ratio than the other products, management might want to discontinue it. Product A, however, actually contributes $20,000 to the company's total profit picture.

Most methods used to distribute fixed costs to products confuse cost-volume-profit relations, for they do not recognize the change in costs and profits produced by a change in volume or product mix. This confusion is eliminated by following the contribution margin principle, which sets apart not only the fixed costs that must be allocated, but also those that are directly assignable to a specific product. Attention is then directed to the margin between sales and variable cost, rather than sales and total cost. Products make a favorable contribution as long as the sales revenue exceeds the related variable cost.

An alternative product should replace the existing one only if idle capacity is not available and only if the alternative product will yield a larger total dollar contribution toward recovering the fixed cost and profit for an equal amount of capacity constraint (e.g., machine hours). Since some fixed costs can be changed in the short run, the analysis must consider any change in fixed cost associated with dropping a product or moving from an existing product to an alternative product. It is assumed, of course, that the added product can be marketed without disturbing the market for other products of the company.

In the case of joint products, the variable as well as the fixed joint costs are best viewed in their relationship to the contribution made by the group of joint products rather than on the basis of an arbitrary allocation to each product (pages 131–132).

DISCUSSION QUESTIONS

1. Define break-even point.

2. (a) Why must the conventional income statement be restated for computation of the break-even point? (b) What type of statement is constructed?

3. What is the contribution margin?

4. State the formulas commonly used to determine the break-even point (a) in dollars and (b) in units.

5. Identify the numbered components of the following break-even chart:

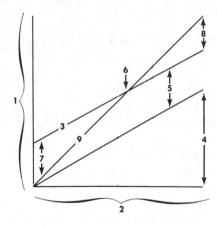

6. Discuss the significance of the concept of the relevant range to break-even analysis.

7. The break-even chart is an excellent planning device. Discuss.

8. Discuss weaknesses inherent in the preparation and uses of break-even analysis.

9. How does the break-even point move when changes occur in (a) variable expense? (b) fixed expense?

10. The break-even chart and the unit profit graph intend to show the same information but seem to differ. How?

11. What is the margin of safety?

12. What is meant by the term "cost-volume-profit relationship?" Why is this relationship important in business management?

13. A price reduction is always accompanied by a proportionate volume increase. Discuss.

14. Why is a cost-volume-profit analysis by products valuable to management?

15. Describe how the contribution of each product to the recovery of fixed expense and to the total profit of a company can be presented in graphic form.

EXERCISES

1. *Break-even analysis. Oliver Company plans to market a new product. Based on its market studies, Oliver estimates that it can sell 5,500 units during the first year. The sales price will be $2 per unit. Variable cost is estimated to be 40% of the sales price. Fixed cost is estimated to be $6,000..*

Required: *Compute the break-even point in dollars and in units.*

2. *Break-even analysis. The 19-- sales of Mercury-Minneapolis Company were $7,640,000. Fixed expense was $2,451,000 and variable expense totaled $4,736,800.*

Required: *Compute (1) the contribution margin, (2) the contribution margin ratio, and (3) the break-even point in dollars.*

3. *Break-even analysis.* The normal capacity of Holmer Company is 18,000 units and the per unit sales price is $2.50. Relevant costs are:

	Variable (Per Unit)	Fixed
Materials	$.70	
Labor	.60	
Factory overhead..............	.175	$2,000
Marketing and administrative....	.20	2,290

Required: *Compute (1) the break-even sales in dollars, (2) the break-even sales in units, and (3) the sales dollars required to produce a profit of $8,250.*

4. *Break-even analysis.* A unit sells for $6.80, variable manufacturing expense is $4.80 per unit, variable marketing expense is 10% of sales, and fixed expense is $28,020.

$144,359

Required: *Compute the break-even point in dollars.*

5. *Unit cost formula.* At 100% capacity, volume is 350 units, variable expense is $742, and fixed expense is $1,008.

Required: *What is the unit cost at 90% capacity?*

6. *Break-even analysis and profit formula.* A month's operations of Wuerflein Company show fixed expense of $9,300, an M/S ratio of 25%, and a C/M ratio of 62%.

Required: *Compute (1) break-even sales, (2) actual sales, and (3) profit for the month.*

7. *Break-even analysis and profit formula.* Operations of Gilley Company for the year disclosed an M/S ratio of 20% and a C/M ratio of 60%. Fixed cost amounted to $30,000.

Required: *Compute (1) break-even sales, (2) the amount of profit, and (3) the contribution margin.*

8. *Cost-volume-profit analysis.* Ship Company is planning to produce and sell 100,000 units of Alt at $4 a unit and 200,000 units of Tude at $3 a unit. Variable costs are 70% of sales for Alt and 80% of sales for Tude.

Required: *If total planned operating profit is $160,000, what must the total fixed cost be?*
(AICPA adapted)

9. *Break-even analysis.* Reggin Specialty Products Company manufactures a product which sells for $5. At present the company produces and sells 50,000 units per year. Unit variable manufacturing and marketing expenses are $2.50 and $.50, respectively. Fixed expenses are $70,000 for factory overhead and $30,000 for marketing and administration.

The sales manager has proposed that the price be increased to $6. To maintain the present sales volume, advertising must be increased. The company's profit objective is 10% of sales.

Required:
   (1) Compute the additional expenditure the company can afford for advertising.
   .(2) Compute the new break-even point in units and dollars, using the $6 sales price and the additional advertising expenditure from requirement (1).   (CGAA adapted)

10. *Break-even analysis.* The income statement for one of Lawrence Company's products shows:

Sales (100 units at $100 a unit)	$10,000
Cost of goods sold:	
Direct labor $1,500	
Direct materials used................................ 1,400	
Variable factory overhead........................... 1,000	
Fixed factory overhead............................. 500	
Total cost of goods sold	4,400
Gross profit	$ 5,600
Marketing expenses:	
Variable .... $ 600	
Fixed... 1,000	
Administrative expenses:	
Variable 500	
Fixed... 1,000	
Total marketing and administrative expenses..........	3,100
Operating income.....................................	$ 2,500

Required: *Compute (1) the break-even point in units, (2) the operating income if sales increase by 25%, and (3) the break-even point in dollars if fixed factory overhead increases by $1,700.* *(AICPA adapted)*

11. *Break-even and patient mix analysis for a hospital.* Donnelly Memorial Hospital records provide the following patient mix data for the year:

Method of Payment	Patient Mix	Average Daily Reimbursement Rate	Average Daily Variable Cost
Self-pay	20%	$120	$40
Private insurance...............	25	120	40
Medicare	30	110	40
Medicaid......................	25	100	40

The annual fixed cost is $1,000,000.

Required:
  (1) Compute the composite break-even point in dollars and inpatient days. (Compute the contribution margin ratio to the nearest percent.)
  (2) Compute the composite break-even point in dollars and inpatient days if the patient mix were 50% self-pay and 50% private insurance patients.

12. *Price decreases and volume increases — elasticity of demand.* Basso Company forecasts next year's sales of Product X to be 50,000 units at a sales price of $10. Management is considering a price reduction to $9 with the expectation that sales and profit will increase. However, the elasticity of demand is questionable, ranging from an estimated low elasticity of only 2,000 additional units sold to a high elasticity of an increase of 30,000 units.

    The variable unit manufacturing cost is estimated to be $5 and the variable non-manufacturing cost is estimated to be 10% of sales revenue. At the high elasticity sales level, annual programmed fixed costs are expected to increase $5,000 and $1,000 for manufacturing and nonmanufacturing costs, respectively.

Required: *Compute the change in the contribution to other fixed cost and to income before income tax if the sales price is reduced and the sales volume increases (a) 2,000 units; (b) 30,000 units.*

PROBLEMS

23-1. Break-even analysis. Bryan Candy Company is a wholesale distributor of candy, serving grocery, convenience, and drug stores in a large metropolitan area. Small but steady growth in sales has been achieved by the company over the past few years, while candy prices have been increasing. The company is formulating its plans for the coming fiscal year. The following data are used to project the current year's aftertax net income of $110,400:

Average sales price per box	$ 4.00
Average variable costs per box:	
Cost of candy..............................	$ 2.00
Marketing..................................	.40
Total	$ 2.40
Annual fixed costs:	
Marketing..................................	$160,000
Administrative.............................	280,000
Total	$440,000

Expected annual sales volume (390,000 boxes), $1,560,000.
Income tax rate, 40%.

Manufacturers of candy have announced that they will increase prices of their products an average of 15% in the coming year due to increases in materials and labor costs. Bryan Candy Company expects that all other costs will remain at the same rates or levels as the current year.

Required:
(1) Compute the break-even point in boxes of candy for the current year.
(2) Compute the sales price per box the company must charge to cover the 15% increase in the cost of candy and still maintain the current contribution margin ratio.
(3) Compute the volume of sales in dollars the company must achieve in the coming year to maintain the same aftertax net income as projected for the current year if the sales price of candy remains at $4 per box and the cost of candy increases 15%.

(CMA adapted)

23-2. Break-even analysis. Maxwell Company manufactures and sells a single product, for which price and cost data are as follows:

Sales price per unit..	$ 25.00
Variable costs per unit:	
Raw materials...	$ 11.00
Direct labor..	5.00
Factory overhead......................................	2.50
Marketing and administrative	1.30
Total variable cost per unit	$ 19.80
Annual fixed costs:	
Factory overhead......................................	$192,000
Marketing and administrative	276,000
	$468,000
Income tax rate	40%

Required:
(1) Compute the break-even point in units.

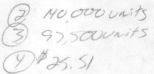

(2) Determine the units to sell in order to earn $156,000 after income tax.
(3) Compute the break-even point in units if direct labor cost increases 8%.
(4) If Maxwell's direct labor cost does increase 8%, determine the per unit sales price to maintain the same contribution margin ratio.   (CMA adapted)

23-3. Break-even analysis; impact of new order. In 19A, Kah-Nee-Ta Company produced and sold 100,000 units of its product at a price of $2.75. The company can increase capacity to produce 125,000 units by increasing fixed cost $5,000 per year. The company receives an order for 15,000 unbranded units to be sold at $2.45 each. With the added volume plus other economies, the plant manager estimates that materials, labor, and variable factory overhead each can be reduced $.02 per unit for all the output. Nonmanufacturing expenses will be unaffected by the added 15,000-unit order. The president of the company wishes to see a projected gross profit statement for next year, assuming that the new order is accepted on January 2, 19B, that there are no other changes in sales volume, and that the economies can be effected.

Data for 19A are as follows:

Sales		$275,000
Cost of goods sold:		
Materials	$80,000	
Labor	62,000	
Variable factory overhead	45,000	
Fixed factory overhead	25,600	
Cost of goods sold		212,600
Gross profit		$ 62,400

Required:
(1) Compute the break-even sales, contribution margin, and C/M ratio, based on 19A data and disregarding nonmanufacturing costs.
(2) Prepare a projected 19B statement of gross profit.
(3) Compute the break-even sales, contribution margin, and C/M ratio, based on projected 19B data and disregarding nonmanufacturing costs. Round the C/M ratio to four decimal places.

23-4. Break-even and cost-volume-profit analysis. Theta Company has analyzed the costs of producing and selling 5,000 units of its sole product to be as follows:

Direct materials	$60,000
Direct labor	40,000
Variable factory overhead	20,000
Fixed factory overhead	30,000
Variable marketing and administrative expenses	10,000
Fixed marketing and administrative expenses	15,000

Required:
(1) Compute the number of units to break even at a per unit sales price of $38.50.
(2) Determine the number of units that must be sold to produce an $18,000 profit, at a $40 per unit sales price.
(3) Determine the price Theta must charge at a 5,000-unit sales level, in order to produce a profit equal to 20% of sales.   (CGAA adapted)

23-5. Cost behavior, break-even, and cost-volume-profit analysis. Fenton Office Equipment Company collected the following data for the second quarter of the year:

	Sales	Cost
April...........................	$70,000	$56,000
May.............................	77,000	59,990
June	85,000	64,550

Required: Compute the following amounts:
(1) The fixed cost and the variable cost per sales dollar.
(2) The contribution margin ratio.
(3) The break-even point.
(4) July profit if sales are $79,000.
(5) August sales if the month's loss is $1,050.

23-6. Break-even and cost-volume-profit analysis. Nisei Electronics produces and markets tape recorders and electronic calculators. Its 19A income statement follows:

Nisei Electronics
Income Statement
For Year Ended December 31, 19A

	Tape Recorders		Electronic Calculators		Total
	Total (000s Omitted)	Per Unit	Total (000s Omitted)	Per Unit	Total (000s Omitted)
Sales......................	$1,050	$15.00	$3,150	$22.50	$4,200.0
Production costs:					
Materials	$ 280	$ 4.00	$ 630	$ 4.50	$ 910.0
Direct labor.....................	140	2.00	420	3.00	560.0
Variable factory overhead	140	2.00	280	2.00	420.0
Fixed factory overhead.............	70	1.00	210	1.50	280.0
Total production cost	$ 630	$ 9.00	$1,540	$11.00	$2,170.0
Gross profit.......................	$ 420	$ 6.00	$1,610	$11.50	$2,030.0
Fixed marketing and administrative expenses					1,040.0
Income before income tax					$ 990.0
Income tax (55%)..					544.5
Net income...					$ 445.5

The tape recorder business has been fairly stable in recent years, and the company has no plans to change the tape recorder price. However, because of increasing competition and market saturation, management has decided to reduce its calculator price to $20, effective January 1, 19B, and to spend an additional $57,000 in 19B for advertising. As a result, Nisei estimates that 80% of its 19B revenue will be from electronic calculator sales. The sales units mix for tape recorders and calculators was 1:2 in 19A and is expected to be 1:3 in 19B at all volume levels. For 19B, materials costs are expected to drop 10% and 20% for the tape recorders and calculators, respectively; however, all direct labor costs are to increase 10%.

Required:
(1) Compute the number of tape recorders and electronic calculators to break even, using 19A data.
(2) Determine the sales dollars required to earn an aftertax profit of 9% on sales, using 19B estimates.
(3) Compute the number of tape recorders and electronic calculators to break even, using 19B estimates.

(CMA adapted)

23-7. Break-even and cost-volume-profit analysis; direct costing. The following data relate to a year's budgeted activity for Martin Corporation, which manufactures one product:

Beginning inventory.	30,000 units
Production.	120,000
Available for sale.	150,000 units
Sales.	110,000
Ending inventory.	40,000 units
Sales price.	$5.00 per unit
Variable manufacturing cost.	1.00
Variable marketing cost.	2.00
Fixed manufacturing cost (based on 100,000 units).	.25
Fixed marketing cost (based on 100,000 units).	.65

A special order is received for 10,000 units, in addition to budgeted sales, to be used in an unrelated market. The total fixed cost remains unchanged within the relevant range of 45,000 units to total capacity of 135,000 units.

Required: Compute the following:
(1) Projected annual break-even sales in units.
(2) Projected operating income for the year from budgeted sales (a) under direct costing; (b) under absorption costing, charging all variances to Cost of Goods Sold.
(3) Price per unit to be charged on the special order, given the original data, so that the operating income will increase by $5,000.
(4) Number of units to be sold to generate a profit equal to 10% of the contribution margin, assuming that the sales price increases by 20%; the variable manufacturing cost increases by 10%; the variable marketing cost remains the same; and the total fixed cost increases to $104,400.   (AICPA adapted)

23-8. Cost-volume-profit analysis. Three companies are each producing and selling annually 10,000 units of a similar product at a unit sales price of $10. The companies have fixed and variable costs as follows:

Company	Fixed Cost	Variable Cost per Unit
.A	$20,000	$6
B	40,000	4
C	60,000	2

Each company contemplates a price cut, from $10 to $8, in the expectation that sales will increase from 10,000 to 15,000 units per year.

Required:
(1) Compute the contribution margin and operating income for each company at the present level of activity.
(2) Compute the contribution margin and operating income for each company at the contemplated price and sales level.
(3) Explain the differences in the answers computed in (1) and (2).
                              (Based on an article in *The Accounting Review*)

23-9. Price decreases and volume increases. Regents Recording Company records and sells phonograph records to outlets across the nation. Competition has increased significantly in recent years, and Regents feels that a price reduction would boost sales volume and operating income.

The following data have been estimated for 19A:

Sales (937,500 units @ $5)	$4,687,500
Variable cost	2,250,000
Fixed cost	2,000,000

Management predicts that an 8% price cut would increase the estimated volume by 20% and that a 15% price cut would lead to a 40% volume increase. Total fixed cost and unit variable cost would not change if the volume increase does not exceed 50%.

Required: Calculate the expected operating income for 19A for each of the following situations: (1) no price cut, (2) an 8% price cut, and (3) a 15% price cut.

23-10. Analysis of price-volume relationships. The income statement for Roscoe Company for the past year is:

Sales (150,000 units @ $30)		$4,500,000
Cost of goods sold:		
Materials	$1,050,000	
Labor	1,500,000	
Variable factory overhead	450,000	
Fixed factory overhead	500,000	3,500,000
Gross profit		$1,000,000
Variable marketing expense	$ 135,000	
Fixed marketing expense	185,000	
Fixed administrative expense	180,000	500,000
Income before income tax		$ 500,000
Income tax		250,000
Net income		$ 250,000

Roscoe is preparing its budget for the coming year and has made the following predictions about cost increases: materials, 5%; labor, 8%; all other costs (including fixed), 6%.

Productive capacity is 200,000 units.

The president has been offered various proposals by the division managers, as follows:

(a) Maintain the present volume and sales price.
(b) Produce and sell at capacity and reduce the unit price to $28.
(c) Raise the unit price to $32, spend an extra $300,000 on advertising, and produce and sell 180,000 units.

Required: Recommend action, based on quantification of alternatives.

(CGAA adapted)

23-11. Price decreases and volume increases. The income statement of Hansen Company for the year ended December 31, 19A, is as follows:

Sales (9,600,000 units)		$160,000,000
Cost of goods sold:		
Direct materials	$38,400,000	
Direct labor	28,800,000	
Factory overhead	48,000,000	115,200,000
Gross profit		$ 44,800,000
Marketing and administrative expenses		28,800,000
Operating income		$ 16,000,000

Production capacity of the installed machinery is 12,000,000 units. Company management is conscious of the high degree of underutilized capacity. It is uncertain, however, whether or not the market will absorb more units of product than at present. The task of assessing product demand was assigned to a marketing research consulting firm. The study made by the consultants predicted the following price-volume relationships:

Sales Price per Unit	Quantity Demanded
$16.00	10,000,000
15.50	12,000,000
14.50	14,000,000
14.25	18,000,000

An analysis of factory overhead reveals that in 19A, fixed factory overhead was $28,800,000 and fixed marketing and administrative expenses were $19,200,000. If new machinery is to be installed for increasing the production capacity to 18,000,000 units, an additional capital expenditure of $100,000,000 is required, resulting in a fixed factory overhead increase of $10,000,000 per year.

Required: Determine the recommended level of activity.

23-12. Use of limiting constraint. Moorehead Manufacturing Company produces two products, for which the following per unit data have been tabulated:

	XV-7	BD-4
Sales price	$4.00	$3.00
Variable manufacturing cost	2.00	1.50
Fixed manufacturing cost	.75	.20
Variable marketing cost	1.00	1.00

Fixed manufacturing cost is applied at a rate of $1 per machine hour.

The sales manager has received a $160,000 increase in the budget allotment for advertising and wants to apply the money on the more profitable product. The products are not substitutes for one another.

Required:
(1) Calculate the minimum increase in sales units and dollars required to offset the advertising increase if the sales manager devotes the entire $160,000 to (a) XV-7, (b) BD-4.
(2) Moorehead has only 100,000 unused machine hours which can be made available to produce either XV-7 or BD-4, but not both. If all the unused machine hours are made available, compute the total estimated contribution margin increase for (a) XV-7, (b) BD-4.   (CMA adapted)

Chapter 24
Differential Cost Analysis

Rrcf

Many management decisions involve:

1. Accepting or refusing certain orders.
2. Reducing the price of a single, special order.
3. Making a price cut in a competitive market.
4. Evaluating make-or-buy alternatives.
5. Expanding, shutting down, or eliminating a facility.
6. Increasing, curtailing, or stopping production of certain products.
7. Determining whether to sell or process further.
8. Choosing among alternate routings in product manufacture.
9. Determining the maximum price that can be paid for raw materials.

Differential cost is the difference in the cost of alternative choices. Differential cost is often referred to as *marginal* or *incremental cost*. The term "marginal cost" is widely used by economists. Engineers generally speak of incremental cost as the added cost incurred when a project or an undertaking is extended beyond its originally intended goal.

Historical costs drawn from the accounting records generally do not give management the differential cost information needed to evaluate alternative courses of action. A flexible budget, however, with its revised current costs for each rise in the capacity level, can be useful in some differential cost analyses. The flexible budget shows the various expenses at different levels of production. It indicates that some expenses increase proportionately with an increase in capacity, while other expenses remain comparatively stationary through various levels of activity.

In the following flexible budget, the $5.40 average unit cost at 60 percent of normal capacity is computed by dividing the total cost at that capacity by the number of units produced ($324,250 ÷ 60,000 units). The total differential cost is determined by subtracting the total estimated cost for one level of activity from that of another level (e.g., $423,400 − $324,250 = $99,150, the differential cost between the 80-percent and 60-percent levels). The differential unit cost is computed by:

1. Subtracting one level of output from the next higher level (80,000 units output at 80 percent minus 60,000 units output at 60 percent = 20,000 units).
2. Dividing the differential cost total between these two levels by the added number of units ($99,150 ÷ 20,000 units = $4.96).

FLEXIBLE BUDGET FOR DIFFERENT RATES OF OUTPUT
(100,000 Units = 100% Normal Capacity)

Capacity	60%	80%	100%	120%
Variable costs				
Direct manufacturing costs:				
Direct materials	$102,000	$136,000	$170,000	$204,000
Direct labor	93,000	124,000	155,000	186,000
Total	$195,000	$260,000	$325,000	$390,000
Indirect manufacturing costs:				
Heat	$ 720	$ 960	$ 1,200	$ 1,440
Light and power	1,440	1,920	2,400	2,880
Repairs and maintenance	2,460	3,280	4,100	4,920
Supplies	1,260	1,680	2,100	2,520
Indirect labor	9,120	12,160	15,200	18,240
Total	$ 15,000	$ 20,000	$ 25,000	$ 30,000
Commercial expenses:				
Clerical help	$ 11,580	$ 15,440	$ 19,300	$ 23,160
Wages, general	6,960	9,280	11,600	13,920
Supplies	1,260	1,680	2,100	2,520
Total	$ 19,800	$ 26,400	$ 33,000	$ 39,600
Fixed costs (within ranges)				
Indirect manufacturing costs:				
Foremen	$ 15,250	$ 20,500	$ 20,500	$ 25,750
Superintendent	15,000	15,000	15,000	17,750
Setup crew	5,000	7,500	7,500	8,500
Depreciation and rent	8,000	9,400	9,400	9,400
Insurance	2,600	2,600	2,600	2,600
Total	$ 45,850	$ 55,000	$ 55,000	$ 64,000
Commercial expenses:				
Executives	$ 28,000	$ 35,000	$ 35,000	$ 40,000
Assistants	11,200	16,400	16,400	19,200
Property tax	3,400	3,400	3,400	3,400
Advertising	6,000	7,200	7,200	8,600
Total	$ 48,600	$ 62,000	$ 62,000	$ 71,200
Total cost	$324,250	$423,400	$500,000	$594,800
Units of output	60,000	80,000	100,000	120,000
Average unit cost	$5.40	$5.29	$5.00	$4.96
Differential cost total		$99,150	$76,600	$94,800
Differential cost per unit		$4.96	$3.83	$4.74

Differential Cost Studies

Differential cost studies deal with the determination of incremental revenue, costs, and margins with regard to alternative uses of fixed facilities or available capacity. In these studies, variable costs are significant, because they usually represent the differential cost. If, however, fixed costs must be increased through the addition of a new machine or rental of additional space, then these costs should be considered differential costs.

The term "fixed" is perhaps a misnomer. If a fixed cost is incurred when temporary additional business, for example, is accepted, it is certainly a variable expense. If it continues, however, it becomes a fixed cost due to its permanent nature. In the latter case, management must be cautioned against a quick decision in favor of additional business, because it might find itself with additional fixed costs and a capacity greater than needed.

Accepting Additional Orders

Differential cost is the cost that must be considered when a decision involves a change in output. The differential cost of added production is the difference between the cost of producing the present smaller output and that of the contemplated, larger output. If available capacity is not fully utilized, a differential cost analysis might indicate the possibility of selling additional output at a figure lower than the existing average unit cost. The new or additional business can be accepted as long as the variable cost is recovered, since any contribution to the recovery of fixed cost and profit is desirable.

To illustrate, assume that a plant has a maximum capacity of 100,000 units, but normal capacity production is set at 80,000 units, or 80 percent of maximum capacity. At this level, the predetermined overhead rate is computed so that fixed expenses are fully absorbed when operating at the 80,000-unit level. If fewer units are produced, unabsorbed fixed overhead results. If more units are produced, fixed overhead is overabsorbed. If this company makes only one unit, its cost would be:

Variable cost	$	5 per unit
Total fixed cost..............		100,000 for this unit
Total......................		$100,005

At normal capacity, the fixed cost per unit is reduced to $1.25 ($100,000 ÷ 80,000 units), and the total cost per unit is:

Variable cost	$5.00
Share of fixed cost	1.25
Total.....................	$6.25

If additional capacity can be utilized to produce an additional 1,000 units, the unit cost of these units—the differential cost—would be only the $5 variable cost, unless the units required additional fixed expense outlays. An income statement comparing present operating results with the total results after additional units are produced and sold might appear as follows:

	Present Business	With Additional Business
Sales	$720,000	$729,000
Variable cost	400,000	405,000
Contribution margin	$320,000	$324,000
Fixed cost	100,000	100,000
Profit[1]	$220,000	$224,000

The additional business requires variable cost only, since the capacity cost (i.e., the fixed cost) indicates that adequate unused capacity is available to handle the additional business. If the 1,000 units are sold at any price above the $5 variable cost, the sale will yield a positive contribution margin.

The illustration above can also be presented in the following manner to highlight the differential revenue of $9,000 and cost of $5,000:

	Present Business	Additional Business	Total
Sales	$720,000	$9,000	$729,000
Variable cost	400,000	5,000	405,000
Contribution margin	$320,000	$4,000	$324,000
Fixed cost	100,000	—0—	100,000
Profit	$220,000	$4,000	$224,000

Reducing the Price of a Special Order

The differential cost aids management in deciding at what price the firm can afford to sell additional goods. To illustrate, assume that a company manufactures 450,000 units, using 90 percent of its normal capacity. The fixed factory overhead is $335,000, which is $.67 ($335,000 ÷ 500,000 units) for each unit manufactured when operations are at 100 percent of normal capacity. The variable factory overhead rate is $.50 per unit. The direct materials cost is $1.80, and the direct labor cost is $1.40 per unit. Each unit sells for $5. Marketing as well as general and administrative expenses are omitted to simplify the illustration. On the basis of these data, the accountant would prepare the following statement:

Sales (450,000 units @ $5)		$2,250,000
Cost of goods sold:		
Direct materials (450,000 units @ $1.80)	$810,000	
Direct labor (450,000 units @ $1.40)	630,000	
Variable factory overhead (450,000 units @ $.50)	225,000	
Fixed factory overhead (450,000 units @ $.67)	301,500	1,966,500
Income from operations		$ 283,500
Unabsorbed fixed factory overhead [(500,000 units— 450,000 units) @ $.67]		33,500
Income from operations (adjusted)		$ 250,000

---

[1]The term "profit" in this discussion denotes operating income before income tax.

The sales department reports that a customer has offered to pay $4.25 per unit for an additional 100,000 units. To make the additional units, an annual rental cost of $10,000 for new equipment would be incurred. The accountant computes the gain or loss on this order as follows:

Sales (100,000 units @ $4.25).......................		$425,000
Cost of goods sold:		
Direct materials (100,000 units @ $1.80).............	$180,000	
Direct labor (100,000 units @ $1.40)	140,000	
Variable factory overhead (100,000 units @ $.50)......	50,000	
Fixed factory overhead (100,000 units @ $.67)	67,000	437,000
Loss on this order...................................		$ 12,000

The accountant's computation would cause management to reject the offer. In this computation, all cost elements use the existing unit costs, and fixed overhead is allocated on the basis of the established rate ($.67 per unit). A second look, however, reveals the following effect of the new order on total factory overhead:

Fixed factory overhead (at present)		$335,000
Fixed factory overhead (because of additional business)..		10,000
Total fixed factory overhead		$345,000
Fixed factory overhead charged into production:		
For 450,000 units (old business)....................	$301,500	
For 100,000 units (additional business)	67,000	368,500
Overabsorbed fixed factory overhead..................		$ 23,500

Instead of underabsorbed fixed factory overhead of $33,500, the additional business would result in overabsorbed factory overhead of $23,500 or a net composite gain of $57,000 ($67,000 − $10,000) in absorbed factory overhead. This $57,000 minus the computed $12,000 loss on the order results in a gain of $45,000, as shown in the following statement, which includes only the differential costs and revenue:

Sales (100,000 units @ $4.25).......................		$425,000
Cost of goods sold:		
Direct materials (100,000 units @ $1.80).............	$180,000	
Direct labor (100,000 units @ $1.40)	140,000	
Variable factory overhead (100,000 units @ $.50)......	50,000	
Additional fixed cost to produce this order............	10,000	380,000
Gain on this order...................................		$ 45,000

The unit cost of the additional units can be computed as follows:

$$\frac{\text{Cost of goods sold}}{\text{Additional units}} = \frac{\$380,000}{100,000} = \$3.80 \text{ per additional unit}$$

Whenever a differential cost analysis leads management to accept an additional order at or above the differential cost, it is assumed that the order is not going to disturb the market of the other products being offered. The additional business may involve a product presently marketed by the firm, or a product that can be manufactured with existing facilities and personnel. If these products are placed in a competitive market, they might have to be marketed at established prices. Otherwise, competitors might retaliate by cutting prices to an unprofitable and therefore undesirable level, considering all relevant cost and market factors. The firm must also be careful not to violate the Robinson-Patman Act and other governmental pricing restrictions.

Make-Or-Buy Decisions

Another phase of alternative actions is the problem of whether to make or buy component parts or a finished product. The importance of the make-or-buy decision is evidenced by the fact that almost all manufacturing firms at some time during the course of their operations will have to make such a decision. The choice of whether to manufacture an item internally or purchase it on the outside can be applied to a wide variety of decisions that are often major determinants of profitability and that can be significant to the company's financial health.

The objective of a make-or-buy decision should be to best utilize the firm's productive and financial resources. The problem often arises in connection with the possible use of idle equipment, idle space, and even idle labor. In such situations, a manager is inclined to consider making certain units instead of buying them in order to utilize existing facilities and to maintain work-force stability. Commitments of new resources may also be involved.

Despite its importance, studies indicate that surprisingly few firms give adequate objective study to their make-or-buy problems.[2] Not only is this type of decision important to the firm, but it is also complicated by a host of factors, both financial (quantitative) and nonfinancial (qualitative) that must be considered. Faced with a make-or-buy decision, the manager should:

1. Consider the quantity, quality, and dependability of supply of the items as well as the technical know-how required, weighing such requirements for both the short-run and long-run period.
2. Compare the cost of making the items with the cost of buying them.
3. Compare the making of the items with possibly more profitable alternative uses that could be made of the firm's own facilities if the items are purchased.
4. Consider differences in the required capital investment and the timing of cash flows (Chapter 26).
5. Adopt a course of action related to the firm's overall policies. Customers' and suppliers' reactions often play a part in these decisions. Retaliation or ill will could result. Whether it is profitable to make or buy depends upon the circumstances surrounding the individual situation.

---

[2]Anthony J. Gambino, *The Make-or-Buy Decision* (New York: National Association of Accountants and Hamilton, Ontario: The Society of Management Accountants of Canada, 1980), pp. 9–10.

The accountant should present a statement that compares the company's cost of making the items with the vendor's price. The statement should present the differential costs of the item as well as a share of existing fixed expenses and a profit figure that places the total cost on a comparable basis. The budget should also be restated to indicate the effect on total costs and total profit when existing fixed costs are allocated to the additional items.

A cost study with only the differential costs and with no allocation of existing fixed overhead or of profit indicates possible cost savings in the short run. In practice, such studies seem to favor the making of the items in the majority of cases. However, if management were asked to sell the items at the differential price, it might be unwilling to do so, since, in the long run, the full cost must be covered and a reasonable profit achieved. Furthermore, if there is only a slight advantage in favor of making, the item will likely be purchased because more reliance will be put on a known cost to buy rather than an estimated cost to make.[3]

A study by the National Association of Accountants makes the following observations about cost considerations:

> To evaluate the alternatives properly, costs to make vs. costs to buy must be based on the same underlying assumptions. Thus, costs for each of the alternatives must be based on the identical product specifications, quantities, and quality standards.
>
> Determination of the "cost to buy" cannot be limited to existing costs shown on supplier invoices. The competitive nature of supplier pricing requires that current optimum third-party prices based upon identical specifications and quantities be used for evaluation of this alternative. There are many examples of lower prices being obtained from suppliers for larger quantities, standardization of specifications, etc., as well as from the use of competitive bids and/or the threat of self-manufacture. All direct and indirect costs of functions and facilities which are properly allocable to the "buy" alternative, under the "full cost" concept, must be considered. Cost to buy must also include the "full cost" to bring the product to the same condition and location as if self-manufactured—including freight, handling, purchasing, incoming inspection, inventory carrying costs, etc.
>
> Determination of the "cost to make" cannot be limited to those identified as manufacturing costs or used in the valuation of inventories. All direct and indirect costs of functions and facilities which are properly allocable to self-manufacture under the "full cost" concept must be considered.
>
> It is concluded that in the case of short-run decisions, differential costs become more significant. However, . . . it is recommended that the long-term and full-cost consideration also be developed. The short-term judgments can then be properly evaluated against the alternative choices which will be required at a later date.
>
> The long-term nature of most make-or-buy decisions requires that cost determinations not only consider present costs but also projections of future costs resulting from inflationary factors, technological changes, productivity, mechanization, etc. More specifically, the projection of the future cost to make and the cost to buy must give full consideration to what the costs "should be" under obtainable conditions and reflect all possible improvements—not just what may be achieved under existing operating conditions.[4]

---

[3]*Ibid.*, p. 21.

[4]*NAA Statement, No. 5,* "Criteria for Make-or-Buy Decisions" (New York: National Association of Accountants, June 21, 1973), pp. 5–8.

Decisions to Shut Down Facilities

Differential cost analysis is also used when a business is confronted with the possibility of a shutdown of both manufacturing and marketing facilities. In the short run, a firm seems to be better off operating than not operating, as long as the products or services sold recover the variable cost and make a contribution toward the recovery of the fixed cost. A shutdown of facilities does not eliminate all costs. Depreciation, interest, property tax, and insurance continue during complete inactivity.

If operations are continued, certain expenses connected with the shutting down of the facilities would be saved. Furthermore, costs that would have to be incurred when a closed facility is reopened can be saved. Management might also consider the investment in the training of the active employees, which would be lost in the event of a shutdown. Morale of other employees, as well as community goodwill, may be adversely affected, and the recruiting and training of new workers would add to present costs. The loss of established markets is also a factor, since reentering a market requires a reeducation of the consumers of the company's products.

To orient management regarding the possible steps to be taken, the accountant might again resort to the flexible budget to determine the effects of continuing operations as long as differential costs or any amount above them can be secured. This does not mean, however, that the volume set in the budget should be considered final. In view of probable prices, the most advantageous operating level can be determined only by considering several different volume levels.

Decisions to Discontinue Products[5]

While an entire facility may not be closed or eliminated, management may decide to discontinue certain individual products because they are producing no profit or an inadequate profit. Decisions to discontinue products require careful analysis of relevant differential cost and revenue data through a structured and continuous product evaluation program. Several benefits can accrue from an effectively administered evaluation program that has as its objective the timely identification of products that should be eliminated or that can be made more profitable through appropriate corrective action. These benefits include:

1. Expanded sales.
2. Increased profits.
3. Reduced inventory levels.
4. Executive time freed for more profitable activities.
5. Important and scarce resources, such as facilities, materials, and labor, made available for more promising projects.

---

[5]This discussion is adapted from Stanley H. Kratchman, Richard T. Hise, and Thomas A. Ulrich, "Management's Decision To Discontinue a Product," *The Journal of Accountancy,* Vol. 139, No. 6, pp. 50–54.

6. Greater management concern with why products get into difficulty or fail, thus enabling the institution of policies that will reduce the rate of product failure.

Care must be taken not only to consider the profitability of the product being analyzed but also to evaluate the extent to which sales of other products will be adversely affected when one product is removed. If the sales decrease of related products is severe enough, it might be desirable to retain the product being scrutinized.

Management needs data that will permit development of warning signals for products that may be in trouble. Such warning signals include:

1. Declining sales volume.
2. Product sales volume decreasing as a percentage of the firm's total sales.
3. Decreasing market share.
4. Malfunctioning of the product or introduction of a superior competitive product.
5. Past sales volume not up to projected amounts.
6. Expected future sales and market potential not favorable.
7. Return on investment below a minimum acceptable level.
8. Variable cost which approaches or exceeds revenue.
9. Various costs as a percentage of sales consistently increasing.
10. Increasingly greater percentage of executive time required.
11. Price which must be constantly lowered to maintain sales.
12. Promotional budgets which must be consistently increased to maintain sales.

Studies have shown that firms often do a poor job of identifying products that are in difficulty and should be eliminated. Probably the major deficiency is the lack of timely, relevant data. To determine what data are required for a successful product monitoring program and its effective implementation and operation, management must draw on the accountant's experience and expertise.

The conditions that bring about the need to evaluate products or facilities may be permanent or even long-term in nature. If profitable alternative asset usage is not foreseen, asset divestment may be needed.

Additional Applications of Differential Cost Analysis

The oil refining industry is characterized by processes that require management to choose between alternatives at various points during the processes. The basic function of oil refining is the separation, extraction, and chemical conversion of the crude oil's component elements, employing skillful utilization of heat, pressure, and catalytic principles. The basic petroleum products are obtained through a physical change caused by the application of heat through a wide temperature range. Within a temperature differential of 300°

(275°F to 575°F), the different liquid products, called fractions, ends, or cuts, pass off as vapors and are then condensed back into liquids. The initial application of heat drives off the lightest fractions — the naphthas and gasoline; the successively heavier fractions, such as kerosene and fuel oil, follow as the temperature rises. This process of vaporizing the crude oil and condensing the gaseous vapors to obtain the various cuts is commonly referred to as primary distillation.

Certain cuts (such as straight-run gasoline) are marketable with but little treating. Other products may undergo further processing in order to make them more salable. Thus, heavier fractions, such as kerosene and fuel oil, may be subjected to cracking, which will cause them to yield more valuable products such as gasoline. Cracking is a process during which, by the use of high temperatures and pressures and perhaps in the presence of a catalyst, a heavy fraction is subjected to destructive distillation and converted to a lighter hydrocarbon possessing different chemical characteristics, one of which is a lower boiling point. The heaviest of the fractions resulting from primary distillation is known as residuum or heavy bottoms. This residuum, after further processing, treating, and blending, forms lubricating oils and ancillary wax or asphalt products.

The management of a refinery must decide what to do with each distillate or fraction and at what stage of refining each should be sold; whether additional fractions should be bought from other refineries and what price should be paid for the additional units; or whether the company should enlarge the plant in order to handle a greater volume. They must also determine what alternate courses should be taken in order to break into the most profitable market at the moment.

The accountant can help management through the preparation of flexible budgets for the secondary operating departments in which further processing might take place. These departmental flexible budgets are called *cost analysis budgets*. They differ from the flexible budget used for control purposes in several respects: (1) all expenses are included in the analysis budget; (2) budgeted expenses of service departments are allocated to operating departments at corresponding capacity levels; and (3) their aim is to discover the departmental differential costs.

The amounts stated for each class of expense at each production level are computed on separate work sheets, in which various individual expenses are separated into their fixed and variable elements. This separation is necessary to arrive at the estimated expenses for each level of production.

Analysis budgets for various activities for the following departments, which represent secondary processing or finishing operations, are prepared:

Treating	Solvent Extraction
Filters and Burners	Wax Specialties
Cracking	Canning
Solvent Dewaxing	Barrel House

The analysis budget for cracking fuel oil in the Cracking Department is as follows:

ANALYSIS BUDGET

Department: Cracking

Period Budgeted: _____ to _____

Supervisor: _____

Normal Capacity (100%) 100,000 gallons through-put of fuel oil

Department and/or Expense Account	Shut-Down	60%	80%	100%	120%
Direct expenses	$6,000	$14,000	$16,000	$17,000	$23,000
Allocated expenses (fixed and variable) .	1,000	2,000	3,000	4,000	6,000
Total cost...........................	$7,000	$16,000	$19,000	$21,000	$29,000
Through-put:					
Totai gallons		60,000	80,000	100,000	120,000
Differential gallons.................		60,000	20,000	20,000	20,000
Differential cost......................		$9,000	$3,000	$2,000	$8,000
Unit differential cost..................		$ .150	$ .150	$ .100	$.4000
Unit average cost....................		$ .267	$ .238	$ .210	$.2417

Cracking analysis budget:
  Present operations, 80% of normal capacity
  Differential cost (80% to 100%) = $.10 per input gallon
Cracking yields: 75% gasoline; 15% residual fuel oil; 10% loss

In the following pages, differential cost analysis is applied to the alternatives which confront the management of an oil refinery. The hypothetical cases, which illustrate the methods that may be employed in solving such problems, can be generalized for other industry settings.[6]

Sell or Process Further. A refiner has on hand 20,000 gallons of fuel oil and must decide whether to sell it as fuel oil or crack it into gasoline and residual fuel oil. The following current prices per gallon are available:

Fuel oil.......... $1.40
Gasoline 1.68

The refiner can then prepare the following differential income computation, utilizing the Cracking Department analysis budget:

Potential revenue — products from cracking:
  Gasoline (15,000 gallons @ $1.68) $25,200
  Fuel oil (3,000 gallons @ $1.40)......................... 4,200
                                                           $29,400
    Less differential cost (20,000 gallons @ $.10) 2,000 $27,400
  Net potential revenue — fuel oil (20,000 gallons @ $1.40) 28,000
  Loss from cracking of fuel oil .... $ 600*

*Not an accounting loss per se, but a loss of profit that would result from an improper choice
  of alternatives.

Thus, judging from a quantitative standpoint, it would be more profitable to sell the 20,000 gallons of fuel oil as such rather than to process them further.

---

[6]Adapted from a study prepared by John L. Fox, later published in *NA(C)A Bulletin*, Vol. XXXI, No. 4, pp. 403–413, under the title, "Cost Analysis Budget to Evaluate Operating Alternatives for Oil Refiners."

Choice of Alternate Routings. A refiner is trying to decide whether to treat and sell the kerosene fraction or to crack it for its gasoline content. The current decision involves 10,000 gallons of raw kerosene. Pertinent available information follows (from an analysis budget for cracking kerosene):

Current prices per gallon:
Kerosene	$1.20
Gasoline	1.68
Fuel oil	1.40

Cracking yields:
Gasoline	85%
Residual fuel oil	5
Loss	10

Differential costs associated with potential gallons through-put of kerosene:
Cracking	$.12 per gallon
Treating	.08

Using the above amounts, the refiner can prepare the following analysis:

Net potential revenue—products from cracking:		
Gasoline (8,500 gallons @ $1.68)	$14,280	
Fuel oil (500 gallons @ $1.40)	700	
	$14,980	
Less differential cost (10,000 gallons @ $.12)	1,200	$13,780
Net potential revenue—kerosene:		
Total revenue (10,000 gallons @ $1.20)	$12,000	
Less differential cost (10,000 gallons @ $.08)	800	11,200
Gain from cracking rather than treating		$ 2,580

In this situation, the more profitable alternative is to crack the kerosene fraction.

Price To Pay for an Intermediate Stock. A refiner has been offered 10,000 gallons of cylinder stock. The usual bargaining process will determine the final price. The refiner is interested in knowing how high a price it can pay and still make a profit. The stock purchased would be processed into conventional bright stock and sold at that stage, since the blending unit for making finished motor oils is currently working at full capacity. Available information is as follows:

Cylinder stock is of such a quality and type that it will probably yield:
  90% bright stock
   5% petrolatum
   5% loss
Current prices: bright stock, $1 per gallon; petrolatum—no market

Differential costs associated with processing 10,000 gallons of cylinder stock through several units (from analysis budgets) are:

Solvent dewaxing	$.06 per gallon
Solvent extracting	.06
Filtering	.03
Total	$.15 per gallon

Using this information, the refiner's position can be analyzed and a bargaining margin can be determined:

Revenue—bright stock (9,000 gallons @ $1)	$9,000
Differential cost (10,000 gallons @ $.15)	1,500
Margin	$7,500
Margin per gallon of cylinder stock	$ .75

The refiner is now ready to bargain for the purchase of the cylinder stock, knowing that a purchase price of $.75 a gallon represents a critical maximum point—to pay more would produce a loss, to pay less would result in a gain. Management can then decide how much profit is required to justify the purchase. Here the concept of *opportunity costs* (page 689) also enters into the final decision. If the available capacity could be more profitably used for another purpose, then perhaps the proposed purchase should not be consummated.

Proposed Construction of Additional Capacity. A refiner discovers that the market for finished neutrals is such that present capacity will not satisfy the demand. The refiner feels certain that an addition to the solvent dewaxing and solvent extracting units would prove profitable. The additional wax distillate stock required would be purchased on the open market at the current rate. However, before going ahead with the construction, the chief accountant is consulted and presents the following information:

Unit differential cost:
    Capacity from 100% (normal) to 120% (increase of 10,000 gallons through-put)
        Solvent Dewaxing Department—$.10 per gallon through-put
        Solvent Extracting Department—$.10 per gallon through-put
Assumed yield from wax distillate:
    90% Viscous neutral
    1.5% Paraffin (8 pounds per gallon)
    8.5% Loss
Current market prices:
    Viscous neutrals—$1.50 per gallon
    Paraffin—$.24 per pound
    Wax distillate stock—$1.20 per gallon*

*Not a published market price but the price management believes it will have to pay to acquire the stock.

Using this information, the following analysis is prepared:

Differential revenue:		
9,000 gallons viscous neutrals @ $1.50	$13,500	
1,200 pounds paraffin @ $.24	288	
	$13,788	
Less cost of wax distillate stock (10,000 gallons @ $1.20)	12,000	
Margin to apply against differential costs		$1,788
Differential costs:		
Solvent Dewaxing Department (10,000 gallons @ $.10)	$ 1,000	
Solvent Extracting Department (10,000 gallons @ $.10)	1,000	2,000
Potential loss from differential production		$ 212

The accountant's analysis indicates that the proposed increase in the productive capacity would not be justified under the stated conditions. Furthermore, even a potential profit should yield a satisfactory return on the additional capital investment.

Quantitative Techniques in Differential Cost Analysis

Differential cost studies must often determine the profitability of the short-run use of available capacity. To aid in these studies, management may use quantitative techniques such as linear programming and probability distributions.

Linear Programming

Differential analyses may become rather involved due to the multiple constraints on production and the number of products possible. The accountant could try numerous combinations to arrive at the incremental revenue and costs associated with each. However, linear programming allows the accountant to determine the optimum course of action when the resource allocation problem is complex and its solution is neither obvious nor feasible by trial and error, guess, or intuition. Chapter 25 is devoted entirely to these important mathematical procedures.

Probability Distributions

The decision-making process is typically based on a single set of assumptions under conditions of certainty, which, in fact, do not generally exist. The problem is usually handled with business judgment and a "feel" for risk and uncertainty tempering the quantitative analysis of relevant data. Much of the difficulty exists because few managers are willing to estimate a probability distribution. Instead, the manager estimates the future event as a single figure or "best guess." More attention is being given, however, to estimates of a range of possible events and the use of probability estimates to allow for risk and uncertainty in order to indicate the likelihood of the incurrence of these events and to calculate useful statistical data.

In some decision-making analyses, a wealth of reasonably reliable historical data permits the assignment of fairly objective probabilities. An example would be the rate of materials usage and the lead time for order filling in computing safety stock. In other cases, probability estimates may be much more subjective, resulting in a probability of occurrence for the most probable, pessimistic, and optimistic assumptions.

To illustrate the use of probability distribution data, assume that a company's contribution margin is $10 per unit sold. A study of a 40-month period indicates highly irregular sales and no specific sales trend. Assuming that past experience is a reasonable basis for future prediction, each possible total contribution margin (conditional value) at each sales level is multiplied by its respective probability in order to compute an expected contribution margin (expected value), as follows:

(1) Unit Sales per Month	(2) Number of Months	(3) Probability	(4) Contribution Margin per Unit	(5) Contribution Margin (Conditional Value) (1) × (4)	(6) Expected Contribution Margin (3) × (5)
4,000	8	8/40 = .20	$10	$40,000	$ 8,000
5,000	10	10/40 = .25	10	50,000	12,500
6,000	12	12/40 = .30	10	60,000	18,000
7,000	6	6/40 = .15	10	70,000	10,500
8,000	4	4/40 = .10	10	80,000	8,000
	40	1.00			$57,000

The expected contribution margin represents the average monthly contribution margin the company should expect, based on past experience. Management is also interested in the risk associated with the expected value. The degree of risk can be measured by computing the standard deviation of the expected value. The *standard deviation* provides a numerical measure of the scatter of the possible values around the average value. The larger the standard deviation, the greater the risk that the actual contribution margin will differ from the expected contribution margin. Computation of the standard deviation is illustrated as follows:

(1) Contribution Margin (Conditional Value)	(2) Difference from Expected Value ($57,000)	(3) (2) Squared	(4) Probability	(5) (3) × (4)
$40,000	$−17,000	$289,000,000	.20	$ 57,800,000
50,000	−7,000	49,000,000	.25	12,250,000
60,000	3,000	9,000,000	.30	2,700,000
70,000	13,000	169,000,000	.15	25,350,000
80,000	23,000	529,000,000	.10	52,900,000
				$151,000,000

Standard deviation = $\sqrt{\$151,000,000}$ = $12,288

If several expected values are involved, e.g., contribution margins for each of several products, their relative risks cannot be compared by simply looking at the standard deviation of each. This comparison problem can be resolved by computing the *coefficient of variation*, which relates the standard deviation for an estimate to the expected value of that estimate, thus allowing for differences in the relative size of expected values.

In the illustration, the coefficient of variation would be computed as follows:

$$\text{Coefficient of variation} = \frac{\text{Standard deviation}}{\text{Expected contribution margin (expected value)}} = \frac{\$12,288}{\$57,000} = .22$$

If another product is analyzed, resulting in an expected contribution margin of $100,000 and a standard deviation of $18,000, the relative risk is less, as indicated by the coefficient of variation of .18 ($18,000 ÷ $100,000), even though the standard deviation is greater.

In this illustration, the possible outcomes are relatively few and thus the probability distribution is discrete. When outcomes can take on any value within a certain range, however, a continuous probability distribution may be a better description of the nature of the problem. As a practical matter, the distribution of outcomes would be assumed to have some common (e.g., normal) shape, which would again permit calculation of the parameters of the distribution of the outcomes, such as the mean and standard deviation.

Use of Probabilities in Strategy Analysis. Probability distributions are especially helpful in selecting the best strategy under conditions of uncertainty. Where several courses of action are available, a payoff table can be constructed to aid in evaluating available alternatives.

For illustrative purposes, assume that the manager of a bakery must decide how many loaves of bread to bake each day. The normal sales price is $1 a loaf. However, the price of bread which is not sold on the day of delivery is reduced to $.30 a loaf. The variable cost of producing and distributing a loaf of bread is $.40. An additional cost of $.10 is incurred for each loaf which is sold at the reduced price. The unit contribution margin is computed as follows:

Regular sales price	$1.00	Reduced sales price.................		$.30
Less variable cost	.40	Less: Variable cost............	$.40	
Unit contribution margin at the		Additional distribution		
regular sales price.............	$ .60	cost.................	.10	.50
		Unit negative contribution margin		
		at reduced sales price		$.20

Over the past 360 days, the company has experienced the following random sales demand (i.e., there are no cycles or trends in sales demand):

Unit Sales per day	Number of Days	Probability
10,000	72	.20
11,000	108	.30
12,000	144	.40
13,000	36	.10
	360	1.00

Assuming that sales demand in the future is expected to be the same as in the past, a payoff table can be constructed. For each production level strategy, (1) the contribution margin (conditional value) for each unit sales possibility is computed and (2) the expected contribution margin (expected value) is determined, as follows:

Production Level Strategy (In Units)	Contribution Margins (Conditional Values) for Sales Unit Possibilities				Expected Contribution Margin (Expected Value) of Each Production Level Strategy
	10,000	11,000	12,000	13,000	
10,000	$6,000*	$6,000	$6,000	$6,000	$6,000
11,000	5,800**	6,600	6,600	6,600	6,440
12,000	5,600	6,400	7,200	7,200	6,640
13,000	5,400	6,200	7,000	7,800	6,520***

*10,000 units at the regular price × $.60 = $6,000
**(10,000 units at the regular price × $.60) − (1,000 units at the reduced price × $.20 negative contribution margin) = $5,800
***(.20 probability × $5,400) + (.30 probability × $6,200) + (.40 probability × $7,000) + (.10 probability × $7,800) = $6,520

In this situation, the best strategy in the long run would be to produce 12,000 loaves of bread each day, because such a strategy would result in the largest average expected profit.

As in the previous illustration, the standard deviation and the coefficient of variation can be computed for each strategy. For example, the computations for the production level strategy of producing 12,000 loaves of bread daily are:

(1) Contribution Margin (Conditional Value)	(2) Difference from Expected Value ($6,640)	(3) (2) Squared	(4) Probability	(5) (3) × (4)
$5,600	$−1,040	$1,081,600	.20	$216,320
6,400	−240	57,600	.30	17,280
7,200	560	313,600	.40	125,440
7,200	560	313,600	.10	31,360
				$390,400

Standard deviation = $\sqrt{\$390,400}$ = $625

Coefficient of variation = $\dfrac{\text{Standard deviation}}{\text{Expected contribution margin (expected value)}}$ = $\dfrac{\$625}{\$6,640}$ = .09

Value of Perfect Information. The opportunity may exist to improve the quality of information for use in selecting the best alternative. Such improvement will require the incurrence of a cost which should be weighed against its information value.

In the illustration on page 684, the value of perfect information is the difference between (1) the average contribution margin if the manager knew the sales volume of loaves of bread for each day in advance (and consequently produced exactly the amount demanded) and (2) the average expected contribution margin using the best strategy under uncertainty. This difference would be the maximum amount that management would be willing to pay to improve its information, perhaps through a market survey or some other source. The value of perfect information is determined as follows:

Unit Sales per Day	Contribution Margin per Unit	Contribution Margin (Conditional Value)	Probability	Expected Contribution Margin
10,000	$.60	$6,000	.20	$1,200
11,000	.60	6,600	.30	1,980
12,000	.60	7,200	.40	2,880
13,000	.60	7,800	.10	780
Expected contribution margin (expected value) with perfect information...				$6,840
Less the expected contribution margin using the best strategy under uncertainty (12,000 units produced per day)...............				6,640
Value of perfect information (on a per-day basis)				$ 200

Thus, management could afford to pay up to $200 per day for perfect information. While perfect information is generally not available, this analysis does serve as an upper limit reference point in considering information value.

Decision Trees. Alternatives and their expected results may be portrayed graphically with the decision tree. This kind of analysis is especially useful when sequential decisions are involved. The *decision tree* highlights decision points, alternatives, estimated results, related probabilities, and expected values. Normally, decision trees are restricted to relatively short-term situations involving one or two years. As more decision points and years are added, decision trees become complex. They can be applied to long-term decisions, but in such cases the time value of money should be included in the analysis.

As an example of the use of decision trees, Davis Recreation Enterprises is faced with the problem of deciding where to locate a ski resort. The search has been narrowed to two locations, either of which would be leased from the owner for one year, with a renewal option. One is within 50 kilometers (30 miles) of a large city. This accessibility makes the site attractive, but its location at an elevation 1 000 meters (3,000 feet) lower than the second site means that the annual snowfall will be less. The other location is 200 kilometers (125 miles) from the city, but the higher elevation will assure better skiing conditions and a longer season.

For each alternative, the conditional values and the expected value for the first year of operations are:

Skiing Weather Conditions	Contribution Margin (Conditional Value)	Probability	Expected Contribution Margin
Close site:			
Favorable	$1,200,000	.6	$720,000
Unfavorable	−200,000	.4	−80,000
			$640,000 expected value
Distant site:			
Favorable	$ 800,000	.6	$480,000
Unfavorable	150,000	.4	60,000
			$540,000 expected value

A one-year decision tree based on these data would appear as follows:

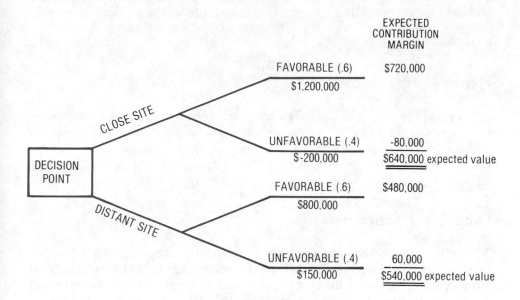

Based on the assumptions and estimates given in the illustration, the company should select the site close to the city, since its expected value is greater than that for the distant site ($640,000 compared to $540,000). However, the decision also will be affected by the decision maker's willingness to accept a negative contribution margin of $200,000 if conditions are unfavorable. The firm may not be in a financial condition that would permit accepting a negative result and, accordingly, may select the lower but safer return of the distant site.

More complex decision trees can be constructed to incorporate additional years and sequential decisions. All sequential decisions are affected by the initial decision. If decisions relating to the second year and beyond can be delayed until more knowledge is available, some of the uncertainty can be eliminated. For example, for the second year, an additional ski lift may be installed at either the close or the distant site, provided favorable skiing weather conditions occurred the first year. If the first year's weather conditions were unfavorable, then funds will be insufficient to permit installing the additional lift, regardless of which site was originally chosen. The decision tree could be extended for the second year with the consideration of (1) a sequential decision as to whether to install an additional lift, assuming favorable weather conditions occurred the first year and (2) continuation through the second year with the existing lift, assuming unfavorable first-year weather conditions.

Monte Carlo Simulation. *Monte Carlo simulation* is a procedure that utilizes statistical sampling techniques in order to obtain a probabilistic approximation of some mathematical or physical problem. The sampling may be drawn from historical data or from estimates. The method is computer oriented, because without the speed of the computer, most Monte Carlo simulation models become impractical.[7]

Other Cost Concepts

To enable management to have useful and meaningful cost data for analysis of costs and profits, several other concepts must be incorporated in the decision-making process. These include long-run implications, cost versus the value of information, opportunity costs, imputed costs, out-of-pocket costs, relevant and irrelevant costs, and sunk costs.

Long-Run Implications

In differential cost analysis, care must be taken to avoid action to maximize short-run profits if such action is likely to be detrimental to the overall company profit objective of long-run profit maximization. The possible conflict between long-run and short-run objectives has been described as follows:

> Because overall company profit objectives are usually long-run objectives, it seems advisable to consider long-run implications of decisions which are intended to maximize short-run profits. To illustrate, addition of a product for the purpose of utilizing capacity which is currently excess may preclude more profitable use of the same capacity at a later date. Likewise, at a time when capacity is temporarily inadequate to meet sales demand, actions to maximize short-run profits (e.g., raising prices, dropping low margin products or customers) may be inconsistent with long-run profit objectives.[8]

Cost vs. Value of Information

Not only which but how much information to collect and analyze must also be determined. Too much information is an inefficient use of resources; too little may increase the likelihood of a poor decision. As illustrated on page 686, the decision to obtain an additional amount of information, whether it is perfect or only a partial improvement, depends on whether the expected differential information value exceeds its differential cost. Of course, management may be forced to make a decision with less information than it would like, simply because there is insufficient time to acquire more information. In some cases, information may not be available even though cost and time constraints would permit its collection.

---

[7]For a comprehensive discussion of Monte Carlo simulation, see James E. Shamblin and G. T. Stevens, Jr., *Operations Research: A Fundamental Approach* (New York: McGraw-Hill Book Company, 1974), pp. 156–182.
[8]Walter B. McFarland, *Concepts for Management Accounting* (New York: National Association of Accountants, 1966), p. 55.

Opportunity Costs

Opportunity costs are the measurable value of an opportunity bypassed by rejecting an alternative use of resources. In the third application of the refinery illustration (page 680), a decision had to be made as to how much profit was required to justify the purchase of the cylinder stock. The concept of opportunity costs enters into the final decision. If the available capacity could be used more profitably for another purpose, then perhaps the intended purchase should not be made. The decision to employ or not to employ the available capacity in favor of one or the other alternative in the future suggests that opportunity costs are also a type of future costs.

Other examples may aid in a better understanding of this concept. The opportunity cost of using a machine to produce one product is the sacrifice of possible earnings from other products that might be produced using the machine. The opportunity costs of the time that owners put into their own businesses are the salaries they could earn elsewhere. Opportunity costs require the measurement of sacrifices associated with alternatives. If a decision requires no sacrifice, there is no opportunity cost.

Imputed Costs

Imputed costs are hypothetical costs representing the cost or value of a resource measured by its use value. Interest on invested capital, rental value of company-owned properties, and salaries of owner-operators of sole proprietorships or partnerships are types of imputed costs. Imputed costs do not involve actual cash outlay, they are not recorded in the books, and they are not considered in a company's regular cost and profit calculations. However, in making comparisons and in reaching a decision, the inclusion of imputed costs is relevant and important.

In contract costing, Cost Accounting Standards provide for inclusion of the imputed cost of capital committed to facilities. Contractors must use an interest rate prescribed by these standards, which indicate that this cost, even though imputed, is relevant for government contract costing. If the contract costs do not include a measure of the imputed cost of money, the result is that cost measurements have made no distinction between contracts with equal amounts of total incurred cost but with vast differences in amounts of facility investments. The imputed interest rate is intended to compensate for the risk-free cost of money and for the impact of inflation. Investment in working capital is excluded.[9] In 1980, the CAS concept of imputed interest was extended to provide for inclusion of the imputed cost of money in the cost of capital assets while being constructed, fabricated, or developed for the contractor's own use.[10]

---

[9]*Standards, Rules and Regulations, Part 414*, "Cost of Money as an Element of the Cost of Facilities Capital" (Washington, D. C.: Cost Accounting Standards Board, 1976).

[10]*Standards, Rules and Regulations, Part 417*, "Cost of Money as an Element of the Cost of Capital Assets Under Construction" (Washington, D.C.: Cost Accounting Standards Board, 1980).

Out-Of-Pocket Costs

The term *out-of-pocket costs,* as opposed to imputed costs, refers to costs which involve cash outlays, either immediately or at some future date. These costs are also often identified as variable or direct costs, because they are the costs relevant to any decision when the total product costs are not pertinent. This cost concept is significant in management's deciding whether a particular venture will at least return the cash expenditures caused by the contemplated business undertaking.

Relevant and Irrelevant Costs

The dictionary defines *relevant* as "bearing upon, or properly applying to, the case in hand; of a nature tending to prove or disprove the matters in issue; pertinent." The application of this definition to the purposes of cost accounting indicates that no single cost figure and concept fits all managerial demands, actions, and decisions. What is necessary is the selection of the appropriate decision model and the kinds of information most useful in implementing the selected model. Differences in the purposes must be recognized and the cost tailored accordingly.

The need for different costs for different purposes is illustrated in Chapter 20 in the discussion of absorption costing and direct costing. This chapter's discussion of cost terms in connection with decision making expresses the relevancy or irrelevancy of a certain cost. Every phase and every decision requires close attention to the inclusion or exclusion of pertinent costs and revenues. The term "relevant," however, is more a statement of the problem than its solution. Costs must be (1) classified in an appropriate manner in order to allow their immediate application to as many situations as feasible, (2) observed and tested in their applicability to a given situation, and (3) perhaps discarded in favor of inflation-adjusted future costs to permit a comparative analysis for the selection of one alternative in contrast with others.

Sunk Costs

The chances for recovery of expenditures made in the past are almost nil. *Sunk costs* are these irrecoverable costs in a given situation. The meaning of a sunk cost will become particularly apparent when a decision must be reached regarding the exchange of an old asset for a new asset (Chapter 26). The undepreciated book balance of the old asset is a sunk cost and entirely irrelevant to the decision-making process except in computing the income tax liability; however, the current exchange value is relevant.

Accountants have been reluctant to exclude sunk costs from their traditional mode of analysis. Although sunk costs play a part in reaching the decision to abandon or continue operations, the essential feature of sunk costs in making managerial decisions is that they may be irrelevant either in whole or in part.

DISCUSSION QUESTIONS

1. Suggest a broad definition of the term "differential cost." What other terms are often used and by whom?

2. Distinguish between marginal cost and marginal costing (or direct costing).

3. Differential costs have also been termed alternative costs. Why are such alternative costs desirable?

4. Differential costs do not correspond to any possible accounting category. Explain.

5. How does the flexible budget assist in the preparation of differential cost analyses?

6. Differential cost studies deal with alternatives that mean not only increased business but also decreased business or even shutdown conditions. Explain.

7. Why is variable cost so important in differential cost studies?

8. When differentially-costed products are marketed, close watch must be kept on their sales trend. Why?

9. Define expected value.

10. Why is the standard deviation of the expected value useful?

11. How is the coefficient of variation used in evaluating the standard deviation?

12. What is the nature of decision trees and how are they used?

13. What is the purpose of Monte Carlo simulation?

14. Define opportunity costs.

15. What are imputed costs?

16. Why are historical costs usually irrelevant for decision making?

17. What are sunk costs?

EXERCISES

1. *Differential cost.* The Baytown Plant of Southwest Company has a normal capacity of 75,000 units per month. At normal capacity, variable cost totals $10 per unit and the monthly fixed cost is $225,000.   *normal capacity 100%*

Required:
   (1) Compute the differential cost of the production between 80% and 90% of normal capacity.
   (2) By increasing fixed cost $10,000 a month, the plant can produce 80,000 units. Compute:
       (a) The differential production cost of these 5,000 units.
       (b) The per unit total production cost. *(Absorption costing)*
       (c) The per unit differential production cost of these 5,000 units.

2. *Analysis of proposed new business.* Saugus Insecticide Company is currently producing and selling 30 000 kilograms of Sta Ded monthly. This volume is 70% of capacity for Sta Ded. A wholesaler outside the Saugus marketing area offers to buy 5 000 kilograms of this product per month on a two-year contract at $1.80 per kilogram, provided the present pinkish color can be changed to green. The product will be marketed under the wholesaler's brand name.

To change the color, a special mixing machine will need to be purchased at a cost of $3,000, but it will have no value at the end of the two-year contract period. Ingredients to change the color in the finished product will cost $.01 per kilogram.

Marketing expense will not be increased if the new business is accepted, but additional administrative expense of $150 per month is estimated. No additional cost for supervision or property tax is contemplated. Additional payroll taxes will be $210.

A monthly income statement for the current operations follows:

Sales.		$72,000
Cost to manufacture:		
Direct materials.	$18,000	
Direct labor	15,000	
Factory overhead:		
Indirect labor.	6,000	
Supervisory labor.	4,000	
Power ($180 fixed).	780	
Supplies.	600	
Maintenance and repair	810	
Depreciation	3,000	
Insurance.	210	
Property tax.	125	
Payroll taxes	1,250	
Cost of goods produced and sold.		49,775
Gross profit		$22,225
Marketing expense.	$11,000	
Administrative expense.	4,500	15,500
Income before income tax		$ 6,725

Required: *Prepare a differential cost analysis to show whether the company should accept the proposed new business.*

3. Acceptance of a special order. *Although Colorado Company has the capacity to produce 16,000 units per month, current plans call for monthly production and sales of only 10,000 units at $15 each. Costs per unit are as follows:*

Direct materials.	$ 5.00
Direct labor	3.00
Variable factory overhead.	.75
Fixed factory overhead	1.50
Variable marketing expense.	.25
Fixed administrative expense	1.00
	$11.50

Required:
  (1) Recommend whether or not the company should accept a special order for 4,000 units @ $10.
  (2) Determine the maximum price Colorado Company should be willing to pay an outside supplier who is interested in manufacturing this product.
  (3) Identify the unit cost figure the company would use in costing inventory, using direct costing.
  (4) Specify the effect on the monthly contribution margin if the sales price were reduced to $14, resulting in a 10% increase in sales volume.   (CGAA adapted)

4. Acceptance of a special order. *Palmer Company has been producing and selling 10,000 units of its product per month, with the following total costs:*

Direct materials.......................................	$20,000
Direct labor	35,000
Variable factory overhead................................	15,000
Fixed factory overhead...................................	24,000
Variable marketing and administrative expenses.............	10,000
Fixed marketing and administrative expenses...............	13,000

The normal sales price is $15 and plant capacity is 18,000 units. The company has received an offer from a special customer who would like to buy exactly 5,000 units of Palmer's product for $9 per unit. Marketing and administrative expenses related to this special order would be $1,500.

Required:

(1) Present computations showing whether or not Palmer should accept this special order.

(2) Determine the effect on the answer to requirement (1) if the plant capacity were only 13,000 units.   (CGAA adapted)

5. Make-or-buy decision. Huntington Company manufactures 10,000 units of Part M-1 annually for use in its production. The following costs are reported:

Direct materials....................................	$ 20,000
Direct labor	55,000
Variable factory overhead..........................	45,000
Fixed factory overhead.............................	70,000
	$190,000

Lufkin Company has offered to sell Huntington 10,000 units of Part M-1 annually for $18 per unit. If Huntington accepts the offer, some of the facilities presently used to manufacture Part M-1 could be rented to a third party at an annual rental of $15,000. Additionally, $4 per unit of the fixed factory overhead applied to Part M-1 would be totally eliminated.

Required: Should Huntington accept Lufkin's offer, and why?   (AICPA adapted)

6. Product alternatives. Schwarz Company sells two products with the following characteristics:

	Product A	Product B
Quantity sold...............	100,000 units	50,000 units
Standard cost per unit:		
Fixed.....................	$10	$20
Variable	10	40
	$20	$60
Sales price per unit	$30	$54

Required:

(1) Compute the profit per unit and in total for each product, assuming that the firm operates at normal capacity and that the standard cost and the actual cost are the same.

(2) Recommend whether the firm should continue its sales of both products, assuming that the fixed cost (in total) will remain the same.

(3) Recommend a decision to either drop Product B or add Product C, assuming that facilities presently committed to B alternatively could be assigned to C, that the two products are mutually exclusive, and that C has the following characteristics:

Quantity sold.	25,000 units
Standard cost per unit:	
Fixed.	$40
Variable	20
	$60
Sales price per unit	$50

(4) Compute the opportunity cost associated with Product B and with Product C.

7. Sell or process further. *Enid Company produces a variety of cleaning compounds and solutions for both industrial and household use. One of its products, a coarse cleaning powder called Grit 337, has a variable manufacturing cost of $1.60 and sells for $2 per pound.*

A small portion of this product's annual production is retained for further processing in the Mixing Department, where it is combined with several other ingredients to form a paste which is marketed as a silver polish selling for $4 per jar. The further processing requires one-fourth pound of Grit 337 per jar; other ingredients, labor, and variable factory overhead associated with further processing cost $2.50 per jar, while unit variable marketing cost is $.30. If a decision were made to cease silver polish production, $5,600 of fixed Mixing Department costs could be avoided.

Required: *Calculate the minimum number of jars of silver polish that must be sold to justify further processing Grit 337.*   *(CMA adapted)*

8. New product analysis. *Helene's, a high fashion women's dress manufacturer, is planning to market a new cocktail dress for the coming season. Helene's supplies retailers in the east and mid-Atlantic states.*

Four yards of material are required to lay out the dress pattern. Some material remains after cutting and can be sold as remnants.

The leftover material could also be used to manufacture a matching cape and handbag. However, if the leftover material is to be used for the cape and handbag, more care will be required in the cutting, which will increase the cutting costs.

The company expects to sell 1,250 dresses if no matching cape and handbag are available. Helene's market research reveals that dress sales will be 20% higher if a matching cape and handbag are available. The market research indicates that the cape and/or handbag will not be sold individually but only as accessories with the dress. The various combinations of dresses, capes, and handbags which are expected to be sold by retailers are as follows:

	Percent of Total
Complete sets of dress, cape, and handbag	70%
Dress and cape	6
Dress and handbag.	15
Dress only	9
Total	100%

The material used in the dress costs $12.50 a yard, or $50 for each dress. The cost of cutting the dress if the cape and handbag are not manufactured is estimated at $20 a dress, and the resulting remnants can be sold for $5 for each dress cut out. If the cape and handbag are to be manufactured, the cutting costs will be increased by $9 per dress. There will be no salable remnants if the capes and handbags are manufactured in the quantities estimated.

The sales prices and the costs to complete the three items once they are cut are as follows:

	Sales Price per Unit	Unit Cost to Complete (Excludes Cost of Material and Cutting Operation)
Dress	$200.00	$80.00
Cape.................................	27.50	19.50
Handbag	9.50	6.50

Required:

(1) *Calculate Helene's differential contribution margin from manufacturing the capes and handbags in conjunction with the dresses.*

(2) *Identify any nonquantifiable factors which could influence Helene's management in this decision.*   *(CMA adapted)*

9. Choice of production method. *Circutech Company is evaluating the use of AZ-17 Photo Resist for the manufacture of printed circuit boards. The major advantages in the utilization of this process versus the present silk-screen method are:*

(a) *Anticipated reduced manufacturing cycle and cost due to elimination of the need for silk circuit screens and shorter operator time to produce circuit boards.*

(b) *Improved ease of registration between front and back patterns.*

(c) *The ability to achieve finer line widths and closer spacing between circuit paths.*

The proposed AZ-17 process is described as follows:

(a) *Fabricate through the completion of the drilling and copper plating of inside holes.*

(b) *Pressure spray AZ-17 Photo Resist on one side, oven bake for 10 minutes, and repeat for other side.*

(c) *Use the photo negative and expose each side for seven minutes in a Nu-Arc Printer.*

(d) *Develop in AZ-17 Developer and proceed through normal operations for making printed circuit board.*

Total direct labor time for the proposed AZ-17 process is 30 minutes.

The original silk-screen method uses a wire mesh stencil film, screening ink, and frames. The direct labor time to prepare the screen for each circuit board is 1½ hours. The direct labor time to screen patterns on the printed wire board is 20 minutes.

The hourly direct labor rate is $6.50. The monthly cost for materials and for equipment rental and operation needed for the proposed process is $4,000 greater than for the silk-screen method, excluding the direct labor.

The company manufactures 20,000 circuit boards annually.

Required: *Compute the annual savings or added cost from changing from the silk-screen method to the new AZ-17 process. (Round off all computations to the nearest dollar.)*

10. *Probability analysis.* *The operator of the corner newsstand wishes to know how many copies of the morning newspaper to stock each day. The newspapers cost $.15 each and are sold for $.20 each. Those unsold at the end of the day have no value. From past experience, the operator has been able to calculate the following probability distribution:*

Number of Papers Sold per Day	Probability
25	.45
30	.35
35	.20

Assume that only the three quantities listed are ever sold and that the occurrences are random events.

Required:

    (1) *What is the average number of papers sold per day? If the operator stocked this average number of papers each day, what would the expected daily contribution margin be?*

    (2) *Compute the standard deviation and the coefficient of variation of the expected value.*   *(CGAA adapted)*

11. *Probability analysis.* *A grocer must decide each morning how many baskets of strawberries to stock that day. The strawberries cost $1 per basket and are sold for $2.50 per basket. Any unsold strawberries at the day's end are given away and therefore are a total loss' to the grocer. From past experience, the grocer is able to provide the following probability distribution of daily demand:*

Number of Baskets	Probability
1	.5
2	.3
3	.2
	1.0

Required:

    (1) *Prepare a payoff table, showing the expected contribution margin for each inventory policy, including identification of the best strategy.*

    (2) *Compute the value of a forecast that would provide the grocer with perfect information on the number of baskets to stock each day.*   *(CGAA adapted)*

PROBLEMS

24-1. **Special order analysis.** Auer Company received an order from Jay Company for a piece of special machinery, but just as the machine was completed, Jay Company defaulted on the order, and forfeited the 10% deposit paid on the $72,500 sales price. Auer's manufacturing manager identified the costs already incurred in the production of the special machinery for Jay as follows:

Direct materials used		$16,600
Direct labor incurred.....................................		21,400
Factory overhead applied:		
Variable	$10,700	
Fixed..	5,350	16,050
Fixed marketing and administrative expenses		5,405
Total cost...		$59,455

Kaytell Corporation would be interested in buying the special machinery if it is reworked to Kaytell's specifications. Auer offered to sell the reworked special machinery to Kaytell for a net price of $68,400. The additional identifiable costs to rework the machinery to the specifications of Kaytell are as follows:

Direct materials	$ 6,200
Direct labor	4,200
	$10,400

A second alternative available to Auer is to convert the special machinery to the standard model, which lists for $62,500. The additional identifiable costs to make the conversion are:

Direct materials	$2,850
Direct labor	3,300
	$6,150

A third alternative for the Auer Company is to sell, as a special order, the machine as is (e.g., without modification) for a net price of $52,000.

The following additional information is available regarding Auer's operations:

(a) The sales commission rate on sales of standard models is 2%, while the sales commission rate on special orders is 3%. All sales commissions are calculated on net sales price (i.e., list price less cash discount, if any).

(b) Normal credit terms for sales of standard models are 2/10, n/30. Customers take the discounts, except in rare instances. Credit terms for special orders are negotiated with the customer.

(c) The application rates for factory overhead and the fixed marketing and administrative costs are as follows:

Factory overhead:
  Variable: 50% of direct labor cost
  Fixed: 25% of direct labor cost
Marketing and administrative:
  Fixed: 10% of the total of direct materials, direct labor, and factory overhead costs

Required:

(1) Compute the dollar contribution that each of the three alternatives will add to Auer's profit.
(2) If Kaytell makes Auer a counteroffer, determine the lowest price Auer should accept from Kaytell.   (CMA adapted)

24-2. Special order analysis. Framar Inc. manufactures automation machinery according to customer specifications. The company is relatively new and has grown each year. Framar operated at about 75% of practical capacity during its most recent fiscal year ended September 30, with operating results as follows:

Sales		$25,000
Less sales commissions		2,500
Net sales		$22,500
Expenses:		
Direct materials		$ 6,000
Direct labor		7,500
Factory overhead — variable:		
Supplies...	$ 625	
Indirect labor	1,500	
Power..	125	2,250
Factory overhead — fixed:		
Supervision..	$ 500	
Depreciation	1,000	1,500
Corporate administration.................................		750
Total expense		$18,000
Income before income tax		$ 4,500
Income tax (40%)...		1,800
Net income		$ 2,700

Framar management has developed a pricing formula based on current operating costs, which are expected to prevail for the next year. This formula was used in developing the following bid for APA Inc.:

Direct materials cost	$ 29,200
Direct labor cost	56,000
Factory overhead calculated at 50% of direct labor	28,000
Corporate overhead calculated at 10% of direct labor	5,600
Total cost, excluding sales commission	$118,800
Add 25% for profit and tax	29,700
Suggested price (with profit) before sales commission	$148,500
Suggested total price (suggested price divided by .9 to adjust for 10% sales commission)	$165,000

Required:

(1) Compute the impact on net income if APA accepts the bid.
(2) Determine the suggested decision if APA is willing to pay only $127,000.
(3) Calculate the lowest price Framar can quote without reducing current net income.
(4) Determine the effect on the most recent fiscal year's profit if all work were done at prices similar to APA's $127,000 counteroffer.   (CMA adapted)

24-3. Comparative cost study to make or buy new product components. Sialkot Surgical Products Company produces diverse lines of surgical instruments. It is considering a proposal, suggested by one of its sales managers, to produce dissection instrument sets for use by medical and premedical students. There is little competition in the market for the instrument sets, and the firm's present sales force could be used for effective distribution coverage. Moreover, the sales manager believes that the company could produce the instruments with the present facilities, except for the addition of certain minor auxiliary equipment.

Company management assigned two members of its Sales Department, two members from the Production Department, and an accounting staff representative to analyze the proposal. The team has assembled the following information:

(a) The proposed dissection instrument sets include:

(1) Dissection knives	3
(2) Scissors	2
(3) Tweezers	2
(4) Scalpels	2
(5) Clamps	4
(6) Glass slides	100
(7) Cover slips	400
(8) Case	1

(b) The market price for such sets ranges from $55 to $65. An estimate of the total annual market demand ranges between 5,000 and 7,000 sets, and Sialkot expects to sell 2,000 sets at $60.

(c) Set components can be purchased from suppliers at the following prices per unit:

(1) Dissection knives	$3.20
(2) Scissors	3.00
(3) Tweezers	2.97
(4) Scalpels	3.05
(5) Clamps	3.28

(6) Glass slides..........................	$ .03
(7) Cover slips..........................	.01
(8) Cases...............................	6.00

(d) Sialkot has the option of manufacturing all of the components, except glass slides, cover slips, and the cases. The remaining components can be grouped into two categories for production and for product costing purposes:
   (1) Group I—dissection knives and scalpels
   (2) Group II—scissors, tweezers, and clamps
(e) Production costs were analyzed to be as follows:

	Group I	Group II
Materials.......................................	1 lb. of steel for 25 units @ $3.27 per lb.	1 lb. of steel for 20 units @ $3.60 per lb.
Labor..	2.5 hrs for 25 units @$9.48 per hr.	2 hrs. for 20 units @ $12.16 per hr.
Variable factory overhead.......................	150% of labor cost	150% of labor cost

(f) Set assembly and packing costs will average $3 per set.
(g) Additional fixed factory overhead directly related to the sets will be $7,040 and $6,000 annually for Groups I and II, respectively.
(h) The new product will have the following amounts of presently existing annual fixed overhead allocated to it:

(1) Group I manufacturing..........................	$4,000
(2) Group II manufacturing	6,000
(3) All other dissection sets' production activity.......	7,000

(i) All sales are FOB Sialkot's plant.

Required: Advise management on the desirability of the proposal, including supporting computations. Compute unit costs to $\frac{1}{10}$ of one cent.

24-4. Evaluating manufacturing alternatives. Satori Corporation has its home office in Ohio and leases factory buildings in Texas, Montana, and Maine, all of which produce the same product. Projection of operations for 19B, the forthcoming year, are:

	Total	Texas	Montana	Maine
Sales..................................	$4,400,000	$2,200,000	$1,400,000	$800,000
Fixed costs:				
Factory............................	$1,100,000	$ 560,000	$ 280,000	$260,000
Administration.....................	350,000	210,000	110,000	30,000
Variable cost.........................	1,450,000	665,000	425,000	360,000
Allocated home office cost	500,000	225,000	175,000	100,000
Total	$3,400,000	$1,660,000	$ 990,000	$750,000
Income before income tax.............	$1,000,000	$ 540,000	$ 410,000	$ 50,000

The sales price per unit is $25.

Because of the marginal results of operations of the factory in Maine, Satori has decided to cease operations and sell that factory's machinery and equipment by the end of 19A. Satori expects that the proceeds from the sale of these assets would be greater than their book value and would cover all termination costs.

Satori, however, would like to continue serving its customers in that area if it is economically feasible and is considering one of the following alternatives:

(a) Expand the operations of the Montana factory by using space presently idle. This move would result in the following changes in that factory's operations:

	Increase over Factory's Current Operations
Sales..........................	50%
Fixed costs:	
Factory.....................	20%
Administration..............	10%

incremental

Under this proposal, the variable cost would be $8 per unit for all units sold.

(b) Enter into a long-term contract with a competitor who will serve that area's customers. This competitor would pay Arcadia a royalty of $4 per unit based on an estimate of 30,000 units being sold.

(c) Close the Maine factory and not expand the operations of the Montana factory. The total home office cost of $500,000 will remain the same under each situation.

Required: Prepare a schedule computing Satori's total income before income tax that would result from each proposal.   (AICPA adapted)

24-5. Elimination of market. Justa Corporation produces and sells three products, A, B, and C. The three products are sold in a local market and in a regional market. At the end of the first quarter of the current year, the following income statement was prepared:

	Total	Local	Regional
Sales.....................................	$1,300,000	$1,000,000	$300,000
Cost of goods sold	1,010,000	775,000	235,000
Gross profit..............................	$ 290,000	$ 225,000	$ 65,000
Marketing expense	$ 105,000	$ 60,000	$ 45,000
Administrative expense....................	52,000	40,000	12,000
	$ 157,000	$ 100,000	$ 57,000
Operating income	$ 133,000	$ 125,000	$ 8,000

Management has expressed special concern with the regional market because of the extremely poor return on sales. This market was entered a year ago because of excess capacity. It was originally believed that the return on sales would improve with time, but after a year, no noticeable improvement can be seen from the results as reported in the quarterly statement.

In attempting to decide whether to eliminate the regional market, the following information has been gathered:

	A	B	C
Sales.....................................	$500,000	$400,000	$400,000
Variable manufacturing expense as a percentage of sales	60%	70%	60%
Variable marketing expense as a percentage of sales	3%	2%	2%

Product	Sales by Markets	
	Local	Regional
A	$400,000	$100,000
B	300,000	100,000
C	300,000	100,000

All fixed expense is based upon a prorated yearly amount. All administrative expense and fixed manufacturing expense are common to the three products and the two markets and are fixed for the period, regardless of whether a market is eliminated. Remaining marketing expense is fixed for the period and separable by market. All separable cost would be eliminated with the dropping of a market.

Required:
(1) Prepare the quarterly income statement, showing contribution margins by markets. Include a total column, combining the two markets.
(2) Assuming that there are no alternative uses for Justa Corporation's present capacity, should the regional market be dropped? Why or why not?
(3) Prepare the quarterly income statement, showing contribution margins by products.
(4) It is believed that a new product to replace Product C could be ready for sale next year if Justa Corporation decides to go ahead with continued research. The new product could be produced by simply converting equipment presently used in producing Product C. This conversion would increase fixed costs by $10,000 per quarter. Calculate the minimum contribution margin per quarter for the new product if Justa Corporation is to be no worse off financially than at present.

(CMA adapted)

24-6. Sell or process further; shutdown of facilities. Novak Chemical Company uses comprehensive annual profit planning procedures to evaluate pricing policies, finalize production decisions, and estimate unit costs for its various products. One particular product group involves two joint products and two by-products. This product group is separately analyzed each year to establish appropriate production and marketing policies.

The two joint products, Alchem-X and Chem-P, emerge at the end of processing in Department 20. Both chemicals can be sold at this split-off point — Alchem-X for $2.50 per unit, and Chem-P for $3 per unit. By-product BY-D20 also emerges at the split-off point in Department 20 and is marketable for $.50 per unit without further processing. Unit costs of preparing this by-product for market are $.03 for freight and $.12 for packaging.

Chem-P is sold without further processing, but Alchem-X is transferred to Department 22 for additional processing into a refined chemical labeled as Alchem-XF. No additional materials are added in Department 22. Alchem-XF is sold for $5 per unit. By-product BY-D22 is created by the additional processing in Department 22, and it can be sold for $.70 per unit. Unit marketing costs for BY-D22 are $.05 for freight and $.15 for packaging.

Novak Chemical Company accounts for by-products by crediting their net realizable value to the production cost of the main products. The market value method is used to allocate the net joint production cost for inventory costing purposes.

A portion of the 19B profit plan established in September, 19A, is as follows:

Production budget:	Chem-P	Alchem-XF
Estimated sales	400,000 units	210,000 units
Planned inventory change	(8,000)	(6,000)
Required production	392,000 units	204,000 units
Minimum production based upon joint output ratio	392,000 units	210,000 units

	BY-D20	BY-D22
By-product output	90,000 units	60,000 units

Manufacturing budget:

	Department 20	Department 22
Materials...	$160,000	—
Cost transferred from Department 20*...................	—	$225,000
Direct labor..	170,000	120,000
Variable factory overhead.............................	180,000	140,800
Fixed factory overhead................................	247,500	188,000
Total..	$757,500	$673,800

*The cost transferred to Department 22 is calculated as follows:

Market value of output:		
Alchem-X (210,000 × $2.50)..................	$ 525,000	31%
Chem-X (392,000 × $3.00)...................	1,176,000	69
Total.............................	$1,701,000	100%
Department 20 cost........................	$ 757,500	
Less by-product (90,000 × $.35)........	31,500	
Net cost....................................	$ 726,000	
Alchem-X............................ 31%	$ 225,000	or $1.07 per unit ($225,000 ÷ 210,000 units)
Chem-X............................ 69	501,000	or $1.28 per unit ($501,000 ÷ 392,000 units)
Allocated net cost................... 100%	$ 726,000	

Marketing expenses budget:

Chem-P...................	$196,000
Alchem-XF...............	105,000

Shortly after this budget was compiled, the company learned that a chemical which would compete with Alchem-XF was to be introduced. The Marketing Department estimated that a price reduction to $3.50 a unit would be required for the Alchem-XF to be sold in present quantities.

The market for Alchem-X will not be affected by the introduction of this new chemical. Consequently, the quantities of Alchem-X which are usually processed into Alchem-XF can be sold at the regular price of $2.50 per unit. The cost for marketing Alchem-X is estimated to be $105,000. If the further processing is terminated, Department 22 will be closed and all costs except $74,800 per year will be eliminated.

Required: Prepare an analysis indicating whether Novak should close Department 22 and sell Alchem-X at the split-off point or continue to process it further in Department 22.   (CMA adapted)

24-7. Evaluation of alternatives for a charitable foundation. J. Watson recently was appointed executive director of a charitable foundation. The foundation raises the money for its activities in a variety of ways, but the most important source of funds is an annual mail campaign. Although large amounts of money are raised each year from this campaign, the year-to-year growth in the amount derived from this solicitation has been lower than expected by the foundation's board. In addition, the board wants the mail campaign to project the image of a well-run and fiscally responsible organization in order to build a base for future contributions. Consequently, the major focus of Watson's first-year efforts will be devoted to the mail campaign.

The campaign takes place in the spring of each year. The foundation staff makes every effort to secure newspaper, radio, and television coverage of the foundation's activities for several weeks before the mailing. In prior years, the foundation has mailed brochures that described its charitable activities to a large number of people and requested contributions from them. The addresses for the mailing are generated from the foundation's own file of past contributors and from mailing lists purchased from brokers.

The foundation staff is considering three alternative brochures for use in the upcoming campaign. All three will be 8½″ × 11″ in size. The simplest and the one sure to be ready and available on a timely basis for bulk mailing is a sheet of white paper with a printed explanation of the foundation's program and a request for funds. A more expensive brochure on colored stock will contain pictures as well as printed copy. However, this brochure may not be ready in time to take advantage of bulk postal rates, but there is no doubt that it can be ready in time for mailing at first-class postal rates. The third alternative would be an elegant, multicolored brochure printed on glossy paper with photographs as well as printed copy. The printer assures the staff that it will be ready on time to meet the first-class mailing schedule, but asks for a delivery date one week later just in case there are production problems.

The foundation staff has assembled the following cost and gross revenue information for mailing the three alternative brochures to 2,000,000 potential contributors:

| Type of Brochure | Brochure Costs | | | | Gross Revenue Potential (000s omitted) | | |
	Design	Type-setting	Unit Paper Cost	Unit Printing Cost	Bulk Mail	First Class	Late First Class
Plain paper	$ 300	$ 100	$.005	$.003	$1,200	—	—
Colored paper	1,000	800	.008	.010	2,000	$2,200	—
Glossy paper	3,000	2,000	.018	.040	—	2,500	$2,200

The postal rates are $.04 per item for bulk mail and $.26 per item for presorted first-class mail. First-class mail is more likely to be delivered on a timely basis than bulk mail. The charge by outside companies who will be hired to handle the mailing is $.01 per unit for the plain and colored paper brochures and $.02 per unit for the glossy paper one.

Required:
    (1) Calculate the net revenue potential for each brochure for each viable mailing alternative.
    (2) The foundation must choose one of the three brochures for this year's campaign. The criteria established by the board—net revenue potential, image as a well-run organization, and image as a fiscally responsible organization—must be considered when making the choice. Evaluate the three alternative brochures in terms of the three criteria.   (CMA adapted)

24-8. Proposed construction of additional capacity. East Lansing Company is considering expanding its production facilities with a building costing $260,000 and equipment costing $84,000. Building and equipment depreciable lives are 25 and 20 years, respectively, with straight-line depreciation and no salvage value. Of the additional depreciation cost, 5% is expected to be allocated to inventories.

The plant addition will increase volume by 50%; the product's sales price is expected to remain the same. The new union contract calls for a 5% increase in wage rates. Because of the increased plant capacity, quantity buying will yield an overall 6% decrease in materials cost, and one additional supervisor must be hired at a salary of $15,000.

The following data pertain to last year:

Sales, 50,000 units @ $10 per unit   Fixed factory overhead, $72,500
Direct materials, $2 per unit   Variable marketing expense, $12,000
Direct labor, $4 per unit   Fixed marketing expense, $7,000
Variable factory overhead, $1.30 per unit

With the volume increase, advertising, which is 10% of present fixed marketing expense, will be increased 25%.

Required: Prepare an analysis estimating the contribution margin and operating income for the present and the proposed plant capacities.

24-9. Make-or-buy decision using probability distribution. Unimat Company manufactures a thermostat designed for effective climatic control of large buildings. The thermostat requires a specialized thermocoupler, purchased from Cosmic Company at $15 each. For the past two years, an average of 10% of the purchased thermocouplers have not met quality requirements; however, the rejection rate is within the range agreed on in the purchase contract.

Unimat has most of the facilities and equipment needed to produce the components. Additional annual fixed cost of only $32,500 would be required. The Engineering Department has designed a manufacturing system which would hold the defective rate to 4 percent. At an annual demand level of 18,000 units, engineering estimates of the probabilities of various variable manufacturing unit costs, including allowance for defective units, are as follows:

Estimated Per Unit Variable Cost	Probability
$10	.1
12	.3
14	.4
16	.2

Required: Prepare a make-or-buy decision analysis, using probability distribution estimates.   (CMA adapted)

24-10. Probability analysis. The owner of Hammer's Clothing Store must decide on the number of men's shirts to order for the coming season. One order must be placed for the entire season. The normal sales price is $12 per shirt; however, unsold shirts at season's end must be sold at half price. The following data are available:

Order Quantity	Unit Sales Price	Unit Cost	Unit Contribution Margin at Regular Price	Unit Loss at Half Price
100	$12.00	$10.00	$2.00	$4.00
200	12.00	9.50	2.50	3.50
300	12.00	9.00	3.00	3.00
400	12.00	8.50	3.50	2.50

Over the past 20 seasons, Hammer has experienced the following sales.

Quantity Sold	Frequency
100	4
200	6
300	8
400	2
	20

The historical sales have occurred at random; i.e., they have exhibited no cycles or trends, and the future is expected to be similar to the past.

Required:
  (1) Prepare a payoff table representing the expected contribution margin of each of the four possible strategies of ordering 100, 200, 300, or 400 shirts, assuming that only the four quantities listed are ever sold.
  (2) Select the best of the four strategies in (1), based on the expected contribution margin.
  (3) Compute the dollar value of perfect information in this problem.

24-11. Probability analysis. Wurst Inc. operates the concession stands at the Tecumseh College football stadium. Tecumseh College has had successful football teams for many years; as a result, the stadium is virtually always filled. From time to time, Wurst has found that its supply of hot dogs is inadequate, while at other times, there has been a surplus. A review of Wurst's sales records for the past ten seasons reveals the following frequency of hot dogs sold:

Hot Dogs	Number of Games
10,000	5
20,000	10
30,000	20
40,000	15
Total	50

Hot dogs that sell for $.50 each cost Wurst $.30 each. Unsold hot dogs are donated to a local orphanage.

Required:
  (1) Prepare a payoff table representing the expected value of each of the four possible strategies of ordering 10,000, 20,000, 30,000, or 40,000 hot dogs, assuming that only the four quantities listed were ever sold and that the occurrences were random events.
  (2) Compute the standard deviation (rounded to the nearest whole number) and the coefficient of variation (rounded to two decimal places) for each of the four possible strategies.
  (3) Select the best of the four strategies in (1), based on the expected value.
  (4) Compute the dollar value of knowing in advance what the sales level would be at each game.
  (5) Compute the standard deviation (rounded to the nearest whole number) and the coefficient of variation (rounded to two decimal places) for the average profit if Wurst knew in advance what the sales level would be at each game.

(CMA adapted)

24-12. Decision tree. The management of Bara Industries is trying to decide whether to build a large, medium, or small plant at a new location. Demand for the company's product in the new area is uncertain, but the marketing manager has assigned probabilities to the three levels of demand. These probabilities, as well as the contribution margins (conditional values—in millions of dollars) for each plant size and demand level, are as follows:

Plant Size	Demand Level High	Moderate	Low
Large	$7	$2	$−1
Medium	$6	$3	0
Small	$5	$4	$ 1
Probability	.3	.5	.2

Required:

(1) Construct a decision tree for the above situation.

(2) Identify the decision preference. (CGAA adapted)

CASES

A. Make-or-buy decision. Until recently, when it discontinued five items, CLK Company manufactured all electrical components that it sold. The items were dropped from the manufacturing process because the unit costs computed by the company's full (absorption) cost system did not provide a sufficient margin to cover shipping and selling costs. The five items are now purchased from other manufacturers at a price which allows CLK to make a very small profit after shipping and selling costs. CLK keeps these items in its product line in order to offer a complete line of electrical components.

The president thought that the switch from manufacture to purchase for the five items would improve profit performance. However, the reverse has occurred. All other factors affecting profits — sales volume, sales prices, and incurred marketing and manufacturing costs — were as expected, so the profit problem can be traced to this decision. Disappointed at recent profitability performance, the president has asked the Controller's Department to reevaluate the decision's financial effects.

The task was assigned to an assistant controller, who has reviewed the data used to reach the decision to purchase rather than manufacture and has concluded that the company should have continued to manufacture the item. In the assistant's opinion, the incorrect decision was made because full cost data rather than direct cost data were used.

Required: Explain the features of direct costing as compared to full costing that make it possible for the assistant controller's conclusion to be correct. (CMA adapted)

B. Analysis of differential business. Silitech Manufacturing, Inc. is presently operating at 50% of normal capacity, producing annually about 50,000 units of a patented electronic component. Silitech recently received an offer from a company in Yokohama, Japan, to purchase 30,000 components at $6 per unit, FOB Silitech's plant. Silitech has not previously sold components in Japan. Budgeted production costs for 50,000 and 80,000 units of output follow:

Units	50,000	80,000
Costs:		
Direct materials	$ 75,000	$120,000
Direct labor	75,000	120,000
Factory overhead	200,000	260,000
Total cost	$350,000	$500,000
Cost per unit	$7.00	$6.25

The sales manager thinks the order should be accepted, even if it results in a loss of $1 per unit, since the sales may build up future markets. The production manager does not wish to have the order accepted, primarily because the order would show a loss of $.25 per unit when computed on the new average unit cost. The treasurer has made a quick computation indicating that accepting the order will actually increase gross profit.

Required:

(1) Determine causes of the drop in cost from $7 per unit to $6.25 per unit when budgeted production increases from 50,000 to 80,000 units.

(2) (a) Explain whether the production manager and/or the treasurer is correct.

     (b) Explain the conclusions of the production manager and the treasurer.

(3) Explain how each of the following may affect the decision to accept or reject the special order:

     (a) The likelihood of repeat special sales and/or all sales to be made at $6 per unit.

     (b) Whether the sales are made to customers operating in two separate, isolated markets or whether the sales are made to customers competing in the same market.   (AICPA adapted)

C. New product proposal. Calco Corporation, a producer and distributor of plastic products for industrial use, is considering a proposal to produce a plastic storage unit designed especially for the consumer market. The product is well suited for Calco's manufacturing process, with no costly machinery modifications or Assembly Department changes required. Adequate manufacturing capacity is available because of recent facility expansion and a leveling of sales growth in its industrial product line.

Management is considering two alternatives for marketing the product. The first is to add this responsibility to Calco's current Marketing Department. The other alternative is to acquire a small, new company named Jasco, Inc. at a nominal cost. This company was started by some former employees of a firm which specialized in marketing plastic products for the consumer market when they lost their jobs because of a merger. Jasco has not yet started operations.

The Product Engineering Department has prepared the following unit manufacturing cost estimate for the new storage unit at both the 100,000- and the 120,000-unit levels of production:

Direct materials.	$14.00
Direct labor	3.50
Factory overhead (25% variable)*	10.00
Total	$27.50

*Total fixed factory overhead will be $750,000 at the 100,000-unit level and $900,000 at the 120,000-unit level.

Calco's Marketing Department has used its experience in the sale of industrial products to develop a proposal for the distribution of the new consumer product. The Marketing Department would be reorganized so that several positions which were scheduled for elimination now would be assigned to the new product. The Marketing Department's forecast of the annual financial results for its proposal to market the storage units is as follows:

Sales (100,000 units @ $45)	$4,500,000
Costs:	
Cost of units sold (100,000 units @ $27.50)	$2,750,000
Marketing costs:	
Positions that were to be eliminated	600,000
Sales commission (5% of sales)	225,000
Advertising program.	400,000
Promotion program	200,000
Share of current Marketing Department's management costs	100,000
Total cost	$4,275,000
Income before income tax	$ 225,000

The Jasco founders also prepared a forecast of the annual financial results, based upon their experience in marketing consumer products. The following forecast was based upon the assumption that Jasco would become part of Calco and be responsible for marketing the storage unit:

Sales (120,000 units @ $50)	$6,000,000
Costs:	
Cost of units sold (120,000 units @ $27.50)	3,300,000
Marketing costs:	
Personnel — sales	660,000
Personnel — sales management	200,000
Commission (10%)	600,000
Advertising program	800,000
Promotion program	200,000
Office rental (the annual rental of a long-term lease already signed by Jasco)	50,000
Total cost	$5,810,000
Income before income tax	$ 190,000

Required:

(1) List factors Calco should consider before entering the consumer products market.

(2) Alter financial forecasts for use in deciding between the alternatives, if Calco decides to enter the consumer market.

(3) Compare the reliability of the two proposals.

(4) Identify the nonquantitative factors Calco should consider when choosing between the alternatives. Indicate whether or not any one of these factors is sufficiently important to warrant selection of one alternative over the other, regardless of the estimated financial effect on profit.   (CMA adapted)

Chapter 25
Linear Programming for Planning and Decision Making

Modern tools and techniques are increasingly used by managers as they seek to make intelligent decisions and control operations. At the heart of management's responsibility is the best or optimum use of limited resources that include money, personnel, materials, facilities, and time. *Linear programming*, a mathematical technique, permits determination of the best use of available resources. It is a valuable aid to management because it provides a systematic and efficient procedure which can be used as a guide in decision making.

Linear Programming and the Maximization of Contribution Margin

The contribution margin is one measure of whether management is making the best use of resources. When the total contribution margin is maximized, management's profit objective should be satisfied.

To illustrate the application of linear programming to the problem of maximizing the contribution margin, assume that a small machine shop manufactures two models, standard and deluxe. Each standard model requires two hours of grinding and four hours of polishing. Each deluxe model requires five hours of grinding and two hours of polishing. The manufacturer has three grinders and two polishers; therefore, in a 40-hour week there are 120 hours of grinding capacity and 80 hours of polishing capacity. There is a contribution margin of $3 on each standard model and $4 on each deluxe model and a ready market for both models. To maximize the total contribution margin, the management must decide on (1) the allocation of the available production capacity to standard and deluxe models and (2) the number of units of each model to produce.

To solve this problem, the symbol x is assigned to the number of standard models and y to the number of deluxe models. The contribution margin from making x standard models and y deluxe models is then $3x + $4y. The contribution margin per unit is the sales price per unit less the unit variable cost that is directly traceable to the product. The total contribution margin is the per unit contribution multiplied by the number of units.

The restrictions on machine capacity are expressed in this manner: to manufacture one standard unit requires two hours of grinding time, so that making x standard models uses $2x$ hours. Similarly, the production of y deluxe models uses $5y$ hours of grinding time. With 120 hours of grinding time available, the grinding capacity is written: $2x + 5y \leq 120$ hours of grinding capacity per week. The limitation on polishing capacity is expressed: $4x + 2y \leq 80$ hours per week.

In summary, the relevant information is:

	Grinding Time	Polishing Time	Contribution Margin
Standard model	2 hours	4 hours	$3
Deluxe model	5	2	4
Plant capacity	120	80	

This information is used in illustrating two basic linear programming techniques — the graphic method and the simplex method.

Graphic Method

When a linear programming problem involves only two variables, a two-dimensional graph can be used to determine the optimal solution. In this example, the x-axis represents the number of standard models, and the y-axis represents the number of deluxe models. The maximum number of each model that can be produced, given the constraints, is determined as follows:

Operation	Maximum Number of Models	
	Standard	Deluxe
Grinding	$\frac{120}{2} = 60$	$\frac{120}{5} = 24$
Polishing...........................	$\frac{80}{4} = 20$	$\frac{80}{2} = 40$

The lowest number in each of the two columns measures the impact of the hours limitations. It appears that at most, the company can produce

20 standard models with a contribution margin of $60 (20 × $3) or 24 deluxe models at a contribution margin of $96 (24 × $4). However, producing a combination of standard and deluxe models may be a better solution.

To determine the combination of production levels in order to maximize the contribution margin, all the constraints are plotted on the graph. In this example, the polishing and grinding constraints are drawn by connecting the points that represent the extremes of production of each model. These points are:

When x = 0:   y ≤ 24 grinding constraint

y ≤ 40 polishing constraint

When y = 0:   x ≤ 60 grinding constraint

x ≤ 20 polishing constraint

The constraints sketched on the graph define the solution space, as follows:

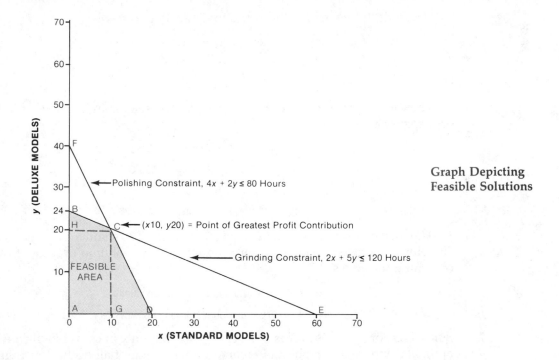

Graph Depicting Feasible Solutions

The solution space represents the area of feasible solutions and is bounded by the lines AB, BC, CD, and AD on the graph. Any combination of standard and deluxe units that falls within the solution space is a feasible solution. However, the best feasible solution, according to a mathematical theorem, is at one of the four corner points. Consequently, all corner point variables must be examined to find the combination which maximizes the contribution margin (CM) of $3x + $4y.

The x and y corner point values can be read from the graph or computed. The x and y values for the corner points B, 24, and D, 20, are extreme points that were used in plotting the constraints. Corner point C values can be computed as follows:

Write the constraints as equalities:

$$2x + 5y = 120$$

$$4x + 2y = 80$$

To find the value of y, multiply the first equation by two and subtract the second equation:

$$
\begin{array}{r}
4x + 10y = 240 \\
-4x - 2y = -80 \\
\hline
8y = 160 \\
y = 20
\end{array}
$$

Substitute the value of y in the first equation and solve for x:

$$2x + 5(20) = 120$$

$$2x = 20$$

$$x = 10$$

The values for x and y and the resulting contribution margin values at each of the corner points are:

A... $(x = 0, y = 0)$; $\$3(0) + \$4(0) = \$0$ CM

B... $(x = 0, y = 24)$; $\$3(0) + \$4(24) = \$96$ CM

C... $(x = 10, y = 20)$; $\$3(10) + \$4(20) = \$110$ CM

D... $(x = 20, y = 0)$; $\$3(20) + \$4(0) = \$60$ CM

The total contribution margin is maximized when 10 standard models and 20 deluxe models are scheduled for production. This solution uses all of the constraint resources:

$$2(10) + 5(20) = 120 \text{ hours grinding constraint}$$

$$4(10) + 2(20) = 80 \text{ hours polishing constraint}$$

Full utilization of all resources will occur, however, only in cases in which the optimal solution is at a point of common intersection of all of the constraint equations in the problem — point C in this example.

Simplex Method

The simplex method is considered one of the basic techniques from which many linear programming techniques are directly or indirectly derived. The *simplex method* is an iterative, stepwise process which approaches an optimum solution in order to reach an objective function of maximization or minimization. Matrix algebra provides the deterministic working tools from which the simplex method was developed, requiring mathematical formulation in describing the problem.

The example described earlier in this chapter is used to illustrate the simplex method. However, before the method can be applied, the following steps must be taken:

1. The relationships which establish the constraints or inequalities must first be expressed in mathematical form. Letting x and y be respectively the quantity of items of the standard model and the deluxe model that are to be manufactured, the system of inequalities or the set of constraints is:

$$2x + 5y \leq 120$$

$$4x + 2y \leq 80$$

Both x and y must be positive values or zero ($x \geq 0$; $y \geq 0$). Although this illustration involves only less-than-or-equal-to type constraints, equal-to and greater-than-or-equal-to type constraints can be encountered in maximization as well as in minimization problems. All three types of constraints are illustrated in the cost minimization example on pages 719–725.

2. The objective function is the total contribution margin the manager can obtain from the two models. A contribution margin of $3 is expected for each standard model and $4 for each deluxe model. The objective function is CM $= 3x + 4y$. The problem is now completely described by mathematical notation.

3. Although the first two steps were the same for the graphic method, the simplex method requires the use of equations, in contrast to the inequalities used by the graphic method. Therefore, the set of inequalities (two less-than-or-equal-to type constraints in this example) must be transformed into a set of equations by introducing slack variables, s_1 and s_2. The use of slack variables involves the addition of an arbitrary variable to one side of the inequality, transforming it into an equality. This arbitrary variable is called a *slack variable*, since it takes up the slack in the inequality. The inequalities rewritten as equalities are:

$$2x + 5y + s_1 = 120$$

$$4x + 2y + s_2 = 80$$

The unit contribution margins of the fictitious products s_1 and s_2 are zero, and the objective equation becomes:

$$\text{Maximize:} \quad CM = 3x + 4y + 0s_1 + 0s_2$$

At this point, the simplex method can be applied and the first matrix or tableau can be set up as follows:

	MIX	0	3	4	0	0	← OBJECTIVE ROW
		QUANTITY	x	y	s_1	s_2	← VARIABLE ROW
0	s_1	120	2	5	1	0	⎤ PROBLEM ROWS
0	s_2	80	4	2	0	1	⎦
		0	−3	−4	0	0	← INDEX ROW

First Simplex
Tableau and
First Solution

↑ OBJECTIVE COLUMN ↑ VARIABLE COLUMN ↑ QUANTITY COLUMN

Explanation and Computations for the First Tableau. The simplex method records the pertinent data in a matrix form known as the *simplex tableau*. The components of a tableau are described in the following paragraphs.

The *objective row* consists of the coefficients of the objective function.

The *variable row* is made up of the notation of the variables of the problem, including slack variables.

The *problem rows* in the first tableau contain the coefficients of the variables in the constraints. Each constraint adds an additional problem row. Variables not included in a constraint are assigned zero coefficients in the problem rows. In subsequent tableaus, new problem row values will be computed.

At each iteration, the *objective column* receives different entries, representing the contribution margin per unit of the variables in the solution.

At each iteration, the *variable column* receives different notations by replacement. These notations, which represent the products to be produced, are the variables used to find the total contribution margin of the particular iteration. In the first matrix, a situation of no production is considered as a starting point in the iterative solution process. For this reason, only slack variables and *artificial variables* (discussed on page 720) are entered in the variable column, and their coefficients in the objective function are recorded in the objective column. As the iterations proceed, by replacement, appropriate values and notations will be entered in the objective and variable columns.

The *quantity column* shows the constant values of the constraints in the first tableau; in subsequent tableaus, it shows the solution mix.

The *index row* carries values computed by the following steps:

1. Multiply the values of the quantity column and those columns to the right of the quantity column by the corresponding value, by rows, of the objective column.
2. Add the results of the products, by rows, of the matrix.
3. Subtract the values in the objective row from the results in Step 2. For this operation, the objective row is assumed to have a zero value in the quantity column. The contribution margin entered in the cell in the quantity column and the index row is zero, a condition valid only

for the first tableau when a situation of no production is considered. In the subsequent matrices, it will be a positive value, denoting the total contribution margin represented by the particular matrix.

The index row for the illustration is determined as follows:

Steps 1 and 2	Step 3
120(0) + 80(0) = 0	0 − 0 = 0
2(0) + 4(0) = 0	0 − 3 = −3
5(0) + 2(0) = 0	0 − 4 = −4
1(0) + 0(0) = 0	0 − 0 = 0
0(0) + 1(0) = 0	0 − 0 = 0

In this first tableau, the slack variables were introduced into the variable column to find an initial feasible solution to the problem. It can be proven mathematically that beginning with positive slack and artificial variables assures a feasible solution. Hence, one possible solution might have s_1 take a value of 120 and s_2 a value of 80. This approach satisfies the constraint, but is undesirable, since the resulting contribution margin is zero.

It is a rule of the simplex method that the optimum solution has not been reached if the index row carries any negative values at the completion of an iteration. Consequently, this first tableau does not carry the optimum solution, since negative values appear in its index row. A second tableau or matrix must now be prepared, step by step, according to the rules of the simplex method.

Explanation and Computations for the Second Tableau. The construction of the second tableau is accomplished through these six steps:

1. Select the *key column,* the one which has the negative number with the highest absolute value in the index row, i.e., that variable whose value will most increase the contribution margin. In the first tableau, the key column is the one formed by the values: 5, 2, and −4.

2. Select the *key row,* the row to be replaced. The key row is the one which contains the

	MIX	0	3	4	0	0
		QUANTITY	x	y	s_1	s_2
0	s_1	120	2	5	1	0
0	s_2	80	4	2	0	1
		0	−3	−4	0	0

First Simplex Tableau

smallest positive ratio obtained by dividing the positive numbers in the problem rows of the key column into the corresponding values, by rows, of the quantity column. The smallest positive ratio identifies the equation which operates as the limiting constraint. In the first tableau, the ratios are 120 ÷ 5 = 24 and 80 ÷ 2 = 40. Since 120 ÷ 5 is the smaller of the two positive ratios, the key row is s_1 — 120, 2, 5, 1, and 0.

3. Select the *key number,* which is the value found in the crossing cell of the key column and the key row. In the example, the key number is 5.

4. Compute the *main row,* which is a computed series of new values replacing the key row of the preceding tableau (in this case, the first tableau). The main row is determined by dividing each amount in Row s_1 (the row being replaced) of the preceding tableau by the key number; i.e., $120 \div 5 = 24$; $2 \div 5 = 2/5$, or 0.4; $5 \div 5 = 1$; $1 \div 5 = 1/5$, or 0.2; $0 \div 5 = 0$. In the second tableau, these are the figures in Row y, which replaces Row s_1.

5. Compute the amounts in all other rows. In this problem, new values are determined for the s_2 row by the following procedure:

Old s_2 Row (First Tableau)		(	Old s_2 Row and y (the Key) Column	×	y Row (Second Tableau)	)	=	Values of New s_2 Row
80	−	(	2	×	24	)	=	32
4	−	(	2	×	0.4	)	=	3.2
2	−	(	2	×	1	)	=	0
0	−	(	2	×	0.2	)	=	−0.4
1	−	(	2	×	0	)	=	1

These computations accomplish (1) the substitution of as much of the deluxe model as is consistent with constraints and (2) the removal of as much s_1 and s_2 as is necessary to provide for the insertion of y (deluxe model) units into the solution. The $4 contribution margin of the deluxe model is placed in the objective column of the y row.

6. Finally, compute the index row:

Steps 1 and 2	Step 3
24 (4) + 32 (0) = 96	96 − 0 = 96
0.4(4) + 3.2(0) = 1.6	1.6 − 3 = −1.4
1 (4) + 0 (0) = 4	4 − 4 = 0
0.2(4) + −0.4(0) = 0.8	0.8 − 0 = 0.8
0 (4) + 1 (0) = 0	0 − 0 = 0

When these steps are completed for the contribution margin maximization illustration, the second tableau appears as follows:

Second Simplex Tableau and Second Solution

This row has been replaced because 24 was the smallest positive ratio computed in Step 2.

	MIX	0 QUANTITY	3 x	4 y	0 s_1	0 s_2	
4	y	24	0.4	1	0.2	0	←MAIN ROW
0	s_2	32	3.2	0	−0.4	1	
		96	−1.4	0	0.8	0	

This second matrix does not contain the optimum solution, since a negative figure, -1.4, still remains in the index row. The contribution margin arising from this model mix is \$96 [4(24) + 0(32)], which is an improvement. However, the second solution indicates that some standard models and \$1.40 (or 7/5 dollars of contribution margin) can be added for each unit of the standard model substituted in this solution.

It is interesting to reflect on the significance of $-7/5$ or -1.4. The original statement of the problem had specified a unit contribution margin of \$3 for the standard model. Now the contribution will increase by only \$1.40 per unit. The significance of the -1.4 is that it measures the net increase of the per unit contribution margin, after allowing for the reduction of the deluxe model represented by y units. That is, all the grinding hours have been committed to produce 24 deluxe models (24 units $\times$ 5 hours grinding time per unit = 120 hours capacity); the standard model cannot be made without sacrificing the deluxe model. The standard model requires 2 hours of grinding time; the deluxe model requires 5 hours of grinding time. To introduce one standard model unit into the product mix, the manufacture of 2/5 (0.4) of one deluxe model unit must be forgone. This figure, 0.4, appears in the column headed "x" on the row representing forgone variable (deluxe) models. If more real variables (i.e., more than two products) were involved, the figures for these variables, appearing in Column x, would have the same meaning as 0.4 has for the deluxe models.

Thus, the manufacturer loses 2/5 of \$4, or \$1.60, by making 2/5 less deluxe models, but gains \$3 from the additional standard models. A loss of \$1.60 and a gain of \$3 results in a net improvement of \$1.40. The final answer, already known from the graphic method illustration, adds \$14 (10 standard models $\times$ 1.4) to the \$96 contribution margin that results from producing 24 deluxe models. However, the total contribution margin of \$110 results from producing 10 standard models (10 $\times$ \$3 = \$30) and 20 deluxe models (20 $\times$ \$4 = \$80). In summary, the -1.4 in the second tableau indicates the amount of increase possible in the contribution margin if one unit of the variable heading that column (the standard model x, in this case) were added to the solution; and the 0.4 value in Column x represents the production of the deluxe model, y, that must be relinquished for each unit of x that is added.

The quantity column was described for the first tableau as showing the constant values of the constraints, i.e., the maximum resources available (grinding and polishing hours in the illustration) for the manufacture of standard and deluxe models. In subsequent tableaus, the quantity column shows the solution mix. Additionally, for a particular iteration in subsequent tableaus, the quantity column shows the constraints that are utilized in an amount different from the constraint's constant value. For example, in the second tableau's quantity column, the number corresponding to the y variable denotes the number of y units in the solution mix (24), and its objective function coefficient of \$4 when multiplied by 24 yields \$96, the value of the solution at this iteration. The number corresponding to the s_2 variable denotes the difference in total polishing hours and those used in the second tableau solution, i.e., 80 hours of available polishing hours less polishing hours used to produce 24 units of y (24×2), or $80 - 48 = 32$. Thus, the number of unused polishing hours is 32. No unused grinding hours, the s_1 variable, are indicated because 24 units of y utilize the entire quantity of available grinding time ($24 \times 5 = 120$ hours).

While this illustration is of less-than-or-equal-to type constraints, a similar interpretation can be made for equal-to type constraints; i.e., the quantity column denotes the difference in the constant value of the constraint and the value used in the tableau's solution mix. For the greater-than-or-equal-to constraint, the quantity column denotes the amount beyond the constraint's minimum requirement that is satisfied by the particular solution mix.

These constraint utilization or satisfaction differences provide useful information, especially in the optimal solution tableau, because management may wish to make decisions to reduce these differences, e.g., by plans to utilize presently unused capacity associated with less-than-or-equal-to constraints.

Explanation and Computations for the Third Tableau. The third tableau is computed by these steps:

	MIX		0	3	4	0	0
		QUANTITY	x	y	s_1	s_2
4	y	24	0.4	1	0.2	0
0	s_2	32	3.2	0	-0.4	1
		96	-1.4	0	0.8	0

Second Simplex Tableau

1. Select the *key column*. This is the column which has the negative number with the highest absolute value in the index row. In the second tableau, the key column is the x column, formed by the values 0.4, 3.2, and -1.4.
2. Select the *key row*, s_2, the row to be replaced by x, which is determined as follows: from the second tableau, for the x row, $24 \div 0.4 = 60$; for the s_2 row, $32 \div 3.2 = 10$. Since 10 is the smaller positive ratio and comes from the s_2 row, s_2 should be replaced by x.
3. Select the *key number*, which is the value 3.2, located in the crossing cell of the key column and the key row of the preceding (second) tableau.
4. Compute the *main row*. The new x row (old s_2 row) figures are determined by dividing each amount in row s_2 of the second tableau by the amount in the x column in row s_2, the key number. The results are: $32 \div 3.2 = 10$; $3.2 \div 3.2 = 1$; $0 \div 3.2 = 0$; $-0.4 \div 3.2 = -0.125$; $1 \div 3.2 = 0.3125$.
5. Compute the amounts in all other rows. The new values of the y row are:

Old y Row (Second Tableau)	−	(Old y Row and x (the Key) Column	×	x Row (Third Tableau)	)	=	Values of New y Row
24	−	(0.4	×	10	)	=	20
0.4	−	(0.4	×	1	)	=	0
1	−	(0.4	×	0	)	=	1
0.2	−	(0.4	×	−0.125	)	=	0.25
0	−	(0.4	×	0.3125	)	=	−0.125

6. Compute the index row:

Steps 1 and 2				Step 3		
20	(4) + 10	(3) = 110		110	− 0 =	110
0	(4) + 1	(3) = 3		3	− 3 =	0
1	(4) + 0	(3) = 4		4	− 4 =	0
0.25	(4) + −0.125	(3) = 0.625		0.625	− 0 =	0.625
−0.125	(4) + 0.3125	(3) = 0.4375		0.4375	− 0 =	0.4375

The third tableau appears as follows:

	MIX	0 QUANTITY	3 x	4 y	0 s_1	0 s_2
4	y	20	0	1	0.250	−0.1250
3	x	10	1	0	−0.125	0.3125
		110	0	0	0.625	0.4375

Third Simplex Tableau and Optimal Solution

There are no negative figures in the index row, which indicates that any further substitutions will not result in an increase in the contribution margin; the optimum solution has been obtained. The optimum strategy is to produce and sell 20 deluxe and 10 standard models for a contribution margin of $110.

Linear Programming and the Minimization of Cost

The previous problem dealt with the maximization of the contribution margin. The simplex method, as well as the graphic method, can also be used in problems whose objective is to minimize variable cost.

To illustrate a cost minimization problem, assume that a pharmaceutical firm is to produce exactly 40 gallons of a mixture in which the basic ingredients, x and y, cost $8 per gallon and $15 per gallon, respectively. No more than 12 gallons of x can be used, and at least 10 gallons of y must be used. The firm wants to minimize cost.

The cost function objective can be written as:

$$C \text{ (cost)} = 8x + 15y$$

The problem illustrates the three types of constraints, =, ≤, and ≥, as follows:

$$x + y = 40$$

$$x \leq 12$$

$$y \geq 10$$

The optimum solution is obvious. Since x is cheaper, as much of it as possible should be used, i.e., 12 gallons. Then enough y, or 28 gallons, should be used to obtain the desired total quantity of 40 gallons.

Simplex Method

In more realistic problems, a solution may not be so obvious, especially if there are many ingredients each having constraints. A simple procedure is needed to generate an optimal solution no matter how complex the problem. The steps toward a solution in the cost minimization problem are similar to those taken in the contribution margin maximization example, where the simplex method was used and slack variables were introduced in order to arrive at the first feasible solution which gave a zero contribution margin.

In addition to the slack variables, a different type of variable known as an artificial variable is introduced. *Artificial variables* allow two types of restrictions or constraints to be treated: the equal-to type and the greater-than-or-equal-to type. Artificial variables are of value only as computational devices in maximization and minimization problems.

In this minimization problem, an artificial variable, a_1, is introduced in the first constraint, which is of the equal-to type. A new equality is written as follows:

$$x + y + a_1 = 40 \text{ gallons}$$

The new ingredient, a_1, must be thought of as a very expensive item which would not be part of the optimum solution. If a costs $999 per gallon, for example, 40 gallons would cost $39,960. This high cost is noted by the coefficient m in the objective function. (For a maximization problem, the notion of a very low contribution margin is denoted by the symbol $-m$.) This symbol is added merely to initiate the simplex method, since the constraint is already an equality.

The second constraint is the less-than-or-equal-to type, and a slack variable, s_1, is added to form an equation: $x + s_1 = 12$ gallons. The s_1 represents the difference between 12 gallons of x and the actual number of gallons of x in the final solution.

The third constraint is the greater-than-or-equal-to type, and a variable, s_2, is introduced to form an equation: $y - s_2 = 10$ gallons. The variable s_2 must be thought of as the amount by which the actual number of gallons of y in the final solution must be reduced to arrive at 10 gallons. For example, if y should be 18 gallons, then s_2 would be 8 gallons ($18 - 8 = 10$ gallons). However, if y

appears in the first solution as 0, then $0 - s_2 = 10$, or $s_2 = -10$. This equation is not feasible because -10 gallons of an ingredient is not possible. To prevent s_2 from entering the first solution, in which only slack and artificial variables are introduced, a second artificial variable, a_2, is utilized. Thus, $y - s_2 + a_2 = 10$ gallons. Similar to a_1, a high cost, m, is assigned to a_2 in the objective function.

As a rule, there must be the same number of entries in the variable (mix) column as there are constraints. Before a_2 is introduced in this example, there are three constraints, one artificial variable, a_1, and two slack variables, s_1 and s_2, of which s_2 has a negative coefficient. The introduction of the artificial variable, a_2, gives a set of four variables, from which the three with positive coefficients, s_1, a_1, and a_2, can be chosen to enter into the variable column of the first tableau.

The new cost equation is:

$$C = 8x + 15y - 0s_2 + ma_1 + 0s_1 + ma_2$$

For minimizing cost, the objective function must be multiplied by -1. This transformed function enters the first tableau as the objective row. The resulting equation is:

$$C = -8x - 15y + 0s_2 - ma_1 - 0s_1 - ma_2$$

The new constraints for the simplex solution are:

$$x + y + a_1 = 40$$
$$x + s_1 = 12$$
$$y - s_2 + a_2 = 10$$

The first tableau can be set up as follows:

	MIX	0	-8	-15	0	$-m$	0	$-m$
		QUANTITY	x	y	s_2	a_1	s_1	a_2
$-m$	a_1	40	1	1	0	1	0	0
0	s_1	12	1	0	0	0	1	0
$-m$	a_2	10	0	1	-1	0	0	1
		$-50m$	$-m+8$	$-2m+15$	m	0	0	0

First Simplex Tableau and First Solution

Explanation and Computations for the First Tableau. The explanation of the arrangement of the tableau is identical with that given for the first tableau of the maximization model. Observe that variables not included in a constraint are assigned zero coefficients in the problem rows. The index row is computed as follows:

Steps 1 and 2		Step 3	
$-m(40) + 0(12) + (-m)(10) =$	$-50m$	$-50m - 0 =$	$-50m$
$-m(1) + 0(1) + (-m)(0) =$	$-m$	$- m - (-8) =$	$-m + 8$
$-m(1) + 0(0) + (-m)(1) =$	$-2m$	$- 2m - (-15) =$	$-2m + 15$
$-m(0) + 0(0) + (-m)(-1) =$	m	$m - 0 =$	m
$-m(1) + 0(0) + (-m)(0) =$	$-m$	$- m - (-m) =$	0
$-m(0) + 0(1) + (-m)(0) =$	0	$0 - 0 =$	0
$-m(0) + 0(0) + (-m)(1) =$	$-m$	$- m - (-m) =$	0

In the simplex method, the optimum solution has not been reached if the index row carries any negative values (except for the quantity column which denotes total cost of this solution) at the completion of an iteration. Consequently, since negative values appear in the index row, the optimum solution has not been found, and a second tableau must be set up.

Explanation and Computations for the Second Tableau. Since the objective is to minimize cost, the key column is found by selecting that column with the negative value having the highest absolute value in the index row, i.e., that variable whose value will most decrease cost. The index row shows only two negative values: $-m + 8$ and $-2m + 15$. Observe that the quantity column value in the index row, $-50m$, is not considered. This figure denotes total cost of this solution and is negative by convention. The negative number with the highest absolute value in the index row is $-2m + 15$; therefore, y is the key column.

	MIX	0	-8	-15	0	$-m$	0	$-m$
		QUANTITY	x	y	s_2	a_1	s_1	a_2
$-m$	a_1	40	1	1	0	1	0	0
0	s_1	12	1	0	0	0	1	0
$-m$	a_2	10	0	1	-1	0	0	1
		$-50m$	$-m+8$	$-2m+15$	m	0	0	0

First Simplex Tableau

The row to be replaced, the key row, is a_2, determined as follows:

a_1 row, $40 \div 1 = 40$

s_1 row, $12 \div 0$ is not considered (not defined mathematically)

a_2 row, $10 \div 1 = 10$

Again, as in the maximization discussion, the smallest positive ratio identifies the equation which operates as the limiting constraint.

Since the key number (the crossing cell of the key column y and the key row a_2) is 1, the values of the main row, y, do not change, as indicated by the following computations: $10 \div 1 = 10$; $0 \div 1 = 0$; $1 \div 1 = 1$; $-1 \div 1 = -1$; $0 \div 1 = 0$; $0 \div 1 = 0$; and $1 \div 1 = 1$.

The values in the other rows are determined as follows:

a_1 Row	s_1 Row
40 − 1(10) = 30	12 − 0(10) = 12
1 − 1(0) = 1	1 − 0(0) = 1
1 − 1(1) = 0	0 − 0(1) = 0
0 − 1(−1) = 1	0 − 0(−1) = 0
1 − 1(0) = 1	0 − 0(0) = 0
0 − 1(0) = 0	1 − 0(0) = 1
0 − 1(1) = −1	0 − 0(1) = 0

Index Row

Steps 1 and 2	Step 3
−m(30) + 0(12) + (−15)(10) = −30m − 150	(−30m − 150) − 0 = −30m − 150
−m(1) + 0(1) + (−15)(0) = −m	−m − (− 8) = −m + 8
−m(0) + 0(0) + (−15)(1) = −15	−15 − (−15) = 0
−m(1) + 0(0) + (−15)(−1) = −m + 15	(−m + 15) − 0 = −m + 15
−m(1) + 0(0) + (−15)(0) = −m	−m − (−m) = 0
−m(0) + 0(1) + (−15)(0) = 0	0 − 0 = 0
−m(−1) + 0(0) + (−15)(1) = m − 15	(m − 15) − (−m) = 2m − 15

The second tableau appears as follows:

	MIX	0	−8	−15	0	−m	0	−m
		QUANTITY	x	y	s_2	a_1	s_1	a_2
−m	a_1	30	1	0	1	1	0	−1
0	s_1	12	1	0	0	0	1	0
−15	y	10	0	1	−1	0	0	1
		−30m−150	−m+8	0	−m+15	0	0	2m−15

Second Simplex Tableau and Second Solution

Since negative values appear in the index row, excluding the quantity column, the optimum solution has not yet been found, and a third tableau must be set up.

Explanation and Computations for the Third Tableau. Since $-m + 8$ is the negative number with the highest absolute value in the index row of the second tableau, x is the key column.

The row to be replaced, the key row, is s_1, determined as follows:

a_1 row, 30 ÷ 1 = 30

s_1 row, 12 ÷ 1 = 12

y row, 10 ÷ 0 is not defined mathematically

The following computations determine the values in the x row that replaces the s_1 row, as well as the values in the other rows:

x Row	a_1 Row	y Row
$12/1 = 12$	$30 - 1 (12) = 18$	$10 - 0 (12) = 10$
$1/1 = 1$	$1 - 1 (1) = 0$	$0 - 0 (1) = 0$
$0/1 = 0$	$0 - 1 (0) = 0$	$1 - 0 (0) = 1$
$0/1 = 0$	$1 - 1 (0) = 1$	$-1 - 0 (0) = -1$
$0/1 = 0$	$1 - 1 (0) = 1$	$0 - 0 (0) = 0$
$1/1 = 1$	$0 - 1 (1) = -1$	$0 - 0 (1) = 0$
$0/1 = 0$	$-1 - 1 (0) = -1$	$1 - 0 (0) = 1$

Index Row

Steps 1 and 2	Step 3
$-m (18) + (-8) (12) + (-15) (10) = -18m - 246$	$(-18m - 246) - 0 = -18m - 246$
$-m (0) + (-8) (1) + (-15) (0) = -8$	$-8 - (-8) = 0$
$-m (0) + (-8) (0) + (-15) (1) = -15$	$-15 - (-15) = 0$
$-m (1) + (-8) (0) + (-15) (-1) = -m + 15$	$(-m + 15) - 0 = -m + 15$
$-m (1) + (-8) (0) + (-15) (0) = -m$	$-m - (-m) = 0$
$-m (-1) + (-8) (1) + (-15) (0) = m - 8$	$(m - 8) - 0 = m - 8$
$-m (-1) + (-8) (0) + (-15) (1) = m - 15$	$(m - 15) - (-m) = 2m - 15$

The third tableau appears as follows:

Third Simplex Tableau and Third Solution

	MIX	0	-8	-15	0	-m	0	-m
		QUANTITY	x	y	s_2	a_1	s_1	a_2
-m	a_1	18	0	0	1	1	-1	-1
-8	x	12	1	0	0	0	1	0
-15	y	10	0	1	-1	0	0	1
		-18m-246	0	0	-m+15	0	m-8	2m-15

Since a negative value, $-m + 15$, appears in the index row, again excluding the quantity column, the optimum solution has not been found, and a fourth tableau must be set up.

Explanation and Computations for the Fourth Tableau. Since $-m + 15$ is the only relevant negative number in the index row of the third tableau, s_2 is the key column.

The smallest positive ratio in the following computation identifies the row to be replaced as a_1.

a_1 row, $18 \div 1 = 18$

x row, $12 \div 0$ is not defined mathematically

y row, $10 \div -1 = -10$

The values in the s_2 row (replacing the a_1 row), the x row, the y row, and the index row are determined as follows:

s_2 Row	x Row	y Row
$18/1 = \quad 18$	$12 - 0(\ 18) = 12$	$10 - (-1)(\ 18) = \quad 28$
$0/1 = \quad 0$	$1 - 0(\ 0) = \ 1$	$0 - (-1)(\ 0) = \quad 0$
$0/1 = \quad 0$	$0 - 0(\ 0) = \ 0$	$1 - (-1)(\ 0) = \quad 1$
$1/1 = \quad 1$	$0 - 0(\ 1) = \ 0$	$-1 - (-1)(\ 1) = \quad 0$
$1/1 = \quad 1$	$0 - 0(\ 1) = \ 0$	$0 - (-1)(\ 1) = \quad 1$
$-1/1 = \ -1$	$1 - 0(-1) = \ 1$	$0 - (-1)(-1) = \ -1$
$-1/1 = \ -1$	$0 - 0(-1) = \ 0$	$1 - (-1)(-1) = \quad 0$

Index Row

Steps 1 and 2	Step 3
$0(18) + (-8)(12) + (-15)(28) = -516$	$-516 - 0 \quad = \quad -516$
$0(\ 0) + (-8)(\ 1) + (-15)(\ 0) = -\ 8$	$-8 \ - (-\ 8) = \quad 0$
$0(\ 0) + (-8)(\ 0) + (-15)(\ 1) = -15$	$-15 \ - (-15) = \quad 0$
$0(\ 1) + (-8)(\ 0) + (-15)(\ 0) = \quad 0$	$0 \quad - 0 \quad = \quad 0$
$0(\ 1) + (-8)(\ 0) + (-15)(\ 1) = -15$	$-15 \ - (-m) = m - 15$
$0(-1) + (-8)(\ 1) + (-15)(-1) = \quad 7$	$7 \quad - 0 \quad = \quad 7$
$0(-1) + (-8)(\ 0) + (-15)(\ 0) = \quad 0$	$0 \quad - (-m) = \quad m$

The fourth tableau appears as follows:

	MIX	0	-8	-15	0	$-m$	0	$-m$
		QUANTITY	x	y	s_2	a_1	s_1	a_2
0	s_2	18	0	0	1	1	-1	-1
-8	x	12	1	0	0	0	1	0
-15	y	28	0	1	0	1	-1	0
		-516	0	0	0	$m-15$	7	m

Fourth Simplex Tableau and the Optimal Solution

No negative values remain in the index row of the fourth tableau, except the minimum cost figure which is negative by convention, -516. The following optimum solution has been reached:

$$
\begin{array}{lr}
12 \text{ gals. of } x \ @ \ \$\ 8 \text{ per gal.} = & \$\ 96 \\
\underline{+28 \text{ gals. of } y \ @ \ \$15 \text{ per gal.}} = & \underline{\ \ 420} \\
\underline{\underline{40 \text{ gals. of mixture}}} & \underline{\underline{\$516 \text{ the lowest cost combination}}}
\end{array}
$$

Graphic Method

The graphic method can be applied to minimization problems in the same manner as illustrated for maximization problems. Again, the constraints define the solution space when they are plotted on the following graph:

Graph Depicting Feasible Solutions

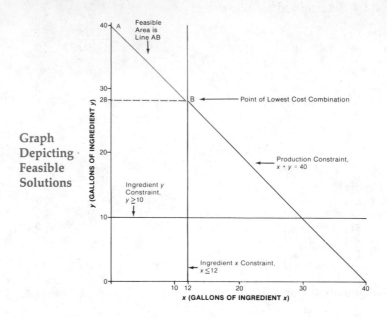

The solution space indicates the area of feasible solutions represented by the line AB. Any combination of x and y that falls within the solution space, line AB, is a feasible solution. However, the best feasible solution is found at one of the corner points, A or B. Consequently, the corner points must be examined to find the combination that minimizes cost, i. e., $8x + $15y.

The values at each of the two corner points are:

A . . . . (x = 0, y = 40); $8(0) + $15(40) = $600 cost

B . . . . (x = 12, y = 28); $8(12) + $15(28) = $516 cost

To minimize cost, the company should use 12 gallons of x and 28 gallons of y at a total cost of $516.

Shadow Prices

The determination of the optimum mix to maximize the contribution margin or to minimize cost assumes a defined set of constraints. It is useful to consider the sensitivity of the solution if a constraint is relaxed. This effect is often referred to as the *shadow price* and simply shows the change in contribution margin, in a contribution margin maximization problem, or the change in cost, in a cost minimization problem, resulting from relaxing a constraint.

To present the idea of shadow prices, the value of additional grinding or polishing hours (from the contribution margin maximization problem previously discussed) can be considered, i.e., the worth of additional grinding and polishing hours.[1] If the machine shop had more grinding or polishing hours, the contribution margin could be increased by using more of each.

The index row of the third, optimal solution, simplex tableau (page 719) shows the shadow prices in the slack variable columns, which are the locations for both $\leq$ and $\geq$ constraints. In this illustration, only $\leq$ constraints are encountered. If there were = constraints, the artificial variable column would be used, with the m value ignored.

The coefficients under the s_1, grinding, and s_2, polishing, slack variable columns give the trade-off in terms of product mix as the constraints are increased or decreased. Thus, one more hour of grinding time will increase the contribution margin by $.625, computed as follows: as one more grinding hour is made available, .25 units of y, deluxe models, with a unit contribution margin of $4 (.25 $\times$ $4 = $1), will replace .125 units of x, standard models, with a $3 unit contribution margin (.125 $\times$ $3 = $.375), for a net contribution margin of $.625 ($1 - $.375 = $.625).

If additional grinding time could be obtained at no increase in unit variable cost, an increase of $.625 contribution margin per grinding hour would result; and as much as $.625 more than the present unit variable cost of grinding time could be incurred before reaching a point at which a zero per unit contribution margin would occur. Thus, overtime hours might be considered. The $.4375 has the same meaning for each hour of polishing time, and in each case the observations assume that the sales price per unit remains unchanged.

The range of hours over which the shadow prices of $.625 and $.4375 for grinding and polishing hours are valid can be found as follows:

1. For the lower limit of the range, divide each unit in the solution mix by the coefficients under the slack variable columns, i.e., the s_1 and s_2 columns. The smallest positive number that results in a column is the maximum decrease for that constraint:

	(1)	(2)	(3)	(4)	(5)
		s_1	s_2	s_1 Grinding	s_2 Polishing
Product	Units	Grinding	Polishing	(1) ÷ (2)	(1) ÷ (3)
y	20	0.250	−0.1250	80	−160
x	10	−0.125	0.3125	−80	32

For the grinding constraint, the decrease is 80 hours. Since the original number of hours available was 120, the lower limit is 40 hours. For the polishing constraint, the decrease is 32 hours. Since 80 hours were originally available, the lower limit is 48 hours.

---

[1]This discussion is adapted from Lanny G. Chasteen, "A Graphical Approach to Linear Programming Shadow Prices," *The Accounting Review,* Vol. XLVII, No. 4, pp. 819–823.

2. For the upper limit of the range, multiply each coefficient by -1 and repeat the Step 1 process. The smallest positive number that results in a column is the maximum increase for that constraint:

Product	(1) Units	(2) s_1 Grinding	(3) s_2 Polishing	(4) s_1 Grinding (1) ÷ (2)	(5) s_2 Polishing (1) ÷ (3)
y	20	−0.250	0.1250	−80	160
x	10	0.125	−0.3125	80	− 32

For the grinding constraint, the maximum increase is 80; and since the original number of hours available was 120, the upper limit is 200 hours. For the polishing constraint, the increase is 160, and the upper limit is 240 hours (160 plus the original constraint of 80 polishing hours).

The limits occur for a constraint because increases or decreases beyond the limits will change the shadow price. In summary, the lower and upper constraint limits for this example are:

	Lower Limit	Upper Limit
Grinding hours	40	200
Polishing hours	48	240

Both the constraints in this example are of the ≤ type. The same method for finding the lower and upper constraint range limits is used for the = type of constraint, except that the coefficients under the artificial variable columns for the = constraints are used in the computations. For a ≥ constraint, the method for finding the lower and upper constraint range limits differs, in that the signs of the coefficients under the slack variable columns for the ≥ constraints are changed in Step 1. With this exception, the procedure is the same.

When there is a zero shadow price (not the case in the above example), there is no defined upper limit for the ≤ type of constraint because there is already more of this constraint available than is required. There is no defined lower limit for the ≥ type of constraint because there is already more of this constraint used than is required.

The lower- and upper-limit computations apply, assuming that only one constraint is to be relaxed, and provided there is a unique solution to the linear programming problem. The limits for cases in which two or more constraints are relaxed simultaneously can be computed following a methodology that is beyond the scope of this discussion.[2]

The described method is equally applicable to cost minimization problems. It should also be observed that the shadow price indicates the opportunity cost of using a resource, such as grinding or polishing hours, for some other purpose. For example, if an hour of grinding time could instead be used to produce some other product at a contribution margin greater than $.625 per

---

[2]This methodology is referred to as *parametric linear programming*. See Frederick S. Hillier and Gerald J. Lieberman, *Introduction to Operations Research, Third Edition* (San Francisco: Holden-Day, Inc., 1980), pp. 688–694.

hour, then use of the grinding hour resource in producing the alternate product would be preferable.

Dynamic Programming

Dynamic programming is an extension of the basic linear programming technique and involves breaking the problem into a set of smaller problems and then reassembling the results of the analysis. It is best suited for the solution of problems requiring interrelated decisions, i.e., decisions that must be made in sequence and that influence future decisions in the sequence.

The procedure involves partial optimization of a portion of the sequence and then connection of the optimized portion to the next in line until the entire sequence is optimized. Thus, the final result is the sum of the result of the immediate decision plus the optimal result from all future decisions.

Dynamic programming is simple in concept but difficult to apply because of the lack of a clear-cut problem formulation and solution method. Each problem requires unique formulation and solution decisions.[3]

Linear Programming Techniques — General Observations

The maximization and minimization studies, together with the exercises and problems presented in this chapter, are realistic examples of the types of problems management faces. By maximizing certain managerial objectives, such as contribution margin and utilization of available labor hours or factory capacity, or by minimizing functions such as cost, weight, materials mix, or time, management's goal can be determined quantitatively. To find a feasible solution, it is necessary to state each situation in mathematical notations. Restrictions or constraints must confine the solution within a well-defined area and appear in the form of equations with nonnegative variables. All data must be deterministic, i.e., involve exact relationships and known factors.

For the accounting community, a definite similarity exists between certain managerial problems and mathematical programming techniques. Furthermore, as other chapters have pointed out, the growing need for and involvement of accounting and cost data in management's planning and decision-making processes are supported and enhanced by these techniques.

The methods for determining the most profitable or optimum use of alternative uses of long-life facilities are presented in Chapter 26. Problems dealing with the short-run uses of facilities or with output having varying combinations of alternative input might be solved by setting down every possible combination of output in order to determine the maximum contribution

---

[3]See *Ibid.*, pp. 266–298.

margin or the minimum cost. Such a procedure, while proven feasible and acceptable, may no longer be necessary. The introduction of newer and more sophisticated decision models allows the accountant to administer the implementation of these models by determining the data needed for their application. When the cases move beyond the possibility of being solved manually or by simple desk or hand calculators, the electronic computer aids the accountant in arriving at a correct and immediate solution.

DISCUSSION QUESTIONS

1. Explain what linear programming is.

2. What is meant by the unit cost in linear programming problems?

3. Examine the graph on page 711 and answer the following questions:
   (a) The area bounded by the lines AB, BC, CD, and AD is called the solution space. Why?
   (b) The triangles BCF and CDE are not part of the solution space. Why?
   (c) What does corner point C mean?
   (d) What is the meaning of the perpendicular line CG and the horizontal line CH?

4. Describe the simplex method.

5. Discuss the components of a simplex tableau.

6. What is the purpose of a slack variable?

7. What is the purpose of an artificial variable?

8. What is a shadow price? Explain its significance.

9. Define dynamic programming.

EXERCISES

1. *Contribution margin maximization—problem formulation.* Golden Hawk Company wants to maximize the profits on Products *a, b,* and *c.* The contribution margin for each product follows:

Product	Contribution Margin
a	$2
b	5
c	4

The production requirements and departmental capacities, by departments, are as follows:

Department	Production Requirement by Product (Hours)			Departmental Capacity (Total Hours)
	a	*b*	*c*	
Assembling	2	3	2	30,000
Painting	1	2	2	38,000
Finishing	2	3	1	28,000

Required: *Formulate the objective function and the constraints.*

2. *Contribution margin maximization — problem formulation. Elon Company manufactures two industrial products: x, which sells for $90 a unit, and y, which sells for $85 a unit. The following production data are available:*

	Amount Required per Unit	
	x	*y*
Direct materials — weekly supply limited to 1,800 pounds at $12 per pound	4 lbs.	2 lbs.
Direct labor:		
Department 1 — weekly supply limited to 10 people at 40 hours each at an hourly rate of $6	2/3 hour	1 hour
Department 2 — weekly supply limited to 15 people at 40 hours each at an hourly rate of $8	1 1/4 hours	1 hour
Machine time:		
Department 1 — weekly capacity limited to 250 hours	1/2 hour	1/2 hour
Department 2 — weekly capacity limited to 300 hours	-0-	1 hour

Elon's factory overhead costs are applied on a plantwide rate per direct labor hour of $12 — $6 variable, $6 fixed.

Required: *Formulate the objective function and the constraints.*   *(CMA adapted)*

3. *Cost minimization — problem formulation. A company seeks to minimize the total cost of Materials a and b. The per pound cost of a is $25 and of b, $10. The two materials are combined to form a product that must weigh 50 pounds. At least 20 pounds of a and no more than 40 pounds of b can be used.*

Required: *Formulate the objective function and the constraints.*

4. *Contribution margin maximization — graphic method. A company has given the following constraints, $8x + 20y \leq 200$ and $4x \leq 60$, and the objective function, $CM = 2x + 10y$.*

Required: *Prepare a graph and determine how many units of x and y to produce to maximize the contribution margin, and the total contribution margin at the optimal solution.*

5. *Product mix contribution margin. The illustration on page 710 assumes that the market for standard and deluxe models was stable and that the $3 and $4 per unit was maintainable for at least the near future. Increased demand for the deluxe model suggests the desirability of raising the price well above the level that produced the original $4 contribution margin.*

Required: *Determine the following:*
  (1) The product mix to be attained if deluxe models are priced to yield a $6 unit contribution margin.
  (2) The product mix to be attained if deluxe models are priced to yield a $10 contribution margin.
  (3) The contribution margin figure per deluxe model to make it possible to abandon production of standard units and operate at less than full capacity, maintaining maximum profits.

6. *Contribution margin maximization — graphic method. Dupree Machine Shop currently manufactures two products, a and b. Four types of machines are used, mills, lathes, drills, and welding, with daily shop capacities of 16, 16, 8, and 8 hours, respectively. Time requirements to produce one unit of each product are:*

Machine	Product	
	a	b
Mills	.1067 hours	.0533 hours
Lathes	.0640	.1067
Drills	None	.0800
Welding	.0267	.0320

Each unit of a and b returns a contribution margin of $2.50.

Required: *Prepare a graph and determine the number of each product to manufacture in order to maximize the contribution margin.*

7. *Contribution margin maximization — graphic and simplex methods; shadow prices. Bayside Boats, a retail outlet, markets two sailboat models, x and y. Model x occupies 140 square feet of floor space and costs $2,400 to Bayside, while y occupies 180 square feet and costs $4,800. For x, the expected contribution margin is $300 per unit, and for y, the expected unit contribution margin is $800. Bayside wishes to limit investment in these two models to $144,000, and available space is limited to 3,600 square feet.*

Required:
(1) *Determine the number of each boat model that should be stocked to maximize the contribution margin, using the graphic and simplex methods.*
(2) *Compute the shadow prices and their lower and upper constraint range limits.*

8. *Contribution margin maximization — graphic and simplex methods; shadow prices. Chasteen Company manufactures two products, Alpha and Beta, that have contribution margins of $10 and $5 per unit, respectively. Each unit of Alpha requires 10 machine hours, while each unit of Beta requires 4 machine hours; 100 machine hours are available. Each unit of Beta requires two units of Material Z, of which 30 units are available.*

Required:
(1) *Determine the units of Alpha and Beta that must be manufactured to maximize the total contribution margin, using the graphic and simplex methods.*
(2) *Compute the shadow prices and their lower and upper constraint range limits.*

9. *Contribution margin maximization — graphic and simplex methods; shadow prices. Snel Nursery is considering the possibility of adding imported fruit trees and oriental yard shrubs to its line of nursery products. The fruit trees have a per unit contribution margin of $6; shrubs, $7. There are 12 square feet available for display. Each tree requires two square feet of space, while each shrub occupies three square feet. In addition, two hours each day are needed to prepare each tree for sale and one hour to prepare each shrub. Due to the many jobs to be performed in the nursery, only eight hours are available each day.*

Required:
(1) *Determine the number of imported fruit trees and oriental yard shrubs that should be stocked each day to maximize the contribution margin, using the graphic and simplex methods.*
(2) *Compute the shadow prices and their lower and upper constraint range limits.*

10. *Cost minimization — graphic and simplex methods; shadow prices. A company produces three products, a, b, and c, which use common materials, x and y. Material x costs $3 per ton and y $4 per ton. The amount of materials required per ton of product and the required weight per ton of product are:*

	Product a	Product b	Product c
Material x	4 lbs.	7 lbs.	1.5 lbs.
Material y	8	2	5
Minimum weight required..................	32	14	15

Required:

(1) Determine the number of tons of each material needed to meet the requirements at minimum cost by (a) the graphic method and (b) the simplex method.

(2) Compute the shadow prices and their lower and upper constraint range limits.

11. *Cost minimization—graphic and simplex methods; shadow prices.* Two additives are mixed with a plastic resin prior to extension into a final product. Over a period of time, empirical relationships were developed to meet quality specifications of the final product. Within the latitude of these relationships, the quantities are varied according to their current cost. Operating costs are not affected by the proportions of the two additives in the product.

The quality relationships per 100 kilograms of product are:

For tensile strength .... $2a + b \geq 1.1$
For flexibility .... $a + 3b \geq 1.5$

Additive a sells for $8 per kg, and b for $5 per kg.

Required:

(1) Determine the most economical (minimum cost) mixture, using the (a) graphic method and (b) simplex method.

(2) Calculate the shadow prices and their lower and upper constraint range limits.

PROBLEMS

25-1. Contribution margin maximization—problem formulation. Excelsion Corporation manufactures and sells two kinds of containers—paperboard and plastic. The company produced and sold 100,000 paperboard containers and 75,000 plastic containers during April. A total of 4,000 and 6,000 direct labor hours were used in producing the paperboard and plastic containers, respectively.

The company has not been able to maintain an inventory of either product, due to the high demand; this situation is expected to continue in the future. Workers can be shifted from the production of paperboard to plastic containers and vice versa, but additional labor is not available in the community. In addition, in the coming months there will be a shortage of plastic material used in the manufacture of the plastic container, due to a labor strike at the facilities of a key supplier. Management has estimated that there will be enough raw material to produce only 60,000 plastic containers during June.

In the following income statement for Excelsion Corporation for April, the costs presented are representative of prior periods and are expected to continue at the same rates or levels in the short-term future.

Excelsion Corporation
Income Statement
For the Month Ended April 30, 19--

	Paperboard Containers	Plastic Containers
Sales	$220,800	$222,900
Less: Returns and allowances	$ 6,360	$ 7,200
Discounts	2,440	3,450
	$ 8,800	$ 10,650
Net sales	$212,000	$212,250
Cost of goods sold:		
Raw materials	$123,000	$120,750
Direct labor	26,000	28,500
Indirect labor (variable with direct labor hours)	4,000	4,500
Depreciation—machinery	14,000	12,250
Depreciation—building	10,000	10,000
Cost of goods sold	$177,000	$176,000
Gross profit	$ 35,000	$ 36,250
Marketing and general expenses:		
General expense—variable	$ 8,000	$ 7,500
General expense—fixed	1,000	1,000
Commissions	11,000	15,750
Total marketing and general expenses	$ 20,000	$ 24,250
Income before income tax	$ 15,000	$ 12,000
Income tax (40%)	6,000	4,800
Net income	$ 9,000	$ 7,200

Required: Formulate (1) the objective function, and (2) the constraint equations.

(CMA adapted)

25-2. Contribution margin maximization—problem formulation. Leastan Company manufactures a line of carpeting which includes a commercial carpet and a residential carpet. Two grades of fiber—heavy duty and regular—are used in manufacturing both types of carpeting. The mix of the two grades differs in each type of carpeting, with the commercial grade using a greater amount of heavy duty fiber.

Leastan will introduce a new line of carpeting in two months to replace the current line. The present fiber in stock will not be used in the new line; therefore, management wants to exhaust the present stock during the last month of production.

Data regarding the current line of commercial and residential carpeting are:

	Commercial	Residential
Sales price per roll	$1,000	$800
Production specifications per roll of carpet:		
Heavy duty fiber	80 lbs.	40 lbs.
Regular fiber	20 lbs.	40 lbs.
Direct labor hours	15 hrs.	15 hrs.
Standard cost per roll of carpet:		
Heavy duty fiber ($3/lb.)	$ 240	$120
Regular fiber ($2/lb.)	40	80
Direct labor ($10/DLH)	150	150
Variable factory overhead	90	90
Fixed factory overhead	180	180
Total standard cost per roll	$ 700	$620

Leastan has 42,000 pounds of heavy duty fiber and 24,000 pounds of regular fiber in stock. All fiber not used in the manufacture of the present types of carpeting during the last month of production can be sold as scrap at $.25 a pound.

There is a maximum of 10,500 direct labor hours available during the month. The labor force can work on either type of carpeting.

Sufficient demand exists for the present line of carpeting so that all quantities produced can be sold.

Required:

(1) Compute the number of rolls of commercial carpet and residential carpet that Leastan must manufacture during the last month of production in order to exhaust completely the heavy duty and regular fiber still in stock.

(2) Explain whether or not the requirement (1) solution quantities can be manufactured during the last month of commercial and residential carpet production.

(3) Explain why linear programming would be useful in this application.

(4) Formulate the objective function and the constraints, so that this problem can be solved by linear programming.   (CMA adapted)

25-3. Contribution margin maximization — graphic method. Argin Inc. makes two kinds of suede leather belts. Belt a is of high quality, while belt b is of somewhat lower quality. The company earns a contribution margin of $7 for each unit of a that is sold and $2 for each unit of b sold. Each unit (belt) of a requires twice as much manufacturing time as a unit of b. Further, if only b is made, Argin has the capacity to manufacture 1,000 units per day. Suede leather is purchased under a long-term contract which makes available enough leather to produce 800 belts per day (a and b combined). Belt a requires a fancy buckle, of which only 400 per day are available; b requires a plain buckle, of which 700 per day are available. The demand for the suede leather belts (a or b) is such that Argin can sell all that it produces.

The following graph displays the constraint functions, based upon the facts presented:

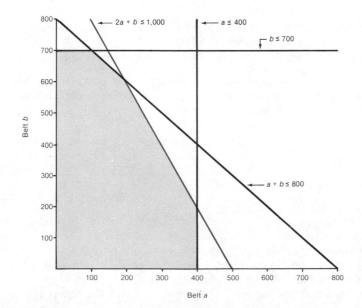

Required: Compute the following:

(1) The number of units of belt *a* and belt *b* that should be produced to maximize the daily contribution margin, using the graph.

(2) The number of units of each of the two belts to be produced each day to maximize the total contribution margin, assuming the same facts, except that the sole supplier of buckles for *a* informs Argin that it will be unable to supply more than 100 fancy buckles per day.

(3) The number of fancy buckles Argin should buy from Texas Buckles Inc. assuming the same facts as in (2), except that Texas Buckles could supply Argin with the additional fancy buckles in 100-unit lots only and the price would be $3.50 more per buckle than Argin is paying now.   (CMA adapted)

25-4. Contribution margin maximization—graphic and simplex methods. Zeus Inc. manufactures two kinds of leather belts—belt *a* (a high-quality belt) and belt *b* (of a lower quality). The respective contribution margins are $4 and $3 per belt. Production of belt *a* requires twice as much time as for belt *b;* and if all belts were of the belt *b* type, Zeus could produce 1,000 per day. The leather supply is sufficient for only 800 belts per day (both belt *a* and belt *b* combined). Belt *a* requires a fancy buckle, and only 400 buckles per day are available for this belt.

Required: Determine the quantity of each type belt to be produced to maximize the contribution margin, using (a) the graphic method and (b) the simplex method.

25-5. Contribution margin maximization—graphic and simplex methods; shadow prices. Sansei Inc. produces two types of promotional fans—oriental and domestic. The contribution margin on oriental fans is $5 per 100; on domestic fans, $4 per 100. Two hundred hours are available for the production of these fans. Two hours are required to produce 100 oriental fans, while one hour is required to produce 100 domestic fans. One pound of paper is required for each 100 fans, whether oriental or domestic. Sansei Inc. has 150 pounds of paper.

Required:

(1) Determine the product mix that provides the maximum contribution margin, using the graphic and simplex methods.

(2) Compute the shadow prices and their lower and upper constraint range limits.

25-6. Contribution margin maximization—graphic and simplex methods; shadow prices. Tarpo Corporation manufactures two products, Trinkets and Gadgets. The information regarding these products is as follows:

Product	Daily Capacities in Units Cutting Department	Daily Capacities in Units Finishing Department	Sales Price per Unit	Variable Cost per Unit
Trinkets	400	240	$50	$30
Gadgets	200	320	70	40

The daily capacities of each department represent the maximum production for either Trinkets or Gadgets. However, any combination of Trinkets and Gadgets can be produced, as long as the maximum capacity of the department is not exceeded; i.e., two Trinkets can be produced in the Cutting Department for each Gadget not produced and three Trinkets can be produced in the Finishing Department for every four Gadgets not produced. Materials shortages prohibit the production of more than 180 Gadgets per day.

Required:
   (1) Prepare a graph that expresses the production relationships stated in the information given.
   (2) Identify and list the graphic locations (coordinates) of the:
       (a) Cutting Department's capacity.
       (b) Production limitations for Gadgets because of the materials shortages.
       (c) Area of feasible production combinations.
   (3) Compute:
       (a) The contribution margin per unit for Trinkets and Gadgets.
       (b) The total contribution margin for each of the points of intersection of lines bounding the feasible production area.
       (c) The best production alternative.
   (4) Determine the best production alternative, using the simplex method.
   (5) Compute the shadow prices and their lower and upper constraint range limits.
   (6) Specify the kinds of decisions for which the contribution margin data are useful.
                                                                (AICPA adapted)

25-7. Cost minimization—graphic and simplex methods; shadow prices. Certain animals at the Southport Zoo must receive an adequate amount of two vitamins in their daily food supply. The minimum daily requirement of Vitamin A is 30 units; of Vitamin B, 50 units.

   One pound of foodstuff x can provide $3\frac{1}{3}\%$ of the minimum daily requirements of A and 4% of B. One pound of y will supply 10% of A and 2% of B requirements. The costs are: x, \$.02 per pound; y, \$.05 per pound.

Required:
   (1) Determine the least possible cost to provide for the minimum requirements of the two vitamins, using the graphic method and the simplex method.
   (2) Compute the shadow prices and their lower and upper constraint range limits.

25-8. Cost minimization—graphic and simplex methods; shadow prices. Deane Pulp Paper Company uses softwood and hardwood pulp as basic materials for producing converter-grade paper. Hardwood is 80% pulp fiber and 20% pulp binder, while softwood is 50% pulp fiber and 50% pulp binder. The cost per pound for hardwood and softwood is \$.50 and \$.40, respectively.

   The company's quality control expert specifies that in order for the product to meet quality standards, each batch must contain at least 12,000 pounds of pulp fiber and at least 6,000 pounds of pulp binder. Because of equipment limitations, the size of a batch cannot exceed 24,000 pounds.

   The production department recently received a new standard from the Cost Department, allowing \$8,200 per batch. The production manager feels that this amount is too low, because such costs have never been less than \$8,400.

Required:
   (1) Determine the hardwood and softwood mix necessary to minimize the cost per batch, using the (a) graphic method and (b) simplex method.
   (2) Compute the shadow prices and their lower and upper constraint range limits.

Chapter 26
Capital Expenditures: Planning, Evaluating, and Controlling

Capital expenditure planning, evaluating, and controlling, sometimes called *capital budgeting,* is the process of planning the continuing investment and reinvestment of an organization's resources and monitoring that investment. Capital expenditures involve long-term commitments of resources to realize future benefits. They reflect basic company objectives and have a significant, long-term effect on the economic well-being of the firm.

In the final analysis, a firm must earn a reasonable return on invested funds. Therefore, considerable attention has been devoted to techniques for evaluating capital expenditure proposals. Yet evaluation is only one essential requirement for the effective administration of a capital expenditure program. Equally important is the effective planning and control of such expenditures, because (1) the long-term commitment increases financial risk, (2) the magnitude of expenditures is substantial and the penalties for unwise decisions are usually severe, and (3) the decisions made in this area provide the structure that supports the operating activities of the firm.

Planning for Capital Expenditures

Planning for capital expenditures consists of relating plans to objectives, structuring the framework, searching for proposals, budgeting the expenditures, and requesting authority for expenditures.

Relating Plans to Objectives

Individual projects must be consistent with objectives and must be capable of being blended into a firm's operations. To achieve this consistency, all levels of an organization need to be conscious of objectives and the different roles played by each level relative to these objectives. Ideally, executive management sets broad objectives; managers of functional activities formulate specific policies and programs for action which, when approved, are executed by operating levels of management. The lower the level at which a decision is authorized, the greater the need for guidelines extending to detailed procedures and standards; investment projects not conducive to such detail require handling at a higher level.

Structuring the Framework

An organization's established capital expenditure framework forms the basis for implementing the capital expenditure program. The framework is important because the very nature of performing tasks implies a sound frame of reference. Several factors influence the molding and revisions of a firm's framework: the company's organizational structure, its philosophy and applications of principles of organization, its size, the nature of its operations, and the characteristics of individual projects.

A company manual may be used to detail policies and procedures and to illustrate forms required for administering the capital expenditure program. Such manuals should be stripped down to helpful levels and should (1) encourage people to work on and submit ideas, (2) focus attention on useful analytical tasks, and (3) facilitate rapid project development and expeditious review.

Searching for Proposals

A capital investment program yields the best results only when the best available proposals are considered and all reasonable alternatives of each proposal have been brought into the analysis for evaluating and screening. Ideas should come from all segments of the enterprise. Persons in the organization should participate in the search activity within the bounds of their technical knowledge and ability, their authority and responsibility, their awareness of operating problems, and existing management guidelines regarding desirable projects. Care must be taken to create and maintain an incentive to search out and bring good projects into the system. This incentive is strong when there is a genuine feeling that all proposals will be reviewed in a fair and objective manner.

Budgeting Capital Expenditures

The capital expenditures budget is typically prepared for a one-year period. It presents management's investment plans at the time the budget is prepared for the coming period.

Some projects never materialize; others are added through amendments to the budget during the budget year. Thus, the budget must be adaptable to changing needs. The capital expenditures budget is not an authorization to commit funds; it merely affords an opportunity to consolidate plans by looking at projects for the total organization, side by side. The capital expenditures budget should be reconciled with the other periodic budgeting activities of the firm, e.g., expense and cash budgets (Chapters 14 and 15), and the annual capital budget should be reconciled with long-range capital investment and operating plans and objectives.

The capital expenditures budget passes through several management levels as it moves toward final approval at the executive management level. It follows that a clear explanation of the content of the approved budget should be transmitted to the various management levels to avoid misunderstandings.

Requesting Authority for Expenditures

The periodic budget is usually an approval of ideas and does not grant automatic approval to commit funds. Authority to commit funds for other than necessary preliminary administrative costs should come by means of an Authority for Expenditure (AFE). The AFE procedure is, in effect, a second look at budgeted projects, based on an up-to-date set of documents justifying and describing the expenditure. The AFE and supporting detail should be originated at the level at which the expenditure will occur, with staff assistance if needed.

Approval of the AFE should be delegated to the organizational level having the necessary competence to make the decision, as opposed to requesting executive management's approval for each AFE. The philosophy of companies varies as to the extent of decentralization of approval authority. The amount, type, and significance of the expenditure should be considered in determining the required level of approval. Required approvals also may be governed by whether certain designated evaluation criteria are met.

During the budget year, periodic reports should be prepared by categories, comparing approved AFE expenditures with the budget. The reports should be prepared for use by the organization levels originating the requests for expenditures as well as those granting approval. Higher echelons find summaries helpful, with out-of-line items reported in detail.

Evaluating Capital Expenditures

Evaluating capital expenditures refers to the basic theory, techniques, and procedures for the appraisal and reappraisal of projects throughout the course of their development. A number of evaluations of a single proposal may be necessary because of:

1. Circumstances that change during the time span from the origin of the project idea to its completion.
2. Alternative solutions of the problem for which the project is designed.
3. Assumptions that vary as to the amount and time pattern of cash flows.

The best available evaluation tools should be used, coupled with an understanding of the risk and danger existing in overreliance on quantitative answers based on many assumptions and estimates. Economic evaluation and related techniques have received prime attention in literature dealing with capital investment programs. The most advanced methods consider the time value of money in computing an estimated return on investment. Many imponderable factors may also affect the decision, e.g., competition, legal requirements, social responsibilities, and emergencies. Furthermore, there is a need to select investments that will keep the firm in balance and be consistent with objectives. The circumstances of each expenditure alternative must be considered in passing judgment on the criteria used. Even then there may be justifiable differences of opinion with respect to governing criteria. The mechanics of various techniques are important, but of still greater importance is their relationship to the overall capital expenditure planning and control process and the need for creative and thoughtful management.

Classification of Capital Expenditures

Capital expenditure projects can be classified as: (1) equipment-replacement expenditures, (2) expansion investments, and (3) improvements of existing products and/or additions of new products. A proposal may involve more than one classification. For example, a firm may consider a proposal to replace an old printing press, whose maintenance cost has become excessive, with a new press that will offer an expanded productive capacity. Also, certain expenditures may be necessary because of tactical or legal requirements, rather than for purely economic reasons: a manufacturer may be forced into the production of a less profitable product because of competitive pressure; recreation facilities may be installed for employee use; or air and water pollution regulations may necessitate an expenditure for a waste disposal unit. Certain projects are musts to the point that use of an evaluation technique is superfluous, e.g., the washout of a section of a railway trestle. Other projects, though indicating an acceptable economic return, may be rejected because of lack of funds, failure to fit into overall objectives, failure to meet other evaluation criteria (such as corner locations for gasoline service stations), or external circumstances (such as current economic conditions or changes in government policies).

Some projects may not be independent of one another and in such cases should be grouped together for evaluation purposes as a compound project. The following quotation illustrates this point:

Contingent or dependent projects can arise, for instance, when acceptance of one proposal is dependent on acceptance of one or more other proposals. One simple example would be the purchase of an extra-long boom for a crane which would be of little value unless the crane itself were also purchased; the latter, however, may be justified on its own. When contingent projects are combined with their independent prerequisites, the combination may be called a compound project. Thus, a compound project may be characterized by the algebraic sum of the payoffs and costs of the component projects plus, perhaps, an interaction term.[1]

Equipment-Replacement Expenditures.   These include both like-for-like and obsolescence replacements. The basis for decision making is future or prospective cost savings, i.e., comparing future costs of old equipment with future costs of new equipment. In addition to comparisons of operating costs, the analysis of future costs requires the determination of the prospective purchase price less any ultimate resale or salvage value. The most difficult problem is to estimate the probable economic life of the new equipment. This is the core of any capital expenditure decision. For the present equipment, the future decline in disposal value must be estimated. The original cost of the present facility is a sunk and irrecoverable cost, totally irrelevant to the decision-making process. Accumulated depreciation is also independent of the company's real future costs. Book values of existing assets are not relevant for the replacement decision, except for possible income tax consequences. For example, an increase or decrease in income tax liability might result from the recognition of a gain or loss, respectively, from the sale, exchange, or abandonment of an asset in the year of disposition. On the other hand, in the case of an exchange of like-kind assets, the income tax effect results from an adjustment to the tax basis of the new asset and the amount of depreciation available for tax purposes, which in turn affects the amount of income tax liability over the depreciable life of the asset. An increase or decrease in income tax liability has a direct effect on cash flow and is, therefore, relevant to the capital expenditure decision.

Expansion Investments.   Expansion investments involve plant enlargement and the invasion of new markets. In these cases, the expected results of doing and not doing the job are compared, with the basis for a decision shifted from cost savings to the expected addition to profits, including the consideration of cash inflow. The added profit is estimated by preparing a projected income statement showing additional revenue and expense over the life of the project. The degree of uncertainty in this type of investment is much greater than in the first category.

Improvements of Existing Products and/or Additions of New Products.   The basis for a decision on projects in this category is strategic; that is, the relative competitive market position compels the firm to make investments. Failure to keep abreast of competitors can cause deterioration of the market share. Since no historical basis for making the decision exists and the return on such

---

[1]H. Martin Weingartner, "Capital Budgeting of Interrelated Projects: Survey and Synthesis," *Management Science*, Vol. XII, No. 7, p. 492.

investments must be based on increasing or maintaining profits in the face of competition, a high degree of sound judgment and business insight is re- quired in making such a decision.

Cost of Capital

The *cost of capital* represents the expected return that investors demand for a given level of risk. Although this discussion is brief, the cost of capital as related to capital expenditures is a complex concept. It may refer to a specific cost of capital from a particular financing effort to provide funds for a specific project. Such use of the concept connotes the marginal cost of capital and implies linkage of the financing and investment decisions. This view has been challenged as a useful concept for allocating capital, however, and the funds available for one or all projects are more generally considered to be a com- mingling of more than one source. Therefore, different costs of capital exist, depending upon the sources. A company could obtain funds from (1) bonds, (2) preferred and common stock, (3) use of retained earnings, and (4) loans from banks. If a company obtains funds by some combination of these sources in order to achieve or maintain a particular capital structure, then the cost of capital (money) is the weighted average cost of each money source. This weighted average considers the joint cost and the desired long-run relative proportions of each type of capital, including inflation's impact, and may be computed as follows:

Funds — Source	Desired Long-Run Proportion of Funds To Be Provided	Aftertax Cost	Weighted Cost
Bonds..........................	.20	.05	.01
Preferred stock...................	.20	.10	.02
Common stock and retained earnings...............	.60	.15	.09
	1.00	Weighted average cost of capital..........	.12 = 12%

The cost of capital for each source is described as follows:

1. The cost of bonds is the aftertax rate of interest, i.e., the pretax rate of interest multiplied by one minus the tax rate.
2. The cost of preferred stock is the dividend per share divided by the present market price.
3. The cost of common stock and retained earnings is the expected earnings per share, after income tax and after preferred dividends are paid, divided by the present market price.[2]

---

[2]Conflicting opinions exist regarding the treatment of the investors' income tax effect on the cost of equity acquired through the retention of earnings.

Inflationary Considerations in Estimating Cash Flows

Just as a company's cost of capital is affected by inflation's impact, so too are estimates of cash flow. In order for the cash flows to be on an equivalent basis with the acceptance criterion, i.e., the weighted average cost of capital, cash flow estimates must include an allowance for the effect of anticipated inflation. To illustrate this effect, assume that Star Company is considering an investment in a project to produce a new product. A sales volume of 1,000 units of the new product is expected for each of the next five years. The planned sales price is $10 per unit and current period cash costs are expected to be $6 per unit, resulting in a net cash inflow of $4 per unit sold. In addition, assume that management expects the general price level to rise at an annual rate of 10 percent. If management believes that its costs will increase at the same rate as inflation and that the sales price of the new product can be increased at the same rate, the estimated cash flows should be adjusted for the effect of inflation as follows:

Year	(1) Unadjusted Estimate of Cash Inflow	(2) General Price-Level Index	(3) Adjusted Estimate of Cash Inflow	(4) Difference (3) − (1)
1	$ 4,000	1.100	$ 4,400	$ 400
2	4,000	1.210	4,840	840
3	4,000	1.331	5,324	1,324
4	4,000	1.464	5,856	1,856
5	4,000	1.610	6,440	2,440
Total	$20,000		$26,860	$6,860

Unless the cash flows are adjusted for inflation's impact, the cash inflows expected over the life of Star Company's project will be understated by $6,860. Such understatement could result in an erroneous rejection of this project. If the impact of inflation is expected to be different for cash inflows and outflows, separate inflation adjustments must be made. For example, such a difference would occur when either the sales price of output or the purchase price of input is to be under a fixed price contract.[3]

Income Tax Considerations in Estimating Cash Flows

The effect of income taxes on cash flows is an important consideration in planning and evaluating capital expenditures. The following paragraphs discuss the tax laws regarding depreciation, the investment tax credit, and interest and taxes during a period of construction.

---

[3]For an elaboration of the effect of inflation in capital budgeting, see Jon W. Bartley, "A NPV Model Modified for Inflation," *Management Accounting*, Vol. LXII, No. 6, pp. 49–52; Debra D. Raiborn and Thomas A. Ratcliffe, "Are You Accounting for Inflation in Your Capital Budgeting Process?," *Management Accounting*, Vol. LXI, No. 3, pp. 19–22; and Allen H. Seed, III, *The Impact of Inflation on Internal Planning and Control* (New York: National Association of Accountants, 1981), pp. 73–78 and 104–105.

Depreciation.   Depreciation is not a cash inflow or outflow. However, depreciation allowed for income tax purposes reduces taxable income and, consequently, tax liability, which is a cash flow.

The Economic Recovery Tax Act of 1981 represents a substantial change in income tax accounting for capital expenditures. A new system for recovering the cost of capital expenditures, referred to as the Accelerated Cost Recovery System (ACRS), is now required for tangible, depreciable property placed in service after 1980. Although required for federal income tax purposes, some states do not allow the ACRS rates in computing state income taxes. ACRS reduces the impact of inflation by significantly accelerating the recovery of capital expenditures. This is done in two ways:

1. By eliminating the useful-life concept and replacing it with a shorter recovery period.
2. By allowing more cost recovery in the earlier years of the recovery period, i.e., accelerated depreciation rates.

Under ACRS, capital expenditures are generally recovered over a period of 3, 5, 10, or 15 years, depending on the type of property:

1. 3-year property — primarily automobiles, light trucks, tangible personal property used in connection with research and development, and certain special tools.
2. 5-year property — primarily machinery and equipment and other tangible personal property not included in the 3-year class.
3. 10-year property — short-lived public utility property, certain short-lived real property, and some others.
4. 15-year public utility property — long-lived public utility property.
5. 15-year real property — depreciable real property (primarily buildings).

For tangible personal property, e.g., machinery and equipment, a full percentage of first-year cost recovery is taken in the year of acquisition, regardless of the time of the year the property is placed in service. However, no cost recovery (depreciation) deduction is allowed in the year of sale or other deposition. In contrast, for buildings and other 15-year real property, the cost recovery deductions allowed in the year of acquisition and disposition are based on the number of months the property was in service during the year. An example of the cost recovery tables is shown on page 746.

Straight-line depreciation and extended recovery periods can be used to slow the rate of recovery, if the taxpayer elects to do so. Regardless of whether straight-line or accelerated cost recovery is used, salvage value is ignored, and depreciation is calculated on the property's tax basis.[4] For property depreci-

---

[4]For income tax purposes, the tax basis is not always cost. For example, in computing the tax basis of a replacement in kind, cost must be adjusted for the gain or loss which was realized but not recognized.

ACRS Recovery Percentages by Property Class

Recovery Year	3-Year	5-Year	10-Year	15-Year Public Utility	Low-Income Housing	Other Real Property
1	25%	15%	8%	5%	13%	12%
2	38	22	14	10	12	10
3	37	21	12	9	10	9
4		21	10	8	9	8
5		21	10	7	8	7
6			10	7	7	6
7			9	6	6	6
8			9	6	5	6
9			9	6	5	6
10			9	6	5	5
11				6	4	5
12				6	4	5
13				6	4	5
14				6	4	5
15				6	4	5
	100%	100%	100%	100%	100%	100%

ated under ACRS, gain which must be recognized on the disposition of the property is treated as ordinary income for tax purposes, except that capital gain treatment applies in the case of buildings which were depreciated by the straight-line method.[5]

ACRS enhances net aftertax cash inflows and should be considered in evaluating capital expenditure projects. Because Congress may make changes in the tax law from time to time, the illustrations and problems in this textbook specify assumed recovery periods and accelerated rates to be used in order to demonstrate the concept. Income tax statutes and regulations should be consulted for current recovery periods and rates.

Investment Tax Credit.   The investment tax credit was originally enacted in 1962 for the purpose of stimulating the economy and generating additional employment by providing an incentive to business to invest and expand. Congress has repealed, reenacted, increased and expanded the investment tax credit to meet varying economic conditions. Although the investment tax credit has not been a stable feature of the income tax law, it is an important capital expenditure consideration during periods when it is available because it reduces income tax expense at the end of a project's first year.

The investment tax credit is available on the acquisition of most tangible property (other than buildings); however, the property's depreciable basis must be reduced by 50 percent of the amount of the credit claimed.[6] The credit

---

[5]In the unlikely event that a loss occurs, the treatment of losses is prescribed by the Internal Revenue Code, Section 1231. Generally, the losses would be pooled with the gains and losses from the sales and exchanges of other Section 1231 assets. If a net gain results from this pooling, the net gain would receive capital gain treatment; however, if a net loss results from the pooling, the net loss would be treated as an ordinary loss.

[6]In lieu of reducing the depreciable basis of the property by 50 percent of the credit taken, the taxpayer may elect to reduce the applicable credit rate by 2 percentage points. See *Internal Revenue Code*, Section 48 (q).

rate is 6 percent of the cost for 3-year recovery property and 10 percent for all other qualified property.[7] If new property is acquired in exchange for a trade-in of an old machine, the qualified cost for purposes of computing the investment tax credit is the tax basis of the old property plus the cash paid. On the other hand, if used property is acquired in a trade-in, the qualified cost is limited to the cash paid for the property.[8]

Construction Period Interest and Taxes. Statement of Financial Accounting Standards, No. 34, "Capitalization of Interest Cost," prescribes capitalization of interest costs incurred in acquiring assets requiring a period of time to be made ready for their intended use, provided the periodic income effect, compared with that of expensing interest, is material. The amount capitalized would be recovered through depreciation over the economic life of the new asset. On the other hand, for federal income tax purposes, both interest and property taxes must be capitalized if paid or accrued during the acquisition or construction period.[9] Furthermore, the tax law limits the capitalization of such costs to the acquisition or construction of real property (e.g., land and buildings). The amount capitalized for tax purposes may be amortized at the rate of 10 percent per year.

In evaluating capital expenditure proposals which involve the acquisition or construction of real property over a period of time, the initial cash outflow would be increased by both interest and taxes incurred during the construction period. Cash inflows in subsequent periods would be increased by the reduction in income taxes that would result from the amortization of the interest and taxes which had been capitalized.

Representative Evaluation Techniques

The following four evaluation techniques are the representative tools in current use: (1) the payback (or payout) period method, (2) the average annual return on investment (or accounting rate of return or financial statement) method, (3) the present value method, and (4) the discounted cash flow (or internal rate of return) method (DCF). None of these methods serves every purpose or every firm. The circumstances and needs of a situation determine the most appropriate techniques to be used. A company may use more than one technique (e.g., payback period and DCF) in evaluating each project; however, the same method or methods should be used uniformly for every project throughout the firm. Confusion could arise if Division A used the discounted cash flow method, while Division B used the average annual re-

---

[7]*Internal Revenue Code*, Section 46 (c) (7).

[8]The total cost of all used property subject to the investment tax credit in a single year is also limited. See *Internal Revenue Code*, Section 48 (c) (2).

[9]*Internal Revenue Code*, Section 189.

turn on investment method. Trying to compare different projects which have been evaluated with different techniques would be like trying to compare apples and oranges. To evaluate alternative projects, the same evaluation techniques must be used.

These evaluation techniques, if thoroughly understood by the analysts who use them, should aid management in exercising judgment and making decisions. Certainly the cost of gathering data and applying the evaluation techniques should be justified in terms of the value to management. Moreover, inaccurate raw data used in the calculations or lack of uniform procedures may yield harmful or misleading conclusions.

For purposes of discussing and illustrating the evaluation methods listed, assume that Diamond Corporation is operating at the limit of the capacity of one of its producing units, and maintenance costs of an existing machine have become excessive. A new machine with greater capacity can be purchased at a cost of $105,000, less a trade-in allowance for the old machine of $10,000, which represents the fair market value of the old machine. Therefore, the initial cash outflow would be $95,000. The old machine has a book value of $5,000, which is also its adjusted basis for tax purposes (i.e., cost or other basis less accumulated depreciation). The net acquisition cost, for both financial accounting and income tax purposes, is $100,000 ($95,000 cash price plus $5,000 book value and tax basis).[10] The expected economic life of the new unit is eight years. Straight-line depreciation is to be used for financial accounting purposes, with an estimated salvage value of $10,000.[11] For tax purposes, however, the property qualifies as five-year property under ACRS and salvage value is ignored.

The estimated differential aftertax cash flow yielded by the utilized additional capacity of the new machine for Diamond Corporation is calculated in the table on page 749. These cash flow estimates include consideration of inflation's impact. In the table, the estimates given in Columns 2 and 3 are

---

[10]Both APB Opinion No. 29 and IRC Section 1031 require that no gain be recognized on the exchange of similar or like-kind assets. The book value or tax basis of the new asset is the value or tax basis of the old asset plus boot given (cash paid to the vendor). Note, however, that if the old asset is sold outright rather than traded in, a $5,000 taxable gain would be realized on the sale ($10,000 sales price less $5,000 tax basis) and the net acquisition cost would be the cash price of $105,000. The initial cash outflow would be $95,000 ($105,000 cash price less $10,000 cash proceeds from the sale of the old asset) plus the tax paid on the $5,000 gain recognized. Regardless of whether the old asset is sold or traded in, the book value of the old asset is a sunk cost and irrelevant to the decision. The aftertax gain on the sale of the old asset is irrelevant, since the proceeds received from the sale must be used to purchase the new asset at a greater cash outflow than would be required if the old asset were traded in. However, the tax liability incurred on the sale of the old asset is relevant, because it could be avoided by trading in the old asset instead of selling it outright. Since a trade-in results in a smaller initial cash outflow than a sale, it is assumed for this illustration.

[11]Generally accepted accounting principles require that the cost of a depreciable asset be allocated to expense over the expected useful life of the asset, even though that period is different from the cost recovery period used for tax purposes. See "AcSEC Position on Tax and Depreciation Lives," *The CPA Letter*, AICPA, Vol. 61, No. 21, p. 3. The method of depreciation and the treatment of estimated salvage value for financial accounting purposes must also comply with generally accepted accounting principles, even though such treatment may differ from that required for tax purposes.

uneven numbers, so that the resulting amounts in Column 8 will be easy to use in subsequent computations.

	DIAMOND CORPORATION — AFTERTAX CASH FLOW						
(1)	(2)	(3)	(4)	(5)	(6)	(7)	(8)
Year	Estimated Cash Savings Relating to Present Capacity (Primarily Maintenance)	Estimated Cash Income Relating to Use of Increased Capacity	Total Cash Inflow (2) + (3)	Tax Depre-ciation*	Taxable Income (Loss) (4) − (5)	Federal and State Income Tax (Reduction) (6) × 48%	Net Aftertax Cash Inflow (4) − (7)
1	$8,705	$20,449	$29,154	$14,250	$14,904	$ (2,846)**	$ 32,000
2	7,113	27,441	34,554	20,900	13,654	6,554	28,000
3	5,835	21,903	27,738	19,950	7,788	3,738	24,000
4	4,226	21,589	25,815	19,950	5,865	2,815	23,000
5	2,485	21,407	23,892	19,950	3,942	1,892	22,000
6	1,270	27,576	28,846	0	28,846	13,846	15,000
7	0	26,923	26,923	0	26,923	12,923	14,000
8	0	28,846	28,846	0	28,846	13,846	15,000
							$173,000
					Cash inflow from salvage at end of economic life		5,200***
							$178,200

*   Tax depreciation is determined by multiplying the depreciable basis of $95,000 by the ACRS percentages provided on page 746 for the five-year property class. The depreciable basis is the acquisition cost of $100,000 reduced by 50 percent of the investment tax credit [50% × ($100,000 × 10%)].

** The tax liability in the first year has been reduced by a 10 percent investment tax credit available on the acquisition cost of $100,000 [($14,904 taxable income × 48% tax) − ($100,000 cost × 10% credit)]. It is assumed that the company has sufficient tax liabilities on income from other sources to absorb the full investment tax credit in the first year. If the company had no taxes on income from other sources, the investment tax credit would reduce income tax in years to which the credit is carried.

*** The salvage value received at the end of the project would be fully taxable because the tax basis would be zero. Thus, the aftertax cash flow would be $5,200 [$10,000 salvage × (1 − .48)]. Note, however, that no tax would be estimated for salvage if management planned to exchange the asset for a replacement in kind.

This example involves both a replacement and an expansion investment, in which the cash outlay is restricted to the cost of the plant asset unit. Some projects require the commitment of working capital for inventories, receivables, etc., as well as expenditures that may not be capitalized. When such commitments and expenditures exist, they should be included as part of the initial investment and, to the extent that they are recoverable, should be shown as cash inflow in the recovery years.

The Payback Period Method. The payback (or payout) period method is widely used in many firms, if only to serve as an initial screening device or to complement the answers of more sophisticated methods. The technique measures the length of time required by the project to recover the initial outlay.[12]

---

[12]The initial outlay used in calculating the payback period should exclude working capital to the extent that the working capital can be recovered through its own liquidation. Investment salvage value at the payback point would further reduce the payback period. Such adjustments result in what is referred to as the "bailout payback."

The calculated payback period is compared with the payback period acceptable to management for projects of the kind being evaluated. The computation for the Diamond Corporation project is:

| | | Recovery of Initial Outlay | | Payback Years |
Year	Cash Flow	Needed	Balance	Required
1	$32,000	$95,000	$63,000	1.00
2	28,000	63,000	35,000	1.00
3	24,000	35,000	11,000	1.00
4	23,000	11,000	0	.48
Total payback period in years				3.48

Because of the effects of variations in business activity, inflation, and accelerated methods of depreciation used for income tax purposes, it is highly unlikely that estimated cash flows for actual projects would be uniform for each year. However, professional examinations, such as the CPA and CMA examinations, may assume uniform cash flows for simplicity in problems requiring the computation of the payback period. In such cases, the payback period can be computed by dividing the cash outflow in the initial period by the annual cash inflow. For example, if the annual cash inflow from the Diamond Corporation capital project were $30,000 each year, the payback period would be 3.17 years ($95,000 initial cash investment ÷ $30,000 annual cash inflow).

The Average Annual Return on Investment Method. This method is sometimes referred to as the accounting rate of return method or the financial statement method. When this method is used, an investment proposal is evaluated by comparing the estimated average annual rate of return on the investment with a target rate of return. The estimated rate of return for the Diamond Corporation project may be computed as follows:

Net income without deduction for depreciation (net aftertax cash
inflow, excluding salvage value) $173,000
Less financial accounting depreciation ($100,000 acquisition
cost less $10,000 salvage value)* 90,000
$ 83,000

Less tax expense on taxable gain from sale of asset at end of
economic life ($10,000 salvage value × 48%) 4,800
Net income over economic life of project .... $ 78,200

*Depreciation is assumed to be the only noncash expense and is thus the only adjustment required in converting from cash flow to accrual basis income.

$$\text{Average annual return on } \textit{original} \text{ investment} = \frac{\text{Net income}}{\text{Economic life}} \div \text{Original investment}$$

$$= \frac{\$78,200}{8 \text{ years}} \div \$100,000$$

$$= 9.775\%$$

Another approach to estimating a project's rate of return is to divide the average annual net income by the average investment rather than the original investment. The computation for the Diamond Corporation project is:

Original investment	$100,000
Investment at end of economic life (salvage value)	10,000
	$110,000
Average investment ($110,000 ÷ 2)..............................	$ 55,000*

*The original book value and the book value at the end of each year can be averaged if the straight-line depreciation method is not used for financial accounting purposes.

$$\text{Average annual return on } \textit{average} \text{ investment} = \frac{\text{Net income}}{\text{Economic life}} \div \text{Average investment}$$

$$= \frac{\$78,200}{8 \text{ years}} \div \$55,000$$

$$= 17.773\%$$

The Present Value Method. A dollar received a year hence is not the equivalent of a dollar received today, because the use of money has a value. To illustrate, if $500 can be invested at 20 percent, $600 will be received a year later ($500 + 20% of $500). The $600 to be received next year has a present value of $500 if 20 percent can be earned ($600 ÷ 120% = $500). The difference of $100 ($600 − $500) represents the time value of money. In line with this idea, the estimated results of an investment proposal can be stated at its present value, i.e., as a cash equivalent at the present time.[13]

Present value tables have been devised to facilitate the application of present value theory. The "Present Value of $1" table on page 777 presents computations to three decimal places and shows today's value, or the present value, of each dollar to be received or paid in the future for various rates of interest and periods of time.[14] By multiplying the appropriate factor obtained

---

[13]The basic formula for present value is:

$$PV = S\left[\frac{1}{(1 + i)^n}\right] \quad \text{or} \quad \left[\frac{S}{(1 + i)^n}\right] \quad \text{or} \quad S(1 + i)^{-n}$$

where PV = present value of future sum of money

S = future sum of money

i = earnings rate for each compounding period

n = number of periods

[14]Ordinary tables, such as those included in this chapter, assume that all cash flows occur at the end of each period and that interest is compounded at the end of each period. Either or both of these assumptions can be varied by the use of calculus so that, instead of assuming that the cash flows occur at the end of each period, they can occur continuously, and interest can be compounded continuously. Although the continuous assumptions often are more representative of actual conditions, the tables in this chapter are more frequently used in practice.

from the table times an expected future cash flow, the present value of the cash flow is easily determined.

The "Present Value of $1 Received or Paid Annually for Each of the Next N Years" table on page 778 shows the present value of a series of $1 periodic receipts or payments. This table is used when the cash flow is estimated to be the same each period. The relationship between this table and the "Present Value of $1" table on page 777 is as follows:

Period	Present Value of $1 at 12%	Present Value of $1 Received or Paid Annually for Each of the Next N Years at 12%
1	.893	.893
2	.797	1.690 (.893 + .797)
3	.712	2.402 (1.690 + .712)
4	.636	3.037 (2.402 + .636)*
5	.567	3.605
6	.507	4.111
7	.452	4.564
8	.404	4.968

*Difference of .001 results from rounding off the results of the formula.

If the flow is uniform, the flow for one period can be multiplied by the cumulative factor to obtain approximately the same answer as by multiplying the individual factors by the flow for each period and totaling the products. For example, if a project costing $20,000 is expected to yield a uniform annual aftertax cash flow of $5,000 for seven years, then the present value of the expected cash inflows, discounted at 12 percent, is $5,000 × 4.564, or $22,820, and the net present value is $2,820 ($22,820 − $20,000).[15]

The present value concept can be applied to the Diamond Corporation problem by discounting at the company's 12 percent estimated cost of capital. Some firms may set as their discount rate something in excess of the cost of capital or use different rates that depend on risk and uncertainty and other characteristics of a particular project. However, for the sake of uniformity for comparison purposes, it seems preferable to discount all proposals at a uniform rate, the cost of capital. Management can interject an allowance for risk and uncertainty and other characteristics peculiar to each specific proposal in the raw data or in the net present value answer.

For assets requiring a period of time to be made ready for use, the initial cash payment marks the project's origin, at which point the discount factor is 1.000. Subsequent cash payments related to the project's acquisition or construction are shown as outflows to be discounted back to the initial cash outflow date, along with net cash inflows associated with the investment's operating use.

The computation for Diamond Corporation is as follows:

---

[15]Although unusual in actual capital expenditure evaluation cases, uniform cash flow analysis is included here because it is occasionally required on professional examinations such as the CPA and CMA examinations.

Year	Cash (Outflow) Inflow	Present Value of $1 at 12%	Net Present Value of Cash Flow
0	$(95,000)	1.000	$(95,000)
1	32,000	.893	28,576
2	28,000	.797	22,316
3	24,000	.712	17,088
4	23,000	.636	14,628
5	22,000	.567	12,474
6	15,000	.507	7,605
7	14,000	.452	6,328
8	20,200*	.404	8,161
		Net present value	$22,176

*$15,000 + $5,200

The positive net present value of $22,176 indicates that the true rate of return is greater than the cost of capital discount rate. A net present value of zero would indicate a rate of return of exactly 12 percent.

A project's useful life is one of the uncertainties often associated with capital expenditure evaluations. Equipment obsolescence or shifts in market demands may occur. The conventional payback method determines the time necessary to recover the initial outlay, without regard to present value considerations. However, management may wish to know the minimum life for a project necessary to recover the original investment and earn a desired rate of return on the investment. The *present value payback* calculation focuses on this question and is computed for Diamond Corporation as follows, using the "net present value of cash flow" figures shown above:

Year	Net Present Value of Cash Flow	Recovery of Initial Outlay Needed	Recovery of Initial Outlay Balance	Present Value Payback Years Required
1	$28,576	$95,000	$66,424	1.0
2	22,316	66,424	44,108	1.0
3	17,088	44,108	27,020	1.0
4	14,628	27,020	12,392	1.0
5	12,474	12,392	0	.99
Total present value payback in years				4.99

Based on the present value of estimated cash flows, 4.99 years will be required to recover the $95,000 original cash investment and earn a desired 12 percent rate of return on the annual unrecovered balance. Additionally, the present value payback will be shortened by the present value of the project's salvage value.

The Discounted Cash Flow (DCF) Method. In the present value method, the discount rate is known or at least predetermined. In the discounted cash flow method, the discount rate is not known but is defined as the rate at which the sum of positive present values equals the sum of negative present values. This discount rate is sometimes referred to as the internal rate of return. Present value theory is used, but the analysis is developed further to determine the discounted rate of return, which is then compared with some standard.

The discounted rate of return for Diamond Corporation can be determined by trial and error, i. e., by computing net present value at various discount rates to find the rate at which the net present value is zero. This computation is illustrated in the following table:

Year	Cash (Outflow) Inflow	Present Value of $1 at 18%	Net Present Value of Cash Flow	Present Value of $1 at 20%	Net Present Value of Cash Flow
0	$(95,000)	1.000	$(95,000)	1.000	$(95,000)
1	32,000	.847	27,104	.833	26,656
2	28,000	.718	20,104	.694	19,432
3	24,000	.609	14,616	.579	13,896
4	23,000	.516	11,868	.482	11,086
5	22,000	.437	9,614	.402	8,844
6	15,000	.370	5,550	.335	5,025
7	14,000	.314	4,396	.279	3,906
8	20,200	.266	5,373	.233	4,707
			$ 3,625		$ (1,448)

The discounted rate is greater than 18 percent and less than 20 percent. The trial-and-error search should continue until adjacent rates in the table are found—one rate yielding a positive net present value with the other rate yielding a negative net present value, and both as close to zero as possible.

Expanded present value tables permit the determination of a net present value nearer zero. However, an approximation is obtainable by interpolation, as follows:

$$18\% + \left[2\% \times \frac{\$3,625}{\$3,625 + \$1,448} \right] = 18\% + [(2\%)(.715)] = 19.43\%$$

The discounted cash flow method permits management to maximize corporate profits by selecting proposals with the highest rates of return, as long as the rates are higher than the company's cost of capital plus management's allowance for risk and uncertainty and individual project characteristics. In most circumstances, the use of the discounted cash flow instead of the present value method at a given interest rate will not seriously alter the ranking of projects.

Note that the rate of return, using either the discounted cash flow method or the present value method, is computed on the basis of the unrecovered cash outflow from period to period, not on the original cash investment. In the illustration, the DCF rate of return of 19.43 percent denotes that, over the eight years, the aftertax cash inflow equals the recovery of the original cash investment plus a return of 19.43 percent on the unrecovered cash investment from period to period. The net present value of $22,176 (page 753) indicates that, over the eight years, this additional amount, or a total of $117,176 ($95,000 + $22,176), could have been spent on the machine; and the original cash investment, plus a return of 12 percent on the unrecovered cash investment from period to period, could still have been recovered.

Advantages and Disadvantages of the Evaluation Techniques. The following lists present several advantages and disadvantages of the four evaluation
techniques that have been discussed.

THE PAYBACK (OR PAYOUT) PERIOD METHOD

Advantages

1. It is simple to compute and easy to understand.
2. It may be used to select those investments yielding a quick return of
   cash, thus placing an emphasis on liquidity.
3. It permits a company to determine the length of time required to
   recapture its original investment, thus offering a possible indicator of
   the degree of risk of each investment. Such an indicator is especially
   useful when the danger of obsolescence is great.
4. It is a widely used method that is certainly an improvement over a
   hunch, rule of thumb, or intuitive method.

Disadvantages

1. It ignores the time value of money. To illustrate this disadvantage,
   assume that the "Net Aftertax Cash Inflow" for Diamond Corporation
   had been: year 1, $62,000; year 2, $16,000; year 3, $14,000; and year
   4, $6,250 — with the same 8-year total. The computation would be:

		Recovery of Initial Outlay		Payback Years
Year	Cash Flow	Needed	Balance	Required
1	$62,000	$95,000	$33,000	1.00
2	16,000	33,000	17,000	1.00
3	14,000	17,000	3,000	1.00
4	6,250	3,000	0	.48
Total payback period in years				3.48

   In both this example and the example on page 750, the payback period is 3.48 years. In this example, however, $30,000 more was re-
   ceived in the first year ($62,000 − $32,000). This situation is more
   desirable from an investment standpoint because money has a time
   value; that is, a dollar is worth more the earlier it is received.
2. It ignores cash flows which may occur beyond the payback period. In
   the example on page 750, the payback period is 3.48 years, the economic life is 8 years, and the "Net Aftertax Cash Inflow" is $178,200.
   Assume that an alternative project indicates a "Net Aftertax Cash
   Inflow" of $95,000 in the first two years and an economic life of
   three years, with "Net Aftertax Cash Inflow" of $10,000 in the third
   year. Although the latter case has a shorter payback period, the original example of a 3.48-year payback and net cash inflow of $178,200
   is more desirable when immediate cash problems are not of critical importance.
3. It fails to consider salvage value which may exist after the payback period.

THE AVERAGE ANNUAL RETURN ON INVESTMENT METHOD

Advantages

1. It facilitates expenditure follow-up due to more readily available data from accounting records.
2. It considers income over the entire life of the project.

Disadvantages

1. It ignores the time value of money. Two projects might have the same average return, yet vary considerably in the pattern of flow of cash. In such a case, the recognition of the time value of money would point to the desirability of the alternative having greater cash flow in the earlier periods.
2. Inflation's effect is expected to be included in cash flow estimates. But a calculation of net income based on historical cost depreciation and the expression of net income as a return on an investment, which is also stated at historical cost, may be quite misleading.
3. The average return on the original investment technique is inapplicable if any of the investment is made after the beginning of the project.

THE PRESENT VALUE METHOD

Advantages

1. It considers the time value of money.
2. It considers cash flow over the entire life of the project.

Disadvantages

1. Some argue that this method is too difficult to compute and to understand.
2. Management must determine a discount rate to be used. However, a well-informed management should already be aware of its cost of capital that should represent the benchmark for discount rate purposes.
3. If projects being compared involve different dollar amounts of investment, the project with more profitable dollars, as computed by the present value method, may not be the better project if it also requires a larger investment. For example, a net present value of $1,000 on an investment of $100,000 is not as economically wise as a net present value of $900 on an investment of $10,000, provided that the $90,000 difference in investments can be used to realize a net present value of at least $101 in other projects. In this case, a net present value index should be used rather than the net present value dollar figure. This index places all competing projects on a comparable basis for the purpose of ranking them. For Diamond Corporation, the computation is:

$$\text{Net present value index} = \frac{\text{Net present value}}{\text{Required investment}} = \frac{\$22,176}{\$95,000} = .233$$

This index simplifies finding the optimum solution for competing projects when the total budget for capital outlays is fixed arbitrarily, because it is possible to rank by percentages rather than absolute dollars.

4. It may be misleading when dealing with alternative projects or limited funds under the condition of unequal lives, in that the alternative with the higher net present value may involve longer economic life to the point that it would be less desirable than an alternative having a shorter life. The problem of dealing with alternatives having unequal lives is discussed on page 758.

THE DISCOUNTED CASH FLOW RATE OF RETURN

Advantages

1. It considers the time value of money.
2. It considers cash flow over the entire life of the project.
3. The percentage figure may have more meaning for management than the net present value or net present value index.
4. The percentage figure allows a generally sound, uniform ranking of projects which require different initial cash outlays and have unequal lives.

Disadvantages

1. Some argue that this method is too difficult to compute and to understand.
2. It implies that cash flow is reinvested at the rate earned by the investment, whereas the present value method implies that cash flow is reinvested at the rate of discount. It is argued that the latter assumption is more reasonable.

Other Situations and Considerations

The following topics related to evaluating capital expenditure proposals require a brief discussion: the error cushion, alternatives having unequal lives, purchase versus leasing, sensitivity analysis, allowance for risk and uncertainty via probability estimates, and computer usage for evaluation analysis.

The Error Cushion.   A project whose estimated desirability is near a cutoff point for the type of project being evaluated affords little cushion for errors. For example, if the management of a chain of automotive muffler shops anticipates that a new location should yield a minimum discounted cash flow of 12 percent, there is obviously a greater cushion for errors when the computed rate of return is 20 percent as opposed to 13 percent. Similarly, when one alternative is clearly superior to others for a particular project, there is a better cushion against errors than when two or more of the best alternatives indicate approximately the same expected results.

Reasonably accurate estimates are desirable in evaluating any project. However, a higher degree of sophistication and care, at a higher cost of obtaining the data, may be necessary to add confidence when the evaluation is close to a cutoff point or when two or more project alternatives yield about the same "best" answer. Conversely, in many cases, the desirability of a project or the selection from alternatives for a particular project will be so obvious that the costs of making sophisticated data estimates and using evaluation techniques are not justified.

Alternatives Having Unequal Lives. An additional difficulty in capital expenditure evaluation arises when alternatives with different economic lives are compared. To illustrate, a firm may be faced with the problem of acquiring equipment for a manufacturing operation. Two alternatives are available: Equipment A, expected to last 18 years, and Equipment B, expected to last 5 years. There are two ways to deal with this problem:

1. Repeat the investment cycle for Equipment B a sufficient number of times to cover the estimated economic life of Equipment A; in the example, 3⅗ times. An estimate of the salvage value of the fourth equipment investment cycle for Equipment B at the end of the life for Equipment A is needed in order to reflect a common termination date.
2. The period considered can be the life of the shorter-life alternative, Equipment B, coupled with an estimate of the recoverable value of Equipment A at the end of 5 years. The analysis would then cover only the five-year period, with the recoverable value of Equipment A being treated as a cash inflow at the end of the period. A serious difficulty rests in the need to estimate a value of the longer-life asset at the end of 5 years. Such an intermediate recoverable value may not be an adequate measure of the service value of the equipment at that point in its useful life.

Purchase vs. Leasing. A lease arrangement may be available as an alternative to investment in a capital asset. This possibility can be evaluated by determining the incremental annual cost of leasing versus purchasing. This cost represents purchasing cost savings which, on an aftertax basis, should be sufficient to yield the desired DCF rate of return on the anticipated purchase price.

In evaluating the leasing and purchasing alternatives, the present value method can be used as an alternative to the DCF method in either of two ways:

1. The net present value of the purchase price and the associated aftertax savings is computed, with the resulting net present value used to evaluate the attractiveness of purchasing versus leasing.
2. The net present values of the purchasing alternative and the leasing alternative cash flows are computed separately, each on an aftertax

basis. The alternative having the more favorable net present value identifies the preferable choice.

Generally, the capital expenditure or investment decision is first justified, followed by the lease or financing decision. The rationale is that the acquisition must be a sound investment before considering the financing strategy and the operating flexibility, obsolescence, and service/maintenance factors associated with leases versus purchases. With a justified capital expenditure in hand, a lease-purchase decision can be made.[16]

Usually the lease is the more expensive alternative, since a lease involves avoiding various ownership risks for which a price must be paid. In such cases, a relevant question then becomes whether or not the extra cost entailed in leasing is worth paying in order to avoid risks of ownership. Management may prefer leasing if it is thereby able to improve balance sheet position by avoiding a purchase liability. Also, the rate of return on capital employed would be enhanced by reducing the investment in capital assets.[17] However, generally accepted accounting principles prescribe rules that require the capitalization and the recording of an associated liability for leases that are determined to be, in effect, purchases.[18]

Sensitivity Analysis.   A comparison of the results of the present value or discounted cash flow techniques with the cost of capital is useful in helping management to arrive at a decision. However, management is never entirely assured, since many estimates enter into quantitative analyses. Any element of the project—revenue, cost, or the investment itself—is subject to variations or changes. Certain estimates are more sensitive to variations than others. Under these circumstances, the analyst must present a variety of possible results using numerous figures, so that management can judge the impact of all possibilities. This type of approach, called *sensitivity analysis*, indicates in graphic or tabular form the effect of one project factor on another.

To illustrate, assume that a new product, X, was developed on the basis of a sales price of $.38 per gallon and at that price, the expected DCF rate of return was 26 percent. An expanded analysis showing the rates of return at sales prices ranging from $.34 to $.41 per gallon would be a form of sensitivity analysis. Variations in price, volume, labor cost, materials cost, and project investment are factors usually considered in such calculations. They are varied

---

[16]William L. Ferrara, *The Lease-Purchase Decison: How Some Companies Make It* (New York: National Association of Accountants; Hamilton, Ontario: The Society of Management Accountants of Canada, 1978), p. 7. For a detailed discussion of the lease-purchase decision model, see William L. Ferrara, James B. Thies, and Mark W. Dirsmith, *The Lease-Purchase Decision* (New York: National Association of Accountants, 1980; Hamilton, Ontario: The Society of Management Accountants of Canada, 1979).

[17]Lawrence A. Gordon, Danny Miller, and Henry Mintzberg, *Normative Models in Managerial Decision-Making* (New York: National Association of Accountants; Hamilton, Ontario: The Society of Industrial Accountants of Canada, 1975), p. 67.

[18]*Statement of Financial Accounting Standards*, No. 13, "Accounting for Leases" (Stamford: Financial Accounting Standards Board, 1976).

singly or in combination. For example, assume that the range of DCF rates of return was based on an assumption that the primary raw material, Z, would cost $.28 per gallon. The range of rates of return with the sales price ranging from $.34 to $.41 per gallon could also be computed if the possible costs of the primary raw material were $.29 and $.27.

The following graph presents this illustration, assuming that a plant having a capacity of five million gallons per year and an economic life of ten years will require a $600,000 investment. Annual sales volume is also assumed to be five million gallons. The DCF rate of return can be read for the various combinations of Product X sales prices and Material Z costs.

Sensitivity Analysis Graph

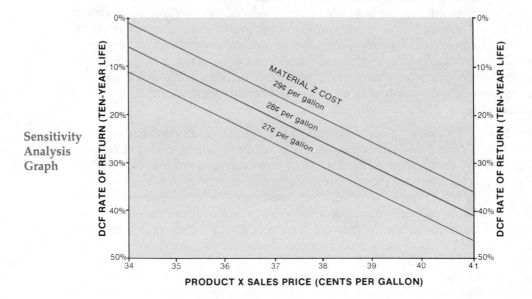

Sensitivity analysis is useful in planning and in a variety of decision-making analyses in which the estimated impact of changed assumptions are relevant, such as in developing long-range plans, the annual budget, break-even and cost-volume-profit analysis, differential cost analysis, and linear programming. The usefulness of data can be further enhanced by injecting probability estimates to allow for risk and uncertainty in order to indicate how likely it appears that the sales price or other factors will vary.

Allowance for Risk and Uncertainty via Probability Estimates. Risk and uncertainty must be considered when cash flows for an investment project are being estimated, because ever-present uncertainty creates a degree of risk in the ultimate occurrence of any set of assumptions used. To assist management in the final decision, the analyst may resort to a presentation of a multilevel project estimate to indicate the possible outcomes, with a probability estimate for each. This risk analysis is an extension of sensitivity analysis.

The following procedure is one possible method for dealing with risk and uncertainty:

1. Determine the net present value of the net cash flows for three different assumptions:
   a. Most probable series of events.
   b. A reasonably pessimistic series of events.
   c. A reasonably optimistic series of events.
2. Assign probabilities to the three net present values, using the best information available or standard weights.
3. The sum of the three expected net present values may be used to represent the expected value of the investment, taking risk and uncertainty into consideration to a limited degree.

This procedure is illustrated as follows:

	Net Present Value (Conditional Value)	Probability	Expected Net Present Value
Most probable (from page 753)	$22,176	.50	$11,088
Pessimistic assumptions	5,000	.30	1,500
Optimistic assumptions	35,000	.20	7,000
Expected net present value (expected value)			$19,588

The standard deviation and coefficient of variation can be computed as follows:

(1) Net Present Value (Conditional Value)	(2) Difference from Expected Value ($19,588)	(3) (2) Squared	(4) Probability	(5) (3) × (4)
$22,176	$ 2,588	6,697,744	.50	$ 3,348,872
5,000	−14,588	212,809,744	.30	63,842,923
35,000	15,412	237,529,744	.20	47,505,949
				$114,697,744

Standard deviation = $\sqrt{\$114,697,744}$ = $10,710

$$\text{Coefficient of variation} = \frac{\$10,710}{\$19,588} = .55$$

Allowing for risk and uncertainty can be further demonstrated by referring to the illustration introduced on page 759 in the discussion of sensitivity analysis. Assume that probability estimates are made as follows:

Material Z Cost	Probability of Occurrence	Product X Sales Price	Probability of Occurrence
$.29	20%	$.39	30%
.28	70	.38	30
.27	10	.37	40
	100%		100%

The annual sales volume is expected to be five million gallons. In this example, the sales price variation is assumed to be independent of materials cost and volume; hence, it may increase, remain the same, or decrease at any of the three Material Z costs. Other sales prices and Material Z costs are assumed to have a zero probability of occurrence. The resulting nine possible outcomes for these assumptions and their related probabilities are:

(1)	(2)	(3)	(4)	(5)	(6)	(7)
Material Z		Product X		Combined Probability (2) × (4)	DCF Rate of Return* (Conditional Value)	Expected DCF Rate of Return (5) × (6)
Cost	Probability	Sales Price	Probability			
	.20	$.39	.30	.06	.26	.0156
$.29	.20	.38	.30	.06	.21	.0126
	.20	.37	.40	.08	.16	.0128
	.70	.39	.30	.21	.31	.0651
.28	.70	.38	.30	.21	.26	.0546
	.70	.37	.40	.28	.21	.0588
	.10	.39	.30	.03	.36	.0108
.27	.10	.38	.30	.03	.31	.0093
	.10	.37	.40	.04	.26	.0104
				1.00		

Expected DCF rate of return (expected value) . . . .   .2500 = 25%

*These rates were read from the graph on page 760.

The standard deviation and coefficient of variation are:

(1) DCF Rate of Return (Conditional Value)	(2) Difference from Expected Value (25%)	(3) (2) Squared	(4) Probability	(5) (3) × (4)
26%	1%	1%	.06	.06%
21	−4	16	.06	.96
16	−9	81	.08	6.48
31	6	36	.21	7.56
26	1	1	.21	.21
21	−4	16	.28	4.48
36	11	121	.03	3.63
31	6	36	.03	1.08
26	1	1	.04	.04
				24.5%

Standard deviation = $\sqrt{24.5\%}$ = 4.9%

Coefficient of variation = $\dfrac{4.9\%}{25\%}$ = .20

Not only is the expected DCF rate of return of 25 percent useful to management, but the cumulative probabilities of realizing a rate of return at least equal to each of the various rates are also useful. Beginning with the highest rate for the nine possibilities, the following cumulative probabilities can be determined:

DCF Rate of Return	Cumulative Probability
36%	.03
31	.27 (.03 + .21 + .03)
26	.58 (.27 + .06 + .21 + .04)
21	.92 (.58 + .06 + .28)
16	1.00 (.92 + .08)

Thus, there is a .03 probability that the rate of return will be 36 percent, a .27 probability that the rate will be at least 31 percent, a .58 probability that the rate will be at least 26 percent, etc.

Many economic variables are not independent of one another; e.g., the materials cost may influence the sales price of the finished product. If there is dependence of the variables, computational procedures must be modified by substituting *conditional probabilities*.

The illustration from the previous page can be used to demonstrate variable dependence when the sales price is presumed to be influenced by materials cost. Assume the same probabilities for Material Z cost as before, but assume that the Product X sales price probabilities will be influenced by Material Z cost as follows:

Product X Sales Price	*Material Z Cost—$.29*	*Material Z Cost—$.28*	*Material Z Cost—$.27*
	Probability of Sales Price		
$.39	60%	40%	20%
.38	30	40	30
.37	10	20	50
	100%	100%	100%

The resulting nine possible outcomes for these assumptions and their related probabilities are summarized as follows. Observe that conditional probabilities have been substituted into Column 4.

(1)	(2)	(3)	(4)	(5)	(6)	(7)
Material Z		Product X		Combined Probability	DCF Rate of Return (Conditional Value)	Expected DCF Rate of Return
Cost	Probability	Sales Price	Conditional Probability	(2) × (4)		(5) × (6)
$.29	.20	$.39	.60	.12	.26	.0312
	.20	.38	.30	.06	.21	.0126
	.20	.37	.10	.02	.16	.0032
.28	.70	.39	.40	.28	.31	.0868
	.70	.38	.40	.28	.26	.0728
	.70	.37	.20	.14	.21	.0294
.27	.10	.39	.20	.02	.36	.0072
	.10	.38	.30	.03	.31	.0093
	.10	.37	.50	.05	.26	.0130
				1.00		

Expected DCF rate of return (expected value) .... .2655 = 26.55%

Again, the standard deviation and coefficient of variation are:

(1) DCF Rate of Return (Conditional Value)	(2) Difference from Expected Value (27%)*	(3) (2) Squared	(4) Probability	(5) (3) × (4)
26%	− 1%	1%	.12	.12%
21	− 6	36	.06	2.16
16	−11	121	.02	2.42
31	4	16	.28	4.48
26	− 1	1	.28	.28
21	− 6	36	.14	5.04
36	9	81	.02	1.62
31	4	16	.03	.48
26	− 1	1	.05	.05
				16.65%

*26.55% rounded = 27%

$$\text{Standard deviation} = \sqrt{16.65\%} = 4.1\%$$

$$\text{Coefficient of variation} = \frac{4.1\%}{26.55\%} = .15$$

Computer Usage for Evaluation Analysis. Electronic data processing equipment offers the analyst an opportunity to expand the investment evaluation analysis beyond a mere handful of manual computations. The computer permits the creation of numerous models that simulate various possibilities of expected results. The main purpose of the simulation process is to improve the quality of management's decisions by offering new and more reliable information and guidance. Whenever the key factors in a business problem are susceptible to various patterns of variations, the use of models and simulation will be especially helpful. It should be understood that even the most sophisticated and computerized analytical methods do not relieve management of the all-important task of making the final decision.

Controlling Capital Expenditures

The phase of controlling capital expenditures consists of (1) control and review of a project while it is in process and (2) follow-up or post-completion audit of project results.

Control While in Process

When a project or a series of projects has finally been approved, methods, techniques, and procedures must be set in motion to permit the control and review of all project elements (costs, time, quality, and quantity) until completion. Control responsibility should be clearly designated, recognizing the necessity of assistance from and coordination with many individuals and groups, including those external to the company. Actual results should be compared with approved plans and evaluation results. Variations or trends toward deviations from plans should be reported promptly to responsible authorities in order to facilitate corrective action as quickly as possible. Day-to-day, on-the-scene observation and up-to-date reports should provide good cost control vehicles. Construction engineers have long used such devices as bar charts for planning and controlling the timing of project activities.

PERT/cost (Chapter 15) utilizes the network scheme to show the inter-relationships of the multiple activities required to complete the average to large-scale project. Any project—the installation of a single large machine, a complex of machinery and equipment, or the construction of a new factory or office building—will involve many diverse tasks. Some of them can be done simultaneously; others must await the completion of preceding activities. PERT/cost offers a clear and all-inclusive picture of the operation as a whole in contrast to the bars on a chart. The use of this technique is particularly appropriate for those evaluation cases where more than one estimate is needed due to risk and uncertainty and there is a desire to expedite and increase the reliability of difficult estimates.

The cost of administering the control phase should be commensurate with the value derived. Overcontrol is an inefficient use of administrative resources.

Follow-Up of Project Results

Follow-up or post-completion audit means comparing and reporting re-sults as related to the outcome predicted when the investment project was evaluated and approved. Follow-up affords a test of the existing planning and control procedure and therein the possibility of reinforcing successful projects, salvaging or terminating failing projects, and improving upon future investment proposals and decisions.

The same techniques used to evaluate the proposed project should be used for follow-up. For example, if the DCF rate of return projected in support of a project proposal is compared, in the follow-up procedure, with the actual average annual return on investment, the comparison could be quite mis-leading. Instead, the projected DCF rate should be compared to a DCF rate based on actual data and a reestimation of future data, thus employing the same evaluation technique in the follow-up as in evaluating the project proposal.

Follow-up should aid in determining the optimal point for project aban-donment. For example, if the present value of estimated aftertax cash flows for a project's remaining life is less than the aftertax disposal value, it should be abandoned.

Generally, actual work in the area of follow-up lags behind advances made in other capital expenditure phases. Common hindrances to follow-up proce-dures are management's unwillingness to incur additional administrative costs, difficulty of quantifying the results of certain types of investments, apparent failure of the accounting or cost system to produce needed informa-tion, lack of personnel qualified to perform the follow-up tasks, and resent-ment by those being audited.

Value received as related to the cost of obtaining the follow-up information should determine the extent of the follow-up. For uniformity, efficiency, and independent review, management should designate a centralized group to prescribe procedures and audit the performance of the follow-up activity. The assembled data should be utilized as a control device and be reported to the controlling levels of management. Out-of-line results should then trigger corrective action in harmony with the management by exception principle.

DISCUSSION QUESTIONS

1. Explain the nature of capital expenditure planning and control.

2. Why are effective planning and control of capital expenditures important?

3. Differentiate between the economic and physical life of a project.

4. Describe the procedure for computing the weighted average cost of capital.
(CMA adapted)

5. Why would a firm use its weighted average cost of capital as the hurdle rate (minimum rate) for a project investment decision, rather than the specific marginal cost of funds?

6. (a) Is depreciation deducted for tax purposes likely to differ from book (or financial accounting) depreciation? Explain.
   (b) Should book depreciation be considered in estimating the future cash flows from a proposed project? Explain.
   (c) Should tax depreciation be considered in estimating the future cash flows from a proposed project? Explain.

7. Financial accounting data are not entirely suitable for use in evaluating capital expenditures. Explain.
(AICPA adapted)

8. Define the payback (or payout) period method.

9. How do the two average annual return on investment methods differ?

10. Modern capital expenditure evaluation uses the present value concept. Explain this concept.

11. What is the basic difference between the payback method and the present value method?
(AICPA adapted)

12. Virginia Company invested in a four-year project, with an expected rate of return of 10%. Annual cash inflow from the project, net of income tax, was estimated to be: year 1, $4,000; year 2, $4,400; year 3, $4,800; year 4, $5,200. Assuming a positive net present value of $1,000, what was the amount of the original investment?
(AICPA adapted)

13. Hilltop Company invested $100,000 in a two-year project. Hilltop's expected DCF rate of return was 12%. The cash flow, net of income tax, was $40,000 for the first year. Assuming that the DCF rate of return was exactly 12%, what was the cash flow, net of income tax, for the second year of the project?
(AICPA adapted)

14. Discuss the difference between the net present value and the discounted cash flow rate of return methods.

15. Both the present value method and the discounted cash flow method assume that the earnings produced by a project are reinvested in the company. However, each approach assumes a different rate of return at which earnings are reinvested. Describe the rate of return assumed in each of the two approaches and discuss which of the assumed rates is more realistic.
(CGAA adapted)

16. Define sensitivity analysis.

17. Distinguish between independent and conditional probabilities.

18. Discuss benefits to be derived from a follow-up of project results.
(CMA adapted)

EXERCISES

1. *Cost of capital.* Babcock Company wishes to compute a weighted average cost of capital for use in evaluating capital expenditure proposals. Earnings, capital structure, and current market prices of the company's securities are:

Earnings

Earnings before interest and income tax............................	$210,000
Interest expense on bonds..	30,000
Pretax earnings	$180,000
Income tax (assume 45% tax rate).................................	81,000
Aftertax earnings	$ 99,000
Preferred stock dividends..	24,000
Earnings available to common stockholders........................	$ 75,000
Common stock dividends	30,000
Increase in retained earnings	$ 45,000

Capital structure

Mortgage bonds, 10%, 10 years...................................	$ 300,000
Preferred stock, 12%, $100 par value	200,000
Common stock, no par, 50,000 shares outstanding	350,000
Retained earnings (equity of common stockholders)	150,000
	$1,000,000

Market prices of the company's securities

Preferred stock...	$96
Common stock	10

Required: Determine the cost of capital, using the method illustrated in the chapter.

2. *Cost of capital.* Electro Tool Company, a manufacturer of diamond drilling, cutting, and grinding tools, has $1,000,000 of its 8% bond issue maturing next month. To meet this debt, an additional $1,000,000 must be raised, and one proposal under consideration is the sale and leaseback of the company's general office building.

The building would be sold to FHR Inc. for $1,000,000 and leased back on a 25-year lease, with annual payments of $110,168, permitting the lessor to recover its investment and earn 10% on the investment. Electro Tool will pay all maintenance costs, property taxes, and insurance and will reacquire the building at the end of the lease period for a nominal payment.

The current capital structure is:

Capital Component	Amount	Pretax Component Cost
Bonds (including amount to be retired next month).............................	$5,000,000	8.0%
Preferred stock (market value)	1,000,000	9.0
Common stock and retained earnings (market value)	4,000,000	12.5

Electro Tool's income tax rate is 40%.

Required: Compute the weighted average cost of capital before and after the bond retirement and the sale-leaseback transaction.   *(CMA adapted)*

3. *Payback and average annual return on investment methods.* Plastics Inc. is considering the purchase of a $40,000 machine, which will be depreciated on the straight-line basis over an eight-year period with no salvage value for both book and tax purposes. The machine is expected to generate net cash inflow before income tax of $12,000 a year. Assume that the income tax rate is 40% and there is no investment tax credit.

Required:
   (1) Determine the payback period.
   (2) What is the average annual return on original investment?   *(AICPA adapted)*

4. *Investment analysis; uniform cash flow.* Apex Company is evaluating a capital budgeting proposal, requiring an initial investment of $30,000. The project will have a six-year life. The aftertax annual cash inflow due to this investment is $10,000. The desired rate of return is 15%.

Required:
   (1) What is the payback period?
   (2) Compute the net present value of the project.
   (3) What amount would Apex have had to have invested five years ago, at 15% compounded annually, to have $30,000 now?   *(AICPA adapted)*

5. *Equipment investment analysis; net present value and present value index.* Futura Corporation is considering purchasing a new press, requiring an immediate $100,000 cash outlay. The new press is expected to increase annual net aftertax cash receipts by $40,000 for the next three years, after which it will be sold for $30,000, after taxes. The company desires a mimimum return of 16% on invested capital.

Required:
   (1) Compute the net present value of the project.
   (2) Compute the net present value index.

6. *Effect of depreciation methods on cash flow.* More Corporation is planning to acquire a machine for one of its projects at a cost of $100,000. The machine has an economic life of eight years, but since it is five-year-class property under ACRS, the entire cost will be recovered for tax purposes in five years. The company's cost of capital rate is 14%, and the income tax rate is 40%.

Required: Determine the present value of the income tax benefits which result from the use of the ACRS recovery percentages as opposed to the straight-line depreciation alternative over the same recovery period. (Ignore the potential effect of the investment tax credit on the depreciable basis for income tax purposes.)

7. *Effect of inflation on investment decision.* McLoud Company is evaluating a capital budgeting proposal which will require an initial cash investment of $60,000. The project will have a five-year life. The net aftertax cash inflows from the project, before any adjustment for the effects of inflation, are expected to be as follows:

Year	Unadjusted Estimate of Cash Inflows
1	$20,000
2	18,000
3	16,000
4	10,000
5	10,000

No salvage is expected at the end of the project. Cash inflows are expected to increase at the anticipated inflation rate of 10% each year. The company's cost of capital rate is 15%.

Required:
    (1) *Compute the estimated cash inflow for each year, adjusted for the anticipated effects of inflation.*
    (2) *Determine the net present value of the cash flows before and after the adjustment for the anticipated effects of inflation.*

  8. *Equipment replacement analysis. Kipling Company purchased a special machine one year ago at a cost of $10,000. At that time, the machine was estimated to have a useful life of 6 years and a $500 disposal value. An ACRS tax deduction of $1,500 was taken in the year of acquisition. The annual cash operating cost is approximately $20,100.*

    A new machine that has just come on the market will do the same job but with an annual cash operating cost of only $16,000. This new machine costs $17,000 and has an estimated life of 5 years with no expected salvage value. The old machine could be used as a trade-in at an allowance of $5,000. The tax basis of the old machine is $8,500.

    The new machine qualifies as five-year property under ACRS, and the income tax rate is 40%. The company's cost of capital is 12%.

Required: *Make a recommendation to management, based on the DCF rate of return. (Ignore the investment tax credit in your computations.)*

  9. *Net present value and DCF rate of return reinvestment assumption. Aftertax cash flows adjusted for effects of inflation for two mutually exclusive projects (with economic lives of 5 years each) are:*

Year	Project A	Project B
0	$(15,000)	$(15,000)
1	5,000	0
2	5,000	0
3	5,000	0
4	5,000	0
5	5,000	35,000

The company's cost of capital is 15%.

Required:
    (1) *Compute the discounted cash flow rate of return for each project.*
    (2) *Determine the net present value for each project.*
    (3) *Which project should be selected?*

  10. *Allowing for risk and uncertainty in present value calculations. The administrator of Portland Municipal Hospital is considering the purchase of new operating room equipment at a cost of $7,500. The surgical staff has furnished the following estimates of useful life and cost savings. Each useful life estimate is independent of each cost savings estimate.*

Years of Estimated Useful Life	Probability of Occurrence	Aftertax Estimated Cost Savings	Probability of Occurrence
4	.25	$1,900	.30
5	.50	2,000	.40
6	.25	2,100	.30
	1.00		1.00

Required:
(1) *Compute the net present value, allowing for risk and uncertainty and using a 10% discount rate. (Round computations to the nearest dollar.)*
(2) *Compute the standard deviation and the coefficient of variation (rounded to two decimal places) for the present value calculations of estimated cost savings before deducting the investment.*

PROBLEMS

26-1. Capital expenditure analysis. Vekany Steel Company is considering a process computer for improved production control in its Tin Mill Department. This department receives coils of cold rolled steel from another department of the company. It further reduces the gage of this steel in its own five-stand tandem cold strip mill. The coils of steel, now much thinner in gage, pass through a continuous annealing line, where the strip is heated to 1300 degrees Fahrenheit and allowed to cool slowly in an atmosphere of inert gas. The strip is then cleaned in a pickling line before it moves to the electrolytic tinning line. This last process deposits a thin coating of tin on the continuously moving strip. The coiled tin plate is then shipped to customers in the canning industry.

The Tin Mill Department estimates that the proposed process computer will require an investment of $2,200,000. Resulting aftertax cash savings from reduced costs of labor, materials, utilities, and scrap losses over the useful life of the computer are estimated to be:

Year	Amount
1	$ 300,000
2	350,000
3	400,000
4	450,000
5	500,000
6	550,000
7	600,000
8	650,000
9	700,000
10	750,000
	$5,250,000

Required: With respect to the proposed capital expenditure, compute the following:
(1) The payout period.
(2) The average annual return on original investment, rounded to the nearest $\frac{1}{10}$ of 1%.
(3) The average annual return on average investment, rounded to the nearest $\frac{1}{10}$ of 1%.
(4) The net present value at an assumed 14% cost of capital.
(5) The discounted cash flow rate of return.

26-2. Comparison of equipment alternatives. Two machines are being evaluated for possible acquisition by the Maxwell Corporation. Forecasts relating to the two machines are:

	Machine 1	Machine 2
Purchase price	$ 500,000	$ 600,000
Estimated economic life	8 years	8 years
Estimated salvage value	none	none
Annual aftertax cash benefit:		
Year 1	$ 125,000	$ 50,000
Year 2	125,000	75,000
Year 3	125,000	100,000
Year 4	125,000	125,000
Year 5	125,000	150,000
Year 6	125,000	200,000
Year 7	125,000	300,000
Year 8	125,000	400,000
Total cash benefit	$1,000,000	$1,400,000

Required: For each equipment alternative, compute the following:
(1) The payback period.
(2) The average annual return on original investment, rounded to the nearest ¹⁄₁₀ of 1%.
(3) The average annual return on average investment, rounded to the nearest ¹⁄₁₀ of 1%.
(4) The net present value and the net present value index, rounded to three decimal places, using an assumed 15% cost of capital.
(5) The discounted cash flow rate of return.

26-3. Feasibility study. Slalom Inc. is considering a proposed addition to its Hidden Valley, Colorado, ski lift facilities, which will require an investment of $1,300,000 and will have a 5-year useful life with no salvage value. The investment tax credit is available on all of the proposed property acquisition at the rate of 10% of cost. The income tax rate is 40%. The company has sufficient income from other sources to absorb any losses that might be generated from the proposed addition to its facilities in the year in which the loss is incurred. The estimated revenue and expenses over the life of the project, adjusted for the effects of inflation, are:

Estimated Revenue and Expenses
(thousands of dollars)

	Year					
	1	2	3	4	5	Total
Revenue	$ 500	$1,000	$2,000	$2,500	$3,000	$9,000
Cash expenses	475	887	$1,461	1,891	1,931	6,645
Net pretax cash inflow	$ 25	$ 113	$ 539	$ 609	$1,069	$2,355
Tax depreciation	185	273	259	259	259	1,235
Taxable income (loss)	$(160)	$ (160)	$ 280	$ 350	$ 810	$1,120
Income tax expense	$ (64)	$ (64)	$ 112	$ 140	$ 324	$ 448
Investment tax credit	(130)	0	0	0	0	(130)
Income tax net of credit	$(194)	$ (64)	$ 112	$ 140	$ 324	$ 318

Required: With respect to the proposed addition, compute the following:
(1) The payback period.
(2) The average annual return on original investment, rounded to the nearest ¹⁄₁₀ of 1%.
(3) The average annual return on average investment, rounded to the nearest ¹⁄₁₀ of 1%.   *(continued)*

(4) The net present value and the net present value index, rounded to three decimal places, at an assumed 12% cost of capital.
(5) The present value payback period.
(6) The discounted cash flow rate of return.

26-4. Investment analysis with inflation adjustment. How Company is considering the purchase of a giant press costing $100,000. The estimated cash benefits before considering income tax and the effects of inflation follow:

Year	Cash Benefit
1	$25,000
2	25,000
3	25,000
4	25,000
5	25,000
6	20,000
7	20,000
8	15,000
9	15,000
10	10,000

For financial accounting purposes, the press is to be depreciated on a straight-line basis over a period of 10 years, with no expected salvage value. For tax purposes, however, the press will be depreciated under ACRS over a period of 5 years. An investment tax credit in the amount of 10% of the cost of the press is available in the first year. The company's tax rate is 40%. The annual inflation rate is expected to be 10% for the planning period.

Required: Adjust the cash flows for the expected effects of inflation (round the price-level index used to two decimal places) and compute each of the following:
(1) Payback period in years.
(2) Average annual return on original investment.
(3) Average annual return on average investment.
(4) Net present value and the net present value index at an assumed 20% cost of capital.
(5) Present value payback in years.
(6) Discounted cash flow rate of return.

26-5. Purchase vs. leasing. Wheary Enterprises plans to operate a sightseeing boat along the Charles River in Boston. In negotiating the purchase of a new vessel from Yachts Dynamic Inc., Wheary learned that Yachts Dynamic would lease the boat to them as an alternative to selling it outright. Through such an arrangement, Wheary would not pay the $2,200,000 purchase price but would lease for $180,000 annually. Wheary expects the boat to last for 20 years, when its salvage value would be $200,000. For tax purposes, however, the boat would be 5-year property (i.e., the cost of the boat would be recovered under ACRS over a 5-year period).

The annual net cash inflow, excluding any consideration of lease payments and income tax, is expected to be $600,000. The company's income tax rate is 40%, and its cost of capital is 14%. A 10% investment tax credit is available only if the boat is purchased. Wheary has sufficient tax liabilities from other income sources to fully absorb all of the investment tax credit available in the first year.

Required: Make a recommendation to purchase or lease the boat, using the present value method to evaluate each alternative.

26-6. Make, buy, or lease. Edwards Corporation is a manufacturing concern that produces and sells a wide range of products. The company not only mass produces a number of products and equipment components, but is also capable of producing special-purpose manufacturing equipment to customer specifications.

The firm is considering adding a new product, with an estimated five-year market life, to one of its product lines. More equipment will be required to produce the new product. There are three alternative ways to acquire the needed equipment: (1) purchase general-purpose equipment, (2) lease general-purpose equipment, or (3) build special-purpose equipment. A fourth alternative, purchase of the special-purpose equipment, has been ruled out because it would be prohibitively expensive.

The general-purpose equipment can be purchased for $125,000. The equipment has an estimated salvage of $15,000 at the end of its useful life of ten years. After five years, the equipment can be used elsewhere in the plant or be sold for $40,000.

Alternatively, the general-purpose equipment can be acquired by a five-year lease for $40,000 annual rent. The lessor will assume all responsibility for taxes, insurance, and maintenance.

Special-purpose equipment can be constructed by the Contract Equipment Department of the Edwards Corporation. While the department is operating at a level which is normal for the time of year, it is below full capacity. The department could produce the equipment without interfering with its regular revenue-producing activities.

The estimated departmental costs for the construction of the special-purpose equipment are:

Materials and parts............................	$ 75,000
Direct labor....................................	60,000
Variable factory overhead (50% of DL).............	30,000
Fixed factory overhead (25% of DL)..............	15,000
Total	$180,000

Corporation general and administrative costs average 20% of the labor cost.

Engineering and management studies provide the following revenue and cost estimates (excluding lease payments and depreciation) for producing the new product, depending upon the equipment used:

	General-Purpose Equipment		Self-Con-structed Equipment
	Leased	Purchased	
Unit selling price.........................	$5.00	$5.00	$5.00
Unit production costs:			
Materials	$1.80	$1.80	$1.70
Variable conversion cost	1.65	1.65	1.40
Total unit production cost..............	$3.45	$3.45	$3.10
Unit contribution margin...................	$1.55	$1.55	$1.90
Estimated unit volume.....................	40,000	40,000	40,000
Estimated total contribution margin	$62,000	$62,000	$76,000
Other costs:			
Supervision............................	$16,000	$16,000	$17,000
Property taxes and insurance.............	—	3,000	5,000
Maintenance...........................	—	3,000	2,000
Total	$16,000	$22,000	$24,000

For tax purposes, the company will depreciate both the general-purpose machine and the special-purpose machine over five years under ACRS. The salvage value of the special-purpose equipment at the end of five years is estimated to be $30,000.

The company uses an aftertax cost of capital of 14%. Its income tax rate is 40%. A 10% investment tax credit is available on the full cost of the property if it is purchased or constructed, but no credit is available if the property is leased.

Required:
   (1) Calculate the net present value for each of the three alternatives that Edwards Corporation has at its disposal.
   (2) Explain which, if any, of the three options Edwards Corporation should select.   (CMA adapted)

26-7. Equipment feasibility study with allowance for risk and uncertainty. The plant manager of Ostende Corporation is confronted with a need to purchase a machine. Machine A will cost $5,000, Machine B's initial cost will be $10,000, and each machine has an estimated life of 3 years. However, an analysis of the operating costs associated with each of the machines reveals that the cost per unit with Machine A is $1 and with Machine B is $.50, excluding depreciation. The product's sales price is $4.

Estimates of the probability of the number of units required for each of the next 3 years, based in part upon analysis of the past and in part on the manager's best appraisal of the future, are as follows:

Annual Requirements	Probability of Occurrence
2,000	.2
3,000	.6
5,000	.2

Required:
   (1) Compute the net present value for each of the three activity levels for Machines A and B, using a discount rate of 6%.
   (2) Determine the expected net present value for each machine. (Ignore income tax considerations.)
   (3) Compute the standard deviation and coefficient of variation for each machine, rounding data used to the nearest dollar.

26-8. New product analysis considering risk and uncertainty; net present value. Grant Enterprises designs and manufactures toys. Past experience indicates that the product life cycle of a toy is 5 years. Promotional advertising produces large sales in the early years, but there is a substantial sales decline in the final year of a toy's life.

A new toy has been developed, and the following sales projections were made by carefully evaluating its consumer demand:

Consumer Demand for New Toy	Probability of Occurrence	Estimated Sales in Thousands of Dollars				
		Year 1	Year 2	Year 3	Year 4	Year 5
Most probable	60%	$1,000	$1,500	$2,000	$1,200	$ 600
Pessimistic	30%	300	400	500	300	200
Optimistic	10%	1,500	2,000	3,000	2,500	1,000

Variable costs are estimated at 30% of the sales price. Special machinery must be purchased at a cost of $1,100,000 and will be installed in an unused portion of the factory, which Grant has unsuccessfully been trying to rent for several years at $50,000 per year, with no prospects for future utilization. Fixed costs (excluding depreciation) of a cash-flow nature are estimated at $60,000 per year on the new toy. The new machinery is to be depreciated by the straight-line method for financial accounting purposes, with an estimated salvage value of $100,000, and will be sold at the end of the fifth year. Advertising and promotional expenses will total $200,000 in the first year, $300,000 in the second year, and $100,000 in the third, fourth, and fifth years.

A 10% investment tax credit is available on the entire purchase price of the machinery. The machinery is 5-year class property under ACRS and will be depreciated by the most accelerated method available for income tax purposes. The income tax rate is 40%, and the company has sufficient income taxes from other activities to absorb all of the investment tax credit available in the first year.

Required:
(1) Prepare a schedule of the new toy's probable sales for each year.
(2) Prepare a schedule of the aftertax cash inflows from the new toy's sales for each of the five years involved and from the disposition of the machinery at the end of the fifth year.
(3) Prepare a schedule of the net present value of the net cash flows, assuming a minimum desired rate of return of 12%.   (AICPA adapted)

CASES

A. Relevant data for investment decision. Clewash Linen Supply Company provides laundered items to various commercial and service establishments in a large city. Clewash is scheduled to acquire some new cleaning equipment in mid-19A, which would enable the company to increase the volume of laundry it handles without any increase in labor costs. In addition, the estimated maintenance costs in terms of pounds of laundry processed would be reduced slightly.

The new equipment was justified not only on the basis of reduced cost but also on the basis of expected increase in demand starting in late 19A. However, since the original forecast was prepared, several potential new customers have either delayed or discontinued their own expansion plans in the market area serviced by Clewash, and the most recent forecast indicates that no great increase in demand can be expected until late 19B or early 19C.

Required: Identify and explain factors which tend to indicate whether the investment should be made as scheduled or delayed.   (CMA adapted)

B. Decentralization and the management of capital expenditures. Judy Knight founded the Newworld Company over thirty years ago. Although she has relied heavily upon advice from other members of management, Knight has made all of the important decisions for the company. Newworld has been successful, experiencing steady growth in its early years and very rapid growth in recent years. During this period of rapid growth, Knight has experienced difficulty in keeping up with the many decisions that needed to be made. She feels that she is losing control of the company's progress.

Regular discussions regarding her concern have been held with George Armet, the company executive vice-president. As a result of these discussions, Armet has studied possible alternative organizational structures to the present highly centralized functional organization.

In a carefully prepared proposal, Armet recommended that the company reorganize according to its two product lines, because the technology and marketing methods are quite different. The plastic products require different manufacturing skills and equipment from the brass products. The change could be accomplished easily because the products are manufactured in different plants. The marketing effort is also segregated along product lines within the sales function. The number of executive positions would not change, although the duties of the positions would change. There would no longer be the need for a vice-president for manufacturing or a vice-president for sales. Those positions would be replaced with a vice-president for each of the two product lines. Armet acknowledges that there may be personnel problems at the executive management level, because the current vice-presidents may not be competent to manage within the new structure.

Armet's proposal also contained the recommendation that some of the decision-making power, long held by Knight, be transferred to the new vice-presidents. Armet argued that this would be good for the company. The vice-presidents would be more aware of the problems and solution alternatives of their respective product lines because they are closer to the operations. Fewer decisions would be required of each new vice-president than now are required of Knight. This should reduce the time between problem recognition and implementation of the solution. Armet further argued that distributing the decision-making power would improve the creativity and spirit of company management.

Knight is intrigued by the proposal and the prospect that it would make the company more manageable. However, the proposal did not spell out clearly which decisions should be transferred and which should remain with the president. Knight requested Armet to prepare a supplemental memorandum specifying the decisions to be delegated to the vice-presidents.

The supplemental memorandum presented the recommended decision areas, explaining in each case how the new vice-presidents would be closer to the situation and thereby be able to make prompt, sound decisions. The following list summarizes Armet's recommendations:

(1) Sales
    (a) Price policy
    (b) Promotional strategy
    (c) Credit policy
(2) Operations
    (a) Manufacturing procedures
    (b) Labor negotiations
(3) Development of existing product lines
(4) Capital investment decision—up to amounts not exceeding the division "depreciation flow" plus 25% of its "aftertax income" (excluding ventures into new fields).

The corporate management (Knight and Armet) would be responsible for overall corporate development. Also, they would allocate the remaining available cash flow for dividends, for investment projects above the limits prescribed, and for investment into new ventures.

Required:
(1) Does the company have the characteristics needed for decentralized profit centers? Explain.
(2) Knight believes that the proposal, as presented, will not work. In Knight's judgment, the corporate level management will be unable to control effectively the destiny of the firm because the proposal grants too much investment freedom to the new divisions. Do you agree with Knight that effective control over the future of the firm cannot be maintained at the corporate level if the capital rationing is shared in the manner specified in the proposal? Support your answer with appropriate discussion, including a recommended alternative procedure if you agree with Knight.   (CMA adapted)

PRESENT VALUE OF $1

Future Years	1%	2%	4%	6%	8%	10%	12%	14%	15%	16%	18%	20%	22%	24%	25%	26%	28%	30%	35%	40%	45%	50%
1	.990	.980	.962	.943	.926	.909	.893	.877	.870	.862	.847	.833	.820	.806	.800	.794	.781	.769	.741	.714	.690	.667
2	.980	.961	.925	.890	.857	.826	.797	.769	.756	.743	.718	.694	.672	.650	.640	.630	.610	.592	.549	.510	.476	.444
3	.971	.942	.889	.840	.794	.751	.712	.675	.658	.641	.609	.579	.551	.524	.512	.500	.477	.455	.406	.364	.328	.296
4	.961	.924	.855	.792	.735	.683	.636	.592	.572	.552	.516	.482	.451	.423	.410	.397	.373	.350	.301	.260	.226	.198
5	.951	.906	.822	.747	.681	.621	.567	.519	.497	.476	.437	.402	.370	.341	.328	.315	.291	.269	.223	.186	.156	.132
6	.942	.888	.790	.705	.630	.564	.507	.456	.432	.410	.370	.335	.303	.275	.262	.250	.227	.207	.165	.133	.108	.088
7	.933	.871	.760	.665	.583	.513	.452	.400	.376	.354	.314	.279	.249	.222	.210	.198	.178	.159	.122	.095	.074	.059
8	.923	.853	.731	.627	.540	.467	.404	.351	.327	.305	.266	.233	.204	.179	.168	.157	.139	.123	.091	.068	.051	.039
9	.914	.837	.703	.592	.500	.424	.361	.308	.284	.263	.225	.194	.167	.144	.134	.125	.108	.094	.067	.048	.035	.026
10	.905	.820	.676	.558	.463	.386	.322	.270	.247	.227	.191	.162	.137	.116	.107	.099	.085	.073	.050	.035	.024	.017
11	.896	.804	.650	.527	.429	.350	.287	.237	.215	.195	.162	.135	.112	.094	.086	.079	.066	.056	.037	.025	.017	.012
12	.887	.788	.625	.497	.397	.319	.257	.208	.187	.168	.137	.112	.092	.076	.069	.062	.052	.043	.027	.018	.012	.008
13	.879	.773	.601	.469	.368	.290	.229	.182	.163	.145	.116	.093	.075	.061	.055	.050	.040	.033	.020	.013	.008	.005
14	.870	.758	.577	.442	.340	.263	.205	.160	.141	.125	.099	.078	.062	.049	.044	.039	.032	.025	.015	.009	.006	.003
15	.861	.743	.555	.417	.315	.239	.183	.140	.123	.108	.084	.065	.051	.040	.035	.031	.025	.020	.011	.006	.004	.002
16	.853	.728	.534	.394	.292	.218	.163	.123	.107	.093	.071	.054	.042	.032	.028	.025	.019	.015	.008	.005	.003	.002
17	.844	.714	.513	.371	.270	.198	.146	.108	.093	.080	.060	.045	.034	.026	.023	.020	.015	.012	.006	.003	.002	.001
18	.836	.700	.494	.350	.250	.180	.130	.095	.081	.069	.051	.038	.028	.021	.018	.016	.012	.009	.005	.002	.001	.001
19	.828	.686	.475	.331	.232	.164	.116	.083	.070	.060	.043	.031	.023	.017	.014	.012	.009	.007	.003	.002	.001	.001
20	.820	.673	.456	.312	.215	.149	.104	.073	.061	.051	.037	.026	.019	.014	.012	.010	.007	.005	.002	.001	.001	
21	.811	.660	.439	.294	.199	.135	.093	.064	.053	.044	.031	.022	.015	.011	.009	.008	.006	.004	.002	.001		
22	.803	.647	.422	.278	.184	.123	.083	.056	.046	.038	.026	.018	.013	.009	.007	.006	.004	.003	.001	.001		
23	.795	.634	.406	.262	.170	.112	.074	.049	.040	.033	.022	.015	.010	.007	.006	.005	.003	.002	.001			
24	.788	.622	.390	.247	.158	.102	.066	.043	.035	.028	.019	.013	.008	.006	.005	.004	.003	.002	.001			
25	.780	.610	.375	.233	.146	.092	.059	.038	.030	.024	.016	.010	.007	.005	.004	.003	.002	.001	.001			
26	.772	.598	.361	.220	.135	.084	.053	.033	.026	.021	.014	.009	.006	.004	.003	.002	.002	.001				
27	.764	.586	.347	.207	.125	.076	.047	.029	.023	.018	.011	.007	.005	.003	.002	.002	.001	.001				
28	.757	.574	.333	.196	.116	.069	.042	.026	.020	.016	.010	.006	.004	.002	.002	.002	.001	.001				
29	.749	.563	.321	.185	.107	.063	.037	.022	.017	.014	.008	.005	.003	.002	.002	.001	.001					
30	.742	.552	.308	.174	.099	.057	.033	.020	.015	.012	.007	.004	.003	.002	.001	.001	.001					
40	.672	.453	.208	.097	.046	.022	.011	.005	.004	.003	.001	.001										
50	.608	.372	.141	.054	.021	.009	.003	.001	.001	.001												

PRESENT VALUE OF $1 RECEIVED OR PAID ANNUALLY FOR EACH OF THE NEXT N YEARS

Future Years	1%	2%	4%	6%	8%	10%	12%	14%	15%	16%	18%	20%	22%	24%	25%	26%	28%	30%	35%	40%	45%	50%
1	.990	.980	.962	.943	.926	.909	.893	.877	.870	.862	.847	.833	.820	.806	.800	.794	.781	.769	.741	.714	.690	.667
2	1.970	1.942	1.886	1.833	1.783	1.736	1.690	1.647	1.626	1.605	1.566	1.528	1.492	1.457	1.440	1.424	1.392	1.361	1.289	1.224	1.165	1.111
3	2.941	2.884	2.775	2.673	2.577	2.487	2.402	2.322	2.283	2.246	2.174	2.106	2.042	1.981	1.952	1.923	1.868	1.816	1.696	1.589	1.493	1.407
4	3.902	3.808	3.630	3.465	3.312	3.170	3.037	2.914	2.855	2.798	2.690	2.589	2.494	2.404	2.362	2.320	2.241	2.166	1.997	1.849	1.720	1.605
5	4.853	4.713	4.452	4.212	3.993	3.791	3.605	3.433	3.352	3.274	3.127	2.991	2.864	2.745	2.689	2.635	2.532	2.436	2.220	2.035	1.876	1.737
6	5.795	5.601	5.242	4.917	4.623	4.355	4.111	3.889	3.784	3.685	3.498	3.326	3.167	3.020	2.951	2.885	2.759	2.643	2.385	2.168	1.983	1.824
7	6.728	6.472	6.002	5.582	5.206	4.868	4.564	4.288	4.160	4.039	3.812	3.605	3.416	3.242	3.161	3.083	2.937	2.802	2.508	2.263	2.057	1.883
8	7.652	7.325	6.733	6.210	5.747	5.335	4.968	4.639	4.487	4.344	4.078	3.837	3.619	3.421	3.329	3.241	3.076	2.925	2.598	2.331	2.108	1.922
9	8.566	8.163	7.435	6.802	6.247	5.759	5.328	4.946	4.772	4.607	4.303	4.031	3.786	3.566	3.463	3.366	3.184	3.019	2.665	2.379	2.144	1.948
10	9.471	8.983	8.111	7.360	6.710	6.145	5.650	5.216	5.019	4.833	4.494	4.192	3.923	3.682	3.571	3.465	3.269	3.092	2.715	2.414	2.168	1.965
11	10.368	9.787	8.760	7.887	7.139	6.495	5.988	5.453	5.234	5.029	4.656	4.327	4.035	3.776	3.656	3.544	3.335	3.147	2.752	2.438	2.185	1.977
12	11.255	10.575	9.385	8.384	7.536	6.814	6.194	5.660	5.421	5.197	4.793	4.439	4.127	3.851	3.725	3.606	3.387	3.190	2.779	2.456	2.196	1.985
13	12.134	11.348	9.986	8.853	7.904	7.103	6.424	5.842	5.583	5.342	4.910	4.533	4.203	3.912	3.780	3.656	3.427	3.223	2.799	2.468	2.204	1.990
14	13.004	12.106	10.563	9.295	8.244	7.367	6.628	6.002	5.724	5.468	5.008	4.611	4.265	3.962	3.824	3.695	3.459	3.249	2.814	2.477	2.210	1.993
15	13.865	12.849	11.118	9.712	8.559	7.606	6.811	6.142	5.847	5.575	5.092	4.675	4.315	4.001	3.859	3.726	3.483	3.268	2.825	2.484	2.214	1.995
16	14.718	13.578	11.652	10.106	8.851	7.824	6.974	6.265	5.954	5.669	5.162	4.730	4.357	4.033	3.887	3.751	3.503	3.283	2.834	2.489	2.216	1.997
17	15.562	14.292	12.166	10.477	9.122	8.022	7.120	6.373	6.047	5.749	5.222	4.775	4.391	4.059	3.910	3.771	3.518	3.295	2.840	2.492	2.218	1.998
18	16.398	14.992	12.659	10.828	9.372	8.201	7.250	6.467	6.128	5.818	5.273	4.812	4.419	4.080	3.928	3.786	3.529	3.304	2.844	2.494	2.219	1.999
19	17.226	15.678	13.134	11.158	9.604	8.365	7.366	6.550	6.198	5.877	5.316	4.844	4.442	4.097	3.942	3.799	3.539	3.311	2.848	2.496	2.220	1.999
20	18.046	16.351	13.590	11.470	9.818	8.514	7.469	6.623	6.259	5.929	5.353	4.870	4.460	4.110	3.954	3.808	3.546	3.316	2.850	2.497	2.221	1.999
21	18.857	17.011	14.029	11.764	10.017	8.649	7.562	6.687	6.312	5.973	5.384	4.891	4.476	4.121	3.963	3.816	3.551	3.320	2.852	2.498	2.221	2.000
22	19.660	17.658	14.451	12.042	10.201	8.772	7.645	6.743	6.359	6.011	5.410	4.909	4.488	4.130	3.970	3.822	3.556	3.323	2.853	2.498	2.222	2.000
23	20.456	18.292	14.857	12.303	10.371	8.883	7.718	6.792	6.399	6.044	5.432	4.925	4.499	4.137	3.976	3.827	3.559	3.325	2.854	2.499	2.222	2.000
24	21.243	18.914	15.247	12.550	10.529	8.985	7.784	6.835	6.434	6.073	5.451	4.937	4.507	4.143	3.981	3.831	3.562	3.327	2.855	2.499	2.222	2.000
25	22.023	19.523	15.622	12.783	10.675	9.077	7.843	6.873	6.464	6.097	5.467	4.948	4.514	4.147	3.985	3.834	3.564	3.329	2.856	2.499	2.222	2.000
26	22.795	20.121	15.983	13.003	10.810	9.161	7.896	6.906	6.491	6.118	5.480	4.956	4.520	4.151	3.988	3.837	3.566	3.330	2.856	2.500	2.222	2.000
27	23.560	20.707	16.330	13.211	10.935	9.237	7.943	6.935	6.514	6.136	5.492	4.964	4.524	4.154	3.990	3.839	3.567	3.331	2.856	2.500	2.222	2.000
28	24.316	21.281	16.663	13.406	11.051	9.307	7.984	6.961	6.534	6.152	5.502	4.970	4.528	4.157	3.992	3.840	3.568	3.331	2.857	2.500	2.222	2.000
29	25.066	21.844	16.984	13.591	11.158	9.370	8.022	6.983	6.551	6.166	5.510	4.975	4.531	4.159	3.994	3.841	3.569	3.332	2.857	2.500	2.222	2.000
30	25.808	22.396	17.292	13.765	11.258	9.427	8.055	7.003	6.566	6.177	5.517	4.979	4.534	4.160	3.995	3.842	3.569	3.332	2.857	2.500	2.222	2.000
40	32.835	27.355	19.793	15.046	11.925	9.779	8.244	7.105	6.642	6.234	5.548	4.997	4.544	4.166	3.999	3.846	3.571	3.333	2.857	2.500	2.222	2.000
50	39.196	31.424	21.482	15.762	12.234	9.915	8.304	7.133	6.661	6.246	5.554	4.999	4.545	4.167	4.000	3.846	3.571	3.333	2.857	2.500	2.222	2.000

INDEX